Lecture Notes in Computer Science 3101

Commenced Publication in 1973
Founding and Former Series Editors:
Gerhard Goos, Juris Hartmanis, and Jan van Leeuwen

Masood Masoodian   Steve Jones
Bill Rogers (Eds.)

Computer Human Interaction

6th Asia Pacific Conference, APCHI 2004
Rotorua, New Zealand, June 29 - July 2, 2004
Proceedings

 Springer

Volume Editors

Masood Masoodian
Steve Jones
Bill Rogers
University of Waikato, Department of Computer Science
Private Bag 3105, Hamilton, New Zealand
E-mail: {M.Masoodian,stevej,coms0108}@cs.waikato.ac.nz

Library of Congress Control Number: 2004108030

CR Subject Classification (1998): H.5.2, H.5.3, C.2.4, H.4, H.3, I.2, I.3.6, K.4.3, K.8

ISSN 0302-9743
ISBN 3-540-22312-6 Springer-Verlag Berlin Heidelberg New York

Springer-Verlag is a part of Springer Science+Business Media

springeronline.com

© Springer-Verlag Berlin Heidelberg 2004
Printed in Germany

Typesetting: Camera-ready by author, data conversion by Boller Mediendesign
Printed on acid-free paper   SPIN: 11014447   06/3142   5 4 3 2 1 0

Preface

APCHI 2004 was the sixth Asia-Pacific Conference on Computer-Human Interaction, and was the first APCHI to be held in New Zealand. This conference series provides opportunities for HCI researchers and practitioners in the Asia-Pacific and beyond to gather to explore ideas, exchange and share experiences, and further build the HCI network in this region. APCHI 2004 was a truly international event, with presenters representing 17 countries. This year APCHI also incorporated the fifth SIGCHI New Zealand Symposium on Computer-Human Interaction.

A total of 69 papers were accepted for inclusion in the proceedings – 56 long papers and 13 short papers. Submissions were subject to a strict, double-blind peer-review process. The research topics cover the spectrum of HCI, including human factors and ergonomics, user interface tools and technologies, mobile and ubiquitous computing, visualization, augmented reality, collaborative systems, internationalization and cultural issues, and more. APCHI also included a doctoral consortium, allowing 10 doctoral students from across the globe to meet and discuss their work in an interdisciplinary workshop with leading researchers and fellow students. Additionally, five tutorials were offered in association with the conference.

The conference was also privileged to have two distinguished keynote speakers: Don Norman (www.jnd.com) and Susan Dray (www.dray.com). Don Norman's invited talk focussed on 'emotional design': the application of recent research on human affect and emotion to the design of products that are easier to use because they are also interesting and beautiful. Susan Dray's research combines expertise in interface evaluation and usability with a cross-cultural and organizational perspective.

The quality of this year's APCHI was the joint achievement of many people. We would like to thank all those who worked so hard to make APCHI a success: the referees for their time and effort generously donated to the reviewing process; the program committee for organizing the reviewing process, the presentations, and of course this volume of proceedings; the steering committee for their support of the APCHI series; and the local organizing committee for their excellent work in bringing the conference to fruition. Finally, we thank the authors and presenters as well as the APCHI 2004 attendees, whose contribution and participation were the crucial ingredients of an exciting and productive conference.

April 2004   Sally Jo Cunningham, Matt Jones

Organizing Committee

Conference Chairs	Sally Jo Cunningham, Matt Jones
Program Chairs	Steve Jones, Bill Rogers
Tutorials	Masood Masoodian, Anette Olsson
Doctoral Consortium	Chris Knowles, Peter Thomas
Treasurer	Kirsten Thomson
Venue and Logistics	Lyn Hunt, Aparna Krishnan, Beryl Plimmer
Marketing and PR	Lyn Hunt, Maree Talmage
Sponsorship	George Buchanan, Dave Nichols
Website	Dana McKay
Proceedings	Masood Masoodian

Steering Committee

Masaaki Kurosu
Lim Kee Yong

Program Committee

Elisabeth André	University of Augsburg
Mark Apperley	University of Waikato
Russell Beale	University of Birmingham
Mark Billinghurst	HIT Lab
Ann Blandford	Middlesex University
George Buchanan	Middlesex University
Richard Butterworth	Middlesex University
Adrian Cheok	National University of Sinagpore
Elizabeth Churchill	FXPAL
Andy Cockburn	University of Canterbury
Sally Jo Cunningham	University of Waikato
Suzanne Currie	Navman
Guozhong Dai	Institute of Software
Ernest Edmonds	University of Technology, Sydney
Peter Grierson	ANZ Bank
John Grundy	University of Auckland
Carl Gutwin	University of Saskatchewan
Masahito Hirakawa	Shimane University
Steve Howard	University of Melbourne
Matt Jones	University of Waikato
Steve Jones	University of Waikato
Elizabeth Kemp	Massey University
Chris Knowles	University of Waikato
Panu Korhonen	Nokia Research Centre
Aparna Krishnan	University of Waikato

Jonathan Lazar	Towson University
Kee Yong Lim	Nanyang Technological University
Christopher Lueg	University of Technology, Sydney
Saturnino Luz	Trinity College Dublin
Robert Macredie	Brunel University
Gary Marsden	University of Capetown
Masood Masoodian	University of Waikato
Dana McKay	University of Waikato
Dave Nichols	University of Waikato
Anette Olsson	University of Waikato
Fabio Paterno	CNR, Italy
Chris Phillips	Massey University
Chui Yoon Ping	Nanyang Technological University
Beryl Plimmer	University of Auckland
Patrick Rau	Chung Yuan Christian University
David Redmiles	University of California at Irvine
Bill Rogers	University of Waikato
Yuzuru Tanaka	Hokkaido University
Yin Leng Theng	Nanyang Technological University
Bruce Thomas	University of South Australia
Peter Thomas	Middlesex University
Kirsten Thomson	University of Waikato
Mike Twidale	University of Illinois
Stephen Viller	University of Queensland
Kwang Yun Wohn	Korean Institute of Science and Technology
Candy Wong	DoCoMo Labs
William Wong	Middlesex University
Kim Jin Woo	Yonsei University
Toshiki Yamaoka	Wakayama University
Michiaki Yasumura	Keio University
Alvin Yeo	UNIMAS, Malaysia

Sponsors

Department of Computer Science, University of Waikato
University of Waikato Usability Laboratory
IFIP Technical Committee No. 13 on Human-Computer Interaction (IFIP TC.13)
ACM SIGCHI, New Zealand Chapter (SIGCHI-NZ)
COMPUTERWORLD
Human Interface Technology Laboratory New Zealand (HITLabNZ)
Orbit Corporate Travel

Table of Contents

Full Papers

A Simple and Novel Method for Skin Detection and Face Locating and
Tracking 1
Saleh A. Al-Shehri

Operation-Support System for Transportable Earth Station Using
Augmented Reality 9
Kikuo Asai, Noritaka Osawa, Yuji Y. Sugimoto, Kimio Kondo

Real-World Oriented Access Control Method with a Displayed Password . 19
Yuji Ayatsuka, Michimune Kohno, Jun Rekimoto

Evolutionary Approaches to Visualisation and Knowledge Discovery 30
Russell Beale, Andy Pryke, Robert J. Hendley

Creating a Framework for Situated Way-Finding Research 40
Nicola J. Bidwell, Christopher P. Luey

Extending Tree-Maps to Three Dimensions: A Comparative Study 50
Thomas Bladh, David A. Carr, Jeremiah Scholl

Creative Expertise and Collaborative Technology Design 60
Linda Candy, Ernest Edmonds

Does DOF Separation on Elastic Devices Improve User 3D Steering
Task Performance? 70
Géry Casiez, Patricia Plénacoste, Christophe Chaillou

Collaborative Interactions on 3D Display for Multi-user Game
Environments 81
Jeong-Dan Choi, Byung-Tae Jang, Chi-Jeong Hwang

Age Differences in Rendezvousing: 18-30s Vs. 31-45s 91
Martin Colbert

Specification and Generation of Model 2 Web Interfaces 101
Dirk Draheim, Gerald Weber

Metaphors for Electronic Music Production in *Reason* and *Live* 111
Matthew Duignan, James Noble, Pippin Barr, Robert Biddle

Extending the Perceptual User Interface to Recognise Movement 121
Richard Green

Real-Time Color Gamut Mapping Architecture and Implementation for
Color-Blind People 133
Dongil Han

Tangible Teleconferencing 143
Jeorg Hauber, Mark Billinghurst, Holger Regenbrecht

Our Ubiquitous Computing Home Inside: A Practical Approach
Emerging into House and Home..................................... 153
Soichiro Iga, Saiko Ohno

A Study of an EMG-controlled HCI Method by Clenching Teeth 163
Hyuk Jeong, Jong-Sung Kim, Jin-Seong Choi

Performance Analysis for User Interface in Real-Time Ubiquitous
Information Network 171
Yung Bok Kim, Mira Kwak, Dong-sub Cho

Envisioning Mobile Information Services: Combining User- and
Technology-Centered Design.. 180
Jesper Kjeldskov, Steve Howard

Supporting Work Activities in Healthcare by Mobile Electronic Patient
Records.. 191
Jesper Kjeldskov, Mikael B. Skov

Design of Chording Gloves as a Text Input Device 201
*Seongil Lee, Sang Hyuk Hong, Jae Wook Jeon, Hoo-Gon Choi,
Hyoukryeol Choi*

Designing Explorable Interaction Based on Users' Knowledge: A Case
Study on a Multi-functional Printer Application 211
Dong-Seok Lee, Douglas Jihoon Kim, Un Sik Byun

The Automatic Generation of a Graphical Dialogue Model from Delphi
Source Code.. 221
Lei Li, Chris Phillips, Chris Scogings

NetWorker: A Practical Web-Based Tool to Support the
Collect-Compare-Choose Cycle 231
Paul Lyons, Chris Phillips, Elizabeth Kemp, Jaimee Alam

Nine Tools for Generating Harmonious Colour Schemes 241
Paul Lyons, Giovanni Moretti

A Practical Set of Culture Dimensions for Global User-Interface
Development 252
Aaron Marcus, Valentina-Johanna Baumgartner

Towards a General Model for Assisting Navigation 262
Mike McGavin, James Noble, Robert Biddle, Judy Brown

inlineLink: Realization of Inline Expansion Link Methods on a
Conventional Web Browser 272
Motoki Miura, Buntarou Shizuki, Jiro Tanaka

Chromotome: A 3D Interface for Exploring Colour Space 283
Giovanni Moretti, Paul Lyons, Mark Wilson

Commercial Success by Looking for Desire Lines 293
Carl Myhill

Steering Law in an Environment of Spatially Coupled Style with
Matters of Pointer Size and Trajectory Width 305
Satoshi Naito, Yoshifumi Kitamura, Fumio Kishino

Design of Information Visualization of Ubiquitous Environment for a
Wearable Display 317
Makoto Obayashi, Hiroyuki Nishiyama, Fumio Mizoguchi

Perceiving Tools in 3D Sculpting 328
Jyrki Parviainen, Nina Sainio, Roope Raisamo

A Tripartite Framework for Working Memory Processes................ 338
Peter J. Patsula

Designing for Flow in a Complex Activity 349
Jon M. Pearce, Steve Howard

Enhancing Interactive Graph Manipulation Tools with Tactile Feedback . 359
Jukka Raisamo, Roope Raisamo

HCI Practices and the Work of Information Architects................ 369
Toni Robertson, Cindy Hewlett

User Model of Navigation 379
Corina Sas

An Interface for Input the Object Region Using the Hand Chroma Key .. 389
Shuhei Sato, Etsuya Shibayama, Shin Takahashi

Menu-Selection-Based Japanese Input Method with Consonants for
Pen-Based Computers 399
Daisuke Sato, Buntarou Shizuki, Motoki Miura, Jiro Tanaka

Framework for Interpreting Handwritten Strokes Using Grammars 409
Buntarou Shizuki, Kazuhisa Iizuka, Jiro Tanaka

A Rapidly Adaptive Collaborative Ubiquitous Computing Environment
to Allow Passive Detection of Marked Objects 420
Hannah Slay, Bruce Thomas, Rudi Vernik, Wayne Piekarski

The Misrepresentation of Use in Technology Demonstrations 431
Wally Smith

An Implementation for Capturing Clickable Moving Objects 441
*Toshiharu Sugawara, Satoshi Kurihara, Shigemi Aoyagi, Koji Sato,
Toshihiro Takada*

A Prototyping Framework for Mobile Text Entry Research 451
Sanju Sunny, Yow Kin Choong

The Effect of Color Coding for the Characters on Computer Keyboards
for Multilingual Input Using Modeless Methods 461
Kuo-Hao Eric Tang, Li-Chen Tsai

Extended Godzilla: Free-Form 3D-Object Design by Sketching and
Modifying Seven Primitives at Single 2D-3D Seamless Display 471
Shun'ichi Tano, Yoichiro Komatsu, Mitsuru Iwata

Quantitative Analysis of Human Behavior and Implied User Interface
in 3D Sketching 481
Shun'ichi Tano, Toshiko Matsumoto, Mitsuru Iwata

What Are You Looking At? Newest Findings from an Empirical Study
of Group Awareness 491
Minh Hong Tran, Gitesh K. Raikundalia, Yun Yang

Cultural Usability in the Globalisation of News Portal 501
Tina Wai Chi Tsui, John Paynter

Collecting, Organizing, and Managing Non-contextualised Data by
Using MVML to Develop a Human-Computer Interface 511
Michael Verhaart, John Jamieson, Kinshuk

Common Industry Format: Meeting Educational Objectives and
Student Needs? 521
Karola von Baggo, Lorraine Johnston, Oliver Burmeister, Todd Bentley

Accessibility: A Tool for Usability Evaluation 531
Daniel Woo, Joji Mori

The Degree of Usability from Selected DVD Menus and Their
Navigational Systems 540
Guy Wood-Bradley, Malcolm Campbell

OPR-LENS: Operation-Lens System for Supporting a Manipulation of
Information Appliances 550
Takumi Yamaguchi, Haruya Shiba, Kazunori Shimamura

A Novel Locomotion Interface with Independent Planar and Footpad
Devices for Virtual Walking 560
Jungwon Yoon, Jeha Ryu

Short Papers

Designing Intelligent Environments – User Perceptions on Information
Sharing 570
Craig Chatfield, Jonna Häkkilä

Sony EyeToy™: Developing Mental Models for 3-D Interaction in a
2-D Gaming Environment 575
Geanbry Demming

Face and Body Gesture Analysis for Multimodal HCI 583
Hatice Gunes, Massimo Piccardi, Tony Jan

Ambulance Dispatch Complexity and Dispatcher Decision Strategies:
Implications for Interface Design 589
Jared Hayes, Antoni Moore, George Benwell, B.L. William Wong

Supporting Group Learning Using a Digital Whiteboard 594
Raymond Kemp, Elizabeth Kemp, Thevalojinie Mohanarajah

Verifying the Field of View Afforded to the Pilot due to Cockpit
Design, Stature, and Aerodrome Design Parameters 599
Eugene Aik Min Khoo, Kee Yong Lim

Creative Information Seeking and Interface Design 604
*Shu-Shing Lee, Yin-Leng Theng, Dion Hoe-Lian Goh,
Schubert Shou-Boon Foo*

Connecting the User View with the System View of Requirements 610
Ralph R. Miller, Scott P. Overmyer

Recourse for Guiding Didactical Creators in the Development of
Accessible e-Learning Material 615
Valeria Mirabella, Stephen Kimani, Tiziana Catarci

DIANE^{nx}: Modelling Exploration in the Web Context 620
Aaron Mullane, Sandrine Balbo

Factors Influencing User Selection of WWW Sitemaps 625
Chris J. Pilgrim, Gitte Lindgaard, Ying K. Leung

ViewPoint: A Zoomable User Interface for Integrating Expressive
Systems 631
Darryl Singh, Mitra Nataraj, Rick Mugridge

Passing on Good Practice: Interface Design for Older Users 636
Mary Zajicek

Doctoral Consortium

Interfaces That Adapt like Humans 641
Samuel Alexander, Abdolhossein Sarrafzadeh

Designers Search Strategies Influenced by the Interaction with
Information Retrieval Systems (IRS): Within the Early Stages of the
Design Process 646
Caroline Francis

Personal Digital Document Management 651
Sarah Henderson

A Study of the Impact of Collaborative Tools on the Effectiveness of
Clinical Pathology Conferences 656
Bridget Kane, Saturnino Luz

Physical Computing – Representations of Human Movement in
Human-Computer Interaction 661
Astrid Twenebowa Larssen

Creative Interface Design for Information Seeking 666
Shu-Shing Lee

Understanding Interaction Experience in Mobile Learning 672
Fariza Hanis Abdul Razak

User Experience in Interactive Computer Game Development 675
Tracey Sellar

Using Patterns to Guide User Interface Development 682
Elizabeth G. Todd

Multimodal Cues for Object Manipulation in Augmented and Virtual
Environments 687
Mihaela A. Zahariev

Author Index 693

Operation-Support System for Transportable Earth Station Using Augmented Reality

Kikuo Asai[1,2], Noritaka Osawa[1,2], Yuji Y. Sugimoto[1], and Kimio Kondo[1,2]

[1] National Institute of Multimedia Education
{asai,osawa,yuji,kkondo}@nime.ac.jp
http://www.nime.ac.jp/index-e.html
[2] The Graduate University of Advanced Study
2-12 Wakaba, Mihama-ku, Chiba 261-0014, Japan

Abstract. We have developed a prototype system for supporting operation of a transportable earth station using augmented reality technology, and have had a preliminary experiment for investigating properties of the operation-support system. It was not easy for non-technical staffs to treat the equipments they saw for the first time. The operation-support system gives us information on how to manage the pieces of equipment, using a see-through HMD. The equipment is distinguished with a marker. The automatic voice also lets the user know the identified equipment, and the voice attention works to reduce a mistake of operation. To simplify authoring of multimedia data for the instruction, the Web browser in information presentation was adopted for using the existent resources. The result of the experiment suggested that the system improved reliability of information acquisition, obtaining information of what a user sees.

1 Introduction

Augmented reality (AR) gives us a new type of man-machine interface in which information displayed with a head-mounted display (HMD). AR facilitates understanding or enhances recognition by superimposing virtual objects onto a real scene that is viewed by a user. One of the advantages, which is viewpoint-based interaction, and recent advance of tracking stability [1] have yielded various applications such as computer-assisted instruction [2], virtual prototyping in engineering [3], architectural design [4], education [5], and entertainments [6]. We used AR as alternative to the conventional instruction manual for supporting operation of a transportable earth station. Fig. 1 shows an HMD and a compact camera of the prototype system.

The inter-university satellite network called Space Collaboration System (SCS) [7,8] was established in October 1996. Since then, it has been used for distance lectures and academic meetings in higher education, exchanging audio and video signals. SCS now links 150 VSAT (very small aperture terminal) stations at universities and institutes. The network was further extended in 1999 with development of a transportable earth station that provided essentially the same functionality as the original VSAT on campus but can be transported throughout Japan, allowing us to have a telecommunication infrastructure in the isolated areas such as mountains and islands.

M. Masoodian et al. (Eds.): APCHI 2004, LNCS 3101, pp. 9-18, 2004.
© Springer-Verlag Berlin Heidelberg 2004

A Simple and Novel Method for Skin Detection and Face Locating and Tracking

Saleh A. Al-Shehri

P.O.Box 20219, Aseer Reigon, Al-Wadyeen, Saudi Arabia
SaaaS101@hotmail.com

Abstract. In many computer vision applications such as human-computer interaction (HCI) and human-motion tracking (HMT), face detection is considered the main step which is also the first step. To detect faces, skin color is considered the most appropriate feature to use. A simple arithmetic on RGB color space components is used in this paper to extract the skin. Elliptical shape fitting is used to locate the face. Then template matching is used to locate the eyes. A very good result is achieved using our simple algorithm. Up to our knowledge, we believe that our skin detection method is one of the most efficient methods being used today.

1 Introduction

Using skin color for face detection has taken the attraction of many researchers and become the subject of their researches [1-12]. Authors in [13] tabulated the major methods of face detection. A survey of human faces detection and recognition is given in [14]. Some image pixels values will be in skin and none-skin regions at the same time. This fact makes it very difficult to perfectly make the right decision for these pixels. Some researchers used the color histogram for skin detection [6,15]. Prior knowledge of skin color clustering and shape information are used to perform pixel level classification [1,2,5,10-12,16,17]. Different researchers used different color spaces [18]. In addition to skin color, geometric properties of faces were used to construct a method for face detection [1,2,9]. Generic algorithm and eigenfaces also used for faces detection [19]. Skin color classification using two discriminates namely: linear discriminate and Mahalanchin distance were presented in [7]. Fischer linear discriminate was used also with color-based segmentation [3]. Building skin color model by subtracting two adjacent image frames as a first step is presented in [6]. The rest of this paper is organized as follows: the main method for skin detection is presented in section 2 whereas steps of face detection and eye locating are discussed in section 3. Section 4 contains the results of applying our algorithm on three faces database [20-22]. A summary is given in section 5.

M. Masoodian et al. (Eds.): APCHI 2004, LNCS 3101, pp. 1-8, 2004.
© Springer-Verlag Berlin Heidelberg 2004

2 Skin Detection

Large number of image sources produces the needed images in RGB format. In many researches, the authors claim that other color spaces such as CIF-x, HSV are more appropriate than the RGB space [2,7,13,16,18]. It was shown that this is not true [11,23]. This implies that the transformation form RGB color to another color space is an extra processing step. Brand, J. stated that R/G > 1 and   the red color is the predominant color in the human skin color [11]. This property in addition to other equations has been used to classify the skin color pixels. Our main observation is that when G component is subtracted from R component of the RGB color representation the pixels values for none-skin become relatively small whereas for skin pixels values are high. It is supposed that the image quality and resolution is sufficient enough. The next step is to automatically separate the two regions representing skin and none-skin regions. We need to find the best two values where the R-G values for the skin pixels reside. We observed that all R-G values are relatively small except for the skin pixels. We used tanh() function to saturates all R-G values. We recognized that R-G values start increasing sharply at the skin boundary pixels to give tanh() value of 1 which means that R-G is about 20. So we picked a lower threshold value of skin R-G values to be 20. By practice, we found the upper limit to be 80. We used Matlab 6.1 running on 1.7 GHZ CPU with 256 MB of RAM. The following summarizes the skin detection process:
- acquire an image in RGB
- calculate R-G
- if 20 < R-G < 80 then R-G pixel is a skin otherwise non-skin

According to [13,15] most of the face databases designed for face recognition, usually contain grayscale images. Whereas collected images from WWW have properties that make them suitable for experiments [15]. So, we have chosen our test images to be from WWW and from different face databases to provide us with more generality [20-22]. Figure 1 (a-d) show the image of a human face before and after skin detection. This method can be used also with complex background as shown in figure 2 and figure 3.

3 Face and Eyes Locating and Tracking

After locating the skin region the largest object which is supposed to be the face is located. Its centroid , majoraxis and minoraxis lengths are determined. The best fitting ellipse is calculated. Objects with semi-skin color may be classified as skin objects which will produce some errors in the skin color classification process. In addition, the neck is not covered most of the time. To reduce the effect of these problems, some image properties can be used. First, the face is an elliptical. Second, the face will be most probably in the upper part of the human in a given image.

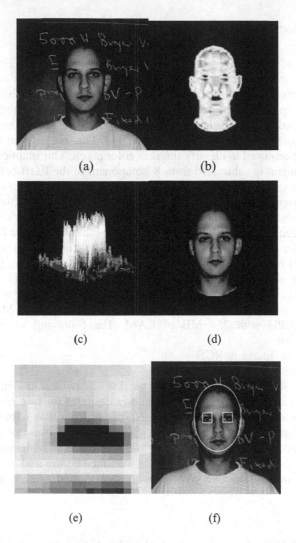

Fig. 1. Face locating. (a) original image. (b) R-G image. (c) R-G image in mesh style.(d) skin detection. (e) the used template. (f) face and eyes after detection

This is true for most of the applications that require skin detection. Also, there is a content relation between the height and the width of the human faces [1,19]. The centroid is then shifted a little upper which produce better ellipse fitting. The following summarizes the face locating steps:
  - connected objects are found
  - area, centroid, minoraxis and majoraxis are calculated for all objects
  - the object with largest area is the candidate face
  - centroid, minoraxis and majoraxis with the face's property that
    (majoraxis = 1.4 x minoraxis) are used for ellipse fitting

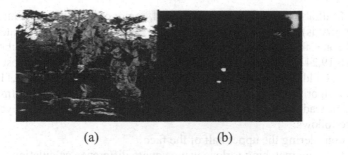

(a)   (b)

Fig. 2. Images with small areas of skin can be processed too. (a) original image. (b) image after skin detection where face and hand are at the center

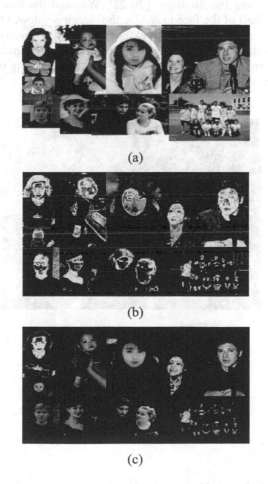

(a)

(b)

(c)

Fig. 3. Skin detection with complex background. (a) original image. (b) R-G image. (C) image after skin detection. Some detection errors can be seen

Simple MatLab functions such as bwLabel, regionprop(for area, centroid, majorAxis and minorAxis) were used in the above process. Once the face is located the next step is to locate the eyes. There are several methods which can be reviewed in [4,7,9,16,19,24]. Template matching is considered one the most famous one. However, building a good eye template is not a trivial step [3,4,7,10,11,16,24]. Using our R-G algorithm, we did not need to build our eye template form many sample images. Instead, one image is enough to manually construct a good eye template. The steps are follows:

- considering the upper half of the face
- template matching is done using square difference calculation
- the two minimas are the centers of the two eyes

Figure 4   shows the result of using this eye template and a larger template to locate the eyes of people using the databases [20-22]. We used the fact that the eyes are located in the upper half of the face to reduce the search window. Our simple method for face tracking is just to locate the best elliptical face as we briefly did then apply it for every frame. By this method the face will be tracked more rapidly and accurately. Figure 1 (e and f) show the template which was constructed using one image and the result of face and eyes detection.

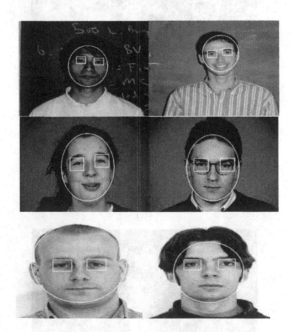

Fig. 4. Some people images after face and eyes locating

4   Results and Discussion

After applying our method to 67 faces images collected from [20-22], we reached more than 96% in face locating and 76% in eyes locating. Table 1 summarizes the results of the detection rate and average execution time of each stage. The execution time is very promising keeping in mind that we used MatLab which is an interpreted language. Butter results can be achieved by using high level languages such as C/C++. The detection rate percentage of face locating is measured simply by testing if the face in a given image is surrounded by an ellipse. For measuring the eyes locating efficiency, we calculated the number of eyes which were correctly located. Our test images have people with different skin tones. The experiments were successful with this all kinds of skin tones. Figure 5 shows the result of such experiment. For eyes location step, some methods are evaluated in the literature [3,4,8,13,16-17]. However, up to our knowledge, our R-G eye template is a novel method since only one R-G image is used. So, higher eye locating rate can be achieved by using more accurate eye template. In case of low or high illumination, our method does not work well except when the image is very clear. The effect of such illumination can be removed by some methods. However, it was proven that doing so will not produce improvements [23].

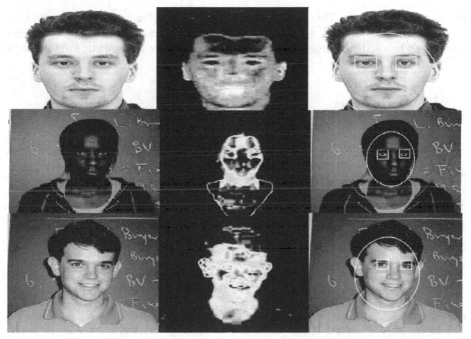

Fig. 5. Experiment of images with different illumination and people with different skin tones

5   Conclusion

In this paper we presented a simple and novel yet efficient method for human skin detection. This method depends on the R and G components of the RGB color space representation. Face in a given image was located using ellipse fitting after skin detection step. One image of a given human faces database was used to construct

Table 1. The experiment results showing detection rate and execution time for different face databases

	DataBase1 image size 175 X 143	DataBase2 image size 262 X 262	DataBase3 image size 528 X 416	Totals
Face DR	**100 %**	**97 %**	**90 %**	**96 %**
Eyes DR	**90 %**	**71 %**	**79 %**	**76 %**
Avg. time of skin detection (seconds)	**0.01**	**0.03**	**0.08**	**0.04**
Avg. time of face locating (seconds)	**0.05**	**0.10**	**0.42**	**0.19**
Avg. time of eyes locating (seconds)	**0.40**	**0.73**	**7.08**	**2.76**

primitive eye template. This template was used to locate the eyes of the human faces in the database. We think that our method is considered one of the best methods which can be used for large number of application since it eliminates the overhead pre-processing.

References

1. Araki, Y. Shimada, N. and Shirai, Y., Face Detection and Face Direction Estimation Using Color and Shape Features, Proc. of ICMA2000, pp. 351-355, Osaka, September 2000.
2. Sobottka, K. and Pitas, I., Extraction of Facial Regions and Features Using Color and Shape Information, Proc. 13th IAPR, pp. 421-425, 1996
3. Senior, A., Face and Feature Finding For a Face Recognition System, In Proceeding of the Second International Conference on Audio- and Video-Based Biometric Person Authentication, pp. 154-159, Washington D. C., March 1999.
4. Veeraraghavan, H. and Papanikolopoulos, N., Detecting Driver Fatigue Through the Use of Advanced Face Monitoring Techniques, ITS Institute, Report CTS 01-05, September 2001
5. Terrillon, J., David, M. and Akamatsu, S., Automatic Detection of Human Faces in Natural Scene Images by Use of a Skin Color Model and of Invariant Moments, Proc. IEEE Int. Conf. on Automatic Face and Gesture Recognition, pp. 112-117, Japan, April 1998
6. Kawato, S. and Ohya, J., Automatic Skin-Color Distribution Extraction for Face Detection and Tracking, ICSP2000 The 5th Int. Conf. on Signal Processing, vol. II, pp. 1415-1418, Beijin, China, August 2000
7. Ahlberg, J., A System for Face Localization and Facial Feature Extraction, Linköping University, report LiTH-TSY-R-2172, July 1999
8. Wu, H., Chen, Q. and Yachida, M., Face Detection From Color Images Using a Fuzzy Pattern Matching Method, IEEE Trans. Pattern Anal. Machine Intell., vol. 21, no. 6, pp. 557-563, June 1999
9. Vezhnevets, V., Face and Facial Feature Tracking for Natural Human-Computer Interface, Graphicon 2002, Russia, September 2002.
10. Yang, J. and Waibel, A., Tracking Human Faces in Real-Time, Technical Report CMU-CS-95-210, CMU, November 1995

11. Brand, J., Visual Speech For Speaker Recognition and Robust Face Detection, Ph.D. Thesis, Department of Electrical and Electronic Engineering, University of Wales Swansea, May 2001
12. Yang, J., Lu, W. and Waibel, A., Skin-Color Modeling and Adaptation, proc. of 3rd Asian Conference on Computer Vision (ACCV'98), vol. 11, pp. 687-694, Hong Kong, China, January 1998
13. Hsu, R., Abdel-Mottaleb, M. and Jain, A., Face Detection in Color Images, IEEE Trans. Pattern Analysis and Machine Intelligence, vol. 24, no. 5, pp. 696-706, May 2002
14. Yang, M., Ahuja, N. and Kriegman, D., Detecting Faces in Images : A Survey, IEEE Transaction on Pattern Analysis and Machine Intelligence (PAMI), vol. 24, no. 1, pp. 34-58, 2002
15. Jones, M. and Rehg, J., Skin Color Modeling and Detection, hp-labs, Cambridge Research Laboratory, June 2002.
16. Kashima, H., Hongo, H., Kato, K. and Yamamoto, k., A Robust Iris Detection Method of Facial and Eye Movement, VI2001 Vision Interface Annual Conference, Ottawa, Canada, June 2001
17. Wang, J., Head-Pose and Eye-Gaze Determination for Human-Machine Interaction, Ph.D. Thesis, School of Electrical and Electronic Engineering, Nanyang Technological University, Singapore, 2001
18. Zarit, B., Super, B. and Quek, F. Comparison of Five Color Models in Skin Pixel Classification, Proc. Of the International Workshop on Recognition, Analysis and Tracking of Faces and Gestures in Real-Time Systems, pp. 58-63, Greece, September 1999
19. Wong, K., Lam, K. and Siu, W., An Efficient Algorithm for Human Face Detection and Facial Feature Extraction Under Different Conditions, Pattern Recognition 34(2001) 1993-2004, 2001
20. http://www.cs.cmu.edu/afs/cs/academic/class/ 17651-f01/www/faces.html.
21. M2VTS Face database, http://www.tele.ucl.ac. be / M2VTS/
22. Psychological Image collection at http://pics.psych.stir.ac.uk
23. Shine, M., Chang, K. and Tsap, L., Does Colorspace Transformation Make Any Difference on Skin Detection?, IEEE Workshop on Application of Computer Vision, Orlando, Florida, December 2002
24. Yuille, A., Cohen, D. and Hallinan, P., Feature Extraction From Faces Using Deformable Templates, Proc. CVPR, pp. 104-109, 1989

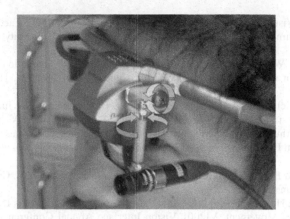

Fig. 1. HMD with a compact camera of the operation-support system.

We designed the transportable earth station so that non-technical staffs could manage the equipments in cooperation with a technician at a Hub station. However, it was not easy for non-technical staffs to treat the equipments they saw for the first time, though an instruction manual was prepared in detail. The main reason for that is to have few opportunities of training in advance. For now, we send out a technician to set up the equipments in preparation for satellite communications.

Providing users with instruction manuals on how to operate or repair an unfamiliar piece of equipment offers excellent prospects as an application for AR. The general purpose of a manual is to assist in learning how to use some product or device, or to illustrate a range of functional capabilities of the device. Recently, digital manuals that make effective use of multimedia content while improving searchability by means of link and jump functions have become increasingly commonplace. Taking the advantages, we believe that the operation-support system enables non-technical staffs to train the setting in advance and to treat the equipments, resulting in no longer being necessary to send out an expert technician on site.

2 Related Work

AR systems were developed first at a pilot project where they were used to train an industrial manufacturing process [9]. Exploiting ability to intuitively present information and potential to interactively manipulate what a user sees [10], AR applications have been extended across a wide range of different areas [11]. Especially since the ARToolkit has been developed [12,13], we saw widespread use of AR implemented into real-time interactive multimedia systems. The ARToolkit is a C/OpenGL-based open-source library, and has achieved high accuracy and stability of detecting and tracking objects with square markers using image processing.

AR is considered to be a promising approach to human-computer interaction in information presentation, and many researches have been done on how effectively the required information is accessed. There is a big issue on scene augmentation in assembly of a mechanical object from its components. An interactive evaluation tool has been developed for efficiently presenting annotations for assembly domain [14]. This research focused on assembly sequence to guide an operator through each step. However, the fixed sequence cannot manage situations without expectation. The concept of online-guided maintenance is introduced in order to cope with the varied situations [15]. The knowledge conditional on the machine type and its current state is conveyed to the maintenance site via a WWW link. Information is also sent back to the manufacturer on the machine status and the maintenance steps performed.

The need of an authoring tool for AR applications was pointed out in order to facilitate content creation and reproduction [16]. An AR media language (ARML) was proposed, so that application content can be authored without troublesome care of AR devices and data formats. In the assembly process, an authoring system of assembly instructor has been developed, which provides an intuitive way for authors to create new assembly instructions [17]. There is often a well-defined way for complex assembly such as hierarchical structures, and the process to find the way is also complicated. The authoring system allowed fast implementation and flexible reconfiguration of the composed elements.

Although AR applications have potential for human-computer interaction enhancing situational awareness of the real world, we have few empirical studies about its effectiveness. AR instructions in an assembly task have explored their effectiveness [18]. They showed evidence to support the proposition that AR systems improve the task performance, but more user studies are needed to confirm the potential. The task was based on assembly of Duplo blocks, but not to manage complicated equipments. We developed an AR instruction system for supporting operation of the transportable earth station, and made a simple user study for investigating properties of the developed operation-support system.

3   Design of Operation-Support System

3.1   Transportable Earth Station

The VSAT stations have been built on campuses, and the use is limited in the campuses. To dissolve the limitation, a transportable earth station was conceived in 1999 as a way to extend the network to outside the campuses. Fig. 2 (a) shows a photograph of the transportable earth station. The transportable earth station has the same basic functions and capabilities as the fixed VSAT stations. It can be transported anywhere and enables users to participate in the videoconferencing sessions with SCS. To support these basic functions, the van carries transmitting-receiving equipments, video coding machines, a GPS-based automatic satellite acquisition system, and cabling to carry audio, video, and control signals.

A number of tasks must be done before the transportable earth station can be used for satellite communications. The UAT (uplink access test) involves operation of the transmitters and receivers shown in Fig. 2 (b), and this requires some specialized expertise. Although there is a detailed manual available that explains the procedures, a technician is sent in order to do the testing on site. We need training in advance for making the appropriate settings and adjustments within limited time, but the training

12   Kikuo Asai et al.

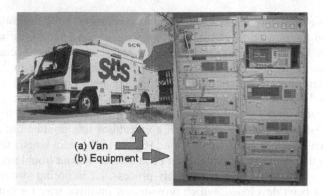

Fig. 2. SCS transportable earth station.

is quite difficult because it must be done only with printed manuals. This led us to develop the operation-support system that permits non-technical staffs to make the training and perform the UAT procedures by working together with a technician at the Hub station.

3.2 System Configuration

Fig. 3 shows a schematic overview of the operation-support system for the transportable earth station. Images of what an operator sees are captured by a compact camera and sent to a PC by way of the DV converter. The registered markers are put on the equipments of the transmitters and receivers, and each marker is detected in the video scene using ARToolkit. If the detected marker is found on the registered list, the marker identifies the piece of equipment. Once the equipment to be set up is identified, the appropriate instructions are presented to the operator through the optical see-through HMD. At the same time, the name of the equipment is stated out loud using a recorded voice to alert the operator and make sure he is working on the right piece of equipment. If the instructions require more than one page, pages are turned using a track ball. A thumb button turns a page forward and a forefinger button turns a page backward.

A compact camera is attached to the see-through HMD, as shown in Fig. 1. The camera can be adjusted on the two axes: up-down and left-right, so that the point where an operator looks matches that on the video presented in the HMD. The markers consist of a capital alphabetic letter followed by a number enclosed in a square surrounded by a black frame of 30 mm on each side. Any recognizable combination of characters or numbers would work, but we choose this particular scheme because the asymmetry makes it easy distinguish up and down. Each individual piece of equipment is distinguished by a unique alpha-numeric combination. When more than one marker appear in the same video scene, the one near the image center has higher priority.

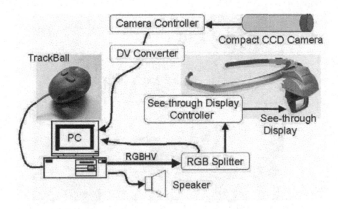

Fig. 3. System Configuration.

Pages presented to the see-through HMD are formatted in HTML, which has a great merit that a Web browser can be used for displaying information. The basic page configuration consists of three pages for each piece of equipment: precautions that must be taken before running the equipment, actual operating instructions, and a page pointing to the next piece of equipment to be operated. The documents of the instructions were based on an existent paper manual. The operator turns pages by clicking the buttons of the track ball. 28 markers were prepared for identification of the pieces of equipment.

3.3 Implementation

The software is functionally divided into a "Marker Recognition Tool" and "Display Application." The former uses ARToolkit as an image processing tool, and detect a marker identifying the piece of equipment. The latter uses a Web browser, and display the information that corresponds to the recognized marker.

Fig. 4 is a screenshot showing the information that is presented regarding the power meter. The documents are presented at the whole screen area of the see-through HMD without counting layout of the real scene. The marker number and the name of the equipment are shown up at the top of the page. The entire procedure is shown as green text, with the specific part to be acted upon highlighted in red. The operator can easily verify what equipment instructions are being displayed from the marker number.

Table 1 shows key specifications of the implemented camera and see-through HMD. The frame rate of the video is roughly 30 frames per second using a Pentium4 2.8 GHz PC with 512 MB memory. The see-through HMD simulates a 13-inches (diagonal) screen at a viewing distance of 60 cm and has a fixed focal point that is not identical with the real scene. It is also necessary to consider the illumination inside the van. A darker interior is better for displaying clear, legible text using an optical see-through HMD. However when the interior is too dark, then the camera images become less clear and marker detection and recognition accuracy diminishes. When the illumination environment is the same as that where the markers have been registered, no recognition error is observed at the viewing distance within 80 cm.

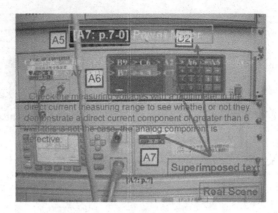

Fig. 4. Screenshot of information presented regarding the power meter.

Table 1. Specifications of video and see-through HMD.

Video camera	
TV scheme	NTSC standard
Effective pixels	768 x 494
Effective area	4.8 mm (H) x 3.36 mm (V)
Vertical operation frequency	59.94 Hz
Camera head weight	8 g (not include the hook)
Lens	Dia. 12 mm, f = 12mm
See-through HMD	
No. pixels	800 x 600
Vertical scanning frequency	60 Hz
HMD weight	75 g (not include the cable weight)

Since the content is written in HTML format, various functions and capabilities can be used when they are supported in the Web browser. The recorded voice in a supplemental role is generated speaking the name of the equipment out loud.

4   User Study

We conducted a preliminary experiment in order to investigate what properties the support system has on operation of the transportable earth station and to identify what functions and parts should be improved. In the experiment, the operation-support system is compared with a paper manual, assuming that the both are used for training of actual operation (Fig. 5). Most of people would think that operation training helps them treat pieces of equipment smoothly and have prospects for the actual operation. We made a subjective evaluation with a 5-step rating of the characteristics listed in Table 2 and open-ended comments on aspects of the operation-support system and the paper manual.

Fig. 5. Experimental setups: (a) paper manual and (b) operation-support system.

Table 2. Questionnaire.

Number	Item
1	It is easy to manipulate the instructions.
2	It has to accustom to the use.
3	The instructions are presented intelligibly.
4	You get accurate information.
5	You do not make a mistake.
6	You know what part you manipulate in the whole.
7	You search what you want.
8	You do not have strange feeling.
9	You feel fatigued after using the instructions.
10	Operation is enjoyable.

4.1 Method

Eleven adults (five women and six men aged 20-46 years) participated in the experiment. All the subjects had normal vision and no experience on operation of the transportable earth station.

On a trial with the operation-support system, a full-size picture of the pieces of equipment are presented in front of a participant, and a distinction marker is attached to each equipment in the picture. A participant views the pieces of equipment in the picture, obtaining information provided by statements superimposed with the see-through HMD and voice from PC speakers. The participant manipulates a trackball for scrolling and turning pages of the instructions. On a trial with the paper manual, on the other hand, instructions are presented with sentences and figures. A participant reads the sentences and sees the figures, obtaining information how to operate the pieces of equipment. The information contained in the instructions is basically the same between the operation-support system and the paper manual.

Six participants began with a trial using the operation-support system, and the others began with that using the paper manual. The participants were instructed to adjust position of the see-through HMD and direction of the compact camera, so that virtual imagery is accurately overlaid on the real world. Following the adjustment, the participants were instructed to see the full-size picture of the pieces of equipment and gaze a marker in the picture. They read statements in the see-through HMD and tried to understand what the statements meant. The trial with the paper manual was performed after the trial with the operation-support system. They were questioned about the usability immediately after finishing the trials.

4.2   Results and Discussion

Fig. 6 shows result of the questionnaire. The marks (A) and (B) correspond to trials of the paper manual and operation-support system, respectively. The value of the solid square is the average of the 5-step rating between the participants, and the length of the bar is the standard deviation. There is a statistically significant difference ($p<0.01$) between (A) and (B) at the item 10. The items 4, 8, and 9 have a trend toward significance ($p<0.05$). There is no significant difference at the other items.

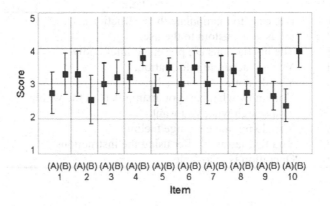

Fig. 6. Result of the questionnaire.

Based on studies of a relationship between spatial location and working memory [19], we expected that AR-based training system would be better in preparation than printed manuals, because users can remember the information tied in with the location of each piece of equipment. However, we did not observe any indication for the merit. It was too difficult for the participants to understand the contents in the operation instruction, and they had not even heard of names of the equipments. So the significant advantage in enjoyment (item: 10) in (B) comparing with (A) does not imply good presentation with the operation-support system but only curiosity about the see-through HMD, though the system may improve users' motivation for the training.

In terms of information acquisition (items 4 and 5), the trial with (B) received good scores. This is consistent with some open-ended comments that the operation-support system has good advantage for getting information of the equipment a user views. Moreover, we verified that it is very easy to go back and redo an operation or check a setting. We then expected that the operation-support system is good at searching for information a user would like to get, but there is no indication about searchability of information. One participant pointed out that it was difficult to search a location of the equipment that he would like to know, though the recorded voice worked well for identifying equipment and to urge caution in performing certain procedures.

The operation-support system lost scores in the items 2, 8, and 9. This is due to instability of displaying pages, that is, a user can get information of the equipment he/she views, but the head has to be fixed. Otherwise, the information presented at the see-through HMD has changed quickly based on the neighboring markers. Half of the participants reported necessity of function that a page is fixed during reading the instructions once a piece of equipment was identified.

5 Conclusions

We have described a developed prototype system for support of setting up and operating the SCS transportable earth station. The system not only simplifies running the equipment by freeing the operator's hands from having to hold and flip through a printed manual, it also facilities smooth operation by quickly presenting the exact information needed to set up and run the equipment and promises through the use of audible warnings to eliminate or reduce operational errors. This system will enable non-technical staffs to set up and run the transportable earth station by working with a technician located back at the Hub station but without having to dispatch an expert to the remote site.

Next we plan to conduct trials to assess how well the system actually works for running the transportable earth station equipment and further improve the stability and operability of the system. There are many kinds of precision instrument where there simply is no blank space on the instrument where a marker can be attached, so we plan to investigate alternative positional alignment methods that do not involve markers. The future work also includes agent installation that would make it possible to quickly present appropriate instructions for setting up and operating instrument when the status changes.

Acknowledgments

This work was supported in part by the Grant-in-Aid for Scientific Research (14580250, 15500653).

References

1.   R. Azuma, Y. Baillot, R. Behringer, S. Feiner, S. Julier, B. MacIntyre, Recent advances in augmented reality, IEEE Computer Graphics & Applications (2001) 34-47.
2.   S. Feiner, B. MacIntyre, and D. Seligmann, Knowledge-based augmented reality, Communications of the ACM, 36 (1993) 52—62.
3.   ARVIKA, Homepage: http://www.arvika.de/www/e/home/home.htm, as of Jan. 2004.

4.   A. Webster, S. Feiner, B. MacIntyre, W. Massie, and T. Krueger, Augmented reality in architectural construction, inspection, and renovation, Proc. ASCE 3rd Congress on Computing in Civil Engineering (1996) 913-919.
5.   H. Kaufmann, D. Schmalstieg, and M. Wagner, Construct3D: A virtual reality application for mathematics and geometry education, Education and information Technologies, Kluwer Academic Publishers, 5 (2000) 263-276.
6.   C. Stapleton, C. Hughes, M. Moshell, P. Micikevicius, and M. Altman, Applying mixed reality to entertainment, IEEE Computer, 35 (2002) 122-124.
7.   Space Collaboration System, Homepage: http://www.nime.ac.jp/scs/index_e.html, as of Jan. 2004.
8.   K.Tanaka, and K.Kondo, Configuration of inter-university satellite network "Space Collaboration System," IEICE Transactions on Information & System, J82-D-I (1999) 581-588.
9.   T. Caudel, aand D. Mizell, Augmented reality: An application of heads-up display technology to manual manufacturing processes, Proc. Hawaii International Conference on Systems Sciences (1992) 659-669.
10. R. Behringer, G. Klinker, and D. Mizell (Ed.), Augmented reality: Placing artificial objects in real scenes (1999).
11. H. Tamura, H. Yamamoto, and A. Katayama, Mixed reality: Future dreams seen at the border between real and virtual worlds, Computer Graphics & Applications, 21 (2001) 64-70.
12. H.Kato, M. Billinghurst, I. Poupyrev, K. Imamoto, K. Tachibana, Virtual object manipulation on a table-top AR environment, Proc. ISAR 2000 (2000) 111-119.
13. M. Billinghurst, H.Kato, M. Billinghurst, I. Poupyrev, The MagicBook: Moving seamlessly between reality and virtuality, IEEE Computer Graphics and Applications (2001) 2-4.
14. R. Sharma, and J. Molineros, Computer vision-based augmented reality for guiding manual assembly, Presence: Teleoperators and Virtual Environments, 6 (1997) 292-317.
15. H. Lipson, M. Shpitalni, F. Kimura, and I. Goncharenko, Online product maintenance by web-based augmented reality, New Tools and Workflow for Product Development (1998) 131-143.
16. U. Neumann, and A. Majoros, Cognitive, performance, and Systems issues for augmented reality applications in manufacturing and maintenance, Proc. IEEE VRAIS'98 (1998) 4-11.
17. J. Zauner, M. Haller, and A. Brandl, Authoring of a mixed reality assemply instructor for hierarchical structures, Proc ISMAR 2003 (2003) 237-246.
18. A. Tang, C. Owen, F. Biocca, and W. Mou, Comparative Effectiveness of augmented reality in object assembly, Proc CHI 2003 (2003) 73-80.
19. D. Kirsh, The intelligent use of space, Artificial Intelligence, 73 (1995) 31-68.

Real-World Oriented Access Control Method with a Displayed Password

Yuji Ayatsuka, Michimune Kohno, and Jun Rekimoto

Interaction Laboratory, Sony Computer Science Laboratories, Inc.
3–14–13 Higashi-Gotanda, Shinagawa-ku, Tokyo, 141–0022, Japan
{aya, mkohno, rekimoto}@csl.sony.co.jp

Abstract. Access control within a ubiquitous networking environment is a critical issue. Traditional access control methods have mainly relied on the authentication of registered users or devices, and security issues arise if visitors are permitted to use networked resources in an office and have accessibility to other resources. We propose a new access control method that uses frequently changing passwords which are displayed beside the resource. This method provides real-world-oriented access control over an internet without any need for special hardware such as sensors.

1 Introduction

Network infrastructure has been extensively developed and now provides a convenient computing environment. In particular, flexible network access is available through wireless network devices such as those based on IEEE802.11a/b/g or mobile phones. We can access the Internet from almost anywhere in our offices or homes, or even outdoors.

The extensive use of various wireless network devices has also created a complex network environment. The geographical proximity of computing devices is not always consistent with the network proximity. Somebody connecting to the Internet through a PC via an office LAN can also access the Internet through a mobile phone via a completely different network at the same time. Logical network topology can also be complicated. One's home PC can virtually participate in an office LAN over the Internet with Virtual Private Network (VPN) technology. Some VPN tools isolate a PC connecting to a remote LAN from other computing devices in its own LAN. We call such an environment an *intertwined network environment*.

Our need to be careful about security and access control can lead to some strange sources of inconvenience in an intertwined environment. For example, we do not want visitors to have access to all resources on our office LAN, though we may allow a visitor to print out a document with a local network printer. Typically, the visitor must ask someone in the office to print the data stored on his mobile PC, and this data needs to be printed from removable media such as a memory card, even if the visitor's PC is equipped with a network device or can access the Internet via a mobile phone. Another example is that sombody using a VPN tool to log-in to his/her office LAN from home has to close the connection to print out a document with a home network printer.

This inconvenience can be easily eliminated with a low-maintenance method that gives a user, especially a visitor, temporary permission to use the resource over the

M. Masoodian et al. (Eds.): APCHI 2004, LNCS 3101, pp. 19–29, 2004.
© Springer-Verlag Berlin Heidelberg 2004

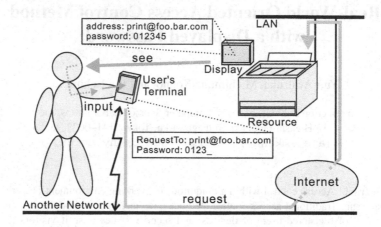

Fig. 1. Concept of ShownPass

global network. However, traditional access control methods are based on registration or network topology. Registration-based methods incur high-maintenance costs in the case of visitors since the system administrator must add and remove the user's account and password, or the MAC address of the user's terminal when the visitor arrives and leaves. Similarly, topology-based methods are not an effective means of providing visitors with partial access to network resources.

We propose a paradigm where access permission is given only to users who are physically near the resource. With visitors, we can usually assume that someone who is allowed to approach the resource should also be allowed to use it. This application of real-world context can be achieved without special hardware such as sensors.

We introduce a new low-cost location-based method of access control — called *ShownPass* — that uses a randomly generated and regularly changing password which is displayed near or on the resource. Any user who can *see* the current password can *use* the resource, even from outside the LAN. After a user leaves the resource's immediate vicinity, he/she cannot use the resource anymore because the password frequently changes. This paper describes the details of this method and its application. We discuss the method's characteristics, relation to existing methods, and extension.

2   ShownPass

Traditional access control methods on a network have mainly focused on authenticating the registered user or device. Another approach has been based on network topology. Both approaches have ignored the real-world context. However, this context can be utilized to impose natural restrictions on use of a resource, especially for temporary use in an intertwined network environment. In most situations, we can assume that anyone who is allowed to approach a resource should also be allowed to use it.

The use of information that cannot be accessed remotely, but can easily be accessed at the resource's immediate location allows us to verify that the user is near the resource.

We can install a local display that shows a randomly generated and regularly changing password on or near the resource. Any user who can *see* the current password can *use* the resource. He or she sends a request with the password to the resource, and the resource will process the request if it is accompanied by the correct password.

Note that the path used to transmit the request does not matter. A user can use a resource even from outside the LAN. When the user leaves the resource's immediate location, he/she cannot use it anymore because the password is frequently changed. Of particular interest is that the password, which would normally be hidden in other situations, is publicly shown and that is why we call it *ShownPass*.

ShownPass only requires a small area for the resource to display the password. Neither the resource nor the user's terminal needs any special devices such as sensors; thus many existing resources and terminals can benefit from ShownPass without having to be modified. Passwords are generated for each resource, so that access for one resource is independent of other resources. It is an easy and secure way to allow visitors to use limited resources in an office.

Password Long passwords are tedious for users to input. In addition, as passwords change frequently, they do not need to be long. Four to eight alphanumeric characters are sufficient for most situations. While an attacker may try all possible passwords after a password has changed, such an attack will be easily detected because the receipt of many requests within a short period will be exceptional for a resource with ShownPass. Moreover, to tighten security even more, a password can be invalidated unless the user physically operates the resource (e.g., pushes a button).

The user's terminal issues a request to the resource with the password. The password can be used in the authentication phase in the protocol, or be attached to the request as additional data. When the resource (or the server that manages the resource) receives the request, it checks the password. If the password is valid the request is processed, otherwise it is deleted. For added convenience, it is best to accept the previous password as well as the current password, because the password might change during the transaction.

Any error messages will appear on the resource and not on the user's terminal. This prevents an attacker from knowing whether the attack has been successful. Of course, a valid user at the resource can easily see the messages.

Application Area ShownPass is not an alternative to traditional authentication methods, but an additional option. ShownPass is a suitable way to provide a visitor with access for a limited time, allowing one-time access for tasks such as printing data or displaying a presentation document on a screen. A system administrator can easily allow visitors (who can access the Internet with their own terminals via a mobile phone or a guest segment) in a meeting room to access resources in that room, but without giving them access to resources outside the room. Traditional mechanisms to control such location-based access are costly. Our method also allows users to temporarily bridge networks which are logically separated because of use of a VPN tool.

Other access control or authentication methods can be used with ShownPass. Registered users may be allowed to use resources in the office without passwords through

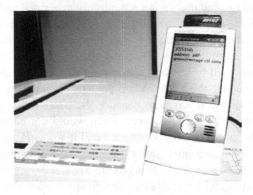

Fig. 2. Printer with ShownPass

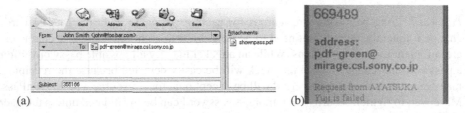

(a)   (b)

Fig. 3. Sending a Request with a Password (a) and the ShownPass Display Showing an Error (b)

terminals connected to a LAN. However, an administrator can also provide a resource that requires both registration and the ShownPass password.

Because ShownPass is based on the physical security around the resource it should not be used where anyone can approach it or have an unrestricted view of it. If a resource is highly protected to control physical access, ShownPass, especially when combined with other access control methods, provides a higher level of security. In such a case, the request itself should be protected by encryption.

3   Implementation

We implemented an e-mail-based ShownPass system. The system generates a password and shows it on a display. The user sees it and sends a request by e-mail with the password included in the subject field. The system checks the subject field in the received e-mail and if a correct password (either the current password or the previous password) is given, the system processes the request.

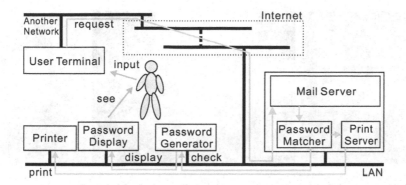

Fig. 4. Architecture for a Printer with ShownPass.

3.1 Printer Operation with ShownPass

Figure 2 shows a normal network printer with ShownPass (available in usual manner to other PCs on LAN), and the password is being displayed on an affixed PDA (PocketPC). The display also shows the e-mail address to which requests should be sent.

A user can print a PDF (Portable Document Format) document by sending an e-mail with the document as an attached file and the password on the display (Figure 3(a)). This password consists of six digits and is changed every three minutes. Error messages appear only on the display (Figure 3(b)), so that anyone trying to access the printer from a remote location cannot see the responses.

Figure 4 shows the architecture for the system. A mail server (qmail on a PC with Linux) invokes a password authentication program for every request that arrives. The authentication program communicates with the password manager, checks valid passwords, and then executes a printing program if the request is accepted. The password manager sends the current password to the display besides the printer. It also sends status messages (including error messages), if there are any.

3.2 Bulletin Board with ShownPass

Figure 5 shows another example application with ShownPass. It is a networked bulletin board, called ChatScape[1], which is installed in our office. Staff can post messages with still images from the ChatScape terminal on their PCs, and we also allow visitors to our office to leave messages with their mobile phones (the rightmost photo in Figure 5) or PCs if they are in front of the ChatScape wall display.

In this implementation, a user has to engage in a physical act to see the current password, while an e-mail address to send the request is always displayed. A set of vibration sensors is installed on the wall to detect and locate knocks on the wall[3]. When a knock is detected at a specified place, a password composed of four digits or an asterisk (*) or a hash mark (#) is briefly shown.

Figure 6 shows the architecture for this system. It is simpler than that for a printer, because ChatScape itslef manages the password. The user sends a message including a

Fig. 5. Networked Bulletin Board with ShownPass, and a Mobile Phone Posting a Message to It

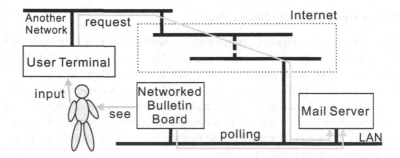

Fig. 6. Architecture for a Bulletin Board with ShownPass

photograph as an attached file. ChatScape checks its mail spool at a specified interval (shorter than the password alternation interval). A request with a valid password is accepted and displayed by the ChatScape terminal. A request with an invalid password is simply deleted.

3.3   Other Possible Applications

A networked display directly connected to an Ethernet or a wireless LAN would be a good application for ShownPass. A display in a meeting room can be used only by users in the room, without providing a separate subnet. The base station of a wireless LAN, such as an IEEE802.11a/b/g device, is another example. Transient wireless services for customers in shops can be easily enabled with ShownPass.

4   Discussion and Comparison

Separated Communication Line for Authentication   One of the key advantages of ShownPass is that a password can be transmitted to the user via a separate channel

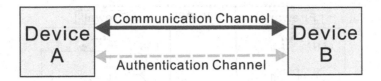

Fig. 7. Communication Channel and Authentication Channel

from the normal communication channel on which the request is sent. Such a combination of different channels produces a useful, intuitive, and secure user interface in a ubiquitous network environment or an intertwined network environment.

Figure 7 shows the new communication model we are proposing that ensures both usability and security[6]. An important feature of this model is that the authentication channel has physical restrictions representative of real-world conditions; e.g., device proximity. In other words, the authentication channel takes into account human factors. ShownPass is one application of this model where the authentication channel is highly dependent on the user.

The idea of transmitting a password or some identifying information via a separate channel has been used unconsciously by many people for a long time. For example, a reservation number is given when one uses an automatic telephone reservation system. Prize competitions on television programs that rely on conventional mail or telephone communication may require keywords that are announced during the programs. When strangers plan to meet for the first time in a public place, they often give each other some identifying information (brown hair, very tall, wearing a blue shirt, and so on) over the phone. Our model is a formalization of these traditional methods, and ShownPass is a new computerized application of these methods.

Encryption Our first prototype system did not use encryption so that it could work with existing terminals without the need for special software. In practice, if a request needs to be protected the user should use encryption techniques in addition to ShownPass. This is because ShownPass is not a data protection method, but an access control method for a resource. The password given by ShownPass, however, could be used as an encryption key. Of course, the password in such a case would then have to be sufficiently long to prevent cracking.

Automatic Password Alternation Some commercial one-time password generator pads (e.g., RSA SecurID tokens) provide passwords that periodically change. In this case, the pad and server are synchronized to generate the same password at the same time, so that the server can authenticate a user who has a valid pad. It can be considered a kind of virtual authentication channel established by sharing an algorithm to generate passwords, a seed of random numbers, a time, and so on.

ShownPass can be simulated with a one-time password generator pad system, by placing the pad besides the resource. The pad then represents the user's location, rather than the user who owns it.

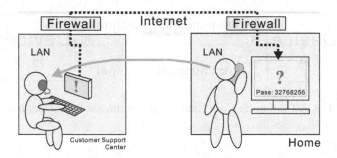

Fig. 8. Temporary Remote Access with ShownPass

Comparison with a Near-field Wireless Network An *ad hoc* network using near-field wireless communication media such as Bluetooth[4] or IrDA[5] can be used as a location-restricted channel for a resource. However, there are various problems with the solution.

First, it is usually difficult to control and recognize the range because radio waves are invisible and can go through walls. A user issuing an inquiry message may find many devices in addition to the one which he/she wants to use. With IrDA, the available range is quite limited so it is inconvenient for sending large amount of data. Second, there is still a registration problem because the user must be allowed to use the wireless infrastructure, and may not be allowed to use all the resources with near-field wireless communication media. A Bluetooth device would require a PIN (Personal Identification Number) code for security reasons. Third, both the terminal and resource have to be equipped for the same near-field wireless communication medium. This is possible, but in reality is often not the case. In addition, a near-field network itself is one of elements that compose an intertwined network environment.

However, ShownPass makes it relatively easy to control the area where visitors are allowed access, because it is based on visibility. A visitor can easily distinguish the resource that he/she is allowed to use, as there is a password display nearby. It can be used for many existing networking terminals and resources without the need for new or additional hardware. It is interesting that such location-restricted access can be achieved without a near-field network.

Moreover, the area can be flexibly extended via audio, video, or other media. For example, a user can allow another person who is talking with him/her on the telephone or through a video conference system (using dedicated communication lines) to print a document from his/her printer by revealing a password and an e-mail address.

This extendibility enables a secure remote maintenance service. A customer (who may be a novice user) can pass on the current password of his/her home network device to the customer support center by telephone (Figure 8). The support staff can remotely connect to the device with the password to service it. The support staff can be given only the limited access needed for maintenance, rather than full access. After the session, the staff cannot connect again unless the customer gives them a new password, because the password is automatically changed. Another important point here is that the ShownPass authentication process is easy for users to understand, so even novices users can confidently give such temporary permission.

On the other hand, a near-field wireless network can also be utilized as an authentication channel if its range is very limited. We have also developed a user interface system that selects a target to connect to based on device proximity[10]. We use an RF tag system to detect the proximity. Security related issues regarding this interface are discussed in another paper[6].

Control Related to Visibility Access control based on visibility is easy for an administrator to control and check, and it is intuitively recognizable by the user. An administrator can stop resource use by simply ceasing password generation or, more simply, hiding the password display. It is also easy to check the ShownPass status.

Interaction based on visibility also enables other intuitive user interfaces. For example, we have developed the Gaze-Link interface to enable intuitive selection of a connection target on network[2]. Gaze-Link uses a camera on a mobile terminal and a visual marker called CyberCode[9] on the connection target. A user wanting to connect his/her mobile device to a nearby device aims the camera at the target to see it on the mobile terminal. The target address is then retrieved from the ID of the CyberCode. In this process, the user does not need to know the network address or name of the target.

Physically Restricted Access The SpaceTag system[12] introduces access control based on the user's global location. That is, it allows access to local information related to a specified area only if the user is within that area. Commercial location-based information services utilizing mobile phones are also now in operation. These systems detect the user's global position by GPS (Global Positioning System) or the ID of the base station to which the user is currently connected. A ShownPass-like mechanism can be implemented on these systems. However, a global server will have to manage all location information to ensure the user's location is close to the resource.

Beacons carried by users[14] or installed in environments [11,7] and their receivers can be used to make up indoor positioning system. In this case a ShownPass-like system can be implemented by adding a password to the data to be transmitted.

Some real-world-oriented user interfaces, e.g., Pick-and-Drop[8] and media-Blocks[13], enable us to handle virtual data as physical objects. Such interfaces inherently control access through physical restrictions. Unfortunately, they cannot be applied to traditional terminals and resources without hardware modifications, and we have to consider the security issue when we want to transfer data between LANs.

Other Physical Restrictions A special device called a hardware key, or a dongle, is used to protect programs or data from illegal access. Lending a dongle to a visitor to access a specified resource is one way to place physical restrictions on temporary access. However, physically managing these dongles is difficult and costly. In addition, a dongle is designed for a specific platform and has a specific connector. For example, one for a parallel port on a PC cannot be connected to a PDA. A virtual rather than a physical key is used in the ShownPass system, so management costs are low and keys are adaptable to many kinds of terminal.

Variation of ShownPass There are many possible variations of ShownPass itself. For example, a password can be generated by a user or a user's terminal instead of a resource. In this case, a user has to input the password directly to a resource to be used, and send request data with the password via the network. While the physical condition is more restricted than in the case of normal ShownPass (because it requires not only proximity but also physical contact with the resource), a major drawback of this idea is that it requires every resource to have some sort of input device like a keypad.

5   Conclusion

The ShownPass system utilizes a real-world context to control access to a networked resource in an intertwined network environment without special hardware such as sensors. In this system, a locally viewable display for the resource shows a password, which is frequently changed, so that any user who can see the current password can use the resource, even from a (possibly mobile) terminal connected to a different network.

We have done a sample implementation using e-mail where even mobile phones could be used to operate the system without additional hardware. We have also tested the use of ShownPass in printer and networked bulletin board applications. As the use of networked electronic appliances continues to spread, the potential area of application for ShownPass will grow. We plan to develop other applications using ShownPass to further verify its effectiveness.

References

1. Y. Ayatsuka, N. Matsushita, and J. Rekimoto. ChatScape: a visual informal communication tool in communities. In *CHI 2001 Extended Abstracts*, pages 327–328. ACM, April 2001.
2. Y. Ayatsuka, N. Matsushita, and J. Rekimoto. Gaze-link: A new metaphor of real-world oriented user interface (in Japanese). *IPSJ Journal*, 42(6):1330–1337, June 2001.
3. Y. Ayatsuka and J. Rekimoto. Real-world oriented application with a simple knock location device (in Japanese). In *Interactive System and Software IX, Proceedings of WISS2001*, pages 191–196. JSSST, Kindaikagakusha, December 2001.
4. Bluetooth. http://www.bluetooth.com.
5. IrDA. http://www.irda.org.
6. M. Kohno, K. Cho, Y. Ayatsuka, and J. Rekimoto. A security model with user interface techniques for ubiquitous computing (in Japanese). In *Proceedings of Internet Conference 2002*, pages 43–51. JSSST, November 2002.
7. S. Long, D. Aust, G. Abowd, and C. Atkeson. Cyberguide: Prototyping context-aware mobile applications. In *CHI'96 Conference Companion*, pages 293–294, 1996.
8. J. Rekimoto. Pick-and-drop: A direct manipulation technique for multiple computer environments. In *UIST '97*, pages 31–39, October 1997.
9. J. Rekimoto. Matrix: A realitime object identification and registration method for augmented reality. In *Asia Pacific Computer Human Interaction 1998 (APCHI'98)*, pages 63–68. IEEE Computer Society, July 1998.
10. J. Rekimoto, Y. Ayatsuka, M. Kohno, and H. Oba. Proximal interactions: A direct manipulation technique for wireless networking. In *Ninth IFIP TC13 International Conference on Human-Computer Interaction (INTERACT 2003), to appear*, September 2003.

11. J. Rekimoto and K. Nagao. The world through the computer: Computer augmented interaction with real world environments. In *UIST '95*, pages 29–36, November 1995.
12. H. Tarumi, K. Morishita, M. Nakao, and Y. Kambayashi. SpaceTag: An overlaid virtual system and its application. In *Proc. International Conference on Multimedia Computing and Systems (ICMCS'99) Vol.1*, pages 207–212, 1999.
13. B. Ullmer, H. Ishii, and D. Glas. mediaBlocks: Physical Containers,Transports, and Controls for Online Media. In *SIGGRAPH '98 Proceedings*, pages 379–386, 1998.
14. R. Want, A. Hopper, V. Falcão, and J. Gibbons. The active badge location system. *ACM Transactions on Information Systems*, 10(1):91–102, January 1992.

Evolutionary Approaches to Visualisation and Knowledge Discovery

Russell Beale, Andy Pryke, and Robert J. Hendley

School of Computer Science, The University of Birmingham, Birmingham, B15 2TT, UK
{R.Beale, A.N.Pryke, R.J.Hendley}@cs.bham.ac.uk
http://www.cs.bham.ac.uk/{~rxb, ~anp, ~rjh}

Abstract. Haiku is a data mining system which combines the best properties of human and machine discovery. An self organising visualisation system is coupled with a genetic algorithm to provide an interactive, flexible system. Visualisation of data allows the human visual system to identify areas of interest, such as clusters, outliers or trends. A genetic algorithm based machine learning algorithm can then be used to explain the patterns identified visually. The explanations (in rule form) can be biased to be short or long; contain all the characteristics of a cluster or just those needed to predict membership; or concentrate on accuracy or on coverage of the data.

This paper describes both the visualisation system and the machine learning component, with a focus on the interactive nature of the data mining process, and provides case studies to demonstrate the capabilities of the system.

1 Introduction

In data mining, or knowledge discovery, we are essentially faced with a mass of data that we are trying to make sense of. We are looking for something "interesting". Quite what "interesting" is hard to define - one day it is the general trend that most of the data follows that we are intrigued by - the next it is why there are a few outliers to that trend. In order for a data mining to be generically useful to us, it must therefore have some way in which we can indicate what is interesting and what is not, and for that to be dynamic and changeable.

The second issue to address is that, once we can ask the question appropriately, we need to be able to understand the answers that the system gives us. It is therefore important that the responses of the system are represented in ways that we can understand.

Thirdly, we should recognise the relative strengths of users and computers. The human visual system is exceptionally good at clustering, at recognising patterns and trends, even in the presence of noise and distortion. Computer systems are exceptionally good at crunching numbers, producing exact parameterisations and exploring large numbers of alternatives.

An ideal data mining system should, we would argue, offer the above characteristics and use the best features of both the user and the computer in producing its an-

M. Masoodian et al. (Eds.): APCHI 2004, LNCS 3101, pp. 30-39, 2004.

swers. This leads us towards a system that will be interactive, in order to be flexible and capable of focusing on current interests. It should use visualisation techniques to offer the user the opportunity to do both perceptual clustering and trend analysis, and to offer a mechanism for feeding back the results of machine-based data mining. It should have a data mining engine that is powerful, effective, and which can produce humanly-comprehensible results as well.

The Haiku system was developed with these principles in mind, and offers a symbiotic system that couples interactive 3-d dynamic visualisation technology with a novel genetic algorithm.

2 Visualisation

The visualisation engine used in the Haiku system provides an abstract 3-d perspective of multi-dimensional data based on the Hyper system[7,8,9] for force based visualisation. The visualisation consists of nodes and links, whose properties are given by the parameters of the data. Data elements affect parameters such as node size, mass, link strength and elasticity, and so on. Multiple elements can affect one parameter, or a subset of parameters can be chosen.

Many forms of data can be visualised in Haiku. Typical data for data mining consists of a number of individual "items" (representing, for example, customers) each with the same number of numerical and/or nominal attributes. This is similar to standard dimension reduction methods used for solely numerical data such as Projection Pursuit [5] and Multi Dimensional Scaling [6], but applicable to data with a mix of nominal and numeric fields. What is required for Haiku visualisation is that a similarity can be calculated between any two items. The similarity metric should match an intuitive view of the similarity of two items. In most cases, a simple and standard distance measure performs well.

To create the visualisation, nodes are initially scattered randomly into the 3d space, with their associated links. Movement in this space is determined by a set of rules similar to the laws of physics. Links want to assume a particular length, determined by similarity between item nodes. They pull inwards until they reach that length, or push outwards if they are compressed, just as a spring does in the real world. Nodes repel each other, based on their mass. This whole approach can be seen as a force directed graph visualisation. This initial state is then allowed to evolve, and the links and nodes shuffle themselves around until they reach a low energy, steady state. The reasoning behind these choices of effects are that we want similar item nodes to be near to each other, and unrelated item nodes to be far away. The repulsive force between nodes is used to spreads them out.

The physics of the space are adjustable, but are chosen so that a steady state solution can be reached that is static - this is unlike the real world, in which a steady state exists that involves motion, such as we see in planetary orbits.

The system effectively reduces the data dimensionality to 3D. However, unlike traditional dimension reduction methods, there is no pre-defined mapping between the higher and lower dimensional spaces.

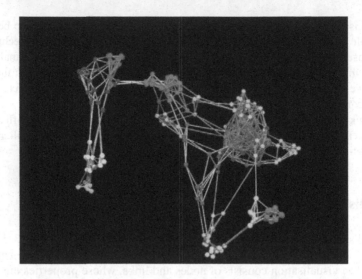

Figure 1. Nodes and links self-organised into stable structure.

Computationally, the process scales exponentially with the number of links, which is usually proportional to the number of data points. For small datasets (up to ~1000 nodes) the process can be allowed to run in real time. For larger data-sets there need to be a number of optimisations: only considering the strongest links, introducing locality of influence and so on.

2.1 Perception-Oriented Visualisation

The interface provides full 3D control of the structure, from zooming in and out, moving smoothly through the system (flyby), rotating it in 3D, and jumping to specific points, all controlled with the mouse.

Some typical structures emerge, recognisable across many datasets. These include clusters of similar items, outlying items not in any particular cluster, and internal structures within perceived clusters. For example, the data may be seen as divided into two main groups, both of which contain a number of sub-groups. Examples of data visualisation are shown in the case studies (Sections 4.1 and 4.2).

2.2 Interaction with the Data Visualisation

When features of interest are seen in the visual respresentation of the data they can be selected using the mouse. This opens up a number of possibilities:
- Data identification
- Revisualisation
- Explanation

The simplest of these (Data identification) is to view the identity or details of items in the feature, or export this information to a file for later use.

Another option is re-visualise the dataset without the selected data or indeed to focus in and only visualise the selected data. This can be used to exclude distorting outliers, or to concentrate on the interactions within an area of interest. Of course, we can data mine the whole dataset without doing this, the approach taken by many other systems. One of the features of the Haiku system is this interactive indication of the things that we are currently interested in, and the subsequent focussing of the knowledge discovery process on categorising/distinguishing that data.

A key feature of the system is that this user selection process takes full advantage of the abilities of our visual system: humans are exceptionally good at picking up gross features of visual representations[10]. Our abilities have evolved to work well in the presence of noise, of missing or obscured data, and we are able to pick out both simple lines and curves as well as more complex features such as spirals and undulating waves or planes. By allowing user input into the knowledge discovery process, we can effectively use a highly efficient system very quickly as well as reducing the work that the computational system has to do.

The most striking feature of the system is its ability to "explain" why features of interest exist. Typical questions when looking at a visual representation of data are: "Why are these items out on their own?", "What are the characteristics of this cluster?", "How do these two groups of items differ?". Answers to these types of question are generated by applying a machine learning component.

The interaction works as follows: First, a group or number of groups is selected. Then the option to explain the groups is selected. The user answers a small number of questions about their preferences for the explanation (short/long) (Highly accurate / characteristic) etc. The system returns a set of rules describing the features selected.

As an alternative, the classic machine learning system C4.5 [4] may be used to generate classification rules. Other data mining systems may be applied by saving the selected feature information to a csv file.

3 Genetic Algorithms for Data Mining

We use a genetic algorithm (GA) approach for a number of reasons. Firstly is that a GA is able to effectively explore a large search space, and modern computing power means we can take advantage of this within a reasonable timeframe. Secondly, one of the key design features is to produce a system that has humanly-comprehensible results. Rules are inherently much more understandable than decision trees or probabilistic or statistical descriptions.

Thirdly, the genetic algorithm aims to discover rules and rulesets which optimise an objective function ("fitness"), and manipulation of this allows us to explore different areas of the search space. For example, we can strongly penalise rules that give false positive in order to obtain rules that can be used to determine the class of new data examples. Alternatively, we can bias the system towards rules which indicate the typical characteristics of items in a group, whether these characteristics are shared with another group or not. In addition short rules are going to be easier to comprehend than longer ones, but longer rules reveal more information. Again, we can allow the user to choose which they would prefer by controlling the fitness function. Initially we might prefer short rules, in order to get an overview. As the Haiku system is interactive and iterative, when we have this higher level of comprehension, we can repeat the process whilst allowing the rules to become longer and hence more detailed.

We use a special type of GA that evolves rules; these produce terms to describe the underlying data of the form:

IF term OP value | range (AND ...) THEN term OP value | range (AND ...)

where term is a class from the dataset, OP is one of the standard comparison operators ($<, >, =, \leq, \geq$), value is a numeric or symbolic value, and range is a numeric range. A typical rule would therefore be:

```
IF colour = red & texture= soft & size < 3.2 THEN fruit = strawberry
```

There are three situations that are of particular interest to us; classification, when the left hand side of the equation tries to predict a single class (usually known) on the right hand side; characterisation when the system tries to find rules that describe portions of the dataset; and association which detects correlations in attribute values within a portion of the dataset.

The algorithm follows fairly typical genetic algorithmic approaches in its implementation, but with specialised mutation and crossover operators, in order to explore the space effectively.

We start with a number of random rules created using values from the data. The rules population is then evolved based on how well they perform. The fittest rules are taken as the basis for the next population, with crossover creating new rules from clauses of previously successful rules. Mutation is specialised: for ranges of values it can expand or contract that range, for numbers it can increase or decrease them, for operators it can substitute them with others.

Statistically principled comparisons showed that this technique is at least as good as conventional machine learning at classification [1], but has advantages over the more conventional approaches in that it can discover characteristics and associations too.

3.1 Feedback

The results from the GA can be fed back into the visualisation to give extra insight into their relationships with the data.. Identified clusters can be coloured, for example, or rules added and linked to the data that they classify, as in Figure 2.

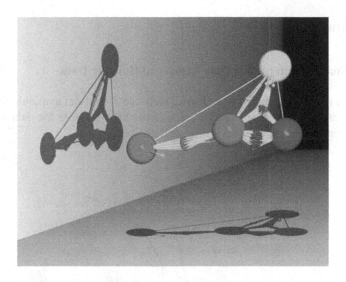

Figure 2. Rules and classified data

In this figure, rules are the large purple, fuschia and green spheres, with the data being the smaller spheres. The white links between rules serve to keep them apart, whilst the cyan links are between the rules and the data that is covered by the rule. The visualisation has reorganised itself to show these relationships clearly. We have additionally coloured the data according to its correct classification.

A number of things are immediately apparent from this visualisation, much more easily than would the case from a textual description. On the very left of the figure, one rule, the fuschia sphere, covers exactly the same data as the other fuchsia sphere, except it also misclassifies one green data point. But the rightmost fuchsia rule, whilst correctly classifying all the fuchsia data also misclassifies much of the other data as well. On the right hand side, the purple rule does well in one sense ; it covers all its data. However it also misclassified by matching some green and fuchsia data. The green rule at the top has mixed results.

It is interesting to note that as this visualisation depends only on the relationship between knowledge (e.g. classification rule) and data, it can be applied to a very wide range of discoveries, including those made by non-symbolic systems such as neural networks.

The system is fully interactive, in that the user can now identify different characteristics and instruct the GA to describe them, and so the process continues.

This synergy of abilities between the rapid, parallel exploration of the structure space by the computer and the user's innate pattern recognition abilities and interest in different aspects of the data produces a very powerful and flexible system.

4 Case Studies

4.1 Case Study 1: Interactive Data Mining of Housing Data

The Boston Housing Data [3] is a classic, well known dataset available from the UCI Machine Learning repository [2]. Haiku was used to visualise the data and the complex clustering shown in figure 3 was revealed.

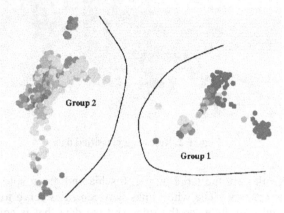

Figure 3. Selection of clusters

Two fairly distinct groups of data are visible, which show smaller internal features such as sub-groups. The two main groups were selected using the mouse, and short, accurate, classification rules were requested from the data mining system.. These rules are shown below:

```
Bounds_river=true -> GROUP_1
Accuracy: 100% Coverage: 43%

PropLargeDevelop = 0.0 AND 9.9 <= older_properties_percent <= 100.0 AND
Pupil_teacher_ratio = 20.2 -> GROUP_1
Accuracy: 94% Coverage: 83%

Bounds_river=false AND 4 <= Highway_access <= 8 -> GROUP_2
Accuracy: 100% Coverage: 77%

Bounds_river=false AND 264 <= Tax_rate <= 403 -> GROUP_2
Accuracy: 100% Coverage:69%

2.02 < Industry_proportion <= 3.41 -> GROUP_2
Accuracy: 98% Coverage: 13%

5.68 <= Lower_status_percent <= 6.56 -> GROUP_2
Accuracy: 96% Coverage: 75%

Bounds_river=false -> GROUP_2
Accuracy: 73% Coverage: 100%
```

This case study illustrates the following: The interactive visual discovery approach has revealed new structure in the data by visual clustering. We have used human visual perception to determine features of interest, and application of a data mining algorithm has generated concrete information about these "soft" discoveries. Together, interactive data mining has delivered increased knowledge about a well known dataset.

4.2 Case Study 2: Applying HAIKU to Telecoms Data

4.2.1 Justification
Massive ammounts of data are generated from monitoring telecommunications switching. Even a small company may make many thousands of phone calls during a year. Telecommunications companies have a mountain of data originally collected for billing purposes. Telecoms data reflects business behaviour, so is likely to contain complex patterns. For this reason, Haiku was applied to mine this data mountain.

4.2.2 Data
The data considered detailed the calling number, recipient number and duration of phone calls to and from businesses in a medium sized town. Other information available included business sector and sales chanels. All identity data was anonymized.

4.2.3 Call Patterns of High Usage Companies

Visualisation
   A number of companies with particularly high numbers of calls were identified. These were visualised separately to identify patterns within the calls of individual company.
   Figure 4 shows a clustering of calls from a single company. The most immediately obvious feature is the "blue wave" to the right of the image. This has been labelled "A". Also visible are various other structures, including the two cluster labelled "B" and "C"

Discoveries
   After identifying these features, we then asked the system to "explain" their characteristics. The following rules were discovered by the system, and translated into sentence form for clarity.
- All calls in group A are to directory enquiries.
    - Further investigation, selecting parts of the "blue wave" showed that the wave structure was arranged by hour of day in one dimension and day of week in the other.
- Within group B, about 70% of calls are to two numbers. 90% of allcalls to these numbers fall into the group B. Almost all of the remaining 30% of calls in group B are to another two numbers.

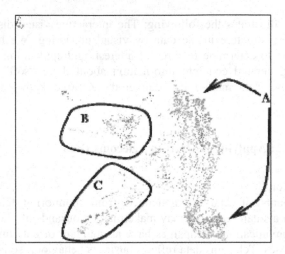

Figure 4. visualisation of call data from one site

- Most long distance ISDN calls are in group B. All but one call in the group has these properties. Most calls in the group are also charged at the same rate.
- About 80% of Group C calls are ISDN calls, and about 10% are from Payphones. About one third occur between 21:00 and 22:59, and about one half start at 15 minutes past the hour. Most are long distance calls. About 50% of the calls are very long, lasting between 8 and 15.5 hours.

For this dataset, Haiku discovers some very interesting facts about the calling patterns of a company. Notice that we can produce short, comprehensible rules that cover a significant portion of the dataset, which are intrinsically much more usable than detailed descriptions of 100% of the data. These insights can then be used by the company to optimise their phone usage, or, as for this study, to feed back to the telecoms company some concepts for marketing and billing strategies.

5 Conclusion

The Haiku system for information visualisation and explanation provides a useful interface for interactive data mining. By interacting with a virtual data space created dynamically from the data properties, greater insight can be gained than by using standard machine learning based data mining. It allows users to explore features visually, to direct the computer to generate explanations and to evaluate the results of their exploration, again in the visual domain. This combination of intuitive and knowledge driven exploration with the mechanical power of the learning algorithms provides a much richer environment and can lead to a deeper understanding of the domain.

Acknowledgements

This work was partially supported by grants from British Telecom, Integral Solutions Ltd and British Maritime Technology. Thanks to Nick Drew and Bob Hendley for their work on the visualisation parts of the system, and to colleagues for their comments and help.

References

1. Pryke, Andy (1998). Data Mining using Genetic Algorithms and Interactive Visualisation (Ph.D Thesis), The University of Birmingham.
2. Blake, C.L. & Merz, C.J. (1998). UCI Repository of machine learning databases [http://www.ics.uci.edu/~mlearn/MLRepository.html]. Irvine, CA: University of California, Department of Information and Computer Science
3. Quinlan,R. (1993). Combining Instance-Based and Model-Based Learning. In Proceedings on the Tenth International Conference of Machine Learning, 236-243, University of Massachusetts, Amherst. Morgan Kaufmann.
4. Quinlan, R. (1992) C4.5: Programs for Machine Learning", Morgan Kaufmann.
5. Friedman, J. H. and Tukey, J. W. , A projection pursuit algorithm for exploratory data analysis, IEEE Trans. Computers, c-23(9) (1974), 881.
6. T. F. Cox and M. A. A. Cox (1994). , Multidimensional Scaling., Chapman & Hall, London.
7. Hendley, RJ, Drew, N, Beale, R, Wood, AM. Narcissus: visualising information. *Readings in information visualization*. pp503-511. eds Stuart Card, Jock Mackinlay, Ben Shneiderman. January 1999
8. Beale, R, McNab, RJ, Witten, IH. "Visualising sequences of queries: a new tool for information retrieval." 1997 Proc IEEE Conf on Information Visualisation, pp 57-62, London, England, August.
9. Wood, A.M., Drew, N.S., Beale, R., and Hendley, R.J.(1995) "HyperSpace: Web Browsing with Visualisation." *Third International World-Wide Web Conference Poster Proceeding*, Darmstadt Germany, pp. 21–25; April.
10. Bocker, H.D., Fischer, G., and Nieper, H. 1986. The enhancement of understanding through visual representations, ACM Proceedings of the SIGCHI conference on Human factors in computing systems, pp. 44–50

Creating a Framework for
Situated Way-Finding Research

Nicola J. Bidwell and Christopher P. Lueg

School of IT, Charles Darwin University, Darwin, NT, Australia
{nicola.bidwell, christopher.lueg}@cdu.edu.au

Abstract. Preliminary themes to scaffold an investigative framework supporting human navigation from a egocentric (viewer-centered) perspective are described. These emerge from prototyping a mobile information appliance that supports, and is ecologically compatible with, human vision-based navigation and acquirement of spatial knowledge during movement through the physical world. The device assists a person finding his/her way from an origin to a destination by providing route information between images of landmarks, presented as they would be seen when walking rather than from an abstract map-type view. The use of the device in a foreign, built environment of the scale of a small university campus is illustrated and related to its use as a community authored resource. Emerging themes, such as the proximity, alignment and spatial separation of "ready-to-hand" landmarks, are discussed. Suggestions for further exploration are proposed and related to intersubjective and cross-cultural differences in communicating and using information for piloting navigation.

1   Introduction

A person in a foreign environment can often successfully navigate to a place by using information, communicated by a person more familiar with that environment, to pilot. Piloting refers to performing a goal-directed path using distinctive environmental features, or landmarks, in conjunction with an itinerary deduced from the spatial relations between current and destination locations [1]. Here, we discuss themes arising from our first endeavours in developing a mobile information appliance that supports, and is ecologically compatible with, human vision-based piloting and acquirement of spatial knowledge while walking through the physical world. The appliance assists a person finding his/her way from an origin to a destination by providing directions which refer to a viewer-centered, rather than an abstract, aerial, map-type, view of the surrounding environment. Supporting the user's natural predisposition for recognizing places and following paths between places helps circumvent some of the complexity issues associated with developing devices based on detailed three-dimensional spatial models of the environment, for example traditional virtual/mixed realities. Further, it affords the potential for a community authored resource in which the details of paths between places, provided by members, refer to a repository of images of landmarks.

M. Masoodian et al. (Eds.): APCHI 2004, LNCS 3101, pp. 40–49, 2004.

We present, for formative purposes, a scenario illustrating the motivations for our research and outline aspects of the ecology of human navigation situated in the real physical world. Next, we relate these to the design and testing of a prototype appliance which supports wayfinding from a viewer-centered perspective. We then discuss themes emerging from our preliminary field experiments and their implications for establishing an investigative framework for supporting human navigation by piloting. We conclude by indicating the future direction of our research.

2 A Usage Scenario

Fig. 1. Images presented by the way-finder with the instruction (a) When you get off the bus facing the big white building look LEFT; (b) Go up the steps between the two white buildings

Fig. 2. Images presented by the way-finder with the instructions (a) Go UNDER the link bridge towards the sun canopies; (b) Do NOT pass under the sun canopies, look RIGHT when you get to them

Peter Schroulig, a visiting professor, arrives at the only university in Australia's Northern Territory on the first day of his sabbatical. Equipped with a personal digital assistant (PDA) loaded with a digital way-finder, he hops off the bus at the university stop (Figure 1a). The way-finder contains a file, downloaded from the web site of his host Belinda Willco, comprising images of distinctive features of the university campus and its environs and route instructions for paths between them. Belinda created the file by customizing resources selected from a way-finding library authored by members of the university community. Peter selects "university bus stop" when prompted to enter his current location, consults Belinda's last email and enters "Belinda's office" as his destination. The way-finder instructs Peter to look to his left and presents an image of two large white buildings where the corner of one obscures the other and there are a few steps leading to a path in between. Peter looks across to his left to see the buildings which match those in the image (Figure 1b) and clicks "OK". The way-finder returns the instruction for Peter to ascend the steps and follow the path between these buildings. At the same time it presents an image containing, in the upper half, a mirrored overhead building link bridge in the foreground and, in the lower half, a white sun canopy further away. As Peter rounds to the left of the nearer white building he notices the link bridge, and behind it a sun canopy, so he walks towards the link bridge and clicks "OK" when under it (Figure 2a). The way-finder zooms into the sun canopy to indicate that he should proceed directly to it and instructs Peter to look right on reaching the sun canopy (Figure 2b).

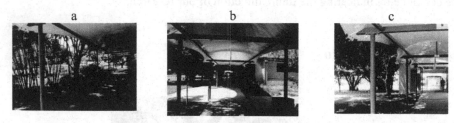

Fig. 3. Images presented by the way-finder with the instructions (a) Walk along the path UNDER the sun canopy; (b) Go PAST the blue wall to your right; (c) Go PAST the red pillars of building 22 and turn LEFT at the junction in the footpath

Peter proceeds, following and interacting with the wayfinder's series of instructions and images, he walks along the footpath beneath the canopy (Figure 3) until he reaches a junction. At the junction the wayfinder instructs him to turn left and presents an image of a building supporting a satellite dish in the background (Figure 4a) which enters Peter's view of the real world shortly after he has turned left. He passes the water feature corresponding to the next image (Figure 4b), sees an imposing link bridge ahead of him (Figure 4c) and walks towards its left hand side (Figure 4d).

Fig. 4. Images presented by the way-finder with the instructions (a) CONTINUE on the footpath with the satellite dishes to your right; (b) PASS the water feature to your right; (c) Go TOWARDS the large link bridge following the footpath you are on; (d) Go UNDER the right hand linked building

Once past the link bridge the campus becomes less dense with buildings and, with the wayfinder guiding his path, Peter clicks "OK" as he passes, to his far right, the sun canopy and some distinctive red buildings (Figures 5 a & b). The wayfinder indicates that when he sees the unusual "cyclone-proof" architecture of sciences he should be outside Belinda's office (Figure 5c). Peter notices the sign to his left denotes that the less imposing building close-by is "41", clicks "destination reached", enters the building and follows signs to Belinda's office in time for coffee.

a
b
c

Fig. 5. Images presented by the way-finder with the instructions: (a) Stay on the footpath PAST the sun canopy to your right; (b) Stay on the footpath PAST the red box-like buildings to your right; (c) The Science building is ahead to your right, you are now OUTSIDE Belinda's building

3 Research Background

People first acquire the spatial knowledge to navigate successfully from their direct experience of an environment rather than symbolically [2]. This knowledge allows humans to navigate transparently, without reference to symbols, canonical directions, or alignment with the Euclidean properties of the world (e.g. distance walked). Humans walking in the world draw upon allocentric (object-centered) and egocentric (viewer-centred) frames of reference from perspectives that are independent or relative to their vantage point, respectively. Unlike the extrinsic referents of maps these do not require orientation knowledge.

Mobile navigation at the scale of interest may be supported using landmark information alone or, together with route knowledge, for piloting. In navigation by landmarks salient distinctive visual cues at intermittent points along a route are used to determine both the path to the destination and current location relative to the path [3]. The importance of humans' conception of space as a collection of familiar landmarks has been shown phenomenologically [4], behaviorally, for example for newcomers to a city [5] and cognitively [6, 7]. Route knowledge requires spatio-temporally relating a specific sequence of landmarks (e.g. the steps taken to move between landmarks) into a chronotopic structure. People learn the order of landmarks in a route rapidly and earlier than the landmark's actual location.

Narratives of spatial layout suggest how frames of reference vary with the scale of a person's experience in the environment. People tend to describe groups of rooms and buildings in towns allocentrically by mental route and features of a room egocentrically by "gaze tours" with deictic references, such as "in front of" or "to the left of" [8]. In contrast, people tend to describe larger features of towns by "survey" using canonical direction terms (e.g. North, South). It takes significant time for people to configure a cognitive map [9] of their survey knowledge, not least because space on a larger scale requires longer exploration. This internal representation entails constructing a mental model of the interrelationships among places with extrinsic frame of reference. The mental model, which may be map-like [10] or conceptually more abstract [11] is imprecise and qualitative and requires association with landmarks to act as an index [1].

The majority of mobile navigation systems seem to focus on an extrinsic perspective and appear better suited to larger scale navigation or assisting a person with some familiarity with the location. For example, systems implemented as headmounted displays, such as WalkMap [12] or handheld devices, such as Cyberguide [13], pictorially represent the user's position on a map. Limited representations of an intrinsic perspective of the environment have been implemented in the mobile tour GUIDE [14] and Tourist Guide [15]. In these, digital images of key tourist attractions were used to relate a user's perspective to the extrinsic perspective map.

We propose a way-finder application which presents route information between images of landmarks, presented as they would be seen when walking. Relative and intrinsic, rather than extrinsic, perspectives of the environment appear better suited to the 50% of people preferring to memorise and use route information rather than maps [16] and more "ready-to-hand when situated in the context of walking. Relative or intrinsic representational perspectives would reduce the cognitive steps of transposing a person's mental model of their environment, based on their current perspective of the real world, to a map. They may also assist in circumventing current limitations of global positioning systems (GPS) [17]. Further, relative or intrinsic perspectives might allow use of the appliance in areas that are not yet covered by sufficiently detailed maps (e.g. Arnhem Land) or where extrinsic maps are limited by geographical constraints (e.g. vertical planes of canyons or in underground caves).

Combining images and route information may extend possibilities for sharing navigation information. Individuals in a community, such as university staff or students, could contribute navigation information by uploading to the web route information to their choice of destinations that relates to a local library of landmark images. Relative and intrinsic perspectives of the environment appear to be less prone to the intersubjective and cultural constraints of a map's symbolic traditions. Further, customization of the resource offers adaptability to cultural and language biases for egocentric or allocentric referents [18]. To our knowledge, understandings of landmarks to learn, apply and communicate navigation information have focused on the memorability of real [4] or computer-mediated environments [19] environments.

3.1 Design of an Exploratory Prototype

To develop an investigative framework for design we explored a prototype application *in situ*. The prototype, developed by the first author used MS Windows Explorer slide show viewer running on a HP Tablet PC TC1000 to present a series of images of landmarks each preceded by a textual route instruction. It was tested by the second author to navigate naturalistically Charles Darwin University's Casuarina campus.

The first author decided on a simple route, described here in the useage scenario, along footpaths to a building known to be a likely destination for the test author. Fifteen digital photographs of various features along the route were taken with a Kodak CX330 3.1 megapixels with 3x optical zoom using landscape adjustment. The features were chosen for seeming to be distinctive or at turning points in the route. Eight photographs were of proximal features, taken at distances of 5-15M, and of 2-4M in height, approximating to one storey of a building. Six of the photographs were of distal features, taken at distances 30-60M, of heights greater than 4M, such as whole large buildings. The remaining photograph was of a feature of 2-4M in height taken at a distance of 25M. The images were sequenced according to encountering their constituent landmarks along the route. A handwritten instruction of 8–16 words, captured using MS Windows Scribble Notes and created from memory of the route, preceded each landmark image (Figure 6).

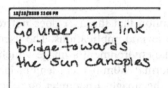

Fig. 6. Sample of route instructions preceding each image in the prototype

Both authors walked the test route together. The tester, who recently arrived at the University and had visited limited parts of the campus, used the prototype while the first author observed and avoided consciously hinting unless required. The discussions in this paper sprung from the observer's notes of tester's explanations of what he was looking at, thinking, doing and feeling while he navigated using the device using the think-aloud-protocol [20] and post-activity analysis and interpretation.

3.2 Themes & Design Implications from Experiences with the Tool

The prototype enabled the tester to navigate to the destination autonomously with the exception of two instances when the observer provided some guidance. Several important themes emerged which bear upon a research framework for situated navigation by piloting and prototype design and development.

Approximately half of the landmarks and their associated textual instructions adequately accounted for the dynamic nature of the tester's frames of reference afforded by the real world as he walked. These tended to be those landmarks which were in close proximity and/or ahead of him as he walked. Many distal landmarks (e.g. large buildings), particularly if aligned parallel to the route, confused despite instructions designed to compensate for this (e.g. Figure 5b). Even highly distinctive buildings at distance appeared "part of the background" (e.g. Figure 5c) and, like proximal landmarks positioned outside of the central region of the image, did not tend to draw attention and afford strong reference frames (e.g. Figure 3b)

The ready-to-hand characteristics of distal and proximal landmarks may relate to intersubjective differences, information paucity in images and the qualitative nature of landmarks in context. Gender differences, for example, may contribute since women (first author and developer of the prototype) take a wider view than men (tester) [21]. The absence, in still images, of cues humans use in the world may have differential affects on the ready-to-hand nature of distal and proximal landmarks. These cues may be visual, such as optical flow field, motion parallax and binocular disparity, or multi-modal, such as aural cues associated with different distances and substrates. Functionally more significant, in addition to physically larger, environmental features are prioritized for learning landmarks [8] and our experiences suggest this relates to what a person notices. While distal large distinctive buildings are indeed physically larger they appeared to have less functional significance for walking between landmarks. We expect this to differ between people, cultures and useage since characteristics of an environment are influenced by a person's schema of spatial context.

Designing with the assumption that the user does not re-orient his/her head from a forward looking focus has several implications. The user may still look at any 25° of the horizontal subtent of the environment's image which represents only 50% of the panorama captured by a normal, 50mm focal length, lens. Where possible the landmark should be central in the image. Encountering a person during our test yielded insights related to specifying regions in a visual field, for example spontaneous communication of a region using hand and body gestures to index specific landmark referents. A prompt, such as an arrow on the image, should direct the user's focus towards landmarks which are relatively small, at a peripheral position or at a height that differs from majority and are not transparently conveyed by the textual description. The system may be additionally advantaged by indicating the correlation between the navigator's own body orientation, for example from input from an integrated flux compass, with information on the camera's canonical orientation captured with the image.

Various observations suggest that the system should synchronously present route instructions, and other topographically relevant textual information, and its associated image. Frequently the tester read the instruction, responded by walking immediately and consequently nearly passed the position for the optimal correspondence between his real world frame of reference and the relevant image. Indeed, on occasion, he became confused and retraced his steps because he referred to the image only after his walking caused it to be obscured by some trees.

Predictability and consistency are salient design principles to support navigating real spaces. Our observations suggest that route instructions should include a metric between landmarks, such as how far apart they are. The landmarks used for our prototype were at irregular distances and were referred to non-relatively by rather parsimonious route instructions. This does not satisfy a user's apparent need to anticipate encountering the next landmark and may compromise trust in the device. For example, the tester interpreted a temporary lack of correspondence between his real world frame of reference and an image to be an error in the prototype rather than requiring him to take a few more steps forward. Various observations indicate that every turn should be associated with an image of a landmark, for example two particular turns were more complex when using the prototype *in situ* than anticipated.

Presenting topographically relevant textual information synchronously with its associated image is a design challenge when screen real estate is limited. The screen size of a Tablet PC, used for our prototype, has sufficient space for adjacently aligning or overlaying instructions on the image, however a PDA's 3.5" screen does not. Embedding hyperlinks in the image could be used to guide attention to the landmark feature and link to the appropriate information.

Our prototype illustrated the potential of several physical constraints in capturing and displaying digital images and sensory constraints in viewing digital images. Our observations support, in agreement with those in virtual environments [7], that landmarks need to be realistic if they are to be transferable to navigation in real places. Photographic images record light intensity and wavelength non-veridically and compress contrast. The majority of images rendered on the Tablet PC afforded a good match to the environment. However, in one image the white wall of a landmark was rendered blue, due to relative glare, and the tester hesitated when using the prototype. The standard 10.4" (resolution 1024 x 768) screen of the Tablet for our prototype was fairly difficult to see in the bright tropical sun and prevented the tester from using sunglasses. We are exploring the extent to which the limited resolution and field of view of a PDA further compromises correspondence between the image and real world.

There are several potential physical and functional contextual adaptation challenges in further developing our prototype. The image capturing and prototype testing shared many similar physical contexts. For example, they both had a similar time of day, weather conditions, seasonal features and numbers of people walking around. We noticed a number of landmarks that may not be visible at night and flora and fauna features that might significantly alter the real world image. The tester obediently followed the prescribed footpath and we did not explore the affect of detours, for example when encountering obstacles or seeking shelter against weather conditions. During the test we unexpectedly engaged, en route, with the person we intended to visit as a goal for the navigation activity. This yielded insights into the vulnerability of a user's ability to re-situate their navigation after a distraction.

Two diverse observations invite us to explore the complementarity between knowledge supporting navigation that is in situ and in the mobile appliance. Characteristics of route information communicated to a user should be compatible with permanent or temporary environmental information en route. On several occasions the tester observed opportunities for locational or semantic information, associated with a landmark, which would enrich the user's sense of orientation. For example, information on sign-posts readable from only one approach direction in the real world could be embedded in the application. This may be particularly useful in less autonomous or unified environments such as towns which contain mixtures of standard and idiosyncratic naming and signposting conventions. It is of interest to examine qualitative differences in landmarks in different environments. Characteristics of landmarks in a university campus, which has a relatively cohesive and homogeneous architecture engineered to support pedestrians, may differ from those in towns which serve diverse purposes and have evolved by gradual synthesis. Landmarks in a built environment, such as a university campus, which presents an image with a distinctive structure featuring places connected by paths and dominated by right angles may be qualitatively different from landmarks in natural environments.

4 Current & Future Work

We seek to elaborate an investigative framework to explore constraints in landmark based navigation which draws on ethnographically and semiotically informed approaches. Our work proceeds in parallel directions which focus on the nature of images of landmarks as communication tools and cross-cultural themes relating to support for piloting navigation. It seems to us that as a consequence these may also yield insights for cyberspace navigation.

To initiate our research in identifying dimensions in human-human communication of landmarks. we are using a race of "pilots and orienteers" as a situated protocol. The object is for the orienteers to follow a pilot's intended route, by using a sequence of photographs taken by pilots across a specified distance anywhere in the university campus. Orienteers will answer a standard set of brief questions, printed on the reverse of each image and record any additional observations. At the end of the way-finding race pilots and orienteers will discuss their experiences and observations.

The influence of intersubjective and cross-cultural differences on the nature and use of landmarks and route information is significant since spatial representations inherently combine both environmental and world order views. One investigative dimension relates to cultural biases in noticing, describing the environment and routes. Different nationalities vary in the richness of descriptions of sites along a route and route directions [22]. The preferential bias of different reference frames by various language communities [8] will influence route descriptions. For example, Australian Aboriginal, Mayan and Japanese languages have exclusively absolute, relative and intrinsic frames of reference, respectively. These investigative dimensions, coupled with the privilege of our own location, might provide opportunities for informing design. We are exploring mutually beneficial opportunities for harnessing alternative navigational strategies by our country's indigenous people. Aboriginal people's narratives of journeys, embedded in the land, seem to both enable navigating a vast continent and nurture specific superiority in locating position schematically and diagrammatically [23].

Acknowledgements

The Tablet PC was awarded to Charles Darwin University under a HP philanthropy grant. NJB expresses thanks to Peter Hall. CPL expresses thanks to Michael Twidale.

References

1. Golledge, R.G.: Precis of "Wayfinding Behavior: Cognitive Mapping and Other Spatial Processes." PSYCOLOQUY 10(36) (1999).
2. Schacter, D.L., Nadel, L.: Varieties of Spatial Memory: A Problem for Cognitive Neuroscience. Perspectives on Cognitive Neuroscience. Oxford, New York (1991)

3. Wickens, C.D.: Spatial Perception and Cognition and the Display of Spatial Information. In: Engineering Psychology and Human Performance. Harper Collins, NY (1992)
4. Lynch, K.: The Image of the City. MIT Press, Cambridge (1960)
5. Thorndyke, P.W.: Performance Models for Spatial and Locational Cognition. Rand, Washington DC (1980)
6. Siegal, A.W., White, S.H.: The Development of Spatial Representations of Large-Scale Environments. In Adv. in Child Dev. and Behav, Vol 10. Academic Press (1975) 10-55
7. Maguire, E.A., Burgess, N., O'Keefe, J.: Human Spatial Navigation: Cognitive Maps, Sexual Dimorphism and Neural Substrates. Curr Op in Neurobiology 9 (1999) 171-177
8. Taylor, H.A., Tversky, B.: Perspectives in Spatial Descriptions. J of Memory and Language Vol 20(5) (1996) 483-496
9. Tolman, E.C.: Cognitive Maps in Rats and Man. Psychol Rev 55 (1948) 189-208
10. Pezdek, K.: Memory for Items and Their Spatial Locations by Young and Elderly Adults. Develop Psych Vol 19(6) (1983) 895-900
11. McNamara, T.P.: Memory View of Space. *Psychology of Learning and Motivation* Vol 27 (1991) 147-186
12. Suomela, R., Roimela, K., Lehikoinen, J.: The Evolution of Perspective in WalkMap. Personal and Ubiquitous Computing 7 (5) (2003) 249-262
13. Abowd, G.D., Atkeson, C.G., Hong, J., Long, S., Kooper, R., Pinkerton, M.: Cyberguide: A Mobile Context-Aware Tour Guide. Wireless Networks 3(5) (1997) 421-433
14. Cheverst, K., Davies, N., Mitchell, K., Friday, A.: Experiences of Developing and Deploying a Context-Aware Tourist Guide: The GUIDE Project. MOBICOM (2000) ACM
15. Simcock, T., Hillenbrand, S.P., Thomas, B.H.: Developing a Location Based Tourist Guide Application. In: Conferences in Research & Practice in IT Vol 21 (2003).
16. Ohmi, M.: How Egocentric and Exocentric Information are Used to Find a Way in Virtual Environments? IIXth Conf of Artificial Reality and Tele-Existence (1998) 196-201
17. Flintham, M., Anastasi, R., Benford, S., Hemmings, T., Crabtree, et al.: Where On-Line Meets On-The-Streets: Experiences with Mobile Mixed Reality Games. Annual ACM SIGCHI Conference on Computer Human Interaction (2003) 569-576
18. Levinson, S.: Frames of Reference and Molyneux's question: Cross-linguistic Evidence. In P. Bloom, M. Peterson, L. Nadel and M. Garrett (eds.), Language and space (1996). MIT Press, Cambridge MA 109-169
19. Vinsen, N.G.: Design Guidelines for Landmarks to Support Navigation in Virtual Environments CHI Papers 15-20 May (1999) 278-285
20. Van Someren, M.W., Barnard, Y.F., Sandberg, J.A.C.: The Think Aloud Method: A Practical Guide to Modelling Cognitive Processes (KBS). Academic Press (1994)
21. Czerwinski, M., Tan, D.S., Robertson, G.G.: Spatial Cognition: Women Take a Wider View. ACM SIGCHI Conf on Human Factors in Computing Systems (2002) 195-202
22. Spencer, C.P., Darvizeh, Z.: Young Children's Place Descriptions, Maps and Route Finding: A Comparison of Nursery School Children in Iran and Britain. Int. Journal of Early Childhood 15 (1983) 26-31
23. Kearins, J.M.: Visual Spatial Memory in Australian Aboriginal Children of Desert Regions. Cognitive Psychology 13 (1981) 434-460

Extending Tree-Maps to Three Dimensions: A Comparative Study

Thomas Bladh, David A. Carr, and Jeremiah Scholl

Department of Computer Science and Electrical Engineering
Luleå University of Technology, SE-971 87 Luleå, Sweden
{tbladh, david, jeremiah}@sm.luth.se
http: //www.sm.luth.se/csee

Abstract. This paper presents StepTree, an information visualization tool designed for depicting hierarchies, such as directory structures. StepTree is similar to the hierarchy-visualization tool, Treemap, in that it uses a rectangular, space-filling methodology, but differs from Treemap in that it employs three-dimensional space, which is used to more clearly convey the structural relationships of the hierarchy. The paper includes an empirical study comparing typical search and analysis tasks using StepTree and Treemap. The study shows that users perform significantly better on tasks related to interpreting structural relationships when using StepTree. In addition, users achieved the same performance with StepTree and Treemap when doing a range of other common interpretative and navigational tasks.

1 Introduction

The most common visualization method used for file system hierarchies is the node-and-indentation style used by the Microsoft Explorer and Nautilus (Linux/Gnome) browsers. Tools of this type are well known and recognized by the vast majority of desktop computer users. But, they have well-known disadvantages. In particular, they do not give an effective overview of large hierarchies because only those areas that are manually expanded are visible at any one time. Also, because nodes are expanded vertically, they require a great deal of scrolling to view the entire hierarchy.

An alternative approach for visualizing file systems is the space-filling approach. This approach is employed in a variety of visualization types including tree-maps [10] and SunBurst [11]. The space-filling approach is more efficient at utilizing screen space than node-and-indentation style visualizations, which leave a large amount of white space unused. The space-filling approach is characterized by subdividing a window into parts representing the branches (directories) and leaves (files) of the tree. The area of these parts is often related to some attribute such as size, which can be aggregated. This approach gives a better overview of the entire hierarchy, especially for the attribute that is mapped to area.

This paper presents StepTree, a tool for displaying hierarchies that relies on the space-filling method and compares it to Treemap version 4.05 – an implementation of tree-maps available from the Human-Computer Interaction Laboratory (HCIL) at the

M. Masoodian et al. (Eds.): APCHI 2004, LNCS 3101, pp. 50-59, 2004.
© Springer-Verlag Berlin Heidelberg 2004

University of Maryland. StepTree is similar to Treemap in that it constructs space-filling displays using a rectangular technique, but differs from Treemap in that it employs three dimensions by stacking each subdirectory on top of its parent directory. The use of three-dimensional space is intended to more clearly convey to users the structural relationships of the hierarchy and gives StepTree an appearance similar to boxes laid out on a warehouse floor, as opposed to the two-dimensional map of rectangles commonly associated with tree-maps.

The rest of this paper is organized as follows: In the next section we discuss related work. This is followed by a more detailed description of StepTree in Section 3. In Section 4 we describe an empirical study of 20 users performing tasks with Step-Tree and Treemap. Finally, we summarize and discuss possible future work in Section 5.

2 Related Work

Shneiderman [10] describes a theoretical foundation for space-filling visualization of hierarchies, including some initial algorithms. Tree-maps are basically nested Venn diagrams where the size of each node (in relation to the whole) is proportional to the size of the file or directory it represents. Tree-maps display hierarchies through enclosure, unlike node-link diagrams, which display hierarchies through connections. Using the two-dimensional, space-filling approach is a clever and simple way of displaying a hierarchy as it allows the contents of an entire structure (or a great deal of it) to be viewed at once. Johnson and Shneiderman [5] offered a more user-centered view of tree-maps that introduced them as an alternative method for viewing large file systems. Their work also introduced basic usability issues requiring additional research. These included the general categories of aesthetics, interactivity, comprehension, and efficient space utilization, which cover topics such as: layout, filtering, zooming (including traversing the hierarchy), coloring and labeling of files. Turo and Johnson [12] presented an empirical study demonstrating the advantages of tree-maps. Their paper included an experiment analyzing 12 users performing tasks with tree-maps in comparison to the Unix tcsh shell, and also an experiment with employees at General Electric Network for Information Exchange using tree-maps on a product hierarchy as compared to using traditional financial reports. Tree-maps outperformed the alternative in both cases. Since their introduction, tree-maps have been used to visualize a wide range of hierarchical structures such as stock portfolios [7], tennis matches [4], and photo collections [1].

After the initial research, two problems remained to be solved. First, the original "slice-and-dice" layout method often presented files of the same size in vastly different shapes having the same area. This made comparisons of size problematic. Second, the flat layout often made it difficult to truly perceive the hierarchy.

A number of improved layout algorithms have been developed to present equal areas in nearly identical shapes. Bruls et al. [3] presents the "squarification" algorithm which packs each directory's rectangle as nearly as possible with rectangles of the same aspect ratio. Squarification uses a greedy approach beginning with the largest children. Figures 1 and 2 show the same data set using the slice-and-dice and squari-

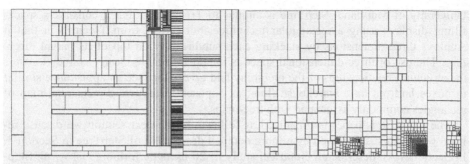

Fig. 1. Tree-map using slice-and-dice layout   **Fig. 2.** Tree-map using squarified layout

fication methods. Bedersen, et. al. [1] present "ordered" tree-maps, which use a family of algorithms based on recursive division of the rectangle into four parts where one is a "pivot" element. Pivots are chosen based on various criteria. Bedersen's paper also summarizes and compares other layout algorithms including quantum tree-maps that are designed to lay out image thumbnails of a standard size.

In order to overcome problems perceiving the hierarchy, van Wijk & van de Wetering propose a shading technique called "cushioning" [14]. Cushioning presents tree-map rectangles as pillows and shades them to enhance edge visibility. This makes the hierarchy more apparent. The SunBurst visualization [11] constructs a radial, space-filling display (Figure 3). It offers users an advantage over tree-maps by more clearly displaying the structure of the hierarchy. SunBurst layers the levels of the hierarchy successively so that the innermost layer corresponds to the tree root and the outermost layer corresponds to the lowest level in the hierarchy. A comparative study showed that SunBurst outperformed tree-maps in tasks related to structural interpretation (e.g., locating the deepest directory). Finally, utilizing the third dimension has been suggested as another approach to help users perceive hierarchal relationships. Two early, 3-dimensional, tree-map-like implementations are FSV [8] and VisFS [9], but neither has been experimentally tested for usability. StepTree was developed to act as a test bed for performing experimental evaluations on the benefits of 3D in tree-map-like graphs. Thus, StepTree follows the design of the Treemap application more closely than FSV and VisFS in order to reduce the number of variables that may alter experimental results.

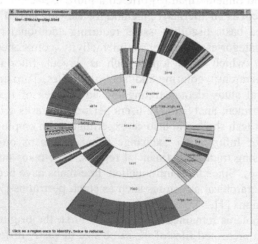

Fig. 3. SunBurst (courtesy of John Stasko)

3 The StepTree Application

StepTree is essentially a tree-map extended into three dimensions by the simple expedient of stacking levels of the tree on top of each other in 3D space. It utilizes the OpenGL API and was developed specifically for the display of file system hierarchies. It currently displays visual mappings of file system metrics such as file size; file and directory changes, and file type. StepTree is intended for use on traditional windows desktops and does not require any special hardware.

Figure 4 shows a screen from StepTree. In addition to size, the display depicts change history and file type. In the figure, files that have been modified within the last three years are solid. Directories that have not been modified are represented with wire frames while unchanged files are simply omitted. Directories containing modified files are also solid. File type is associated with color, a mapping that was fixed for the study and set as close as possible to that of the Treemap application.

StepTree was in part developed to investigate ways of enriching space-filling visualization so that size is less dominant. Often relationships depicted by mapping size to area come at the expense of all other mappings. As the areas of nodes tend to be linked directly to this relationship, some nodes may dominate the view while others may be completely drowned out. If one wants to display change, changes to small files are as important as to large files. A solution to this problem is the optional use of gradual equalization of sibling nodes provided by the layout algorithm (Section 3.1).

StepTree uses a "ghosting" technique to display modified files. If a file has been modified within a specified range, then the node is drawn as a solid. If it has not, it is either drawn as a wire frame (ghosted) or hidden. Ghosting unchanged nodes can be extremely effective, and hiding even more so when trying to spot changes to the file system. Modified files are effectively singled out. Changes are also propagated up in the hierarchy so that a directory is considered modified at the same date as it's most recently modified descendant. This is necessary as StepTree sometimes does not display nodes that are deep in the hierarchy in order to maintain good interactive response. Consequently, undisplayed files that have changed are represented by solid parent directories.

In adapting StepTree for the user study, we devised a new and more restrictive method of interaction with the 3D scene (Section 3.2), added a sidebar with a file type legend tab, a tab for dynamic-query filters, a tab for a traditional file system browser (coupled to the 3D tree-map), and a tab for settings. In addition labels were made translucent.

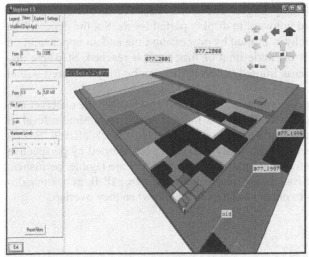

Fig. 4. StepTree

3.1 Layout and Labeling

The graph is laid out by a recursive function where the initial call specifies the root node of the file system subset and the coordinates and dimensions of the box for layout. This function then calls itself once for every child, placing child nodes as dictated by the squarification layout algorithm detailed in [3]. If equalization (redistribution of area), is enabled, it is applied before the node is actually laid out. The equalization step is followed by an "atrophication" step (size reduction of successive levels), in which the child nodes are shrunk to enhance level visibility.

Equalization is implemented in StepTree as a method of redistributing area from large nodes to smaller ones within a group of siblings. Equalization does not change the total area of the group. The equalization function is applied to all members in a sibling group, adjusting their size depending on the global equalization constant, ε.

$$v_{eq} = (1 - \varepsilon)v + \varepsilon\alpha \quad (0 \leq \varepsilon \leq 1) \qquad \text{(Equalization function)}$$

Where: v is the initial area of the child as a fraction of the area of the parent, α is the mean child area fraction for the sibling group, and v_{eq} is the equalized area fraction. Setting equalization to 1 results in a group where all nodes have the same fraction of the parent's area. Setting equalization to 0 results in no change in area distribution.

Small files and empty directories would not be visible without equalization or a similar redistribution function. Equalization, however, distorts the visualization. Two files of equal size might appear to have different sizes if they have different parent directories. Note that in our implementation, the equalization step is followed by an atrophication step where the area used by children is shrunk by a set fraction in relation to the parent in order to expose underlying structure. Both steps can be disabled. Equalization is but one of the many types of distortions that could be applied to a space filling visualization. Previous uses of distortion include, for example, the application of exponential weight functions to exaggerate size differences [13].

The final layout issue is to ensure adequate performance when rotating and moving in real time. While StepTree readily handles about 5,000 nodes on most machines, file systems are often considerably larger. Therefore, we were forced to introduce node pruning. However, we did not want to display partial levels. So, the depth of the displayed portion of the hierarchy is limited by processing time and an upper limit on the number of visible nodes. If the node limit or time limit is reached, StepTree displays a partial 3D tree-map that is limited to levels that can be fully rendered within the limits.

Labels in StepTree are implemented as text flags that always face the observer and always have the same size and orientation. This helps to ensure a minimum level of legibility regardless of how the visualization has been rotated. Labels affixed directly to the surface of the nodes are often arbitrarily truncated and distorted by perspective projection. In order to avoid a forest of labels where few labels are legible, permanent flags are only assigned to the root and its immediate children. All flags are translucent. Translucency also seems to make more labels legible when they overlap.

3.2 Navigation and Interaction

A common problem with 3D visualization is ending up with an unusable view, or as it is termed by Jul and Furnas [6], ending up lost in the "desert fog". This was a problem in StepTree's early versions where view navigation allowed unconstrained flight. The user would frequently navigate into an unfavorable position, be pointed in the wrong direction, and see nothing but a blank screen. From such a view it is difficult if not impossible to draw conclusions as to where to navigate next. To correct this, we elected to use object-centric manipulation of the 3D scene, treating the graph as an object to be manipulated and inspected. Furthermore, we limited the user's freedom to position the graph. It can be rotated around two axes, x and z, but limited to a maximum rotation of 160 degrees. Rotation is also constrained so that some part of the graph is always at the center of the display. The viewpoint's position on the (x, z) plane can be panned. Panning is also constrained so that some part of the graph is always centered. Zooming is accomplished by moving closer to or farther away from the graph along the y-axis and is limited by a set of distance bounds. This combination of constraints on rotating, panning, and zooming seems to have solved the desert-fog problem, but a user study would be required to make sure.

4 User Study

The primary motivation for our study was the relative lack of experiments comparing two- and three-dimensional visualization tools. In order to determine directions for further research on three-dimensional extensions to the tree-map concept, it is important to find out exactly what is the difference in user performance between two-dimensional and three-dimensional tree-maps.

4.1 Experiment Procedure

Twenty students in a Human-Computer Interaction class at Luleå University of Technology volunteered to participate in the experiment. Of these twenty students, one participant was later excluded because he is color-blind. A predetermined color palette was used with both tools, and we felt color-blindness might bias the results. The color-blind student was replaced by a member of the university's computer support group who is of comparable age, education, and computer experience. The participants were between 21 and 35 years old with an average age of 23.3. Most were in their third or fourth year at the university. They had used computers for an average of 10.5 years and currently used computers on average of 30 hours per week. All but one of the participants had 3D game experience averaging slightly less than one hour per week. All participants were right-handed; three were female and 17 were male.

The tests were conducted on a 1.7 GHz Pentium 4 workstation with 256 Megabytes of RAM and running the Windows 2000 operating system. Both Treemap and StepTree were run at a resolution of 1024 by 768 pixels on a 21-inch CRT. For the test, equalization was disabled as it is not available in Treemap, and atrophication was set to 10%. Participants used only the mouse.

The test leader conducted a tutorial session for each tool just before each participant performed the related tasks. Each tutorial session took approximately ten minutes to complete and was followed by a five minute, free-form exploration period during which each participant could try the tool and ask any questions. The actual test began after the five minutes had passed, or earlier if the participant indicated readiness. Before the test the timing procedure was explained to the participant.

Each task was first read out loud followed by the phrase "and you may start now" to indicate the start of timing. At this time the task in question was provided on paper, which was especially important when the task description contained complicated path information. Answers to questions could be given by pointing with the mouse and using a phrase such as "this one", or the answer could be given verbally by naming a file or directory. In addition, a challenge-response procedure was used when an answer was indicated. All verbal interaction and written material was in Swedish, the native language of all test participants and the test leader.

Each participant performed a set of nine tasks with both Treemap and StepTree. Two distinct, but structurally similar, data sets of about a thousand nodes were used. During each test the participant used the first data set with one visualization followed by the second with the other. The order of the visualizations and the mapping between data set and visualization tool were counterbalanced. The tasks were:

1.   Locate the largest file.
2.   Locate the largest file of a certain type.
3.   Locate the directory furthest down in the hierarchy structure.
4.   Locate a file with a certain path.
5.   Determine which of two given directories contains the most files including subdirectories?
6.   Determine which of two given directories is the largest?
7.   Name the most common file type?
8.   Determine in which directory the file I'm pointing at is located?
9.   a) Locate the largest file in a certain directory
      b) Locate the largest file of the same type in the whole hierarchy.

The tasks were chosen as a representative sampling of the types of perceptual and navigational problems a user might run up against when browsing a file system. Tasks were also classified and distributed evenly between the two broad categories of topological tasks and content-related tasks. Tasks 1, 2, and 6 are clearly content-related tasks while tasks 3, 4, and 8 are clearly topological – task 3 strongly so. The remaining tasks 5, 7, and 9 belong in both categories. Exact classification of tasks can be fuzzy. As the number of files grows, and they become more densely packed, one tends to perceive the pattern rather than the exact structural placement of each entity. Topology becomes content. Therefore for tasks 5, 7, and 9, we can argue for both interpretations.

4.2 Hypotheses

Our first hypothesis for the experiment was that Treemap, the two-dimensional tool, would be faster overall and result in fewer errors. This is mainly based on the assumption that the added complication of three-dimensional navigation would have significant adverse effects. In slight contradiction to this overall hypothesis, we hypothesized that the task with a pronounced topological component (Task 3) would benefit from the three-dimensional view, resulting in shorter task times and fewer errors when StepTree is used on this specific task.

4.3 Results and Discussion

Contrary to what we expected, we found no statistical significance in favor of Treemap for all tasks combined. An ANOVA on the effect of tool, tool order, data set, and data set order for total task times, showed $p > 0.05$ by a significant margin in all cases. We did, however, find a statistical significance for the effect of tool type on time ($p = 0.0091$), when we performed an ANOVA looking at the effect of the same factors for just Task 3. Users were in this case significantly faster when they used StepTree. The same test also found a significant effect for data sets ($p = 0.0153$), on task times for Task 3. This effect can be explained by the fact that the deepest directory in data set 2 is less isolated, and thus harder to pick out, than the one in data set 1. Error rates on task 3 also differed significantly ($\chi^2 = 14.54$, df $= 1$, $p < 0.001$), with the fewest errors being made when StepTree was used. Seventeen participants got this question wrong with Treemap, while only five participants were unable to complete this task correctly with StepTree.

Except for performance with Task 3, the performance on the tools was very similar (Figures 5 and 6.) It would seem that mapping depth in the hierarchy to height in the visualization is an effective method for visualizing the topological component of file systems. Users were both faster and less error prone using Step-Tree when looking for the deepest subdirectory.

We also noticed a much higher error rate for Task 7 on data set 1

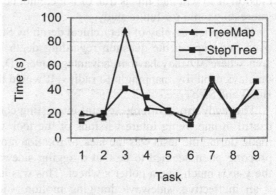

Fig. 5. Mean completion time (seconds) by task

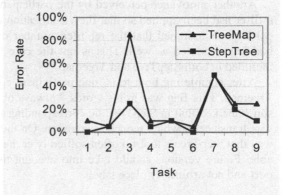

Fig. 6. Error rate by task

than on data set 2. In data set 1 the most common file type (gif) consists primarily of small files. As the participants were inexperienced with space-filling visualizations, many picked the predominate color and answered the question, "Which file type uses the most space?" This illustrates that both visualizations can be misleading and that a greater understanding of the visualization is required to correctly answer some questions.

5   Conclusions and Future Work

The equivalence of StepTree and Treemap on most tasks was unexpected, since 3D interfaces often result in longer task times. However, we may find an explanation for these results in that the interface used in StepTree was designed to be more restricting than traditional 3D interfaces. The limits imposed on zoom, pan, and rotation seem to have been effective in preventing users from getting lost. In addition, the fact that 19 out of the 20 users had previous experience playing 3D games may have helped equalize performance. The gap in usability between 2D and 3D interfaces may close as the average computer user becomes more experienced with 3D. While a clear conclusion as to whether this is true or not cannot be drawn from our experiment, it is an interesting topic for future study.

The explicit display of hierarchical depth by StepTree resulted in a clear advantage over Treemap on the question regarding depth in the hierarchy. This illustrates an area where 3D may have an advantage over 2D. However, SunBurst also explicitly displays depth by mapping it to radius. It would thus be worthwhile to compare Sun-Burst and StepTree.

The study group offered several interesting comments about StepTree that may be useful in improving future versions of the tool. One frequent complaint participants made during the tests was the lack of rotation around the y-axis (vertical axis). Their preconception seemed to be that dragging sideways should rotate the object around the y-axis much like a potter's wheel. This was indicated by the participant's actions – an ineffective, sideways dragging motion – just prior to voicing the complaint. Manipulation of this sort should be added in future versions of the StepTree software.

Another annoyance perceived by the participants was the lack of tight coupling. If a filter had been applied so that the visualization only showed ".gif" files, then many participants assumed that the reported number of nodes in the visualized directory had been updated as well. This is not the case in either application and should be included in both StepTree and Treemap.

After completing both tests, one participant complained about the tool-tip flag in Treemap. This flag was in his words, "always obscuring something". The same person remarked that in StepTree the corresponding flag did not appear immediately and was translucent, which reduced occlusion. On the other hand, a source of complaints was that StepTree's tool-tip often spilled over the edge of the screen and was unreadable. Future versions should take into account the physical dimensions of the view port and not arbitrarily place labels.

6 Acknowledgement

We would like to thank John Stasko for providing the SunBurst figure. Thanks also go to Carl Rollo for proofreading this paper. Finally, special thanks go to the anonymous participants who helped us in our study.

References

1. Bederson, B. B., Shneiderman, B., Wattenberg, M., Ordered and quantum treemaps: making effective use of 2D space to display hierarchies, *ACM Transactions on Graphics*, 21(4), Oct. 2002, 833-854.
2. Bederson, B. B., PhotoMesa: A zoomable image browser using quantum treemaps and bubblemaps, *Proceedings of the 2001 ACM Symposium on User Interface Software and Technology, CHI Letters 3(2)*, Orlando, FL, 11-14 Nov. 2001, 71-80.
3. Bruls, M. Huizing, K. van Wijk, J. J., Squarified treemaps, *Proceeding of Joint Eurographics and IEEE TCVG Symposium on Visualization*, Amsterdam, the Netherlands, 29-30 May 2000, 33-42.
4. Jin, L., Banks, D. C., TennisViewer: a browser for competition trees, *IEEE Computer Graphics and Applications*, 17(4), July/Aug. 1997, 63-65.
5. Johnson, B., Shneiderman, B., Tree-maps: A space-filling approach to the visualization of hierarchical information structures. *Proceedings of IEEE Visualization '91*, San Diego, CA, Oct. 1991, 284-291.
6. Jul, S., Furnas, G. W., Critical zones in desert fog: aids to multiscale navigation, *Proceedings of the 1998 ACM Symposium on User Interface Software and Technology*, San Francisco, CA, Nov. 1998, 97-106.
7. Jungmeister, W. A., Turo, D., Adapting treemaps to stock portfolio visualization, 1992, University of Maryland Center for Automation Research, technical report CAR-TR-648.
8. Richard, G. D., File System Visualizer (FSV), http://fsv.sourceforge.net, Jan. 2004.
9. Schmidt, H., Visual File System (VisFS), http://www.heiko-schmidt.info/project/visfs/visfs_de.html, Jan. 2004.
10. Shneiderman, B., Tree visualization with tree-maps: a 2-D space-filling approach, *ACM Transactions on Graphics*, 11(1), Jan. 1992, 92-99.
11. Stasko, J. Catrambone, R. Guzdial, M., McDonald, K., An evaluation of space-filling information visualizations for depicting hierarchical structures, *International Journal of Human-Computer Studies*, 53(5), Nov. 2000, 663-694.
12. Turo, D., Johnson, B, Improving the visualization of hierarchies with treemaps: design issues and experimentation, *Proceedings of IEEE Visualization '92*, Boston, MA, 19-23 Oct. 1992, 124-131.
13. Turo, D., Hierarchical visualization with Treemaps: making sense of pro basketball data, *ACM CHI '94 Conference Companion*, Boston, MA, 24-28 April 1994, 441-442.
14. van Wijk, J., van de Wetering, H., Cushion treemaps: visualization of hierarchical information, *Proceedings of INFOVIS'99*, San Francisco, CA, 25-26 Oct. 1999, 73-78.

Creative Expertise and Collaborative Technology Design

Linda Candy[1] and Ernest Edmonds[2]

[1]Key Centre of Design Computing and Cognition
Faculty of Architecture, Design Science and Planning
University of Sydney, NSW 2006, Australia
[2] Creativity and Cognition Studios, Faculty of Information Technology
University of Technology, Sydney, NSW 2007, Australia

Abstract. The paper is concerned with increasing our understanding of creative expertise drawing upon studies of collaboration between technologists and artists. The nature of expertise in collaborative creative work is discussed and the implications for support tools considered. Characteristics of a visual programming environment used to support collaboration in the development of interactive digital works are discussed. Such environments provide facilities for sharing representations between experts from different domains and in this way can be used to enable all parties to the collaboration to participate fully in the decision making process.

1 Introduction

Creative people with different areas of expertise frequently work together in professional practice. Enterprises such as film-making and building design and construction require groups of experts to collaborate in the creation of new ideas and artifacts towards the realization of the overall projects. This paper is concerned with increasing our understanding of both creativity and expertise drawing upon studies of creative collaboration between experts from different domains. Creativity is characterized as the invention of new forms that have not been represented or realized in any explicit way. We define *creative expertise* as the application of expertise to previously unidentified problems and the creation of innovative solutions to meet novel situations, in this case interactive digital artworks. We may say that someone possesses creative expertise when they are outstandingly good at finding new forms in a specific domain: for example, an artist might have creative expertise in painting or a software engineer might have creative expertise in object-oriented systems. The paper addresses two main issues: first, the characteristics of collaborative creativity between experts and second, the role of technologies in facilitating successful creative collaboration. In particular, we identify issues about Human-Computer Interaction (HCI) requirements of the software used in such work.

In the studies referred to here, small groups of experts from different domains worked together towards the realization of creative projects defined by artists. A specific focus of the paper is the role of technologists collaborating with artists in the creation of interactive digital works. The term *technologist* is used to designate the

M. Masoodian et al. (Eds.): APCHI 2004, LNCS 3101, pp. 60-69, 2004.

role of designer and implementer of the interactive tools, systems and installations. In the studies described, all the technologists were selected for their expertise in the development and application of various digital hardware and software systems for creative art, music and design. Each person also had a specific area of expertise that was essential for the particular project in which he or she was the primary collaborating partner: for example, expertise in sound analysis software or visual programming languages. The studies took place in the COSTART project (Candy and Edmonds, 2002a). Collaborations between technologists and artists were established initially on the basis that the technologist's role was to provide solutions to specific problems arising out of a proposal determined by the artist partner. Experts with specific skills areas were identified and matched to the people and their projects. It was discovered that the characteristics of experts best suited to working collaboratively in creative contexts extended well beyond having deep knowledge of the field, in this case digital technology. The expert as "solution finder", whilst highly appropriate for traditional consultation and advisory roles, has its limits when he or she ventures into the creative space as a "problem finder" with altogether different demands upon professional expertise. Whether collaborating about the design of an artefact or about a computer program to control an environment, the design intentions and options have to be made explicit and then shared amongst the team. Identifying acceptable ways of doing this is important. In the cases under consideration, software development was at the heart of each project: the representation used for that software and how it contributed to the sharing of ideas was critical to the progress of the work.

2   Practice-Based Research in Collaborative Creativity

In order to understand more fully the issues discussed above, a new approach to the creation of technology-based art was developed. Practice-based research involves two complementary and interdependent processes: innovative technology-based art projects are developed in tandem with observational research activities. The aim of the research is to acquire information that guides change in the existing situation but also to increase our understanding of creative practice and the requirements of future digital technologies. The aim of the practice, on the other hand, is to create new forms of art and technology systems for exhibition in galleries and public places as ends in themselves. The approach involves forming collaborative teams, gathering research data, collating and analyzing the results and disseminating knowledge on the basis of the evidence. The methods used are based upon ethnographic approaches and user-centered techniques. The research aims were to identify the key activities of the creative process and to understand the nature of collaboration in design and development of interactive technology. The artist residency, a familiar experience in the artistic community, is at the heart of the process. However, it is a residency that differs in a number of important respects from the conventional type. In order to maximize the opportunities for acquiring reliable evidence, the data gathering process must be transparent to the research team, all of whose members have significant roles in assessing the feasibility of the prospective studies, facilitating the conduct of the residencies and collecting primary data. The preparation of material is shared across the team and resulting information distributed where it is relevant to decision making. All participants, artists, technologists and observers, kept a daily record of events as they happened. Images and prototypes of work in progress were kept for reference and illustration. Experiences were recorded about what was proposed, discussed, carried through, what stumbling blocks arose, how they were addressed. Perceptions as to whether the ideas were workable, interesting, challenging were noted and whether the collaboration worked well or not. Reflections about whether the technical solutions worked well, or not, were recorded at the time and in follow up interviews and meetings. The many types of data about the activities and outcomes of the art-technology collaborations were assessed. Diaries kept by artists, technologists and observers were collated into a single transcription record for each case. Transcriptions of key meetings and the final interview were documented in a data repository as sound files and text records. The data was compiled and structured in chronologically ordered transcription records for each case. This provided the primary evidence for the extraction of features and descriptors of collaboration and was carried out by different analysts in order to arrive at independent viewpoints. The approach is described in Candy and Edmonds, 2002a.

3   Expertise, Creativity, and Collaboration

When experts collaborate, the incentive to do so may spring from different motivations. In many organizations, the expert's role is to provide a specialized contribution to a complex project in which there may be several other contributing disciplines. Experts identify potential problem areas and bring forward solutions to these in advance of the physical realization of the product. Being an expert implies having special knowledge that confers the status of an authority within a particular community of experts as well as the wider public. The expert is most often called upon to provide insight and analysis based upon an ability to draw rapidly from up to date and pertinent information that can provide appropriate solutions to specified problems. The expert is a specialist rather than a generalist and as such the expertise is based upon recognized strategies, skills and methods that have been developed and honed with experience. In the review by Glaser and Chi (1988), expertise is perceived to be domain specific and whilst experts are good at perceiving large patterns in their own domain and applying the knowledge very quickly, this is for routine work only. Hewett relates some of the known characteristics of expertise to that of the artist embarking on a digital work (Hewett, 2002). He points out that technology expertise involves finding efficient solutions to a given problem and this focus does not easily lend itself to the kind of open exploration that is important in creative practice.

When people collaborate, there is usually a significant degree of self-interest involved: there is a need for something they cannot supply themselves. If the collaborative project is complex and involves difficult tasks, it makes sense to collaborate with someone who possesses complementary knowledge and skills. In that sense, the very basis of collaboration is often *difference*: whilst the parties may both be expert in their own right, the expertise itself comes from different disciplines. Where the context is a creative one, the nature of the creative vision and aspirations play an important role in defining and shaping the role of the expert. Bringing expertise into a collaborative situation involves a process that is different to one of commissioning expertise as a specific contribution to a problem situation. Expertise as a consultative process may take the form of writing a report based on a single visit or series of visits which is then used by the commissioning parties to address the problems identified. Expertise in collaboration, however, involves the development of sustainable relationships between the participating parties as well as the contribution of domain knowledge and skill. In addition, expertise applied in creative contexts requires a degree of motivation and commitment that is intrinsic to the activity, as distinct from being driven by extrinsic factors such as financial incentives. Nickerson's recommendations for improving creativity could be applied equally to expertise (Nickerson, 1999). These are summarized as follows:

- Establish Purpose and Intention
- Build Basic Skills
- Encourage Acquisition of Domain-specific Knowledge
- Stimulate and Reward Curiosity and Exploration
- Build Motivation
- Encourage Confidence and Risk Taking
- Focus on Mastery and Self-Competition
- Promote Supportable Beliefs
- Provide Balance
- Provide Opportunities for Choice and Discovery
- Develop Self Management (Meta-Cognitive Skills)
- Teach Techniques and Strategies for Facilitating Creative Performance

3.1 Creative Expertise and Collaboration

In collaborative work, expert skills are essential contributions to the process and provide the basis for the choice of partners. However, where the work is also creative, those specialised skills, whilst essential for certain tasks, are not enough unless they are combined with other attributes. Being an expert in the conventional sense of the term, i.e. a specialist who has significant levels of knowledge about a well-defined domain, could be a negative thing for creative collaborative work if it operates in such a way as to inhibit contributions from the team. Where the project is of a creative and high-risk kind, expertise that is used to provide answers and solutions to given problems, must be combined with other kinds of personal characteristics. From the studies undertaken, we have identified a set of individual characteristics and other collaboration elements that are necessary for the effective conduct of collaborative creative projects (Candy and Edmonds, 2002b).

In the follow up studies referred to here, the technology experts were selected for their knowledge of digital technology that was applicable to creative work. The range of areas of expertise included design support systems, music analysis and production tools, sound and vision systems as well as a number of programming languages. They also had foundation skills ranging across a number of different disciplines: music, graphic design, product design, business etc. from which they had developed their interests in using and developing digital tools for creative purposes. Educational experience was diverse and no single subject discipline dominated. With employment and further education all were involved in migrating existing knowledge into new areas. Examples of issues that were identified are summarized below.

In one case, both collaborating parties had a high degree of background education, knowledge and experience in common and both were qualified in different areas of music with a mutual interest in electronic music. The technologist was also formally trained in classical music and was able to link music and technology through the skills developed in her music degree.

It was an important selection criterion that the technology collaborators were able to demonstrate openness about artistic work and, therefore, evidence of personal creativity was an important factor. The person who was, on the face of it, the least involved in creative work initially adopted a supportive but artistically detached, approach. That position proved to be hard to sustain and changed as the work developed and the technical challenges grew.

The processes of collaboration depended on the artist as well as the technologist and in some cases that encouraged more creativity on the part of the technologist than others. In one case, it was noted that the technologist felt concerned that his own creativity might be seen as interference in the artist's process. It was not clear, however, that the artist necessarily agreed. So in that sense, an opportunity for personal creativity in a collaborative team can be quite a complex issue.

It proved to be important to ongoing commitment for the technologists to be engaged in something they respected and enjoyed doing. All had different initial reactions to the artistic work itself. In one case, there was an explicit wish to have active engagement with the conceptual basis for the work from the start. In the other two cases, there was a growth of interest during the development process and a wish to be engaged with the ideas behind the work as well as its technical implementation. Where this was achieved there was greater commitment to the fulfillment of the project goals. In a certain sense, this implies a need for "ownership" of the project.

3.2 Creative Expertise and Learning

The ability to learn new techniques in very short time scales was important. The basis for that learning rested in existing skills that were readily transferable. Learning how to use a programming environment such as Visual Basic competently in a matter of two or three days was relatively easy for someone who already knew the C and C++ programming languages. This also applied to knowledge of software applications: for example, using two types of music analysis software could be combined quickly to support experimentation with ways of developing the synthetic language that was the main goal of the artist. These transferable skills were useful in finding practical ways of moving forward in order to progress difficult and ambitious goals. Being able to offer such skills facilitated exploration and discovery in the creative process.

A striking concern that is shared by all of the three technologists discussed here is having an opportunity to learn how to do something that has not been done before. Learning is a central motivator and projects that do not require it tend not to be very stimulating. It is not the case that having high levels of expertise precludes the need to learn something new. In the cases discussed here, the collaborative experience was often explicitly used to generate new problems or situations that brought with them the need to learn a new technique. Sometimes it was even the case that the unexpected, interventions of others, actually stimulated what was seen as the most interesting aspect of the work.

"...but the other interesting thing is that in Athens, without my knowledge the people who organized it put a video camera behind my head and projected it on my screen. And I thought – I didn't know this and I thought I'd played a really rubbish set I was really unhappy with it, the sound was terrible, in fact it did sound terrible it was a lot worse than anywhere else I'd played but the audience loved it, people even came round and said wow that was brilliant and it was because they could see the screen and they could see what I could see which was all the patterns shifting and all the things changing and I had a visual kind of representation of it and which I thought was interesting"

"Yes, so I'm hoping there'll be some new aspect to it.
I'm quite keen to learn something new as well.
You find out something new that's the exciting bit "

The unknown, the new and the challenging tasks seem to be the ones most likely to motivate the expert. In the cases reviewed here, it was the artist's tendency to generate such problems that often gave the collaboration its life and interest to the technologist. Learning new things is inherently interesting to the expert despite their presumed significant existing knowledge.

4   Collaborative Technology Development

In a majority of the COSTART case studies, new software was designed, implemented and evaluated as a collaborative activity between technologists and artists. Each residency project gave rise to an interactive artwork, performance or installation and in five cases, the Max/MSP visual programming language provided the basic software implementation environment (cycling74). The use of the Max/MSP environment enabled the artists, although often not expert programmers, to take an active role in the development of the systems alongside the technologists.

One issue for shared representations arises from the desirable practice of generating software prototypes that the user (in this case the artist) can evaluate. The prototype is typically not something that can or does evolve into the delivered system. It is built in a fast development environment that does not attempt to offer all of the functions or performance desired. Instead, it allows something that looks rather like the intended end result to be made quickly – and then thrown away. The issue is to ensure that a good looking prototype does not lead the user to believe that the work is largely completed when, in point of fact, it has hardly started. One approach is to use an evolutionary approach by working in software development environment that allows rapid change and also provides easy to read representations of the code.

The origin of Max/MSP is in electronic music studios and the forms used are quite easy to understand for musicians who have worked in that context. It turns out that artists working in visual interaction sometimes also find Max/MSP quite understandable without much training (Edmonds et al, 2003).

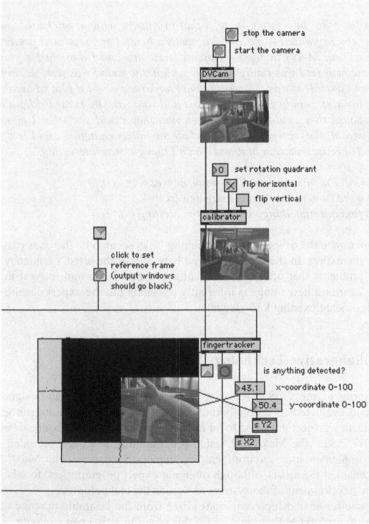

Fig 1. Part of the Max code for one of the artworks

When working with Max/MSP the process of software development is not defined by a linear sequence of distinct stages. Where particular stages can be observed, they are largely determined by separate technological processes. These, in turn, generate software tasks that can be developed in parallel. We also observed that, as the process of making art changed, there was a shift in the allocation of shared responsibility in that the artist was able to engage with technical processes and the technologist was able to contribute to previously aesthetic or artistic content. This sharing of knowledge and crossover of skills is one that can lead to innovation in both art and technology.

4.1 Characteristics of Max/MSP

Max/MSP is a programming system that is largely developed by its user community. It provides an open-ended framework for developing new objects that can be written in the C language. There are several communities of artists and programmers developing new objects, and, as new technologies and approaches to interaction arise, new objects find their way into these communities. It is in this way that Max both 'keeps up with' and contributes to a dialogue between the needs and interests of the artist-programmers and their tools. External and third party objects provide increasingly simple ways of doing complex tasks. For example, what might have been done with several more basic objects, can be achieved with one custom object. The developmental process is not only streamlined, but also the general vocabulary of the user community is extended. As is the case with open system environments, the user interface to this programming environment is largely developed by the user community itself.

Max/MSP provides the facility to integrate low-level system inputs with high-level visual programming tools so that a single software system can be used for the entire process. In the projects studied here, it facilitated the easy integration of separately developed components. In one residency project, the technologist concentrated on developing a system for aural manipulation while the artist concentrated on visual manipulation. When the whole system needed to be evaluated, these two components were easily linked by links drawn on the screen that defined a flow between the two sections. The graphical interface to the programming system was an important contributing factor to the projects.

Max/MSP not only supports but also encourages different ways of approaching technology-based art. It conforms to the needs of the artistic community where different and contradictory strategies are often nurtured. This attitude is especially evident in contemporary practices where emphasis is firmly placed on process as opposed to artifact. In one project, it became clear that Max was able to promote radical methods. Both artist and technologist felt that it removed the constraints of working within the 'top down versus bottom up' approach to making technological art, and in place of this opposition asserted a heterogeneous collection of methods. This is in contrast to a standard software design life cycle in which the user provides the client requirements definition which is carried out by the software development team, the results of which are then evaluated by the user, feedback given and a new version created in response to that feedback. Thus a much more intimate communication and highly iterative user-developer relationship is enabled by this kind of approach.

4.2 Shared Code Representations for Collaboration

In the cases described, Max/MSP, with its graphical representation, was seen to be helpful as a shared form to facilitate the collaboration. The software being developed could be discussed and considered in itself and its definition as well as in terms of simply what it put into effect. However, there is a disadvantage to the use of such shared representations. One of the technologists did not find Max/MSP a representation that gave him sufficient information about the details of what the computer was going to do. That was offered in a more acceptable way by languages such as C or Java. These languages, on the other hand, are quite inappropriate for using as shared representations in multi-disciplinary teams as we find here. Thus we see a tension between the preferred shared representation and the preferred technical representation. One answer, not explored here or more generally to any great extent, at this time, is to facilitate multiple views of the same code. One example that is somewhat in this direction and can be sited is the alternate views of html code in web development environments, such as Dreamweaver, where the user can switch between looking at the web page design, as it will appear to the user, and the code that generates it (Macromedia Dreamweaver). They may also see both views side by side.

During one project, a number of systems that were only obliquely related to his proposal were investigated. It was the discussions that ensued, though, which led to a clear understanding between both parties about, on the one hand, what was required and, on the other hand, what sort of things could be done. A note from the technologist's diary illustrates the process:

> "...after I showed him the ID Studiolab colour database thing we came back to that- a discussion of the people in a orchestra moving about according to some rules- when one moves that causes the others to move in response.
> In this case, it was possible to implement some parts of the newly emerging concepts as the week progressed and this helped the two parties to develop a shared understanding of, and a shared language for describing, the problem at hand."

The need for a shared language in support of collaboration has a very particular implication for complex projects that include significant software development. For the technologist, the implementation language is important and it, or something close to it, is treated as if it was also the description of the design of the system. The team, however, may need the code to be represented from different viewpoints in different notations for the different collaborators.

5   Conclusions

In the increasingly important area of technological expert involvement in creative projects we have seen that there are a number of important human-computer interaction issues that need to be considered. These issues arise primarily from the need to share ideas and potential problem solutions amongst a multi-disciplinary team. The paper has reviewed the issues on the basis of a set of studies of art projects conducted under experimental conditions and has pointed to a way forward in the development of support systems appropriate to such work. Characteristics of the Max/MSP visual programming environment used to support collaboration in the development of interactive digital works were discussed. Such environments provide facilities for sharing representations between experts from different domains and in this way can be used to enable all parties to the collaboration to participate fully in the decision making process.

Acknowledgements

The authors are indebted to the efforts, reflections and comments of the technologists and artists who participated in the second phase of the COSTART project. The work was partly funded by the UK Science and Engineering Research Council.

References

1. Candy, L. and Edmonds, E.A.: Explorations in Art and Technology, Springer Verlag, London (2002a)
2. Candy, L. and Edmonds, E.A.: Modeling Co-Creativity in Art and Technology, In Hewett, T. T. and Kavanagh, T. (eds) Proceedings of the Fourth International Conference on Creativity and Cognition, ACM press: New York (2002b) 134-141
3. Crabtree, A.: Designing Collaborative Systems: A Practical Guide to Ethnography, Springer-Verlag, London Ltd (2003)
4. Cycling74 Max/MSP: http://www.cycling74.com
5. Edmonds, E. A., Candy, L., Fell, M., Knott, R. and Weakley, A.: Macaroni Synthesis: A Creative Multimedia Collaboration. In Banissi, E. et al (eds) Proceedings of Information Visualization 2003, IEEE Computer Society, Los Alamitos, CA. (2003) 646-651
6. Hewett, T.T.: An Observer's Reflections: The Artist Considered as Expert. In Candy and Edmonds, Explorations in Art and Technology Ch13, (2002) 137-144
7. Glaser, R and Chi, M.T. H.: Overview, In Chi, M.T.H., Glaser, R. and and Farr, (eds). The Nature of Expertise. Erlbaum, Hillsdale, NJ (1988)
8. Macromedia Director: http://www.macromedia.com/software/director/
9. Macromedia Dreamweaver: http://www.macromedia.com/software/dreamweaver/
10. Nickerson, R.S.: Enhancing Creativity, In R.J. Sternberg (ed). Handbook of Creativity, Cambridge University Press, Cambridge, UK, (1999) 392-430.

Does DOF Separation on Elastic Devices Improve User 3D Steering Task Performance?

Géry Casiez, Patricia Plénacoste, and Christophe Chaillou

LIFL (UMR CNRS 8022) & INRIA Futurs
Université des Sciences et Technologies de Lille,
59655 Villeneuve d'Ascq, France
{gery.casiez, patricia.plenacoste, christophe.chaillou}@lifl.fr

Abstract. We investigated the use of a new haptic device called the DigiHaptic in a 3D steering task. Unlike other devices intended to interact in 3D with one end-effector, the DigiHaptic has three levers that the user may handle simultaneously or not in elastic mode to rate control objects. We compared it to the SpaceMouse - another elastic device - to evaluate the influence that degrees of freedom (DOF) separation have in terms of accuracy (coordination and errors) and speed (time). The task consisted of steering paths that required the use of two or three DOF simultaneously. We found that users performed faster on the SpaceMouse but were less coordinated and accurate than on the DigiHaptic for the most complicated paths.

1 Introduction

The majority of existing devices for three dimensional interaction have one end-effector that the user manipulates with his hand. They can be isotonic or isometric/elastic depending on their mechanical architecture. The latter are better for rate control rather than position control where the former are better, according to the experiments of Zhai [1]. For example, the PHANToM is an isotonic device that provides an intuitive interaction similar to everyday gestures through the manipulation of a stylus or thimble, and the SpaceMouse [2] is an elastic device to rate control objects in 3D.

Devices for 3D interaction with one end-effector are integral as it is possible to move diagonally across dimensions as defined by Jacob et al. [3]. Nevertheless the user has no individual control on each DOF. If the user moves the device in one particular direction, the pointer will not go exactly in that direction due to human limb limitations. Rice et al [4] observed that controlling six DOF with one hand is difficult. Some teleoperation systems, such as the Shuttle Remote Manipulator require two-handed operation: one hand for rotation control and the other for translation control. In the same way, can we improve 3 DOF devices by subdividing them in multiple lower DOF near fingers?

To evaluate DOF separation in 3D interaction, we have designed a new haptic device called the DigiHaptic proposing a novel interaction concept that consists of the separation and association of the degrees of freedom in an intuitive way to

M. Masoodian et al. (Eds.): APCHI 2004, LNCS 3101, pp. 70–80, 2004.

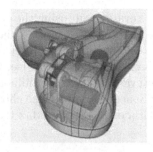 

Fig. 1. The DigiHaptic

three fingers [5]. The device comprises three levers associated with the thumb, forefinger and ring finger as illustrated in figure 1. Each lever is connected to a DC-motor through a thread to provide force feedback or simulate behaviors such as springs on levers [6].

Depending on the motor command, the DigiHaptic can be used in isotonic and elastic mode with force feedback, and in isometric mode. In elastic mode, springs are simulated so as to always return the lever to a neutral position set at equal distances of the lever boundaries. Considering that the user handles each lever over a 60° range, this give 4cm of movement amplitude. Moreover it is possible to adjust spring stiffness from low to high depending on the user preferences.

Although it is a separable device [3], the three DOF can be handled simultaneously. In each mode there is an isomorphism between fingers and object movements. Objects are translated according to the width of the screen (x axis) with thumb, the height of the screen (y axis) with the ring finger and the depth of the screen (z axis) with the forefinger[1]. As there is a direct relationship between the fingers and the object's movements, we hope to make the use of the device intuitive. Objects can also be rotated around the corresponding axis in rotation mode after pressing a switch on the device with the middle finger. In this paper, we only use the translation mode.

In the same way the keyboard is a device with multiple separated end-effectors and the way a person playing a shooting game like Quake uses it shows that separated DOF can be used if arranged in an intuitive manner. In these games the "w" and "s" keys are used to move the character upward and backward and the "s" and "d" keys to move the character left and right.

The DigiHaptic can be used mainly for navigation and manipulation tasks. Questions arise from its use, such as: Can the user coordinate the three levers simultaneously to perform a given task? Does the user perform better with individual control of each DOF?

---

[1] In this paper, we use the following convention (OpenGL convention): x axis is from the viewer's left side to the right side, y axis is the bottom up direction, and z axis is the direction the viewer facing

This paper presents here the DigiHaptic's evaluation (using the elastic mode) and a comparison to the performance of the SpaceMouse (another elastic device) in three dimensional steering tasks - where a user moves a pointer along a pre-defined path in the workspace. In this first evaluation of the device, we used the two elastic devices in rate control mode to evaluate only the influence of DOF separation on the user's performances. The SpaceMouse was also chosen because it is widely used in 3D softwares such as Catia or 3D Studio Max to control the camera position or to manipulate objects.

2   Method

2.1   Experimental Task

The task involved steering in a 3D workspace. In the experiments, subjects were asked to move the 3D cursor (ring or ball) to the beginning of the path and then to steer the path. Participants had to minimize the time elapsed between the beginning and the end of the path and were urged to adjust their speed-accuracy strategy so as to avoid going beyond the path boundaries.

There were three straight paths oriented in different directions we name respectively "A" (path from the front side to the back side), "B" (path from the left down front side to the right up back side), and "C" (path from the left up side to the right down side) and three representations for each path we name respectively "1" (thread with ring), "2" (empty tube with the ball), and "3" (filled tube with the ball) (fig.2). In all conditions, the cursor orientation was automatically oriented perpendicular to the path.

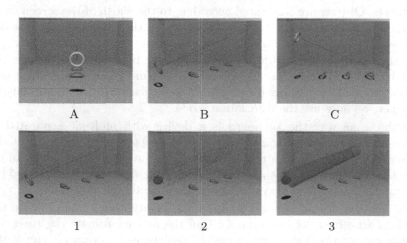

Fig. 2. The three straight paths (up) and the three path representations (down)

We wanted to start with easy paths before trying more complicated ones because subjects were not used to use 3D devices thus complicated paths would not have allowed us to distinguish between the influence of DOF separation and the influence of learning time. That is why we chose three straight paths. The paths orientation were chosen to manipulate two or three DOF on the device to compare if users performed worse with simultaneous use of three DOF than two DOF. The different representations were used especially to ensure that results do not depend on the representation of the path but depend only on the coordination effect.

The experiment was conducted with a desktop 3D virtual environment. In designing the 3D displays, several types of visual cues were chosen like linear perspective, interposition (edge occlusion), shadow of the 3D cursor and rings on the ground which help in the perception of the depth. Rings on the ground were placed at 33%, 66% and 100% of the path length to provide cues regarding the height of the path. We didn't want to use stereo-glasses in this experiment as we wanted to place the subject in natural conditions (computer desktop).

At the beginning of each trial, the 3D cursor (ring or ball) appeared at a random position in red. The subject was asked to bring it to the beginning of the path by matching the 3D cursor to a phantom and was helped by the straight line and the 3D cursor shadow represented on the ground. When the 3D cursor match the phantom, the subject start to steer the path.

During the experiment the phantom, represented in a gray transparency, indicates the last position of the 3D cursor within the tube before it exited the path. It helps the user to know where he has to return the cursor in order to continue in the case he exits the path (fig. 3). When the 3D pointer's center coincided with the path center, it became green. Then the further it went outside the path's center, the darker it became. It became black when it touched the path boundaries (contact) and red when outside the path boundaries (fig. 4).

Ring + thread	Ball + tube	Cursor color
		Green
		Black
		Red

Fig. 3. The cursor in red outside the path and its phantom in gray into the path during a trial

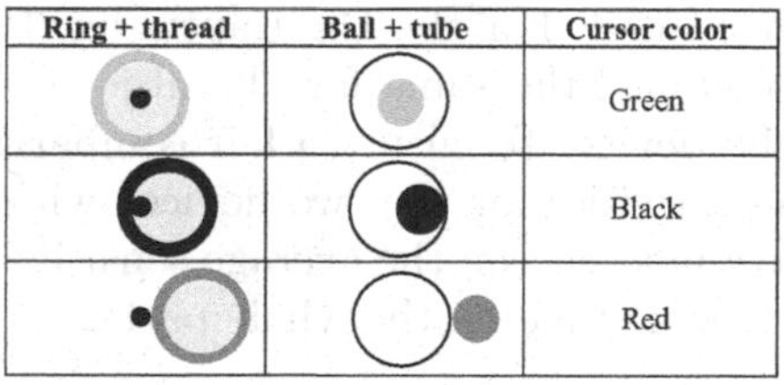

Fig. 4. Cursor colors depending on cursors positions

2.2   Participants

A total of 23 subject volunteers, all normal sighted participated in the study. Most of the participants (19) were right-handed and 4 were left-handed. There were two different groups randomly separated for each device. All subjects used their right hand on both devices. None of the subjects was familiar with the task being investigated or the interface used in this study. None of the subjects had prior experience with the input devices.

2.3 Procedure

The subjects sat in front of the screen at a distance of approximately 70 cm. Tests started after nine warm-up trials. The entire experiment lasted one hour for each subject. Each combination of path and representation was tested with 9 trials. The trials were presented randomly. A dialog box explaining the task was presented at the beginning of the experiment. Subjects were instructed to perform the task as quickly and accurately as possible.

The trial happens like described in section 2.1. The end of each trial was signaled with a short auditory beep and a dialog box indicating the remaining trials to perform. Subjects could thus take a short break before pressing a key to continue.

The number of contacts, exits, steering time, total path length covered and deviations to the path center were recorded approximately every 20 to 30 ms. For each trial, the recording started after the user placed the cursor at the beginning of the path. A between-group design was used in this experiment.

2.4 Apparatus

The experiment was conducted on an Athlon Windows 2000 running a custom-built Visual C++/OpenGL application. The display was a 21-inch monitor, set to 1024x768 resolution. Two input controllers were used: a SpaceMouse Classic and a DigiHaptic used in elastic mode. Both devices were operated in rate control mode. For the DigiHaptic fixed spring stiffness were set on each lever and remained the same for all subjects. No additional force feedback was used on the device. To ensure a fair comparison between the two devices, we tuned the sensitivities for the two devices with two experimented users on each of them. We have chosen the average sensitivity for each device which leads to the lowest steering time on the whole paths.

3 Results and Discussion

3.1 Steering Time

In this steering task experiment, we wish to compare the steering time to the index of difficulty of the path. The mechanics of 2D steering have been studied extensively by Accot and Zhai (e.g.[7,8,9]), who showed that performance can be predicted by an extension to Fitts' Law called the Steering Law [7]. The Steering Law relates completion time to two factors: the length and width of the path. The performance equation is:

$$T = a + b \frac{A}{W} \tag{1}$$

Where T is the completion time, a and b are constants, A is the length of the path, and W is its width. The constants allow consideration of the shape of the path (e.g. circular paths have higher constants than straight paths). The steering law has been shown to accurately predict completion time over several path types, input devices, and task scales. $\frac{A}{W}$ represents the index of difficulty of the path (ID).

Finally, by analogy to Fitts' law, the index of performance IP in a steering task is defined by $IP = 1/b$. This result is usually used for comparing steering performance between different experimental conditions.

The index of difficulty depends on the path and its representation. The ID was calculated by the ratio between the path length (A) and the width (W) (Table 1). W was the path width effectively available for maneuvering. All the lengths taken correspond to the effective dimensions of objects in OpenGL units.

Table 1. Table with the ID for each path and representation

	1	2	3
A	77	12	12
B	100	15	15
C	72	11	11

For each path, the IDs are equal for the second and third representations as the tube and ball diameters are identical. In the first representation, the ring's internal diameter is lower than the ball diameter, which explains the higher ID.

Inevitably participants sometimes stray beyond the specified boundaries. In Zhai's original work all trials with errors were disregarded, which is clearly sub-optimal as it disregards what users were not able to do. If we compare a fast and unreliable device with a slow and reliable device and just use movement times, the outcome unreliable device will always win if we take only into account the correct trials, yet nobody can achieve anything with it. In the experiment, when the user exits the path, he has to bring back the cursor where he exited which gives a time penalty. So we used all trials to test the steering law.

For the DigiHaptic, the steering law proved to hold at all representations with very good regression fitness. The models for steering time were for each representation (in ms) (2)(3)(4).

$$1 : T = -68174 + 1110 \times ID \quad r^2 = 0.999 \tag{2}$$

$$2 : T = -61416 + 6521 \times ID \quad r^2 = 0.999 \tag{3}$$

$$3 : T = -58621 + 6277 \times ID \quad r^2 = 0.999 \tag{4}$$

As a result, the time performance for the DigiHaptic is the highest for the ring and thread (representation "1") while the two other representations are equivalent. Another point is that paths requiring the use of 2 DOF ("A" and "C" paths) or 3 DOF ("B" path) are consistent in steering time compared to the ID of the path. i.e. using two or three fingers has no influence on the steering time. This represents the same difficulty for the user.

For the SpaceMouse, the steering law does not hold for all representations and it is surprising (5)(6)(7). To investigate why, we will compute the coordination efficiency for each device and path in the next section.

$$1 : T = -24993 + 495 \times ID \quad r^2 = 0.744 \tag{5}$$

$$2 : T = -17382 + 2474 \times ID \quad r^2 = 0.666 \tag{6}$$

$$3 : T = -18266 + 2524 \times ID \quad r^2 = 0.745 \tag{7}$$

Results of an analysis of variance (ANOVA) were consistent with the early analysis. The analysis design included the devices conditions (DigiHaptic and SpaceMouse) with repeated measures on the path and representation factors: 3 (path) * 3 (representation). The path factors had three categories: A, B and C (fig. 2). The representation factors had also three categories: 1, 2 and 3 (fig. 2).

Analysis of variance (ANOVA) for mean task steering time revealed a significant effect of the devices (F(1,21)=5.734, $p < 0.0260$). Globally, the test shows that subjects perform the task faster for the SpaceMouse than for the DigiHaptic. The path factor (F(2,42)=70.291, $p < 0.0000$) has a significant effect on task performance. The results on the path show that the "B" and "C" paths require more time than the "A" path both for the DigiHaptic and the SpaceMouse but for all paths they were better for the SpaceMouse. There is also a significant effect of the representation factor (F(2,42)=8.673, $p < 0.0007$). Significant effects were found for both two-way interaction devices * paths (F(2,42)=13.664, $p < 0.0000$) and paths * representations (F(4,84)=4.247, $p < 0.0035$). Figure 5 shows mean task steering time for each paths and devices.

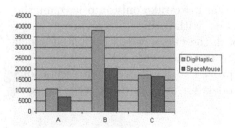

Fig. 5. Mean task steering time (ms) for each path and devices

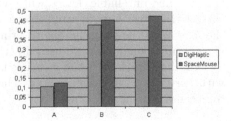

Fig. 6. Efficiency factor for the Space-Mouse and DigiHaptic versus paths

3.2 Coordination Measures

We want to compare how much the user can coordinate the three DOF on the two devices and thus compare whether the DOF separation leads to lower or better coordination. To quantify the DOF coordination, we used the notion of efficiency proposed by Zhai [10] that suppose that the highest DOF coordination is achieved between two points when the path followed is a straight line. Thus the amount of coordination is calculated by:

$$efficiency = \frac{Length\,of\,actual\,path - Length\,of\,shortest\,path}{Length\,of\,shortest\,path} \qquad (8)$$

The lower the efficiency coefficient is the more coordinated the device.

To quantify the coordination for each device, we used the definition of efficiency presented above. Each time, we took the length covered by the user from the start to the end of the path, including the length covered when outside the path after an exit. For each path and representation, the SpaceMouse's efficiency coefficient is always greater than the one of the DigiHaptic (fig. 6), which means there is less coordination on the SpaceMouse. There is no important difference between efficiency factors calculated for the three representations of each path.

The "A" path is the most coordinated one. For the paths "A" and "B", the results are similar for the two devices whereas for the path "C", there is a sharp difference between the two devices. It is surprising that for the SpaceMouse the coordination coefficient of the "C" path is greater than the one of the "B" path although the "C" path is easier than the "B" path. We can hypothesize that the "C" path is responsible for the fact that the SpaceMouse does not fit the steering law. Users had difficulty coordinating the action of pushing down the motion controller while going to the right.

If we compare the "A" and "C" paths both require the use of two DOF, the "A" path get better results for the DigiHaptic and SpaceMouse. We can hypothesize that this is due to the lower slope on the "A" path. For the "B" path, the DigiHaptic is at its least efficiency because the path requires the use of the three DOF at the same time.

3.3 Exits

Figure 7 shows the mean number of exits for each path (A, B and C) with each device. The ANOVA analysis for mean task exits indicates that there is a main effect of path ($F(2,42)=76.811$, $p < 0.0000$). For "A" and "B" paths, the average number of exits is similar for the two devices. Globally, the subject exits more with the "B" path as it is more difficult to coordinate 3 DOF at the same time. One more time, we observe a large difference between the DigiHaptic and the SpaceMouse for the "C" path that concerns this time the average number of exits: users exit more with the SpaceMouse for the "C" path. Indeed there are a significant interaction effects devices * paths ($F(2,42)=6.090$, $p < 0.0047$). These results were consistent with coordination results that implies a coordination problem with width axis ("x") and the height axis ("y") for the SpaceMouse.

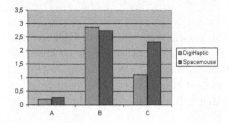
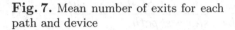

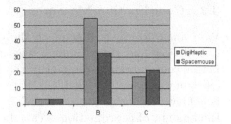

Fig. 7. Mean number of exits for each path and device

Fig. 8. Mean number of contacts for each path and device

3.4   Contacts

Figure 8 shows mean number of contacts for each path and device. The ANOVA on the average number of contacts indicated that there were a significant effect of the path ($F(1,42)= 48.444$, $p < 0.0000$). Significant interaction effects were found for device * path ($F(2,42)= 6.017$, $p < 0.0050$). Finally, there were no significant three-way interactions. The mean number of contacts shows that the "A" path is better than the "B" and "C" paths.

For the "B" path, the average number of exits for the DigiHaptic and Space-Mouse was similar whereas the average number of contacts is more important for the DigiHaptic. We could have expected that the number of exits would have been proportional to the number of contacts. This could imply that the DigiHaptic allows a good control when path boundaries are reached.

The average number of contacts are similar for the DigiHaptic and Space-Mouse for the "C" path whereas we observed that an average number of exits was more important with the SpaceMouse than the DigiHaptic for the "C" path. The results suggest that there is a rate control problem on the SpaceMouse together with the previously discussed coordination problem. We could hypothesize that the rate control problem comes from the low movements amplitude of the motion controller.

4   Conclusion

First of all, the main result is that the DigiHaptic conception allows simultaneous coordination of separated DOF. Otherwise, we have seen that the coordination of two or three DOF leads to the same steering time compared to the ID of the path.

Certainly, we have seen that the DOF separation increase the steering time, nevertheless the DOF separation appears to increase the control on the 3D pointer. For the paths where the number of contacts are similar for the DigiHaptic and the SpaceMouse, the number of exits is more important with the Space-Mouse, and where the number of contacts is more important on the DigiHaptic, the number of exits keeps similar for the two device. So the DOF coordination difficulty that increase the steering time is compensated by a better correction and adjustment of the trajectory.

The coordination efficiency is better on the DigiHaptic than on the Space-Mouse. We believe this is due to the original and ergonomic design of the Digi-Haptic because there is a direct relationship between the fingers and cursors movements. These results can also be explained because the DigiHaptic is more elastic than the SpaceMouse. Thus the DigiHaptic affords richer proprioceptive feedbacks which leads to a better control. In the same way, Poulton indicated that for tracking tasks, spring-loaded controls were best for compensatory tracking in a position control system with a slow ramp target to track [11].

The problem found on the SpaceMouse between the "x" and "y" axis needs further analysis to be deep understood. We have noticed that users keep their wrist motionless. For the movement involved, subjects have to perform a translation movement with the motion controller. Nevertheless the motion controller affordance implicates an involuntary rotation movement.

In future works, we plan to repeat the same study on other more complicated paths to see if the results keep consistent with this study and check if there are other coordination problems with the SpaceMouse.

5 Acknowledgements

This work has been carried out within the framework of the INRIA Alcove project and is supported by the IRCICA (Institut de Recherche sur les Composants logiciels et matériels pour l'Information et la Communication Avancée).

References

1. Shumin Zhai. *Human Performance in Six Degree of Freedom Input Control*. PhD thesis, University of Toronto, 1995.
2. Spacemouse http://www.spacemouse.com.
3. R.J.K. Jacob, L.E. Silbert, C. Mcfarlane, and M.P. Mullen. Integrality and Separability of Input Devices. *ACM Transactions on Computer-Human Interaction*, 1(1):3–26, March 1994.
4. J.R. Rice, J.P. Yorchak, and C.S. Hartley. Capture of satellites having rotational motion. In *Human Factor Society 30th Annual Meeting*, 1986.
5. G. Casiez, P. Plénacoste, C. Chaillou, and B. Semail. The DigiHaptic, a New Three Degrees of Freedom Multi-finger Haptic Device. In *Proceedings of Virtual Reality International Conference*, pages 35–39, May 2003.
6. G. Casiez, P. Plénacoste, C. Chaillou, and B. Semail. Elastic Force Feedback with a New Multi-finger haptic device: The DigiHaptic. In *Proceedings of Eurohaptics*, pages 121–134, July 2003.
7. J. Accot and S. Zhai. Beyond Fitts' Law: Models for Trajectory-Based HCI Tasks. In *Proc. of CHI'97*, pages 295–302, 1997.
8. J. Accot and S. Zhai. Performance Evaluation of Input Devices in Trajectory-Based Tasks: An Application of The Steering Law. In *Proc. of CHI'99*, pages 466–472, 1999.

9. J. Accot and S. Zhai. Scale Effects in Steering Law Tasks. In *Proc of CHI'01*, pages 1–8, 2001.
10. S. Zhai and P. Milgram. Quantifying Coordination in Multiple DOF Movement and Its Application to Evaluating 6 DOF Input Devices. In *Proc. of CHI'98*, pages 320–327, 1998.
11. E.C. Poulton. *Tracking skill and manual control*. New York: Academic Press, 1974.

Collaborative Interactions on 3D Display for Multi-user Game Environments

Jeong-Dan Choi[1], Byung-Tae Jang[1], and Chi-Jeong Hwang[2]

[1] Telematics Solution Research Team, Telematics Research Department,
Electronic and Telecommunications Research Institute,
161 Gajeong-dong, Yuseong-gu, Dajeon, 305-350, Korea
{jdchoi, jbt}@etri.re.kr
[2] Image Processing Laboratory, Computer Engineering Department,
Chungnam National University,
220 Gung-dong, Yuseong-gu, Daejeon, 305-764, Korea
{cjhwang}@ipl.cnu.ac.kr

Abstract. This paper describes a method to integrate VR interfaces on 3D display for multi-user game environments, which addresses the problem of synchronization and calibration multiple devices together to treat game events. The challenge we interest in is how to build and use a low cost 3D display that collaborative interact for multi-user immersive game requirements. In the multi-user VR game, 3D display is an important component that supports immersion to gamer. So our display system is supported by following two methods. Projection-based screen system makes it possible to display on large-sized surface. Stereo sea-through HMD is to produce private area as well as public area: a viewer-oriented and private information display. To accomplish this system, we concrete a multi-projector system for creating a seamless wide-area view, head mounted device to play game, and gesture recognition system for collaborative interactions. Our preliminary system is well suited for jungle hunting as game contents with surround displays running on a PC clusters.

1 Introduction

The most game depends on typical devices such as monitors, keyboard and mouse. While monitors were cost-effective and easy to use, they failed to convey a feeling of immersion to their users. We believe that multi-user VR game display requires a different model, which delivers a sense of presence in the environments, incorporates 3D visualization capabilities, and helps encourage the entertainment. VR technology makes it possible to fulfil its duties by making a user interact with immersive virtual environments (VE) in a natural and intuitive way. This kind of VR system enables developers to create and execute VR applications with visual aspects and interactive responses.

In the visual aspects, large physical size, high-resolution multi-projector displays have the potential to allow users to interact with 3D objects, which can be critical to immersion and perception [1], [2]. The space in front of the display supports natural collaborations among multiple participants simultaneously, which the entire field of

M. Masoodian et al. (Eds.): APCHI 2004, LNCS 3101, pp. 81-90, 2004.

view is guaranteed for each user. And also sea-through head mounted display device make the gamer extremely useful for immersing game contents. And advances in large scale computing have allowed researchers to produce more data than ever, required by very various applications. Today's PC-based graphics accelerators achieve better performance – both in cost and speed. So a cluster of PCs where many or all of the system have 3D accelerators is an attractive approach to building a scalable graphics system [3], [4]. And the multi computer displays are increasingly important for applications such as collaborative computer-aided design, interactive scientific visualization, entertainment, and medical visualization. The high-resolution of the displays enables visualization of highly detailed data sets. So, what we interest in is how to build and use a low cost platform that satisfies these requirements.

2   Our Proposed System Components

This section describes in detail our proposed VR Game system and contents, with some specific game devices. Our system overview is graphically shown in Fig. 1.

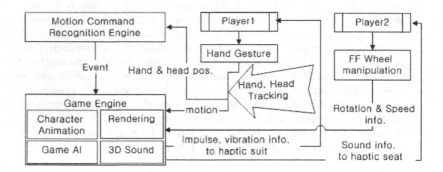

Fig. 1. Our multi-user VR game system overview

Target content is a jungle hunting adventure and on-line role-playing game supported by more than 2 persons. Main system supports surrounded display with PC clusters. And it drives various VR interfaces with DirectX [5] APIs such as haptic jacket, seat and force feedback wheel. One user plays game performing gestures with hand glove. The hand gesture is tracked by magnetic sensor, which is attached hand glove. And then the hand's orientation and positions are transmitted to Motion Recognition Engine. The other user drives the jungle off-road with force feedback steering wheel. The extracted game event is transferred to Rendering and Animation Engine. And the motion of actor is generated with virtual actor on screen in real-time. Player 1 wears see-through HMD and player2 wears polarized glasses. Both players enjoy the jungle hunter with wide stereo screen. So, our topics of several 3D display interfaces and real-time interactions [6], [7], [8] are discussed in the order written.

3 3D Display Interface

The challenge we are interested in is how to build and use a low cost platform that satisfies collaborative interactions on a 3D display environments and learning how to use it to bridge into the immersive VR game environments. We describe our efforts in developing a 3D display for the improvement of collaborative abilities and maximization of entertainment. This section covers three components, large-sized stereo display, sea-through stereo HMD and rendering techniques for creating stereo scenes using common graphics library DirectX.

3.1 Large-Sized Stereo Display

Our projector-based display system is configured as Fig. 2. This 3D stereo system includes LCD projectors with polarized filter and PC clustered rendering systems. The PC rendering system is clustered for synchronization. This clustered system has been developed last year [4].

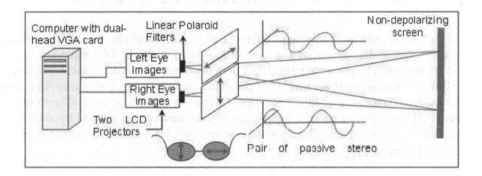

Fig. 2. Configuration of Projector-based 3D stereo display

Each PC transmits the left and right images at the same time. The viewer wears special eyewear comprising with horizontal and vertical filter. The horizontal filter closed the vertical wave and pass through the horizontal wave. In this way, the user with polarization lenses is capable of seeing the stereo. Although a single flat projection display can be used, using multi-projectors display increases the field of view and resolution. But the conveniences of using multi-projectors should solve the extra considerations of synchronization and seamless panoramic view. Especially, since the display surface is shaped arbitrarily, the user must endure watching the distorted game display affected by shape of the surface. If there are cases where a display area for a projector is overlapped with another, theses will cause an irregular game display in terms of intensity. These problems can be fixed by using structured light techniques [9], [10] and intensity blending [9], [10].

Structured Light Technique. We use a set of a reference plane, a arbitrary display surface, a CCD camera and projector pairs, and a laser tracker (see Fig. 3). Each camera and projector pair is used to extract a shape of its corresponding portion of display surface based on a Structured Light Technique. The same projector is also used to project a game content on the display surface.

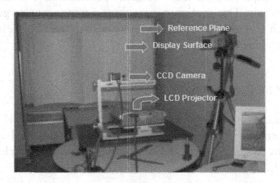

Fig. 3. System configuration of extracting the arbitrary display surface

Projector is used to display an interference pattern on its display area and camera is used to capture the pattern on the area. The Structured Light Technique is a well-known two-wavelength phase shifting interferometer. The basic concept of phase-shifting method is to extract heights of the object surface from an interference pattern created by a phase-shift of interferometer. 4-frame phase-shifting method is normally used, and, from this method, we can acquire four interference patterns by shifting a phase of $\pi/2$ four times. The formula (1) expresses the intensity of acquired interference pattern at (x, y).

$$I_p(x,y) = I_0(x,y)\{1 + \gamma(x,y)\cos[\phi(x,y) + \Delta]\} \tag{1}$$

$I_0(x,y)$ is an average moiré intensity at (x, y), $\gamma(x,y)$ is a standardized visibility of moiré interference pattern, Δ is a degree of phase-shifting, and $\phi(x,y)$ is a height of the surface at (x, y). By the 4 frame phase-shifting method, we can get following four different formulas from formula (2).

$$
\begin{aligned}
I_1(x,y) &= I_0(x,y)\{1 + \gamma(x,y)\cos[\phi(x,y)]\}, \\
I_2(x,y) &= I_0(x,y)\{1 + \gamma(x,y)\cos[\phi(x,y) + \pi/2]\}, \\
I_3(x,y) &= I_0(x,y)\{1 + \gamma(x,y)\cos[\phi(x,y) + \pi]\}, \\
I_4(x,y) &= I_0(x,y)\{1 + \gamma(x,y)\cos[\phi(x,y) + 3\pi/2]\}
\end{aligned}
\tag{2}
$$

Therefore, we can acquire the height map of the object surface from $\phi(x, y)$. However, since these heights are calculated from arctangents, there can be ambiguities of height in every 2π. And then two-pass rendering technique is added (see Fig. 4).

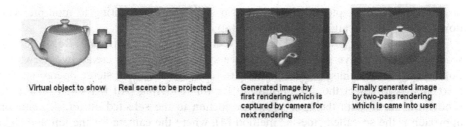

| Virtual object to show | Real scene to be projected | Generated image by first rendering which is captured by camera for next rendering | Finally generated image by two-pass rendering which is came into user |

Fig. 4. Object rendering onto arbitrary display surface

Intensity Blending. This multi-projector display does not rely on an assumption that each projector is dedicated to its unique part of the display surface. Thus, there may be an overlapped display surface area by projectors. When this overlap occurs, the intensity of the overlapped area becomes the sum of intensities of the projectors involved with the area. Thus, this situation produces an irregularity of brightness to the multi-projection display. Our method is to assign each vertex of display surfaces in overlapped area different alpha value depending on the distance to its nearest edge of the display surface. The vertices of an overlapped area in a display surface are same with its corresponding ones in the other display surfaces. The alpha value is expressed as (3).

$$\alpha_i(x,y) = \frac{d_i(x,y)}{\sum_i d_i(x,y)} \tag{3}$$

Fig. 5. Effect of intensity blending: without and with

$\alpha_i(x,y)$ is an alpha value of a vertex at (x,y) which is in the display surface i.
$d_i(x,y)$ is the distance between the vertex and its nearest edge of the display surface i.
Fig. 5 shows a display without the intensity blending and one with it. Cleary one can see the effect of the intensity blending from the overlapping edge.

3.2 Rendering for Stereo Scene Using DirectX

Former multi-head problems are poor API support and duplication of resources such as frame buffer. We implemented multi-head display system with one VGA card having dual-head adapter. DirectX 8.x also supports for rendering to multiple windows through the creation of additional swap chains.

The following explains about creating stereo pairs using Direct3D. Regardless of whether it is an active system or a passive system, one has to create two views for both eyes. The first thing one has to do is initializing buffers for stereo operation. The next step is to select the appropriate buffer for rendering. All that's left now is to render the scene with the appropriate projection to the selected buffer. A common approach is the so called "toe-in" method [4], where the camera for the left and right eye is pointed towards a single focal point and D3DXMatrixPerspectiveFovLH( ) is used (see Fig. 6(a)). However a stereo scene using the "toe-in" method gave a while giving workable stereo pairs is not correct, it also introduces vertical parallax which is most noticeable for objects in the outer field of view. The correct method (see Fig. 6(b)) is to use what is sometimes known as the "parallel axis asymmetric frustum perspective projection". In this case the view vectors for each camera remain parallel and a D3DXMatrixPerspectiveOffCenterLH() is used to describe the perspective projection (see Fig. 6(c)).

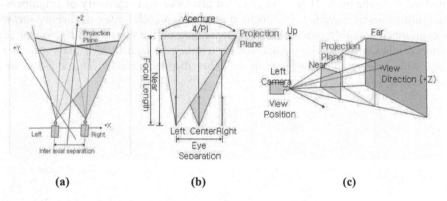

| (a) | (b) | (c) |

Fig. 6. Toe-in(a), Correct(b) method and Perspective view frustum

The following is the procedure for the projection setting. First we set camera and view frustum parameters as follows.

FocalLength : distance from eye to the screen
Aperture : FOV in radians
Near : z value of the near clipping plane
Far : z value of the far clipping plane
EyeSep : ditance between two eyes. Usually set by 1/20 of *FocalLength*

HalfHeight is the half of the height of the near clipping plane and calculated by using the following.

$$HalfHeight = Near * \tan (Aperture / 2) \qquad (4)$$

Next we can set the view matrix and projection matrix for the left eye. The view matrix is set by using D3DXMatrixLookAtLH() and its 3 parameters as follows.

LEyePt : vector(-*EyeSep* / 2, 0, 0)
LLookAtPt : vector(-*EyeSep* / 2, 0, *FocalLength*)
UpVec : vector(0, 1, 0)
D3DXMatrixLookAtLH(matView, *LEyePt, LLookAtPt, UpVec*)

Referring to Fig. 6(b) minimum and maximum x values of the view volume are calculated by using the following euqation.

$$Left = -Aspect * HalfHeight + EyeSep/2 * Near/FocalLength \quad (5)$$
$$Right = Aspect * HalfHeight + EyeSep/2 * Near/FocalLength \quad (6)$$

Where Aspect is the aspect ratio of the rendering window, the projection matrix is set as follows.

D3DXMatrixPerspectiveOffCenterLH(matProj, *Left, Right, -HalfHeight, HalfHeight, Near, Far*)

Finally we can set the view matrix and projection matrix for the right eye similarly using the following parameters.

REyePt : vector(*EyeSep* / 2, 0, 0)
RLookAtPt : vector(*EyeSep* / 2, 0, *FocalLength*)

$$Left = -Aspect * HalfHeight - EyeSep/2 * Near/FocalLength \quad (7)$$
$$Right = Aspect * HalfHeight - EyeSep/2 * Near/FocalLength \quad (8)$$

3.3 See-Through Stereo HMD

And also see-through HMD is used to overlay private information on the contents displaying on the wide screen. There are many situations in which we would like to interact with private objects in the surrounding public contents. An Augmented Reality can make this possible by presenting private information that enriches the public worlds.

HMD is used to determine which weapon is selectable in nearby-space and which object is targeted in far-space. The interface presents two windows to the operator. The first window carries private information. We currently use a navigation menu and selection weapon. And the second window displays surround contents formed through the lenses. Fig. 7. shows the HMD window.

4   User Interactions with Real-Time Virtual Character Animations

A user is displayed as a virtual character in the game. We use a skinned mesh for the character that is stored as an X file, and it is rendered using the Direct3D. For the user's immersion into the game, whenever the user makes a command by gesture, movement of the arm of the virtual character is generated in real-time according to the sensed hand position of the user. For this purpose we implemented a real-time inverse kinematics (IK) routine.

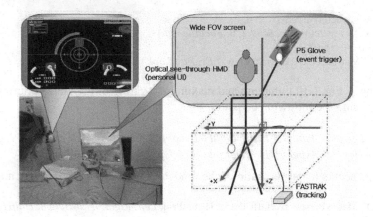

Fig. 7. HMD window and an example of HMD interface

Two kinds of IK solver were implemented. One is an analytic solution for 2-link IK problem (see Fig. 8) and the other is for multi-links by using the inverse rate control.

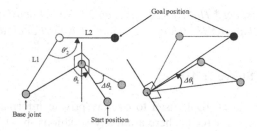

Fig. 8. 2-step algorithm for 2-link IK problem

In the figure the light gray balls represent joints, black ones represent the goal position for the end-effecter, and the dotted line represents the expected configuration after each step. We assume the links are arms in the following explanations. Our 2-step IK solution for the 2-link case consists of finding the incremental transformations for the elbow and the shoulder. If an original transformation matrix is R and a new needed incremental transformation is ΔR, then a new transformation matrix becomes ΔR·R. The detailed 2-step algorithm is as follows. First, we calculate the desired elbow angle θ'2 from L1, L2, the goal position, and the base joint position. L1 and L2 are the length of the upper arm and the lower arm, respectively. If we designate L3 as the distance from the base to the goal, θ'2 is given by

$$\theta_2' = \cos^{-1}\left(\frac{L_1^2 + L_2^2 - L_3^2}{2L_1L_2} \right) \tag{9}$$

Δθ2 is (θ'2 - θ2), and the incremental transformation for the elbow, ΔR2, is a rotation by Δθ2 with respect to the axis of rotation that is perpendicular to the plane formed from the three joints.

The second step is positioning the end-effecter to the goal position by adjusting the shoulder joint. This is similar to the first step and $\Delta\theta1$ is calculated. The axis of rotation for $\Delta R1$ is the line perpendicular to the plane formed from the base, the goal position, and the intermediate end-effecter position in the first step. Without additional calculations for exploiting the redundancy in the elbow joint [8], our algorithm produces a fast and natural-looking solution given an initial natural configuration. Initial configuration is restored after each execution of the algorithm to avoid losing the original posture and drifting with an unfeasible posture. Fig. 9 shows some variation poses from the leftmost initial pose by using the 2-step algorithm and virtual characters with several poses by using the 2-step IK.

Fig. 9. Variation poses by using the 2-step IK solver and virtual characters with several poses by using the 2-step IK solver

For the multi-link IK we applied the inverse rate control as in [7]. This method uses the Jacobian matrix and numerical integrations. The process can be abstracted by following equations.

$$x = f(\theta), \ \Delta x = J\Delta\theta \tag{10}$$

$$\Delta\theta = J^{+}\Delta x, \ J^{+} = J^{T}(JJ^{T})-1 \tag{11}$$

Where J is a Jacobian matrix and J+ is a pseudo inverse of J. In order to obtain a real-time result, the multi-link IK routine was formulated to solve an incremental problem i.e. a final configuration becomes the initial configuration of the IK problem at the next frame.

5 Implementation & Conclusions

When used for VR interactions the 3D stereo display is quite immersive. Immersive projection displays can produce stereoscopic images but are less isolating than a HMD. Because of this reason, projection displays have been more suited collaboration than HMDs. So, we use a set of custom designed HMD and large-area display. Not only do projection displays allow multiple users to collaborate more easily, but they also allow a single user to operate VR game contents more comfortably. But Large-area display is more difficult since multi-projectors create overlap area. We currently solve these problems as extracting the screen surface using structured light techniques and intensity blending.

We implemented game interactions for VR safari hunting on 3D display system using various VR devices. We developed projection-based 3D stereo system, rendering using DirectX, and user interactions using real-time virtual character animations. Finally, our current research includes further work on the projector calibration process and extension of the current ideas to handle automatic multiple projectors.

References

1. Dave P. and Dan S. : Quality Evaluation of Projection-Based VR Display. Immersive Projection Technology Workshop. Ames. IA (2000) 19-20
2. Funkhouser, F. and Li, K. : Large-Format Displays. IEEE CG&A Vol. 20, No. 4. (2000) 20-21
3. Brian, W., Constantine, P. and Vasily, L. : Scalable Rendering on PC Clusters. IEEE CG&A (2001), 62-70
4. Jeong-Dan, C., Ki-Jong B. et al. : Synchronization method for Real Time Surround Display using Clustered Systems. ACM Multimedia. (2002) 259-262
5. Microsoft Corporation. DirectX 8.1 programming reference
6. D. Tolani, A. Goswami and N. I. Badler : Real-time Kinematics techniques for anthropomorphic limbs. Graphical Models. Vol. 62, No. 5. (2000) 353-388
7. K. J. Choi and H. S. Ko : On-line Motion Retargetting. Proc. of International Pacific Graphics. (1999) 32-42
8. Pattie M., Bruce B., Trevor D., and Alex P. : The Alive System: Wireless, Full-body Interaction with Autonomous Agents. ACM Multimedia Systems, No. 5. (1997) 105-112
9. Raskar, R.; van Baar, J.; Beardsley, P.; Willwacher, T.; Rao, S.; Forlines, C., iLamps: Geometrically Aware and Self-Configuring Projectors, ACM Transactions on Graphics (TOG), Vol. 22, Issue 3, (2003) 809-818
10. van Baar, J.; Willwacher, T.; Rao, S.; Raskar, R., Seamless Multi-Projector Display on Curved Screens, Eurographics Workshop on Virtual Environments (EGVE), (2003) 281-286

Age Differences in Rendezvousing: 18-30s Vs. 31-45s

Martin Colbert

School of Computing and Information Systems, Kingston University,
Kingston Upon Thames, Surrey, UK KT1 2EE

Abstract. One strategy for increasing the usefulness, ease of use and satisfaction of wireless navigation and related services is to tailor a package of services to meet the requirements of particular user groups. This paper reports a diary study, which compared the rendezvousing performance and behaviour of two age groups - 18-30s and 31-45s. The age groups differed in the following respects: (i) 31-45s more frequently attributed problems rendezvousing to the overrunning of previous activities, and to the spontaneous performance of additional tasks ('side-stepping'); (ii) 31-45s more frequently experienced lost opportunities associated with the failure to meet as initially agreed in the form of personal sacrifices; and (iii) 31-45s more frequently changed plans for the rendezvous. The explanation for these differences suggested by the diaries is that commitments to spouse and children lead 31-45s to pack their lives more tightly with activities than 18-30s. Some implications for tailoring wireless navigation and related services to the 31-45 age group are discussed.

1. Introduction

1.1. Wireless Navigation and Related Services and Rendezvousing

Personal navigation and related services for the general public are gradually being introduced. In 1998, Garmin's NavTalk integrated a GPS (Global Positioning System) unit with a GSM (Global Services for Mobiles) mobile telephone to provide talk, text messaging, Internet access via WAP (Wireless Application Protocol), map displays and routing, with To Do lists, calendars and reminders (www.garmin.com). In 2001, Swedish mobile operator Telia launched their FriendFinder service, in which subscribers (who have been given the necessary permissions) use text messaging, WAP or the Internet to obtain the location of another phone – the ID (identity) of the network cell currently handling that phone (www.openwave.com, 2003). KTF of South Korea offer child-tracking and OAP-tracking (www.guardian.co.uk, 2003). UK operator 02 provide Trafficline - dial 1200 from any 02 mobile to receive a voice-recorded, up-to-date, traffic report for the cell-id of the requesting phone (www.o2.co.uk, 2003). In July 2003, Germany's T-Mobile announced the NaviGate BlueKit service over GPRS – plan your route, then download the map to your phone for a couple of ECUs (www.t-mobile.com, 2003). Other devices and services are currently under development, often in the form of electronic guides that combine navigational tools, with related, position-aware services, such as timetables and route

M. Masoodian et al. (Eds.): APCHI 2004, LNCS 3101, pp. 91-100, 2004.

information, local shops and landmarks, on-line booking and purchasing, and small group communication. For example, PNT (Personal Navigation Tool) is for use over GSM networks, and enabled by WAP [4]. LOL@ (Local Location Assistant) is for use over UMTS (Universal Mobile Telecommunications Services) - a broadband, so-called third generation wireless network [5]).

One context of use for wireless navigation and related services is rendezvousing. A rendezvous, here, is the informal co-ordination of a small group of friends and family. The purpose of a rendezvous is for individuals to come together to participate in a subsequent activity, such as 'to watch a movie', or 'to give the kids a lift home'. Rendezvousers have personal relationships - they are not embodiments of organisational roles. Consequently, rendezvous do not include: formal, or anonymous attendance at institutions, such as 'reporting to the Tax Office for interview' and 'going to my Electronics lecture; business fora, such as Annual General Meetings; or receipts of service, such as 'Pizza delivery'. Previous work has studied the rendezvousing performance of students and the reasons for rendezvousing problems [3]. However, this study did not investigate possible differences between user groups, and so does not support the tailoring of packages of services.

1.2. Tailoring Services to Meet the Needs of Particular User Groups

The use of wireless navigation and related services for rendezvousing is flexible and discretionary. The public is free to choose whether or not they use a service to rendezvous, and, if so, then how they will use that service. The public also has various types of service at their disposal, and some or all of them may assist rendezvousing in particular circumstances. For example, are rendezvouser may solve problems arising from a late arrival, by looking for travel information and at a map. Alternatively, a rendezvouser may talk to, or track other rendezvousers – the option chosen depends upon the rendezvousers' "lifestyle choices". Consequently, the uptake of navigation and related services is greatly influenced by their perceived usability i.e. their perceived usefulness, ease of use and user satisfaction.

One way of improving the usability of navigation and related services is to tailor packages of basic services to meet the requirements of particular user groups, rather than develop a single package for 'the public generally'. Different user groups may have distinctive requirements, reflecting differences in the kinds of task each group tends to perform, the contexts in which they tend to use services, and the qualities of use that they value most.

2. Aims

To set the tailoring of navigation and related services in a productive direction, this paper compares rendezvousing as performed by two age groups – 18-30s and 31-45s. The two groups are compared in terms of task goals, levels of performance, reasons for problems, and planning and communication behaviour. Two age groups were selected for study, because age differences within the general public have often been reported, and are of importance for the development of wireless technology [1, 5].

Better understanding of the differences in rendezvousing as performed by these two age groups may suggest how to tailor a package of services towards one age group. Perhaps, different age groups have rendezvousing problems for different reasons, or prepare for rendezvousing differently. This paper aims to find out.

3. Method

This study uses a diary method to study rendezvousing. A diary method was chosen, because rendezvous events are too rare, private and geographically dispersed for direct observation, and users too easily forget important details of their behaviour to report them accurately long afterwards. Diaries have long been used in user-centred development. The diary used here also generated qualitative data about the nature of rendezvousing, plus quantitative data about users, the tasks and performance.

3.1. Participants

The participants in the study were 39 students from the School of Computing and Information Systems, Kingston University. The aim of selecting participants was to obtain a sample that was balanced in terms of sex, and also large in size, despite the fact that the vast majority of students in the School are male. Between January 2001 and April 2002, students who took a module in Human-Computer Interaction completed a diary as a minor part of coursework exercises. Three classes were set this coursework - the final year undergraduate classes of 2001 and 2002, and the class for post-graduates on a conversion course in 2002. At the outset of the study, a large number of machine-readable response sheets were printed, and then used as part of the diaries. After setting the coursework to 3 classes, there were not enough machine readable-sheets to set the coursework to a fourth class. 22 female students completed a diary and consented to its anonymous use here - 4 undergraduates in 2001, 6 undergraduates in 2002 and 12 post-graduates in 2002. The diaries of 22 male students were then selected from the appropriate course module year, to match the female participants as closely as possible in terms of age, ethnic background, marital status, number of children, and mobile phone ownership.

Of this set of 44 participants, 5 did not state their age, and so were excluded from this analysis. Of the 39 participants remaining, 30 were between 18 and 30 years old and 9 were between 31 and 45 years old. The mean age of participants in the 18-30 group was 22 years 9 months, and, in the 31-45 group, the mean age was 36 years.

Both the 18-30 group and the 31-45s comprised approximately equal numbers of males and females. Both groups also comprised individuals who, almost without exception, owned a mobile telephone, had access to a fixed phone, possessed an e-mail account in addition to their university account, and were registered as full-time students (see Table 1). Also, all participants lived within commuting distance of

Kingston Upon Thames, a suburb of London, UK. However, the 18-30 and 31-45 age groups were not identical in the following respects:
- the 31-45 group comprised a higher proportion of married individuals, a higher proportion of individuals with children, and a higher proportion of post-graduate students;
- the 18-30 group comprised a higher proportion of frequent mobile phone users, and a higher proportion of students from an Asian or Far-Eastern ethnic background.

Although the 18-30 and 31-45 age groups match each other in many respects, then, the match is not perfect.

Table 1. Participants: characteristics of 18-30 and 31-45 age groups

Characteristics	Age Groups	
	18-30	31-45
Sex (ratio male:female)	1:1	4:5
Mean age (yrs mths)	22 yrs 9 mths	36 yrs
Ethnic Background	11:12:2:2:3	5:2:2:0:0
(Ratio White:Asian:Afro-Carib:FarEast: Other)		
Married (%)	3%	44%
Have Children (%)	3%	56%
On Postgraduate Course (%)	50%	66%
Full-time study (%)	97%	100%
Amount of Additional Paid Work (hrs/wk)	8 hrs	5 hrs
Own Mobile Phone (%)	93%	78%
Have Access to Fixed Phone (%)	83%	100%
Have Additional E-Mail (%)	97%	100%
Frequent User of Mobile Phone (% >10calls/wk)	60%	30%
Frequent User of Fixed Phone (% >10 calls/wk)	30%	38%

3.2. Diaries

Post-graduates kept diaries about their own rendezvousing behaviour for a one-week period in January. Undergraduates kept diaries for two, one-week periods, the first week in February, the second week was in April. To be consistent with the post-graduates, only February entries for undergraduates are used here. This sample of the student year is of interest, because it approximates to the term-time routine, and so accounts for most of the year. However, it does not include vacations (when students may be working, or have returned to their parental home) and only collects data during the winter (which is not suitable for some activities, modes of travel, clothing etc).

Participants made one diary entry for each rendezvous event they attended. Each entry comprised: (i) an open-ended, narrative description in the diary keeper's own words of what happened, and why; and (ii) the diary keeper's responses to a questionnaire, which asked for specific details of each rendezvous event. This questionnaire comprised 37 questions about the event, outcomes, and usage and user experience of communication before and during the rendezvous.

3.3. Procedure

At the outset of the study, all students were given an overview of future position-aware, computing and communications for mobile devices, and were introduced to the aims of the study and the obligations of diary keeping. To illustrate the kind of services that could be developed, participants examined fixed-access Web sites that provide map, transport and venue information, such as www.multimap.com, and londontransport.co.uk. A possible future service was also described, which enabled each member of a small group to display on their mobile telephone the positions of other group members, superimposed upon an annotated map. At the end of the diary-keeping period, diary keepers also completed a further form, which summarised their diary and its completeness. Questionnaire responses were processed automatically by an Ocular Reading Machine. This machine generated a text file of responses, which was checked manually before being read into statistical analysis software.

4. Results

This section presents results in terms of rendezvousing tasks, rendezvousing outcomes, usage of communication services and user experience of communication. Significant differences between age groups are listed in Table 2. Statistical significance was calculated using an independent-samples, two-tailed 't'-test, when comparing numerical data, and the Chi^2 test, when comparing frequency data.

4.1. Rendezvousing Tasks

Both 18-30s and 31-45s reported, on average, just over 5 rendezvous per week. 18-20s reported 5.6 rendezvous per week and 31-45s reported 5.1 per week. This rate of rendezvousing is very similar to the rate obtained by a pilot study. It also means that the results reported in this paper are based upon 168 rendezvous reported by 18-30s and 46 rendezvous reported by 31-45s.

18-30s and 31-45s were not significantly different in terms of the mean size of the rendezvous - the mean number of other rendezvousers involved, including the diary keeper, was 3.7 people for both groups. An initial inspection of the means suggested that 31-45s might be more likely to meet members of their immediate family (partners or children) than 18-30s (50% vs 22%), less likely to meet close friends (50% vs 65%), and more likely to meet at places where they had met before (78% vs 61%). However, these means are not significantly different (sig. = 0.102, 0.109 and 0.100 respectively).

4.2. Rendezvousing Outcomes

Both groups reported that they met as initially agreed about 50% of the time. Again, this rate of 'success' is very similar to the rate reported in previous studies. An initial inspection of the means for occurrence of stress and lost opportunity[1] as a result of failing to meet as agreed, suggest that 31-45s might be more likely to report stress (60% vs. 49%) and lost opportunity (57% vs 44%). However, these means are not significantly different (sig. = 0.112 and 0.152 respectively).

Generally speaking, the 18-30s and 31-45s were not significantly different in terms of the frequency with which problems rendezvousing were attributed to various possible causes, such as disruption of the mode of travel, poor planning, and lack of geographic information etc. However, 31-45s were more likely to attribute problems rendezvousing to the overrunning of previous activities (sig. = 0.50) and to the spontaneous performance of additional tasks aka "side stepping"[2] [7](sig. = 0.002).

When stress or lost opportunity occurred, the levels of stress or lost opportunity reported by 18-30s and 31-45s were not different (approx. 2.3 and 2.0 respectively). Also, when lost opportunity occurred, the frequency with which various kinds of lost opportunity[3] were reported generally did not differ between groups. However, 31-45s reported making individual sacrifices more often (sig. = 0.008) i.e. in order to rendezvous, 31-45s were more likely to report curtailing or not performing other activities.

4.3. Usage and User Experience of Communication

18-30s and 31-45s were not different in terms of the mean number of communications before or during the rendezvous, or the proportion of communications made via the telephone or voicemail. However, 31-45s were more likely to change the plan for the rendezvous before or during itself (sig. = 0.008)(see Table 2). Compared to 18-30s, 31-45s were particularly likely to change plan twice. 31-45s were also more likely to use e-mail at some point during the rendezvous, and less likely to use text messaging (sig. = 0.006 and sig. = 0.022 respectively).

The groups were not different in terms of user experience of communication[4] before or during the rendezvous.

---

[1] Lost opportunity, here, refers to the loss of not doing what the participant would have done, had the rendezvouzers met as initially agreed.

[2] For example, taking the opportunity to call in at the shops on the way to the rendezvous point.

[3] Kinds of lost opportunity, here, include restructing the post-rendezvous activity, reduced participation in this activity by one or more rendezvousers, non –participation in the activity, or cancellation of the whole activity.

[4] User experience, here, refers to ratings for satisfaction, frustration, mental effort, disruption, convenience, and social acceptability of communication.

Table 2. Age Differences Rendezvousing.

Measure	18-30s	31-45s	significance
Frequency rendezvousing problems attributed to over-running of previous activity	21%	39%	Sig. = 0.500
Frequency rendezvousing problems attributed to spon-taneous additional tasks	5%	17%	Sig. = 0.002
Frequency lost opportunities take the form of personal sacrifices	7%	22%	Sig. = 0.008
Frequency with which plan changes before or during a rendezvous	No. Changes 0 | 1 | 2 | >2 44% 35% 9% 11%	No. Changes 0 | 1 | 2 | >2 37% 24% 28% 9%	Sig. = 0.008
Mean number of communi-cations via e-mail per ren-dezvous	0.40	0.91	Sig. = 0.006
Proportion of communica-tions via text messaging	1.23	0.70	Sig. = 0.022

5. Discussion

5.1. Age Differences in Rendezvousing

Overall, then, rendezvousing by 31-45s differs from rendezvousing by 18-30s, in the following ways:

(i)   31-45s more frequently attribute problems to the overrunning of previous activities, and to taking the opportunity to perform additional, spontane-ous tasks ('side-stepping');

(ii)   31-45s more frequently lose opportunities in the form of individual sacri-fices;

(iii)   31-45s more frequently change the plan for the rendezvous; and

(iv)   31-45s communicated less frequently via text messaging than 18-30s, and more frequently via e-mail than 18-30s.

Free text entries in the diaries suggested that differences (i), (ii) and (iii) arise, be-cause 31-45s have commitments to spouse and children, and so pack [2] their daily life with planned activities more tightly than 18-30s. Previous activities are seen to overrun, because a 31-45s day is packed so tightly that there is no 'slack' in the sys-tem, and so a delay departing has a knock-on effect upon later rendezvous. The day of an 18-30, in contrast, is less tightly packed, and so they are more able to absorb the impact of a delayed departure. 'Side-stepping' is seen as a more frequent cause of problems by 31-45s, because side-stepping is a good technique for increasing personal 'productivity' (the ratio of time devoted to 'productive activity' to 'unproductive' travelling is increased), so side-stepping may occur more frequently in this age group. For 18-30s, if side-stepping is necessary, it is less likely to be problematic, because there is more 'slack' in the system. Lost opportunities are more often perceived in the form of personal sacrifices by 31-45s, because 31-45s are more aware of the activities they could have packed in to the time they actually 'wasted' failing to meet as agreed. 18-30s, in contrast, do not see, for example, waiting around for someone else to turn up that way. The plan for a rendezvous is more likely to change with 31-45s, because 31-45s need to keep adjusting their plans to optimise the packing of activities in time and space. For example, "My son has decided to go to Scouts this evening, so if we put the meeting back a little, I can drop him off on the way to you.". 18-30s change plan less often, because they do not seek to pack daily lives so tightly. The reason 31-45s pack their daily lives more tightly, seems to be the commitments they have to spouse and children (see Table 1).

Diaries revealed that e-mail usage was almost exclusively desk-top PC to desk-top PC. Some users had phones which could send and receive e-mail, but they tended not to use this feature. Difference (iv) arose for two reasons. First, 31-45s were more predictably at their desks, and so cheaply and almost immediately reached by e-mail. Second, 31-45s had yet to adopt text messaging to the extent of 18-30s, and continued to rely upon the fixed communication infrastructure to a greater extent (see figures for mobile phone ownership and usage in Table 1.).

5.2. Further Studies

In this study, only 9 participants were in the 31-45s group, compared to 30 in the 18-30 age group. It is possible that, because of the smaller size of the 31-45 group, this study did not identify all the differences in rendezvousing that actually exist. If future studies involved more 31-45s, perhaps mean values for stress and lost opportunity, and the relative frequency of rendezvous of different types, could be estimated more accurately, and additional differences revealed (see significance values in Results).

The participant profile in Table 1. also identifies two possible confounding factors for this study - ethnic background and mobile phone ownership. It is possible that some of the differences reported here are in part due to ethnic background and mobile phone ownership. Although diary entries did not suggest such effects, further studies may confirm their absence.

Further studies may also seek to confirm, or disconfirm hypotheses about the lifestyles of 18-30s and 31-45s implicit in the explanation for age differences reported. For example, are the daily lives of 31-45s really more tightly packed with planned activities than 18-30s? Is side stepping actually more frequent amongst 31-45s? Additional, specific questions in the questionnaire, together with interviews before or after diary keeping, may help answer these questions.

5.3. Tailoring Navigation and Related Services to 31-45s

The aim of this diary study was to set the tailoring of packages of navigation and related services for 31-45s in a suitable direction. Further observational and inter-view-based studies are needed to pursue a particular line of enquiry. 31-45s are of interest, because products tailored to the 18-30s already exist, notably those which package mobile telephony with sending text messages, and playing computer games and music. The discussion considers, first, the target of tailoring (possible services), and second, the process of tailoring (design scenarios and criteria).

The study suggests that tailoring a package of navigation and related services to 31-45s should consider placing greater emphasis on services that support side-stepping. 'Locator' services, which to find the nearest ATM ("cash") machine, or shop, already exist and directly support side-stepping. Other services could also support side-stepping. In the 'Position-aware reminder service' in Figure 1, a user first notes down a task to perform, and where he or she would like to perform it on a map-based 'To Do List'. The user is reminded about this task later, when they hap-pen to pass close enough to the planned task location to side-step to it. Or perhaps map-based displays of planned activities alone would help 31-45s to perceive addi-tional opportunities to sidestep themselves. The combination of 'tracking', locator and reminder services might be useful – one rendezvouser is then able ask another rendezvousers to side-step for them.

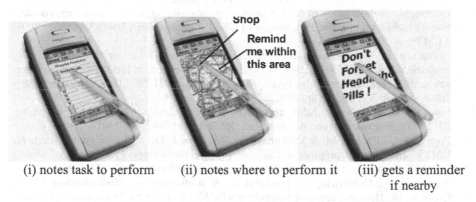

(i) notes task to perform   (ii) notes where to perform it   (iii) gets a reminder
if nearby

Fig. 1. Possible map-based side-stepping utility

Another response, less related to navigation, is to simply enable 'virtual side-stepping' i.e. to enable rendezvousers to take the opportunity to perform tasks re-motely and electronically, should they ever find themselves 'waiting around'. Diaries suggested that 31-45s side-stepped to do some shopping, or drop off a book, or dis-cuss coursework with someone else (no playing arcade games, or taking photographs of themselves here!). This suggests placing greater emphasis upon various kinds of service for performing domestic or work related tasks, such as remotely checking the contents of your fridge, updating a family diary, communicating with work mates etc..

This study also suggests designing with rendezvous scenarios that offer the oppor-tunity for side-stepping, such as "Today, you want to do the following chores: get some headache pills for your teenage daughter; drop your form in at the Post Office; collect your spouse from the railway station; meet Bob for a chat", rather than just "Today, you are to collect your spouse from the train station".   Tailoring may also apply criteria that focus upon packing daily life with activities, such as amount of unproductive, "down-time" saved per day.

6. Conclusions

This study identified some differences in rendezvousing between 18-30s and 31-45s. These differences may be used to tailor packages of navigation and related services to 31-45s. It is hoped that greater use and usability of these packages will result.

References

1.   Berg., S., Talyor, A. S. & Harper, R. Mobile phones for the next generation: device designs for teenagers. In Proceedings of CHI 2003 (Ft. Lauderdale, FL USA). ACM Press Boston, 2003, 433-440
2.   Carlstein, T., Parkes, D & Thrift, N.: Human Activity and Time Geography: Timing Space and Spacing Time (vol 2). Edward Arnold, London, 1978.
3.   Colbert, M.: A diary study of rendezvousing: implications for position-aware communication for mobile groups. In: Proceedings of GROUP'01, (Boulder, USA, September 2001) ACM Press, 2001, 15-23.
4.   Chincholle, D., Goldstein, M., Nyberg, M. and Eriksson, M.: Lost or found? A usability evaluation of a mobile navigation and location-based service, in Human-Computer Interaction with Mobile Devices.In: Proceedings of Mobile HCI 2002 (Pisa Italy, September 2002) Springer-Verlag, Berlin, 2002, 211-224.
5.   Ling, R.: Teen Girls and Adolescent Men: Two sub-cultures of the mobile telephone. Kjeller, Telenor research and development. R&D Report r34/2001, 2001.
6.   Poposchil, G., Umlauf, M. & Michlmayr, E.: Designing Lol@, a Mobile Tourist Guide for UMTS. In: Human-Computer Interaction with Mobile Devices, Proceedings of Mobile HCI 2002 (Pisa Italy, September 2002). Springer-Verlag Berlin, 2002, 155-169.
7.   Tamminen, S., Oulasvirta, A., Toiskalio, K. & Kankainen, A.: Understanding Mobile Contexts. In: Human-Computer Interaction with Mobile Devices, Proceedings of Mobile HCI 2003 (Verona Italy, September 2003). Springer-Verlag Berlin, 2003.

Specification and Generation
of Model 2 Web Interfaces

Dirk Draheim[1] and Gerald Weber[2]

[1] Institute of Computer Science
Free University Berlin
Germany
draheim@inf.fu-berlin.de
[2] Department of Computer Science
The University of Auckland
New Zealand
g.weber@cs.auckland.ac.nz

Abstract. We describe the language and tool Angie for the type-safe specification of Web presentation layers and the subsequent generation of an executable interface prototype. A textual description of a Web based dialogue can be directly expressed in the proposed language and is then automatically mapped onto a system structure in compliance with currently discussed Web design patterns like the Model 2 architecture. The Angie tool bridges between specification and implementation level in a different way than other approaches in the same area. The proposed language directly supports the system metaphor of form-oriented analysis, namely the system model as a bipartite state machine.

1 Introduction

We introduce the language and tool Angie for the specification of submit/response style systems and the subsequent generation of an executable interface prototype.

Web interaction based on HTML forms is untyped. In many common Web presentation frameworks this leaves the programmer with a considerable number of tasks like type conversion, which are moreover error prone. Angie frees the programmer from these tasks by introducing a clean abstraction layer and offering a generator tool based on this abstraction layer. Moreover, Angie supports the recommended Model 2 architecture. For this purpose the language Angie uses the system metaphor of form-oriented analysis [10,8], in which the system is modeled as a bipartite state machine. A description of a Web interface in the Angie language is independent of particular target languages or even particular frameworks for this architecture. Angie rather focuses on the principles of the HTML interaction model itself, not the platform for generating dynamic HTML. An Angie document allows the generation of Web presentation layers in compliance with the Model 2 architecture for arbitrary platforms, depending on the available code generators for the Angie compiler. A Java generator is provided, a PHP generator is planned. However, Angie integrates specifically well with advanced server pages technologies like NSP [5,6]. The reverse engineering tool JSPick [9] can be considered as the counterpart of Angie, because JSPick takes a JSP-based actual system and retrieves a typed specification.

M. Masoodian et al. (Eds.): APCHI 2004, LNCS 3101, pp. 101–110, 2004.
© Springer-Verlag Berlin Heidelberg 2004

On the syntax level the Angie approach offers different formats. In this papers we use for the sake of readability the C/Java like format, an XML format is however available as well.

Our running example system is a form-based seminar registration system as it is suited for a single course. The screen shots of the system are shown in Figure 1. The front page shows the students registered so far and contains links to the different interaction options. New students can register themselves. From the homepage, students already registered can change or delete their registration. Each link leads to a new page specific for the chosen option. We now introduce our notion of page transition diagrams, which we call *page diagrams*. This diagram type is intended to introduce the modeler into the Angie viewpoint of HTML dialogues in a hands-on fashion. It is especially suited as a starting point for the discussion with the domain expert about the intended task of the system. A page diagram as shown in Figure 1 describes a system as consisting of a finite set of pages, each page offering a finite number of interaction options.

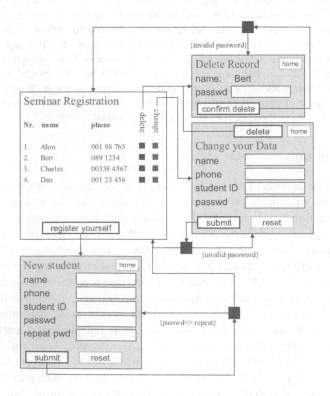

Fig. 1. Page diagram of the online seminar registration system.

A textual description of this system as a so called form storyboard can be directly expressed in Angie, and is then automatically mapped onto a system structure in compliance with currently discussed Web design patterns like the Model 2 architecture. The Angie tool bridges between specification and implementation level, therefore we give also an outline of the targeted technology, namely the JSP technology for implementing Web interfaces. We discuss the properties and problems of this technology for submit/response style systems.

2 Shortcomings of Common Web Presentation Frameworks

The advantages of Angie are best appreciated from the standpoint of the design phase. We describe why the working developer of servlet-based Web interfaces can gain advantages for everyday problems by using Angie.

The HTML form standard offers an untyped, text-based remote call mechanism, which is used as the standard parameter passing mechanism for dynamic Web sites. This mechanism is commonly, but not quite correctly, referred to as CGI parameter mechanism. We prefer *HTML form parameters* in the following as precise term for those parameters. The mechanism can be used in HTTP links as well. Hence the user of a HTTP dialogue can be viewed as invoking methods on the system via the browser.

But consider now e.g. Java Server Pages (JSP) and servlets [13]. Servlets and JSPs give access to HTML form parameter passing through an object-oriented mechanism, yet still in the style of the original CGI (Common Gateway Interface). Commonly accepted documentation and testing concepts, when used naively in the context of developing a servlet-based ultra-thin client tier, may consider only the purely technical parameters (HTTPRequest, HTTPResponse) instead of the parameters significant for business logic.

In the formal language called Angie each servlet or JSP is seen as a method with the form parameters as parameter list. Such a method is called a dialogue method.

Each result page offers the user the choice between different calls to dialogue methods as the next step in the dialogue. Dialogue methods can be called by links or forms. Forms can be seen as editable method calls offered to the user.

Angie allows specifying the links and forms contained in a page. The syntax of these declarations is derived from the Java method syntax. From each specified method declaration and call the generator will produce appropriate code templates as described below. The template generator maps each dialogue method to one JSP.

2.1 Model 2 Architecture

The Model 2 architecture is a recommended good practice for Web presentation layer design. A detailed discussion of the Model 2 Architecture can be found in [6]. In the Model 2 architecture, the user request is directed at a first dialogue method, the so called front component, which executes business logic. Dependent on the outcome, the front component redirects the request to other dialogue methods, the result pages. Note therefore that one JSP will potentially yield as many different result pages as it has redirect directives.

3   Introduction to the Viewpoint of Angie

Angie provides a typed view on Web interfaces. Each page method creates an own type of result page. In page diagrams the type of the currently shown page represents at the same time the state of the user session. The page diagram is therefore a proper state transition diagram. At this point we see the impact of the two-staged interaction paradigm: Only the page changes are modeled as state transitions in the page diagram. The state transition diagram is a coarse grained state transition since it depicts only page change as state change. This is a major difference in contrast to common user interface modeling with state transitions [17,16], where the fine-grained page interaction is modeled. But the most crucial observation we have to make, which immediately opens the conceptual path to form storyboards, is the observation that system response may be conditional: a single page change triggered by the user can result in different response pages, depending on the system state. A typical case is that either the regular response page or an error page is shown. Hence page diagrams as an interface prototype notation offer also conditional transitions. An example is the submission of a registration form in the diagram. The transition has a branching point depicted by a square from which different branches lead to different response pages. These branches are annotated with the conditions under which they occur. The branching points are called server actions.

Such a system can formally still be seen as a state transition diagram, and for this purpose we introduce a more abstract diagram, the form storyboard. Form storyboards take the understanding of submit/response style applications a step further by introducing into the system model one of the major conceptual cornerstones of form-oriented analysis: in form storyboards the system is seen as a bipartite state transition diagram. The bipartite state machine is the basic structure of form storyboards as can be seen in Figure 2. In this view the system is alternating between two kinds of states. The first kind of states corresponds to the pages of the system as before. These states are called client pages; they are depicted by rounded rectangles. The system remains in such a client page state until the user triggers a page change. In that moment the record with her previous input is sent to the system. The type of this record, as one can see in Figure 2, is specified within the rectangles depicting the second kind of states. They represent the systems action in response to a page change and are therefore called server actions. These states are left automatically by the system and lead to a new client page.

In Angie, form storyboards can be directly expressed, and the bipartite structure of the specification is checked by the Angie tool. Both kinds of states in the form storyboard are specified as dialogue methods in Angie. The client pages are declared with the keyword page and the server actions are declared with the keyword action. The bipartite structure of the form storyboard matches with the so called Model 2 Design pattern, and therefore supports current state-of-the-art Web interface development.

4   The Language Angie

The language Angie is a specification language for HTML dialogues. Its type system and syntax are oriented towards Java. Angie allows the specification of an HTML dialogue as a textual representation of a form storyboard. A whole Web interface is specified in Angie in a single source file.

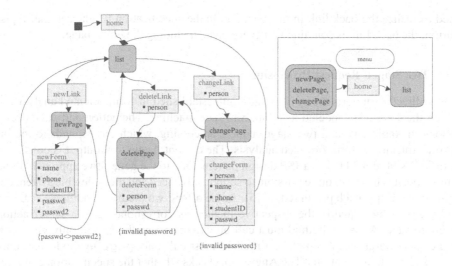

Fig. 2. Form storyboard for the seminar registration system

The Angie compiler performs static type checking on this specification and the code generator generates JSP templates, containing protected regions. The JSP templates can be completed by inserting custom code into the protected regions.

Each dialogue method has a fixed parameter set. The method construct in Angie is again similar to the method syntax in Java. The type checking requires, that the signatures of method definition and invocation is matching, i.e. that the parameter list matches and that the single parameters have the same type. Angie currently supports Strings, integers and Booleans.

In the body of Angie's method construct, the programmer has to specify all links and forms which will be offered by the result page of this method. Since links and forms enable calls of dialogue methods, their declarations resemble method calls. They start with the keywords link or form, they get a label, which enables references to them, and finally they have a method call syntax, e.g.

```
link myLabel calls myGroup.myMethod(myActPar1,..,myActParN).
```

For links, the actual parameters are names of variables. Angie generates a protected region in which variables with these names are accessible (the declaration is placed in front of the protected region). The custom code should assign values to these variables. In the code subsequent to the protected region, these variables are used to construct an appropriate HTML link code.

In form declarations each actual parameter is a pair of the widget type that will be generated and a variable name. The values of these variables are used to provide the default values within the widgets.

These link or form declarations serve as specifications of the possible next actions the user can take.

The example also shows the usage of the menu construct. This construct may contain link and form declarations, which will be included on every result page. It is used to realize the back link in the example. In the specification for the seminar registration, the back link is contained on every page, including the home page.

4.1 Two Staged Request Processing

Angie directly supports the system paradigm established in form-oriented analysis, in which the system is modeled as a bipartite state machine. The action and page declarations in Angie enable a two-stage request processing, which corresponds to the bipartite structure of form-oriented analysis. The current Angie tool output is consistent with SUNs Model 2 [13] as a JSP design pattern. Due to the generative approach of the Angie tool it is however quite possible to support advanced and more flexible system designs like the approach presented in [5]. Angie offers two method modifiers, `action` and `page`, which qualify the respective method as corresponding to a server action or client page. A `page` method must call only `action` methods, and only via `link` or `form` declarations. An `action` method must call only `page` methods, and only via `redirect` declarations. The Angie tool checks whether the specification complies with the given rules, and whether all methods have a modifier.

4.2 Generation of Code

The language Angie serves as a formal specification language, but also as input to the Angie tool, a type checker and generator. The Angie tool performs the following static checks:

- It checks whether all calls to methods (in the result pages of other methods) have correct parameter sets. This is important, especially for forms. Here the tool checks whether the widgets chosen in each actual parameter matches the type of the corresponding formal parameter.
- It checks syntactically whether every `action` calls only `page` targets via `redirect` declarations, and whether every `page` calls only `action` targets via `link` or `form` declarations.

For correct input, the Angie generator produces the following output code:

- For each method it produces one JSP with the same name. Within that JSP it produces code which performs runtime type checking whether the method is called with the correct parameters, and converts the parameters to Java local variables with the same name as the formal parameters in the Angie file. Subsequently it creates a protected region which can be used as a method body for the Java code.
- For every `link` or `form` declaration in the Angie method body it creates HTML code, giving a form or link which offers a correct call to the corresponding method. Within that HTML code, the Angie tool again creates protected regions for each HTML parameter, defining where to insert Java code which produces actual parameters. Similarly, it creates redirect directives for the redirect declarations in the method body.
- The Angie tool produces comments, structuring the generated code.

4.3   The Seminar Registration System in Angie

We now give a part of the Angie code for the running example, the seminar registration system. The code specifies the home page and the change subdialogue. The subdialogues for deleting and new entries are similar, we see the calls to their methods e.g. on the homepage.

```
menu {
    link home    calls home()
}
action home() {
    redirect list()
}
page list() {
    link delete calls deleteLink(personId)
  or link change calls changeLink(personId)
  or link change calls newLink()
}
action changeLink(int selectedId) {
    redirect changePage(selectedId)
}
page changePage(Person person) {
    link delete calls deleteLink(personId)
  or form submit calls changeForm(HIDDEN personId,
                                  TEXTFIELD name,
                                  TEXTFIELD phone,
                                  TEXTFIELD studentID,
                                  PASSWORD passwd)
}
action changeForm(int person, String name, String phone,
               int studentID, Password passwd) {
    redirect changePage(personId)
  or redirect list()
}
//  ... further specifications omitted
```

5   The Position of Angie Within Related Technologies

In comparison with other tools Angie can be seen to be on the declarative side, while other tools typically fall on a rather operational side.

We can see that if we compare Angie with Web presentation frameworks; Angie does not prescribe architecture [11] or design, even if it goes very well with concrete technologies. This is our very aim in making an abstraction; we want to have added value for the concrete technology, yet we do not want to be tied to that. In that sense the high level language like Angie directly supports an architecture like SUNs Model2 JSP architecture[13]. As one may check against these two examples, our proposal neither encourages nor discourages concrete architectures or designs. Instead, it starts as a best practice for documenting JSP-based systems and ends up as a development discipline for such systems. This is in contrast to, for example, the Struts framework [4], which leads to very particular Model 2 architectures only. Struts suggests dynamic type checking. Angie on the other hand consequently performs static type checking and ensures that the resulting system is statically well typed [1].

In comparing tools like Angie one has to be aware of the precise task this tool is designed for. It has nothing to do with e.g. Web authoring tools, which are more related to content management systems, another important technology class. Such tools typically also achieve a certain abstraction level, but this targets questions of information modularity, as expressed in description languages like WebML [2].

It is interesting to compare Angie with interactive Tools, e.g. Wizards [18] and graphical IDE's. From the software engineering standpoint the important advantage of Angie is, that you have a formal specification in form of the Angie source code, while in the case of Wizards you have only the resulting system.

The functionality of Angie is different from tools like [12], which provide an interconnection between different language paradigms like HTML and SQL. Angie takes one signature specification and generates code in the different paradigms, Java and HTML, according to this signature specification.

With respect to performance, the use of Angie leads to almost no overhead. The main function of Angie is not to generate Java statements, but to generate matching HTML and Java signatures. Additionally Angie generates conversion code and dynamic type checking, which serves as an additional firewall against invalid calls to the system. This code must be provided in any stable system implementation, even if Angie is not used.

6   Conclusion

As starting point for our contribution we have observed:

- HTTP offers a page based dialogue paradigm.
- HTML forms introduce a remote call mechanism with key-value lists as parameter sets.
- Servlets do not enforce strong typing, they do not control overloading.
- The servlet mechanism has no inbuilt rejection mechanism for invalid requests (no runtime type checking).
- Naive Java documentation misses the point for servlets.

We proposed specification guidelines based on a formal language Angie and a template generator taking Angie as input. Our main paradigm is that we view a system with HTML interface as a static object that is described by its signature. The use of Angie offers the following advantages:

- A type system for HTTP requests connected to the Java type system, and support for the enforcement of this type system.
- Generation of runtime type checks according to the type system.
- Support for Model 2 Architecture, based on the System paradigm of Form Oriented Analysis.

– Generation of HTTP requests in compliance with the type system.
– Generation of a variety of input forms for each signature as well as generation of links.

Appendix: Angie Grammar

We present here a simplified syntax, which defines a superset of the Angie language.

```
syntax    ::= <LOCATION> <EQUALS> <LOCATOR> methods ( menu )?
methods ::= ( method )*
method  ::=
  ( <ACTION> | <PAGE> )? <IDENTIFIER> <OPEN> parameters <CLOSE>
  <CURLYOPEN> ( calls )? <CURLYCLOSE>
parameters ::= ( parameter ( <COMMA> parameter )* )?
parameter  ::=
  ( ( <BOOLEAN> <IDENTIFIER> )
  |( ( <INT> | <STRING> )
     ( ( <ARRAYOPEN> <ARRAYCLOSE> <IDENTIFIER> )
       |( <IDENTIFIER> ( <ARRAYOPEN> <ARRAYCLOSE> )? ) ) ) )
calls    ::= ( call ( <OR> call )* )
call     ::= ( link | form | redirect )
redirect ::=
  <REDIRECT> <IDENTIFIER>
  <OPEN> actualLinkParameters <CLOSE>
link ::=
  <LINK> <IDENTIFIER> <CALLS>  <IDENTIFIER>
  <OPEN> actualLinkParameters <CLOSE>
actualLinkParameters ::=
   ( <IDENTIFIER> ( <COMMA> <IDENTIFIER> )* )?
form ::=
  <FORM> <IDENTIFIER> <CALLS>  <IDENTIFIER>
  <OPEN> actualFormParameters <CLOSE>
actualFormParameters ::=
  ( actualFormParameter ( <COMMA> actualFormParameter )* )?
actualFormParameter ::=
  ( <TEXT> | <TEXTAREA> | <CHECKBOX> | <RADIO> | <COMBOBOX> |
    <MULTIPLELIST> | <HIDDEN> ) <IDENTIFIER>
menu ::= <MENU> <CURLYOPEN> calls <CURLYCLOSE>
```

References

1. Luca Cardelli. Type systems. In: Handbook of Computer Science and Engineering. CRC Press, 1997
2. S. Ceri, P. Fraternali, S. Paraboschi. Web Modeling Language, (WebML): a modeling language for designing Web sites. Proceedings of the 9 th. International World Wide Web Conference, Elsevier, 2000, pp.137-157.
3. E.J. Chikofsky, J.H. Reverse Engineering and Design Recovery: A Taxonomy. IEEE Software, pp. 13-17, 1990.

4. Malcolm Davis. Struts, an open-source MVC implementation. IBM developerWorks, February 2001
5. Dirk Draheim and Gerald Weber. Strongly Typed Server Pages. In: Proceedings of The Fifth Workshop on Next Generation Information Technologies and Systems, LNCS 2382, Springer, June 2002.
6. Dirk Draheim, Elfriede Fehr and Gerald Weber. Improving the Web Presentation Layer Architecture. In (X. Zhou, Y. Zhang, M.E. Orlowska, Editors): Web Technologies and Applications. LNCS 2642, Springer, 2003.
7. Dirk Draheim and Gerald Weber. Storyboarding Form-Based Interfaces. In: Proceedings of INTERACT 2003 - Ninth IFIP TC13 International Conference on Human-Computer Interaction. IOS Press, 2003.
8. Dirk Draheim and Gerald Weber. Modeling Submit/Response Style Systems with Form Charts and Dialogue Constraints. Workshop on Human Computer Interface for Semantic Web and Web Applications. LNCS 2889, pp. 267 - 278, Springer, 2003.
9. Dirk Draheim, Elfriede Fehr and Gerald Weber. JSPick - A Server Pages Design Recovery Tool. In: Proceedings of CSMR 2003 - 7th European Conference on Software Maintenance and Reengineering. IEEE Press, 2003.
10. Dirk Draheim and Gerald Weber. Form-Oriented Analysis, Springer, 2004, to appear.
11. Nicholas Kassem and the Enterprise Team. Designing Enterprise Applications with the Java 2 Platform, Enterprise Edition. Sun Microsystems, 2000
12. Tam Nguyen, V. Srinivasan. Accessing Relational Databases from the World Wide Web. Proceedings of the 1996 ACM SIGMOD, 1996
13. Eduardo Pelegri-Llopart, Larry Cable. Java Server Pages Specification, v.1.1. Sun Press, 1999
14. James Rumbaugh, Ivar Jacobson, Grady Booch. The Unified Modeling Language - Reference Manual. Addison-Wesley, 1999
15. John Vlissides. The Hollywood Principle. C++ Report, vol. 8, Feb. 1996
16. P. Vilain, D. Schwabe, C.S. de Souza. A Diagrammatic Tool for Representing User Interaction in UML. Lecture Notes in Computer Science 1939, Proc. UML'2000, York, 2000
17. A.I. Wasserman. Extending State Transition Diagrams for the Specification of Human-Computer Interaction. IEEE Transaction on Software Engineering, vol. SE-11, no. 8, IEEE, 1985, pp. 699-713.
18. James R. Borck. WebSphere Studio Application Developer 4.0. In: JavaWorld, March 2003.

Metaphors for Electronic Music Production in *Reason* and *Live*

Matthew Duignan[1], James Noble[1], Pippin Barr[1], and Robert Biddle[2]

[1] School of Mathematics and Computing Sciences
Victoria University of Wellington, New Zealand
Matthew.Duignan@mcs.vuw.ac.nz
[2] Human Oriented Technology Laboratory
Carleton University, Ottawa, Canada
Robert_Biddle@carleton.ca

Abstract. Electronic music production was originally accomplished using a variety of electronic components and conventional analogue recording techniques. Both the electronic components and the recording equipment are now being replaced by computer software. In this paper we present a comparative study of two popular new systems, *Reason* and *Live*, concentrating on the role of user-interface metaphors. We compare the two systems, identify the key ways metaphor is used, and describe how it affects usability of the systems focusing on the role that user-interface metaphor play in their design.

1 Introduction

Electronic music production was originally accomplished using a variety of electronic components and conventional analogue recording techniques. Now both the electronic components and the recording equipment are being replaced by computer software. We are interested in the user interface design for such software, and in this paper we present a comparative study of two popular new systems, *Reason* and *Live*, concentrating on the role of user-interface metaphors.

Most electronic music systems have similar functional structure, regardless of whether they are hardware or software. As sources of audio signals, there are *sound generators*, which can include synthesisers, recorded sound "loop" players, or drum machines. There are also *effects processors*, which filter, distort, compress, or otherwise modify an audio signal. To combine audio signals, *mixers* are used, that allow selection of sources, and setting of audio signal levels. Finally, there are *sequencers*, that control audio source behaviour over time.

We are interested in the design of electronic music software in particular both because the domain is highly specific and complex, and because elements of electronic music systems are essentially specialised programming systems. Our previous work in this area has focused on corpus analysis of one very specialised system for sound synthesis [1,2,3] . Much existing computer music software utilises interface metaphor to a striking degree. Recently, we have been working towards a principled model to guide understanding interface metaphor. This paper is a case study which utilises a simplified

M. Masoodian et al. (Eds.): APCHI 2004, LNCS 3101, pp. 111–120, 2004.
© Springer-Verlag Berlin Heidelberg 2004

version of our framework. This serves the dual purpose of illuminating some of the interesting ways in which interface metaphor is being used in commercial software, and also acts as a proof of concept for our analytical model.

2   Metaphor

The concept of a user-interface metaphor is one which is widely known in the field of human-computer interaction and often utilised in the process of user-interface design. There has been advocacy and acceptance [4,5,6,7], and also expressions of caution [8,9], and many other points of view. Many metaphors, such as the desktop metaphor and the trash-can metaphor, have become ubiquitous. In recent work, we have developed a principled model for understanding and evaluating user interface metaphor. In particular, we have explored the philosophical and semiotic foundations of user interface metaphor [10] , and suggested heuristics based on the principles that can provide guidance for development and evaluation of user interface metaphors [11,12].

In this paper we will explore the user interfaces of the two music systems using our heuristics to identify and evaluate their key metaphors. For each of the two systems, we first provide a general overview. We then identify several of the key metaphors involved in the interface. For each, we name the metaphor in small capitals (e.g. THE DATA IS A DOCUMENT) following the convention of Lakoff and Johnson [13]. We then identify the *representaman* of the metaphor; this involves the graphical and language elements that suggest the presence of the metaphor, and is a key idea from the semiotics of Pierce upon which our principled model is based [10]. Lastly we evaluate the metaphor , considering the issues that affect usability. We focus primarily on *structural* metaphors, where the structure of a real-world object is used to frame process elements in the user interface. The subset of the heuristics from our model that we consider follow. During our discussion of Live and Reason, these metaphors will be referred to where appropriate as H*n*:

1. *When choosing metaphors based on real world objects consider the real world usability issues for insight into interface usability.*
2. *When using orientational metaphors, make sure they fit into the overall framework defined by that orientation.*
3. *When using new metaphors, carefully indicate the UI metaphorical entailments to the user.*
4. *When using conventional metaphors, be careful to indicate any deviation from the accepted set of metaphorical entailments.*
5. *Aim to use as many metaphorical entailments as possible while still keeping a firm focus on actual functionality.*
6. *Represent only those affordances of the vehicle which have an implemented function in the user-interface.*
7. *As far as possible make sure that metaphors are coherent with one another.*
8. *Ensure metaphors do not inhibit access to any functionality.*
9. *Always address the aspects of the system* not *explained by metaphors.*
10. *Harness the user's experience to help identifying useful vehicles.*

11. *Allow expert users to circumvent the metaphorical means of achieving tasks where such circumvention would increase task efficiency.*

3   Reason

Reason [14], aims to bring physical electronic music hardware into the realm of software. Reason emulates hardware synthesisers, mixers, samplers, drum-machines, loop players, and various effects units on general purpose computers. In Reason, each of these components are presented to the user as graphical versions of their real world equivalents, with the knobs, buttons, LEDs, cables and switches of physical hardware all reproduced.

In the physical world, electronic music hardware such as synthesisers, samplers, equalisers, effects units, and various other components are designed to be mounted vertically in standard sized racks. As a general rule, the controls for these components are situated on the face of the rack, while the sockets for wiring them together are on the rear. Reason reproduces this, with its interface dominated by a rack. Each of Reason's components are stacked vertically in this rack. Pressing the *TAB* key flips the rack around, exposing the cabling connecting the various components together. Reason's rack interface is shown on the left of figure 1, and the rear cable connection interface is shown on the right.

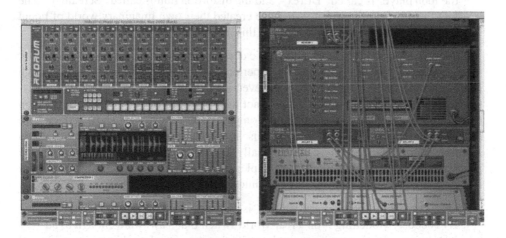

Fig. 1. Reason's user interface.

Metaphor: REASON IS A RACK

- *Graphical* The left and right hand sides of the window have a graphical depiction of the metal framework of a hardware rack. Devices in the rack have screws or rivets attaching them to the rack.
- *Language* The Options menu has a "Toggle Rack Front/Rear" item.

The entire design of Reason is based on the idea that it is "a virtual studio rack" [14]. While the idea of rack-based electronic music components is something that many users will be familiar with (H10), it seems that there could be unresolved issues regarding the real world usability of racks (H1). Constraining users to a rack may create undue complexity for the user as all components must be set-up vertically. This makes it difficult for users to layout components in ways that make sense to them, and that reduce the overlaying of cables. Other products such as the Nord Modular [15] and Reaktor [16] do allow arbitrary layout of components in a two dimensional space [1] (H17). While hardware racks make sense in the physical world for physical reasons, it does not follow that a metaphor of a rack will be the best solution in the software domain.

Metaphor: A COMPONENT IS A DEVICE

– *Graphical* The appearance of each of the components are modelled very closely on physical hardware. Knobs, switches, power plugs, fuses, serial numbers and manufacturing dates are all depicted.
– *Language* The back of Reason's components feature text such as:
    WARNING: To reduce the risk of fire or electrical shock, do not expose this equipment to rain or moisture...
Another curious use of language contributing to the device metaphor is that each device has been given its own branding. The drum-machine is called "Redrum", the loop player is called "Dr:rex", and the distortion unit is called "Scream 4". The fact that Propellerhead Software have created their own imaginary world of brand name hardware shows the strength of this metaphor.

Using the metaphor of a physical music device is consistent with the rack metaphor (H7), and utilises many users existing experience with music hardware (H10) through Reason's very literal interpretation. However, it seems that the real world usability issues of electronic music hardware may not have been taken fully into consideration (H1). For example, the "Redrum Drum Computer" device can only show sixteen time steps of a single drum part at a time, because it only has room for sixteen buttons. Even a simple four bar drum pattern will typically take up thirty-two time steps. The same problem is evident in the following example, where a reviewer becomes irritated with Reason's use of awkward switches in the interface [17]:

One thing that annoyed me slightly is the awkward bypass switch for the RV70000...Modelling it on a real-world switch that's awkward enough to adjust even when it's a real one surely isn't what the virtual world's supposed to be like!

Additionally, Reason's devices have depictions of superfluous switches and cables that cannot be manipulated in the interface (H6). It is possible that this could lead to some confusion for new users. Using hardware interface interaction models, rather than those standardly employed in graphical user interfaces leads to problems illustrated by the following [17]:

The eight virtual pots around the display are used to adjust those parameters, so unfortunately no easy life dragging graphics around the display.

Metaphor: THE CONNECTION BETWEEN DEVICES IS A CABLE

– *Graphical* The devices have jack cable style input and output sockets. The cables hang between these sockets and shake when they are moved.
– *Language* The Options menu has a "Show Cables" item.

The use of cables makes intuitive sense for a component connection metaphor, especially considering the extensive use of the hardware metaphor in the devices they are connecting (H7). One clear problem that emerges from the cable metaphor comes back to the use of the rack metaphor. The constraints that the rack puts on layout, coupled with the opaque appearance and non-intelligent hanging of cables is the source of very real problems (H1). Comments such as the following begin to illustrate the disadvantages of the metaphor:

> The rack flips round to display the kind of spaghetti hell you would usually associate with a hardware set-up — [17]

Another consequence of the cable metaphor is that it conflicts with other potential systems of device organisation that might be more effective (H11):

> The sequencer can trigger pattern changes in pattern-based modules, but you cannot switch sounds using program changes, and the sound modules aren't multitimbral. To work around those limitations, you must run multiple instances of the modules. Doing that doesn't appear to affect processing much, but it can make for potentially unwieldy rack configurations. *I would prefer a true matrix-switching setup, but that would probably interfere with the cabling metaphor.*" — [18] Emphasis added.

4 Live

Live by Ableton [19] is designed to "blur the separation between recording, composition and performance" [19]. It is principally a loop and sample playing tool, providing beat matching and real time audio warping, while also allowing audio input from Rewire [20] compatible audio software and the system's audio hardware. Its interface has two main views, the *session* view and the *arranger* view.

Session The session view, shown to the left in figure 2, takes the general form of a mixing desk. It is broken into a series of vertical tracks, each of which have their own volume faders, and other audio controls. Running horizontally along the top of the mixer are a number of rows called *scenes*. A scene consists of a number of slots for audio clips, each of which corresponds to a track. Triggering a scene causes all of the scene's audio clips to begin playing through the mixer. The user can drag and drop additional audio clips from a directory browser into scenes at any time.

Arranger The arranger view, shown on the right of figure 2, consists of a time-based view of the tracks. Unlike the session view, in this view tracks are long shallow strips laid out vertically: time now occupies the horizontal axis. The user can drag audio clips into the arranger, record audio from a sound source, or capture the output from

Fig. 2. Live's interface consisting of the Session view (left) and Arranger view (right).

interacting with Live's session view. The user can also automate a track's effects and other parameters in the arranger by reshaping graphs which are overlaid on the track.

Effects In either the session or arranger view, when the user clicks on a track, the effects associated with that track are displayed. This can be seen in the lower area of the arranger in figure 2. Effects take the output of a track, and perform various parameterised audio transformations in real time. To add an effect to a track, the user can drag and drop it from the effects library folder on the left into the track's effects area.

Audio clip When the user selects an audio clip in either the session or arranger views, an interface for manipulating the clip is displayed. This can be seen in the lower area of the session view in figure 2. The user can then modify the audio clip's various parameters. This includes the ability to *warp* the audio clip to change its inherent timing. The warping engine stretches and squeezes the audio without altering its pitch.

Metaphor: THE SESSION VIEW IS A MIXER

- *Graphical* The display has the important components and layout of an audio mixer. This includes a number of audio channels with volume faders, send controls, and a master channel.
- *Language* The Info View describes the area as the "Session Mixer"

The mixer is a very conventional metaphor in computer music tools. As Live's entire session view is based around the mixer metaphor, this takes advantage of many users' prior knowledge of how mixing desks work (H10). For example, each track on the mixer can be sent to one or more *send tracks* via the "Sends" volume controls. In Live, there is an absence of visual cues pointing to the fact that the send tracks are conceptually different from the regular tracks. Also, there is no visual indication of the signal flow from regular tracks to send tracks, other than a corresponding number or the first letter of the send track name sitting beside each send control. This is where prior knowledge of the metaphor becomes important, as users familiar with mixers will be able to rapidly identify and utilise this functionality (H10). One key place where Live does not follow an entailment of the metaphor can be seen again with the audio send functionality. Live only displays as many send volume controls as there are actual send tracks. The user can interactively add new send tracks, and each regular track will gain a new send volume control dynamically. This can be compared to Reason's mixer, which closely follows the real world.

Metaphor: THE ARRANGER IS A MULTITRACK RECORDER

- *Graphical* The main display of the Arranger is a series of horizontal *tracks*. These show both the audio content, and controls for each track. Each track can be independently manipulated and controlled.
- *Language* The term "tracks" is used throughout the interface.

This metaphor is used very commonly in computer music recording and writing software. The multitrack recorder metaphor allows multiple tracks of audio to be recorded into the system, and then played back simultaneously. Track parameters such as volume and panning can be controlled independently of other tracks, affecting the playback of the given track. Typically, multitrack systems allow the user to *automate* track parameters over time. Live's multitracking system allows all of this.

Live's use of the multitrack recording metaphor is interesting in that it is in tension with Live's direct support of loop and sample style composition (H7). The multitrack recorder metaphor is ideal for supporting the recording and arrangement of music featuring real world instruments. However, while most sample and loop based music will be built from multiple drum tracks and bass tracks etc., the ability to throw arbitrary audio clips into the mix live does not mean that these clips should belong to a particular track.

Metaphor: AN EFFECT IS A DEVICE

- *Graphical* The effects have abstract representations of typical device controls, such as knobs, switches and faders.
- *Language* The interface refers to them as devices. They also have what Live refers to as "Factory Settings".

The use of the effects device metaphor will suggest to users familiar with effects devices that they can be "plugged in" to other components, and that the effects will have settings that can be manipulated (H10). However, the metaphor is kept at a quite abstract level. Instead of wiring an effect up between an arbitrary sound source and destination, Live simply provides a mechanism to associate an instance of an effect device with a particular track. This is analogous to *effect inserts* in real world mixers. This means that you are limited to as many effects processing flows as you have tracks. This issue is discussed further in section 5.

Metaphor: SOUND IS A WAVE FORM

- *Graphical* When a user selects an audio clip, a waveform representation of the audio is shown in the sample display area. This can be seen in the lower part of the session view in figure 2. The arranger view also shows waveforms as representations of the audio clips, placing a graphic of the waveforms in the time and track where the audio is located.

The waveform is a conventional metaphor for computer tools that deal with audio. Originating from oscilloscope displays, this metaphor is based on its component orientational metaphors AMPLITUDE IS WIDTH and THE PASSAGE OF TIME IS RIGHT. As this is such a common metaphor, the majority of non-novice users should be able to utilise their understanding of waveforms in Live's interface (H10). This metaphor is of central importance in Live as it serves as the principle interface for flexible real-time audio warping. When a user selects an audio clip, a detailed display of the audio is shown as a waveform. The user can use *warp markers* to tell Live where they want the beats of the bar to be in relation to the shape of the waveform. For example, if the user sees a large jump in the width of the waveform, they may deduce that this is the kick-drum they can hear when they play the sample. If they want the kick-drum to land on the third beat of the bar, they can drag the warp marker labelled *3* onto the large jump. However, this begins to break down the orientational metaphor of THE PASSAGE OF TIME IS TO THE RIGHT. Because time, as the user perceives it, is now indicated by the location of the warp markers, rather than by horizontal position, the usage of the waveform metaphor is deviating from its accepted set of behaviours (H4). While this interface is comprehensible, we would expect an alternative interface that preserved the accepted behaviour of the waveform metaphor might be more appropriate and intuitive.

5   Comparison

Live and Reason solve similar problems with a mix of comparable and differing techniques. The following sections compare these techniques with a focus on how metaphors are utilised.

Shared conventional metaphors Reason and Live share a large number of conventional metaphors. Both utilise the knob metaphor, where the user clicks on a knob and drags up or down, which causes the knob to rotate. A convention has developed in music interfaces where UP IS CLOCKWISE and DOWN IS ANTI-CLOCKWISE, in line with corresponding metaphors for the parameters that the knob is controlling. Both applications also feature the mixer metaphor as an important part of their organisation, including the standard fader volume control which can be moved vertically to modify volume. These interfaces include the knob, fader and mixer metaphors, as well as the button metaphor. There are a large number of other minor metaphors that Live and Reason have in common, but it is not practical to enumerate them all here.

Music hardware metaphors Both Reason and Live utilise electronic music hardware metaphors. While Live's interface uses these metaphors to a lesser extent, the example of Live's mixer send tracks, discussed in section 4, shows that it is also dependent on leveraging peoples real world knowledge. What may become a problem is that as music software becomes increasingly powerful, it is likely that it will begin to replace music hardware altogether. An important question that must be answered to validate the dependence on music hardware metaphors is: what proportion of new and potential users have prior experience with music hardware?

Realism Vs. Abstraction Both Reason and Live incorporate hardware metaphors into their interfaces. However, the obvious difference between them is how tightly they mimic their real world counterparts. Reason closely follows its hardware counterparts, while Live takes a more abstract approach, and this is apparent in the visual cues of their interfaces. The attention to visual accuracy in Reason's interface is a strong cue that the behaviour of the interface will match physical hardware devices.

One example of Live and Reason's different approaches can be seen in how Live associates effects devices with a particular track. This utilises a common approach used in user interfaces where one element is shown as a property of parent element. In Live, when you select a track, the effect properties of that track are shown. Contrasted with Reason, where all effects are on the screen at all times, linked by a complicated network of cabling, it is clear that Live has a more elegant approach that is conventional in software interfaces.

The principle problem with Reason's literal approach is that you keep all of the disadvantages of physical hardware, without utilising the advantages that software interfaces offer. The example of Live's dynamic mixer, compared to Reason's static "physical" mixer is an example of how Live exploits the flexible nature of software while Reason sticks to resemblance. The latter may be less useful, but it can still generate enthusiasm [17]:

> The cables even jiggled as you moved them. This in itself was a nice touch, but more importantly illustrated the kind of over-engineering and attention to detail we've come to expect from this Swedish software company.

6   Conclusions

The new applications *Reason* and *Live* show that metaphor is still an important part of real world interface design. In this paper, we have used our semiotic theory of metaphors, and the heuristics derived from that theory, to compare and contrast *Reason* and *Live*, two integrated electronic music production systems. We chose electronic music production for this study as it is a relatively new application area, and so the metaphors found in its user interfaces have not yet succumbed to conventionality. We demonstrated that our analyses were able to uncover significant similarities and differences between the two tools and the way they utilised metaphor. More importantly, we were also able to provide principled rationales to explain these similarities and differences. We expect these analyses could assist musicians trying to make sense of some of the interface design decisions found in Reason and Live; more pragmatically, we believe they will be applicable to the designers of next-generation electronic music production systems, as well as to any interface designer who intends to utilise metaphor.

References

1. James Noble and Robert Biddle. *Software Visualization, K. Zhang(Ed.)*, chapter Visual Program Visualisation. Kluwer, 2003.
2. James Noble and Robert Biddle. Visualising 1,051 visual programs: Module choice and layout in nord modular patch language. In John Grundy and Paul Calder, editors, *User Interfaces 2002*. Australian Computer Society, 2002.

3. James Noble and Robert Biddle. Program visualisation for visual programs. In Peter Eades and Tim Pattison, editors, *Information Visualisation 2001*. Australian Computer Society, 2001.
4. Jeff Johnson, Teresa L. Roberts, William Verplank, David C. Smith, Charles H. Irby, Marian Beard, and Keven Mackey. The Xerox Star: A retrospective. *IEEE Computer*, 22(9):11–29, September 1989.
5. Steven Johnson. *Interface Culture: How New Technology Transforms the Way We Create and Communicate*. Harper SanFrancisco, 1997.
6. Apple Computer, Inc. Staff. *Macintosh Human Interface Guidelines*. Addison-Wesley, 1992.
7. Microsoft Corporation. *The Windows Interface Guidelines for Software Design: An Application Design Guide*. Microsoft Press, 1995.
8. John M. Carroll and Robert L. Mack. Learning to use a word processor: By doing, by thinking, and by knowing. In Ronald M. Baecker, Jonathan Grudin, William A. S. Buxtin, and Saul Greenberg, editors, *Readings in Human-Computer Interaction: Toward the Year 2000*, pages 698–717. Morgan Kaufmann Publishers, Inc., 1995.
9. Donald A. Norman. *The Invisible Computer*. The MIT Press, 1998.
10. Pippin Barr, James Noble, and Robert Biddle. *Virtual, Distributed and Flexible Organisations*, chapter A Semiotic Model of User-Interface Metaphor. Kluwer Academic Publishers, 2003.
11. Pippin Barr, Robert Biddle, and James Noble. A taxonomy of user interface metaphors. In *Proceedings of SIGCHI-NZ Symposium On Computer-Human Interaction (CHINZ 2002)*, Hamilton, New Zealand, 2002.
12. Pippin Barr. User-interface metaphors in theory and practise. Master's thesis, Victoria University of Wellington, 2003.
13. George Lakoff and Mark Johnson. *Metaphors We Live By*. The University of Chicago Press, 1980.
14. Propellerhead Software. Reason, 2003.
    http://www.propellerhead.se/products/reason/.
15. Clavia Digital Musical Instruments. Nord modular & nord micro modular, 2003.
    http://www.clavia.se/nordmodular/index.htm.
16. Native Instruments. Reaktor 4 - the future of sound, 2003.
    http://www.native-instruments.com/index.php?reaktor4_us.
17. Future Music. Propellerhead reason 2.5. *Future Music*, FM136:30–37, June 2003.
18. Jeff Burger. Propellerhead reason 1.0 (mac/win). *Electronic Musician*, 17 i7:164, July 2001.
19. Ableton. Live: The audio sequencing instrument, 2003.
    http://www.ableton.com/index.php?main=live.
20. Propellerhead Software. Rewire, 2003.
    http://www.propellerhead.se/products/rewire/.

Extending the Perceptual User Interface to Recognise Movement

Richard Green

Computer Science, University of Canterbury,
Christchurch 8020, New Zealand
richard.green@canterbury.ac.nz

Abstract. Perceptual User Interfaces (PUIs) automatically extract user input from natural and implicit components of human activity such as gestures, direction of gaze, facial expression and body movement. This paper presents a Continuous Human Movement Recognition (CHMR) system for recognising a large range of specific movement skills from continuous 3D full-body motion. A new methodology defines an alphabet of dynemes, units of full-body movement skills, to enable recognition of diverse skills. Using multiple Hidden Markov Models, the CHMR system attempts to infer the movement skill that could have produced the observed sequence of dynemes. This approach enables the CHMR system to track and recognise hundreds of full-body movement skills from gait to twisting summersaults. This extends the perceptual user interface beyond frontal posing or only tracking one hand to recognise and understand full-body movement in terms of everyday activities.

1. Introduction

Research and commercial interest in the design and development of Perceptual User Interfaces (PUIs) is growing rapidly. This paper provides a technical analysis of the problems associated with accurately recognising and tracking body and limb position, and describes a Continuous Human Movement Recognition (CHMR) system that is based on a generalisable "dyneme" model of human movement. Although our focus is on the technical challenges of recognising movement, doing so is the first component in many of the new breed of PUIs. Beyond merely driving an avatar by tracking joint angles, this research extends PUIs to more effectively interact with humans by recognising activities from full body motion. This activity aware PUI now needs to know when each skill begins and ends with such temporal segmentation enabling recognition of hundreds of skills to progress PUIs to activity understanding.

The CHMR framework (Figure 1) forms a basis for recognising and understanding full-body movement in 3D for a large diverse range of movement skills.

Human movement is commercially[1] tracked by requiring subjects to wear joint markers/identifiers, an approach with has the disadvantage of significant set up time.

---

[1] Commercially available trackers are listed at www.hitl.washington.edu/scivw/tracker-faq.html

M. Masoodian et al. (Eds.): APCHI 2004, LNCS 3101, pp. 121-132, 2004.
© Springer-Verlag Berlin Heidelberg 2004

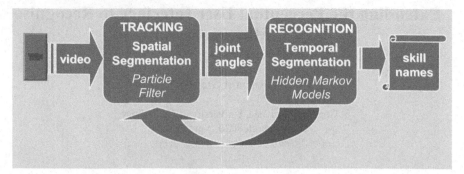

Figure 1. Overview of the continuous human movement recognition framework.

Such an invasive approach to tracking has barely changed since it was developed in the 1970s. Using a less invasive approach free of markers, computer vision research into tracking and recognising full-body human motion has so far been mainly limited to gait or frontal posing [21]. Various approaches for tracking the whole body have been proposed in the image processing literature using a variety of 2D and 3D shape models and image models as listed in Table 1.

Authors	Shape model	Image model
Hogg	Cylinders	Edge
Rohr	Cylinders	Edge
Gavrila & Davis	Superquadrics	Edge
Drummond & Cipolla	Conics	Edge
Goncalves et al.	Cones	Edge
Kakadiaris & Metaxas	Deformable	Edge
Wren & Pentland	2D colour blobs	Skin colour blobs
Ju et al.	Patches (2D)	Flow
Bregler & Malik	Cylinders	Flow
Wang et al.	Cylinders	Flow
Cham & Rehg	Patches (2D)	Template
Wachter & Nagel	Cones	Flow + Edge
Plänkers & Fua	Deformable	Silhouette + Disparity
Deutscher et al.	Cones	Edge + Silhouette
Brand	Outline	Silhouette moments
Rosales & Sclaroff	Outline	Silhouette moments
Liebowitz & Carlsson	Outline	Hand-marked joints
Taylor	Outline	Hand-marked joints
Leventon & Freeman	Outline	Hand-marked joints

Table 1 Comparison of different human body models.

Computer-human PUIs will become increasingly effective as computers more accurately recognise and understand full-body movement in terms of everyday activities. Stokoe began recognising human movement in the 1970s by constructing sign language gestures (signs) from hand location, shape and movement and assumed that these three components occur concurrently with no sequential contrast (independent variation of these components within a single sign). Ten years later Liddel and Johnson used sequential contrast and introduced the movement-hold model. In the early 1990s Yamato et al began using HMMs to recognise tennis strokes. Recognition accuracy rose as high as 99.2% in Starner and Pentland's work in 1996. Constituent components of movement have been named cheremes [33], phonemes [37] and movemes [3].

Author   - **Recognition approach**
Stokoe 78 – transcription: sign = location (tab) + hand shape (dez) + movement (sig)
Tamura and Kawasaki 88 - cheremes to recognise 20 Japanese signs
Liddell and Johnson 89 - use sequences of tab,dez,sig => Movement-Hold model
Yamato, Ohya and Ishii 92 - HMM recognises 6 diff tennis strokes for 3 people
Schlenzig, Hunter and Jain 94 - recognises 3 gestures, *hello, goodbye* and *rotate*
Waldron and Kim 95 - ANN recognises small set of signs
Kadous 96 - recognises 95 Auslan signs with data gloves – 80% accuracy
Grobel and Assam 97 - ANN recognise finger spelling - 242 signs, coloured gloves
Starner and Pentland 96 - HMM recognises 40 signs in 2D, constrained grammar
Nam and Wohn 96 - HMM very small set of gestures in 3D – movement primes
Liang and Ouhyoung 98 - 250 Taiwanese signs, continuous, temporal discontinuities
Vogler & Metaxis 97 - HMM continuous 53 signs, models transitions between signs
Vogler & Metaxis 98 - HMM continuous 53 signs, word context with CV geometrics
Vogler & Metaxas 99 - 22 signs, define tab,dez,sig as phonemes - one hand

Table 2 Human movement recognition research.

As can be seen from Table 2, most movement recognition research has been limited to frontal posing of a constrained range of partial-body motion usually only tracking the 2D location of one hand. By contrast, this paper describes a computer vision based PUI framework that recognises continuous full-body motion of hundreds of different movement skills. The full-body movement skills in this study are constructed from an alphabet of 35 *dynemes* – the smallest contrastive dynamic units of human movement. Using a novel framework of multiple HMMs the recognition process attempts to infer the human movement skill that could have produced the observed sequence of dynemes.

Because the temporal variation of related joints and other parameters also contains information that helps the recognition process infer dynemes, the system computes and appends the temporal derivatives and second derivatives of these features to form the final *motion vector* for each video frame. Hence the motion vector includes joint angles (32 DOF), body location and orientation (6 DOF), centre of mass (3 DOF), principle axis (2 DOF) all with first and second derivatives.

2. Recognition

To simplify the design, it is assumed that the CHMR system contains a limited set of possible human movement skills. This approach restricts the search for possible skill sequences to those skills listed in the skill model, which lists the candidate skills and provides dynemes – an alphabet of granules of human motion – for the composition of each skill. The current skill model contains hundreds of skills where the length of the skill sequence being performed is unknown. If M represents the number of human movement skills in the skill model, the CHMR system could hypothesise M^N possible skill sequences for a skill sequence of length N. However these skill sequences are not equally likely to occur due to the biomechanical constraints of human motion. For example, the skill sequence *stand jump lie* is much more likely than *stand lie jump* (as it is difficult to jump while lying down). Given an observed sequence of motion vectors y_1^T, the recognition process attempts to find the skill sequence $\hat{s}_1^N$ that maximises this skill sequence's probability:

$$\hat{s}_1^N = \arg\max_{s_1^N} p(s_1^N \mid y_1^T) \equiv \arg\max_{s_1^N} p(y_1^T \mid s_1^N) p(s_1^N) \qquad (1)$$

This approach applies Bayes' law and ignores the denominator term to maximise the product of two terms: the probability of the motion vectors given the skill sequence and the probability of the skill sequence itself. The CHMR framework described by this equation is illustrated below in Figure 2 where, using motion vectors from the tracking process, the recognition process uses the dyneme, skill, context and activity models to construct a hypothesis for interpreting a video sequence.

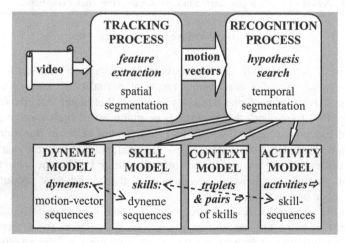

Figure 2   Continuous human movement recognition system. The dyneme, skill, context and activity models construct a hypothesis for interpreting a video sequence.

In the tracking process, motion vectors are extracted from the video stream. In the recognition process, the search hypothesises a probable movement skill sequence using four models:

- the *dyneme model* models the relationship between the motion vectors and the dynemes.
- the *skill model* defines the possible movement skills that the search can hypothesise, representing each movement skill as a linear sequence of dynemes;
- the *context model* models the semantic structure of movement by modelling the probability of sequences of skills simplified to only triplets or pairs of skills as discussed in Section 2.3 below.
- The *activity model* defines the possible human movement activities that the search can hypothesise, representing each activity as a linear sequence of skills (not limited to only triplets or pairs as in the context model).

Three principle components comprise the basic hypothesis search: a dyneme model, a skill model and a context model.

2.1 Dyneme Model

As the phoneme is a phonetic unit of human speech, so the dyneme is a dynamic unit of human motion. The word *dyneme* is derived from the Greek *dynamikos* "powerful", from *dynamis* "power", from *dynasthai* "to be able" and in this context refers to motion. This is similar to the phoneme being derived from *phono* meaning sound and with *eme* inferring the smallest contrastive unit. Thus *dyn-eme* is the smallest contrastive unit of movement. The movement skills in this study are constructed from an alphabet of 35 dynemes which HMMs use to recognise the skills. This approach has been inspired by the paradigm of the phoneme as used by the continuous speech recognition research community where pronunciation of the English language is constructed from approximately 50 phonemes

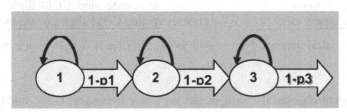

Figure 3 Hidden Markov Model for a dyneme. State transition probabilities *p1, p2, p3* govern possible transitions between states.

Figure 3 shows a HMM for a dyneme. A set of *state transition probabilities* – p_1, p_2 and p_3 – governs the possible transitions between states. They specify the probability of going from one state at time t to another state at time $t + 1$. The motion vectors emitted while making a particular transition represent the characteristics for the human movement at that point, which vary corresponding to different executions of the dyneme. A *probability distribution* or *probability density function* models this variation. The functions – $p(y|1)$, $p(y|2)$ and $p(y|3)$ – can be different for different transitions. These distributions are modelled as parametric distributions – a mixture of multidimensional Gaussians. A centre-of-mass (COM) category of dyneme is illustrated in the biomechanics PUI in Figure 4a where each running step is delimited by

COM minima. A full $360°$ rotation of the principle axis during a cartwheel in Figure 4b illustrates a rotation dyneme category.

Figure 4. Biomechanics PUI overlaying COM parameters during running and principle-axis parameters through a cartwheel.

2.2 Skill Model

The typical skill model shown in Table 3 lists each skill's possible executions, constructed from dynemes. An individual movement skill can have multiple forms of execution which complicates recognition.

Movement Skill	Dyneme
walk	step (right), step (left)
walk	step (left), step (right)
handstand from stand	step, rotate-fwd (180^0)
jump	knee-extension, COM-flight
backward salto	knee-extension, COM-flight, rotate-bwd (360^0)

Table 3   Typical minimal dyneme skill model (with the skill *walk* having two alternative executions)

The system chooses the skill model on a task-dependent basis, trading off skill-model size with skill coverage. Although a search through many videos can easily find dyneme sequences representing commonly used skills in various sources, unusual skills in highly specific situations may require manual specification of the dyneme sequence. In fact the initial definition of skills in terms of dynemes involved extensive manual specification in this research.

2.3 Context Model

The search for the most likely skill sequence in Equation 1 requires the computation of two terms, $p(y_1^T \mid s_1^N)$ and $p(s_1^N)$. The second of these computations is the *context model* which assigns a probability to a sequence of skills, s_1^N. The simplest way to determine such a probability would be to compute the relative frequencies of different skill sequences. However, the number of different sequences grows exponentially with the length of the skill sequence, making this approach infeasible.

A typical approximation assumes that the probability of the current skill depends on the previous one or two skills only, so that the computation can approximate the probability of the skill sequence as:

$$p(s_1^N) \approx p(s_1)p(s_2|s_1) \prod_{i=3}^{i=N} p(s_i|s_{i-1},s_{i-2}) \qquad (2)$$

where $p(s_i|s_{i-1},s_{i-2})$ can be estimated by counting the relative frequencies of skill triplets:

$$p(s_i|s_{i-1},s_{i-2}) \approx N(s_i,s_{i-1},s_{i-2}) / N(s_{i-1},s_{i-2}) \qquad (3)$$

Here, N refers to the associated event's relative frequency. This context model was trained using hundreds of skills to estimate $p(s_i|s_{i-1},s_{i-2})$. Even then, many skill pairs and triplets do not occur in the training videos, so the computation must smooth the probability estimates to avoid zeros in the probability assignment [13].

2.4 Activity Model

Research into human activities generally represents an activity as a single skill such as *walk, run, turn, sit,* and *stand* [31]. This is problematic since human activities are often more complex consisting of a sequence of many possible skills. An activity can be more accurately defined as a sequence of one or more core skills. This research seeks to broaden the distinction between activity and skill. The CHMR activity model in Part I defines possible human movement activities that the search can hypothesise, representing each activity as a sequence of one or more core skills.

For example, making a coffee consists of the minimum sequence "spoon-coffee, pour-water". Many other potential skills exist in the make-coffee sequence with *pre-skills* such as "boil-water, get-cup, get-spoon" and *post-skills* such as "stir-coffee, carry-cup". Therefore a set of zero or more related pre and post skills are associated with each activity to enable the temporal grouping of skills relating to a particular activity. In this way, not only are a sequence of motion vectors temporally segmented into a skill, but a sequence of skills can be temporally segmented into an activity.

2.5 Hypothesis Search

The hypothesis search seeks the skill sequence with the highest likelihood given the model's input features and parameters [13]. Because the number of skill sequences increases exponentially with the skill sequence's length, the search might seem at first to be an intractable problem for anything other than short skill sequences from a small lexicon of skills. However, because the model has only local probabilistic dependencies the system can incrementally search through the hypothesis in a left-to-right fashion and discard most candidates with no loss in optimality.

Although the number of states in the context model can theoretically grow as the square of the number of skills in the skill model, many skill triplets never actually occur in the training data. The smoothing operation backs off to skill pair and single skill estimators, substantially reducing size. To speed up the recursive process, the system conducts a *beam search*, which makes additional approximations such as retaining only hypotheses that fall within threshold of the maximum score in any time frame.

Given a time-series, the Viterbi algorithm computes the most probable hidden state sequence; the forward-backward algorithm computes the data likelihood and expected sufficient statistics of hidden events such as state transitions and occupancies. These statistics are used in Baum-Welch parameter re-estimation to maximise the likelihood of the model given the data. The expectation-maximisation (EM) algorithm for HMMs consists of forward-backward analysis and Baum-Welch re-estimation iterated to convergence at a local likelihood maximum.

Brand [2] replaced the Baum-Welch formula with parameter estimators that minimise entropy to avoid the local optima. However, with hundreds of movement skill samples it is felt that the research in this paper avoided this pitfall with a sufficiently large sample size. Viterbi alignment is applied to the training data followed by Baum-Welch re-estimation. Rather than the rule based grammar model common in speech processing, a context model is trained from the movement skill data set. The Hidden Markov Model Tool Kit[2] (HTK) version 3.2 is used to support these dyneme, skill and context models.

3. Performance

Hundreds of skills were tracked and classified using a 1.8GHz, 640MB RAM Pentium IV platform processing 24 bit colour within the Microsoft DirectX 9 environment under Windows XP. The video sequences were captured with a JVC DVL-9800 digital video camera at 30 fps, 720 by 480 pixel resolution. Each person moved in front of a stationary camera with a static background and static lighting conditions. Only one person was in frame at any one time. Tracking began when the whole body was visible which enabled initialisation of the clone-body-model.

The skill error rate quantifies CHMR system performance by expressing, as a percentage, the ratio of the number of skill errors to the number of skills in the reference training set. Depending on the task, CHMR system skill error rates can vary by an order of magnitude. The CHMR system results are based on a set of a total of 840 movement patterns, from walking to twisting saltos. From this, an independent test set of 200 skills were selected leaving 640 in the training set. Training and testing skills were performed by the same subjects. These were successfully tracked, recognised and evaluated with their respective biomechanical components quantified where a skill error rate of 4.5% was achieved.

Recognition was processed using the (Microsoft owned) Cambridge University Engineering Department HMM Tool Kit (HTK) with 96.8% recognition accuracy on the training set alone and a more meaningful 95.5% recognition accuracy for the independent test set where H=194, D=7, S=9, I=3, N=200 (H=correct, D=Deletion, S=Substitution, I=Insertion, N=test set, Accuracy=(H-I)/N). 3.5% of the skills were ignored (deletion errors) and 4.5% were incorrectly recognised as other skills (substitution errors). There was only about 1.5% insertion errors – that is incorrectly inserting/recognising a skill between other skills.

---

[2] An excellent discussion of HMMs and application of Viterbi alignment and Baum-Welch re-estimation can be found in the extensive HTK documentation of HTKBook: http://htk.eng.cam.ac.uk/docs/docs.shtml

The HTK performed Viterbi alignment on the training data followed by Baum-Welch re-estimation with a context model for the movement skills. Although the recognition itself was faster than real-time at about 120 fps, the tracking of 32 DOF with particle filtering was computationally expensive using up to 16 seconds per frame.

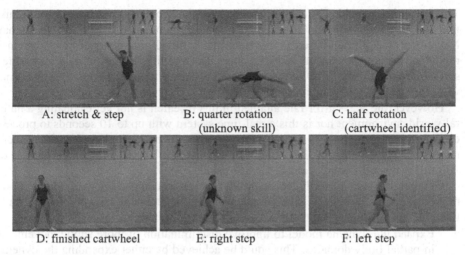

| A: stretch & step | B: quarter rotation (unknown skill) | C: half rotation (cartwheel identified) |
| D: finished cartwheel | E: right step | F: left step |

Figure 5 A PUI coaching system recognising stretching into a cartwheel followed by steps.

This PUI augments each picture with four overlaid tiles displaying CHMR processing steps:

- Tile 1: Principle axis through the body.
- Tile 2: Body frame of reference (normalised to the vertical).
- Tile 3: Motion vector trace (subset displayed).
- Tile 4: Recognising *step*, *stretch* and *cartwheel* indicated by stick figures with respective snapshots of the skills.

Figure 5 illustrates a coach PUI system recognising the sequence of skills *stretch & step, cartwheel, step* and *step* from continuous movement. As each skill is recognised, the scene is augmented with a snapshot of the corresponding pose displayed in the fourth tile. Below each snapshot is a stick figure representing an internal identification of the recognised skill. Notice that the cartwheel is not recognised after the first quarter rotation. Only after the second quarter rotation is the skill identified as probably a cartwheel. This PUI system enables, for example, a list of all cartwheels across training sessions to be compared for tracking progress. Figure 4a illustrates another PUI coaching system augmented by biomechanical data.

The activity aware aspect of a PUI was also investigated by testing the CHMR on a set of five activities performed, each by three people: coffee (making a coffee), computer (entering an office and using a computer), tidy (picking an object off the floor and placing it on a desk), snoop (entering an office, looking in a specific direction and exiting), and break (standing up, walking around, sitting down). This sample size is too small for the activity error rate of 0% to be significant and reflects the skill recognition result of 4.5% skill error rate

4. Conclusions

This paper has provided a technical analysis of the problems of accurately recognising and tracking body and limb position, and demonstrated a Continuous Human Movement Recognition based PUI system that is based on a generalisable "dyneme" model of human movement. A PUI system successfully recognised and augmented skills and activities with a 95.5% recognition accuracy to validate this CHMR framework and the dyneme paradigm.

However, the 4.5% error rate attained in this research is not yet evaluating a natural world environment nor is this a real-time system with up to 10 seconds to process each frame. Although this 95.5% recognition rate was not as high as the 99.2% accuracy Starner and Pentland [31] achieved recognising 40 signs, a larger test sample of 200 full-body skills were evaluated in this paper.

Generalisation to a user independent PUI system encompassing many partial body movement domains such as sign language should be attainable. To progress towards this goal, the following improvements seem most important:

- Expand the dyneme model to improve discrimination of more subtle movements in partial-body domains. This could be achieved by either expanding the dyneme alphabet or having domain dependent dyneme alphabets layered hierarchically below the full-body movement dynemes.
- Enhance tracking granularity using cameras with a higher frame rate.

So far PUIs with constrained partial-body motion such as sign language have been ignored. Incorporating partial-body movement domains into the full-body skill recognition PUI system is an interesting challenge. Can the dyneme model simply be extended to incorporate a larger alphabet of dynemes or is there a need for sub-domain dyneme models for maximum discrimination within each domain? The answers to such questions may be the key to developing a general purpose unconstrained skill recognition PUI system. Many PUIs automatically extract user input from natural and implicit components of human activity such as gestures, direction of gaze and facial expression. Although our focus has been on the technical challenges of recognising general movement, doing so is the first component in many of the new breed of PUIs.

5. References

[1]   N I Badler, C B Phillips, B L Webber, *Simulating humans*, Oxford University Press, New York, NY, 1993.
[2]   M Brand, V Kettnaker, Discovery and segmentation of activities in video, *IEEE Transactions on Pattern Analysis and Machine Intelligence*, 22(8), August 2000.
[3]   C Bregler, Learning and recognizing human dynamics in video sequences, *IEEE Conference on Computer Vision and Pattern Recognition*, CVPR, 1997.
[4]   C Bregler, J Malik, Tracking people with twists and exponential maps, *IEEE Conference on Computer Vision and Pattern Recognition*, CVPR, 8–15, 1998.

[5]   T J Cham, J M Rehg, A multiple hypothesis approach to figure tracking, *IEEE Conference on Computer Vision and Pattern Recognition*, CVPR, 1: 239–245, 1999.

[6]   T Drummond, R Cipolla, Real-time tracking of highly articulated structures in the presence of noisy measurements, *IEEE International Conference on Computer Vision*, ICCV, 2: 315–320, 2001.

[7]   D M Gavrila, L A Davis, 3-D model-based tracking of humans in action: a multi-view approach, *IEEE Conference on Computer Vision and Pattern Recognition*, CVPR, 73–80, 1996.

[8]   L Goncalves, E Di Bernardo, E Ursella, P Perona, Monocular tracking of the human arm in 3D, *IEEE International Conference on Computer Vision*, ICCV, 764–770, 1995.

[9]   K Grobel, M Assam, Isolated sign language recognition using hidden Markov models, *IEEE International Conference on Systems, Man and Cybernetics*, 162–167, Orlando, 1997.

[10] D Herbison-Evans, R D Green, A Butt, Computer Animation with NUDES in Dance and Physical Education, *Australian Computer Science Communications*, 4(1): 324-331, 1982.

[11] D C Hogg, Model-based vision: A program to see a walking person, *Image and Vision Computing*, 1(1): 5–20, 1983.

[12] A Hutchinson-Guest, *Choreo-Graphics; A Comparison of Dance Notation Systems from the Fifteenth Century to the Present*, Gordon and Breach, New York, 1989.

[13] F Jelinek, *Statistical Methods for Speech Recognition*, MIT Press, Cambridge, Mass., 1999.

[14] S X Ju, M J Black, Y Yacoob, Cardboard people: A parameterized model of articulated motion, *IEEE International Conference on Automatic Face and Gesture Recognition*, 38–44, 1996.

[15] M W Kadous, Machine recognition of Auslan signs using PowerGloves: Towards large-lexicon recognition of sign language, *Workshop on the Integration of Gesture in Language and Speech*, WIGLS, 165–74, Applied Science and Engineering Laboratories, Newark, 1996.

[16] I Kakadiaris, D Metaxas, Model-based estimation of 3D human motion with occlusion based on active multi-viewpoint selection, *IEEE Conference on Computer Vision and Pattern Recognition*, CVPR, 81–87, 1996.

[17] M E Leventon, W T Freeman, Bayesian estimation of 3-d human motion from an image sequence, *TR–98–06*, Mitsubishi Electric Research Lab, Cambridge, 1998.

[18] R H Liang, M Ouhyoung, A real-time continuous gesture recognition system for sign language, *Third International Conference on Automatic Face and Gesture Recognition*, 558–565, Nara, 1998.

[19] S K Liddell, R E Johnson, American Sign Language: the phonological base, *Sign Language Studies*, 64: 195–277, 1989.

[20] D Liebowitz, S Carlsson, Uncalibrated motion capture exploiting articulated structure constraints, *IEEE International Conference on Computer Vision*, ICCV, 2001.

[21] T B Moeslund, E Granum, A survey of computer vision-based human motion capture, *Computer Vision and Image Understanding* 18: 231–268, 2001.

[22] Y Nam and K Y Wohn, Recognition of space-time hand-gestures using hidden Markov model, *ACM Symposium on Virtual Reality Software and Technology*, 1996.

[23] A Pentland, B Horowitz, Recovery of nonrigid motion and structure, *IEEE Transactions on PAMI*, 13: 730-742, 1991.

[24] S Pheasant, *Bodyspace. Anthropometry, Ergonomics and the Design of Work*, Taylor & Francis, 1996.

[25] R Plänkers, P Fua, Articulated soft objects for video-based body modeling, *IEEE International Conference on Computer Vision*, ICCV, 1: 394–401, 2001.

[26] J M Rehg, T Kanade, Model-based tracking of self-occluding articulated objects, *Fifth International Conference on Computer Vision*, 612-617, 1995.

[27] J Rittscher, A Blake, S J Roberts, Towards the automatic analysis of complex human body motions, *Image and Vision Computing*, 20(12): 905-916, 2002.

[28] K Rohr, Towards model-based recognition of human movements in image sequences, *CVGIP - Image Understanding* 59(1): 94–115, 1994.

[29] R Rosales, S Sclaroff, Inferring body pose without tracking body parts, *IEEE Conference on Computer Vision and Pattern Recognition*, CVPR, 2000.

[30] J Schlenzig, E Hunter, R Jain, Recursive identification of gesture inputers using hidden Markov models, *Second Annual Conference on Applications of Computer Vision*, 187–194, 1994.

[31] T Starner, A Pentland, Real-time American Sign Language recognition from video using Hidden Markov Models, *Technical Report 375*, MIT Media Laboratory, 1996.

[32] W C Stokoe, *Sign Language Structure: An Outline of the Visual Communication System of the American Deaf*, Studies in Linguistics: Occasional Papers 8. Linstok Press, Silver Spring, MD, 1960. Revised 1978.

[33] S Tamura, S Kawasaki, Recognition of sign language motion images, *Pattern Recognition*, 31: 343-353, 1988.

[34] C J Taylor, Reconstruction of articulated objects from point correspondences in a single articulated image, *IEEE Conference on Computer Vision and Pattern Recognition*, CVPR, 586–591, 2000.

[35] C Vogler, D Metaxas, Adapting hidden Markov models for ASL recognition by using three-dimensional computer vision methods, *IEEE International Conference on Systems, Man and Cybernetics*, 156–161, Orlando, 1997.

[36] C Vogler, D Metaxas, ASL recognition based on a coupling between HMMs and 3D motion analysis, *IEEE International Conference on Computer Vision*, 363–369, Mumbai, 1998.

[37] C Vogler, D Metaxas, Toward scalability in ASL recognition: breaking down signs into phonemes, *Gesture Workshop 99*, Gif-sur-Yvette, 1999.

[38] S Wachter, H Nagel, Tracking of persons in monocular image sequences, *Computer Vision and Image Understanding* 74(3): 174–192, 1999.

[39] M B Waldron, S Kim, Isolated ASL sign recognition system for deaf persons, *IEEE Transactions on Rehabilitation Engineering*, 3(3): 261–71, 1995.

[40] J Wang, G Lorette, P Bouthemy, Analysis of human motion: A modelbased approach, *Scandinavian Conference on Image Analysis*, SCIA, 2: 1142–1149, 1991.

[41] C Wren, A Azarbayejani, T Darrell, A Pentland, "Pfinder: Real-time tracking of the human body", *IEEE Transactions on PAMI*, 19(7): 780-785, 1997.

[42] J Yamato, J Ohya, K Ishii, Recognizing human action in time-sequential images using hidden Markov models, *IEEE International Conference on Computer Vision*, ICCV, 379–385, 1992.

Real-Time Color Gamut Mapping Architecture and Implementation for Color-Blind People

Dongil Han

Department of Computer Engineering, Sejong University
98 Gunja-Dong, Gwangjin-Gu, Seoul, Korea
Tel: +82-2-3408-3751
Fax: +82-2-3408-3321
dihan@sejong.ac.kr

Abstract. A novel color gamut mapping method and architecture is described. The color gamut mapping allows versatile color display devices to generate transformed colors so that certain colors which are confused can be recognized by the color-blind users. And real-time hardware architecture for color gamut mapping is also described. The concept of three-dimensional reduced resolution look-up table is proposed and applied for color gamut mapping. The proposed architecture greatly reduces the required memory size and computational loads compared to the conventional methods and it is suitable for real-time applications. The proposed real-time architecture can easily be implemented in high-speed color display applications especially for color-blind users. The experimental results show that the proposed method is successfully used for color transform, which enables confused colors to be differentiated.

1 Introduction

Recently, several kinds of color display devices such as LCD(Liquid-crystal display), PDP(Plasma Display Panel) are developed and used for color information display purposes. When one in twelve men have some measurable degree of color vision deficiency, the use of certain colors in certain ways can cause difficulty in recognizing color information. The conventional approach uses special color palette [1] for web site design or differences in shading [2] for document design. But these approaches must be used at initial stage of web design or documentation and it is hardly applicable to existing documents or web sites.

In this paper, the color gamut mapping method that is widely used for enhancing color reproduction quality between PC monitor and printing devices is adapted for color transformation of display devices. And real-time hardware architecture for color gamut mapping is also proposed and described.

The conventional approach for adjusting display characteristics uses three one-dimensional look-up tables for Red, Blue and Green component adjustment. But this one dimensional look-up table cannot correct display color gamut precisely for the color-blind users. There are many color gamut mapping algorithms which can be used for reducing any differences that might exist between the sets of colors obtainable on different display devices and different printing devices [3] - [8].

M. Masoodian et al. (Eds.): APCHI 2004, LNCS 3101, pp. 133-142, 2004.

The lightness mapping and multiple anchor points are proposed by Lee [3]. The lightness mapping minimizes the lightness difference of the maximum chroma between two gamuts and produces the linear tone in bright and dark regions. In the chroma mapping, a separate mapping method that utilizes multiple anchor points with constant slopes plus a fixed anchor point is used to maintain the maximum chroma and produce a uniform tonal dynamic range.

Three-dimensional gamma-compression gamut mapping algorithm (GMA) is proposed by Chen [4]. This article describes the 3D GMA based on the concept of Image-to-Device (I-D). It is shown that the GMA coupled with 3D gamut compression and multi-mapping directions resulted in the better rendition than 2D nonlinear GMA.

As discussed above, lots of outstanding color mapping algorithms for reducing the gamut differences have been proposed for enhancing the color reproduction quality between PC monitor and printer devices. But all of these mapping algorithms are very difficult to use in the high-speed display color gamut mapping applications.

In this paper, a general-purpose gamut mapping method and a real-time hardware architecture are proposed. The proposed hardware architecture offers a method for representing vivid color images as perceived with a color deficiency. And the concept of three-dimensional reduced resolution look-up table is proposed and successfully adopted for color gamut mapping.

2   Reduced Resolution Look-Up Table

The popular color space which is used in color management system and color gamut mapping is CIE L*a*b* color space. The L*a*b* color space is now the most popular uniform color space. Though, this color space is not a directly displayable format, its gamut encompasses the entire visible spectrum and can represent accurately the colors of any display, print, or input device.

But most of the display devices use RGB color space. The RGB color space is a linear color space that formally uses three types of phosphors as a primary and generates composite color images by using the linear combinations of the primary colors. Thus display gamut mapping method requires RGB to L*a*b* color space conversion, gamut mapping, and L*a*b* to RGB color space conversion function, sequentially. For high-speed display applications, we can consider several approaches. First, we can consider implementing two color space conversion functions and the gamut mapping function, individually. The color space conversion function among RGB, YCbCr, YIQ, YUV, XYZ color space requires 3x3 matrix operation and can be implemented easily. But the RGB to L*a*b* color conversion requires RGB to XYZ and XYZ to L*a*b* color space conversion sequentially. The RGB to XYZ color space conversion can be easily calculated by using 3x3 matrix multiplication. However, XYZ to L*a*b* color space conversion requires very complex and highly nonlinear equations [9]. Thus, RGB to L*a*b* conversion requires highly nonlinear conversion function and it is difficult to implement in high-speed applications.

Most of the gamut-mapping algorithms also require very complex mapping functions. Furthermore, the color gamut-mapping algorithm could be changed and upgraded lately in order to fix possible problems and defects. In this case, the hardwired solution could not adapt the necessary modifications.

The second approach for real-time implementation, we can consider a 3-dimensional look-up table which can convert two color space conversion rules and gamut mapping rules into single mapping rule and can define all mapping functions for each red, green and blue input and output pair. Thus, in setup stage, the mapping function is loaded into 3-dimensional look-up table. And, in normal stage, it can generate transformed R_{out}, G_{out} and B_{out} image data for each R_{in}, G_{in} and B_{in} image input. In this case, the gamut mapping rule itself can be loaded in flexible manner and render the architecture for adapting the modification and upgrade of gamut-mapping rules. But major disadvantage of this approach is that the required memory space could be calculated as 256 x 256 x 256 x 3 bytes = 50,331,648 bytes. Such large amount of memory cannot be used in real-time color gamut mapping application.

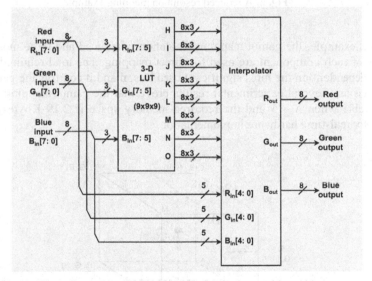

Fig. 1. The 3-dimensional reduced resolution look-up table architecture

In this paper, the concept of three-dimensional reduced resolution look-up table (RRLT) is introduced. The 3-dimensional look-up table is successfully implemented by reducing the mapping resolution of each look-up table components. The reduced resolution look-up table itself does not deteriorate the image quality and it just affects the mapping quality. Figure 1 shows the block diagram of the proposed RRLT. As shown in figure 2, each R, G, B component is divided into 8 intervals. Three most significant bits of each component are used for selecting the corresponding cube position and generating the eight mapping values of each vertex of the cube. Five least significant bits of each component are used for interpolating the new mapping value for each R, G and B input image.

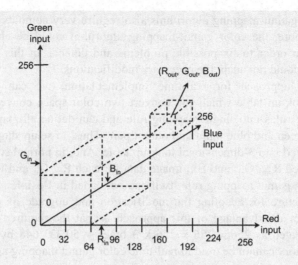

Fig. 2. A reduced resolution mapping example

In this example, the gamut mapping resolution is reduced and three most significant bits of each component are used for direct mapping. The total required memory space is dependent on the most significant used bits, n and it controls the gamut mapping precision. Several experimental results prove that the gamut mapping precision is achievable when n = 3 and the required memory space is 2.19 Kbytes and it is suitable for real-time hardware implementation.

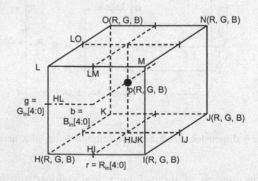

Fig. 3. Three-dimensional interpolation scheme

When n = 3, as shown in figure 2, nine positions are required for storing direct mapping values for each red, green, and blue input image. The mapping values are also composed of new Red, Green, Blue output triplet. Therefore 9x9x9x3 = 2.19 Kbytes memory space is required for constructing reduced resolution look-up table.

The final gamut-mapped R_{out}, G_{out}, B_{out} values are calculated by 3-dimensional interpolator as shown in figure 1. In this case, using the 3-bit MSB information for each

R_{in}, G_{in}, and B_{in} triplet, the 3-D LUT generates gamut-mapping values of eight vertex points that encompass the R_{in}, G_{in}, and B_{in} input triplet.

The interpolation scheme is shown in figure 3. The eight vertex data and the five least significant bits of each component are used to determine the internal cube position and the final mapping value. A simple consecutive bi-linear interpolation for each component can generate new mapping value at the image input position 'p'. The direct mapping value H(R, G, B) and I(R, G, B) from the 3-D LUT and $R_{in}[4:0]$ value are used for calculating HI(R, G, B) value which denotes the new gamut mapping value in HI position. The KJ(R, G, B) value can be calculated at the same manner. Thus, if we let the gamut mapping function of each components be $gm_{component}(.)$, the final gamut mapping value of red signal at 'p' point can be calculated as follows.

$$R_{HI} = (R_H \times (32 - r) + R_I \times r) / 32 \tag{1}$$

$$R_{KJ} = (R_K \times (32 - r) + R_J \times r) / 32 . \tag{2}$$

Here

$$r = R_{in}[4:0] \tag{3}$$

$$R_H = gm_{red}(H(R,G,B)) \tag{4}$$

$$R_I = gm_{red}(I(R,G,B)) . \tag{5}$$

In the second step,

$$R_{HIJK} = (R_{HI} \times (32 - b) + R_{KJ} \times b) / 32 , \tag{6}$$

Finally, we can get

$$R_p = (R_{HIJK} \times (32 - g) + R_{LMNO} \times g) / 32 , \tag{7}$$

here

$$b = B_{in}[4:0] \tag{8}$$

$$g = G_{in}[4:0] . \tag{9}$$

The green and blue mapping values are calculated as the same way. The simple integer operations are sufficient for generating the final mapping values.

3 Real-Time Architecture

The proposed 3-dimensional RRLT architecture, described in the previous section, is not suitable to be directly implemented in the real-time hardware. For calculating the new mapping value at 'p' point, the red, green, and blue mapping value of 8 vertex points are required simultaneously in hardware implementation. Thus, this 3-dimensional calculation procedure is improved by one-dimensional decomposition.

In this paper, the 3-D LUT block in figure 1 is implemented by using an address decoder, eight one-dimensional look-up tables and a data switch as shown in figure 4. The 9x9x9 = 729 vertex points are separated and stored into eight one-dimensional look-up tables. For example, the mapping values of Rin [7:5] = 0, Gin [7:5] = 0, Bin [7:5] = 0 position is stored into first address of look-up table 0(LUT0).

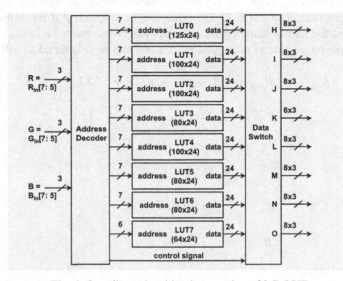

Fig. 4. One-dimensional implementation of 3-D LUT

And the mapping value of R_{in} [7:5] = 1, G_{in} [7:5] = 0, B_{in} [7:5] = 0 position is stored into first address of look-up table 1(LUT1). The eight vertex points that include the origin are stored into the first address of eight one-dimensional look-up tables. In this manner, the 729 vertex points can be store into 8 one-dimensional look-up table. An example address decoding logic for LUT0 is shown in equation (10).

$$LUT0\_address = (R+1)/2 + 5*((G+1)/2) + 25*((B+1)/2). \tag{10}$$

Here,

$$R = R_{in}[7:5], G = G_{in}[7:5], B = B_{in}[7:5] \tag{11}$$

This addressing logic enables us to use eight one-dimensional look-up tables instead of one three-dimensional look-up table.

3.1   Initial Gamut Mapping Data Setup

In the setup stage, arbitrary gamut mapping rules can be loaded into the 3-D RRLT. The address decoder selects the proper look-up table and its address for all R= R_{in}

[7:5], G= G_{in} [7:5], B= B_{in} [7:5] input values. The address decoding logic can be described as follows.

$$LUT0\_address = (R+1)/2 + 5*((G+1)/2) + 25*((B+1)/2) \qquad (12)$$

$$LUT1\_address = (R\ )/2 + 4*((G+1)/2) + 20*((B+1)/2) \qquad (13)$$

$$LUT2\_address = (R+1)/2 + 5*((G\ )/2) + 20*((B+1)/2) \qquad (14)$$

$$LUT3\_address = (R\ )/2 + 4*((G\ )/2) + 16*((B+1)/2) \qquad (15)$$

$$LUT4\_address = (R+1)/2 + 5*((G+1)/2) + 25*((B\ )/2) \qquad (16)$$

$$LUT5\_address = (R\ )/2 + 4*((G+1)/2) + 20*((B\ )/2) \qquad (17)$$

$$LUT6\_address = (R+1)/2 + 5*((G\ )/2) + 20*((B\ )/2) \qquad (18)$$

$$LUT7\_address = (R\ )/2 + 4*((G\ )/2) + 16*((B\ )/2) \qquad (19)$$

For interpolation, extra mapping values when R_{in} = 256, G_{in} = 256, B_{in} = 256 must be loaded into the look-up table. These mapping values are used for interpolating the mapping values when an input image is located at the outer cube position of 3-D LUT. The simple integer operations are applied to the address generation logic.

3.2 Real-Time Color Gamut Mapping

For any input values, 8-vertex points that come from the vertex of cube that encompass the input triplet can be generated from the eight one-dimensional look-up tables. For example, let us consider a R_{in} = 10, G_{in} = 10, and B_{in} = 10 input. In this case, a cube that encompasses the origin is selected. For proper operation, LUT0 generates mapping values in H point, and LUT1, LUT2, LUT3 generate mapping values in I, J, K points, respectively. But, let's consider another example, the R_{in} = 10, G_{in} = 40, B_{in} = 10 input case. From the figure 2 and figure 3, we can find that the LUT0, LUT1, LUT2, and LUT3 generate mapping values in J, K, H, I point, respectively.

Thus, the final problem of this architecture is that generated mapping data cube positions for any input can be changed arbitrary. As discussed in the previous paragraph, LUT0 can generate mapping data of H and J position of cube and it is dependent on the input value. And each LUT can generate all positions of cube vertex. Thus the data switch block in figure 4 changes all mapping data positions to a fixed position. This reduces the complexity of the 3-D interpolator.

The address decoding logic for real-time gamut is the same as that of the initial gamut mapping data setup. The same equation as in (12) ~ (19) is used for real-time gamut mapping.

4 Experimental Results

The proposed hardware architecture is implemented in VHDL and FPGA hardware. Using the implemented hardware, many still images and moving images are tested. The total memory and logic gates are described in Table 1.

The color gamut mapping algorithm [8] which stretches the blue component of display gamut is used for color transformation test. Table 2 shows the sample mapping rules. Figure 5 shows the result of real-time color gamut mapping. We can notice that the gamut mapped image shows more natural color compared to the original image.

Table 1. The used gate count for implementing 3-D RRLT

	Memory	Logic	Total
Gate count	47,303	45,658	92,961

Table 2. Gamut mapping data example

R_{in}	G_{in}	B_{in}	R_{out}	G_{out}	B_{out}
0x00	0x00	0x00	0x02	0x1b	0x13
0x00	0x00	0x20	0x02	0x16	0x24
0x00	0x00	0x40	0x02	0x11	0x48
...	...	...	...	...	...
0x00	0x00	0xe0	0x02	0x1f	0xff
0x00	0x00	0xff	0x02	0x24	0xff
0x00	0x20	0x00	0x02	0x24	0x17
0x00	0x20	0x20	0x02	0x23	0x24
0x00	0x20	0x40	0x02	0x22	0x48
...	...	...	...	...	...

(a) Original image   (b) Gamut mapped image

Fig. 5. A gamut mapping result

Ishihara's color deficiency test plate is used for another color transformation test. Figure 6 is a disappearing type digit plate seen as 16 by normal people and 16 is disappeared by those with red-green blind and totally color-blind people.

A gamut mapping rule that depresses red, yellow, and orange color components and stretches the green component is applied to the color plate. Figure 7 shows the result of color gamut mapping. The number 16 can be seen with red-green blind and even with totally color-blind people.

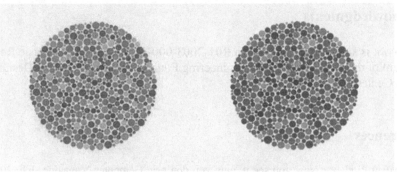

Fig. 6. A color plate 16 and its monochrome version

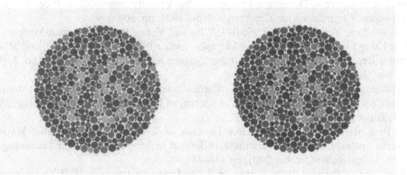

Fig. 7. A gamut mapped color plate 16 and its monochrome version

5 Conclusion

The color gamut mapping method that is used for enhancing the color reproduction quality between PC monitor and printer devices is adopted for real-time display quality enhancement and color transformation of display devices. For high-speed processing and affordable hardware integration, the concept of three-dimensional reduced resolution look-up table is proposed and successfully implemented for color gamut mapping.

The properly chosen color transformation rules implemented in the display devices enable color-blind people to differentiate colored document that is not properly prepared for them. And, the proposed color mapping architecture can be used for constructing display devices especially for color-blind people.

The proposed architecture is not dependent on the gamut mapping algorithm and arbitrary gamut mapping rules, for example rules for red-blind or green-blind, can be accommodated by the proposed 3-dimensional reduced resolution look-up table. And it can be easily implemented in the real time with reasonable system cost. The number for intervals for approximating the three-dimensional look-up table can be modified and selected by affordable memory size and required color mapping precision.

Acknowledgments

This work is supported by grant No R01-2003-000-10785-0 from the Basic Research Program of the Korea Science & Engineering Foundation, and by the IC Design Education Center.

References

1. Christian Rigden, : Now you see it, now you don't. in Computer Magazine, July 2002, pp. 104-105.
2. Laurel Kay Grove, : Document Design for the Visually Impaired. in Proc. International Professional Communication Conference, Nov. 1991, pp. 304-309.
3. Chae-Soo Lee, Yang-Woo Park, Seok-Je Cho and Yeong-Ho Ha, : Gamut Mapping Algorithm Using Lightness Mapping and Multiple Anchor Points for Linear Tone and Maximum Chroma Reproduction. in Journal of Image Science and Technology, Vol. 45, no. 3, pp.209-223, May/June 2001.
4. Hung-Shing Chen and Hiroaki Kotera: Three-dimensional Gamut Mapping Method Based on the Concept of Image Dependence. in Journal of Image Science and Technology, Vol. 46, no. 1, January/February 2002, pp44-52
5. Raja Bala, Ricardo deQueiroz, Reiner Eschach, and Wencheng Wu: Gamut Mapping to Preserve Spatial Luminance Variations. in Journal of Image Science and Technology, Vol. 45, no. 5, September/October 2001, pp.436-443
6. B. Pham and G. Pringle: Color Correction for an Image Sequence. in IEEE Computer Graphics and Applications, 1995, pp.38-42
7. H. Haneishi, K. Miyata, H. Yaguchi and Y. Miyake, : A New Method for Color Correction in Hardcopy from CRT Images. in Journal of Image Science and Technology, Vol. 37, no. 1, pp.30-36, 1993.
8. Byoung-Ho Kang, Jan Morovic, M. Ronnier Luo, and Maeng-Sub Cho, : Gamut Compression and Extension Algorithms Based on Observer Experimental Data. in ETRI Journal, Vol. 25, no. 3, 2003, pp.156-170
9. Phil Green, Lindsay MacDonald, : Color Engineering – Achieving Device Independent Colour. in John Wiley & Son Ltd, West Sussex England, 2002.

Tangible Teleconferencing

Jeorg Hauber[1], Mark Billinghurst[1], Holger Regenbrecht[2]

[1]Human Interface Technology Lab (New Zealand), University of Canterbury,
Private Bag 4800, Christchurch, New Zealand
{jeorg.hauber/mark.billinghurst}@hitlabnz.org
[2]DaimlerChrysler AG, P.O.Box 2360,
89013 Ulm, Germany
Holger.Regenbrecht@DaimlerChrysler.Com

Abstract. This paper describes a teleconferencing application that uses real objects to interact with virtual on-screen content. A variety of tangible interaction techniques can be used to load, translate, rotate and scale shared virtual models. In addition, snapshots of real documents can be easily introduced into the system and enlarged using a tangible lens. We describe the teleconferencing interface and present results from a pilot user study.

1 Introduction

The ultimate goal of teleconferencing systems is to enable remote people to work together as easily as if they are face to face. Unfortunately this is still far from being achieved. For example, with an audio only interface such as ThunderWire [7], participants are unable to exchange non-verbal cues, while with desktop video conferencing there is often a lack of spatial cues [14]. Even in high end immersive virtual environments such as GreenSpace [10] remote users are represented as virtual avatars that cannot display all the nuances of face to face communication.

In a face to face meeting real objects and interactions with the real world play an important role [6]. However, with current technology it is difficult to bring elements of the real world into a remote communication space. In most video conferencing applications users cannot share real documents, or manipulate tangible objects.

In this paper we describe a virtual conferencing space that uses tangible interaction techniques [8] to bridge between the real and virtual spaces. Our goal is to bring real documents and objects into screen-based collaborative environments.

2 Related Work

Over the past decade teleconferencing options have increased. People can now use cell phones, on-line chat services or free video conferencing suites such as Microsoft's NetMeeting. More sophisticated users may have access to desktop virtual conferencing spaces in which they can navigate through an on-screen virtual space.

M. Masoodian et al. (Eds.): APCHI 2004, LNCS 3101, pp. 143-152, 2004.

Computer supported collaborative work (CSCW) systems vary widely in the functions they provide. Some applications such as IBM Lotus Notes or Microsoft Outlook utilize the desktop metaphor from today's graphical user interfaces and bring them into a distributed, collaborative context. The main shortcoming of these systems is their lack of synchronous, distributed communication. Often, simultaneous telephone conferencing is needed to substitute for this lack of synchronicity.

Recent video conferencing systems overcome this limitation by partially integrating CSCW content (e.g. chat and whiteboard) with synchronous video and audio. In most cases, application or 2D data sharing is offered as an option. These systems are typically used in special rooms or facilities in large companies. Although able to share audio and video data, there is often limited ability to interact with three dimensional virtual content or share spatial cues.

Collaborative virtual environments do connect distributed users in a three-dimensional shared graphical environment [2, 5]. These environments can be highly realistic and vivid, but are mostly synthetic or abstract and cannot really be a substitute for real world communication. For example, the representations of the users are either symbolic or as virtual avatars (dynamic 3D geometry). Neither are able to convey the non-verbal nuances of real face to face conversation.

In projects such as the "Office of the future" work [12] remote participants and places are integrated into one shared environment. A similar approach to integrating participants in a spatial simulation of reality is project VIRTUE [9]. Here, a combination of advanced computer vision and computer graphics methods are used to provide a comprehensive system for video conferencing. With this system the impression is created that three remote participants actually sit around the same table.

Although developments have been made in collaborative interfaces that share natural audio and visual cues between remote users, there has been less work on incorporating real objects into the interface. Projects such as Psybench [4] and inTouch [3] allow remote users to move real objects together. In these cases the focus is on remote control of physical objects, rather than using physical objects to control virtual information.

Unlike this previous work, our research combines elements of tangible user interface design with a desktop virtual environment conferencing interface. In this way we can seamlessly link real and virtual worlds in a collaborative setting. In the next section we describe the cAR/PE! interface that our work is based on, and then we present our tangible conferencing interface.

3   The cAR/PE! Conferencing Space

Our work is an enhancement of the cAR/PE! desktop collaborative virtual environment [13]. This is software that runs on a desktop computer with a web camera attached, showing a three dimensional virtual conference room environment (see figure 1). Remote users are shown as virtual avatars in the conferencing space with live video texturing onto their virtual representations.

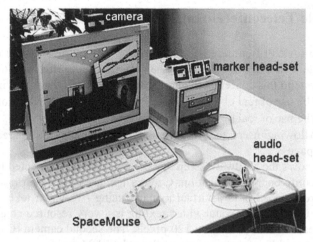

Fig. 1. The cAR/PE! interface

The cAR/PE! interface allows multiple remote participants to communicate over a network in an environment simulating a traditional face-to-face meeting. Integrated into the virtual environment are live video streams of the participants spatially arranged around a virtual table, a large virtual presentation screen for 2D display, and shared 3D virtual models (figure 2). In the center of the room there is table on which alternative 3D virtual models can be placed. Each participant can change his/her view into the virtual environment using a SpaceMouse input device. User movements are transmitted to the other participants and used to control the orientation of the virtual video avatars. Thus each user can see where the other participants are looking.

Fig. 2. The cAR/PE! virtual environment

The cAR/PE! application is written in C++ and uses the OpenInventor graphics library [11] for its 3D graphics components and interaction. It runs on the Microsoft Windows operating system. Although designed for low-end hardware, cAR/PE! represents the state-of-the art in desktop collaborative virtual environments.

4   Tangible Teleconferencing

Although the cAR/PE! conferencing space supports intuitive spatial conferencing it still creates an artificial separation between the real and virtual worlds. Our research goal was to extend this conferencing application to support the following:

- The use of real objects to load three-dimensional virtual content
- The use of real objects to manipulate virtual content
- Allowing users to bring real documents into the shared conferencing space

Figure 3 shows the hardware setup. Two web-cams are connected to a desktop PC running the conferencing application. Camera 1 is used for capturing the user's face. Its images are mapped onto a virtual avatar's using live video texturing (Figure 4). Permanently updating the avatar video texture is a very resource consuming task, so the camera resolution is just 160 x 120 pixels. The second camera (Camera 2) is used for detecting tangible interaction objects. It is placed 24 cm above the table and points down at a marker on the table. When objects are moved in front of this marker they are detected by the camera. The camera is used to take high quality snapshots so its resolution is set to 800 x 600 pixels.

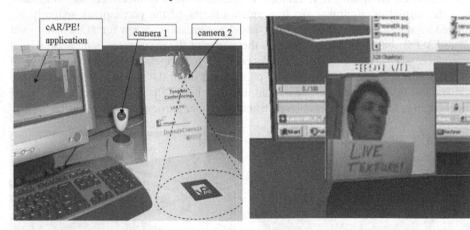

Fig. 3: Tangible conferencing hardware setup   **Fig. 4:** Avatar with live video texture

4.1   Model Loading

In our collaborative interface we first needed an intuitive way to load virtual models into the conferencing space. This is accomplished through the use of small square cardboard model markers Each of these markers is associated with a different virtual model. When a marker is placed under the desktop camera (camera 2), the ARToolKit tracking library [2] is used to recognize the pattern on the marker and load the appropriate 3D model into the conferencing space. When different model markers are in view of the camera the individual virtual models associated with them are loaded onto the table in the virtual conferencing space. Thus the markers allow users to easily load a variety of different virtual models.

4.2 Model Manipulation

Once models have been loaded into the conferencing space they can be manipulated using a different set of tangible interface objects. In our work we have explored two different approaches to model manipulation:

- *Mouse based:* Tangible markers are used to attach virtual manipulators to the model which the user can then interact with using mouse input.
- *Tool-based:* Physical tools are used to select the manipulation mode and also perform the virtual object manipulation.

4.2.1 Mouse-Based Manipulation

We enable users to rotate, translate, and scale the virtual models by using three manipulation markers. When these markers are placed on top of a model marker, an Open-Inventor manipulator widget appears on the virtual model. This allows a user to perform mouse- and keyboard-operated manipulations to the virtual model.

Placing a translation marker over the model marker representing a red car causes a virtual translation widget to appear over the car model. Selecting the widget with the mouse allows a user to freely translate the model (figure 5a). Similarly, placing a rotation/scaling marker over the car model marker causes the rotation/scaling widget to appear (figure 5b). When different model markers are in view different virtual manipulators appear on the models on the table in the virtual space

Fig. 5a: Model translation   **Fig. 5b:** Model rotation

4.2.2 Tool-Based Manipulation

As an alternative to using marker and mouse/keyboard input we also explored the use of physical tools that could be used for model translation, rotation and scaling.

Translation: The translation tool can be used to move a model along all three axes in space. The tool consists of a ARToolKit marker attached to a handle. When this is held under the desktop camera the motion of the tool is mapped onto the virtual model (Figure 6). A distance vector is calculated between the current tool position and its initial position. This vector is used to update the positon of the virtual model. Thus the translation tool is a relative input device. For example, when the marker is moved upwards after being detected, the virtual object will start moving upwards as well. The translation speed itself depends on the distance to the initial position; a large offset causes a fast translation while a small offset produces slow motion. Six virtual arrow cones are shown around the model to give visual feedback about the direction and amount of the actual translation speed. The diameter of every cone is used as an indicator for the amount of translation speed component.

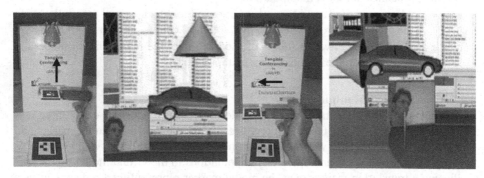

Fig. 6: Tool-based model translation

Rotation: The Rotation tool (figure 7) can be used to rotate a model about its x- y- or z-axis in space. The tool consists of three markers that are arranged in a triangular shape. Each marker represents one of the three rotation axes. Once one of the markers is held under the dekstop camera, rotation about the corresponding axis begins. The speed and direction can be controlled by the distance of the tool to the camera. For example, if the rotation tool is close to the camera with the z-axis marker facing the camera, the virtual model will start rotating clockwise about the z-axis. As the tool is moved away the rotation speed decreases until it finally reverses its direction.

Fig. 7: The rotation tool   **Fig. 8:** The scaling tool

Scaling: Model scaling is achieved by using a physical tool shaped like a magnifying glass and placing it under the desktop camera (figure 8). The scale tool's initial position is detected and stored and as the user moves the tool, the relative distance to the camera is calculated and used to determine a scale-factor that is applied to the virtual model. The closer the scale tool is to the camera, the more the model is scaled.

4.3 Incorporating Real Documents

The final functionality we wanted to add to the interface was the ability to bring real documents into the virtual environment. The document we want to capture is placed inside a folder with a marker on the cover (figure 9). If the closed folder is brought into the tangible interaction space, the marker is detected and a virtual model of the document pops up on the table. In this way a virtual representation of the real document can easily be loaded into the cAR\PE! environment.

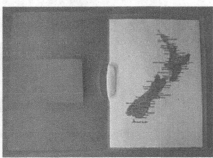

Fig. 9: The Document folder

Photo Texture: After the document model is loaded into the scene the user is able to take a snapshot of the real document and display this as a texture map on the surface of the virtual document model. When the real folder is opened the cover marker is no longer visible and our software knows to take a picture of the document and texture map it onto the virtual model (figure 10). This allows the user to share text or pictures from any real document with another person in the cAR/PE! environment.

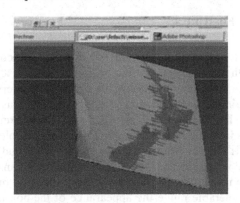

Fig. 10: Document Image Loading

Shared Snapshot: If the user wants to share a document he or she can show a large snapshot on the virtual projection screen where it is visible to everyone. To do this he or she has to move the virtual document model close to the projection wall and open the real folder. The photo snapshot now appears on the projection wall.

Our software also allows the user to immediately add physical annotations to the shared document view with conventional pens . To update the shared snapshot all the user has to do is close and reopen the document folder. So the user can write on the document and have those annotations appear in the cAR\PE! environment (figure 11).

Fig. 11: Adding Annotations

Texture Zooming: For some tasks the user may want to zoom into part of a document to share a closer view. The user can magnify and move the image texture with the scale tool. Holding the scale tool over the real document enlarges the virtual image texture shown on the projection wall. The closer the scale tools is to the camera, the bigger the texture's updated zoom factor. By moving the tool the user can also pan around the texture. Thus with these two techniques it is easy for the user to pan and zoom into any part of the document image.

5 User Feedback

In order to test the usability of our interface we conducted a simple pilot usability study with nine subjects. At the beginning of each test, every participant was given a 30 minute introduction on how the different markers and tools were supposed to be used. During this introduction, every participant was allowed to try the markers/tools and make himself or herself familiar with the different forms of actions they affected. After this introduction, two simple tasks were completed with the interface.

Task1: Object Manipulation: A car model had to be loaded into the scene and then manipulated so that it would fit into a semi-transparent box which was placed on a podium next to the virtual table. Once the car's orientation, position and size was within a tolerable range the appearance of the box turned from red to green and the task was completed. In order to perform the manipulation, the participants chose between the mouse- based manipulation technique or the fully tangible tools.

Task 2: Document Annotation: In the second task the participants were asked to reconstruct a snapshot that showed a finished Tic Tac Toe game. A shared snapshot had to be created from a real document with an incomplete Tic Tac Toe board, physical annotations had to be added and the image had to be magnified.

After the tasks were completed, we asked the participants how easy it was to learn how to use the various interface elements, and how well they felt they could use the interface. They filled out a simple survey where they were asked to rate ease of learning and ease of interaction for each tool on a scale of 1 to 7 (1 was *'not very easy'* and 7 was *'very easy'*). They were also timed how long to complete each task.

5.1 Results

In general subjects found the interface easy to use and were able to complete the tasks relatively quickly. The time for the completion of the manipulation task averaged 5 minutes, while the document task ould be completed in 3 minutes.

The Translation- tool and the Scaling-tool were rated as very easy to learn by most of the participants, with average scores of 6.2 and 6.3 respectively. The translation tool was also thought to be relatively easy to use, with an average grade of 5.1. The subjects especially liked the high sensitivity of the tool and the visual feedback showing the actual motion in space.

However the Rotation-tool was found to be not as easy to learn, receiving an average score of 5.7. It was also graded as less usable with an average score of only 4.4. Many subjects commented that this was because of the unnatural mapping of a translation movement to a rotation. It was difficult to mentally map up and down motion of the tool to clockwise and counter-clockwise rotation of the virtual model. Users almost always tried to rotate the virtual model by initially turning the model marker itself, suggesting an interesting direction for further interaction analysis.

In terms of document interaction, most of the subjects liked the folder metaphor and could immediately understand how to update snapshots and add annotations. Adding annotations was given average score of 6.1 on the ease of use scale.

Eight of the nine subjects thought that the use of physical objects as controls was helpful. Furthermore, when they had to decide between using mouse-based or tool-based operations for model manipulation, six out of nine participants preferred the fully tangible tools. This may have been due to the difficulty of mouse selection of the virtual manipulators. For example, the translation-tool allowed simultaneous movement along all three axes in space. In contrast, the mouse-based translation-tool "handlebox", only allows the models to be translated along a single axis.

6 Conclusions

The main theme of our work is to seamlessly blend elements of the real world with shared digital content in a desktop collaborative virtual environment. With the tools that we have developed people can use real objects to place virtual models into the cAR/PE! environment and to translate, rotate and scale these models. In addition we have developed document interaction tools that enable users to bring real documents into the virtual environment, and annotate the documents using pen and pencil. In this way we hope to make CSCW systems easier to use and to reach more potential users.

We also completed an initial pilot study that highlighted some of the advantages and disadvantages of our system. Users felt that the system was easy to learn because of use of real object interaction, and preferred tangible tools were over combined maker and mouse interaction. However they found the rotation tool difficult to use and also sometimes had trouble with failure with the computer vision marker detection.

This feedback has given us some good directions for future work. We next plan on completing a more rigorous user study and building further intuitive tangible interaction methods based on the results from this study.

7 References

1. ARToolKit website: http://www.hitl.washington.edu/artoolkit/
2. Benford, S. D., Brown, C. C., Reynard, G. T. and Greenhalgh, C. M (1996): "Shared Spaces: Transportation, Artificiality and Spatiality", In Proceedings of CSCW '96, Nov. 16th -20th, 1996, New York, NY: ACM Press.
3. Brave, S., and Dahley, D. inTouch: a medium for haptic interpersonal communication. Extended Abstracts of CHI'97 (Atlanta GA, Mach 1997). ACM Press, 363-364.
4. Brave, S., Ishii, H. and Dahley, A., Tangible Interfaces for Remote Collaboration and Communication , in Proceedings of CSCW '98, (Seattle, Washington USA, November 1998), ACM Press, pp. 169-178.
5. Frecon, E., Smith, G., Steed, A., Stenius, M., Stahl, O. (2001) An Overview of the COVEN Platform, Presence: Teleoperators and Virtual Environments, 10(1), February 2001, pp. 109-127 , MIT Press
6. Garfinkel, H. (1967) Studies in Ethnomethodology. Englewood Cliffs, NJ: Prentice-Hall.
7. Hindus, D., Ackerman, M., Mainwaring, S., Starr, B. Thunderwire: A Field study of an Audio-Only Media Space. In Proceedings of CSCW '96, Nov. 16th -20th, 1996, New York, NY: ACM Press.
8. Ishii, H., Ullmer, B. Tangible Bits: Towards Seamless Interfaces between People, Bits and Atoms. In proceedings of CHI 97, Atlanta, Georgia, USA, ACM Press, 1997, pp. 234-241.
9. Kauff, P. & Schreer, O. (2002). An Immersive 3D Video-Conferencing System Using Shared Virtual Team User Environments. ACM Collaborative Environments, CVE 2002, Bonn, Germany, Sept./Oct. 2002.
10. Mandeville, J., Davidson, J., Campbell, D., Dahl, A., Schwartz, P., and Furness, T. A Shared Virtual Environment for Architectural Design Review. In CVE '96 Workshop Proceedings, 19-20th September 1996, Nottingham, Great Britain.
11. OpenInventor website: http://oss.sgi.com/projects/inventor/
12. Raskar R., Welch, G., Cutts, M., Lake, A., Stesin, L., and Fuchs, H. (1998). The Office of the Future : A Unified Approach to Image-Based Modeling and Spatially Immersive Displays. "ACM SIGGRAPH 1998, Orlando FL
13. Regenbrecht, Ott, C., Wagner, M., H., Lum, T., Kohler, P., Wilke, W., Mueller, E. (2003). An Augmented Virtuality Approach to 3D Videoconferencing. International Symposium on Mixed and Augmented Reality, Tokyo/Japan, October 2003.
14. Sellen, A., Buxton, B. Using Spatial Cues to Improve Videoconferencing. In Proceedings CHI '92, May 3-7, 1992, ACM: New York , pp. 651-652.

Our Ubiquitous Computing Home Inside: A Practical Approach Emerging into House and Home

Soichiro Iga and Saiko Ohno

[1] Keio University, Keio Research Institute at SFC, 252-8520,
5322 Endo, Fujisawa, Kanagawa, Japan
{igaiga, sai}@sfc.keio.ac.jp
http://home.q00.itscom.net/ouchi/

Abstract. To make practical ubiquitous computing environment for everyday activities especially for house and home, the environment has to be proactively managed by the users at home themselves. This paper introduces an "Our Ubiquitous Computing Home Inside Project" and outlines some of our user-centered information architecture and interaction technique to provide practical ubiquitous computing environment at home. We have implemented two proto-type systems called Coordi and Collenda to demonstrate our approach, and applied these to clothing coordination task. The result shows that the systems were proven to be useful for managing information and for decision-making.

1 Introduction

The notion of "smart homes" that seamlessly interconnect computerized artifacts in which we are surrounded by is one of the promising applications of ubiquitous computing research and development.

In the last several years, many research efforts have been done in both academia and industry in designing ubiquitous technologies for house and home [6]. The Aware Home project demonstrates an infrastructure to aid in the rapid development of context aware applications by providing a living laboratory [7]. Easy Living project focuses on the development of the architecture and technologies for an intelligent environment that contains many devices that work together to provide users access to information and services [2]. This project provides a middleware to dynamically program the communication between the intelligent artifacts. This kind of middleware approach to manage distributed computerized artifacts can also be seen in Context-aware toolkit [4] or Metaglue [3]. Other approaches are to design interactive home gadgets to support domestic duties rather than providing infrastructure itself. Counter Intelligence group focuses on dynamic activities done in kitchen, and developing many novel electrical kitchen devices [8]. Digital family portrait provides awareness among geographically distant family members by network connected interactive photo frames [9]. Peek-a-drawer is taking similar approach by interactive cabinets that distant family members could see inside the cabinet each other [11]. Magic Wardrobe connects a digitally augmented wardrobe directly to online stores to show clothing products that are potentially of interest to the user [12].

M. Masoodian et al. (Eds.): APCHI 2004, LNCS 3101, pp. 153-162, 2004.
© Springer-Verlag Berlin Heidelberg 2004

Although aforementioned approaches meet the needs of upcoming ubiquitous smart home environments, it can be said that they lack a basic respect to give the users primary role to create and manage their information by the users themselves.

In this paper, we propose a user-centric framework for managing and manipulating information that would occur at home. We firstly categorize information into "contents" and "events". Contents represent actual entities of information where so-called "clothing, food and housing" can be included. Events represent temporal schedule like birthdays, memorial days, trips, and so on. We then report on two prototype systems called "Coordi" and "Collenda". Coordi is a database management system to manage information that come about at home and it has an audio/visual interactive user interface to handle information stored in the system. Collenda is a calendar-based schedule management system that imports information managed in a Coordi system. We also demonstrate a clothing coordination application system to test our prototype systems. We finally discuss on our future research topics and conclude.

2   OUCHI (Our Ubiquitous Computing Home Inside) Project

We are experimentally practicing a ubiquitous computing situation at actual home. The project is called OUCHI (Our Ubiquitous Computing Home Inside) Project. The aim of this project is to naturally augment house and home environments with information technology without building a special laboratory setup that wire everywhere around the home.

Most of the former smart home approach can be said to be technology-driven that drawing on the concept of what a novel information technology can bring significant benefits to house and home. In contrast, we are taking rather user-centric approach in which house and home are initially uncolored - unwired. We provide an information architecture where we can proactively manage information, and we can gradually add a bit of novel information technologies when the needs arise. We are skeptical about too much hot-wired "jack-in-a-box home" approach and we think that installing various preplanned embedded mechanisms does not worth the cost. House and home grows up with the growth of the dwellers in it, and the information infrastructure also has to grow accordingly with the needs of the people inside home.

There are two main human-computer interaction research efforts that have to be made to realize this kind of concept: an exploration of a design of information architecture that fits to home, and a provision of interaction technique that the actual home users can easily manipulate their information. We would discuss on each issues in later sections.

3   Designing Information of Home: Contents and Events

Key to the success of practical smart homes is to make information environment to be able to proactively be managed by the users themselves. Information that arouse from home tends to be much lifestyle-oriented of the users, and they differ among individuals. So, there would need some way of managing information that would be much lifestyle-oriented of the users.

We categorized information into "contents" and "events". Figure 1 shows the general idea of this classification. Contents represent actual entities of information. Every information which has entities would be categorized in this factor, where so-called "clothing, food and housing" can be included. Events represent temporal schedule like birthdays, memorial days, trips, and so on. However, events themselves do not have entities, we can recognize them as sensuously cohesive information that assemble pointers to entity information.

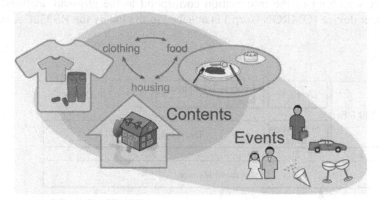

Fig.1. Two main factors in designing information of home: Contents and Events. Contents represent actual entities of information where so-called 'clothing, food and housing' can be included. Events represent temporal schedule like birthdays, memorial days, trips, and so on.

4   The Systems: Coordi and Collenda

We implemented two prototype systems called Coordi and Collenda. Coordi (Coordinator Database Management System) is an interactive multimedia database management system to coordinate and manage information that comes about at home. It has an audio/visual interactive user interface to handle information stored in the system. Collenda (Collectable Calendar System) is a calendar-based schedule management system that assembles and imports information managed in a Coordi system and in other network services.

The both systems are implemented in Microsoft Visual Basic and run on Microsoft Windows XP operating system. Output data of both systems are represented in XML-based language that can be exchanged each other.

4.1   Coordi

Figure 2 shows the architecture of the Coordi system. To give a quick view, the system is made up of two parts: a database management part and a user interface part. The database management part consists of a contents data repository to store actual entity of the contents, and a meta-data repository to store relationship among the contents information. Meta-data are represented in XML-based language. The user interface part consists of APIs to control data in a database management system, and a graphical user interface, which is to provide an interactive surface for the user to manipulate visually represented data. Multimedia data like images and audios are captured through external information input interface, for example, a digital camera and a microphone, and took into the database using the database control APIs. The Collenda system can communicate with the Coordi through these APIs. The user interface part also has a RFID control to link RFID tags and visually represented data to simplify searching of the information correspond to the physical artifacts. RFID reader/writer device (OMRON Corp.) is attached to the PC by the RS232C serial port.

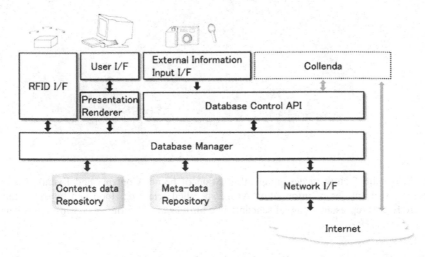

Fig.2. Coordi system architecture

In Fig.3 we show a possible graphical user interface of the Coordi system. Information stored in database management part is represented in an icon, which is shown in the center region. The region is scalable so that the user can zoom in and out depending on the numbers of the icons. Lines that are drawn between the icons are called "link" which show the relationship among the visually represented data. The user can manually create link information simply by drawing lines between the visual icons.

There are two ways to search information items stored in the system. One is by incremental text-based search. The user can find particular information by simply typing keyword. Another is by RFID tags. If the user associated a particular item with a RFID tag, he or she can find item of his or her choice just by holding the tag up closer to a RFID reader device, which is attached to the PC.

The user can capture snapshots of physical artifacts through a small camera attached to the PC. The color distribution and texture of captured images are automatically analyzed and the results of analysis are stored associated with the captured images. Color distribution is calculated by HSV color space. Texture is analyzed by rate of change of gray scale images sampled from the center region of the captured image.

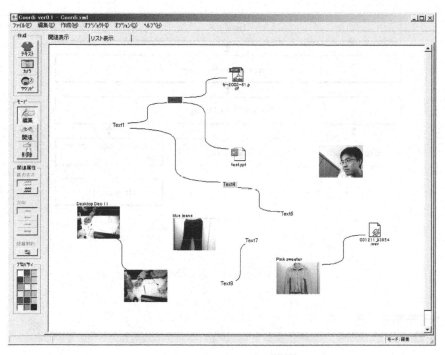

Fig.3. Graphical user interface of Coordi system: Information stored in the database management system is represented as visual icon objects. Relevant objects can be linked through the lines, which can be manually created by simply drawing lines between the objects.

Audio information like the user's voices or sounds can also be captured and the result data file would be presented in a file icon.

4.2 Collenda

Figure 4 shows the architecture of Collenda system. Schedule data for each day are deployed in events data manager and they are stored in events data repository in XML format. External information like weather forecast information or the date of national holidays are collected through the network and associated with the schedule information, which the events data manager stores. The data stored in Coordi database can be obtained through the Coordi APIs so that previously captured data in the Coordi system can be associated with the related events information which Collenda contains.

The user can edit events data through the calendar-styled graphical user interface, which is shown in Fig.5. The system can handle short texts, files, images, and URLs. Those data are visually represented in thumbnails and icons in corresponding date. The system supports drag and drop operation so that the user can easily incorporate information stored in the PCs.

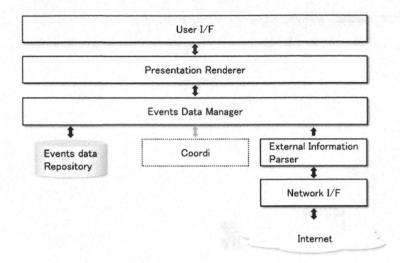

Fig.4. Collenda system architecture

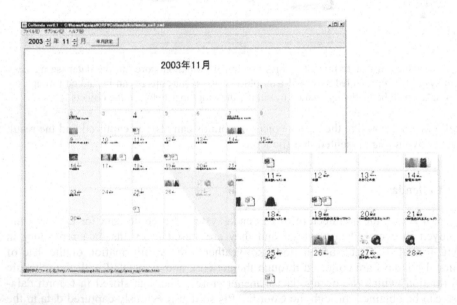

Fig.5. Graphical user interface of Collenda system: The user can manage information which is related to the events by calendar-styled graphical user interface.

While relative concerns among dates are important in checking schedules, Collenda gives a zoom-able user interface of viewing and editing data (Fig.6). Each object is rendered in fluid and dynamic distortion-oriented views that the user can browse neighbor dates while focusing on the particular one. Drag and drop operation of the information among the days and months is also dynamically rendered.

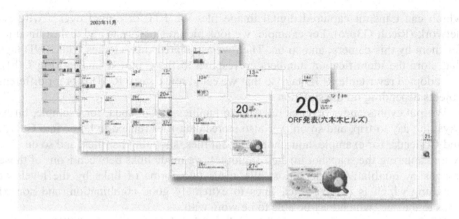

Fig.6. Zoom-able user interface of Collenda system: Information is represented in a fluid and dynamic distortion-oriented zooming view.

5   Application Example - Clothing Coordination System

We developed a clothing coordination application system to demonstrate performances of Coordi and Collenda. Clothes have strong ties to the events information, for example, we choose formal clothes for formal affairs, the casual one otherwise. We consciously and subconsciously select appropriate attire, which is suitable for the events. General idea of this demonstration system is to record snapshot images of clothes, link between the images that match well, and support making decision of which clothes to wear.

| (a) System appearance | (b)System in use |

Fig.7. Configuration of a clothing coordination application: (a) the user captures a snapshot image of a particular physical artifact by cameras; (b) the user associates the captured image with the artifact by holding the artifact up to the RFID reader. Notice that a small RFID tag is embedded in the artifact.

We captured a number of images of clothes and artifacts by a small camera attached to the PC (Fig.7 (a)). Images can also be obtained through a digital camera which can transmit captured digital image files via FTP or e-mail over a wireless network (Ricoh G3pro). For example, we took pictures of guests and dishes lined up for them by this camera, and so on. Then we associated each clothes with RFID tags that store the identification numbers correspond to the captured images (Fig.7 (b)). We adopted rewritable RFID tags so that we could reuse same RFID tags for different objects depending on the situation.

We put events and schedules relevant to families in Collenda, for example, birthdays, the day to trip, and so on. We also stored data files related to home into Coordi and Collenda, for example, household account files, shopping list files, and so on. After capturing the snapshot images of clothes, we made links between icons of those images by qualitative observation. We made two forms of links by the levels of matching which is to give thick lines to extremely good combination, and normal lines to the one, which may be able to be worn with.

When the user types the name of the color of the clothes or put the RFID tag closer to the RFID reader, the corresponding visual icon would be high-lighted and zoomed in the distortion-oriented view. The system also provides a sound feedback according to the combinations of the levels of the matching between high-lighted icons. The system synthesizes a major key chord for the good combinations, a minor key chord for the matching that can be worn with, and inharmonic tones for the bad combinations. The tone timbre of the sound changes according to the air temperature of the day, which the Collenda system acquired from the external weather forecast web site.

The Collenda stores events information, which are scheduled on a particular day and the clothes information, which are selected in the Coordi can be incorporated into the Collenda. This will enable the user to link between events and the clothes, which the user wore.

6 User Experience and Discussion

We are in the process of conducting formal field tests, although we have been actually utilizing the clothing coordination system for three months. During this trial use, the number of the objects stored in the Coordi system was 34 (23 for clothes, 5 for events, 6 for document files) and the number of the links among those objects were 48. The number of the events stored in the Collenda system was 33.

From the experiences of using the system, we observed many contexts of the system supporting making decision. One example is the user changed clothes which he once picked out because he found that he was wearing same clothes last week when meeting the person scheduled to meet on the very day.

Another example is that the user chose clothes by the weather forecast information. While the system displays the air temperature of current date by sound, the user realized that the clothes he was going to wear were not proper to the temperature of that day without any glancing of the PC monitor.

Some researches have shown that organizing information by time improves users' performance in retrieval tasks [1][10]. We think that important basis in information platform for home is to provide the information space where the user can independently relate information together. In this mean, the Coordi system provides a way to manage relationship among the actual contents and the Collenda system provides a way to relate contents with the events information. Information retrieval task can be enhanced with our fusion approach that is to not only associate contents with the events, but also to link between related contents themselves.

Obviously, our approach can be applied not only to the coordination of the clothing, but also to other information management application, for example, recorded recipe data for cooking, manage purchased amount for household accounting, and so on.

There is some room for improvement though. One problem is the cost of entering information. In our current prototype system, the user has to manually capture the snapshot images of the clothes and input clothes data, which he or she has actually chosen. We believe that RFID technique can be applied to automatically gathering profile information of the clothes and making entries of what the user worn on the particular day by putting RFID reader devices to the doors and the like. In the future, with the advent of EPC (Electronic Product Code) and smart tags, we believe that it would be possible to automatically assemble thumbnail images of the artifacts, and to track in real-time where they are, and how they have been used [5]. Another problem is the scalability issues. It was visually imperceptible for the user to understand which link goes with what, when the number of the objects increased. We should introduce some kind of grouping among the analogous objects to reduce the link operation for individual objects which have same properties to be handled by the user.

7 Conclusion

We have proposed a user-centric framework to manage information of house and home by providing a database management system and an interactive user interface to manipulate information of home. We categorized information at home into contents and events where the users can manage their information in much lifestyle-oriented ways. We implemented two prototype systems, Coordi and Collenda, and demonstrated a clothing coordination application. Our user experiences show that these prototype systems can support decision-making, which is to leverage relationships among contents and events.

Future work will continue to refine our systems and to carry out much precise field tests.

Acknowledgement

We would like to thank Prof. Michiaki Yasumura at Keio University of his continual guidance and encouragements to this work.

References

1. Adcock, J., Cooper, M., Doherty, J., Foote, J., Girgensohn, A., Wilcox, L.: Managing Digital Memories with the FXPAL Photo Application. ACM Multimedia 2003 (2003) 598-599
2. Brumitt, B., Meyers, B., Krumm, J., Kern, A., Shafer, S.: Easy Living: Technologies for Intelligent Environments. Handheld and Ubiquitous Computing (2000) 12-27
3. Cohen, M., Phillips, B., Warshawsky, N., Weisman, L., Peters, S., and Finin, P.: Meeting the Computational Needs of Intelligent Environments: The Metaglue System. MANSE'99 (1999) 201-212
4. Dey, A., Salber, D., and Abowd, G.D.: A Conceptual Framework and a Toolkit for Supporting the Rapid Prototyping of Context-Aware Applications. Human-Computer Interaction (HCI) Journal, Volume 16 (2-4) (2001) 97-166
5. EPC global: [on-line] http://www.epcglobalinc.org/
6. Iga, S. and Yasumura, M.: Attachable Computer: Augmentation of Electric Household Appliances by Portable Fit-up Computer. IPSJ Journal, Vol.40 No.2 (1999) 381-388
7. Kidd, C.D., Orr, R., Abowd, G.D., Atkeson, C.G., Essa, I.A., MacIntyre, B., Mynatt, E.D., Starner, T., and Newstetter, W.: The Aware Home: A Living Laboratory for Ubiquitous Computing Research. CoBuild'99 (1999) 191-198
8. MIT Media Lab Counter Intelligence Group: [on-line] http://www.media.mit.edu/ci/ (1999)
9. Mynatt, E.D., Rowan, J., Craighill, S. and Jacobs, A.: Digital family portraits: Providing peace of mind for extended family members. ACM CHI 2001 (2001) 333-340
10. Rekimoto, J.: Time-Machine Computing: A Time-centric Approach for the Information Environment. ACM UIST'99 (1999) 45-54
11. Siio, I., Rawan, J., and Mynatt, E.: Peek-a-drawer: communication by furniture. Conference Extended Abstracts on Human Factors in Computer Systems (ACM CHI 2002) (2002) 582-583
12. Wan, W.: Magic Wardrobe: Situated Shopping from Your own Bedroom. Personal and Ubiquitous Computing, Volume 4, Number 4 (2000) 234-237

A Study of an EMG-controlled HCI Method by Clenching Teeth

Hyuk Jeong, Jong-Sung Kim, Jin-Seong Choi

Digital Content Research Division,
Electronics and Telecommunications Research Institute
161 Kajeong-dong, Yuseong-gu, Daejeon, Korea
{jay, joskim, jin1025}@etri.re.kr

Abstract. In this paper, a new Human-Computer-Interaction (HCI) method for a quadriplegic, which is controlled by clenching teeth, is proposed. By simple combination of two clenching patterns, seven instructions including rest, up, down, left and right as well as click and double click actions are made for the control of a pointing device. The control source is EMGs (electromyograms), which are generated by clenching teeth and acquired on two temporal muscles in one's forehead. For easy-to-wear, the prototype device is designed for attaching EMG electrodes on a forehead by using a headband. Stochastic values such as difference absolute mean value are used for feature extractions and Fuzzy Min-Max Neural Network (FMMNN) is used for classifying clenching patterns. The usefulness of the proposed system is confirmed by the user test.

1 Introduction

Human Computer Interaction (HCI) technology by using bioelectric signals such as an electromyogram (EMG), an electroencephalogram (EEG) and an electrooculogram (EOG) is considered to alternatives to conventional input devices such as a keyboard or a mouse. Among these bioelectric signals, EMGs can be used as control source for an intuitive and natural HCI because EMGs represent electrical activity of muscles. Also, EMGs can be easily acquired on a skin with easy-to-apply surface electrodes.

An EMG is a bioelectric signal generated by using a muscle. The amplitude of an EMG ranges from 0 to 10 mV (peak-to-peak) and the usable energy of the signal is limited to the 0 to 500 Hz frequency range [1]. An EMG can be acquired on the skin near to a muscle by differential amplification in order to eliminate the noise signal. An EMG electrode should be placed between a motor point and the tendon insertion and along the longitudinal midline of the muscle [2].

Input devices for amputees using EMGs generated by wrist motions have been studied on the several researches [3-6]. Also, a method to control a transport for the handicapped such as a wheelchair by performing head rotation was suggested [7]. However, there are few methods helping to operate a computer for a quadriplegic by using EMGs.

The purpose of this study is the development of the EMG-controlled input device to operate a computer for a quadriplegic by clenching teeth. A method and a prototype

M. Masoodian et al. (Eds.): APCHI 2004, LNCS 3101, pp. 163-170, 2004.
© Springer-Verlag Berlin Heidelberg 2004

device for attaching electrodes on a forehead are provided. Also, definitions of actions and the EMG signal processing methods are described for classifying clenching patterns.

2   A Method to Attach EMG Electrodes

A quadriplegic cannot use muscles below his head. Among muscles in the head, a pair of temporal muscles can be a good candidate for control source in operating a computer. Temporal muscles are near the sides of one's forehead and activated by clenching teeth.

By considering wearability of electrodes and basic knowledge in anatomy, two positions on the surface of a forehead were chosen for attaching electrodes. For easy-to-wear, we designed the prototype device for attaching EMG electrodes on a forehead by using headband. The prototype device for attaching EMG electrodes is shown in Fig. 1. The device is a headband type and it is wearable. The electrodes, the DE-2.1 of Delsys Inc. are used in this study. The electrode, the DE-2.1 does not need an adhesive and it is suitable for wearability. The electrodes are attached on the mounting band by using Velcro tapes and the position of an electrode can be easily adjusted.

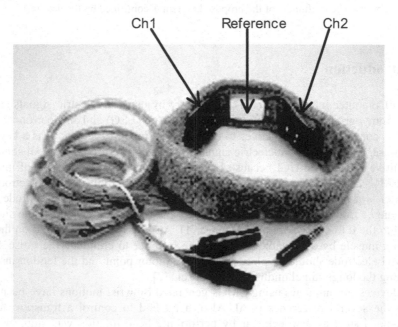

Fig. 1. The prototype device for attaching EMG electrodes. (Ch1: left temporal muscle, Ch2: right temporal muscle, reference: reference electrode)

Fig. 2 shows the situation in wearing the prototype device for attaching the electrodes. In Fig. 2, the locations of the EMG electrodes are marked. The reference electrode is attached on the center of the forehead.

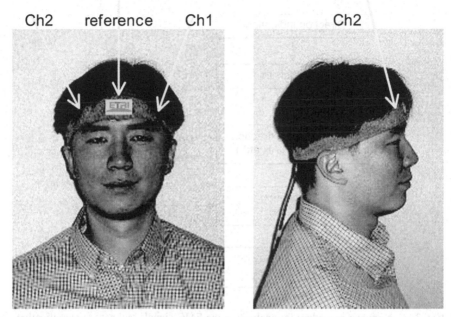

Fig. 2. The situation in wearing the prototype device for attaching the electrodes. The words represent the locations of EMG electrodes. (Ch1: left temporal muscle, Ch2: right temporal muscle, reference: reference electrode)

3 EMG Signal Processing Methods

Our system is developed for assisting a mouse operation. In order to operate a computer by using a mouse, at least following seven input commands are needed. These are the rest, the horizontal movement (left or right), the vertical movement (up or down), the selection (click) and the execution (double click).

From the assumption that one can clench his teeth partly (left or right), the four basic actions, which are the rest, clenching one's left teeth, clenching one's right teeth and clenching one's all teeth, are classified at first. Then we compose the seven commands for operating a mouse by combination of the four basic clenching actions.

In this section, the EMG signal processing methods are described for classifying the four basic clenching actions. In order to classify the four basic clenching actions, the procedures such as direction indication, data acquisition, feature extraction and pattern learning are needed. Fig. 3 shows the schematic diagram for classifying the four basic clenching actions. After the specific direction signal is shown on a display, a subject, who attaches EMG electrodes on one's forehead, clench the related parts of his teeth. From the EMG signals acquired by a data acquisition system, the features of the signals are extracted. Then, learning the patterns is carried out. The parameters, which are learned in the learning process, are used for classifying new signals into four basic clenching actions.

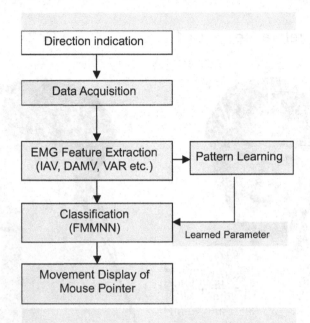

Fig. 3: A schematic procedure for analysis of the EMG signals and pattern classification

Fig. 4 is an example scene of the program for displaying the indicated direction and acquiring the EMG signals. The color of the direction symbol in the figure is changed according to the given direction. After the specific direction, a subject should clench one's left teeth, right teeth or all teeth. If the circle located in the center is turned on, the subject has a rest. If the left or right direction symbol is turned on, one has to clench one's left or right teeth, respectively. If the left and right symbols are simultaneously turned on, he has to clench his all teeth. Then the EMG signals due to the specified clenching patterns can be acquired.

EMG signals are acquired from a subject by repeating each clenching actions about two times. The duration for indicating the pre-defined motion is fixed to about 5 second. Since it is hard to determine the start point of clenching actions in pattern learning, the first 500 ms data acquired after indicating a direction, are not used in the pattern learning. The indication for clenching actions can be shown up sequentially or randomly. The program can control the sampling frequency, the data acquisition time and so on.

The Bagnoli-4 of Delsys Inc. amplifies the EMG signals by 1000 times. For data acquisition and processing, PCI-MIO-16E of National Instrument Inc. is used. The 1024 Hz and 12 bit sampling is conducted in analogue-to-digital converting.

The features extracted from the EMG signals are used as the input vectors in learning and classifying the patterns. The features used in this study are as follows:

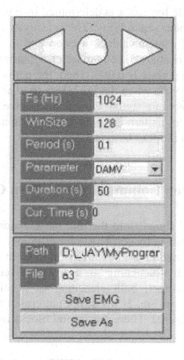

Fig. 4. An example scene of executing program to acquire the EMG signals by the clenching actions according to a direction.

• Integral Absolute Value (IAV): The IAV is calculated for each window of data according to the following equation:

$$IAV = \frac{1}{N}\sum_{i=1}^{N}|x(i)|, \tag{1}$$

where x is data within the window and N is window length.

• Difference Absolute Mean Value (DAMV): The DAMV is calculated for each window of data according to the following equation:

$$DAMV = \frac{1}{N-1}\sum_{i=2}^{N}|x(i) - x(i-1)|. \tag{2}$$

Since the EMG with duration of 100 ms or more can be assumed statically stable [8], the window length is set to 125 ms. The features at each time block are used as the input vector for pattern learning.
For learning and classifying the patterns, the Fuzzy Min-Max Neural Network (FMMNN) algorithm [9] is used. The FMMNN is a kind of supervised learning neural network classifier. Each class is described as summation of several hyperbox,

which is a fuzzy set, and the hyperbox is determined by n dimensional min-max value. The FMMNN has a nonlinear separability. The sensitivity parameter in the FMMNN controls the decay rate of a membership function and the value 4 is chosen as the sensitivity parameter in this study. The number of hyperbox at each class is 100 and the increment degree of hyperbox is 0.005. Then, the pattern recognition rate of each clenching actions is above 90% when the DAMV is used as the feature. Since IAV or DAMV represents the power of a signal, these features give a similar recognition rate. The parameters calculated in pattern learning are saved in a file and they are used for classifying new signal into the four basic actions.

4   Generation of Seven Commands from Two Clenching Patterns

After classifying the EMG signals into the four basic actions, we compose the seven commands for operating mouse by combination of the four basic clenching actions. A left teeth clenching is defined as a left movement, a right teeth clenching as a right movement, left teeth double-clenching as a down movement, right teeth double-clenching as an up movement, both clenching as a selection and both double-clenching as an execution. In Fig. 5, the seven patterns for representing seven input commands are briefly described. There are several blocks in black, white or shaded in the figure.

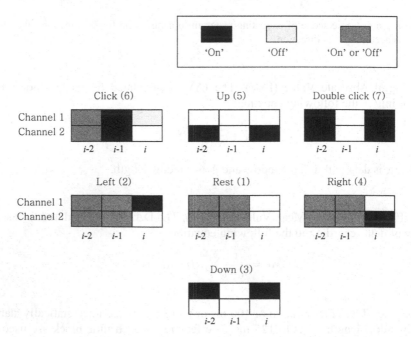

Fig. 5. A schematic diagram for generation of seven commands for operating a mouse. The black box and the white box represent clenching state and non-clenching state, respectively. The shaded box can represent any state. The index of 'i', 'i-1' and 'i-2' represent i^{th}, i-1th and i-2th block of the series respectively. The number in the parentheses is the given pattern number.

In the figure, the black box and the white box represent the activation state and the rest state of the specified temporal muscle, respectively. The shaded box does not care what the pattern is. If the classified pattern at i^{th} step is left clenching, the block of channel 1 is marked in black and the block of channel 2 is marked in white. If the classified pattern is right clenching, only the block of channel 2 is marked in black and the block of channel 2 is marked in black. After following this procedure, seven commands for operating mouse can be made.

5   Simulation of Operating Mouse

The Fig. 6 shows a scene in the demonstration program for the EMG-controlled graphic interface. The left part in the figure is an area for illustrating the movement of a mouse pointer and the right part is an area for showing the control parameters such as the sampling frequency and the feature type. After loading the learned parameters and activating the program, one controls the position of pointer by clenching teeth. If all teeth are simultaneously clenched, the symbol of mouse pointer is changed. This action can be used for the instruction of execution in a window operating system.

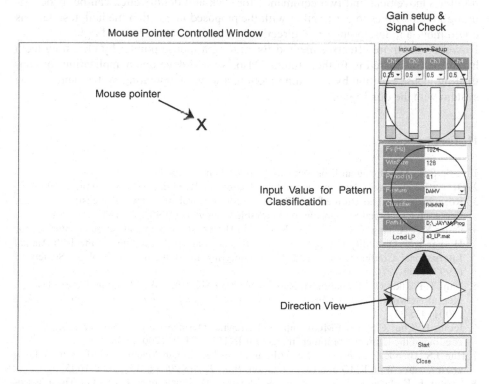

Fig. 6. An example scene in executing the program for demonstration of the EMG-controlled graphic interface.

The user test was conducted with five persons. The test users were not handicapped but they are forced not to move their bodies. The averaged recognition rate about the basic four patterns is about 94%. The test users could easily move the mouse pointer in the horizontal direction. However, they have some difficulties to move the mouse pointer in the vertical direction at the beginning. It took times to get familiar with the proposed interaction method. In further study, the more effective method for moving a mouse pointer by clenching teeth has to be considered.

6 Summary

In this study, a new EMG-controlled HCI method for a quadriplegic by clenching teeth is proposed. EMGs generated by clenching teeth are acquired on two temporal muscles in one's forehead. For easy-to-wear, the prototype device for attaching EMG electrodes on a forehead is designed by using a headband and conventional sensors. Stochastic values such as difference absolute mean value are used for feature extractions and Fuzzy Min-Max Neural Network (FMMNN) is used for classifying clenching patterns.

By simple combination of two clenching patterns, five commands for a mouse pointer's movement and two commands for click and double click can be made. Although it took times to get familiar with the proposed interaction method, test persons could move a mouse pointer in 4 directions such as up, down, left and right.

However, the more effective method for moving a mouse pointer by clenching teeth has to be considered in further studies. Also, we will develop an application for controlling mouse position by clenching teeth in a window operating system and test the system with the quadriplegic.

References

1. Park, S.H., The Biosignal Processing and Application, Edtech (1999)
2. Delsys Inc., Surface Electromyography: Detection and Recording, Delsys Tutorial (1996)
3. Rosenberg, R., The Biofeedback Pointer: EMG Control of a Two Dimensional Pointer, Second International Symposium on Wearable Computers (1998) 162-163
4. Tarng Y.H., Chang, G.C., Lai, J.S., Kuo, T.S., Design of the Human/Computer Interface for Human with Disability Using Myoelectric Signal Control, Proceedings of the 19th Annual International Conference of the IEEE Engineering in Medicine and Biology Society, 5 (1997) 1909-1910
5. Tsuji T, Fukuda O, Murakami M, Kaneko M., An EMG Controlled Pointing Device Using a Neural Network, *Transactions of the Society of Instrument and Control Engineers*, 37, 5 (2001) 425-31
6. Jeong H, Choi C.S, An EMG-Controlled Graphic Interface Considering Wearability, Proceeding of the Human-Computer Interaction-INTERACT'03 (2003) 958-961
7. Han J.S., Bien Z. Z., Kim D.J., Lee H.E. and Kim J.S. Human-Machine Interface for Wheelchair Control With EMG and Its Evaluation. *Proc. EMBS 2003* (2003) 1602-1605
8. Delagi, E. F., Iazzetti, J., Perotto, A., & Morrison, D., Anatomical Guide For The Electromyographer, *The Limbs and Trunk*, Springfield (1994)
9. Simpson, P. K., Fuzzy Min-Max Neural Networks-Part 1: Classification, *IEEE Trans, On Neural Networks*, 3, 5 (1992) 776-786

Performance Analysis for User Interface in Real-Time Ubiquitous Information Network

Yung Bok Kim[1], Mira Kwak[2], and Dong-sub Cho[2]

[1] Dept of Computer Engineering, Sejong University,
Gunja-Dong, Gwangjin-Gu, Seoul, Republic of Korea
yungbkim@sejong.ac.kr
[2] Dept. of Computer Science and Engineering, Ewha Womans University,
Daehyun-Dong, Seodaemun-Gu, Seoul, Republic of Korea
mirakwak@ieee.org, dscho@ewha.ac.kr

Abstract. The Web server for knowledge and information should be unified as a center for real-time information network in the ubiquitous computing environment. We studied the performance analysis for HCI (human-computer interaction) user interface in real-time ubiquitous information network based on wired and mobile Internet. We show an empirical performance analysis and metrics for user interface, at the customer's perspective, on the basis of simple implementation of the unified information portal accessible with single character domain names.

1 Introduction

Two breakthrough inventions formed the information society's foundation: computers and telecommunications, which play roles similar to those that the steam engine and electricity played during the industrial revolution [1]. The hybrid technology of the above two inventions, Internet penetrates deeply in normal life and business; and the two ways, wired Internet and mobile Internet should be unified with worldwidely convenient HCI user interface for convenience as well as integrity of consistent information. The Web server is the appropriate as a role center for unified information service and the client mobile devices become very important for HCI in ubiquitous computing environment. Let's briefly look over the recent technologies and services using Web services.

For the objective of user interface for unified information portal in the ubiquitous information network, we considered several aspects about the Web server as follows. The performance of a World Wide Web (WWW) server became a central issue in providing ubiquitous, reliable, and efficient information system for ubiquitous information services. The performance issues in the World Wide Web servers were studied [2], and the mechanisms to reduce the number of packets exchanged in an HTTP transaction were presented. For wired Internet using HTML for PCs, and for mobile Internet using WML, mHTML or HDML for mobile phones, the management of Web server becomes more difficult; and Hwang et al. studied the case of WAP site [3]. The wireless, mobile Web promises to provide users with anytime, anywhere access

M. Masoodian et al. (Eds.): APCHI 2004, LNCS 3101, pp. 171-179, 2004.

to the same information; ubiquitous Web access should also facilitate greater acceptance of new services that are specialized for mobile use [4].

Here, we have studied the performance of the unified information portal with inexpensive Web server. At first, we discuss the issues about performance of mobile Internet. For the mobile phone Internet, as one of major protocols, the WAP protocol has been used a lot, especially in Korea and many other countries, and WAP browsers, with WAP 1.0 to WAP 2.0 version, have been implemented in many mobile phone devices. The ubiquitous mobile computing [5] was discussed in the current environment with a plethora of mobile devices, and introduced several challenges, e.g. authentication, profiles and personalization, performance, etc. The challenged performance is what the bottlenecks in the application architecture or the content path are.

We studied new performance analysis methodology for ubiquitous information network, based on the user's perspective beyond the computer networking, i.e. at the customer's view-point in this ubiquitous computing environment. We introduce the new performance analysis for real-time unified portal for world-wide information network based on wired and mobile Internet, especially about HCI (human-computer interaction) user interface at the customer's perspective. We will discuss the importance of the mobile user interface with the results from real implementation of a unified portal for ubiquitous information network, e.g. Korean information network as an example of a ubiquitous information network using PCs as well as handheld mobile phones.

We studied the important performance metric, delay, that is broken down into several metrics at the user's perspective. We studied the performance metric, delay, not only with the time in the network and server, but also with the spent time by user and the input time with keypads for URL or for notification of information. We studied also the relationship of performance metrics to order the dominating factors in the overall performance at the user's perspective to impress the importance of fast user interface especially in the mobile computing environment.

2   Real-Time Unified Portal and User Interface

The unified Web server for information processing should have the capability of showing the appropriate contents, i.e. the HTML contents for wired Internet as well as the mobile contents for many different kinds of mobile devices, e.g. WML, mHTML, HDML. For unified service, there are several constraints compared to the contents for the wired Internet. First of all, we should consider the various kinds of mobile devices as well as the browsers; each of those devices may have different capabilities in terms of the image and melody. Therefore the development and application environment for HCI user interface with new technologies are very different from the existing wired Internet mainly based on the almost unified browser, MS Explorer.

We implemented the unified portal of Korean information network for wired Internet for PC and wireless Internet for mobile devices, as ubiquitous information network beyond the computer networking. The size of contents is below 1.5Kbyte as a WML deck, which is the transmission packet unit in the WAP environment; and even for the wired Internet we considered the same content for unified service, but the size generated by HTML editor is around 5KByte. We used single Web server as a unified portal service for the simplicity of management and the cost-effectiveness of information processing. This method gives the effectiveness and efficiency for the notification of information and utilization of resources, in terms of the bandwidth for communication and the size of required disk storage for information to store.

To access the unified portal pervasively, the user interface should be as convenient as possible even for typing-in the domain names or URL; because the just first step for Web service with wired/mobile Internet (especially, mobile case) is typing-in the URL of the Web site offering the requested information. About the user interface, the following Table 1 shows the average of the keypad press number in the case of a Korean mobile phone model. Based on the assumption of single alphabet character; this is analyzed at the user's point of view. For writing the business information in real-time way, the user's typing speed of character is one of important performance factors, especially with the mobile phone.

Table 1. Average number of keypad pressing for user interface (a Korean model)

Press number	Alphabet	Probability	(Mean) press number
1 time	a, d, g, j, m, p, t, w	8/26	8/26
2 times	b, e, h, k, n, q, u, x	8/26	16/26
3 times	c, f, i, l, o, r, v, y	8/26	24/26
4 times	s, z	2/26	8/26
	Average number of keypad pressing for single alphabet		56/26≈2.15

In the Table 1, the model shows the average about 2.15. Among many other models from other vendors in Korea, a model by Samsung in Korea shows that the average keypad pressing number is about 2.04. In the case of single Korean character composed of one consonant and one vowel, over 4 keypad pressing numbers even for simple Korean character are required, that means inconvenient keypad pressing is required for the mobile phone user interface.

The English domain name is at least consisted of several alphabet characters; that means the averaged keypad pressing number for single alphabet character is the same as we discussed above. Therefore the minimum bound of keypad pressing number for English domain names composed of several alphabets will be the multiple of the above keypad pressing number at least because of the shift key. For example, to type-in our unified portal site 'ktrip.net', the actual keypad pressing number with the LG-i1500 model is around 20 including the mode change from Korean mode to the English mode; in the case of the portal site 'yahoo.com', the keypad pressing number is around 22 as well. The number of keypad pressing '.net' itself is 6 and the keypad pressing number for '.com' itself is 8 for both LG models. For Korean domain '.kr', the required keypad pressing number is 6.

For user interface in the real-time information network, even the input of characters becomes important for retrieval of information or registration of information, especially with keypad in the mobile phone for information processing. To access the unified portal ubiquitously, the user interface should be as convenient as possible even for typing-in the domain names or URLs, or information. For writing the information in real-time way, the user's typing speed of characters, e.g. Korean characters, is one of important performance factors, especially with the mobile phone. Over 4 keypad pressing numbers, even for simplest Korean character composed of one consonant and one vowel is required, that means inconvenient keypad pressing is required for the mobile phone user. Even for the case of typing URLs, the Korean domain name is consisted of several characters where each character is at least composed of one consonant and one vowel. Therefore the minimum bound of keypad pressing number for Korean domain names, in the case of several Korean characters, will be the multiple of the above keypad pressing number.

3 Performance Analysis at Customer's Perspective

The performance analysis at the user's viewpoint may be different from the conventional analysis methodology. However, we should investigate this new approach, because the environment has been changed a lot, especially in terms of the interactivity of customers with mobile devices for information processing in the ubiquitous computing environment. In this paper, we studied the new performance analysis at the user's viewpoint for the real world; and this approach might give rather realistic insight for HCI user interface. The real-time application, getting required information as well as writing information in the wired Internet and mobile Internet environment, will be considered.

We studied the important performance metric, delay, at the user's perspective. We studied the performance metric, delay, not only with the time in the network and server, but also with the spent time by user and the input time with keypads for URL or information for notification.

For the mobile user, let's assume that the random variables, the round-trip response time for user's single interaction in a session, from user to the contents in database through wired/mobile Internet before next interaction, with mobile phone is r_m, which is composed of the time for user's preparation to get mobile phone in his hand is U_m (we can use this random variable as metrics for *Ubiquity* with the *mean* and *standard deviation*); the time spent with mobile phone to do appropriate action for service is D_m; the aggregate time to the Web Server after the mobile device through wired/mobile Internet for mobile service is S_m (the conventional network time is embedded here); the time depending upon mobile contents is C_m.

The session time may be dependent on this content retrieval or registration, and there may be several back and forth iterations. However we simply use the aggregate time instead of breaking them down, then

$$r_m = r'_m + r_{mback} = U_m + D_m + S_m + C_m + r_{mback}. \tag{1}$$

The returning round trip time, from the content retrieval time to the requesting user through Web server and wired/mobile Internet using mobile device, is r_{mback}.

Among the above random variables without subscript for mobile, i.e. the performance metrics, (U, D, S, C) for mobile user and PC user, the most dominating factor, i.e. the random variable, may be different from person to person. At first, for the fair comparison, let's assume that the same person is using the same content in the same server with the same device. Then, we can order the dominating random variables, after estimation with an implementation for information network with the unified server, http://ktrip.net [6]. The previous works for computer networking have been mainly focused on the analysis of the time about S, but we suggest the overall performance metric, delay, i.e. the response time r, instead of the partial and minor delay S, in ubiquitous information network for the ubiquitous computing environment beyond the computer networking.

In Fig. 2, the overall time delay by user, device, network, server and contents are shown and broken down as follow; user's preparation time, U_1; time with client's device, D_1 and D'_1; time in network and Web server, S_1 and S'_1; user's time for understanding and readiness, U_2; time with client's device, D_2 and D'_2; time in network and Web server, S_2 and S'_2; time for reading contents in the database server, $C_{1(Read)}$; time for writing contents in the database server, $C_{1(Write)}$; user's preparation time for understanding and readiness, U_3; time for writing contents with client's device, D_3 and D'_3; time in network and Web server, S_3 and S'_3; user's preparation time for understanding and readiness, U_4; time for finishing the business session with client's device, D_4; time in network and Web server, S_4.

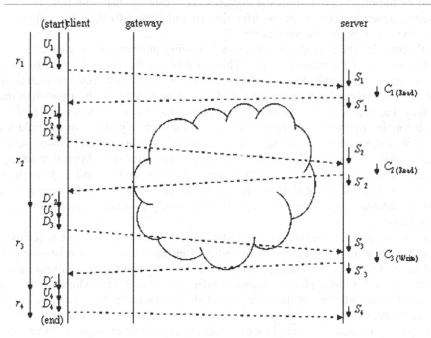

Fig. 1. Overall time delay for a session

From the Fig. 1, for mobile user, a performance metric, the response time for ith transaction at the user's viewpoint is

$$r_i = U_i + D_i + D'_i + S_i + S'_i + C_i. \qquad (2)$$

and the overall performance metric, i.e. the overall delay for a session is

$$\sum_{i=1}^{n} r_i \,. \tag{3}$$

In this session the dominating factor is U_i and D_i in normal network and server, considering the recent stable network. We considered the packet size to be independent from the network traffic condition as well as the simple service in the Web server to be independent from the load of the Web server.

For the real-time application using wired Internet and mobile Internet, the dominating factor and the variance of that random variable should be bounded within the deterministic response time. To be deterministic for real-time application, the user should be skilled, the user interface of device should be convenient, the network should be stable if possible, the server should be efficient and have high performance for the dedicated application, and finally the contents for information processing should be simple as possible with simplified and efficient format. The bandwidth requirement for wireless or mobile Internet should be as little as possible to be immune to the network traffic condition; also that will be good in terms of degradation caused by the other rich multimedia contents. The user's preparation time U will be shortened depending upon the proliferation of ubiquitous devices for information processing, e.g. mobile Internet devices.

Let's consider the average of the keypad pressing number for the case of Korean mobile phone model discussed before. This is related to the device time D. Based on the assumption of single Korean character composed of one consonant and one vowel; this is analyzed at the user's point of view. For writing the information in real-time way, the user's typing speed of Korean character is one of important performance factors in any mobile Internet services with the mobile phone. For example with the simplest Korean character composed of one consonant and one vowel, several Korean mobile phone models showed that the average number of keypad pressing is around 4~5 for the mentioned single Korean character and around 2~3 for single English alphabet, including shift key for next character. This is also serious dominating factor related to the time, D, especially for writing contents of information with mobile phone.

We studied to order the dominating factors in the overall performance at the user's perspective. We found that there were some difference between the relationship for wired Internet with PC (discussed later, $U > D > C > S$) and the relationship for mobile Internet with mobile phone (discussed later, $U > D > S > C$). Therefore the user interface design with the mobile device in the ubiquitous computing environment (i.e. U becomes smaller as the ubiquity increases) is most important to decrease the time D that is heavily related to the HCI mobile user interface. For example, the Pen Phone introduce by Siemens in the Cebit 2004 is a sort of mobile device that reduces the device time D, especially for writing messages

We discuss the above relationships more in the following chapter after real implementation.

4 Implementation and Empirical Results

The real-time information network for ubiquitous information services beyond the computer networking, here Korean information network, is based on wired or mobile Internet, many single Korean character domains for fast access of the required Korean domain name with simple single character, the required information or advertisement can be registered in any time and any place using wired or mobile Internet [6] in the unified Web server for ubiquitous information service, i.e. the 'ktrip.net'. The implemented system is as follows; for the operating system, MS Windows 2000 server; for wired and mobile Internet Web services, MS IIS 5.0 Web server and ASP 3.0; for DBMS, MS SQL server; for the mobile markup language, WML for SK Telecom, mHTML for KTF, HDML for LG Telecom. The E1 (2.048Mbps) Internet communication line to the Web server, i.e. the unified portal, for both wired and mobile Internet service, is being used, because this E1 or T1 line is most popular and cost effective for many small and medium sized companies. As we discussed already, the size of Web page for unified service was considered below 1.5Kbyte, i.e. between 500Byte and 1.5Kbyte of compiled WAP binary, to minimize the dependency of the overall performance to the shared and stochastically varying network traffic; also the Web server is dedicated to minimize the server load, and dedicated for the unified portal of Korean information network as an example. For the cost-effectiveness, we chose the most common and inexpensive server available, and the E1 line which is one of the most common communication lines for Web service in Korea.

The speed of real-time registration of business advertisement as well as the speed of access of special information for various communities is fast enough for real application for ubiquitous information services. Moreover, the effectiveness and efficiency of storage for advertisement and information is being anticipated if we consider the inefficient worldwide applications, e.g. various community sites, home pages for small companies, or inconvenient notification bulletin boards, as far as the consumed disk storage, operation and administration are concerned.

Considering the performance of the unified portal, we can make the processing time deterministic in the Web server for contents, where the deterministic time is possible with the deterministic size of packet, below around 1.5Kbyte, i.e. below one WML deck size for the old models of mobile phone.

The average response time after Ping command from wired PC to the unified server (ktrip.net) directly, or via A site (Web forwarding service server A of domain registrar), or via B site (similarly, the Web forwarding service server B of domain registrar) is around 30msec, 223msec, and 221msec, respectively.

The following Fig. 2 shows the mean and standard deviation of 100 samples, we can observe that the response time at wired PC is fastest and stable with little deviation, the averaged response time with mobile phone Internet is around 12 seconds with about 2 seconds standard deviation, the other two cases with wired PC via the intermediate server in domain registrar office show that depending upon the intermediate server the mean and deviation of the response time become very different. The size of one Web page for wired Internet is around 25Kbyte, and the notations are marked with Via A and Via B in Fig. 2, here we show that direct IP service without domain name resolution is much faster. The size of Web page for the wired Internet

accessed by the domain name 'ktrip.net' is about 5Kbyte, and the size of the mobile
Web page (not-compiled) is about 1.5Kbyte, that become about 1Kbyte after compil-
ing to WAP binary file. This type of information processing with mobile Internet will
be popular because of the simplicity and mobility for any information processing
models.

From Fig. 2, we can conclude that the network and server response time for Ping
command is much shorter than the content retrieval time in the server. The mobile
1.5Kbyte content retrieval time with mobile Internet is about 10 seconds longer than
the wired (PC) 5Kbyte content retrieval time because of the elapsed time with the
gateway, and this time is related to the network time (in WAP gateway and in mobile
system) instead of time in server.

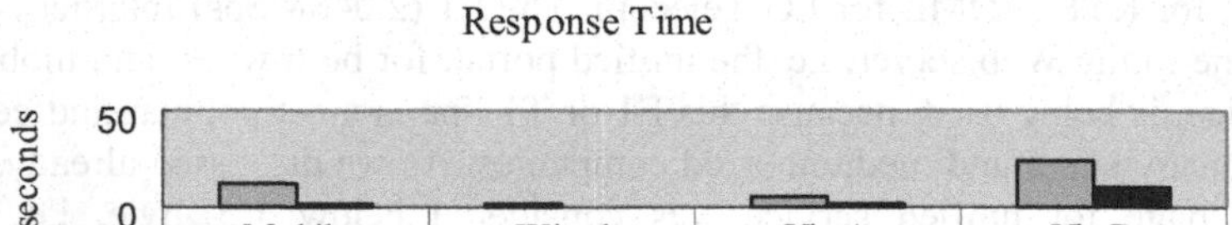

Response Time

		Mobile	Wired	Via A	Via B
□ Mean		12.11	1.94	6.02	23.85
■ Std		1.96	0.3	1.64	10.1

Mobile/Wired Internet

Fig. 2. Response time (mean and standard deviation)

From the Fig. 2, we could get the relationship between S and C. First, with the PC
using wired Internet, the time S may be considered rather short period (around
5~30msec with Ping, which is related to the S; but with 5Kbyte Web page for PC the
response time is around 2~3 seconds, which is related to the S and C, here C is much
larger than S); and with PC, for larger contents (over 20Kbyte, in our case), the server
time is longer than the shorter packet (below 5Kbyte). Secondly, with recent mobile
phone using mobile Internet (for short packets below 1.5Kbyte and even around
5Kbyte), the response time is around 12 seconds with little deviation through the
WAP gateway; therefore the time S is longer than C, where S includes the elapsed
time at the gateway in the mobile Internet.

Therefore, we may order the dominating factors in the overall performance at the
user's perspective for information processing as follows. In general, the relationship
for wired Internet with PC could be $U > D > C > S$; and the relationship for mobile
Internet with mobile phone could be $U > D > S > C$, without subscript notation. Here,
we need to decrease the major times U and D, as well as the network and server (minor) time S (or C). For another example to reduce time the device time, D, and as
Internet URLs for unified mobile service, we used around 1000 *single Korean character*.net URLs to find information as well as to notify information directly from the
unified information DB in the portal, with the indexed key of single character. The
Korean domain name is a sort of multi-lingual domain names, which are worldwidely being in service by Verisign since the end of the year of 2002, and we used
some of the Korean domain names for ubiquitous Korean information network.

5 Conclusion

The performance analysis for user interface design in ubiquitous information network with the wired and mobile Internet, considering the effective response time with efficient investment was studied for unified information service in the ubiquitous computing environment. The overall performance analysis for user interface in ubiquitous information network at the customer's perspective was studied for assuring the real-time requirement with the unified portal, including the statistical analysis based on the empirical results. With more ubiquitous network environment (i.e. the decrease of the user time, U), the HCI user interface time in the device, D will become more critical, thus we need more efficient mobile user interface for any information processing, especially using mobile Internet with mobile devices like handheld phone. For further future works, the voice application in the ubiquitous information network will be added for the real-time retrieval of information as well as for real-time registration of information or advertisement to reduce the dominating times, i.e. the discussed user time and device time, in the aggregate performance metric, round-trip delay in session time. In the ubiquitous computing environment, e.g. even in the driving car as well as during overseas-travel, we can retrieve information as well as giving information in real-time way with convenient user interface at the suggested unified information portal in the ubiquitous information network.

References

1. Cellary, W.: The Profession's Role in the Global Information Society. IEEE Computer (September 2003) 122-124
2. Nahum, E., Barzilai, T., Kandlur, D.D.: Performance Issues in WWW Servers. IEEE Transactions on Networking, Vol. 10, No. 1 (February 2002) 2-11
3. Hwang, G., Tseng, J.C.R., Huang, S.: I-WAP: An Intelligent WAP Site Management System. IEEE Transactions on Mobile Computing, Vol. 1, No. 2 (April-June 2002) 82-95
4. Pashtan, A., Kollipara, S., Pearce, M.: Adapting Content for Wireless Web Services. IEEE Internet Computing (September-October 2003) 79-85
5. Chen, Y.R., Petrie, C.: Ubiquitous Mobile Computing. IEEE Internet Computing, (March-April 2003) 16-17
6. Ubiquitous Information Network Site (test site), Korean Information Network Web site: http://ktrip.net

Envisioning Mobile Information Services: Combining User- and Technology-Centered Design

Jesper Kjeldskov and Steve Howard

Department of Information Systems
The University of Melbourne
Parkville, Victoria 3010, Australia
jesper@cs.auc.dk, showard@unimelb.edu.au

Abstract. We provide a meta-commentary on two approaches used for designing context-dependent mobile devices. On the basis of a 'user-centered' approach, consisting of interviews, observation of current practice and enactment of future scenarios in context, a number of non-functional design sketches were developed. While these sketches reflected a rich understanding of current work practices, they were little more than abstract speculations about future practice; *lacking in detail on usability and feasibility, and being largely reactive to current problem situations*. Conducted in parallel, the technology-centered study informed the design and implementation of a mature functional prototype. This facilitated a comprehensive usability evaluation revealing a series of technical challenges and problems related to mobile use. Though the technology-centered approach provided detailed input for refining the prototype, and an initial provocative break with current practice, it was less useful in supplying further original alternatives; *post-evaluation, the design discussion was largely reactive to the current prototype*. In concert, the two approaches complement each other well; the user-centered approach grounding design in current practice, in all its contextual complexity, and the technology-centered approach providing a counterpoint in technically detailed expressions of future possibilities.

1 Introduction

Mobile, pervasive and ubiquitous computing constitutes a challenge for human-computer interaction design. Like other emerging technologies, these technologies are characterized by being different from traditional desktop computers in their physical appearance and the contexts in which they are used. Consequently, they often imply interaction dissimilar from how computers are usually operated and are used for purposes beyond office and home computing. Many traditional approaches to HCI design are evolutionary and based on iterations of analysis, design, implementation and testing. These methods have proven valuable in relation to the development of computer systems with high usability based on well-known and widely adopted technologies such as desktop workstations and the Internet. In the light of emerging technologies, however, interaction design research has been stimulated into the development and use of design approaches that are less analytic and more creative. These approaches supplement traditional HCI methods by introducing an explicit focus on

M. Masoodian et al. (Eds.): APCHI 2004, LNCS 3101, pp. 180-190, 2004.
© Springer-Verlag Berlin Heidelberg 2004

envisioning future technology and its use – so called 'blue-sky' research. The fundamental assumption is that just like the introduction of personal computing and computer networks have led to huge and unexpected changes in the work and leisure activities of many people, so will mobile, pervasive and ubiquitous computing in the decades to come. As the potential use of these technologies is, however, still unknown, researchers must develop new concepts and ideas for future technology: what it may look like, what it may be used for, and how people may interact with it.

HCI research promotes two overall approaches to concept design for emerging technologies: 1) experiments driven by the opportunities offered by new technology and 2) user-centered design driven by field studies. While a recent literature survey [7] shows a tendency towards mobile HCI being driven by technology- rather than user-centered approaches, growing attention has lately been brought to concept development methods focusing on present and envisioned future user activities. Much of this research has its roots in the Participatory Design tradition [2], and is motivated by the observation that "we can make amazing things, technically, but arc often at a loss to understand what to make", as stated by Vygotsky [12]. In response to this, new methods are introducing techniques from theatre, such as actors, props and role-playing to HCI research. Sato and Salvador [11] suggests a focus group approach modified to involve actors and an active audience acting-out use of existing and non-existing product concepts. The benefits from this approach are that the theatre approach creates a strong context with focus on interaction as well as an improvisational space for the participating users. However, it is also noted that it can be difficult for users to be creative and articulate on non-existing products in fictive use scenarios. Inspired by this work, Howard et al. [3] have experimented with the use of 'endowed props' providing the design team with a means of directing the discourse between science- and plausible-fiction. Extending this line of thought, Iacucci et al. [5] presents techniques where enacting the use of future technology is a part of a board game or takes place in the real world (the SPES technique), thus restricting discourse by means of a game master or the constraints of real life activity.

These and related techniques indicate a plausible approach to interaction design for emerging technologies. However, they are to a large extent disconnected from real technology. While on one side this frees designers from the technological constraints of the present, it also inhibits the exploration of new technological potentials and may blind insight into limitations of present and emerging technology. Hence, Rogers et al. [10] promotes that instead of choosing between a user- and a technology-centered approach, blue-sky research should explicitly involve both playful visions of technology in their social context and innovation through 'technology inspiration'.

On the basis of this discussion, this paper presents a research project in which a user- and a technology-centered approach were combined for envisioning design of mobile information services for the same problem domain. The first section describes the motivation and methodological design of the project. Following this, the details of the user- and the technology-centered approaches are described and discussed. This includes a description of the empirical methods used, the designs produced and the evaluations conducted. Finally, the interplay between the two approaches is discussed and directions for further research are outlined.

2 Supporting Use of Public Transport by Mobile Computing

Between October 2002 and April 2003 we conducted a research project focusing on the potential use of context-aware mobile computing for supporting the use of public transportation in Melbourne, Australia. The project was motivated by discussions among consultants and sales staff of a large IT company about alternatives to the use of cars for traveling in city meetings with clients. In large cities where traffic is often very dense, traveling by car can be highly time-consuming, necessitating much planning. Using Melbourne's tram-based public transport would not only be more environmental, but might also be more effective if supported by a mobile information service providing travelers with relevant information at the right time and place. Over the course of six months, a team consisting of three senior researchers, five Ph.D. students, two research assistants and an industrial interaction designer worked on different parts of the project. The first author of this paper managed the project and participated in the majority of activities. The researchers were all involved in HCI design for mobile computing but had different specific individual research interests ranging from ethnographic user-studies to prototype development and usability evaluation. On the basis of the different points of interest, the project consisted of two parallel tracks of research: a user- and a technology-centered track (figure 1).

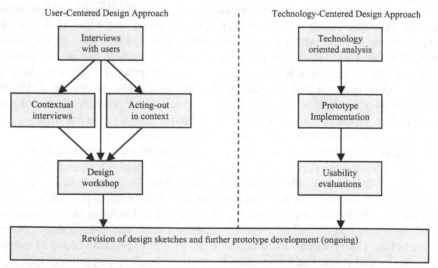

Fig. 1. Combining user- (left) and technology- (right) centered approaches to interaction design

The user-centered track grew out of the initiating discussions with the IT professionals. The technology-centered track grew out of an already ongoing activity to develop a mobile route-planning service for the tram system of Melbourne. The researchers in each track remained mutually unaware of each other's activities for the first 3 months of the project. Thus the user studies were conducted without any knowledge of the prototype development and the design of the first experimental prototype was not informed by the empirical user studies. Following the design workshop, researchers joined across the tracks and conducted a usability evaluation of the prototype. Finally, the outcomes from the two tracks of research were merged. The following sections describe the activities in the two parallel tracks in detail.

3 The User-Centered Approach

Based on the discussion above, we designed a user study to investigate into the current and possible future work practices of our nomadic users. In order to construct a rich understanding of travel and work practices, and building on project members' experience with techniques for acting-out future scenarios from previous research [3] we combined three empirical methods: 1) Semi-structured interviews with users (at the office), 2) Contextual interviews and observation of current practice (driving cars in city), and 3) Acting-out future scenarios in context (on board trams in city)

These methods all involved users talking about their perceptions, activities and needs. While the semi-structured interviews were separated from context, the contextual interviews and acting-out sessions took place while the users were carrying out real work activities. During the contextual interviews and acting-out sessions, we observed current practice, including the use of different artifacts in relation to the work activities being carried out. In the acting-out sessions we furthermore provided a series of non-functional props to assist the users' imagination. The three methods and a summary of their primary outcomes are described below.

3.1 Interviews

To establish the context, four semi-structured interviews were conducted with the IT professionals, who frequently traveled for work activities in the city. The interviews focused on the users' perceptions of pros and cons of traveling by car and tram. Each interview was conducted by a pair of researchers and lasted 30-60 minutes.

It was clear from the interviews that the users were willing to use public transport when attending meetings in the city, but that the use of the local tram system had a number of limitations. Firstly, uncertainties were related to route planning: which routes to take, when to change trams, how many changes would be needed, would there be a wait at each change, how close was the tram stop to the desired destination...? Often users would tend towards their car, or a taxi, if tram changes were needed, or if the journey was to an unfamiliar destination. Being able to predict the time of arrival of the tram rather precisely was seen as critical. The interviewees attempted to avoid being either late or too early (thus wasting time for their clients, or themselves respectively). To assist in timely arrival at appointments the interviewees needed to know exactly when to leave their office in order to arrive at their meeting just at the right time. When using the car this estimation was reportedly done based on knowledge about normal traffic conditions in the city and was not very precise. Uncertainty about combining routes, trams not running on schedule, finding the nearest stop and having to walk all constituted barriers to tram use.

3.2 Contextual Interviews and Observation of Current Practice

Following the interviews, the next phase consisted of observing and enquiring into current practice (figure 2). Here we were trying to understand both hurdles and enablers to car and tram travel. The observations were conducted by shadowing the users during travel from their offices to meetings in the city. One researcher asked questions about pros and cons of using trams while another video taped the session.

Fig. 2. Contextual interview and observation of current practice

From the observations we learned that, although driving to meetings in the city could be rather time consuming, the car was seen as flexible and provided a useful 'office on the move', a semi-private space for limited work activities. Thus time spent in the car was not necessarily 'wasted' time but often used for preparing the upcoming meeting or coordinating other activities over the phone.

3.3 Acting-Out in Context

The final phase of our field study consisted of a number of sessions in which our nomadic users acted-out future scenarios of using mobile information technology to support travel by tram (figure 3). The acting-out approach was adapted from previous research by project participants [3].

When acting-out a future scenario, people are asked to envision and enact situations involving future use of technology, based on an overall frame of context and supported by simple props which are attributed the desired functionality. For

Fig. 3. Acting-out in context

the present project, the original approach was modified in a number of ways, resembling aspects of the SPES technique [5]. First, real users instead of actors did the acting-out. Secondly, the acting-out was done in context: using the trams for attending a real meeting in the city instead of performing fictive tasks in a studio. Two researchers facilitated the sessions and took notes; a third recorded the sessions on video.

From the acting-out sessions we learned a lot about information needs and desires and how these varied across different situations and locations. Also criteria for assessing the appropriateness of different form factors were revealed, for example the need for privacy when working in a public space. Specifically, the acting-out in context sessions revealed that before catching a tram into the city, estimation of travel time was essential to determine when to go. On the tram, the primary information needed was when and where to get off and what to do next. In addition, users envisioned that they could prepare a meeting, browse the Internet or listen to music. One user also envisioned that the device would automatically buy an electronic ticket from the tram.

3.4 Design Workshop

Following the field studies, we conducted a one-day design workshop. The purpose of this was to recap and discuss the outcome of the empirical user studies and to produce a number of ideas for mobile systems supporting current and/or envisioned future practice. The workshop involved three senior researchers, three Ph.D. students, two research assistants and one industrial interaction designer. The latter managed the workshop in collaboration with the first author. First the three teams of researchers who had conducted the interviews, contextual interviews and acting-out sessions presented their findings. This was followed by a one-hour joint discussion. The participants were then divided into three groups, mixed so that they did not resemble the teams who did the user studies. The groups then spent 2½ hour on producing a design sketch of their own choice. No restriction was put on their focus, but the design had to address issues identified in the user studies. Following this, each group presented their design sketches using whiteboards and paper drawings. The workshop resulted in four design concepts. The ideas were highly creative and diverse: from a foldable mobile office to an MP3 player with voice-based route-planning, capabilities for presenting PowerPoint slides and wireless connectivity to stationary I/O devices at the customer's site. The envisioned concepts all addressed different aspects and challenges of the mobile work activities studied and were informed by both input from the interviews, the contextual interviews and the sessions of acting-out. Due to limited resources and time, only one of the concepts, described in detail below, was developed further.

3.5 TramMate

TramMate supports the use of public transportation by means of a context-aware mobile calendar application. On the basis of the field study, the basic idea of Tram-Mate is to 1) relate traveling information directly to appointments, 2) provide route planning for the tram system based on current location 3) alert when it is time to depart, and 4) provide easy access to travel time, walking distance and number of route changes. Elaborating on ideas of context awareness [1] and indexicality [8], the interface of TramMate is indexed to contextual factors such as time, location, and activity [6].

Fig. 4. Refined design sketches for TramMate

The rationale behind TramMate is not to impose too much additional complexity on the user. Accomplishing this, an extended electronic calendar provides dynamic route planning information related to the user's schedule for the day. TramMate thus requires very little additional interaction. When a new appointment is made, the user is asked to specify the physical location of it, following which TramMate schedules a time slot for getting there. When an appointment is coming up, this timeslot adjusts itself in accordance with the location of the user and the estimated time needed to get there based on real time information about the public transport system (figure 4 left). Apart from specifying the first step of the route plan, the calendar view also provides additional details on the suggested route: estimated travel time, required walking distance and the number of route changes. During traveling, the TramMate timeslot continuously updates itself with information about the next leg of the route. From the calendar view, the user also has access to a screen providing his current location on a map with directions to the nearest tram stop. This screen also outlines the full route (figure 4 center). Based on the time required to walk from the user's current location to the first tram stop, TramMate notifies when it is time to leave in order to make the appointment. The reminder contains simple information about the appointment, what tram to catch, how soon it leaves, where it leaves from and how to get there (figure 4 right). On the tram, TramMate notifies when to get off and what next step to take. Arriving at the destination, a map provides the location of the appointment.

4   The Technology-Centered Approach

In parallel with the user-centered approach, researchers at the University of Melbourne's Department of Geomatics conducted a technology-centered track of research with the purpose of developing a functional prototype for Melbourne's tram system. The prototype addressed the same overall use-situation involving nomadic workers in the city that motivated the user study, but was not influenced by the findings in this track of research. Instead, it was driven by a desire to explore the potentials for providing location-based route planning on GPS and GPRS enabled handheld computers.

The prototype had a number of differences from and similarities to the TramMate concept. The prototype was similar in providing route-planning facilities for the tram system based on the user's current location as a mix of textual instructions and annotated maps. However, it provided a fundamentally different user interface, requiring the user to actively look up travel information rather than relating it to planned activities, and did not alert the user before or while in transit. Also, the prototype did not automatically reflect contextual changes such as the user changing location. This was only taken into account when the user actively looked up timetable information.

4.1   Usability Evaluations

Whereas the design sketches produced in the workshop were non-functional, the prototype enabled us to study the use of real technology. We conducted two usability evaluations of the prototype: in the field and in a usability lab, involving ten subjects.

The evaluations were identical in terms of tasks and the profiles of test subjects. The subjects had to complete three realistic tasks involving route planning while traveling to appointments in the city derived from the user studies with IT professionals.

Fig. 5. Field evaluation   **Fig. 6.** Laboratory evaluation

The field evaluation focused on use in realistic settings. The test subjects had to lookup necessary information on the device according to the tasks and then perform the tasks "for real" (e.g. catching a tram to a specific destination). The prototype accessed live timetable information on Internet but GPS positioning had to be simulated. One researcher encouraged thinking-aloud, one took notes and one recorded the evaluation on video (figure 5). In the laboratory evaluation, the subjects were seated at a desk, with the mobile device in their hand (figure 6). To ensure a good video recording, the subject held the device within a limited area indicated on the table. Two researchers observed through a one-way mirror and took notes.

Studying the use of real technology revealed a number of problems concerning the design of context-aware mobile information services for supporting the use of the tram system. Overall, two critical and nine serious themes of usability problems were revealed [9]. One of the major problems identified concerned *the relation between information in the system and in the world*. During use, the context changed constantly; the users moved, the trams moved, time went by etc. While this was to some extent reflected in the system, the granularity of this relation was not sufficient. Consequently, the information on the screen would often be often 'out of sync' with the real world. Another major problem concerned the *graphical design of maps*. All users wanted to use the maps a lot. However, the maps turned out to have three significant limitations. Firstly, the level of detail was generally not appropriate. Either the screen would be cluttered or it would provide second to no information. Secondly, the maps lacked annotation of key information such as landmarks and precise indication of the user's location, route and destination. Thirdly, the users had serious problems relating the orientation of the map to the real world and would frequently rotate the device. As a consequence, screen text was often viewed upside down.

Other problems identified included difficulties entering data while being mobile, missing vital information due to lack of visual attention, and lack of functional transparency when information on the screen changed to reflect contextual changes.

5 Discussion and Conclusions

It is interesting to compare the outcomes of the two parallel tracks of R&D. The user-centered design approach facilitated the development of design concepts representing considerable insight into present work practices, and some speculations about the future not envisioned by the prototype designers. However, the usability and feasibility of these concepts were unclear. The technology-centered approach revealed specific technical challenges and problems related to the design and use of context-aware mobile information services not considered in the user-studies. However, aside from the initial visionary prototype, the technology-centered approach largely provided input for refining the implemented design rather than informing original alternatives, thus endorsing a trial-and-error approach [7].

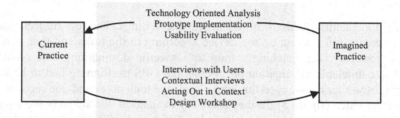

Fig. 7. Interleaving user- (bottom) and technology- (top) centered interaction design

With careful interleaving however, the two approaches complemented each other in the revision of design sketches and development of further prototypes by providing both playful visions and technology inspiration based on a mix of contextual richness and technical detail. Fig. 7 illustrates this interleaving, describing design as the exploration of the relation between an understanding of current practice (acquired in this case through the interviews and contextual interviews) and speculations about future practice (expressed as the technology prototype, and explored in the evaluations).

In the technology-centered approach, usability evaluation is used as a way of examining the impact, on current practice, of technology prototypes. Design proceeds by 'imposing' the design on the current situation of use during the evaluations, thereby exploring the design's impact on that use. In the user-centered approach, design moves from an understanding of current practice to imagined future use, thus driving design with user needs. Employing both a user- and technology-centred approach, results in a design process that attempts the co-evolution of an understanding of both current and future use, delivering innovative technology that is grounded in use [4].

The technology-centered approach informed the revision of the TramMate concept by identifying those envisioned design solutions that were challenging to implement or simply not feasible. Some examples may illustrate the interplay between the approaches. The critical user need (clear from the user-centered study) of maintaining a close relation between the system and the real world was not to be satisfied by the granularity of current GPS technology (clear from the evaluations of the technical prototype); especially on trams, other means of positioning would be required. Further, studying use of real technology showed that requirements for the user to devote their full attention to the device were excessive, as envisaged in the acting-out sessions. Also, an unexpected amount of effort would have to be put into the design of the maps; including pointers to landmarks, reflecting the orientation of the user etc. Finally, additional functionality was suggested such as manual timetable lookup. The user-centered approach assisted in the revision of the prototype by indicating and prioritizing information needs, outlining realistic use scenarios and proposing a novel interaction design concept integrating the system into another application. In short, the user-studies taught us a lot about what the system should do, while the evaluations of the prototype provided valuable insight into what could be done and feedback on the usability of what a specific design solution did do.

The presented project points towards many opportunities for future research. On a system design level, the revised design concepts should be implemented and evaluated. On the methodological level, it would, among others, be interesting to enquire into the potentials of managing discourse in blue-sky research envisioning future design concepts by introducing functional prototypes into acting-out sessions.

Acknowledgements

Thanks to colleagues on the TramMate project: Jennie Carroll, John Murphy, Jeni Paay and Frank Vetere (user-centered component), Connor Graham, Sonja Pedell and Jessica Davies (technology-centered approach). Thanks also go to professionals who participated in the user studies and to the usability evaluation test subjects.

References

1. Cheverst K., Davies N., Mitchell K., Friday A. and Efstratio C. (2000) Developing a Context-Aware Electronic Tourist Guide: Some Issues and Experiences. Proceedings of CHI'00, The Netherlands, ACM
2. Greenbaum J. and Kyng M. (eds.) (1991) *Design at Work: Cooperative Design of Computer Systems.* London, Lawrence Erlbaum Associates
3. Howard S., Carroll Jennie., Murphy J. and Peck J. (2002) Endowed props in scenario based design. Proceedings of NordiCHI'02, Denmark, ACM
4. Howard, S., Carroll, Jennie., Murphy, J., and Peck, J. 2002, Managing Innovation in Scenario Based Design. In Proceedings of Human Factors 2002, Melbourne.
5. Iacucci, G., Kuutti, K. and Ranta, M. (2000) On the Move with a Magic Thing: Role Playing in Concept Design of Mobile Services and Devices. Proceedings of DIS'00, ACM
6. Kjeldskov J., Howard S., Murphy J., Carroll Jennie., Vetere F. and Graham C. (2003) Designing TramMate - a context aware mobile system supporting use of public transportation. Proceedings of DUX'03, San Francisco, CA, ACM
7. Kjeldskov J. and Graham C. (2003) A Review of MobileHCI Research Methods. Proceedings of Mobile HCI'03, Italy. Lecture Notes in Computer Science, Springer-Verlag
8. Kjeldskov J. (2002) Just-In-Place Information for Mobile Device Interfaces. Proceedings of Mobile HCI'02, Italy, Lecture Notes in Computer Science, Springer-Verlag

9.   Pedell S., Graham C., Kjeldskov J. and Davies J. (2003) Mobile Evaluation: What the Metadata and the data told us. Proceedings of OzCHI 2003, Brisbane, Australia
10. Rogers Y., Scaife M., Harris E., et al. (2002) Things aren't what they seem to be: innovation through technology inspiration. Proceedings of DIS'02, London, ACM
11. Sato S. and Salvador T. (1999) Methods & tools: Playacting and focus troupes: theater techniques for creating quick, intense, immersive, and engaging focus group sessions. Interactions of the ACM, 6 (5), pp 35-41
12. Vygotsky L. (1978) *Mind in Society*. MIT Press, Cambridge, MA

Supporting Work Activities in Healthcare by Mobile Electronic Patient Records

Jesper Kjeldskov and Mikael B. Skov

Aalborg University
Department of Computer Science
DK-9220 Aalborg East, Denmark
{jesper, dubois}@cs.auc.dk

Abstract. Supporting work activities in healthcare is highly complex and challenging. This paper outlines the findings from a usability study of a commercial PC based electronic patient record (EPR) system at a large Danish hospital and presents our experiences with the design of a mobile counterpart. First, a number of challenges in relation to the use of traditional desktop-based EPR systems in healthcare were identified. Secondly, a mobile context-aware prototype was designed and implemented, which automatically keeps track of contextual factors such as the physical location of patients and staff, upcoming appointments etc. The usability of the mobile EPR prototype was evaluated in a laboratory as well as in relation to carrying out real work activities at the hospital. Our results indicate that mobile EPR systems can support work activities in healthcare, but that interaction design of such systems must be carefully thought out and evaluated. Specifically, our findings challenge the view of context-awareness being a universally useful paradigm for mobile HCI.

1 Introduction

An electronic patient record (EPR) is a collection of information about a single patient's history in a hospital. The hospital personnel use the record to diagnose diseases, and to document and coordinate treatment. Within the last 20 years, a considerable amount of effort has been devoted to the development of electronic patient record systems. The primary motivation for this effort is that unlike paper-based patient records, electronic patient records will be accessible to all relevant persons independent of time and location.

The design of electronic patient records is a huge challenge for the HCI community, raising a wide range of still unanswered questions related to issues such as screen layout, interaction design, and integration into work processes. Where should the systems be located and who should enter the data? How do we make sure that input is complete and accurate? How are the different work processes in healthcare structured and coordinated? What is the most useful way of displaying and accessing the vast quantity of patient data? [4]. In the light of these questions, a lot of research has been published in the HCI literature about EPR systems and how to meet challenges related to design and use of computer system in healthcare. Specifically, much

M. Masoodian et al. (Eds.): APCHI 2004, LNCS 3101, pp. 191–200, 2004.

attention has been given to issues such as information sharing [5], support for cooperation [6] and privacy [12]. While much of this research is based on studies on the use of traditional paper-based patient records, suggesting viable electronic counterparts, however, little research has been published based on studies that inquire into the use of the mass of EPR systems already in use.

In Denmark, there is currently an extensive focus on electronic patient records. The government has decided that by 2005 all Danish hospitals must have replaced the traditional paper-based patient records with electronic ones. However, it is up the regional authorities to decide on the details of deployment. Thus a number of pilot projects are currently in progress with the aim of developing and evaluating electronic patient record systems (see e.g. [2]). In relation to a regional Danish research program entitled "The Digital Hospital" we have studied the use of a commercial EPR system currently in use at a large hospital (IBM IPJ 2.3). In addition to this, an experimental mobile EPR prototype extending the current system's functionality was designed and evaluated. Driving this study, we were concerned with the following research questions: 1) what challenges characterize the use of contemporary electronic patient record systems? 2) How can these challenges be met by improved interaction design?

This paper outlines the findings from the usability evaluation of IBM's PC based EPR system IPJ 2.3 and presents our preliminary experiences with the usability of a mobile counterpart. The paper is structured in the following way. First, we present our initiating usability evaluation. The findings from this evaluation are then outlined as a number of themes describing problems and advantages encountered during use. Subsequently, we present the design of the experimental mobile EPR prototype system, and present the results of a field- and lab-based evaluation of its usability. Finally, we discuss the findings from the usability evaluations of the mobile EPR prototype in the light of the themes identified in the evaluation of the stationary EPR system.

2 Electronic Patient Record Usability

We conducted a usability evaluation of IBM's electronic patient record system IPJ 2.3 currently in use at the Hospital of Frederikshavn, Denmark. The evaluation was carried out in a dedicated usability laboratory at the University of Aalborg over a period of two days in May 2002. The evaluation involved two elements: 1) a think-aloud evaluation with the purpose of identifying usability problems in the electronic patient record system and 2) a series of interviews with the purpose of gaining insight into the integration of the electronic patient record into the work of the nurses.

Preparation: Prior to the evaluation, the research team inquired thoroughly into the work activities at the hospital related to the use of patient records. This was done through observation at the hospital and interviews with key personnel. Also, the research team investigated into the functionality of the electronic patient record system to be evaluated. Based on this, scenarios of use of the system and a number of tasks for the evaluation were produced in collaboration with personnel at the hospital.

Test subjects: The evaluation involved eight trained nurses from the Hospital of Frederikshavn. All nurses were women, aged between 31 and 54 years of age with professional work experience ranging from 2 to 31 years. All nurses had attended a course on the IPJ 2.3 system prior to the test amounting to between 14 and 30 hours but none of them had used the system in their daily work. They characterized themselves as novices or beginners in relation to the use of IT in general.

Tasks: The purpose of the usability evaluation was to investigate how the EPR system supports typical work activities for nurses at the hospital. Based on our scenarios, we designed three tasks that were centered on the core purpose of the system such as retrieving information about patients, registering information about treatments, making treatment notes, and entering measurements.

Procedure: The test was based on the think-aloud protocol [13], [11]. The interviews were semi-structured, based on a list of questions and a number of issues that could be raised. Evaluations and interviews were conducted over two days. Each nurse first used the system to solve the tasks. After this, four randomly selected nurses were interviewed about their work and their opinions about the system as well as its integration in and influence on their work.

Test setting: All evaluations and interviews were conducted in a dedicated usability laboratory. A test monitor observed the test subjects, encouraged them to think aloud and asked questions for clarification. Two additional researchers operated the video equipment and took notes in a separate control room. The computer used was a standard PC with a 19" screen and a standard mouse and keyboard matching the hardware used on the hospital.

Data Collection: All evaluation sessions were recorded on digital video. Two remotely controlled motorized cameras captured overall and close-up views of the test subject and test monitor. The image on the PC screen was converted to composite video and mixed with the camera images to one composite video signal.

Data analysis: Following the evaluations a log file was produced from each test. Each of the three researchers then used the video recordings and these log files as empirical foundation for producing three individual lists of usability problems. These lists were then merged to one. The severity of the identified problems was rated as critical, serious or cosmetic based on the guidelines proposed by Molich [9]. The rating was done individually and followed by negotiation in cases of disagreement.

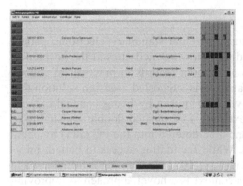

Fig. 1. Electronic patient record: List of patients on the ward.

Fig. 2. Electronic patient record: detailed information about a specific patient.

2.1 Findings

The evaluation of the electronic patient record identified a substantial amount of usability problems. The total was 75 usability problems distributed on 9 critical, 39 serious and 27 cosmetic problems [8]. These 75 usability problems relate to various concerns of human-computer interaction, e.g. finding information, storing information, complexity of screen layouts. On the other hand, the usability test also identified a number of strengths in the interface of the electronic patient record, e.g. easy registration of values, well integrated in the work activities, good overview of the patients in the ward. The following three themes reflect more abstract concerns of the usability of the electronic patient record.

Mobility. During the usability evaluation and in the interview afterwards, most nurses would stress concerns about being mobile while working with the system. Meeting this challenge, the use of laptop computers rather than desktop workstations had been suggested and discussed at the hospital. However, most of the nurses stated that they would find it impossible or unfeasible to carry a laptop computer around the ward every time they were to conduct work tasks away from their office. One problem was the size of the laptop, as they would also have to carry other instruments.

Complexity. Another overall concern or problem was complexity and fragmentation of information. Most nurses found it difficult to locate the necessary patient information as they were solving tasks. This sometimes led to inadequate or incomplete task completion. Hence, the nurses would be insecure whether they had found the right information and whether they had succeeded in finding all relevant information.

Work Relation. Most nurses experienced problems in the laboratory due to the fact that they had difficulties in relating the test-tasks to carrying out of real work activities. The problem was that they would typically use different kinds of information in the "real life" to determine how to solve a problem, e.g. the visible condition of a patient. Another concern related to the fact that the system only partially reflected the current work task, making it difficult to the test subjects to find or store information.

3 MobileWARD

Motivated by the findings from our evaluation of the stationary electronic patient record system, a field study was conducted into the work activities at the hospital of Frederikshavn related to the use of electronic patient records in practice. In concert with the findings from the usability evaluation, this suggested a design solution that 1) supported the highly mobile work activities of nurses by being handheld, 2) reduced complexity by adapting to its context and 3) eliminated double registering of information (first written down on paper and then entered into the PC later) by being integrated with the existing patient record. While facilitating access to patient information at the 'point of care' is not a new idea [1, 10, 15], adapting information and functionality in a mobile EPR system to its context is a novel approach to improving the usability of such systems, which has not yet been investigated thoroughly. On the basis of the findings from the usability evaluation and subsequent field study, an experimental prototype of a handheld context-aware EPR system for supporting the morning procedure, was designed and implemented [6]. The system is described briefly below.

3.1 Architecture

MobileWARD is designed for a Compaq iPAQ 3630 running the Microsoft® Pock-etPC operating system. The system uses a Wireless Local Area Network (wLAN) for network communication. The system was implemented in Microsoft embedded Visual Basic 3.0. For the experimental prototype of MobileWARD, context awareness was simulated by means of a "context control center" application. The control center runs on a separate iPAQ connected to the wireless network. Through this application, an operator can trigger "context events" in MobileWARD, simulating that the user has entered a specific room, scanned the barcode on a specific patient etc. This approach was chosen to facilitate early evaluation of the experimental design solution without having to worry about the technical challenges of context sensing. In later versions of the system, real sensing of the environment will be implemented where promising. For discussions on how to sense environments see for example [3] or [14].

3.2 Interface Design

MobileWARD is designed to support work tasks during morning procedure at the hospital ward. The design is based on two basic concepts. First, the system is designed to reflect the context of the user in the sense that it is able to sense and react to a number of changes in the environment. Secondly, as the use of a pen for typing in information would sometimes be inappropriate because the nurses would often use the system while being mobile or engaged in other activities, the interface design incorporates a visual layout with large-scale buttons that enables finger-based interaction through the touch-screen of the iPAQ.

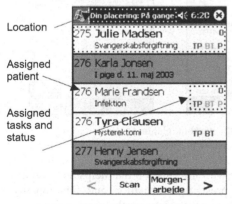

Fig. 3. MobileWARD. Patient lists

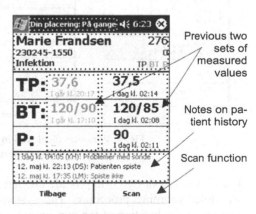

Fig. 4. MobileWARD. Patient information

MobileWARD is context-aware in the sense that the system recognises the location of the nurse and presents information and functionality accordingly. Before visiting assigned patients, the nurses often want to get an overview of the specific information about each patient, e.g. previous measured values. This typical takes place at the nurse's office or in the corridor. The windows related to these locations are shown in figure 3 and 4. When in the corridor, the system by default displays all the patients on the wards. The patient list is ordered by ward number. Patients assigned for morning procedure are shown with a white background and the names of patients assigned to the nurse using the system are boldfaced (e.g. "Julie Madsen" and "Tyra Clausen" on figure 3). At the top of all windows, the nurse can see their current physical location as interpreted by the system. In the example on figure 3, the nurse is in the corridor ("på gangen"). For each patient, MobileWARD provides information about previous tasks, upcoming tasks and upcoming operations. The indicators TP (temperature), BT (blood pressure) and P (pulse) show the measurements that the nurse has to perform. The indicators are either presented with red text (value still to be measured) or green text (value already measured). Above the three indicators, an "O" indicates an upcoming operation (within 24 hours), which usually requires that the patient should fast and be prepared for operation. If the nurse wants to view data about a specific patient, she can click on one of the patients on the list. This will open the window shown on figure 4, displaying the name and personal identification number of the patient, the previous two sets of temperature, blood pressure, and pulse measurements taken as well as written notes regarding the treatment of the patient. This window is accessible at any time and location. Thus the nurse can choose to look up more specific details about each patient while located in the corridor or in the office. In order to enter new data into the system, the nurse has to scan the barcode identification tag on the patient's wristband using the "scan" function in the bottom of the screen. This is described further below.

Fig. 5. Windows displayed in the ward in relation to the tasks of measuring temperature, blood pressure, and pulse.

The aim of this design is to provide the nurse with information that helps her plan the scheduled morning procedure. The system presents information and functionality adapted to the location of the nurse and the time of the day. Furthermore, the system knows the status of each patient and represents already measured values and values yet to be measured by simple colour codes.

When the nurse enters a ward, the system automatically displays a different set of information. This is illustrated in figure 5. At the top of the screen, the nurse can see her physical location as interpreted by the system (e.g. ward 276). Below this, information about the patients on the current ward is presented, resembling the information available on the patient list displayed in the corridor, with the addition of a graphical representation of the physical location of the patient's respective beds. In this way, MobileWARD aims at presenting only relevant information to the nurse, e.g. by excluding patients from other wards. Like in the corridor, data about the patients is available by clicking on their names (or on their bed-icon). At the bottom of the screen, the nurse can activate the barcode scanner ("scan") used to identify a patient prior to entering data into the system. After having scanned a patient, the nurse can type in measured values (figure 5, center). This window shows previous measurements of values and provides functionality for typing in new values. By clicking the new value button ("ny"), the system displays a window for entering new values (figure 5, right). Below the personal information (name and personal identification number), date and time is shown. In the gray box, the nurse can input the measured value by editing the shown value. This is done by pressing the large sized buttons on the screen with a finger. The number shown by default is the latest measurement. The reason for this is that the latest measure is most likely to be close to the newest one. If there is a huge difference, this is clearly signaled to the nurse, as she will have to perform more button presses than usual, providing an implicit opportunity to see whether, e.g. the temperature for a given patient is rising or falling. The Save button stores the value in the database along with the date, time, and user identification. Furthermore, the system updates the status of the task as having been carried out.

3.3 Usability Evaluation of MobileWARD

We designed and conducted two different usability evaluations of the mobile EPR system MobileWARD. The evaluations were similar as they involved trained, registered nurses as test subjects, who should conduct standard morning work routines. However, they were different in their setting and data collection. The participating subjects were between 27 and 54 years old and they had diverse experiences with nursing. All of them were novices with the use of handheld computers.

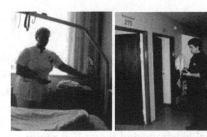

Fig. 6. Laboratory evaluation   **Fig. 7.** Evaluation at the hospital

The first evaluation took place at the usability laboratory at Aalborg University. The idea of this evaluation was to evaluate the mobile system in an environment where we could closely monitor all actions and situations (figure 6). Three test subjects participated in the study. They were all given a series of tasks to perform while using the system, and were asked to think-aloud. Three students acted as patients for the evaluation. One researcher acted as test monitor while another controlled the video equipment in the control room. The second evaluation took place at the Hospital of Frederikshavn. The field evaluation focused on using the system in a realistic environment and took place during evening procedure with real patients. Prior the evaluation, data on the patients at the ward was entered into the system. The use of the system was not controlled by task assignments but the nurses were asked to use it for registering the data they would be measured during the evening procedure (figure 7).

3.4 Findings

In a preliminary analysis of the evaluations, we have identified a total of 16 usability problems. These problems can be divided into three categories, concerning *interaction, mobility, and context-awareness*. First, interaction problems concerned nurses having problems with interacting with the system or understanding the interface. E.g. one nurse did not know the semantics of the keyboard for typing in textual notes about patients. Specifically, she felt insecure about the buttons "Tab", "Caps" and "Shift" as she would expect them to be "tablets", "capsules" and "shift medication". Secondly, other problems concerned aspects of mobility and working conditions, e.g. one nurse was concerned about putting the mobile device in her pocket. She was afraid that she would accidentally click some buttons while walking and she stated that it would be impossible to carry the device in the hand at all times. Another problem related to mobility and working conditions was the fact that one nurse feared that the device could spread bacteria from patient to patient. Thus, she did not want to place the device on the patient's bedside table or on the bed. Thirdly, some problems concerned aspects of context-awareness, e.g. the automatic adaptation of the interface to location. One of the nurses was reading information on the device while walking into the ward and got confused when the interface suddenly changed its content without notice or without her trigger anything.

4 Discussion

Through a usability evaluation of a traditional electronic patient record, we identified a number of important issues to consider when supporting work tasks in health care namely mobility, complexity, and work tasks.

Mobility. We found that mobility issues were important in professional nursing work activities. Nurses would normally find themselves visiting patients in different physical locations and they often require several kinds of information for more work tasks. We attempted to support mobility through a relatively small, handheld device that could be carried around by the nurses (potentially in their pockets) while visiting patients or conducting other work tasks. The idea of having a mobile device was adapted by all nurses in our evaluation. However, the nurses would switch between reading/storing information on the device and conducting work tasks without the device e.g. taking measurements from patients. Hence, having the device in the hands all the time would be impossible and thus, they would occasionally need to put away or lay down the device. Some of them requested functionalities that would allow them to lock the screen.

Complexity. Another important issue identified in our first evaluation was problems related to complexity and fragmentation of information. Most nurses experienced problems in locating relevant and adequate information in the traditional electronic patient record. This was mainly due to extensive amount of different types of information on each screen (figure 2). As a result, they occasionally failed to notice relevant or even critical information on e.g. patients and scheduled operations. On the mobile device, we aimed at presenting much less information at a time to address this problem. The nurses found no severe complexity problems while using the mobile device. However, they would occasionally request more information than could be fitted into the screen at one time. Exploiting context-awareness, e.g. physical location of users and patients, furthermore reduced the complexity of information. Thus, we were, for example, able to present information about patients close by only.

Work Relation. From the usability evaluation and field studies, we found that nurses would typically require very specific information based on current work tasks and activities. The traditional electronic patient record did not fully support this but presented too much, too little, or too fragmented information. In the mobile EPR prototype, we again utilized context-awareness in different ways as a mean for determining the work task of the nurses. However, this also introduced some pitfalls as nurses would sometimes miss reminders presented on the screen because they their focus was engaged elsewhere. Furthermore, some nurses became confused or even annoyed by the automatic adaptation of information on the screen to their physical location. Thus, the idea of context-awareness would not always support the nurses' work activities. On the contrary, it was sometimes seen as an obstacle to interacting with the system.

5 Conclusions

Supporting work activities in healthcare has been found to be a highly complex and challenging task [2]. We have conducted a study with two aims. First, we identified important issues in supporting work tasks in healthcare through the evaluation of a traditional desktop-based electronic patient record. Secondly, a mobile electronic patient record prototype that would address the identified challenges from the first evaluation was designed, implemented, and evaluated. The mobile prototype utilized context-awareness as a key means for supporting the nurses' use of the EPR system. Our results indicate that work tasks can be supported through a mobile, handheld device, but that healthcare work is highly complex which needs further investigations. Also, our findings have challenged the prevalent view of context-awareness as a universally useful paradigm for interacting with mobile computer systems.

Acknowledgements

The authors thank all test subjects who participated in the usability evaluations and the Hospital of Frederikshavn for kind collaboration throughout the project. The usability evaluations were conducted in collaboration with Jan Stage, Benedikte Skibsted Als and Rune Thaarup Høegh. MobileWARD was designed by Rune Thaarup Høegh, Karsten Kryger Hansen and Søren Lauritsen.

References

1. Arshad, U., Mascolo, C. And Mellor, M. (2003) Exploiting Mobile Computing in Healthcare. In Demo Session of the 3rd International Workshop on Smart Appliances, ICDCS03
2. Bardram, J., Kjær, T. A. K., and Nielsen, C. (2003) Supporting Local Mobility in Healthcare by Application Roaming among Heterogeneous Devices. In Proceedings of Mobile HCI'03, Springer-Verlag, LNCS
3. Bohnenberger, T., Jameson, A., Krüger, A., and Butz, A. (2002) Location-Aware Shopping Assiatnce: Evaluation of a Decision-Theoretic Approach. In Proceedings of Mobile HCI'02, Springer-Verlag, LNCS, pp. 155-169
4. Brinck, T. And York, G. (1998) User Interfaces for Computer-Based Patient Records. In Proceedings of CHI'98, ACM
5. Grimson, J. And Grimson, W. (2000) The SI Challenge in Health Care. Communications of the ACM 43(6), pp. 49-55
6. Hansen, K. K. Høegh, R. T. and Lauritsen, S. (2003) Making Context-Awareness (at) Work. June, 2003, Aalborg University
7. Kaplan, S. M. and Fitzpatrick, G. (1997) Designing Support for Remote Intensive-Care Telehealth using the Locales Framework. In Proceedings of DIS'97, ACM
8. Kjeldskov, J., Skov, M. B. and Stage, J. (2002) Usability Evaluation of IBM IPJ 2.3 Electronic Patient Record (in Danish), June, 2002, Aalborg University
9. Molich, R. (2000) *Usable Web Design* (In Danish). Ingeniøren | bøger
10. Morton, S. and Bukhres, O. (1997) Utilizing mobile computing in the Wishard Memorial Hospital ambulatory service. In Proceedings of SAC'97, ACM
11. Nielsen, J. (1993) Usability Engineering. Morgan Kaufmann
12. Rindfleish, T. C (1997) Privacy, Information Technology, and Health Care. Communications of the ACM 40(8), pp. 93-100
13. Rubin, J. (1994) Handbook of Usability Testing. Wiley
14. Schilit, B. N. and Theimer, M. M. (1994) Disseminating Active Map information to Mobile Hosts. In IEEE Network, Vol. 8(5), pp. 22-32
15. Urban, M. and Kunath, M (2002) Design, Deployment and Evaluation of a Clinical Information System which uses Mobile Computers and Workstations. In Proceedings of the 2nd conference on Mobiles Computing in der Medizin, Heidelberg

Design of Chording Gloves as a Text Input Device

Seongil Lee[1], Sang Hyuk Hong[1], Jae Wook Jeon[2],
Hoo-Gon Choi[1], and Hyoukryeol Choi[3]

[1] Sungkyunkwan University, School of Systems Management Engineering,
440-746 Suwon, Korea
{silee, skkie96, hgchoi}@skku.ac.kr
http://www.springer.de/comp/lncs/index.html
[2] Sungkyunkwan University, School of Information and Communication Engineering,
440-746 Suwon, Korea
jwjeon@skku.ac.kr
[3] Sungkyunkwan University, School of Mechanical Engineering,
440-746 Suwon, Korea
hrchoi@skku.ac.kr

Abstract. A chording input device for text input was developed in a Glove-typed interface using all the joints of the four fingers and thumbs of both hands. The glove-based device works for input of Korean characters as well as Roman- alphabet, Braille characters, and numbers using mode conversion among the respective keymaps. To minimize finger force and fatigue from repeated finger motions, input switch was made of conductible silicon ink, which is easy to apply to any type of surface, light, and enduring. The chording gloves showed comparable performances in Korean text input tasks with input keypads of mobile phones, but proved to be inferior to conventional keyboards. Subjects' performance showed that the chording gloves can input approximately 108 characters per minute in Korean, but needs further ergonomic consideration to reduce keying errors. The chording gloves developed in the study can be used with common computing devices such as PCs and PDAs in mobile environments.

1 Introduction

Keyboards have been used as an important input device to computers. The increase in use of small portable electronic products such as PDAs, cellular phones, and other wearable computing devices requires some type of external input devices for convenient and error-free typing. Conventional keyboards do not meet the needs of portability for these small electronic devices, resulting in many alternatives in the form of flexible or folding keyboards, keypads, and stylus.

This paper proposes a portable chord keyboard in the form of gloves that can provide mobile users with accessibility and usability to computing devices. Gloves equipped with a wireless communication module can be a good input device to computers since the hands and fingers are the most dominantly used parts of the body. Therefore, humans can naturally develop unique and effortless strategies for interfac-

M. Masoodian et al. (Eds.): APCHI 2004, LNCS 3101, pp. 201-210, 2004.

ing with machines. In other words, hands do not have to hold and manipulate interfacing devices, but hands can be the interfacing devices themselves.

1.1 Chord Keyboard

Several types of glove-based devices recognizing hand gestures or contact gestures directly have been widely proposed as input devices to computers. These devices are well suited for use in a mobile environment because the gloves can be worn instead of just being used to hold a device, are lightweight and easy to store and carry. It is, however, difficult to recognize enough separate gestures to allow useful text input. Some glove-based input devices, though, have capabilities to make decent text input in addition to their intended functions of gesture recognition and space navigation. Pinch Gloves [1] are glove-based input devices designed for use in virtual environments, mainly for 3D navigation, and N-fingers [5] is a finger-based interaction technique for wearable computers also utilizing finger pinching. Pinching is basically the motion of making a contact between the tip of thumb and a fingertip of the same hand. It uses lightweight gloves with conductive cloth on each fingertip that sense when two or more fingers are touching. Pinch Gloves use the same key layout with the QWERTY keyboard, and the "inner" characters that are placed in the center columns of the QWERTY keyboard such as "g"and "h" are selected by wrist rotating motion that could be detected by motion trackers attached to the gloves.

For use of many small portable electronic products, chord keyboards have also been proposed as input devices [2-12]. A chord keyboard is a keyboard that takes simultaneous multiple key pressings at a time to form a character in the same way that a chord is made on a piano. In chord keyboards, the user presses multiple key combinations, mainly two-letter combinations, to enter an input instead of using one key for each character. Pressing combinations of keys in this way is called chording [6, 9]. Since chord keyboards require only a small number of keys, they do not need large space, nor the many keys of regular keyboards such as the QWERTY keyboard. For example, the Handkey Twiddler is a one-handed chord keyboard with only 12 keys for fingertips and a ring of control keys under the thumb, and the Microwriter with only 6 keys [2]. With a typical two-handed chord keyboard, most Braille writers have a keyboard of only six keys and a space bar for all the Braille characters. These keys can be pushed one at a time or together at the same time to form Braille symbols for visually impaired people.

Rosenberg and Slater [9, 10] proposed a glove-based chording input device called the chording glove to combine the portability of a contact glove with the benefits of a chord keyboard. In their chording glove, the keys of a chord keyboard were mounted on the fingers of a glove and the characters were associated with all the chords, following a *keymap*. Their design of the keymap for the chording glove for Roman-alphabetic text input left room for improvement according to the experimental results. Finge Ring [3] is another type of chord keyboard that uses finger movements with rings on the fingers instead of wearing gloves. Pratt [8] also designed a device-independent input device and language code called "thumbcode" using chording gloves targeting for PDAs. For extensive review on chord keyboards, see Noyes [6].

All the previous works on glove-based input devices, however, lack consideration for accessibility and usability in mobile computing environments. They were intended to be used with general computers and even in virtual worlds. This paper solely investigates the utilities, functionality, and usability of the chording gloves as a text input device to mobile computers. In this paper, the chording gloves are also compared with other text input devices for the purpose of providing text input capabilities for mobile devices.

2 System Structure

The design of chording gloves and its controller began with the arrangement of the sensors on the gloves which function as keys. The interface of the system is based on the human-friendly nature of finger movements, particularly finger flexion.

2.1 Layout

A pair of chording gloves developed in the study which use finger motions of pinching to make input is shown in Fig. 1. An input can be made by contacts between the tip of thumb and character keys on the other fingertips or phalanges. Chording is possible by making contacts between the tip of thumb and two or more fingertips in parallel, i.e., simultaneously. Twelve character keys are placed on the fingertips as well as on all the phalanges of fingers on the palm side of leather gloves. The keys are made of conductible silicon ink applied to each part between the joints of the fingers with the rectangle of 1.5 cm by 1.3 cm. The keys become "pressed" once the voltage through the silicon ink rises above 3.5 V with contact with the ground attached on the Thumb. The voltage outputs of chord gloves are connected to an embedded controller that translates chord information into its corresponding character.

Fig. 1. Finger motions for making input using the chording gloves. Input can be made by simple pinching (left), by chording using two fingertips at the same time (center), and by touching the mid-phalanx (right).

2.2 Controller

The 16F874 microprocessor is used for controlling and analyzing the signals from the chording gloves. The controller also works for functions of converting the signals to text codes and sending them to PC or PDA through a RS232C serial port, or an IrDA wireless adapter. The controller works with a 9V battery. The voltage outputs of chording gloves are sent to an embedded system that translates chord information into its corresponding code, character, or number. The chord glove-based input device can be used in connection with computers or PDAs directly as a portable keyboard.

2.3 Keymap

The Korean as well as the Roman-alphabet, and numbers can be entered according to each keymap developed. The keymap for Korean input, however, follows a different mapping scheme from conventional keyboards and uses chording for generating diphthongs and some consonants. A keymap for the Roman-alphabet generally follows the similar arrangement of alphabet-finger mapping of the QWERTY keyboard, except some chordings for generating some letters such as "t" and "y", the letters located in the center of the conventional QWERTY keyboard (Fig. 2).

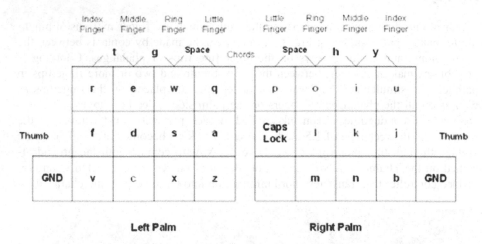

Fig. 2. The Roman-alphabet keymap. Characters such as "t", "g", "h", "y", and "space" can be keyed in by chording. Pinching the "t" and "n" keys at the same time also generates a chord for "-tion".

3 Human Performance and Usability Evaluation

Experiments were performed to measure the input speed and accuracy for text input using the chording gloves. Since most Korean students are not familiar with English-style typing, all the performances were measured using the Korean keymap. Performances on the chording gloves, as well as on the other popular text input devices – conventional keyboard and keypad of mobile phones – were measured for comparison. Upon the completion of text input tests, the chording gloves were also compared against existing text input devices in terms of usability through a survey with partici-pating subjects.

3.1 Text Input Experiment

Subject. Ten college students (five males and five females) participated in the text input experiment. All the subjects had previous experiences in use of computer key-board (average use of 55 minutes per day), and a keypad of mobile phones manufac-tured in Korea for sending and storing short text messages (average use of 5 times per day). The average age of the subjects was 22.8 years old. All the subjects were right-handed.

Apparatus. Three types of text input devices were used: the chording gloves with a Korean keymap, a conventional QWERTY keyboard upon which Korean "Hangul" code is assigned, and a keypad of the most popular cellular phone models sold in Korea. The chording gloves were connected to a notebook computer for the experiment. The models of the mobile phones used in the experiment were Samsung's SPH-X2700 with "Chun-Jee-In" text input interface, and LG's SD-2100 with "EZ-Hangul" interface. Seven subjects used the SPH-X2700 and three used the SD-2100. Subjects used their own mobile phones for the experiments.

Learning. Subjects were trained to use the chording gloves to make a text input using short pre-defined sentences. The training sessions for the chording gloves consisted of 10 sessions, each of which lasted for 4 hours a day. A new sentence was used for each training session. Therefore a total of 40 hours was devoted to training for each subject. Subjects were able to memorize the complete set of chords in Korean in a period ranging from an hour to two hours during the first training session. For the keyboard and keypad of mobile phones, only one brief practice session for about an hour was given since all the subjects were quite familiar with keyboard and the keypads of their own mobile phones.

Procedure. Upon completion of training sessions and when the subjects felt comfortable with each device, a new sentence was given for performance test. The sentence used in the performance test consisted of 270 Korean characters including spaces. A total time to input the whole sentence was measured for 10 times along with the error rate for each device using the same sentence without practice. Text input time was later converted to input speed in terms of cpm(characters per minute) for statistical analysis. An average was calculated for each measure. Subject started with a device to input the given sentences, then switched to the second device to input the same sentences, and then to the third device for the same sentences in a trial session. The device order was counterbalanced for each trial session for each subject to eliminate the order effect.

Results. The learning effect for the chording gloves in terms of input speed and error rate is shown in Fig. 3. As is shown in the graph, input speed was still increasing while error rate seemed approaching the plateau after 40 hours of extensive training. It would be reasonable to say that more performance improvement in terms of input speed can be expected with time.

The results of the text input experiments are summarized in Table 1. A one-way ANOVA was performed on the input speed and error rate. There were significant differences in both input speed ($\underline{F}$= 64.04, p< 0.001) and error rate ($\underline{F}$= 10.12, p< 0.01) among the input devices. All these differences resulted from the superior performances from keyboard compared to the other input devices. In further analysis, no significant difference could be found between the chording gloves and the keypad of mobile phones in input speed (p> 0.1), but error rate was significantly higher for the chording gloves than for the keypad of mobile phones (Duncan $\underline{t}$= 4.18, p< 0.05).

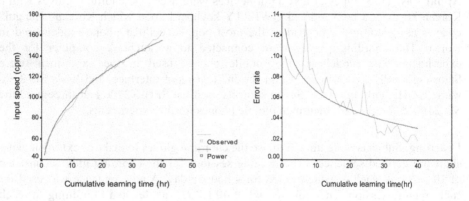

Fig. 3. The learning effect for the chording gloves. Mean of input speed (left) and error rate (right) with training time.

Table 1. Keying performance (mean and standard deviation) of Korean characters for each input device.

	Chording Gloves	Keyboard	Phone Keypad
Input Speed , cpm	108.3 ± 23.5	388.0 ± 124.4	94.8 ± 26.4
Error Rate, %	8 ± 6	1 ± 1	3 ± 1

Discussion. For text input tasks, the keyboard was by far the better device than the others in performance, probably due to subjects' long term exposure to the interface and experience accumulation. Chording gloves, though, seemed to provide comparable performances taking into account the subjects' lack of training and previous experiences.

However, the fact that the chording gloves resulted in significantly more errors in text input compared to the other devices needs to be noted. Most of the errors from the chording gloves were missed entries, which means that the input was not correctly made due to poor contact. Considering that the silicon ink can conduct electricity with a very light touch, the poor contact seemed to be the result from the discrepancy between subject's hand and the glove size. While there was not a significant lag in speed, which suggests that the interface may still be user-friendly, the design of gloves and contact mechanisms still need improvement in ergonomics.

3.2 Usability Evaluation

Subjects' perceived ratings were measured for usability evaluation after the text input experiments. Each subject rated for all the input devices used for the experiments based upon the following four categories using a 5-point scale. The subject was asked to rate "5" if he/she thought a device provided maximum usability in each category, and to rate "1" if he/she thought the device had very poor usability. The subjective ratings on usability in the aspects of portability, learnability, functionality, and overall satisfaction for mobile use are displayed in Fig. 4.

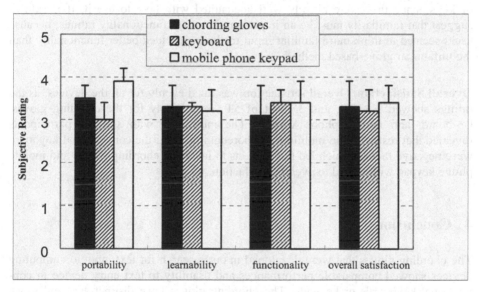

Fig. 4. Mean subjective ratings on usability of chording gloves, conventional keyboard, and mobile phone keypad.

Portability. Subjects were asked to rate the portability of the devices, where 5 indicates the maximum portability. Subjects who participated in the text input experiment rated the chording gloves 3.5, mobile phone keypad 3.8, and the keyboard 3.0 for portability. Subjects expected that the chording gloves' light weight and non-rigid form could provide good portability. The fact that mobile phones are always carried with them seemed to signify good portability for subjects. However, considering that the keyboard is not portable at all and is still rated 3.0 out of 5.0, other truly portable devices seemed to be relatively underrated.

Learnability. The learnability for both the chording gloves and keyboard was rated 3.3 while that for the mobile phone keypad was 3.2 out of 5.0. Subjects seemed to take much longer to learn the complex text keymap of chording gloves. The learnability for the chording gloves seemed to be rated higher than expected, considering that the gloves required extensive learning to memorize all the chords for generating certain texts, without any marking on the keys. According to interviews with subjects, they still found the input mechanism of the chording gloves easier to learn than expected, and fun to use.

Functionality. The functionality for the chording glove, keyboard, and mobile phone keypad was rated 3.1, 3.4, and 3.4, respectively. Since the chording gloves have fewer keys and lots of chording were needed for use of function keys which are not visibly marked on the gloves, subjects seemed to be easily confused and thought that the functionality was not fully provided. It seemed that subjects thought the functionality of mobile phone keypad was relatively good even with limited number of keys, since they were already well acquainted with how to use it. It is safe to suggest that familiarity must be an important factor for functionality ratings, because users seemed to think more familiar input methods provided better functionality than the unfamiliar glove-based method.

Overall Satisfaction. Overall satisfaction was rated evenly for all the devices, as the ratings showed 3.3, 3.2, and 3.4 out of 5.0, respectively for the chording gloves, keyboard, and mobile phone keypad. The interviews with selected participants revealed that restriction in mobility and boredom in using the conventional keyboard were negative factors which led the subjects to favor the chording gloves and mobile phone keypad with regard to overall satisfaction.

4 Conclusion

The chording gloves that were developed in our research for text input to computing devices showed comparable performances and usability to text entry device in conventional keyboards or keypads. The chording gloves have distinct size and space advantages over both conventional keyboards and keypads.

In order to develop a keymap for the chord keyboards, either a strong spatial correspondence to the visual shape of the typed character should be used, or a strong link to a well-built semantic knowledge base should be created [3, 6]. The keymap for our chording gloves is quite simple and easy to learn because of its similar arrangement with the already familiar QWERTY keyboard. The keymap can be altered at any time to satisfy any user's requirement. This would provide much flexibility in terms of usability. In addition, the chording gloves have advantages in portability and fast learning. It is lightweight, and can be easily carried, and takes less space than any other text entry device. Since we always use our fingers and hands in daily life, to enter codes in combination, by touching the thumb and other fingers together, can be easy to remember and natural to perform.

The chording gloves also have flaws that must be corrected. Since the gloves have limited number of keys compared with keyboards, extensive usage of mode change is needed for executing control functions such as "enter" and "backspace" while making text input. The mode switch is currently performed by a chord using three fingers. The chording gloves also require extensive training, apparently more than 40 hours, and give users a load on the working memory due to the absence of markings on the keys. As was discussed in the text input experiment, the gloves need to be tailored to each user to minimize the discrepancy between the user's hand and the glove's size.

Typing with two hands for hand-held devices brings up an issue of true mobility, too. Currently, a one-hand chord glove is being developed for text entry and control functions since at least one hand needs to be free for other daily activities while holding to or accessing to small mobile computing devices; so that it provides better portability and usability.

We can conclude that the chording gloves developed in this study can contribute to (1) convenient access to computing devices by mobile users, and (2) expanded usage of universal input device in ubiquitous computing environment; so that anyone can store and retrieve information anywhere, in any form, and with any coding techniques.

Acknowledgement

This study was supported by Grants 2001-s-152 and 2002-s-131 from Advanced Technology Program of Institute of Information Technology Assessment, Daejeon, Korea.

References

1. Bowman, D. A., Wingrave, C. A., Campbell, J. M., Ly, V. Q.: Using Pinch Gloves for both Natural and Abstract Interaction Techniques in Virtual Environments. In: Human-Computer Interaction; Proceedings of the HCI International 2001, Lawrence Erlbaum Associates, (2001) 629-633
2. Endfield, C.: A typewriter in your pocket. Computer Weekly, 11 May (1978) 4
3. Fukumoto, M., Tonomura, Y.: "Body Coupled Finge Ring": Wireless Wearable Keyboard. In: Proceedings of CHI '97 (Atlanta GA, March 1997), ACM Press, (1997) 22-27
4. Gopher, D., Raij, D.: Typing With a Two-Hand Chord Keyboard: Will the QWERTY Become Obsolete? IEEE Trans. On Systems, Man, and Cybernetics, 18(4) (1988) 601–609
5. Lehikoinen, J., Roykkee, M.; N-fingers: a finger-based interaction technique for wearable computers. Interacting with Computers, 13 (2001) 601-625
6. Noyes, J.: Chord keyboards. Applied Ergonomics, 14(1) (1983) 55-59
7. Porosnak, K. M.: Keys and Keyboards. In: Helander, M. (ed.): Handbook of Human-Computer Interaction, Elsevier, New York (1988) 475-494.
8. Pratt, V.: Thumbcode: A Device-Independent Digital Sign Language. In: Proceedings of the 13th Annual IEEE Symposium on Logic in Computer Science, Brunswick, NJ (1998)
9. Rosenberg, R.: Computing without Mice and Keyboards: Text and Graphic Input Devices for Mobile Computing. Doctoral Dissertation. University College London (1998)

10. Rosenberg, R., Slater, M.: The Chording Glove: A Glove-Based Text Input Device. IEEE Trans. On Systems, Man, and Cybernetics-Part C: Applications and Reviews, 29(2) (1999) 186-191
11. Sturman, D., Zeltzer, D.: A Survey of Glove-based Input. IEEE Computer Graphics & Applications, Jan (1994) 30-39
12. Weber, G.: Reading and pointing-New interaction methods for Braille displays. In: Edwards, A. (ed.): Extra-Ordinary Human-Computer Interaction, Cambridge University Press, Cambridge (1995) 183-200

Designing Explorable Interaction Based on Users' Knowledge: A Case Study on a Multi-functional Printer Application

Dong-Seok Lee[1], Douglas Jihoon Kim[2], Un Sik Byun[3]

[1] Software Solution Lab., Digital Media R&D Center, Samsung Electronics.
416, Maetan-3Dong, Yeongtong-Gu, Suwon, Korea 442-742.
[2] Corporate Design Center, Samsung Electronics. 14th Fl., Joong-Ang Ilbo Bldg.,
7 Soonwah-Dong, Chung-Gu, Seoul, Korea 100-759
[3] Printer Design Group, Samsung Electronics. 11th Fl., Joong-Ang Ilbo Bldg.
{david.ds.lee, doug.kim, ui.byun}@samsung.com

Abstract. Many studies on exploratory learning advocate that the label-following heuristic is the user's basic and strongest exploration strategy (Polson, 1988). According to various observational studies, users exploit their prior knowledge when label-following fails. Their prior knowledge is classified by Yoon and Park's (1997) task knowledge types (Lee and Yoon, 2000; Lee et al., 2001). This paper deals with how that knowledge guides users' exploration. A framework for exploratory learning is suggested, which defines exploration as bi-directional search both from user goals and interface widgets. A case study shows that the framework assists designers to identify the source of usability problems and helps inspire design alternatives based on gathered users' knowledge. Usability evaluation shows that the design alternatives resulted in better performance and user satisfaction.

1 Introduction

People need to interact with products to carry out everyday tasks, like sending a fax, watching a DVD, or buying an airline ticket at a website. A great body of research supports the view that users of interactive systems rely on the method of exploratory learning [1]. In other words, users will interact with a system right away and learn how the system works just by using it. Shrager and Klahr [2] showed that subjects were indeed able to learn a novel computing system. Chursh [3] reported that only 9% of the users read the printed users' guides and 11% read the printed tutorials.

Designing easy-to-use interaction has already been one of the important requirements for recent interactive systems. One promising approach for user-centered interaction design is providing an *explorable* interaction where users muddle through tasks. Explorable interaction is valuable to a company because it reduces costs as an alternative to training and knowledge [4] and promotes market competitiveness.

We can easily find that some users learn a system simply by using it without any instruction. People inherently have an exploration ability that lets them figure out how a system works. For example, people have little trouble staying in a different city

M. Masoodian et al. (Eds.): APCHI 2004, LNCS 3101, pp. 211-220, 2004.
© Springer-Verlag Berlin Heidelberg 2004

because of their exploration ability. They can find a restaurant, a grocery store, or an information center. Van Ootendorp and Walbeehm [5] support this view by pointing out that there is a substantial similarity among all systems on some abstract level. However, users sometimes can not learn how to use a system by themselves. This paper addresses what makes the difference of successful exploration and how explorable interaction design can be supported.

2   A Framework of Exploratory Learning

2.1 User Knowledge Guides Exploration

Two observational studies on a PDA and on e-commerce websites [6] [7] found that (1) users rely on label-following heuristics (2) when label-following heuristics comes to an impasse, they depend on every clue from their prior experience, (3) computer-illiterate users exhibited extreme label-following behavior, (4) computer-literate users efficiently and effectively exploited their knowledge to show better performance, and (5) the knowledge that makes exploration different can be classified by Yoon's [8] types of task knowledge, which are defined as goals-means structure of tasks, organization of tasks/operations, natural orders among tasks/operations, control patterns, and operation images. Table 1 shows the types of user knowledge and some instances found in the observations.

Table 1. Users' knowledge exploited during exploration

Users' Knowledge Type	Instances Found in the Observations
Goal-means structure of tasks	– Launch application first, then perform tasks – Make a memo sheet, then enter contents
Organization of tasks/operations	– Where a memo application is provided, an address and schedule application is also provided. – The operation for deleting a memo/address is available at the object level
Natural orders among tasks	– Select a memo/address, then delete it – Login first, then shop for items
Control patterns	– Adjust parameters, then confirm – Toggle patterns for power on/off
Operation image	– The meaning of 'Application' and 'Record' – The icon button and drop-down menus

Polson and Lewis [1] suggest hill-climbing, back chaining, and label-following heuristics as exploration strategies. However, there are no studies about what triggers these strategies. Users of novel interactive systems tend to use the processes of planning, sub-goaling, schema, and cognitive leaps. For example, if a user knows the object/action paradigm, then he/she will first selects the associated object and then looks for the appropriate menu item or button. In this case, the knowledge of the object/action paradigm facilitates a hill-climbing strategy. This paper asserts that the knowledge facilitates an informational process that results in a diversity of behaviors as follows.

- The goal-means structure of tasks enables users to create a sub-goal. Recursively executing a sub-goal leads to hill-climbing, back chaining or progression in both directions. Most of the experienced users can generate sub-goals and have a planned sequence for a solution.
- Users organized and managed the relationships among tasks/operations in terms of semantic affinity and whole-part relationship [8] [9]. The organization of tasks can generate some similar level alternatives, exhibiting the side-goaling strategy. When similar tasks/operations are executed, users expect that the procedure will be similar and the related interface objects will be found on the same level.
- Natural orders exist among tasks on some abstract level. People form a schema/script when objects or situations posses similar characteristics. When the sub-goals are generated, the natural orders among them determine the temporal order of a planned solution sequence. For example, a user must select an object first and then perform an action to the object in the Windows environment.
- Familiar control patterns reduce the cognitive complexity by simplifying a task procedure. Some patterns are commonly used to control objects so users can progress to the next operation automatically.
- Operation images let users recall the required subtasks or operations in an inductive way. The observations showed that knowing what the label, shape, location, or color of the interface widget leads to efficient and corrective exploration. For example, the link located in top-right corner of the display on a PDA reminds the users to select an appropriate category.

2.2 A Framework of Exploratory Learning

Users can perform a task by interacting with a system in order to achieve a goal. During this interaction, the users' knowledge is active and guides the users' exploration. In this context, exploration can be defined as making a connection between the users' goals and the interface widgets with a reference to prior knowledge. If the users' goals are at the top level of abstraction during interaction, then the interface widgets are at the bottom. If users can find the appropriate interface widgets for their goal, a direct connection is made and the users can achieve their goal without any difficulty. However, the interfaces of current systems are not wide enough to accommodate all the interface widget for all the users' goals, resulting in some hidden tasks. Therefore, a direct connection between some user goals and interface widgets are impossible. Yoon [9] suggested that somewhere in the middle is a *design construct* where tasks, subtasks, syntax, semantic operations, and decision makings are located. The users' opportunistic behavior of exploration can be explained with this design construct. Some examples are (1) interface objects remind users of appropriate tasks/subtasks, (2) users' knowledge of a goal-means structure can formulate subtasks and that can be executed recursively and (3) users take hints from information about task similarity, expecting related tasks to have similar syntax.

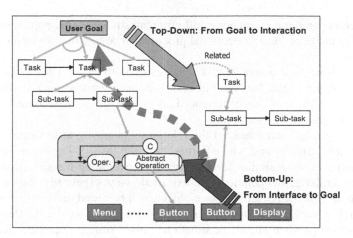

Fig. 1. Suggested framework of exploratory learning

To summarize, this paper suggests a framework for the strategies of exploratory learning (Fig. 1). Contrary to task-based researchers' top-down approach (from tasks to interface) and designers' bottom-up approach (from interface to task) to explore the problem space, users explore the problem space from both directions in order to generate an interaction between goals and interface objects. This framework consists of user goals, tasks, sub-goals/sub-tasks, operations, feedback, abstract operations, temporal relations, and interface widgets. The users' knowledge can be represented in the framework with design construct and links among them. The opportunistic behavior of users results from searching in a more efficient and effective way. This framework attempts to capture the users' opportunistic behavior.

The framework is based on the users' bi-directional approach for exploration. The users' behavioral tendency should be reflected in an interaction design. That means if a task cannot be accomplished only by label-following heuristics, then there must be at least one association to the users' knowledge, which pops into users' mind and can guide the next step of exploration. In order to provide an association, it is required to identify and represent the users' knowledge. Table 2 introduces how the knowledge can be identified and represented. Note that representing the knowledge is required for managing design complexity, communicating with co-developers, and documenting design decisions.

Table 2. Identifying and representing the users' knowledge

Types of Users' Knowledge	Identifying	Representing
Goal-means structure of tasks	Card sorting (grouping)	Task tree
Organization of tasks/operations	Card sorting (grouping)	Similarity diagram, dendrogram
Natural orders among tasks	Card sorting (sequencing)	Flowcharts, OCD
Control patterns	Market survey	Flowcharts, OCD
Operation image	Questionnaire	Dictionary

3   Designing Explorable Interaction of a MFP Application

3.1   Domain Introduction

With the introduction of the Multi Functional Printer (MFP), the ability for a single product to scan, print, copy and fax has become an attractive tool to both home and small office users. The MFP application enables these functions by offering users the tools to complete their tasks. Since the product offers multiple functions and a variety of workflows, a clear interaction design is necessary for a productive user experience.

The existing version of the Samsung MFP application was developed without having an understanding of its users. As a result, a number of customers had voiced their dissatisfaction with the product, specifically about the difficulty of its use. Understanding that the usability of products was a priority, the consumer feedback prompted a usability evaluation.

3.2   Usability Evaluation

The usability of the MFP application was evaluated as a comparative usability test between Samsung and a major competitor to identify and benchmark the issues with usability. Twelve experienced users of an MFP, with 7 months to 3 years experience, participated in the testing. Using both applications, they were asked to perform 4 basic tasks: print, copy, scan and fax. Verbal and behavioral protocols were collected and analyzed to measure tasks times and the level of frustration. The results found that there were serious usability problems in both applications. Written usability test reports and recorded movie clips were presented to stakeholders of the application in order to inform them of the situation.

After the test, a series of discussions were conducted to identify the major problems and the strategies to solve them. A proposed framework was developed to visualize the steps that were not explorable and unrelated to the users' knowledge. For example, it was found in the usability testing that participants had difficulty scanning a document, cropping the image and then sending it as an email. As Fig. 3 denotes, participants had minimal resistance when performing the first two operations using the label-following heuristics by pressing the buttons 'Scan Wizard' and 'Scan to Email'. However, frustration began when the application did not match the users' knowledge. One participant started the scan task and then relied on his prior-knowledge to direct his actions. The user expected to see a preview of the scanned document. But instead, he saw a different image with several buttons options, including 'Scan' and 'Prescan'. The user was puzzled and then pressed the 'Scan' button. This started the page scanning process and the user failed to complete the task.

It was concluded from the usability evaluation that the current version of the MFP application did not follow user-centered heuristics, but instead reflected an engineering mindset. In order for the next version to successfully address the usability issues and provide an easy-to-use product to its customers, it was necessary to conduct user research to identify the users' knowledge.

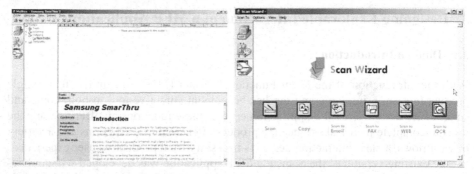

Fig. 2. Current version of the Samsung MFP application

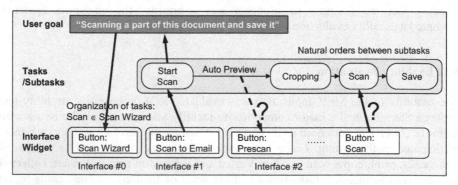

Fig. 3. Scanning a document then sending it as an email in the existing version

3.3 Identifying Users' Knowledge

The goal of conducting user research was to gather data in order to construct a model of the users and their knowledge when interacting with an MFP application. The research involved (1) card sorting, (2) card sequencing and (3) competitive benchmarking.

The strategy involved beginning with user research at the beginning of the design process, followed by iterative user evaluations of the concept during the development of the design. Since the application was planned to release internationally, it was critical to gather data from an international audience. Since Korean users were only available for the initial interviews, it was decided that a hypothetical mental model could be constructed from these users and then tested with an international audience to validate the conclusions. The tests were conducted at the Samsung User Centered Design Lab in Seoul, Korea in June 2003. The five participants were between the ages of 28-33, had prior experience with an MFP, and were comfortable in the Windows OS environment.

The card sorting technique was selected to help the team identify the users' understanding of hierarchical structures in an MFP application. Since the tests were originally designed with international participants in mind, the team made the decision to use a software-based card sorting and cluster analysis program. This strategy allowed the team to easily administer the tests in multiple languages while also giving them tools to perform a cluster analysis of all the user data, regardless of language. It was concluded that most users (1) perceived the MFP application as different functions and workflows, (2) defined categories using the primary functions of the product, and (3) grouped similar workflows together.

The card sequencing technique was developed to observe the users' sequence of actions while completing a task. It was important for the team to understand what functions the user would expect to use and where the user would expect to find them. Additionally, it was important to understand the sequence in which the users would perform an action to complete a task. The tasks were also written without including the names of specific functions to avoid making suggestions about methods to complete a task. The users can be grouped into three user types – 'The Controller', 'The Manager' and 'The Hybrid'. Table 3 summarizes the user types and their characteristics.

Table 3. User groups and their characteristics

User Group	Characteristics
The Controller	– User viewed the software as a way to control the hardware.
	– User preferred wizards to facilitate the tasks.
	– User had no concern with archiving or managing images.
The Manager	– User viewed the software as a system to input, manage and output objects.
	– User preferred an object/action interaction model.
	– User wanted to archive and managing images.
The Hybrid	– User viewed software as a system to input, manage and output objects.
	– User preferred wizards to facilitate tasks.
	– User wanted to archive and managing images using an object/action OS interaction model.

Table 4. Existing interaction models and idioms

Interaction Model	Characteristics
Wizard	– The user is presented a control panel that gives direct access to a series of wizards to complete a task.
	– The interaction focuses more on workflow and less on content management.
Manager	– The user is presented with a manager style interface where objects can be imported and exported.
	– The interaction focuses more on content management.

Finally, the technique of competitive benchmarking was used to identify interaction models and idioms that exist in the current market. Since the users have had prior experience with an MFP application, this data would be helpful in identifying the users' existing knowledge and expectations. After benchmarking three of the competitors MFP applications, a number of standards were identified. The conclusions are presented in Table 4.

3.4 Interaction Design

After the analysis of the user data, an interaction design was developed, focusing on 'The Hybrid' user type and drawing from the 'Wizard' and 'Manager' interaction models. The new design uses the concept of a dynamic application window (Fig. 4) that applies the idiom of the control panel as its global navigation. This approach gives the user access to the primary functions, while providing context during a workflow sequence.

When a function is selected, the control panel expands to reveal a secondary navigation of hidden workflows. When one of these sub-tasks is selected, the control panel expands to present the navigation and tools to complete the selected workflow. These workflows are designed with a unique navigation that operates like a wizard giving novice users the ability to complete their tasks linearly, but also offers experienced users the ability to navigate using more of a direct method. When the task is complete, the wizard collapses transforming the UI back into the control panel. Additionally, the application lets the user manage, manipulate and share their content using an object/action interaction method.

3.5 Discussion

During the design process, the team conducted a usability evaluation in the US, the UK and France. Eighteen users from the different countries participated to evaluate both the existing product and the design concepts of the new project. Two versions of a Flash prototype were developed to present two different design approaches of the same concept. Issues dealing with terminology, navigation, and workflow were also addressed in the evaluation.

The results showed that the design concept was well received by the users. Many responded favorably to the simplicity and clarity of the new design in comparison to the previous version. The users offered their opinions about the terminology and provided their unique associates based on national differences.

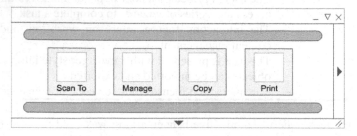

Fig. 4. The control panel of the new prototype

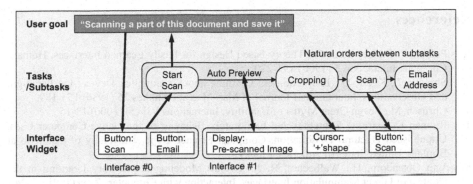

Fig. 5. Scanning a document then sending it as an email in the new version

When addressing navigation and workflow, it was discovered that each prototype offered different benefits depending on the task. Because low fidelity prototypes were used, a great deal of design insight was gathered from the users and was taken into consideration in the evolution of the design. Both concepts were re-examined and the final design integrated the positives from each.

The proposed framework shows that the newer version of the application is easier to use. Fig. 5 illustrates that the task 'Scan' can now be achieved without much difficulty. Right time and right place feedback, cursor shape, and buttons help the users to accomplish their task easily. The results of the international usability testing also demonstrated that all subjects could accomplish the basic tasks successfully without much frustration.

4   Conclusion

This study attempts to identify the types of users' knowledge exploited when exploring novel interactive systems and how this knowledge guides their exploration. A framework for exploratory learning is presented based on the users' bi-directional exploratory behavior. The case study shows that this knowledge and the proposed framework can help interaction designers create an explorable interaction. The results of the case study also illustrate that the framework is useful to identify usability problems and can inspire design alternatives. The proposed framework will be refined through series of further case studies.

Acknowledgements

- Many thanks to Ms. Kyoung Soon Oh and Mr. Bong Uk Im for supporting user-centered design.

References

1. Polson, P. G., Lewis, C. H.: Theory-based Design for Easily Learned Interfaces. Human-Computer Interaction 5 (1990) 191-220.
2. Shrager, J., Klahr, D.: Instructionless Learning about a Complex Device: the Paradigm and Observations. International Journal of Man-Machine Studies 25 (1986) 153-189.
3. Chrusch, M.: Seven Great Myths of Usability. Interactions VII (5) (2000) 13-16.
4. Rieman J.: Learning Strategies and Exploratory Behavior of Interactive Computer Uses, Unpublished Doctoral Dissertation. Computer Science Dept., University of Colorado at Boulder, United States of America. (2000)
5. Van Ootendorp, H., Walbeehm, B. J.: Toward Modeling Exploratory Learning in the Context of Direct Manipulation Interfaces. Interacting with Computers 7 (1) (1995), 3-24.
6. Lee, D.-S., Yoon, W. C.: Exploratory Behavior of Computer-literate User in Interactive System. In: Proceedings of the third Asia-Pacific Conference on Industrial Engineering and Management Systems, Hong Kong, 20-22 December, 2000. pp. 637-641.
7. Lee, D.-S., Cha, S. I., Yoon, W. C.: An Observation of Exploratory Learning on E-commerce Homepages. In: Proceedings of 2001 Conference of Ergonomics Society of Korea, Ansan, Korea, 20 April, 2001.
8. Yoon, W. C., Park, J.: User Interface Design and Evaluation based on Task Analysis. In: Proceedings of the 14th International Conference on Production Research, Osaka, Japan, 4-8 August, 1997. pp. 598-601.
9. Yoon, W. C.: Task-Interface Matching: How we May Design User Interfaces. In: Proceedings of the XVth Triennial Congress of the International Ergonomics Association (IEA 2003), Seoul, Korea, 24-29 August, 2003.

The Automatic Generation of a Graphical Dialogue Model from Delphi Source Code

Lei Li[1], Chris Phillips[2], and Chris Scogings[3]

[1]Department of Computer Science, University of Auckland,
Auckland, New Zealand
L.Li@cs.auckland.ac.nz
[2]Institute of Information Sciences & Technology, Massey University,
Palmerston North, New Zealand
c.phillips@massey.ac.nz
[3]Institute of Information and Mathematical Sciences, Massey University,
Auckland, New Zealand
C.Scogings@massey.ac.nz

Abstract. A shortcoming of current user interface builders is that while they permit the designer to construct the visible user interface, they provide no model of the interaction. This paper describes how a Lean Cuisine+ graphical dialogue model of the behaviour of a graphical user interface (GUI) can be automatically generated from Delphi source code. The model is produced in a file format which is compatible with SELCU, an experimental support environment for Lean Cuisine+. SELCU provides for viewing, printing and editing of the model, which can be used to analyse the interaction.

1 Introduction

Dialogue models can make a useful contribution to user interface design. They provide a behavioural description of the dialogue at a level removed from the visible user interface. This description can be subjected to analysis, for example to check that all tasks uncovered at the requirements stage are supported by the system and that they can be carried out in an efficient manner.

A shortcoming of current user interface builders is that while they permit the designer to program the visible user interface, they provide no model of the interaction. However, the information contained in the source files which specify the user interface could be analysed to produce such a model. In addition to supporting analysis of the interaction, the dialogue model so generated would provide useful documentation.

Lean Cuisine+ [1, 2] is a semi-formal graphical notation for describing the external behaviour of event-based graphical user interfaces (GUIs). A software environment, SELCU, has been developed for Lean Cuisine+ [3] which permits dialogue models to be manually constructed and edited using a drag and drop approach. The research being reported in this paper is concerned with the *automatic* generation of Lean Cuisine+ dialogue models of user interface behaviour from Delphi source code. The

M. Masoodian et al. (Eds.): APCHI 2004, LNCS 3101, pp. 221–230, 2004.

models are produced in a textual file format which is compatible with the SELCU application.

In Section 2, the Lean Cuisine+ notation and its support environment SELCU, are briefly described. Section 3 describes the requirements of the auto-generation software, and the Delphi components which can be handled. Some implementation details are provided. In Section 4 a case study which demonstrates the software in action is presented. Section 5 reviews the research and outlines further work.

2 Lean Cuisine+ and Its Support Environment

Examples of graphical notations applied to dialogue description over the past 20 years include state transition networks [4], petri nets [5], statecharts [6], and Lean Cuisine+ [3]. A review appears in [7].

Lean Cuisine+ was developed expressly for describing the behaviour of graphical user interfaces, and is unique in providing for the description of task sequences within the context of the dialogue structure. Lean Cuisine+ is a development and extension of the Lean Cuisine notation [8]. In a Lean Cuisine+ specification, an interface is described in terms of a set of selectable primitives, called menemes, arranged in a tree structure, and a set of constraints over these primitives. A meneme can represent an object, action, value or state. At any time, a meneme is either selected or not selected, and is either available or not available for excitation. This gives rise to four possible meneme states.

Menemes may be grouped into sub-dialogues to any level of nesting. The grouping of menemes within sub-dialogues places constraints on their behaviour. The grouping may be either mutually exclusive (1 from N) or mutually compatible (M from N). Menemes may be real or virtual. Real menemes represent specific selectable options. Non-terminal real menemes are headers to further sub-dialogues. Virtual menemes are always non-terminal and are used to partition a sub-dialogue. They are not available for selection. Examples illustrating these basic constructs appear in Section 3.

Further behaviour is captured in three ways: through the use of meneme modifier symbols on the diagram (for example, a meneme may be designated as 'deselect only'); through conditions for selection associated with menemes; and via selection triggers. Triggers visually link menemes, showing system selections in response to user events. They are overlayed on the base tree diagram. A further layer, the task layer provides a bridge between task and dialogue modelling. Each user task (sequence of related sub-tasks) can be represented in Lean Cuisine+ as an overlay of linked menemes superimposed on the base diagram, thus showing the task within the context of the dialogue. Figure 1 shows a simple example of a Lean Cuisine+ diagram displayed within the SELCU environment. It includes a task overlay Open Folder, and a trigger which deselects a window following user selection of Close.

2.1 The SELCU Support Environment

A software environment (SELCU) has been developed for Lean Cuisine+ [3]. It is a prototype system and is subject to revision and upgrading as new Lean Cuisine+

features are evolved. SELCU aims to provide a platform for the efficient production of Lean Cuisine+ dialogue models and provides for the creation, display, editing, storage and printing of diagrams. Where possible the tool supports a 'drag and drop' approach and any part of a diagram can be directly selected. SELCU data files have been organised as simple text files that can be easily generated by other applications. SELCU is a Windows-based package that will run on Windows®2000 or similar. It has been developed in Microsoft Visual C++®6.0 using Microsoft Foundation Classes.

Figure 1 illustrates the SELCU user interface in use with a typical Lean Cuisine+ diagram under construction in the work area, which is surrounded by toolbars and status information. To the left of the work area is the SELCU toolbar. This provides options relating directly to the construction and editing of Lean Cuisine+ diagrams in the work area. These options include creating a new meneme, constructing a mutually compatible or mutually exclusive subdialogue grouping, constructing a trigger, constructing a task sequence, modifying an existing task sequence, and hiding or displaying selected objects.

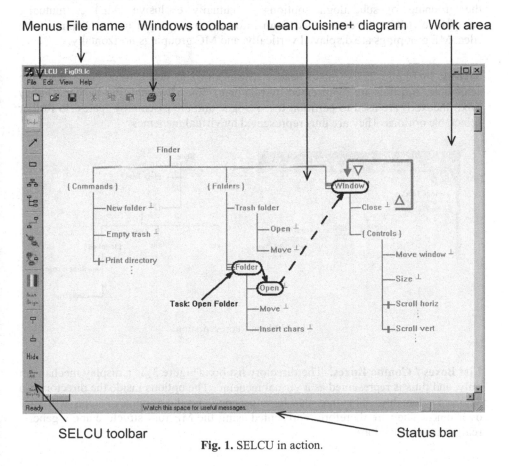

Fig. 1. SELCU in action.

3 The Auto-Generation Software

The wider purpose of this research is to explore the possibility of automatically generating behavioural descriptions of GUIs constructed using proprietary software development environments. Delphi has been chosen as representative of this class of software. The auto-generation software accepts Delphi source files as input, extracting information relating to user interface components and their inter-relationships, and translating this information into an equivalent Lean Cuisine+ dialogue model expressed as a SELCU-compatible textual source file [9].

3.1 Delphi Components and Their Translation into Lean Cuisine+

The Delphi IDE includes an Object Pascal compiler and interactive component toolkit [10]. Some widely used Delphi components and their Lean Cuisine+ visual counterparts are described below. It should be noted in relation to these examples that the grouping of subdialogue options – mutually exclusive (ME) or mutually compatible (MC) – is determined from information contained in the Delphi source files. ME groupings are displayed vertically, and MC groupings horizontally.

Menus. In Figure 2, the menu header (Style) and leaf nodes (e.g. Bold, Italic) are selectable, and thus are represented by real menemes. The menu sub-headers (Fancy Text, Indexed) are used to partition the dialogue and are essentially 'gates' to further selectable options. They are thus represented by virtual menemes.

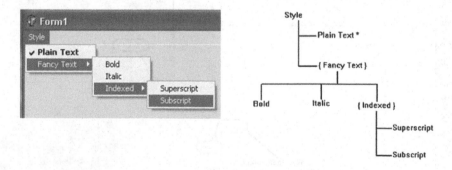

Fig 2: Menu Representation.

List Boxes / Combo Boxes. The directory list box (Figure 3) is a display mechanism only, and thus is represented as a virtual meneme. The options inside the directory are ME and selectable. They are also homogeneous and the number of items will vary over time. They are therefore represented using the ME fork structure and a generic real meneme (Directory).

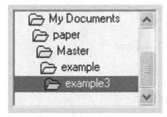 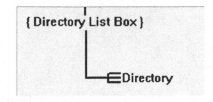

Fig 3: List Box Representation.

Radio Groups. In the radio group (Figure 4), the group header is a display mechanism represented as a virtual meneme, and the selectable options inside the group box (Timetable, Clash List) are represented by real menemes. The options are ME.

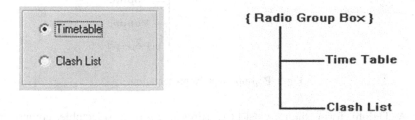

Fig 4: Radio Group Representation.

Check Boxes. The check box header (Figure 5) is a display mechanism represented by a virtual meneme, and the selectable options inside the check box (Lectures etc) are represented by real menemes. The options are MC.

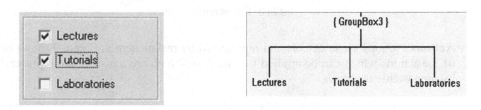

Fig 5: Check Box Representation.

Buttons: Buttons are represented as real menemes, denoting the fact that they are selectable (They may of course be unselectable at certain points in a dialogue). Following selection, many buttons return automatically to an unselected state. They are represented by Monostable menemes ($\perp$) (as in the case of Print in Figure 6).

Fig 6: Button Representation.

Pop-up Menus. In Figure 7, the pop-up menu (Popup Menu1) is selectable by the user and is represented by a real meneme. The leaf-nodes (Popup1 etc) are also selectable, are ME, and are represented as real menemes.

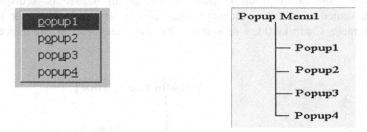

Fig 7: Pop-up Menu Representation.

Forms. A Delphi form such as SELCU (Figure 8) is a selectable component represented by a real (root node) meneme. In a multi-forms system, one form may generate another form (which will remain invisible until selected).

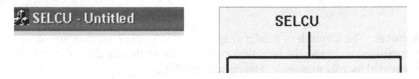

Fig 8: Forms representation.

Actions. Actions are selectable and represented by real menemes. Figure 9 shows two of the actions which can be applied to a window – both are transient and represented by monostable menemes.

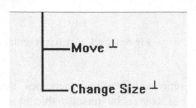

Fig 9: Representation of Actions.

Data Input Boxes. In Figure 10, the input box Input Date is directly manipulable, and is represented by a real meneme. Selectable actions such as Insert, Delete or Modify are represented by real menemes (which are also monostable).

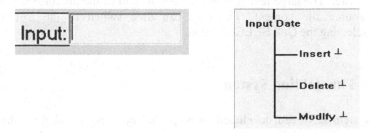

Fig 10: Representation of Data Input Box.

3.2 Implementation Issues

The Delphi code is analysed in two passes. The first pass examines the *.dfm file, extracting meneme names, and building the basic Lean Cuisine+ tree structure of menemes in the form of a temporary text file held in memory. The second pass examines the *.pas file, extracting further meneme attributes (for example whether they are real or virtual), and additional logical relationships between menemes (for example triggers). The final output from the analysis is a SELCU-compatible source file containing a textual representation of the Lean Cuisine+ diagram.

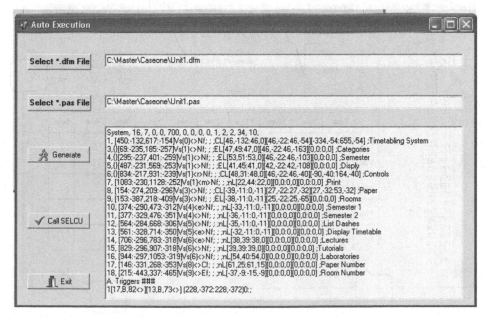

Fig 11: GUI for the Auto-Generation Software.

The GUI for the auto-generation software is shown in Figure 11. The button sequence (from top to bottom) indicates the process order. Once the files have been identified, the user selects the **Generate** button to initiate the creation of the SELCU-compatible source file. The large text area in the bottom-right of the interface is used to display the source file content. The user can then switch to the SELCU environment by selecting the **Call SELCU** button.

4 Case Study: Timetabling System

An interactive system has been developed to help students design and print their academic timetable. For a selected semester, the user can choose to show any combination of lectures times, tutorial times and laboratory times. The timetable can be printed. The graphical user interface for this system is shown in figure 12. It allows users to select a category – Papers or Rooms (A), a Semester (B) and Session Types (C). There are inbuilt constraints or behaviours relating to the selectable options: only one of the generic category options (Papers, Rooms) can be selected at any time; only one of the room numbers can be selected at any time; several paper numbers can be selected at the same time; only one of the semester options can be selected at any time; any combination of session types can be selected at the same time (**Lecture** is the default). When the user selects a paper number, the system will automatically display the selected paper's timetable (E). Users can switch between two display options – **Timetable** and **Clash List** (D), and can also print the screen information at any time (F).

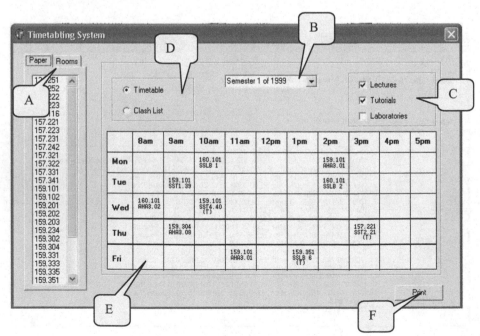

Fig 12: Timetabling System GUI.

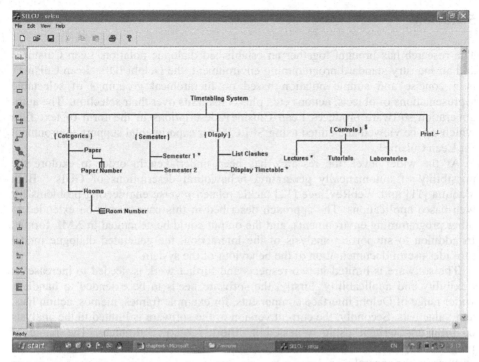

Fig 13: Lean Cuisine+ Representation of the Timetabling System GUI Displayed within the SELCU Environment.

The GUI for the Timetabling application was developed using the Delphi 6.0 IDE. Figure 11 shows in the large window the SELCU-compatible text file generated by the auto-generation software from this Delphi code. Figure 13 above shows the equivalent graphical representation of this, as displayed by the SELCU application following selection of the Call SELCU button.

The Lean Cuisine+ diagram is made up of five mutually compatible sub-dialogues, four of which are headed by virtual menemes: {Categories}, {Semester}, {Display} and {Controls}. Only the Print subdialogue is directly selectable by the user. The options within each of these subdialogues are grouped to reflect the behaviours which have been extracted from the Delphi code.

Further constraints are captured through the use of meneme modifier symbols. For example, {Controls} is shown as a required choice group (§) with Lectures as the default (*). Print is represented by a monostable meneme (⊥). The fork symbols within the {Categories} sub-dialogue are used to denote generic options, which are mutually compatible in the case of Paper Number (several paper numbers can be selected at any time) and mutually exclusive in the case of Room Number.

Although not shown in Figure 13, a trigger exists between Paper Number and Display Timetable to reflect the fact that when the user selects a paper number, the system will automatically display the selected paper's timetable (as defined earlier). Within SELCU, triggers are displayed on request over a dimmed tree diagram.

5 Review

The research has brought together an established dialogue notation, Lean Cuisine+, and an industry standard programming environment, the Delphi IDE. Lean Cuisine+ is a concise and simple notation based on hierarchical groupings of selectable representations of objects, actions etc., plus constraints over their selection. The auto-generation software produces Lean Cuisine+ descriptions in the form of text files which can be viewed and edited using SELCU, an experimental support environment for Lean Cuisine+.

At the wider level, the research has been undertaken in order to explore the possibility of automatically generating behavioural descriptions of GUIs. Both Vaquita [11] and WebRevEnge [12] tackle related reverse engineering problems for web-based applications. The approach described in this paper could be extended to other programming environments, and the output could be generated in XML format. In addition to supporting analysis of the interaction, the generated dialogue model provides useful documentation of the behaviour of the system.

The software is limited in two respects and further work is needed to increase its flexibility and applicability. Firstly, the software needs to be extended to handle a wider range of Delphi interface components, for example frames, memos, action lists, and value lists. Secondly, the current version of the software is limited to the analysis of programs written using a nested if...then... else... structure. The range of programming styles capable of being analyzed needs to be extended to make the software more general.

References

1. Phillips, C.H.E. (1995): Lean Cuisine+: An Executable Graphical Notation for Describing Direct Manipulation Interfaces, *Interacting with Computers*, **7**, 1, 49-71.
2. Scogings, C.J. (2000): The Lean Cuisine+ notation revised. *Research Letters in the Information & Mathematical Sciences* 2000 (1). Massey University, New Zealand. 17-23.
3. Scogings, C.J. (2003): *The Integration of Task and Dialogue Modelling in the Early Stages of User Interface Design*, PhD Thesis, Massey University, New Zealand.
4. Jacob, R.J.K. (1985): A State Transition Diagram Language for Visual Programming, *IEEE Comput.*, **18**, 51-59.
5. Peterson, J.L. (1977): Petri Nets, *ACM Comput. Surv.*, **9**, 3, 223-252.
6. Harel, D. (1988): On Visual Formalisms, *Commun. ACM*, **31**, 5, 514-530.
7. Phillips, C.H.E. (1994): Review of Graphical Notations for Specifying Direct Manipulation Interfaces. *Interacting with Computers*, **6**, 4, 411-431.
8. Apperley, M.D. & Spence, R. (1989): Lean Cuisine: A Low-Fat Notation for Menus, *Interact. with Comput.*, **1**, 1, 43-68.
9. Li, L. (2003): The Automatic Generation and Execution of Lean Cuisine+ Specifications, MSc thesis, Massey University, New Zealand.
10. Jacobson, J.Q. (1999): *Delphi Developer's Guide to OpenGL*, Wordware Publishing Inc..
11. Vaquita (2004), Belgian Laboratory of Computer-Human Interaction, accessed at: http://www.isys.ucl.ac.be/bchi/research/vaquita.htm
12. WebRevEnge (2004): ISTI, Italian National Research Council (CNR), accessed at: http://giove.cnuce.cnr.it/webrevenge/

NetWorker: A Practical Web-Based Tool to Support the Collect-Compare-Choose Cycle

Paul Lyons, Chris Phillips, Elizabeth Kemp, and Jaimee Alam

Institute of Information Sciences and Technology, Massey University, Private Bag 11-222,
Palmerston North, New Zealand
(p.lyons,c.phillips,e.kemp)@massey.ac.nz, jaimee_2@hotmail.com

Abstract. An earlier paper has covered the development of a paper prototype of
NetWorker, a tool designed to facilitate a Web usage referred to as the Collect-
Compare-Choose cycle. Here we describe an initial implementation of the tool,
a small scale evaluation, and modifications that were implemented subsequent
to the evaluation. NetWorker is a PC application with a single window
containing multiple web browsers and a text pane. It allows users to download
and view pages from multiple web-sites in parallel, to drag text from the web
pages into a working area (the WorkPad) and to edit and rearrange information
within the WorkPad. The browsers and the WorkPad can be rearranged in
various ways to make optimum use of the available screen space.

1   Introduction

An earlier paper [1] described a paper prototype of a tool designed to support Web
users who need to make decisions based on comparisons between items of
information collected from multiple web-sites. This style of Web usage has been
called the Collect-Compare-Choose cycle [2]. Here, we briefly review the background
to the tool, and describe an initial implementation called NetWorker, a small scale
evaluation of this implementation, and subsequent modifications.

A study of Web usage by Morrison et al. [3] indicated that, for 51% of the users
surveyed, it was important to evaluate multiple products or answers to make
decisions. Indeed 71% of the respondents were searching for multiple pieces of
information. When reviewing the significance of this study, Nielsen [2] observed that
it appeared to be almost three times as important for users to find multiple pieces of
information as it was for them to locate single pieces of information. Currently
available browsers provide good support for users who wish to access single
locations, but none for users who need to make decisions based on information from
multiple web-sites. As Nielsen noted, Morrison et al.'s study used the critical incident
method, which is not intended to provide a complete overview of user activities. In
spite of this restricted focus, the study pinpointed the importance of supporting the
Collect-Compare-Choose cycle.

The *Collect* phase of this cycle involves accessing a series of web-sites, assessing
the quality and relevance of the contents of each site, and retaining a reference to
suitable sites.

M. Masoodian et al. (Eds.): APCHI 2004, LNCS 3101, pp. 231–240, 2004.
© Springer-Verlag Berlin Heidelberg 2004

The *Compare* phase involves viewing information from more than one web-site on the screen, moving relevant information to the support tool, where it can be rearranged into a format which facilitates comparative analysis, and performing the comparative analysis in this single workspace.

The *Choose* phase involves returning to the original web-site to implement a decision, by making a purchase, for example. Note that the phases of the cycle do not have to be performed in a strict sequence.

2   Requirements of the Tool

There are various metasites that will compare prices for users on the dimension of interest. Expedia, [4] for instance, enables people to compare airfares, hotel rates, etc. PriceSpy [5] lists prices for computer equipment from a number of suppliers and it includes links back to the suppliers' sites for ordering purposes. However, Expedia does not access Tourist Board sites to obtain information about the views of those who have already stayed in the hotels. Similarly, PriceSpy does not include a review, for example, of the cheapest piece of equipment. Such metasites still cannot handle the situation where a user needs to access a variety of information.

Bearing in mind the facilities available in the tools already on the market and the support needed for handling the content from multiple web-sites, the following requirements were initially identified:

Functional Requirements
The tool should:
- permit the user to access and then keep references to several web-sites;
- permit the user to view content from more than one web-site at a time;
- provide the user with a working area (a 'WorkPad') onto which web content can be pasted, URLs can be referenced, notes can be made, and calculations carried out;
- permit the user to switch focus between web-sites, and between web-sites and the WorkPad;
- allow the user to control the number of windows to be displayed at any time;
- permit the user to switch between vertical and horizontal arrangement of windows, to suit the information being browsed;
- provide for system placement of windows, with window size(s) being a function of the number of windows being displayed at any time, and the chosen orientation (horizontal or vertical).

Non-functional Requirements
The user interface of the tool must
- be consistent with the user interface of the browser;
- provide for each of the following functions to be carried out by the user in a single operation:

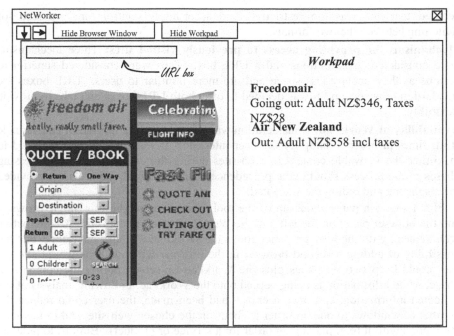

Fig. 1. Paper prototype of the interface - horizontal alignment of the two main panels

- opening browser windows;
- opening web-sites;
- switching focus between displayed web-sites;
- switching focus between displayed web-sites and the WorkPad;
- revisiting previously accessed web-sites;
- changing the number of windows being displayed;
- switching between vertical and horizontal arrangement of windows;
- transferring web content to the work pad;
- make the system status clear to the user at all times;
- provide user help and support.

3 Early Prototyping

Early development of the tool concentrated on low fidelity or paper prototypes. These are most commonly based on sketches or drawings of screens [6]. During this phase, design decisions were made in regard to a number of the requirements outlined above:

Number of web-sites viewable at any time: As the number of on-screen sites increases, so the viewable content area of each site decreases. It was decided that two sites provided the best compromise.

Horizontal and vertical window arrangement: Consideration was given to providing only vertical arrangement in order to simplify the user interface. It was decided that this was too restrictive, and accordingly controls are provided for switching between the two formats.

Mechanisms for providing access to previously visited sites: Three mechanisms were considered: tabs, buttons and a URL box. Tabs were considered superior to buttons as they occupy less space and are more familiar to users. URL boxes are standard in browsers and it was decided to offer both URL boxes and tabs to provide flexibility.

Availability of WorkPad: Consideration was given to having the WorkPad available at all times in order to simplify the user interface. It was decided that the need to maximize the viewable content of web-sites during the comparison and processing phases of the process should take precedence, and accordingly controls are provided for displaying and hiding the WorkPad.

Fig. 1 shows a paper mock-up of the tool. This diagram shows a single browser, and the browser panel on the left and the WorkPad panel on the right. An alternative arrangement, with the browser panel above the WorkPad was also envisaged, and the possibility of adding a second browser in the browser window. This would allow a user could keep two web-sites plus the WorkPad on-screen during the comparison phase, while information is being copied onto the WorkPad. Following analysis of the collected information, and once a choice had been made, the user could reduce the number of windows to one, in order to focus on the chosen web-site, and to facilitate interaction with it (e.g. placing an order for a service or product). Buttons to hide the WorkPad and a browser window are shown on the toolbar to the right of the arrow buttons.

4   First Delphi Prototype

A prototype, called NetWorker, was written in Object Pascal, using version 7 of Borland's Delphi IDE [7]. The main window for this prototype, shown in Fig. 2, is divided into three areas; interface controls are shown across the top of the window, and web browser and WorkPad areas appear below these controls. The layout of the lower part of the window is quite flexible; the browser panel and the WorkPad panel can be arranged vertically or horizontally; the number of browsers can be varied between zero and two; an individual browser can be maximised (hiding other browsers and the WorkPad); the WorkPad can be maximised (hiding the browsers).

After loading a page, the user can drag text from the browser into the WorkPad, and edit it there. Whenever the user loads a webpage, its URL is added to a tab at the top of the browser window, and to a drop-down list associated with the URL box, so that the user can subsequently reload a page. The complete URL history is available in each browser, and survives the closure of all browsers.

This version of NetWorker lacked some of the common features of commercial browsers such as "back," "forward," and "reload" buttons.

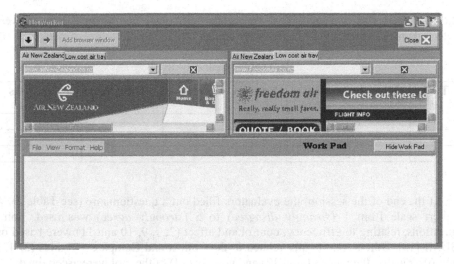

Fig. 2. The first version of NetWorker. It displays several controls at the top of the window -
arrows for toggling between horizontal and vertical window layout, a button for adding another
browser, and a close button to terminate the application. Here, the user has added a second
browser, loaded a webpage into each of the browsers, and clicked on the right arrow to align
the browsers from left to right. Each browser window has a URL box and its own close button.
The bottom half of the window is occupied by the WorkPad, with several (unimplemented)
menu options and a minimise control.

5   Evaluation

It is important to identify the goals of an evaluation [8, 9]. We wished to identify the
prototype's strengths and weaknesses [10]. Suitable protocols include observation and
timing of users' actions [11], "think aloud," and jargon-free, specific, positively-
worded [9] questionnaires, with a user population of five to twelve [10].

Five evaluators, representative of people who regularly use the web (three
Computer Science postgraduate students and two Computer Science staff members)
evaluated NetWorker. They were told that the system was being evaluated, and not
their actions. The evaluation procedures were fully explained in advance and the
evaluators' informed consent was obtained. Documentation about NetWorker was
provided and the evaluators were allowed to explore the system for about a quarter of
an hour before the evaluation proper began.

The evaluators were asked to carry out three typical web-related tasks – (1) to find
the most competitive price for the collector's edition of "The Lord of the Rings,"
where payment could be made by international credit card, (2) to find the most
competitive home loan available, and (3) to find a cheap motel room with specified
services in a certain location. Evaluators were told that they had 10 minutes to
complete a task. They were observed and asked to "think aloud." Their comments
were recorded. No usability laboratory was available, so an observer made notes
about their actions. The sessions were timed and the observer noted how many times

the WorkPad was accessed, how frequently horizontal and vertical layouts were selected and whether new browsers were added.

Table 1: Task statistics

Task #	Mean time (mins)	Number succeeded	Total WorkPad accesses
1	8.96	3	8
2	6.14	5	10
3	7.2	4	10

At the end of the session, the evaluators filled out a questionnaire (see Table 2). A Likert scale from 1 (*strongly disagree*) to 5 (*strongly agree*) was used. Some questions, relating to efficiency, control and affect (2, 7, 9, 10 and 11) were based on SUMI [12]. Others specifically related to the Collect and Compare activities (3, 4, 5 and 6). Finally, the value (1 and 12) and novelty (13) of the tool were ascertained.

6   Results

Table 1 shows that the mean time for carrying out task 1 substantially exceeded the mean time for tasks 2 and 3, and that two of the five evaluators failed to complete it. The WorkPad was used regularly - 28 accesses overall with a mean of 5.6 times. Only three of the evaluators selected a second browser window. The others copied information from a page to the WorkPad and then loaded another page into the same window. Four of the five selected both the vertical and horizontal layout at some time in the proceedings. The fifth always used the default vertical layout.

Whilst the sample is very small, some trends emerged (Table 2). The results for the questionnaire showed that the median for item 12 was five, indicating that most of the users *strongly agreed* with the proposition that the tool would be useful for personal or academic activities. The users *disagreed* with the statement that the tool was similar to other tools used. The medians for items 1, 2, 3, 4, 6, 8 and 9 were all four, indicating an overall level of satisfaction. The users were not so happy about *referring back to web-sites, making the software do exactly what they wanted* and *arranging the work space to meet their needs* (all with a median of three). Speed was not an issue though, as users *disagreed* with the proposition that the software responded too slowly.

Analysis of the transcripts and open-ended questions revealed some problems. All evaluators wanted to be able to directly resize a window/WorkPad. Four mentioned the lack of a "back" button. Two amplified this, noting that the interface lacked typical browser features. Three people did not like the fact that the last level visited in a web-site could not be accessed. Instead the initial URL was accessed. Two people complained that they had to log in to both NetWorker and Internet Explorer. Finally, two people noted that the close button was duplicated. When asked to comment on aspects of the tool that they really liked, four users mentioned the WorkPad facility and three the value of being able to return to previously visited web-sites. Finally two of the five users appreciated the option of using two browser windows.

Table 2: Questionnaire responses

Item Number	Item	Median
1	It is clear what the purpose of the tool is	4
2	It is clear how to use the tool and move from one part of the task to another	4
3	It is easy to collect and view web-sites using the tool	4
4	It is easy to compare multiple web-sites using the tool	4
5	It is easy to refer back to visited web-sites	3
6	It is easy to copy important information	4
7	It is easy to make the software do exactly what you want	3
8	The work space of the tool can be arranged to my needs	4
9	The labels and icons on the buttons can be clearly read and are understandable	4
10	The tool has an attractive presentation	3
11	The software responds too slowly to inputs	2
12	The tool will be useful to my academic or personal activities on the Net	5
13	The tool is similar to other tools I have used	2

7   Current Version

Informal discussion with the evaluators led to the incorporation of several improvements (see Fig 3). These are detailed below:

Tool tips: The evaluators had previously had no experience with tools that allow a user to create and destroy multiple web browser windows; one did not understand the controls for accomplishing these tasks. Accordingly, all the controls now display a brief description of their function, whenever the cursor hovers over them for 2.5s.

Close buttons: The evaluation version of the software sported two types of close button – one for closing the whole application, and one (replicated in each browser window) for closing individual browser windows. Although the background colours of these buttons differed, users confused them. Accordingly, the application-close button now shows the caption "Close NetWorker," and the browser-close button now shows the caption "Close This Browser." The tool tips referred to above are also active for these buttons.

Maximise WorkPad: In the evaluation version of the software, there was a button on the WorkPad that contained the caption "Hide WorkPad" when the WorkPad was on display, and "Show WorkPad," when the WorkPad had been minimised. Users did not feel comfortable with these captions, and they have been changed to "Minimise WorkPad" and "Restore WorkPad," and Windows standard icons for minimise and restore buttons have been added.

Source Button: Users felt that it would be useful to display the URL for the page from which a piece of information had been transferred to the WorkPad. A button with the caption "Source" has been added to the WorkPad which adds the URL to the text shown in the WorkPad.

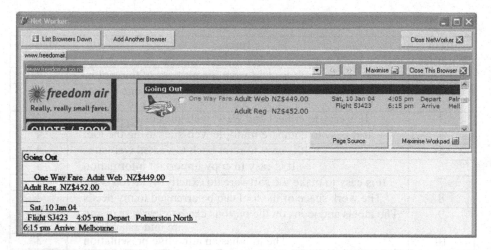

Fig. 3. The static appearance of the interface produced in response to the user evaluation

Tile Browsers button: The buttons for tiling browsers horizontally and vertically contained right- and down-pointing arrows respectively, but otherwise gave no indication of their purpose, and were ill understood by the evaluators. They were replaced by a single button. When the browsers are tiled vertically the button contains the caption "Tile browsers across" and a right-pointing arrow. When the browsers are tiled horizontally, it contains the caption "Tile browsers down" and a down-pointing arrow.

Maximise browsers feature: When all three NetWorker windows - two browsers and a workpad area – were on display, users sometimes found that web pages were too large to fit comfortably into the available space. Accordingly, "Maximise" buttons have been added to the browser windows and to the WorkPad. When one of these buttons is pressed, its window takes over the complete display region. The button changes to a "Restore" button, which returns the display to its former appearance.

Smooth Transitions: Transitions from one screen layout to another are no longer instantaneous, but morph smoothly. Although this modification was not requested, the implementers feel there was an unacceptable cognitive load associated with the instantaneous transitions, and this has been reduced significantly.

Multiple Browsers: The restriction to two browsers has been lifted.

Resizable windows: The browser and WorkPad panels can now be directly resized

Colour: Background colour has been changed from the Windows standard beige to a more interesting blue.

Fig. 3 shows an abbreviated image of the updated interface, with all the static changes – buttons, icons, etc. – visible.

8   Discussion

The terms *browsing* and *surfing* imply a certain degree of aimlessness about the way users navigate the Web. Although we surmise that nearly all users, at least occasionally, allow serendipity to govern their traversal of the Web, many engage in a more purposeful behaviour pattern called Collect-Compare-Choose. NetWorker has been designed to provide a greater degree of support for the Collect-Compare-Choose cycle than conventional browsers.

A small-scale evaluation of NetWorker has produced two types of result. First, users felt that the tool would benefit from a number of improvements - most of which have now been incorporated - to its interface and capabilities. Secondly, the subjects felt quite strongly that NetWorker was unlike other tools they had used, and that they would be likely to use such a tool in their academic and personal activities.

A tool such as NetWorker does not perform hitherto impossible functions. Rather, it integrates, and therefore simplifies an approach to Web-based information processing that can be achieved in a more circuitous fashion by a combination of other tools.

9   Future Work

The software described in this paper is in a very early stage of development; it was intended to act as a tool for experimenting with the look and feel of an interface paradigm combining multiple browser windows and a workpad. However, time for implementing the software was severely limited and the interesting new functionality was implemented at the cost of a number of familiar browser and editor functions.

Users tend to have a holistic approach to evaluating software and were, understandably, critical of these omissions. Accordingly, future versions of NetWorker will incorporate such obvious features as back and forward buttons for the browser, and methods to implement the menu items shown in the WorkPad.

A related problem concerned returning to pages that had previously been displayed in a browser tab; when a user opens a page in a NetWorker browser tab, then navigates to other pages by clicking on hyperlinks, the URL stored by the software for that page is not updated. Consequently, if the browser reloads, the page that appears is the one that was first loaded. Users found this particularly annoying, and in future versions, a history of URLs for the tab will be implemented. Thus the tab will be able to be reloaded with the page associated with the most recent URL, and back and forward functions, as described in the previous paragraph, will be supported by the same mechanism.

Some problems with the interface remain; for example, some web-sites, when queried, produce results in popup windows. It will not necessarily be obvious to a naïve user that information can be dragged from a popup window into the WorkPad just as effectively as from a browser within NetWorker. Further, when information is dragged from a web browser into a RichEdit box, it sometimes displays as text, sometimes as a mixture of text and table, and sometimes as a mixture of body text, table, and HTML. A more reliable way of displaying text alone will need to be found.

One of the features in the original list of functional requirements has not been incorporated into the current implementation; there is no facility for performing calculations using values from websites (calculating sales tax, for example). Adding this feature to the system could prove something of a challenge, in terms of designing an intuitive user interface, and in terms of cleaning up the text dragged from a web page. Such text may or may not incorporate HTML, and any HTML it contains may be malformed. For example, tags may not be terminated, or contextual tags that should surround the text (table layout information, for example) may be missing.

References

[1]   Collect, Compare, Choose: Supporting the decision making cycle on the web, *Proc of CHINZ'03*, ACM, Dunedin, New Zealand, 3-4 July 2003, 33-38.
[2]   Nielson, J., (2001): The 3Cs of Critical Web Use: Collect, Compare, Choose, Available at http://www.useit.com/alertbox/20010415.html, April 15, 2001
[3]   Morrison, J.B., Pirolli, P., and Card, S.K. (2001): A Taxonomic Analysis of What World Wide Web Activities Significantly Impact People's Decisions and Actions., Interactive poster, presented at the Association for Computing Machinery's *Conference on Human Factors in Computing Systems*, Seattle, March 31 - April 5, (2001).
[4]   www.expedia.com: Accessed 8 Sept 2003.
[5]   www.PriceSpy.co.nz: Accessed 8 Sept 2003.
[6]   Rettig, M. (1994): Prototyping for Tiny Fingers, *CACM*, 37, No 4, 21-28, 1994.
[7]   Borland   Software   Corporation,   Delphi   Version   7.0   (Build   4.453): http://www.borland.com © 1983-2002.
[8]   Shneiderman, B., (1997): *Designing the User Interface: Strategies for Effective Human-Computer Interaction*, 3rd ed., Reading, Mass, Addison-Wesley.
[9]   Preece, J, Rogers, Y, Sharp, H, (2002): *Interaction Design* NY, Wiley.
[10] Dumas J.S and Redish J.C. (1999); Exeter, Intellect.
[11] Preece, J, Rogers, Y, Sharp, H, Benyon, D, Holland, S, and Carey, T, (1994): *Human Computer Interaction*. Reading, Mass, Addison-Wesley.
[12] Porteous M., Kirakowski J. and Corbett M. (1993): *SUMI User Handbook*, Human Factors Research group, University College, Cork.

Nine Tools for Generating Harmonious Colour Schemes [1]

Paul Lyons and Giovanni Moretti

Institute of Information Sciences and Technology, Massey University, Private Bag 11-222,
Palmerston North, New Zealand,
(P.Lyons,G.Moretti)@massey.ac.nz

Abstract. We survey a number of tools that have been developed for generating sets of colours according to commonly accepted rules for colour harmony. Informal manual techniques for generating harmonious sets of colours have been known and used for at least a century. Although superficially simple, they have not been precise techniques, as pigment-based and dye-based colouring techniques are not susceptible to accurate measurement, in terms of area of colour used or mathematical relationships between colours, and mathematical analysis does not appeal strongly to the design community. Now the historical separation between engineering and design has narrowed. First, the development of colour television brought numerical precision into colour specification. Secondly, in computers, the medium for colour representation and the tool for calculating colour parameters have been integrated. Consequently, it has also become feasible to derive sets of harmonious colours automatically.

1   Introduction

This research is part of a long-term investigation into techniques for selecting harmonious groups of colours for computer interfaces. The current focus is on designing an interface visualisation that facilitates exploration of a colour space. After a brief description of the background to the work, we present a survey of existing interfaces in tools for choosing colours using colour harmony heuristics.

1.1   Colour Selection Is Important

Colour is ubiquitous. We see its strong subliminal effects in many areas. For example:

- Advertisers are skilled in combining colours for effect. They imply urgency with light, saturated primaries, and sophistication with carefully selected tertiaries [1].
- Political parties - indeed whole political ideologies - are summed up by a single colour ("The Greens," and that 1950s clarion call: "Better dead than red")
- Colour-coding is used by many graphic artists to make a diagram's components more recognizable than if they were identified solely by shape or by name

---

[1] in full colour at www-ist.massey.ac.nz/plyons/papers/Lyons and Moretti 2004 (Nine Tools).pdf

M. Masoodian et al. (Eds.): APCHI 2004, LNCS 3101, pp. 241-251, 2004.
© Springer-Verlag Berlin Heidelberg 2004

- In the workplace, colours are found to have significant effects on productivity. Greens are often used for their restful effect, but poorly chosen greens can induce nausea, and reduce productivity. Areas of strong colours can cause eye fatigue [2].

In general, interfaces with garish colours are undesirable; users should be able to concentrate on the task at hand, without being conscious of the appearance of the interface. That is, it should be perceptually visible, but cognitively invisible.

1.2   Colour Selection Has Become Even More Important

There are more colours available now than there used to be. Once, our environment was mostly made up of natural materials with inherently harmonious colours. Now it is largely manufactured; we are free, indeed *obliged* to choose, the colours of everything, including computer interfaces, from a range of thousands.

1.3   Colour Selection Is Difficult

Colour space is large. Even acknowledged masters of the area have trouble exploring it. Josiah Wedgewood, for example, performed over 10,000 experiments to find the best pale blue to contrast with the white decoration on his jasper ware [2]. Colour specialists specify colours in terms of a 3D colour solid with hue, saturation and brightness axes, but most non-specialists aren't familiar with 3D colour spaces, and have difficulty correlating a particular colour with a location in the space, and finding sets of points in the space that exhibit desirable colour relationships.

1.4   Colour Interactions Are Important

Colours never occur in isolation. Our perception of a colour is invariably influenced by simultaneous contrast, which is caused by the way our perceptual system exaggerates differences between adjacent parts of an image. For example, an orange background makes red areas appear yellower, and yellow areas appear redder [3].

1.5   Computer Programmers Are Not Colour Designers

GUI interfaces involve visual design, by definition. Their features differ in size and importance so they are often colour-coded for differentiation. Overlapping screen objects need to be clearly distinguishable. In addition, as interfaces are often used for long periods, poorly designed colour schemes will lead to user fatigue.

Software developers are rarely skilled in considering all these factors. They are more likely to choose colours on the basis of their individual attractiveness. Not only are most system designers amateurs in designing for colour, but many senior designers "grew up" using software designed to run on 16-colour or 256-colour hardware. Worse, just about the time when designers started using 24-bit colour in applications, the World Wide Web rose to prominence. Web designers had to allow for outdated user hardware, and they standardised on a 216-colour "websafe" palette [4], that delayed the universal use of full-colour interfaces.

To summarise:
- colour selection is important for computer applications
- colour selection is difficult
- colour selection for interfaces concerns interaction more than individual colours
- computer application developers are not trained in colour choice or interaction
- computer applications developers have been inured to garish colour schemes

2   Computer-Aided Selection of Harmonious Colour Sets

Informal manual techniques for generating harmonious sets of colours have been known for at least a century [5, 6]. They are generally based on geometric relationships within a colour wheel. A set of colours will be harmonious if the members of the set are chosen: from a small range of hues near each other on the colour wheel (analogous harmony); from a full saturation base hue and the colours obtained by mixing the base hue with white (tints), black, (shades), grey (tones) (monochromatic harmony); from a range of greys (achromatic harmony) from a base hue and the hue directly opposite it on the colour wheel (complementary harmony); from a base hue and colours close to, and equidistant on the colour wheel from its complement (split complementary harmony); from a base hue and two others chosen so that the three colours form an equilateral triangle on the colour wheel (triad harmony), from a set of four colours equidistant around the colour wheel (tetrad harmony); from a set of colours disposed on an oval around the colour wheel (polyadic harmony). Such heuristics seem vague but are widely recognised as ways of achieving harmonious colour combinations [2-4, 6-11] Many writers attribute these heuristics to Johannes Itten [5] of the Bauhaus (1919-1933) design school, but most of them are common coin amongst artists, and they certainly antedate the Bauhaus. For example, Albert Munsell [6] published all of these heuristics, around 1905.

Fig. 1 shows two view of the L*u*v* colour solid [12], a 3D colour space like Munsell's, but mathematically tractable). Munsell held that an image would be harmonious if it was centred on grey (Itten also used this criterion at a descriptive level rather than as a rigorous mathematical technique). Munsell's criterion can be summarised thus:

$$\sum_{n=1}^{c} (CS_n \cdot A_n) = 0$$

Munsell based his colour harmony heuristic on a more sophisticated three-dimensional solid, based firmly in empirical measurements of human colour perception. (

where   c is the number of colours in the image
CS_n, (the colour strength of colour$_n$) = saturation$_n$ x lightness$_n$
A is the area of colour$_c$
and the scales are chosen so that mid-grey has a saturation and lightness of 0

For example, a small area of light, high saturation red (with a high CS) would balance a larger area of low saturation, dark green (with low CS). This approach is much more powerful than Itten's simple colour wheel heuristics, but it requires measurements of hue, saturation, lightness, and area for each colour in an image. The technique was largely ignored the twentieth century in favour of Itten's heuristics.

Engineering and design have converged significantly since Munsell's seminal work. Precision and mathematical tractability were brought into colour specification by the development of colour television, and computers have made the calculations trivial. Consequently, it has also become feasible to derive sets of harmonious colours automatically using Munsell's techniques. Here we report the results of a survey to determine the extent to which mathematical modelling of colour harmony has been incorporated into commonly available tools for generating harmonious sets of colours.

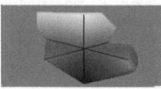

Fig. 1: External and cutaway views of the L*u*v* perceptually uniform colour solid.

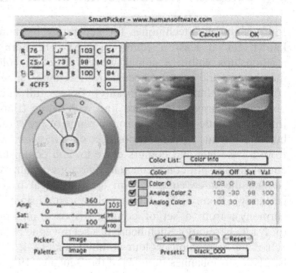

Fig. 2: SmartPicker, a CW/RW (Colour Wheel/Rotating Wireframe) interface

3   The Survey

While researching techniques for specifying sets of harmonious colours for computer interfaces, we searched for colour selection tools that take account of colour harmony heuristics. Here we survey features related to colour harmony in the tools we found.

Most of the applications show a colour circle overlaid by a rotary wireframe in the shape of one of the abstract schemes. We denote this interface style as **CW/RW** (Colour Wheel/Rotary Wireframe).

In most cases, the colour circle is affected by the three-primary-colour technology of CRTs; primary colours use one phosphor, secondary colours use two. Thus, unless the software normalises the brightness of the secondary colours (cyan, magenta, and yellow) they are significantly brighter than the primaries. This produces a set of light coloured "spokes" representing the secondary colours, oriented at 120^0 with respect to each other. We say that such interfaces use an **unnormalised colour circle**.

None of the tools provide real-time update of a user-generated image, though several have a built-in selection of representative images that are updated when the user chooses a new set of colours

3.1   SmartPicker: A Typical CWRW Interface

SmartPicker [13] is a plugin for Photoshop that runs under MacOS 9 and X. It produces sets of colours conforming to analogous, complementary, split complementary, monochromatic, tetradic and triadic colour schemes via a CW/RW interface with an unnormalised colour circle. The points where the wireframe intersects the colour circle specify the components of a concrete colour scheme, and the user rotates the wireframe to choose a new set of colours.

In SmartPicker, slider controls are provided for specifying the lightness and saturation after the hue selection stage. The number of colours is restricted to three.

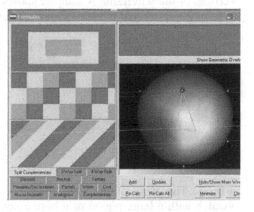

Fig. 3: The ColourSchemer interface produces a colour "wheel" tailored to a user-specified base colour in the top left corner of the 16-colour square

Fig. 4: ColorSchemes produces 13 types of colour scheme based on the choice of base colour from a wheel showing the surface of the colour space

3.2   ColorSchemer

Colorschemer [14] allows the user to specify a base colour, shown in the swatch on the left hand side, and at the top left of the square of colours in Fig. 3, It then fills in the remaining fifteen locations in the square with other colours related to the base colour by the rules of colour harmony. Eleven of the other colours are distributed in colour-wheel-order order around the square, with the top left hand corner occupied by the base colour, and the four central positions occupied by lighter and darker versions of the base colour, and lighter and darker version of its complement. The user can thus easily select a colour scheme based on one of the standard colours schemes. However, the number of colours in a colour scheme produced by the system is restricted to three or four. If more colours could be chosen, they would not harmonise.

3.3   ColorSchemes

ColorSchemes [15] uses a variant of the CW/RW interface (Fig. 4). The circular view is more than a circle of hues; it shows the complete exterior of a spherical colour solid. From the centre of the circle to half the radius, the interface shows the sphere from above, with the white pole at the centre. Beyond that point, it shows the "skin" of the lower half, stretched so that the black pole forms the circumference of the circle. The user interacts with this display by choosing a base colour, and the software displays a set of (full saturation) colours that correspond to the user's choice of one of colour scheme from a set of eleven. A wireframe corresponding to the chosen scheme can be superimposed on the colour circle by selecting "Show Geometric Overlay," and the user can changes any of the colours in the scheme by repositioning any of the vertices of the wireframe A sampler shows the selected colours in a geometric pattern that, in the opinion of the authors, effectively disguises the harmony of the colours.

 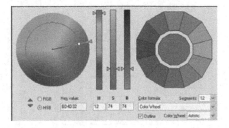

Fig. 5: The HP Colour Wheel displays a swatch with a large region of a base colour and smaller regions of harmonious colours corresponding to a particular colour scheme (here, a tetradic scheme)

Fig 6: ColorImpact's wheel allows simultaneous alteration of hue and saturation, with instant feedback on sliders and a colour palette.

3.4   HP Colour Wheel

The HP Colour Wheel [16] is an applet that displays an unnormalised CW/RW image with complementary, split complementary, analogous, triadic, and tetradic colour schemes (see Fig. 5). The user can rotate the wireframe around the circle and a set of colours corresponding to the colour will be displayed in the area to the right of the colour circle. Sliders alongside the colour wheel allow the user to change the saturation and brightness of the colour set that is generated as a whole. There is no facility for changing the brightness or saturation of individual colours.

3.5   ColorImpact

ColorImpact [17] has a CW/RW interface with an elegant control (the small white circular handle shown in Fig 6 where a radial line and a black circle intersect) that allows both the hue and saturation of a base colour to be specified simultaneously. Although a number of interfaces provide a visualisation that allows simultaneous specification of hue and saturation, the explicit representation of both polar coordinates (the radial line shows the angular coordinate and the black circle shows the length coordinate) works as a visual feedback mechanism that lends a feeling of control that is out of all proportion to its simplicity. The elegance of the interface is further enhanced by immediate feedback between this control and the Hue and Saturation sliders; the colour wheel does not alter brightness, so there is no interaction between the handle on the colour wheel and the brightness slider.

The application generates a polygonal palette – the number of sectors can vary between three and thirty-six – containing colours harmonised with the base colour calculated according to a "formula." The formulae incorporate the usual complementary, split complementary, monochromatic schemes, and a number of others that are more ambitious. However, these are not presented in the context of the colour space (even a simplistic colour wheel), and it is difficult to correlate a "formula" (see Tetrad 2, below) and the heuristic that was used to generate it.

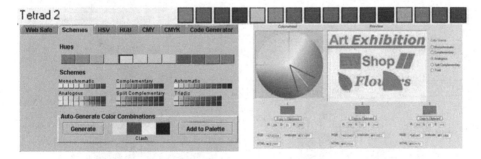

Fig. 7: ColorWrite's interface presents colours from various colour schemes; the user can add colours from any of these schemes to a palette.

Fig. 8: The wireframe in Life Software's CW/RW Colour Wheel is extensible; it allows the user to select a range of lightnesses. The grey lines at 9 and 12 o'clock are artefacts

3.6   ColorWrite

Colorwrite [18] presents the user with a range of full-saturation hues (Fig. 7). When the user selects a hue, the software generates six colour schemes. The monochromatic range, for example, comprises nine colours with the same hue as the user's base colour, and a range of lightnesses. Other schemes follow a similar pattern, except that analogous and split complementary schemes have two ranges of colours in addition to the base hue. There are other tabs in which the base colour can be specified in HSV, RGB, etc. units.

After experiencing a number of other, colour wheel-based applications, it was interesting to test ColorWrite, which, lacking a CW/RW interface, forces the user to model the behaviour of the colour selection heuristic cognitively. The underlying behaviour of the two types of application is of course the same; a CW/RW system, doesn't really rely on the rigidity of a rotating wire shape to define a consistent relationship between positions on a colour wheel. Nor does the application sample the colours at the ends of wireframe when it comes to rest. CW/RW applications replace pondering with perception. It is surprisingly unsettling to be forced to return to pondering, and the user feels that the application is running by "magic."

3.7   Life Software Color Wheel

Life Software's Color Wheel [19] has an interesting feature that makes it more intuitive to use. At heart, it is a CW/RW system with an unnormalised colour wheel (Fig. 8), but unlike the others, its colour wheel represents two dimensions of the colour space, lightness and hue[2], *and* the user can extend the wireframe (so that the colours chosen are full-saturation hues) or contract it (so that the colours are light, low saturation colours, typically called pastels[3]). This makes the software more intuitive to use than some of the other colour choice interfaces – even though the number of colours chosen is restricted to three.

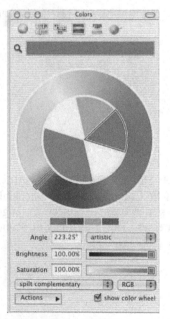

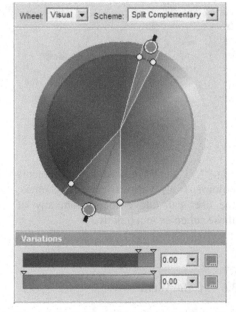

Fig. 9: Painter's Picker can replace Apple's MacOS colour picker

Fig. 10 Color Wheel Pro can be configured to specify hue ranges

---

[2] The lightness range is not complete; all the colours displayed have a minimum value of 255 for at least one of R, G, and B, so only hues and tints are displayed; there are no shades.

[3] though real pastels incorporate some of the highest concentrations of pigment in any painting medium, and can thus be more highly saturated than most paints

3.8   Painter's Picker

The oddly named Painter's Picker [20] is an alternative to the Apple Color Picker in MacOS X. It does not explicitly show a colour scheme wireframe but it is essentially a conventional CW/RW system (Fig. 9). Its main distinguishing features are its MacOS compatability, its fourteen colour schemes and two types of colour wheel, one based on the RGB primaries, another on artist's RYB primaries. Though the latter does not orient the CMY secondaries at 120^0 to each other, the wheel is still unnormalised; the secondaries are brighter than the primaries, for technical reasons explained earlier.

3.9   Color Wheel Pro

Color Wheel Pro [21], (Fig. 10) is a more than usually customisable CW/RW interface. Three features set it apart. First, each "colour" chosen is a range of hue, lightness and saturation. Secondly, the wireframe shape of a scheme is capable of some customisation. For example, the angle subtended at the centre of the colour wheel by a pair of analogous colours can be varied from 0^0 to 120^0. Thirdly, the colour scheme is presented on a realistic image at a realistic size (*much reduced in the adjacent inset*). This combination of controls generates a set of colour regions from which the user can select individual colours, or colour ranges which can be used as a gradated fill. The system automatically chooses a range of saturation and lightness for each colour region. The user may increase or decrease the range.

4   Discussion

The use of colour wheels for colour harmony derives from the spectral model of *light* that Newton developed as a result of his famous prism experiments [22]. But *colour* is a complex psycho-perceptual construct: in the retina, ganglia transform signals from S, M, and L^4 retinal cones into values on orthogonal red-green, blue-yellow, and light-dark axes. Further processing in the visual cortex converts these into a sensation that requires three dimensions - hue, saturation and brightness – to characterise it adequately [2, 12].

Although the colour-set selectors reviewed here often incorporate separate controls dedicated to saturation and brightness, most of them use an underlying model of the colour universe that is one dimensional[5]. Indeed, the help system for Color Wheel Pro, the last application surveyed, includes this interesting assertion:

> *Color theory analyzes only the relationships of pure colors, it does not take color lightness and saturation into account. While your color scheme can use any tints, shades, and tones, color theory pays attention only to the hue component.*

---

[4] Short-, medium-, and long-wavelength-sensitive (loosely, blue-, green-, and red-sensing) cones
[5] A colour *wheel* with no information encoded in its radial dimension - as in most of the surveyed applications – can perhaps be thought of as a 1½D representation.

The developers of most of the applications surveyed seem to labour under the same misapprehension. Such a simplification based on Itten's theories of colour harmony[6] was perhaps justifiable when designers and artists used brushes. However, now that the design medium is the computer, Albert Munsell's earlier and more sophisticated theory [6] that accounts for saturation, lightness and area of colours, is viable.

All of the surveyed applications that display colour wheels are non-linear, because their colour wheels are unnormalised. In addition, they do not account for the fact that the human perceptual system does not accord all full saturation hues the same brightness. Ideally, all full saturation hues would occur on the equator of a spherical colour solid. In fact, Munsell's experiments showed that full saturation yellow, red and blue are (respectively) brighter, darker, and darker than full saturation green. And full saturation yellow, red and blue are respectively more, less and less saturated than full saturation green. Thus a *perceptually uniform* colour solid is a rather bulbous-looking blob. Only if the colour space is represented as this shape will the neat geometrical wire frames reliably generate harmonious sets of colours.

It is our view that the tools surveyed fall short in several respects. They do not allow for technologically-generated inconsistencies in the colour wheels they use. Their visualisations do not display the full three-dimensional structure of the colour universe. Consequently they do not make it easy to position colour choices in the three-dimensional colour space, or to change colour choices in real time. Although most of them allow the user to visualise colour harmony heuristics as simple wire frames, they do not maintain a constant relationship between point-to-point distances on a wireframe and colour differences as experienced by humans. None will update a user-supplied image in real time, though several have a selection of built-in images that they recolour each time the user tries a new set of colours.

References

1.   Danger, E.P., *Using Colour to Sell*. 1968: Gower Press.

2.   Birren, F., *Colour*. 1980: Mitchell Beazley Arts House.

3.   Chevreul, M.E., *The Principles of Harmony and Contrast of Colours and their Applications to the Arts*. 1839.

4.   Hess, R., *The Safety Palette*. 1996, Microsoft Developer Network Online.

5.   Itten, J., *The Art of Color*. 1970: Wiley.

6.   Birren, F., *MUNSELL: A Grammar of Color*. 1969: Van Nostrand-Reinhold.

7.   Graves, M., *Color Fundamentals*. 1952: McGraw-Hill.

8.   Birren, F., *The Elements of Color*. 1970: Van Nostrand Reinhold.

9.   Clulow, F.W., *Colour, Its Principles and Applications*. 1972, London: Fountain Press.

10.   Arnheim, R., *Art and Visual Perception*. 1974: University of California Press.

---

[6] Itten was clearly aware that colour harmony heuristics could be based on the geometry of 3D colour spaces, but in his discussions he ignored the implications of this almost completely.

11.   von Goethe, J., *Theory of Colours*. 1997: MIT Press.

12.   Travis, D., *Effective Color Displays: Theory and Practice*. 1991: Academic Press 1991.

13.   HumanSoftware, *SmartPicker*.

14.   Epstein, A., 2002, *Color Schemer* **2.5.1**, downloaded from www.colorSchemer.com,

15.   Oken, E., Patton, G., Can You Imagine Software, 1999, *ColorSchemes* **1.0.0.2**, downloaded from http://oken3d.com/html/tips.html,

16.   HP, *HP Colour Wheel* downloaded from http://h40099.bbn-stage.europe.hp.com/country/za/eng/color/art_hp_colour_wheel.html,

17.   Grøntoft, T., TigerColor, 2000, *ColorImpact* downloaded from downloaded from www.tigercolor.com,

18.   Pomeroy, P., Adaptive Software, 2002, *ColorWrite* downloaded from http://www.adaptiveview.com/cw/,

19.   Triantafyllou, A., Life Software, *ColorWheel* downloaded from http://www.lifesoftplus.com/Colorwheel/,

20.   Software, O.J., Old Jewel Software, *Painter's Picker* **1.1.2**, downloaded from http://www.oldjewelsoftware.com/ppicker/,

21.   *Color Wheel Pro* QSK Software Group, **2.0**, downloaded from http://www.color-wheel-pro.com/,

22.   Newton, I., *The New Theory about Light and Colours (quoted in Thayer, H.S., (Ed.) Newton's Philosophy of Nature, Hafner, 1953)*. Philosophical Transactions of the Royal Society, 1672. **80**: p. 3075-3087.

A Practical Set of Culture Dimensions
for Global User-Interface Development

Aaron Marcus[1] and Valentina-Johanna Baumgartner[2]

[1] President, Aaron Marcus and Associates, Inc.
`Aaron.Marcus@AmandA.com`
[2] Analyst/Designer
`vj.baumgartner@mavas.at`

Abstract. User-interface design is influenced by cultural differences. Cultures around the world have different patterns of social behavior and interaction that have led anthropologists and scientists of communication to develop culture models whose dimensions describe these differences. This paper describes an effort to collect expert opinion about these cultural dimensions and how they influence user-interface design. The goal was to determine the most important dimensions. Data collected from over 50 experts in the field of user-interface design are presented in this survey. This paper is an edited extract of a much longer thesis by one of the authors [Baumgartner].

1 Introduction

People from different countries/cultures use user-interfaces (UIs) in different ways, prefer different graphical layouts, and have different expectations and patterns in behavior. Therefore user-interfaces must be adapted to the needs of different locales to provide an optimum user experience. Localization, for example of Web sites or software applications, includes changing metaphors, mental models, navigation, interaction, and appearance [Marcus, 22ff). Much research is done on the topic of localization regarding technical approaches (*e.g.* display different character sets, multi-language handling, and memory-based translation software). To facilitate the work of translators and multi-language site providers, content management systems (CMS) were invented that support different cultures, but only regarding text and translation. In fact, current CMS are not really able to handle most other aspects of content and therefore cultural differences automatically, especially regarding graphical appearance. Today, if a company or organization decides to adapt a UI to a certain culture, much time and money must be spent to accomplish this task well: besides all the terminology/measurement changes and translation, one must hire cultural experts for all the targeted countries to account for all UI-component changes. Nielsen [Nielsen, 1996] admits that international usability engineering is a challenging and often avoided area because of the many issues that have to be covered when one wants to serve an international audience [Nielsen, Engineering, 1]. To facilitate and lower the costs of localizing, the development of a CMS that could handle the expanded requirements of localization would be helpful. To support an eventual development of

M. Masoodian et al. (Eds.): APCHI 2004, LNCS 3101, pp. 252–261, 2004.

such a CMS, it is desirable to identify the most important dimensions of culture regarding UI development. This idea is based on the work Marcus has done using Geert Hofstede's cultural dimensions and applying them to the field of UI design [Marcus and Gould]. This current research seeks to find out if Hofstede's dimensions, or others, are appropriate to use for culture-oriented evaluation of UIs.

Many researchers in the field of anthropology have studied patterns of behavior and thinking that differentiate one culture from another. Some of them have compiled these patterns into culture models. To gather expert opinions about which of the dimensions of these models are important when localizing UIs, a set of dimensions extracted from primary references were presented to experts in the form of a questionnaire. The experts were asked to rank the dimensions according to their perceptions of importance. The outcome of the ranking is the basis of an analysis about which dimensions are important for the field of UI design and why they are important. Clearly, which dimensions are the most important can be controversial. Nearly every participant made statements pointing to this controversy: everything depends on the purpose of the UI and the locale itself. Nevertheless, the goal was to derive a concrete result that provides a basis for further discussion.

2 Culture Dimensions and User-Interface Design

The meaning of the term *culture* is complex and used in different ways among many professions. One of the many definitions found in the *Merriam-Webster OnLine Dictionary* is the following: Culture is "the set of shared attitudes, values, goals, and practices ..." (Webster, online). Del Galdo adds: "In addition, culture can also be affected by nationality, language, history, and level of technical development." [del Galdo, 78]. We can use categories to differentiate one culture or country from others. *Dimensions of culture* are "...categories that organize cultural data." (Hoft, Developing, 41) "The notion of cultural dimensions originated in cross-cultural communication research done by Edward Hall and Florence Kluckhohn and Fred L. Strodtbeck in the 1950s." [Gould *et al*, 3]. Many anthropologists have done research in the field of cultural dimensions. One of the most cited studies is that by Geert Hofstede. In the 1970s and 80s he did a survey at IBM that "dealt mainly with the employees' personal *values* related to work situation..." Within this study he covered 72 national subsidiaries, 38 occupations, 20 languages, all in all about 116,000 people. [Hofstede, Cultures, 251]. Based on this survey he came up with five dimensions of culture. Other anthropologists and communication scientists also did studies or academic research to determine different cultural dimensions.

This present study derives from the work of one co-author (Marcus). Marcus combined the scheme of Hofstede's five cultural dimensions and the scheme of five UI design components to create a five-by-five matrix that allows for 25 fields of interest. An article by Marcus and Gould [Marcus and Gould] points out possible implications of Hofstede's dimensions for UI components. During an internship at Marcus' firm, Baumgartner was involved in a study that attempted to find out if these assumptions match with "real life": *i.e.*, can examples be found in localized Web sites? For this analysis, we attempted to be generally inclusive under constraints of time and chose time and chose reasonably complex, different "B2B" and "B2C" Websites from three different continents (North America, Europe, and Asia). The exact circumstances of each Web site design could not be determined; however, we examined evidence from the sites themselves. The results of this study, presented at IWIPS03 [Marcus and Baumgartner] are the following: (1) The matrix-oriented method helps to organize and analyze data collection and (2) initial observations suggest that cultural habits run deeply and operate even under constraints of global design specifications. In high individualistic and low power-distance countries, variations from standard practice seem likely to be most frequently observed. This study sought to determine which dimensions might be most useful in mapping culture dimensions to UI components. The following authors were selected by informal polling of a limited number of initial experts regarding primary resources. Their works are cited in the References and are commented upon more completely in Baumgartner's thesis [Baumgartner].

Adler, Nancy J.	Kluckhohn, F. R.	Victor, David A.
Condon, John C.	Parsons, Talcott	Wright, Quincy
Hall, Edward T.	Strodtbeck, Fred	Yousef, Fathi S
Hofstede, Geert	Trompenaars, Fons	

As Hoft describes cultural dimensions, they can be divided into two categories: objective and subjective. Objective categories are "easy-to-research cultural differences like political and economic contexts, text directions in writing systems, and differences in the way that you format the time of day, dates, and numbers." Subjective categories cover information "...like value systems, behavioral systems, and intellectual systems..." [Hoft, 41- 42]. This study focuses on subjective categories, because objective categories are easy to extract from a culture, and localization approaches already cover these dimensions. Nevertheless some dimensions that seem to be objective at first (economical progress, or resources a country owns) also are of interest. These dimensions are included for two reasons: (1) the objective categories included in this survey are not yet covered by "normal" localization methods and (2) it was of interested to see if there would be a significant difference in the rating of objective and subjective categories (which turned out to be true). The following are the dimensions used in the survey derived from these sources. A complete description of each, including background, examples, the relation to UI components, and comments from evaluators appear in the thesis [Baumgartner]. Space does not allow for further elaboration or for identifying the experts. As Hoft describes cultural dimensions, they can be divided into two categories: objective and subjective. Objective categories are "easy-to-research cultural differences like political and economic contexts, text directions in writing systems, and differences in the way that you format the time of day, dates, and numbers." Subjective categories cover information "...like value systems, behavioral systems, and intellectual systems..." [Hoft, 41- 42]. This study focuses on subjective categories, because objective categories are easy to extract from a culture, and localization approaches already cover these dimensions. Nevertheless some dimensions that seem to be objective at first (economical progress, or resources a country owns) also are of interest. These dimensions are included for two reasons: (1) the objective categories included in this survey are not yet covered by "normal" localization methods and (2) it was of interested to see if there would be a significant difference in the rating of objective and subjective categories (which turned out to be true).

The following are the dimensions used in the survey derived from these sources. A complete description of each, including background, examples, the relation to UI components, and comments from evaluators appear in the thesis [Baumgartner]. Space does not allow for further elaboration or for identifying the experts.

Achievement vs. ascription	Gender roles	Property
Activity orientation	Human nature orientation	Resources
Affective vs. neutral	Individualism vs. collectivism	Space
Authority conception	Instrumental vs. expressive	Specific vs. diffuse
Context	Internal vs. external control	Technological development
Degree of power	International trade commun	Time orientation
Economic progress	Long- vs. short-time orient.	Time perception
Experience of technology	Meaning of life	Uncertainty avoidance
Face-saving	Nonverbal communication	Universalism vs. particularism
	Political decentralization	
	Power distance	

3 Survey, Results, and Ideas for Practical Use

After studying the described 29 dimensions by nine authors, a questionnaire was compiled that described the dimensions briefly. This questionnaire became a tool to get expert opinion quickly and in a structured form. Although the questionnaire might appear like one produced for a quantitative study (use of a Likert Scale), the real purpose was to get ideas about thinking directions of UI designers and analysts, which were obtained through an online questionnaire. The questionnaire gained background information about the participants, presented brief descriptions of each dimension and the rating system, listed the dimensions to be rated, and provided fields for extra comments by participants. To find out if the structure of the questionnaire was appropriate and the estimated time to fill out the form was correct, a pretest was conducted with a group of UI design students at the Fachhochschule Joanneum, Graz, Austria. In order to get valuable input for the survey, experts were contacted in four ways: research within specialized literature to find expert's names combined with Internet research for email addresses, mailing lists in the field of UI design and cultural matters, relevant companies, and relevant conference. Regarding feedback, personal contact and contact via expert mailing lists were the most efficient and effective.

The objective for the survey was to get 30 expert opinions. By the deadline for the survey 57 experts had completed the questionnaire. The participants are from 21 different countries across the world (Australia, Austria, Belgium, Canada, China, Cyprus, Egypt, France, Germany, Hungary, India, Japan, Mexico, Netherlands, Pakistan, Scotland, South Africa, Switzerland, Sweden, UK, and the United States). 19 respondees work in a different country from which they were born (and raised) in. Approximately 43% of the participants originally came from North America and 39% form Europe. They currently work in North America (47%) and Europe (37%). Regarding the participants experience in the field of UI design, 27 had 3-7 years and 14 had 7-11 years of experience. The participants are from more than 40 different institutions including global companies (*e.g.*, Siemens, PeopleSoft, and Ogilvy), universities (Kanda University of International Studies, Stanford University, The George Washington University) and many smaller, specialized companies.

The expert's comments on the survey were positive. Many mentioned that the set of 29 dimensions itself would form a helpful tool in their future work to understand cultural differences. The statement "None of them seemed unimportant" by one expert confirms this impression. However, at least three experts stated that these cultural dimensions do not really have influence on their daily work. This attitude seems ascribable to cultural ignorance, but this opinion must be validated through further research. As already stated, nearly everyone mentioned that "everything depends" on the purpose of the UI itself and the domain of the users. To analyze the data from a statistical point of view is risky; as stated earlier, the study is basically a qualitative one, not quantitative. Concepts like deviation and variance in the raw data are not very meaningful. Ordinal values must be considered instead of metrical. Thus we include a factor analysis, as shown in Figure 1.

The boxplot in Figure 1 tries to visualize the distribution of expert ratings. To analyze ordinal values, parameters like first quartile (Q1), third quartile (Q3), minimum (min), median (med), and maximum (max) are used. A boxplot provides a simple graphical summary of a set of data. It shows a measure of central location (the

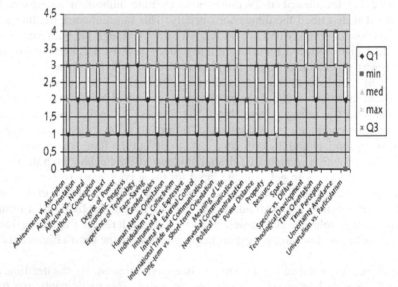

Figure 1. Boxplot or whisker diagram of the data gained through the questionnaire

median), two measures of dispersion (the range and inter-quartile range), the skewness (from the orientation of the median relative to the quartiles) and potential outliers (marked individually). Boxplots are especially useful when comparing two or more sets of data. As stated previously, the survey was intended to deliver directions of thinking; it is not mainly a quantitative survey. The comments most of the participants offered were valuable and gave insight into the expert's mental models and experience. Nearly all participants pointed out that a general opinion on this topic is very hard to provide: "everything depends" was a very common comment. Nevertheless, each of the participants provided a ranking of the dimensions.

To filter out the most important dimensions in a general sense, one draws a "line," which seems best after the dimension of *Authority Conception*. The statistical reasoning for this decision is the following: There are just five dimensions that are clearly located in the space between "very important" (4) and "important" (3): context, environment and technology, technological development, time perception, and uncertainty avoidance. As authority conception is, in the average, still very high and in the statistical ranking of the experts with more than five years of experience even at rank 5, it seemed reasonable to include this dimension in the top five dimensions. The following list summarizes the results for the most important culture dimensions [Baumgartner]:

Table 1: Ranking of the most important cultural dimensions

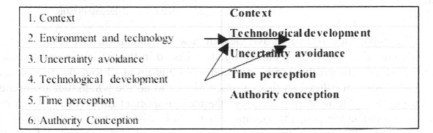

1. Context	Context
2. Environment and technology	Technological development
3. Uncertainty avoidance	Uncertainty avoidance
4. Technological development	Time perception
5. Time perception	Authority conception
6. Authority Conception	

4 Practical Use of the Set

One purpose of this project was to present ideas for how the findings of this survey might be used for practical work. As already stated, it is a very difficult venture to determine the most important dimensions for UI design in general. More research must be done to filter out which dimensions are the most important for special fields of UI design; for example, the design of medical instruments might demand different cultural emphases than a general telecommunication tool. Although it would be ideal if every localization project would take into account all 29 dimensions, this is not likely. Therefore, we provide a grouped and ranked list of dimensions: One purpose of this project was to present ideas for how the findings of this survey might be used for practical work. As already stated, it is a very difficult venture to determine the most important dimensions for UI design in general. More research must be done to filter out which dimensions are the most important for special fields of UI design; for example, the design of medical instruments might demand different cultural emphases than a general telecommunication tool. Although it would be ideal if every localization project would take into account all 29 dimensions, this is not likely. Therefore, we provide a grouped and ranked list of dimensions:

Table 2: Grouped and ranked dimensions

No.	Name	No.	Name
1	D05 Context	10	D12 Individualism vs. collectivism
2	D25 Technological development, D08 Experience of technology	11	D26 Time orientation, D16 Long-term vs. short-term orientation
3	D28 Uncertainty avoidance	12	D29 Universalism vs. particularism
4	D27 Time perception	13	D15 International trade and communication
5	D27 Authority conception, D20 Power distance	14	D10 Gender roles
6	D03 Affective vs. neutral	15	D01 Achievement vs. ascription
7	D09 Face-saving, D24 Specific vs. diffuse, D13 Instrumental vs. expressive	16	D21 Property
		17	D07 Economic progress
8	D02 Activity orientation, D17 Meaning of life	18	D14 Internal vs. external control
		19	D22 Resources
9	D18 Nonverbal communication, D23 Space	20	D06 Degree of power
		21	D11 Human nature orientation
		22	D19 Political decentralization

The list above tries to give an overview of how the dimensions are related to each other and how they could be grouped together. Listed in the order of their statistical average (gained through the expert questionnaire) and grouped together (for reasons to be described later), they can form a practical tool to decide which dimension must be focused on in the next step to cover the most important differences. When one thinks of a localization project, one may need to focus on the top six dimensions of the list. If, suddenly, more money is available for this part of the project and now the project manager must decide which dimension should be focused on next, the list offers a helpful decision support. Tying to group the dimensions above is a very difficult task. One requires more empirical studies about how cultural background influences UI design. Currently, most of the ideas on this issue are based on assumptions. There are still tests and studies to be done to provide valuable material. Nevertheless, we provide groupings and within the following paragraphs describe the reasons for the groupings. The groupings are based on the idea that the problems the UI designer face by paying attention to the dimension might awake similar thoughts and directions of thinking:

Group 1: D08 Experience of technology, D25 Technological development: These are clearly similar in relation to technology.

Group 2: D27 Authority conception, D20 Power distance: As Hoft [Hoft, online] describes these two dimensions as very similar. Although the two dimensions have not been ranked by the experts on similar levels, we can assume that cultural differences in this field have the same impact on UI design as they are so similar.

Group 3: D09 Face-saving, D24 Specific vs. diffuse, D13 Instrumental vs. expressive: all three dimensions cope with the problems of interpersonal relationships. The UI component influenced mainly by these dimensions is interaction and the examples mentioned within the very same chapters point in the direction of community tools. Same impacts on the design of the UIs design are therefore to expect.

Group 4: D02 Activity orientation, D17 Meaning of life: Regarding metaphor building we can assume that societies that focus on material goals value doing more than being, the opposite might be true for spiritual oriented cultures. As already stated, this is just an assumption and has to be verified through more research and convenient tests.

Group 5: D18 Nonverbal communication, D23 Space: The dimension of space is mentioned within the dimension of nonverbal communication, called proxemics.

Group 6: D26 Time orientation, D16 Long-term vs. Short-term orientation: In a way these two dimensions are complementary: The first mainly affects metaphors and navigation, the latter mental models and interaction. Within the statistical ranking of the average value, the two dimensions are followed by each other. The dimensions seem to cover different areas of a society, but some implications on UI design might be the same, for example, future-oriented cultures are likely to be willing to learn how to use a UI if they know that it will be necessary to know how to use it in the future. The same can be true for long-term oriented societies.

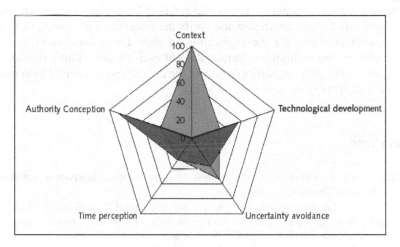

Figure 2: Culture-dimensions pentagon

If we had empirically researched values for all the cultural dimensions mentioned above of a certain country, it would be very easy to generate a tool that could answer the question: "Is it necessary to change the UI for a certain culture/country?" and "Regarding which dimensions must changes be considered?." The basic idea for this tool is the use of star charts in the form of a pentagon, but expandable to more dimensions if needed, depending on how complex the localization project is. The diagram illustrates the cultural values of a targeted culture. Figure 2 shows a theoretical comparison. These diagrams can what changes are necessary and in what dimension, as Smith has demonstrated [Smith] but with different dimensions.

5 Conclusions and Recommendations for Further Research

Generating a set of the most important 7±2 cultural dimensions for localizing UIs is a difficult task. The experts commented that everything depends on knowing the domain and purpose of the UI. Nevertheless, this survey sought to rank culture dimensions in relation to UI design components and to filter out the most important ones, the five dimensions of Context, Technological development, Uncertainty avoidance, Time perception, and Authority conception. Moreover, the original thesis work of Baumgartner provides a compilation of 29 culture dimensions annotated with detailed descriptions and concrete examples of what influence they have on certain domains of UI, and showing the UI design components that are especially affected. The practical result is a grouped and ranked list of cultural dimensions that could form a decision making tool kit in a localization process. A second possible use of the findings is the idea of a diagram tool that could facilitate determining the culture-related changes necessary for localizing to a specific target country. We have also suggested the concept of a culturebase that could automatically or semi-automatically handle cultural changes for content management systems based on these dimensions. In the future, determining the top dimensions for special fields of UI design might be an interesting area of study that could contribute and verify the findings of this work. Developing a database with examples for the implication on each design component by each cultural dimension and gathering cultural values of each country/culture through empirical research could be a supporting work for the culturebase concept. Much remains to be researched. This study is a start.

References

1. Adler, Nancy J.: International dimensions of organizational behavior Cincinnati, Ohio: South-Western/Thomson Learning, 2002.
2. Baumgartner, Valentina-Joanna: A Practical Set of Cultural Dimensions for User-Interface Analysis and Design. Thesis, Fachhochschule Joanneum, Graz, Austria 2003. http://www.mavas.at/val/education05_thesis00.asp
3. Condon, John C., and Yousef, Fathi S.: An Introduction to Intercultural Communication. Indianapolis: Bobbs-Merrill, 1981.
4. del Galdo, Elisa: Culture and Design, In: del Galdo, Elisa M. / Nielsen, Jakob: International User-Interfaces, New York: John Wiley & Sons, 1996, 74-87.
5. Fernandes, Tony: Global Interface Design. A Guide to Designing International User-Interfaces, San Diego, Ca: Acad. Press, 1995.
6. Gould, Emilie W./ Zakaria, Norhayati / Yusof, Shafiz Affendi Mohd: Think Globally, Act Locally: The Role of Culture in Localizing Web Sites for Global Competition, http://www.rpi.edu/~goulde/Abstract.doc, 16 May 2003
7. Hall, Edward T.: Beyond culture, New York: Doubleday 1989.
8. Hall, Edward T.: The dance of life. The Other Dimension of Time, New York: Doubleday 1989.
9. Hall, Edward T.: The hidden dimension, New York: Anchor Books 1990.
10. Hall, Edward T.: The silent language, New York: Doubleday 1990.

11. Hofstede, Geert: Cultures and Organizations: Software of the Mind, London: McGraw-Hill 1991.

12. Hoft, Nancy L.: Communicating the Risks of Natural Hazards: The World-At-Large Is At Stake. http://www.world-ready.com/volcano.htm#power, 15 May 2003

13. Hoft, Nancy L.: Developing a Cultural Model, In: Del Galdo, Elisa M. / Nielsen, Jakob: International User-Interfaces, New York: John Wiley & Sons, 1996, 41-73.

14. Kluckhohn, Florence Rockwood / Strodtbeck, Fred L.: Variations in value orientations, Evanston: Row, Peterson 1961.

15. Laurel, Brenda: Introduction, in: Laurel, Brenda (ed): The Art of Human-computer Interface Design, Boston: Addison-Wesley 2001, xi-xiii.

16. Marcus, Aaron et al.: Globalization of User-Interface Design for the Web. http://zing.ncsl.nist.gov/hfweb/proceedings/marcus/index.html, 10. Apr 2003.

17. Marcus, Aaron, and Gould, Emilie W.: Crosscurrents. Cultural Dimensions and Global Web User-Interface Design, in: interactions 7/8 (2000), 32-46.

18. Marcus, Aaron: Graphical User-Interfaces, chapter 19, in: Helander, Martin / Landauer, Thomas K. / Prabhu, Prasad V. (eds): Handbook of Human-Computer Interaction, Amsterdam: Elsevier 1997, 423-444.

19. Nielsen, Jakob: Internat. Usability Engineering. In: Del Galdo, Elisa M., and Nielsen, Jakob: Internat. User-Interfaces, New York: John Wiley & Sons, 1996, 1-19.

20. Parsons, Talcott: Talcott Parsons on institutions and social evolutions. Selected Writings, Ed. Leon R. Mayhew, Chicago: University of Chicago Press, 1987.

21. Smith, Andy, Chang Yu: Quantifying Hofstede and Developing Cultural Fingerprints for Website Acceptability. *Proc.* IWIPS 2003, Berlin, 89-102.

22. Trompenaars, Fons: Riding the waves of culture. Understanding Cultural Diversity in Business. London: Brealey 1995.

23. Victor, David A: Internati. Business Communication, New York: Prentice Hall 1997.

24. Webster's New Collegiate Dictionary, http://www.m-w.com/, 24. Apr 2003.

25. Wright, Quincy: The Study of International Relations, New York, Appleton-Century-Crofts 1955

26. Yetim, Fahri: Call for papers for *Interacting with Computers*. Journal Special Issue: Global Human-Computer Systems, Email, received 2. Dec 2002.

27. Zaharna, R.S.: Overview: Florence Kluckhohn Value Orientations. http://academic2.american.edu/~zaharna/kluckhohn.htm, last visited 26. Apr 2003.

Towards a General Model for Assisting Navigation

Mike McGavin, James Noble, Robert Biddle, and Judy Brown

School of Mathematical and Computing Sciences
Victoria University of Wellington,
New Zealand,
firstname.lastname@mcs.vuw.ac.nz

Abstract. In this paper, we review the principles of navigation, present a general model for supporting navigation in user interface design, and show examples of how the model can be applied. The model has four different properties along which navigational scenarios can be classified. These are: dimensionality, freedom of movement, presentation and reinforcement. We show how use of the model leads to heuristics to help in the design and evaluation of user interfaces that include navigational aspects.

1 Introduction

Navigation, wayfinding, and the act of getting from one place to another: these have been identified as an increasingly important field of study in human-computer interaction [10]. Much navigational research in HCI has sought to apply psychological theories to specific situations, as we relate below, but it is not common to find work on more general principles for user-interfaces to support navigation. In particular, much navigational research in HCI appears to be about the need to efficiently instruct people on *where to go*, *how to move*, or perhaps *how to manipulate* another object. We contend that although these actions may appear different, many of them are similar in the decisions that are made and the types of information processed to make such decisions. For instance, the decision of when to stop turning a radio tuning dial might be compared with the decision of when to stop clicking "next page" hyperlinks on a website. We also contend that navigation takes place in contexts that allow for movement in different dimensions, and that the navigational task determines how much freedom of movement is available within the context.

We believe that it is useful to gain a better understanding of common patterns about navigation because such an understanding can then help to guide future research about specific problems in a more structured way. Furthermore, we believe that by identifying certain common properties that occur in many navigational tasks, heuristics and guidelines can be identified that will help to design more specific solutions to specific navigational problems.

In this paper, we argue for a single consistent high level model that encompasses many different occurrences of navigation. We present our model, showing how it highlights what we believe to be the major factors of "instructing somebody where to go" in general terms, and outline some case studies of how to apply the model. Observations about these case studies are also shown to demonstrate the possibility of developing

M. Masoodian et al. (Eds.): APCHI 2004, LNCS 3101, pp. 262–271, 2004.

heuristics, and we follow this with an example of how a user interface could be designed by using the model. The conclusions then review the usefulness of our model and present our intentions for future work.

The eventual intent of this model is to assist in designing user interfaces that involve navigation. The content of this paper does not discuss design in detail. Instead we focus on introducing the model, demonstrating how it can be applied to better understand existing interfaces. Where appropriate, we also discuss why certain parts of the model are important for design.

2   Research About Navigation

The word "navigation" is used to describe a broad range of activities, but most such activities are similar in nature. For example, a workshop with attendees from many disciplines [10] identified four main components that generally determine navigation as it is applied today. Navigation involves *locomotion* between one place and another as an *incremental real time process* while *decision making* is taking place. Navigation also happens within a *context*, which is some kind of space that can be moved within. As well as navigation in physical space, the context can also be an "information space" [2]. Browsing the web, for example, is an example of navigating information space.

2.1   Tasks

A key part of navigation is the task. A task may be "to stay on the road", or "to find text on the web about the current weather in London". Tasks can also be hierarchical. For instance, a task is made up of sub-tasks, which are made of more sub-tasks, and so on. This claim is consistent with the *decision plans* described by Passini [17, p53], who claims that people form a hierarchical plan as a prerequisite to wayfinding activities. Having made a decision to go to work, one must also make decisions to leave the house, walk to the car, and drive to work. These tasks again can be divided into more sub-tasks. Such plans are also dynamic in nature — if the car doesn't start, one might need to change their plan and walk to the bus stop instead. Navigation occurs because of a task, even if navigation was not the original intent.

2.2   Movement from Place to Place

Past research, especially in the field of psychology, has investigated and presented theories of how people get from one place to another. A well known model for large scale navigation is the Landmark, Route and Survey model [19] that describes how people use these three main factors to move from place to place.

The well supported theory of cognitive maps, first proposed by Tolman [20], proposes that people and animals mentally store a spatial representation of an area. Although referred to as a map, it is generally agreed that the map is not a literal representation of the world [6,7]. Johns has proposed that cognitive maps could be used to help people remember information by presenting it spatially [9], and this is consistent with Chen and Czerwinski's observation that people built cognitive maps of interactively presented graph data [5]. The published research and literature of cognitive maps is extensive. For further reading, an excellent starting point is the summary provided by Kitchin [11].

Such maps are not always necessary for navigation. Route knowledge is about following cues, or known procedures on encountering landmarks along the route. It is about looking for certain signs in the surrounding environment, knowing what turns to take, and when to take them. Using route knowledge normally doesn't result in a spatial understanding of the area, as noted by Hunt and Waller [8, p23] and supported by Moeser [16]. When used appropriately, however, sign following can provide a very fast way to get between points A and B, as demonstrated by Butler et al. [3].

Another theory that deals with particular instances of navigation is dead reckoning. Dead reckoning navigation relies largely on egocentric information, such as internally measuring distance travelled and angles turned. Lewis has observed dead reckoning techniques used by both Australian Aborigines [12] and Polynesian travellers [13]. A subset of dead reckoning known as "path integration", where the subject primarily keeps track of a homing position rather than the complete route taken, is common among dogs [4,15] and geese [21]. In contrast, it has been suggested that congenitally blind humans form a representation of the entire path travelled, such that it becomes more difficult to locate the starting point as the outbound path becomes more complex [14].

Although these theories explain different methods of getting from place to place, a common theme is that they involve the assessment of information to make decisions about *where to go*. The information may come from a cognitive map, from signs along the route or from egocentric interpretations. The structure and meaning of this information allows a synthesis of the different movement models, as we present in the next section.

3   A General Model of Navigation

This section presents the essential elements of our high level model. The model considers the *context* in which a particular instance of navigation takes place, and the *freedom of movement* of the intended task. It then considers two properties of the signs that are used to accomplish the task, referred to as the *presentation axis* and the *reinforcement axis*.

3.1   Dimensions of Context Space

The *context* space being navigated can be described in terms of its dimensional constraints. The easiest demonstration is in physical space, which can often be divided into categories such as one dimension, two dimensions and three dimensions.

Turning a dial, pushing a lever or scrolling a document up and down, where only two directions of movement are logical, are examples of one dimensional contexts. Two dimensional contexts could be the movement of eyes over a street map, or walking over the surface of the Earth. Yet another class of context is present when a third dimension of depth is involved, such as a bird flying through the sky or a surgeon manipulating a scapel during an operation.

Not every context can be expressed in such simple terms, however. Dimensional constraints can also be affected by other limiting features that restrict movement more arbitrarily, such as walls. This is clearer when describing information space, which often cannot be grouped into broad categories such as the number of dimensions. More relevant is the arrangement of possible exit points and available routes between locations. For example, a small website that contains many heavily inter-linked pages creates a situation where the subject is more free to move from one place to another. Conversely, a large site with very few links between pages may require more movement to traverse from one side of the site to another.

The dimensionality of a context can most easily be defined as the *possibility of movement*. If a context being navigated reduces the possibility of moving beyond certain points, it has lower dimensionality. It is important to consider the context when designing a user interface, because the context defines all of the places where a subject can possibly move, whether correct for the required task or not.

3.2   Freedom of Movement

The *freedom of movement* describes how "free" a subject is to determine their own path *according to the task*. This is distinct from the context, since it describes the constraints of the task rather than the constraints of the world being navigated. A *looser* freedom of movement describes when the subject can choose their own path towards the end goal. A *stricter* freedom of movement describes when the subject must follow a very specific path. With a looser freedom of movement, there are a larger number of successful routes that a subject can take to reach the goal.

If searching the web for certain information, for instance, the task does not dictate a specific route that the user needs to take in order to reach the destination. This denotes a *looser* freedom of movement. Navigating a labyrinth, on the other hand, probably requires a very specific route to be taken in order to reach the goal, denoting a *stricter* freedom of movement. It is important to consider the freedom of movement of tasks when designing a user interface, because it defines the *correct path or paths* that the subject should follow to successfully complete the task.

3.3   Two Axes of Navigation

Our model contains two separate axes to categorise the signs that are used to indicate a direction. The *presentation axis* describes how the information is received by the subject.

– **Active** presentation occurs when the subject is made aware of the sign at any time or can discover it through some superficial action, such as looking at an available indicator.
– **Passive** presentation requires the subject must attempt to move to discover the sign.

The *reinforcement axis* describes if the information is interpreted as telling the subject where to go, or telling the subject where to avoid.

- **Positive** reinforcement indicates a correct direction.
- **Negative** reinforcement indicates an incorrect direction.

As will be shown in the following case studies, these axes can be used to generally describe information that is being used for navigational purposes. ie. Is a subject being informed of where to go, or of where not to go? Does the subject receive this information in advance, or is movement required?

The two axes are important to consider when designing because they describe the *nature* of the signs that are used to instruct a subject of where to go.

4   Case Studies

We believe that it is possible to develop guidelines and heuristics that describe how to construct navigational systems, based on the tasks that will be required. In this section we present some scenarios and derive sample guidelines. We then present an example of a possible user interface design process.

4.1   Scenarios

Animals on a farm must stay within the limits of a designated field. They can openly roam within the field with a *looser freedom of movement*, but may not stray beyond specified boundaries. The first measure taken by the farmer to specify this is to build a fence around the perimeter of the field. The farmer hopes the animals will recognise that they may not walk through the fence, and therefore stay within the bounds of the field. As long as it is recognised as being a boundary, the fence presents an *active presentation* of *negative reinforcement*.

When driving along the highway, lines mark both the lanes and the edges of the road. The driver can see these lines and remain within the designated lane. The lines are another example of *active presentation* of *negative reinforcement*, but this time used with a *stricter freedom of movement*. They provide a predictable structure of where traffic should flow, which helps to prevent accidents.

> **Observation:** *Active presentation* of *negative reinforcement* may work when the task has a *loose freedom of movement* but the subject is restricted from specific locations.

> **Observation:** *Active presentation* of *negative reinforcement* may also be useful for marking edges when a *strict freedom of movement* is required.

Some animals on the farm may not understand or recognise the fence and will try to walk through it or break it down. To cover for these situations the farmer might install an electric fence. When touching it, the animal receives an electric shock, informing it to stay away from the fence. Because the animal needed to attempt movement before receiving the message, the electric shock provides *passive presentation* of *negative reinforcement*, indicating to the animal that it was a bad idea.

If the driver's attention is momentarily diverted on the highway, the driver may stray towards the edge of the road. Luckily however, "rumble lines" are installed on the edge of the road. As the wheels touch the edge, a strong vibration rattles the car, alerting the driver to straighten up and return to the lane.

> **Observation:** When *active presentation* of signs is not available or cannot be understood, more urgent *passive presentation* of signs may be an appropriate alternative.

Academic research is spread over many thousands of publications, indicating a *large context*. One method of learning about a topic could be to simply read everything available on that topic with a *looser freedom of movement*, hoping to stumble on research that is relevant. Finding useful research through such luck describes *passive presentation* of *positive reinforcement* about the current location. This method is often impractical due to time constraints, however, since most available information is unlikely to be useful, yet would still be traversed. Instead, researchers use indexes, citations and search engines for *active presentation* to find *positive reinforcement* about where to look and *negative reinforcement* about where to avoid, creating a *stricter freedom of movement*.

> **Observation:** A *stricter freedom of movement* may apply within a *large context* if most locations are undesirable.

> **Observation:** *Active presentation* of signs can be used to more efficiently guide a subject through a *larger context* with a *stricter freedom of movement*.

A common way to browse the web is to follow cues (in the form of links), that lead to wanted information. The user locates links that present *active positive* hints, indicating that they lead to an interesting page. The user also notes links that present *active negative* hints, indicating that they don't lead to an interesting page. Combining this knowledge may help the user to make more definite decisions about the best place to go.

Internet filtering software is a method that some parents use to prevent children from viewing questionable websites. If the user attempts to view a disallowed website, the software interjects and tells the user that it is blocked. The interjection is *passive presentation* of *negative reinforcement*, because the user had to attempt movement before discovering that it was disallowed. As long as there are only a small number of disallowed websites nearby, the user will not encounter them often. If the user is in a region of the web that has many blocked websites, trying to locate sites that aren't blocked could become tedious since attempted browsing of those sites is needed to discover if they are available.

> **Observation:** *Positive* and *negative* reinforcement may be used simultaneously to more clearly present a path to a desired location.

> **Observation:** *Passive presentation* of *negative reinforcement* is reasonable when the context is large and the disallowed locations are few, but may become tedious if there are many disallowed locations.

An alternative to simply following links to find information on the web is to use a search engine. After searching for a term, the search engine presents a list of pages that provide relevant information. Instead of having to browse the whole web searching for relevant information, the user can now investigate a more restricted list of likely locations, presented down the page. Effectively, the search engine has reduced the possible movement to irrelevant locations in the web, so that most available exit points lead to useful information.

When automobiles were new, it was not unusual for them to be arbitrarily driven over terrain with few constraints and a *looser freedom of movement.* More recently it has become undesirable for cars to be driven in some places, which may be damaged or destroyed if vehicles were to drive over them. City streets are now imposed upon the landscape to define for drivers where they should drive their vehicles. City streets are to the landscape what search engines are to the web. They *reduce the dimensions* of the available landscape so that drivers can't move outside of certain constraints. Although this prevents some actions like driving directly between points A and B, it also prevents drivers from driving on places that shouldn't be driven on.

> **Observation:** When the *context* being navigated is large, *reducing the dimensionality of the context* by removing access to irrelevant or protected locations makes navigation easier.

Car navigational devices can provide *active presentation* of *positive reinforcement* that informs drivers of where to go, given in terms of where the roads are. For example, such a device may inform the driver to turn left at the upcoming intersection. This is largely possible because of the structure of the city streets, which allows instructions such as "take the next turn left" to be meaningful.

The manual focusing dial on a camera lens can be moved in only two directions, indicating a *context of low dimensionality.* When focusing the lens, a photographer turns the focus dial experimentally to see if the focus gets better or worse in that direction. If the image doesn't get sharper, he tries the other direction. If it does get sharper, he continues turning it in that direction until it passes the sharpest focus, at which point he moves it more carefully back to the focused position. The signs that the photographer looks at are *passively presented*, as he simply keeps moving the dial until it is seen to be in the right place. Little effort is needed for the photographer to move the focus dial, and there is only a small context in which it can be moved.

> **Observation:** Signs may be easier to present when the context has *less dimensionality* is present, because with less possible movement within the context there are less possible meanings.

> **Observation:** When the *context* being navigated has a *low dimensionality* and movement takes little effort, *passive presentation* of *positive reinforcement* may be preferred.

4.2   A Preliminary Example of Design

As these case studies suggest, the model can also be considered for designing an interface. Consider a designer who wishes to develop a computerised interface to inform a user of where in the sky to direct an astronomical telescope. The designer could first consider that by its design, the user is able to push the telescope to point towards nearly any direction in the sky. This indicates a loose dimensionality of the context being navigated. The designer may then consider a typical task, which could be to locate a requested star — a specific location in the sky. If the user wished to learn about nearby star patterns, it might be useful for the interface to provide directions for a specific route that went through other interesting night-sky objects on the way, denoting a stricter freedom of movement for the task. Alternatively the user might wish to have more control over the route taken, simply wanting to be continuously informed of the relative location of the star at the end of the route, denoting a looser freedom of movement. By consciously taking into account such considerations the designer can better consider whether to actively provide information about how to get to the star, or to passively inform the user whenever they move their telescope away from an appropriate course.

5   Conclusions

In this paper we reviewed previous specific models for navigation, described our general model, and demonstrated some applications of it in practice. The model itself emphasises several key points about determining a system of instructions:

1. Different contexts may have differing constraints determining how much movement is physically or logically possible. (The context's *dimensionality*.)
2. A given task is carried out within a context. It may impose either strict or loose constraints, depending on how accurately a subject is required to move during the task. (The *freedom of movement*.)
3. We can tell subjects where to go, or where to avoid. (The *reinforcement* axis.)
4. Subjects can either be informed outright, or be required to discover information through movement. (The *presentation* axis.)

While many traditional models focus on how people interact with the environment, our model focuses on how to arrange interfaces to assist navigation from a design perspective. The model itself is high level and does not cover specific instances or methods of giving instructions. Information could be provided as a voice informing the subject where to go, an arrow pointing to a location, a series of beeps for the subject to interpret, or an internally generated cue derived from considering currents on the ocean and making a decision. The decision about specifically how such information should be presented is a separate area of research, and one that has received a significant amount of attention already. We believe, however, that our model provides a different perspective on how to consider the information that is being made available for navigational purposes.

A further area that we are interested in pursuing is the application of semiotics research in combination with this model, and the role that semiosis plays in generating navigational information and instructions. Existing terminology that is commonly used in navigation, such as landmarks, does not immediately translate to signs and directional information. In this way, the subject might generate their own cues through a process of semiosis, as described by Peirce [18, v2] and others, and similar to the way users interpret user interface metaphors [1].

Interwoven with the case studies in section 4 were examples of heuristic guidelines that we have observed, although future work is necessary to develop a more comprehensive list of guidelines. Heuristics would have many potential uses for user interface design, as was demonstrated with the telescope interface example. In particular they would help designers to develop specific interfaces for solving specific navigational problems. A clear area of future work is therefore to further develop heuristics that may apply for user interfaces, based on these properties of navigation. Such heuristics could potentially be extended into a navigation-based methodology for developing user interfaces.

References

1. Pippin Barr, James Noble, and Robert Biddle. *Virtual, Distributed and Flexible Organisations*, chapter A Semiotic Model of User-Interface Metaphor. Kluwer Academic Publishers, 2003.
2. David R. Benyon. Beyond navigation as metaphor. In *Proceedings of 2nd EuroDL conference*, Crete, 1998.
3. D. L. Butler, A. L. Acquino, A. A. Hijsong, and P. A. Scott. Wayfinding by newcomers in a complex building. *Human Factors: The Journal of the Human Factors Society*, 35(1):159–173, 1993.
4. Nicole Chapius and Christian Varlet. Short cuts by dogs in natural surroundings. *The Quarterly Journal of Experimental Psychology*, 39B:49–64, 1987.
5. Chaomei Chen and Mary Czerwinski. Spatial ability and visual navigation: An empirical study. *The New Review for Hypertext and Multimedia*, 3:40–66, 1997.
6. Roger M. Downs. Maps and mapping as metaphors for spatial representation. In Lynn S. Liben, Arthur H. Patterson, and Nora Newcombe, editors, *Spatial representation and behavior across the life span: theory and application*, chapter 6, pages 143–166. New York Academic Press, New York, 1981.
7. R. A. Hart and G. T. Moore. The development of spatial cognition: A review. In R. M. Downs and D. Stea, editors, *Image and Environment: Cognitive Mapping and Spatial Behavior*, chapter 14, pages 246–295. Aldine, Chicago, 1973.
8. Earl Hunt and David Waller. Orientation and wayfinding: A review. Technical report, University of Washington, 1999.
9. Cathryn Johns. Spatial learning: Cognitive mapping in abstract virtual environments. In *Proceedings of Afrigraph 2003*, pages 7–16, Cape Town, South Africa, February 2003. AFRIGRAPH.
10. Susanne Jul and George W. Furnas. Navigation in electronic worlds: A CHI 97 Workshop. In Steven Pemberton, editor, *ACM SIGCHI Bulletin*, volume 29, pages 44–49. ACM, ACM Press, New York, NY, USA, October 1997. Also available online at http://www.si.umich.edu/ furnas/Papers/Nav97_Report.pdf.
11. R. M. Kitchin. Cognitive maps: What they are and why study them? *Journal of Environmental Psychology*, 14(1):1–19, 1994.

12. David Lewis. Observations on route finding and spatial orientation among the aboriginal peoples of the western desert region of central australia. *Oceania*, 46(4):249–282, 1976.

13. David Lewis. *We, the Navigators: The Ancient Art of Landfinding in the Pacific*. The University Press of Hawaii, Honolulu, 2nd edition, 1994.

14. Jack M. Loomis, Roberta L. Klatzky, Reginald G. Golledge, Joseph G. Cicinelli, James W. Pellegrino, and Phyllis A. Fry. Nonvisual navigation by blind and sighted: Assessment of path integration ability. *Journal of Experimental Psychology: General*, 122(1):73–91, 1993.

15. H. Mittelstaedt and M. L. Mittelstaedt. Homing by path integration. In F. Papi and Hans G. Wallraff, editors, *Avian Navigation: International Symposium on Avian Navigation (ISAN) held at Tirrenia (Pisa), September 11-14, 1981*, pages 290–297. Berlin; New York: Springer-Verlag, 1982.

16. Shannon D. Moeser. Cognitive mapping in a complex building. *Environment and Behavior*, 20(1):21–49, 1988.

17. Romedi Passini. *Wayfinding in Architecture*. New York : Van Nostrand Reinhold, 1984.

18. Charles Sanders Peirce. *Collected Papers of Charles Sanders Peirce*. Cambridge: Harvard University Press, 1931-58.

19. A. W. Siegel and S. H. White. The development of spatial representations of large-scale environments. *Advances in Child Development and Behavior*, 10:9–55, 1975.

20. Edward Tolman. Cognitive maps in rats and men. *Psychological Review*, 55(4):198–208, July 1948.

21. Ursula von Saint Paul. Do geese use path integration for walking home? In F. Papi and Hans G. Wallraff, editors, *Avian Navigation: International Symposium on Avian Navigation (ISAN) held at Tirrenia (Pisa), September 11-14, 1981*, pages 298–307. Berlin; New York: Springer-Verlag, 1982.

inlineLink: Realization of Inline Expansion Link Methods on a Conventional Web Browser

Motoki Miura, Buntarou Shizuki, and Jiro Tanaka

Institute of Information Sciences and Electronics, University of Tsukuba
1-1-1 Tennodai, Tsukuba, Ibaraki, 305-8573, Japan
{miuramo,shizuki,jiro}@iplab.is.tsukuba.ac.jp

Abstract. Conventional web browsing displays a web page inside of a window. In conventional web browsing, following a link replaces the previous document entirely, and the readers tend to lose the context. We have developed a system inlineLink, which applies an in-line, expansion-link method to web browsing. This in-line expansion inserts the linked document after the link anchor text. The inlineLink provides navigation mechanisms such as automatic animated scrolling, zooming, and index jumping in order to reduce the scrolling tasks while handling longer, inlined documents. We have adopted Dynamic HTML to implement the inline expansion functions. Casual users can try them on conventional web browsers. The results of our experiment prove the advantages of inlineLink in both click counts and mouse movement.

1 Introduction

Clicking on a link anchor is the most popular and fundamental operation in following links in conventional web browsers. The operation normally replaces the current document with the linked document of the window. When a reader needs to pay attention to both the current and the linked document simultaneously, the reader may choose the "open link in new window" operation to keep both documents open by window duplication. This operation is frequently selected because the linked document is closely related to the current document.

Although the open link in new window operation is effective, the duplicated window usually overlaps the current window. The reader must then change the size and location of the new, and possibly the old window, by dragging the mouse to display both documents. These operations for window management severely distract the reader reading the documents. Alternatively, the reader can drag the link anchor and drop it into another window. The operation enables the reader to specify a target window to be displayed intuitively. This operation, however, only works well if two or more windows have already been arranged on the screen. While reading the documents, the reader is still forced, however, to remember the relationships between the link anchors and the windows in which they are displayed.

M. Masoodian et al. (Eds.): APCHI 2004, LNCS 3101, pp. 272–282, 2004.

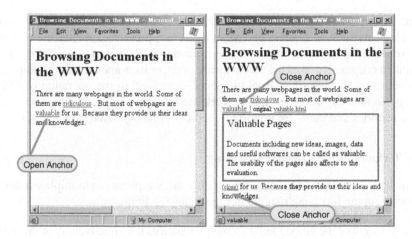

Fig. 1. An example behavior of "activity anchors" in inlineLink

2   Method

To solve these problems, we designed an in-line, expansion-link method and developed "inlineLink"[6], a technique that realizes the in-line, expansion-link method on conventional web browsers.

2.1   In-line, Expansion-Link Method

The in-line, expansion-link method represents a linked document. The linked document is inserted near its link anchor for easy display. In-line expansion is described as "replacement-buttons" in Guide[1], developed by Peter Brown in 1982. When a reader presses the replacement-button, the button or display is altered by the related documents. The reader can then refer to the detail of the document.

Guide handles particular hypertext contents, whereas we applied the replacement-button mechanism to the web documents written in HTML. To enable this function, we developed the "inlineLink" technique. With this technique, anchors in a normal web document are changed to "activity anchors," which perform special functions. The primary activity anchors are "open anchor" and "close anchor." When the open anchor (Figure 1 left) is selected, the linked document is inserted below the anchor. The open anchor then becomes the close anchor. An extra close anchor is deployed at the end of the linked document (Figure 1 right). When one of the close anchors is selected, the linked document and the extra close anchor are removed. The close anchor then reverts to the open anchor. These activity anchors enable the reader to control the appearance of the linked document.

2.2   Representation of Linked Document

In inlineLink, a representation of a linked document insertion is different from Guide, where the replaced document is embedded without any borders. Consequently, the document region is ambiguous. In inlineLink, the inserted document is surrounded by visual elements such as borders and alignments to represent explicitly the regions and their relationship to the document. The explicit representation of region and structure in the linked document makes the reader aware of its position and the relationship between the document. Because the visual elements correspond to the operation of following links performed by the reader, it may work as a history or map of the browsing activity. These histories and maps are important facilities of navigational support[7]D

2.3   Techniques for Effective Browsing

The in-line, expansion-link method can reduce the complexity of multiple window management, but the browsing method has the following limitations.

1. The length of the embedded document influences the effectiveness of the page representation. If the document length is longer, most of the document below the open anchor is obscured.
2. The nested documents generated by repetitive insertion increase. The new, longer document may increase not only the trouble of scrolling but also navigation difficulty. Understanding the whole document structure thus becomes more difficult.

To overcome these limitations, we applied two techniques to inlineLink: (1) partial insertion and (2) navigational support.

Partial Insertion   Partial insertion displays the linked document within the limited height of the embedded internal frame (see Figure 2). The partial insertion technique in inlineLink is effective in the following cases: (a) the area necessary for displaying the linked document is greater than the height of the browser window; (b) the part of the link-base document below the open anchor is crucial for the concurrent browsing task; and (c) displaying an arbitrary part of the linked page is more appropriate for the reader. The reader can change the insertion mode by selecting special activity anchors labeled "partial" or "whole." The height of the region can also be adjusted by selecting special activity anchors labeled "expand" or "shrink" (see Figure 2).

Navigation Supports   Navigation supports reduces difficulties in moving around in longer documents, and in perceiving the current position of the view port. We have prepared three functions for supporting navigation in inlineLink.

(1) Automatic adjustable scrolling function   When the reader selects the open anchor in a lower view-port area, the greater part of the embedded document will not be shown on the screen. To resolve this, we introduced the automatic, adjustable-scrolling function. This function scrolls the whole document upward to make the embedded document visible after insertion. Consequently, the embedded document is placed in the middle of the view port. This function is feasible because the action of anchor selection indicates that the reader takes interest in the linked document, and will focus on the document. If the height of the embedded document is greater than the window height, the top of

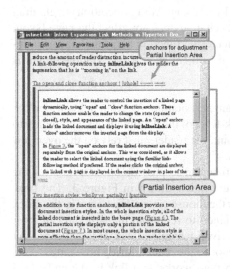

Fig. 2. Partial insertion

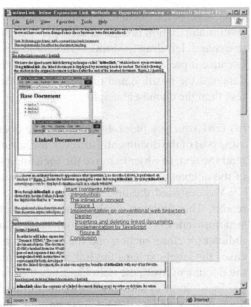

Fig. 3. Zoomed-out document view and a link structure index.

the embedded document is adjusted to the "ceiling" of the view port. In such cases, the inlineLink method has an advantage over conventional browsing because the reader can easily look at the relationship of the documents with a few scrolls. Without the automatic-scrolling function, the reader needs to scroll down (raise the document) frequently after selecting open anchors.

We assigned two additional operations to the embedded document. Clicking on the embedded document causes adjustable scrolling the same as the selection of an open anchor. Double-clicking on the embedded document closes the document. The former operation should lessen the reader's concerns about scrolling. The latter operation allows the reader to dismiss the embedded document instantly if the mouse is located over the document.

To reduce the cognitive efforts, the adjustable scrolling is animated. In addition to inserting the open anchors, we applied animation to the close anchors. When the close anchor is selected, the embedded document shrinks until it disappears. If the original open anchor is located above the view port, the inlineLink scrolls the document downward to reveal the open anchor. These techniques make it easier for the reader to concentrate on the document.

(2) Document-zooming function When the reader repeatedly selects open anchors, the document is nested, and becomes longer. Understanding of the longer document becomes more difficult. To alleviate the length problem, we applied the document-zooming function. The document-zooming function enables users to manipulate the

zoom level of the document. Figure 3 shrinks the original document by 70%. The zoom-level manipulation is continuously performed by horizontal drag operations (right drag to expand, left drag to shrink). The zoom-level change does not affect the page layout because it preserves the position of the new line. This function helps the reader to understand the position and the structure of the document even if the window height is less than the document height.

(3) Link structure indexing function The document-zooming function helps widen the view port of the document. However, the shrink-level of the document has a boundary to read the text. In order to move the focusing point, the reader must rely on the overview of the document for finding the target position.

We designed the link structure indexing function to provide an overview for the reader. This function displays the link-structure index shown in Figure 3. The link-structure index is shown as a pop-up layer near the mouse cursor. Each item in the index indicates a close anchor, and the items are aligned to represent the structure. In most cases the label explains the linked document. Even when the label does not represent the document itself, the item identifies the anchor to the reader during browsing.

In addition to showing the structure, each item works as a link to the embedded document. When a reader selects an item, the view port of the document scrolls with an animated effect similar to the selection of an open anchor. In the current design of inlineLink, selection of the pop-up layer of the link structure index is assigned to a keyboard shortcut.

3   Implementation

We developed the inlineLink technique to enable both readers and page-content producers to easily browse using the in-line expansion-link method. We employed Dynamic HTML technology for enabling insertion and deletion on a conventional web browser. The document objects are specified based on the DOM[2] and standardized by the W3C. Using Dynamic HTML technology, a script written in a language such as JavaScript can handle the document based on the DOM. However, this approach may limit design for visual representation when compared with an implementation that is tightly coupled with a browser system. We regard portability and popularity as equally important when using the in-line expansion-link method.

3.1   Processes of Insertion and Deletion

The fundamental activities of inlineLink are insertion and deletion, corresponding to an open anchor and a close anchor respectively. These characteristics are implemented by the following two processes.

1. Retrieve source of the linked document
2. Replace source of the document.

It should be noted that deletion does not require retrieval, while inlineLink only requires replacement. To retrieve the arbitrary linked-document source, we utilize an "inline frame" element (iframe) defined by HTML 4.0 Transitional DTD[10]. To replace the source of the document, we used insert_page() and remove_page() functions in JScript. The technical details of these function are described in [6].

3.2 How to Convert inlineLink Documents

To browse an HTML document with the in-line expansion-link method, anchors in the document should be replaced with the open anchor. In addition to replacing the anchors, the document should import the inlineLink script to enable insert_page() and remove_page() functions.

One plain solution to fulfill these condition is to use a rewriting filter that converts an ordinary HTML page into an inlineLink page. However, we believe the original HTML source should be kept as it is, since the pre-conversion of the source may reduce its simplicity and maintainability. Accordingly, we have prepared the following two methods to dynamically convert an HTML source.

Script of inlineLink (by Content Producers) The inlineLink script is equipped with a dynamic anchor rewriting function. The built-in function converts an ordinary anchor into an open anchor before the source is pasted into the div element.

The content producer can provide an inlineLink-enabled page by preparing a "meta-index page." The meta-index page includes an open anchor to the original index page. The content producer does not have to convert the original anchors in either the index page or the other contents. The readers can choose their favorite type of document by entering either the original index page or the meta-index page. If the reader chooses the meta-index page, the anchor tags in the linked page are automatically replaced as open anchors. The replacement is a trivial task performed as a local process. The replacement is performed recursively so that the reader can continue browsing with inlineLink.

On-Demand Conversion with inlineLink Servlet (by Readers) The method in the above section (3.2) applies when the content producer has prepared the meta-index pages. If no meta-index page is presented, the reader cannot utilize the in-line version of the content.

We have implemented an inlineLink Servlet that converts anchors in the HTML source from an arbitrary site into open anchors. The converter Servlet (inlineServlet) obtains the source of the requested URI. Then it parses the source with our HTML parser. The inlineServlet converts ordinary anchors into open anchors, and replaces URIs in each anchor as requests for the inlineServlet. As a result, all requests from anchors converted by the inlineServlet go through the inlineServlet. Since an inlineServlet is designed to work with a common servlet container, the reader can install an inlineServlet at any computers including a PC.

With the inlineServlet bootstrap page, the reader only needs to specify the URI in the form and press the [convert] button. The reader can continue browsing with in-line expansion-link method because the page content of each request is converted by the inlineServlet. Furthermore, the reader can bookmark the URI including the request to the inlineServlet.

4   Experiments

To measure the effectiveness of the inlineLink in page browsing tasks, we performed a usability and performance study on 12 subjects. We conducted the usability test on an 850 MHz portable notebook PC powered by Windows 2000, with 384MB RAM, XGA display (1024×768 pixels), and a two-button mouse with a wheel.

Microsoft Internet Explorer (IE) 6.0 performed all tasks. We maximized the IE window, showing the standard buttons. We then compared the following three conditions.

- [normal] is the basic feature of the IE. Subjects were allowed to use "back" and "forward" button.
- [inline] is the in-line expansion-link method. Subjects used the inlineLink without an automatically adjustable scrolling function.
- [inline (adjust)] is similar to the [inline], but subjects browsed the inlineLink document with the automatic adjustment scrolling function.

To record the data, we developed a tiny counter tool[1] that hooks Windows' system events. We measured (1) the number of mouse button clicks, (2) the distance of mouse-pointer move, (3) the distance of the mouse pointer drag, (4) the amount of wheel rotation, and (5) working time.

Experiment 1 (Glossary)   We prepared a CGI-based glossary site to evaluate the inlineLink while browsing relatively short web documents. The glossary includes computer and internet terms. An anchor represents the inlineLink term in the glossary, which is written in Japanese. We asked each subject to answer 12 questions. Each question is designed so that the subject must refer to at least two explanations of terms. An example question is "Which organization was established earlier, ISO or IEC?" The subjects start with a page that includes the questions and links to the related terms. The height of the document, which inserts all related terms, is up to six times greater than the height of the browser window.

Experiment 2 (StyleGuide)   To measure the effects of a greater number of documents, we employed a Japanese translation of "Style Guide for Online Hypertext" authored by Tim Berners-Lee[2]. The document consists of 28 pages, 23 of which can be followed by index. Others are supplemental topics followed by a description of the document. The height of the document, which inserts all document, is about 50 times greater than the height of the browser window.

We prepared 15 questions divided into three subtasks. The first 10 questions simply require finding the sentences in lines. The last five questions require a detailed understanding of the document. An example question is "What is the ideal length of a title in characters?" A subject must answer by referencing the sentence in the document, "The title should be less than 64 characters in length."

---

[1] http://www.iplab.is.tsukuba.ac.jp/˜miuramo/wheelcounter/
[2] http://www.kanzaki.com/docs/Style/ (translation)
  http://www.w3.org/Provider/Style/ (original)

Table 1. Result of paired t-test

Experiments	methods compared	mouse click	mouse move	time	wheel up	wheel down	mouse drag	significant border (5%)
Glossary	normal - inline	+4.52	+3.47	(+1.65)	-2.40	-4.37	+3.05	1.80
Glossary	normal - adjust	+4.62	+3.31	(+1.15)	(-1.60)	(-1.72)	+2.96	1.80
Glossary	inline - adjust	(+0.32)	(+0.71)	(-0.46)	(+0.53)	+2.12	(-0.89)	1.80
StyleGuide	normal - inline	(+0.93)	+2.12	(+1.12)	(-0.36)	(+0.62)	(+1.74)	1.80
StyleGuide	normal - adjust	(-0.26)	(+1.26)	(+0.04)	-2.52	(+0.30)	+2.38	1.80
StyleGuide	inline - adjust	(-1.38)	(-1.66)	(-1.41)	-2.06	(-0.45)	(+1.30)	1.80

Observations and results First we described the activities of subjects after observation. During the test, the height of the working window with inlineLink was two to three times greater than the window height in the Glossary. In the StyleGuide, the height was 10 to 20 times greater than the window height.

In the [normal] method, subjects were allowed to utilize any mouse operations including open link in new window, move/resize of window, and drag the anchor and drop it to another window. As a result, half of the subjects chose the "open link in new window" operation in the Glossary. The subjects who opened one window and dropped anchors could effectively finish the tasks. The subjects who opened more than one window took much more time in management tasks such as moving, resizing, and overlapping. Some subjects lost the original window while handling other similar windows.

Table 1 indicates the result of the paired t-test ($p = 0.05$). The t-values without parentheses indicate the significance between two compared methods. The "+" mark represents results that show the right-hand method is better (less) than the left-hand method, whereas the "−" shows the opposite.

In the Glossary task, both [inline] and [inline(adjust)] significantly reduced the mouse click count ($t = 4.52, p = 0.05$) and the distance of the mouse move ($t = 3.47, p = 0.05$). The reason may depend on the ratio of linked-document height to window height. In the Glossary task, few subjects closed the inserted documents.

In the StyleGuide task, only the [inline] method reduces the distance of the mouse move significantly ($t = 2.12, p = 0.05$). One of the reasons why [inline] did not decrease the mouse click count in the StyleGuide is that some participants frequently used "closing by double click" instead of using the close anchor. In the [inline(adjust)] task, the automatic scrolling function may generate a gap between the mouse pointer and the close anchor. The gap encourages double clicking and discourages selection of the close anchor.

Although the average working time tended to decrease with the inlineLink, the data does not illustrate the significance of using our technique. In our experiment, each task completion time included some extra working time such as reading, understanding and forgetting, besides the pure operating time. The extra working time may distort the effects.

In the StyleGuide task, the [inline(adjust)] method significantly increased the mouse wheel rotation ($t = 2.52, p = 0.05$). The reason of this phenomenon is that the subjects tried to scroll upward against the automatic scrolling. In the Glossary task, the wheel rotation significantly increased (upward $t = 2.40$, downward $t = 4.37$) with the [inline] method. This result does not indicate the disadvantage in the inlineLink method because the Glossary document is too short to display the scroll bars with the [normal] method. In the StyleGuide document, the wheel rotations are frequently used even in the [normal] method. The amount of the downward wheel rotation with the inlineLink method is restrained to minimize the significance. As an exception, the upward wheel rotation increased with the [inline(adjust)] method in the StyleGuide task. The result derives from the insufficiency of the automatic scrolling function. The downward scrolling at insertion is straightforward, whereas the upward scrolling at deletion has not been tuned for these experiments, so the subjects should perform some wheel-up operations after the deletion.

To summarize the results of the experiments, the in-line link method significantly reduced the mouse click counts and the distance of the mouse movements where the embedded documents were short. The automatic scrolling function also reduced the amount of downward wheel rotations.

After the experiments, we interviewed the subjects. Some subjects commented that the automatic upward scrolling at deletion is necessary. Most of the subjects answered that "double click to close" is feasible, but a few subjects said that there is an alternative for mapping close functions. The comments regarding the effectiveness of the inlineLink include "useful if the embedded document is shorter" and "I might switch from [normal] to [inline] depending on the situation."

5   Related Works

LinkPreview[5] produces a pop-up balloon window to display a thumbnail of the linked document near the anchor when the pointer is over the anchor. HyperScout Linktool[9] takes a similar approach. It produces a pop-up balloon window that contains information about the linked page, such as its title, author, language, time last visited, and server status. Neither of these approaches supports reading of hierarchically organized hypertexts. In contrast, the inlineLink technique allows readers to read multiple pages in a hypertext hierarchy by inserting two or more linked pages into the current one.

Fluid Links[11,12] proposed several kinds of displays to add information about a linked page. The inlineLink uses a portable implementation technique that produces an effect similar to Fluid Link's *inlining* without any modification to the web browser.

SmallBrowse[8] is a Programming by Example (PBE) system that suggests a link to be selected by considering the reader's web browsing history. The targeted display of this system is a small display such as a PDA. SmallBrowse reduces the selection tasks by indicating predicted links as pop-up windows called "tip help." The objective of the SmallBrowse is similar to that of inlineLink. SmallBrowse works effectively, especially for recurrent browsing, whereas inlineLink can control the granularity of the browsing information specialized for structured documents.

The Elastic Windows[3,4] method allows readers to open, close, or replace pages as required to support typical browsing tasks. For example, a single operation can open multiple windows, each corresponding to a link on the current page. All of the windows are displayed simultaneously, and the placement and size of the windows are automatically set as part of the operation. This operation allows the reader to browse effectively, while at the same time eliminating a considerable number of step-by-step operations such as "following a link" and selecting the "Back" or "Forward" buttons. Elastic Windows thus successfully removes a significant number of tedious window operations. However, readers have to remember the relationship between the pages that are shown in the multiple windows, and the reader can only select the one operation that is most appropriate for him. In our approach, relationships are explicit, since every linked document is inserted directly into the current page right after its anchor. Also, since the representation is so simple, the reader only has to choose between the opening and closing operations.

6 Conclusions

We described the in-line, expansion-link method and inlineLink, which applies the method to commonly used web documents. Using the inlineLink significantly reduces the use of the "Back" button while browsing a web document is. The feature is quite simple but powerful and effective in enabling readers to concentrate on the context of the web document itself. As the inlineLink is designed to work on conventional web browsers and web documents, the readers can easily apply the interface for their browsing tasks. The empirical study revealed the advantage of the inlineLink that can reduce both the number of mouse button clicks and the distance of the mouse movement.

The inlincLink scripts and servlets are available from the following URI.
http://www.iplab.is.tsukuba.ac.jp/~miuramo/inlinelink/

References

1. P. J. Brown. Turning Ideas into Products: The Guide System. In *Hypertext'87 Proceedings*, pages 33–40, Nov. 1987.
2. Document Object Model (DOM) Level 2 Specification. (Web Page), May 2000. http://www.w3.org/TR/DOM-Level-2/cover.html.
3. E. Kandogan and B. Shneiderman. Elastic Windows: A Hierarchical Multi-Window World-Wide Web Browser. In *Proceedings of the 10th annual ACM Symposium on User Interface Software and Technology (UIST'97)*, pages 169–177, Oct. 1997.
4. E. Kandogan and B. Shneiderman. Elastic Windows: Evaluation of Multi-Window Operations. In *conference proceedings on Human factors in computing systems (CHI'97)*, pages 250–257, Mar. 1997.
5. T. Kopetzky and M. Mühlhäuser. Visual Preview for Link Traversal on the WWW. In *Proceedings of the 8th International World Wide Web Conference (WWW8) / Computer Networks 31 (11-16)*, pages 1525–1532, 1999.
6. M. Miura, B. Shizuki, and J. Tanaka. inlineLink: Inline Expansion Link Methods in Hypertext Browsing. In *Proceedings of 2nd International Conference on Internet Computing (IC'2001)*, volume II, pages 653–659, June 2001.
7. J. Nielsen. *Multimedia and Hypertext: The Internet and Beyond*, chapter 9, pages 247–278. AP Professional, 1995.
8. A. Sugiura. Web Browsing by Example. In H. Lieberman, editor, *Your Wish is My Command – Programming by Example –*, chapter 4, pages 61–85. Morgan Kaufmann Publishers, 2001.

9. H. W. R. Weinreich and W. Lamersdorf. Concepts for Improved Visualization of Web Link Attributes. In *Proceedings of the 9th International World Wide Web Conference (WWW9) / Computer Networks 33 (1-6)*, pages 403–416, 2000.
10. World Wide Web Consortium (W3C). HTML 4.01 Specification. (Web Page), Dec. 1999. http://www.w3.org/TR/html401/.
11. P. T. Zellweger, B.-W. Chang, and J. Mackinlay. Fluid Links for Informed and Incremental Link Transitions. In *Proceedings of HyperText'98*, pages 50–57, 1998.
12. P. T. Zellweger, S. H. Regli, J. D. Mackinlay, and B.-W. Chang. The Impact of Fluid Documents on Reading and Browsing: An Observational Study. In *Proceedings of the CHI 2000 conference on Human factors in computing systems (CHI'00)*, pages 249–256, Apr. 2000.

Chromotome: A 3D Interface for Exploring Colour Space[1]

Giovanni Moretti, Paul Lyons, and Mark Wilson

Institute of Information Sciences and Technology, Massey University, Private Bag 11-222,
Palmerston North, New Zealand,
P.Lyons/G.Moretti@massey.ac.nz

Abstract. When continuous 3D shapes or enclosed structures, such as solid objects or skeletons, are mapped onto a 2D screen, simplifications such as hulls and wire frames are suitable visualization tools, because most or all of the information is concentrated along discontinuities that occupy only a small proportion of the space. Visualizing a colour space is more difficult. Colour spaces are three-dimensional solids with no discontinuities, and every point in such a space represents a unique colour. A colour space visualization tool must therefore facilitate the exploration of a *solid, continuous, three-dimensional* shape. Here we describe Chromotome, a software tool that has been developed for this purpose. Chromotome provides a cutaway view of a spherical colour space, and has controls for rotating the space (to alter the hues displayed), for altering the shape of the cutaway, and for visualizing sets of colours positioned according to simple geometrical relationships within the space.

1 Introduction

The authors are developing the Colour Harmoniser [1], a tool that assists users to select groups of harmonious colours for use in computer interfaces. It calculates an abstract colour scheme, based on several parameters associated with the components of the interface. The Colour Harmoniser needs an interface component that will enable the user to visualise and explore the three-dimensional colour space. The present paper describes Chromotome, the first prototype of that component.

1.1 The Colour Harmoniser

Conventional heuristics for choosing colour scheme are often represented as simple rigid wireframe shapes overlaid onto a colour circle. The wireframes correspond to common rules for colour harmony (lines represent the rules for monochromatic, achromatic, and complementary colour schemes, a Y shape represents split complementary colour schemes, and an oval represents polyadic colour schemes, particularly triadic and tetradic schemes [2]). They can be thought of as a rigid framework for a sort of multi-barrel eyedropper (see Fig. 1); the colours selected are the colours at the points of intersection between the wireframe and the colour circle.

---

[1] In full colour at www-ist.massey.ac.nz/plyons/papers/Moretti Lyons and Wilson 2004.pdf

M. Masoodian et al. (Eds.): APCHI 2004, LNCS 3101, pp. 283-292, 2004.

The Colour Harmoniser presents an *abstract colour scheme* as a set of nodes on a rigid wireframe in a three dimensional colour space. The user can manoeuvre the wireframe within the colour space until, in the user's opinion, the positions of the nodes correspond to a satisfactory set of colours – a *concrete colour scheme* – for the interface components. The development of the Colour Harmoniser has been influenced by the following considerations;

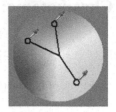

Fig. 1: A wireframe as a "multi-barrel eye-dropper"

- Technological progress (specifically, the development of computers) has made it feasible to use a sophisticated mathematical model of colour harmony to support the generation of a harmonious set of colours.
- Choosing colours is the business of the user, not a mathematical model, so the user should have access to an interface in which prospective sets of colours that are consistent with the model of colour harmony can be seen in the context of the complete colour space, and easily changed.
- Distances in the colour solid and the wireframe used to represent colour schemes should maintain a constant proportionality with respect to human perception of colour differences.
- Choosing a new set of colours should be nearly instantaneous, and the user should instantly see feedback in the real interface.

1.2 Problems with Current Tools

Elsewhere [3], we have noted that the interfaces to currently available tools for selecting harmonious sets of colours [4-11] suffer from a number of drawbacks. First, the colour wheels they use have significant brightness variations, caused by using naïve algorithms for generating the colours on the wheels. These algorithms fail to take into account the fact that CRTs produce the primary colours (Red, Green and Blue) by turning on a single phosphor, and the secondary colours (Cyan, Magenta, and Yellow) by turning on two phosphors [12]. Consequently, the secondaries they display are significantly brighter than the primaries. When wireframes are overlaid on these colour wheels and rotated to produce colours, they will produce colour sets that vary in brightness.

Secondly, their two-dimensional colour wheels do not display the full three-dimensional structure of the colour universe. Though there is still argument about exactly how colour sensations derive from physical input [13], the human perceptual system is generally considered [14, 15] to derive a three dimensional colour sensation *via* a chain of conversions. The spectral power distribution of light entering the eye is converted by cones in the retina into (R, G, B) amplitude signals bounded by the maximum cone response. Still in the retina, ganglia detect linear combinations of the (R, G, B) signals and use these to modulate the frequencies of three electrical spike sequences that can be modelled as a (*dark-bright, red-green, yellow-blue*) triple in a Cartesian coordinate system.

The pulse trains generated by the retinal ganglia enter the brain where they are transferred *via* the Lateral Geniculate Body to the visual cortex. There they are converted into a percept that is usually represented as a point in a bounded 3D space with pair of polar axes (rotational angle representing hue, and radial distance representing saturation) and a Cartesian axis (representing *brightness*), orthogonal to the first two. In the conversion from gangliar space to perceptual space, the orthogonal (*red-green, yellow-blue*) duple has become the polar (*hue, saturation*) duple, and the angular hue dimension of the space roughly corresponds to the periphery of a colour conventional wheel.

Our level of understanding of this chain decreases at the later stages, but there is evidence that hue and saturation are genuine psychological constructs [13]. Each (hue, saturation, brightness) triple in this three-dimensional coordinate system corresponds to a unique colour, except that, at the extremes of the brightness scale, our perception of high saturation colours diminishes, so an accurate representation of the human colour space needs to come to a point at the extremes of light and dark. Colour space is thus often modelled as a sphere or bicone [12].

These symmetrical models broadly conform to our knowledge of human colour perception, but their symmetry, though appealing, has no empirical basis. It is, in fact, contradicted by measurements of human response to colour [16]. In a colour space based on empirical measurements of human subjects, full saturation yellow is positioned above and out from the "equator" (that is, it's brighter and strongly coloured), whereas full saturation blue and red, being less bright and less strongly coloured, occur below and set in from the equator. These corrections to the symmetric "ideal" result in significant warping of both biconical and spherical models.

Of the currently available tools [3] that provide a visualisation of the colour space, most show it as a simple circular colour wheel, and incorporate only the full saturation hues that are dispersed around the "equator" of the colour solid. The more ambitious show a disc with full saturation colours at the periphery and a range of less saturated colours inside, decreasing to grey in the centre. One tool distorts of the skin of the colour sphere, stretching it out to form a disc, with the white pole in the centre, and as the radius increase it successively displays the tints, the full saturation colours, the shades, and finally black distributed around the periphery.

A colour selection algorithm that relies on choosing colours where a wireframe intersects these circles and discs is inherently restricted; the vast majority (over 99%) of perceivable colours are not represented on the colour wheel or disc, so they cannot form part of the colour scheme. A number of the applications provide slider controls that allow the user to alter the saturation and brightness of the colours after their hue has been selected but this is no substitute for seeing them *in situ* in a high quality visualisation. It's precisely the colours that aren't represented in the simple colour wheels – medium and low saturation, intermediate, nameless colours (artists cheat by calling them coloured greys) – that people find most difficult to visualise, to specify, and to distinguish between, but which combine well in colour schemes.

A final problem with the colour selection applications that we have surveyed is that none maintain perceptual uniformity - a pair of fixed points on a wireframe should always appear to have a colour difference of the same magnitude when the wireframe is rotated. As described by Munsell [16], harmonious sets of colour schemes can be automatically produced from conventional monochrome, complementary, split colour complementary and similar heuristics, but for these heuristics to work reliably, they need to take human perception into account. Then, when a wireframe is used as a sort of multi-eyedropper to select a set of colours with a defined geometrical relationship

Fig. 2: The three top images show external views of the L*u*v* colour solid; the others show the Wilson Colour Cutaway at various rotations

in the colour solid, the colour differences between the members of the set will always correspond to identical differences in colour in human perception. This will maintain the differences between differently coloured objects. Mathematical interpolation techniques will not reliably find harmonious sets of colours if distances in the space are not consistently proportional to the only meaningful unit of colour difference, the human JND (Just Noticeable Difference) [17].

Note that perceptual uniformity in colour selection does not have to be enforced by displaying the wireframe in a perceptually uniform colour space (a colour space in which a given distance d in any part of the space, will always correspond to a given multiple of JND units). However, it can alternatively be enforced by displaying a perceptually non-uniform space with a pleasing shape - a spherical space, for example. This space will exhibit various distortions with respect to perceptual uniformity at various locations; if equal distortions are applied to the parts of the wireframe laid over the colour space, then any colours selected from the space by virtue of their position under the wireframe will have a harmonious relationship to each other in undistorted colour space. Although this may seem an unlikely way to enforce perceptual uniformity, it avoids the extremely disconcerting shapes that correspond to an accurate mapping of human colour perception.

An automatic tool for selecting sets of harmonious colours needs to work with a mathematically tractable visualisation of the three-dimensional, perceptually uniform, colour solid. The CIE L*a*b* colour solid is mathematically tractable and approximately perceptually uniform. The tool should be able to project wireframes representing colour heuristics onto the visualisation, and it should be easy to reposition them.

2   The Three 3D Colour Selection Interfaces

We have implemented three experimental interfaces for this task.

2.1 The Wilson Colour Cutaway$_A$

The first of these, the Wilson Colour Cutaway$_A$ [18], Fig. 2, shows a cutaway view of the L*u*v* perceptually uniform colour space [12] based on an image in Faber Birren's encyclopaedic *Color* [14]. The cutaways produced internal surfaces onto which the wireframes representing colour heuristics were to be projected, and the cutaway could be rotated to allow a wireframe to be positioned anywhere in the space. However, the highly asymmetrical shape of the L*u*v* space caused an unexpected problem; when the cutaway view was rotated, various projections on the shape appeared and disappeared from view. The profile alterations that resulted from this (the static images in Fig. 2 convey a muted impression of the extent of this problem) were so distracting as to render the Wilson Colour Cutaway unsuitable.

2.2 Wilson Colour Cutaway$_B$

A second version of the Wilson Colour Cutaway that attempted to make use of the L*u*v* space was also abandoned. This involved trimming off the projecting corners to display only the spherical core of the L*u*v* solid. Unfortunately, the original shape of the L*U*V* colour solid is so bizarre that when only the spherical core was retained, very little remained. And a partial trim, to retain a larger proportion of more highly saturated colours, still produced strange and disquieting shapes when rotated.

2.3 Chromotome

In Chromotome[2], the third interface, we have therefore taken a step back from our original plan to display the highly irregular perceptually uniform colour solid. Chromotome is based on a more conventional, non-perceptually uniform, rotationally symmetric colour sphere.

Chromotome was developed in accordance with the second consideration listed for the Colour Harmoniser in the introduction - that the user should have access to an interface in which prospective sets of colours that are consistent with the model of colour harmony can be seen in the context of the complete colour space, and easily changed.

This presented us with two problems. First, while the human perceptual system can be considered to treat colours as occupying a three-dimensional space, ordinary users and application developers do not have a conscious understanding of the shape of the space, nor the meaning or disposition of the axes within the space. Secondly,

---

[2] The name Chromotome is formed from χρώμα, *chroma*, color + τομος *tomos*, a cut, because the visualization implemented by the tool shows a cutaway view of the three-dimensional colour space.

these target users do not generally wish to learn colour theory or to develop an in-depth familiarity with colour spaces. Consequently, Chromotome has been designed to expose and "explain" the colour space.

2.4 An Exploratory Visualisation

Providing colour users with a visualisation of the interior of a 3D colour solid is a challenging task. Generally, when continuous 3D shapes or enclosed structures, such as solid objects or skeletons, are mapped onto a flat screen, simplifications such as hulls and wire frames are suitable

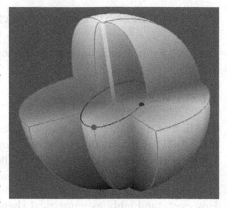

Fig. 3: The Chromotome shows a cutaway view of a colour solid

visualization tools, because most or all of the information in the space is concentrated along discontinuities. We visualise the "space" by visualising the discontinuities, which occupy only a small proportion of the space. Colour spaces are different. The three-dimensional volume of a colour space is information-rich, and feature-poor. It is information-rich because each point in the space specifies a unique colour, and feature-poor because there are no discontinuities that can be visualised as edges. A colour space visualization tool must therefore facilitate the exploration of the interior of a *solid, continuous, three-dimensional* shape.

The Chromotome has been designed to facilitate this task. The cutaway view is designed to give the user an idea of how the colours vary in each of the three dimensions of the space, so that a single control can be used to cycle through all the possible colours in the space. The cutaway view of the solid has been dissected so that it reveals a significant portion of a familiar colour wheel (the "equatorial plane" in Fig. 3). This colour wheel is tilted about at 80^0 to the plane of the screen (though the user can reorient it), so it only occupies a small amount of screen area. The remainder of the display shows vertical cuts through the colour solid up to the White Pole and down to the Black Pole. These show brightness and saturation variations, and, by rotating the hues – a simple mouse interaction - the user can show all possible colours on the vertical surfaces of the visualisation. The colour wheel puts the vertical faces into context, and the vertical faces allow the user to see and choose "difficult" colours in an intelligent fashion. To aid visualisation, a real-time animation, controlled by the mouse, allows the user to view the colour solid from any angle. The slight tilt in Fig. 3 is intentional – the image is easier to interpret when viewed from a slight angle.

The cutaway visualisations also help with the second problem mentioned above - that colour spaces are more difficult to map onto a flat screen than many other three-dimensional shapes, because colour spaces are information-rich, and feature-poor. However, even with the visual cueing given by the cutaways, it has been found beneficial to accentuate the edges with lines. The featurelessness of the space makes the edges difficult to deduce when the image is not being animated. Lines are a simple and effective aid.

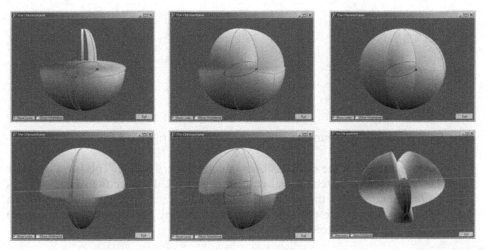

Fig. 4: The cutaway angle can be varied to reveal differing parts of the inside of the colour space, and the space can be viewed from any angle.

2.5 Controlling the Chromotome Visualisation

The user has three ways of controlling the Chromotome interface; altering the viewing angle by rotating the solid, exposing different colours by rotating the colours within the solid, and changing the angle of the cutaway.

The user rotates the colour solid by dragging on the window surface with the left mouse button, and rotates the colour within the solid by dragging on the window surface with the right mouse button. Opening and closing the cutaway angle is currently associated with the thumbwheel on the mouse.

These controls are primitive but the initial investigation has been into the value of the cutaway visualisation. Even with the simplistic controls, the insight and naturalness of using an interactive and animated 3D visualisation as a way of selecting colours has been immediately apparent.

2.6 The Chromotome Geometry

The cutaway visualisation originally produced by Birren lacks a flat surface for displaying the wireframes for split complementary and polyadic colour schemes. A central elliptical region was added to act as a surface, both to "support" the wireframe and to give context to the colours selected by the wireframe. This region (shown in Fig. 3) is created by scooping out the horn that projects up from the "equatorial plane" to form a cutaway that resembles a Sydney Opera House roofline.

Handles on the central ellipse allow it to be tilted from left to right, and from front to back (see Fig. 5). When it is tilted, the "equatorial plane" is redrawn to be coplanar with the ellipse (so strictly, the plane is only equatorial when the ellipse is horizontal).

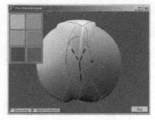

Fig. 5: The angle of wireframe can be tilted from left to right and from front to back

The outer surface of the solid has been maintained as a sphere. This is reassuringly familiar, and when the internal oval is tilted or rotated, disconcerting shape changes like the ones produced by the Wilson Colour Cutaway are avoided. It also provides a larger display surface for the vertical faces to display the intermediate (internal) colours than a biconical projection.

2.7 Using the Chromotome for Harmonious Colour Schemes

The Chromotome interface has been designed to allow the Colour Harmoniser to show colour scheme wireframes on the central ellipse. The axes of the ellipse can be given any orientation within the space, and the surface can display linear, Y-shaped and oval wireframes. Thus any type of harmonious colour scheme, involving colours from anywhere within the space, with any orientation, can be generated.

Colour harmony selectors that use a wireframe overlaid on a simple colour wheel usually generate a restricted set of colours. For example, a split complementary wireframe will commonly generate a colour scheme with three colours, corresponding to the intersection points between the wireframe and the colour wheel. Sometimes a separate palette of colours is generated by the application, but the user does not have a great deal of control over their colour relationships. Because the Chromotome shows the intermediate colours that the wireframe passes through, it will be possible to put an arbitrary number of eyedroppers anywhere along the wireframe and select as many colours as are necessary for the interface. Similarly, the Chromotome allows the ends of the wireframe to occur at low or high saturation colours, so the user has a much greater degree of control of the appearance of the selected colours. The orientation of the ellipse can be altered quickly and simply to update a complete colour scheme.

The images in Fig. 5 show the Chromotome in use. The wireframe illustrated is the Y-shape of a split-complementary colour scheme, with an additional colour being selected from the midpoint of each arm of the Y. Thus the Chromotome is being used to select six colours. As the user changes the orientation of the wireframe, the six selected colours are displayed continuously, in a palette in the upper left corner of the window.

Although the wireframe and the ellipse could be positioned within the colour space independently, fixing the wireframe on the ellipse reduces interface complexity (there are fewer degrees of freedom) and provides context for the colour selected by the wireframe. Tilting the oval front-to-back produces schemes with varying lightness (Fig. 5). Altering the overall size of the oval enables colour schemes of varying saturation to be created.

Two handles (the two dark dots on the edge of the oval in Fig. 3) control its aspect ratio and its tilt. One handle enables the user to change the size and aspect ratio of the oval from a 9:1 ellipse to a circle; the other alters the front-to-back and sideways tilt.

After only a few minutes of experimenting, naïve users can use these controls to vary a colour scheme in a sophisticated way, without endangering the harmony of the scheme.

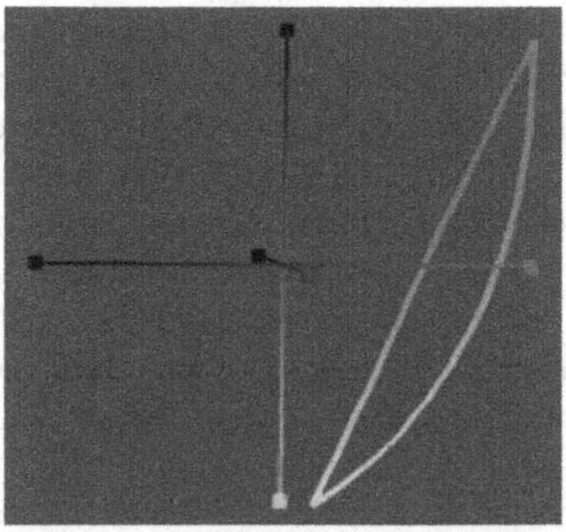

3   Perceptual Uniformity

Fig. 6: A straight line in L*a*b* space becomes a curve in the Chromotome's colour space

The wireframe metaphor is supported by the mathematical technique of interpolation; to generate colours at intermediate points along a wireframe, the Colour Harmoniser interpolates between the colours at the ends of the wireframe. In order for the intermediate colours to appear to fall directly between the colours at the endpoints, the interpolation should occur in a perceptually uniform space such as the CIE's L*a*b* space.

The Chromotome displays a spherical colour space. Fig. 6 shows how a linear interpolation in L*a*b* space (in other words, a perceptually linear wireframe) appears when displayed in this coordinate system. The Colour Harmoniser will achieve perceptual uniformity by mapping straight wireframes in perceptually uniform L*a*b* space into bent wireframes in non-uniform spherical space.

The wireframe for a triadic colour scheme, for example, is an equilateral triangle in L*a*b* space. When projected onto the spherical colour solid, the triangle would no longer be equilateral, and would change continuously as the cutaway rotated beneath it, but a projection back into the perceptually uniform colour space would always be congruent to the original equilateral triangle. Unfortunately, in the spherical visualisation space, the triangle is generally non-planar. This will be addressed by sculpting away the surface of the ellipse where the colour dips below the plane.

4   Conclusion

Chromotome is being developed in two stages. Stage I – discussed in this paper - has resulted in an interface component that shows a wireframe in a cutaway view of a colour solid. It has controls for orienting the solid, and for altering the cutaway shape. The wireframes are perceptually non-uniform shapes; a straight line, a Y, or an ellipse.

In Stage II, the wireframes will be distorted in the display space to conform to a perceptually uniform space, and the cutaway view of the colour solid will become a "sculpted" visualisation that conforms to the shape of the wireframe.

This phased development has allowed us to assess the general concept of the cutaway as a tool for visualising and exploring the colour space, before tackling the more complex programming associated with real-time sculpting of arbitrary curves.

The cutaway view reduces the difficulty of exploring information-rich, feature-poor colour spaces, and makes it possible to orient wireframes anywhere in the space. The freedom and flexibility afforded by the interactive 3D visualisation are difficult to convey in a written document, but are readily apparent with a few minutes of use. The Chromotome display allows the user to explore a large number of possible harmonious colour combinations rapidly.

Although the interface has a large number of degrees of freedom, the immediate visual feedback helps maintain consistency between the state of the software and the user's mental model. More sophisticated, intuitive, pop-up handles have been designed for addition to a future version of the Chromotome. Space restrictions preclude their description here.

References

1.   Moretti, G., Lyons, P.J. Colour Group Selection for Computer Interfaces. in Proc Conf Human Vision and Electronic Imaging (SPIE2000). 2000. San Jose, California.

2.   Itten, J., *The Art of Colour; New York*. 1973: New York: Van Nostrand Reinhold.

3.   Lyons, P. and G. Moretti. Nine Tools for Generating Harmonious Colour Schemes. in Proc APCHI 2004 elsewhere in this volume. 2004. Rotorua, New Zealand: Springer-Verlag.

4.   Epstein, A., 2002, *Color Schemer* **2.5.1**, downloaded from www.colorSchemer.com,

5.   HP, *HP Colour Wheel* downloaded from http://h40099.bbn-stage.europe.hp.com/country/za/eng/color/art_hp_colour_wheel.html,

6.   HumanSoftware, *SmartPicker*.

7.   Pomeroy, P., Adaptive Software, 2002, *ColorWrite* downloaded from http://www.adaptiveview.com/cw/,

8.   Software, O.J., Old Jewel Software, *Painter's Picker* **1.1.2**, downloaded from http://www.oldjewelsoftware.com/ppicker/,

9.   Triantafyllou, A., Life Software, *ColorWheel* downloaded from http://www.lifesoftplus.com/Colorwheel/,

10.   *Color Wheel Pro* QSK Software Group, **2.0**, downloaded from http://www.color-wheel-pro.com/,

11.   Oken, E., Patton, G., Can You Imagine Software, 1999, *ColorSchemes* **1.0.0.2**, downloaded from http://oken3d.com/html/tips.html,

12.   Travis, D., Effective Color Displays: Theory and Practice. 1991: Academic Press 1991.

13.   Jamseon, K., *What Saunders and van Brakel chose to Ignore in Color and Cognition Research*. Commentary in Behavioural and Brain Science, 1997. **20**(2): p. 195-196.

14.   Birren, F., *Colour*. 1980: Mitchell Beazley Arts House.

15.   Wyszecki, G. and Stiles, *Color Science*. 1967: Wiley.

16.   Birren, F., *MUNSELL: A Grammar of Color*. 1969: Van Nostrand-Reinhold.

17.   MacAdam, D.L., *Visual sensitivities to color differences in daylight*. J. Opt. Soc. Am., 1942. **32**: p. 247-273.

18.   Moretti, G., P. Lyons, and M. Wilson. Chromatic Interpolation for Interface Design. in OZCHI 2000. 2000. Sydney, Australia.

Commercial Success by Looking for Desire Lines

Carl Myhill

User Experience Group, GE Network Reliability Products and Services, Energy Services,
Elizabeth House, 1 High Street, Chesterton, Cambridge, UK
carl.myhill@litsl.com, http://www.litsl.com

Abstract. 'Desire Lines' are the ultimate unbiased expression of natural human purpose and refer to tracks worn across grassy spaces, where people naturally walk – regardless of formal pathways. This perfect expression of natural purpose can extend into other interactions in the real world and in the software world.

Rather than trying to understand user needs from a focus group, being alert for desire lines will show you users' actual purpose more directly. Smart companies have an obsession with what is typed into their Search facility, analysing hourly this pure expression of what people want from their sites.

'Normanian Natural Selection' is proposed to describe survival of the fittest design. Companies focusing on desire lines apparent in their products, will be able to successfully adapt them to what their users really want. Perhaps these positive adaptions in design, aligned with human natural purpose, will lead to their greater commercial success.

1   Desire Lines

The term 'Desire Line' originates from the field of urban planning and has been around for almost a hundred years [1]. A desire line normally refers to a worn path showing where people naturally walk. Desire lines are an ultimate expression of human desire or natural purpose. An optimal way to design pathways in accordance with natural human behaviour, is to not design them at all. Simply plant grass seed and let the erosion inform you about where the paths need to be. Stories abound of university campuses being constructed without any pathways to them. Planners responsible earn great respect for their cunning in allowing the desire lines to form before finalizing the construction of the paved pathways. Reconstruction of paths across Central Park in New York was famously based on this approach [2].

Desire lines are such a perfect expression, or rather impression, of human natural purpose that they are the ultimate design pattern for building pathways [3]. Looking at such desire lines as shown in figure 1, it is easy to imagine people, like a line of ants, marching along the route to their goal. In this case, ignoring the formal path off to the left and instead marching over the fence, across the car park and directly towards the entrance to the store.

M. Masoodian et al. (Eds.): APCHI 2004, LNCS 3101, pp. 293-304, 2004.
© Springer-Verlag Berlin Heidelberg 2004

Fig. 1. Photo of desire line towards the entrance to a Cambridge Supermarket built in 2003

2 Extending the Concept of Desire Lines

Desire lines normally refer to pathways across open spaces but they are such perfect impressions of things that humans actually try to do (rather than what they say they are trying to do), that perhaps the concept can be extended. How else can we see the snail trails left by human natural purpose? Can such trails help us design better? To explore these questions, I took a trip into town.

2.1   Speed Humps – 200m

200m into my trip I came upon speed humps, a traffic calming measure designed to slow down motorists. As I watched cars proceed over the humps, like watching a line of ants, I could see a very definite behavior pattern. In figure 2 you can see that the car in the foreground appears parked. In fact, this vehicle is traveling at speed and has swerved into the curbside because the speed humps dip at the edges. The natural desire of certain drivers to maintain their speed over the speed humps leads them to take the path of least resistance, or least bump, to their progress.

Is there a desire line here? The tarmac prevents there being a desire line left carved in the road for all to see. The curbstones display considerable scratching from over zealous speedsters and the wheels of cars getting this slightly wrong will be tell tale. However, in this case, watching the cars, as if a line of ants, is perhaps the clearest approach to seeking the natural human behavior in this situation. A more relevant expression of the consequences of this human or driver desire to maintain speed would be accident statistics. You can clearly see in figure 2 that cars performing this maneuver cut into the curbside so dramatically that any cyclist there would be crushed. It is likely that accident statistics will be blamed on driver error, or cyclists, rather than on the design of the traffic calming measures which cause the problem but these statistics are perhaps the most relevant expression of the consequences of human behavior here.

Fig. 2. Photo of speeding traffic crossing a speed hump, swerving curbside to minimize bump.

2.2   Combined Use Pedestrian and Cycle Bridge – 500m

As I cross the bridge on my bike I can't help noticing the behavior of the ants in their natural purpose. The bridge shown in figure 3 has an exit arrangement with a clear design intent – cyclists to the left; pedestrians to the right (cows to remain on the common, hence the grid). What do the ants do? On the whole, the majority of ants, whether on foot or on a bicycle will traverse the grid. The gate, designed for pedestrians is rarely opened in the natural scheme of things.

Inconsequential or ephemeral desire lines might be broken heels from shoes or angry exchanges between cyclists and pedestrians. The grid perhaps shows indications that it is traversed by other than just cycle tyres but again, in this case, the strongest impression of natural human purpose is gained from observing the ants.

Fig. 3. Photo of an exit to a combined use bridge, which way do the pedestrians go?

2.3   Rising Bollards – 2000m

On to my favorite desire line in town, the rising bollards. The idea behind these traffic measures is to only allow access into the Cambridge's inner ring road to authorized vehicles, such as taxis and buses and delivery vans. Ever increasing numbers of signs tell the unsuspecting tourist not to proceed, some of which can be seen in figure 4.

Fig. 4. Authorized vehicles proceeding over rising bollards.

The desire lines are very easy to see and although recorded as accident statistics, there is no doubt what is to blame for standing in the way of natural human purpose on this occasion. The unsuspecting tourist driving into central Cambridge, on a road that was open to the public only a few years ago, is now baffled with signs. Never mind the signs, the car in front is going this way so it must be ok.

The natural human desire of driving into central Cambridge conspires with befuddling sign posts to lead the unsuspecting 'unauthorized' vehicles over the rising bollards. The bollards will appear sunken if the unsuspecting driver is following an ordinary looking authorized vehicle. It is hard to believe that what happens next to the unsuspecting driver is the complete destruction of their car from the bollard punching upwards as they progress over it. The desire line impression of this context reinforces our understanding of the problem – there is a regular appearance of destroyed cars at the side of the road, and newspaper headlines such as, "Two in hospital after rising bollards hit cars" [6]

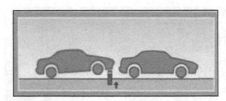

Fig. 5. An unauthorized vehicle is destroyed as it follows an authorized vehicle through the rising bollard. Adapted from [5].

The attitude of those responsible for the bollards is to blame drivers and deny the desire line clearly showing that there is a problem here, "Sue Hewitt, who manages the bollards for Cambridgeshire County Council, admitted she was concerned at the number of accidents at the spot, but insisted drivers were to blame."[6]

The severity of the penalty for people getting this wrong is tremendous but there is no denying the fact that human purpose or desire continues to lead unsuspecting motorists onwards to their destruction. No matter what signposts indicate, people don't expect to be punished for a motoring error by having a huge iron pole punch its way through the bottom of their car!

However much the officials blame the motorists, the desire line tells the actual story of the human behavior in this context.

2.4   Speed Cameras and Speed Warning Signs – 6000m (North or South)

If you head north out of Cambridge you'll soon come upon speed cameras. These cameras will photograph your car registration number plate if you are driving too fast and send you a fine and traffic endorsement through the post (sometimes this can lead to a complete ban).

There is always debate about the intentions of such cameras – do they really want to slow down traffic or just raise funds? Either way, the desire lines are very clear. On sight of a speed camera, people driving speeding cars perceive a THREAT and brake HARD. Desire lines appear in the form of rubber tire tracks on the road, and accident statistics are argued to back up claims that the cameras cause accidents [7]. Natural human behavior in this context is to brake hard.

A design refinement recently introduced was to paint the cameras yellow, so drivers have an earlier warning and can start their excessive braking earlier.

Fig. 6. Cars under heavy braking on noticing speed camera; and skid marks on road next to speed camera

Heading south out of Cambridge, through the village of Hauxton a different kind of approach to slowing traffic has been installed. These are non-threatening speed warning signs which check the speed of the approaching vehicle and only illuminate if the speed limit is being exceeded.

Fig.7. Speed triggered, but unthreatening, speed warning sign

There are no real desire lines relating to the speed warning sign but observing the line of drivers as they pass through this zone is striking. With the polite and non-threatening reminder of the speed limit, the motorists naturally slow down, without sudden braking.

2.5   Back Home – Cook Tops

Back home I am reminded of desire lines in my household products, for example, those relating to cook tops (or hobs). A survey of 400 cook tops [4] found that many available for sale in the UK in 2003 suffered from a poor mapping of controls to elements. This is a well understood design flaw - in 1959 Chapanis and Lindenbaum [8] found hob design layouts yielding errors up to 11% and in 1979 Ray and Ray [9] replicated the results finding errors up to 19%. Even though we've known about this problem for 45 years, the majority of new cook tops designed replicate the bad design.

Does this kind of bad design have a desire line? Perhaps the most obvious desire line would be to look at household fire statistics. A 1997 report by the UK government [10] found cooking to be the second highest cause of household fire. Of these, cookers left unattended represented 75% of the incidents. I wonder for what proportion of those people turned on the wrong burner by mistake?

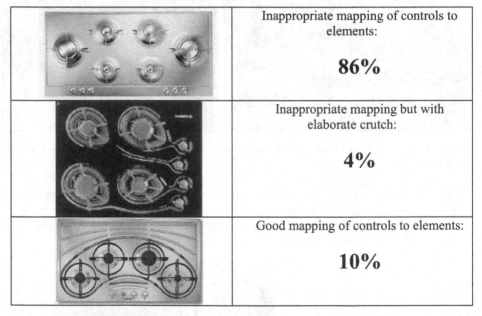

	Inappropriate mapping of controls to elements: **86%**
	Inappropriate mapping but with elaborate crutch: **4%**
	Good mapping of controls to elements: **10%**

Fig. 8. Kinds of cook tops available in the UK in 2003 from [4]

We know there is a design problem here. We know that cookers are a primary cause of household fire. This would seem to be a desire line worth investigating, though as you might expect the government report made no mention of the design of cook tops.

2.6   Desire Lines on Aircraft – Visa Waiver I-94 Form

Extending the concept of desire lines to the real world would not be complete without mentioning the US Visa Waiver form. As aircraft begin their approach into a US destination, flight crews hand out Visa Waiver I-94 forms, warning you not to make a mistake because this can delay you getting through immigration.

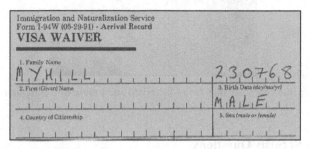

Fig. 9. Spot the desire line across a US Immigration I-94 form

Figure 9. shows the common error – the date of birth is on the wrong line. How often are these forms filled out incorrectly in a way which is clearly obvious from the desire line left on the form itself? Such statistics are not available but it seems a safe bet that the desire lines are ignored. A simple design adaption of this form could fix the problem and could fractionally speed up US immigration procedures. However, this is perhaps not a desire line which is has much commercial significance.

Form design is clearly an area where desire lines have relevance. Researchers know the importance of running pilot studies of forms and questionnaires and very often look for common mistakes, or omissions in how people filled out the pilot questionnaires – they actively seek the desire lines.

Perhaps the most famous case of poor form usability in recent times can be seen from the 'butterfly ballot' desire lines [11]. Mistakes made on the ballot paper created desire lines which probably changed an election result in Florida in 2000!

3 Relating Desire Lines to Computers

Slightly broadening the concept of desire lines from muddy tracks across grass, it is possible to see other impressions of human desire or purpose in the field of computing, many of which could be heeded for commercial advantage.

3.1 Keyboard and Mouse Arrangement

It's not too hard to see the workstation arrangement shown in figure 9 as something analogous to a muddy track across a park. Natural human desire to interact with a computer for the purpose of employment or enjoyment can lead to consequences which are far more undesirable than a muddy track. This is actually my workstation. Repetitive Strain Injury (RSI) has led me to learn how to use the mouse left-handed; the split keyboard forces my hands into a more natural position for typing and the wrist restraint keeps my wrist at a good angle preventing further damage. Whilst not providing any answers, the desire line from this interaction is very clear.

Fig. 10. Desire line computer interface - keyboard and mouse of a computer user with RSI

3.2   Website Security Questions

When my bank asked me for security information for accessing my on-line account, one piece of information was a memorable date. This date was to be typed into a free format text field. It turned out that the security question was a bit harder to remember than just a date – you had to remember the precise string format you used to enter that date. Given the breadth of string formats for entering a valid date, it seems likely that a desire line would form in the bank's logs of security failures.

For illustration, suppose the date were 23/7/1968. Login failures would include the following and many more: 23/07/1968; 23/7/68; 23/07/68; 23 July 1968; 23 July 68; 23rd July 1968.

Some analysis of security check failures in this case would very likely show many people had the correct date, which was the intended security information, but the incorrect string syntax. Attention to this desire line could have quickly improved usability of user access to this on-line bank account.

In this case though, there was another desire line which the bank did observe. I emailed them to explain the problem to them and they fixed it. Actively listening and genuinely acting on user feedback is akin to planting grass seed on a new university campus and watching where the pathways form. This is well recognized good business sense but few companies successful handle these gems of information.

3.3   Software Support Organisations

I recently bought a cup of coffee during a long car journey and after 20 minutes the bottom of the cup started to leak. Interestingly, this company, 'Coffee Nation' had the idea of putting 'Express Yourself' labelling on their cups, asking for feedback. I'm not sure why a company which has vending machines in petrol stations would really be quite so geared up for feedback but in their approach, they are observant for the desire lines.

Too often, support organizations in software companies do the opposite of this – they do a great job of hiding desire lines. Smart support folks solve problems and tell users how to get around problems. They are often not put in a position to influence design, and may not realize a design problem even exists – just more problems with stupid users.

Support organizations, if not attuned to seeking and acting on desire lines, very often spend their entire existence covering them up. The same problem occurs with many customer services teams whose immediate priorities seem to be getting the complaining customer off the phone, rather than deriving any insight from what they are saying. Customer services departments offer routine disinterest in customer feedback. Hiding desire lines in this way is becoming an increasingly risky business in the commercial world. Companies like Coffee Nation already have a competitive advantage from their attention to their product's desire lines.

3.4   Products Which Ask for Feedback – Apple iTunes & Microsoft Windows

There is evidence that some companies are attuned to desire lines. Apple have a menu item on iTunes labeled, 'Provide iTunes Feedback'. Actively seeking direct feedback from users in the actual moment they are using the software is a great way of watching a desire line form. There have to be benefits from observing closely the precise desires of your users at the point where they are being true to their natural desires rather than abstracted out of this context in an interview or focus group. Combined with Apple's reputation for design, and the cult status of their products and wildly loyal customers, it is easy to see that their attention to desire lines will continue to pay off.

Microsoft have a similar idea, when a Windows program crashes a dialog box appears asking you to "send an error report". Somehow I feel uncomfortable about such snooping on my computer but the intention of looking for the effects of actual use of their products, in critical situations like system crashes, has to be a positive move, which will ultimately improve their product design.

3.5   Website Statistics and Search

The beauty of desire lines comes from the fact that their impressions express pure human purpose. Website statistics of various kinds can show you what users are actually doing with your website. Perhaps the most powerful of these is the free format text people type into web search boxes, which creates desire lines showing what people are trying to find on your site. Very smart companies make a great deal of such information, for example the BBC [12],[13] check these desire lines hourly. They adapt other aspects of their web user interface and information structure, such as their subject index, based on what people are typing into the Search facility.

Hill, Holland et al [14] introduced the idea of modeling 'wear' from the physical world (like the bindings of paperbacks) to the digital world to indicate frequency of use of digital objects. They were initially concerned with 'edit wear' and 'read wear' and modeling the frequency with which parts of a document had been read or written. Perhaps the analysis of search terms on a website is a similar concept – 'search term wear'. An example from the BBCi search facility demonstrates this. When Eastenders (a UK soap opera) was removed from the main BBCi index page, it quickly became the top search term typed into the BBCi search facility – this heavy search term wear drove a re-think of Eastenders place in the index!

Overall, website statistics and in particular those relating to search (or search term wear), show a true impression of what a user wants from your website, not what they say they want but what they actually want and what they do. Companies ignoring this information are ignoring their customers at their peril.

3.6   Rate This Page / Was This Review Helpful?

Microsoft and others routinely offer the opportunity to rate a page of information from their online knowledge-base. Did the article help solve your problem? There are desire lines here, though at times I wonder whether this is effectively analyzed, so rarely can I answer in the affirmative.

A more effective rating system is perhaps that adopted by Amazon. Desire lines are captured for the benefit of other users by allowing readers to declare whether they found a particular review helpful or not.

This is another example of actively seeking desire lines in the context of use, also close to the concept of 'read wear' – Amazon clearly lead the way here and seems to be aware that this kind of thing is what keeps them ahead of their competition.

3.7   On-line Help

Online Help facilities within applications often seem to not help much. They typically have no means of allowing the desire line of natural purpose to leave an impression. If you don't find what you want in the help, that information is lost.

Perhaps it is time for designers to invest some time in ensuring that Help systems actually do help by analysing desire lines, particularly what it is users are typing into search boxes. Combine that with a 'rate this page' system and Help systems could evolve.

3.8   Automated Teller Machines (ATMs)

Desire lines surrounding certain ATMs are great fun. There is a standard interaction sequence for ATMs, the user is given their card back before they get the cash (there is even a delay before the cash comes out to allow the user to put their card safely away!). The standard design pattern for this sequence is presumably because when people have their desire satisfied, i.e. getting the cash, they perceive task closure. It is therefore perplexing to discover a lack of adherence to this design pattern in certain ATMs in the USA, which distribute the cash before returning the card. A desire line you might expect in this instance would be a high incidence of lost cards. Such commercial loses would, you would hope, lead to focus on the design of the ATMs but perhaps not always.

4   Normanian Natural Selection

Don Norman has given us many examples of how humans naturally interact with everyday things as well as computers (e.g. The Psychology of Everyday Things [15]).

Extending the urban planning concept of 'desire lines' allows us to look at the tracks left by these natural human interactions in everyday life, and in computing. Somewhat casually drawing further parallels with nature, is it possible to consider that a kind of natural selection is evident in the evolution of design? Capitalist economies arguably have parallels with nature, and in particular, can contribute to the commercial favoring of one design over another. Could the concept of Normanian Natural Selection [4] gain ground, describe commercial design evolution where only slightly successful adaptations are needed for a design to begin to prosper but where unfavorable adaptations die out?

Given 2 identical websites for example, one with the desire line from the search facility analyzed daily and the other ignored, would the former evolve more successfully and ultimately win out in the commercial Normanian Natural Selection stakes? This question seems ridiculous, though it describes the current commercial context of the web very adequately.

5   Concluding Remarks

Expressions of human purpose or desire are all around us, not just available as muddy tracks across open spaces. The urban planning concept of desire lines provides such a perfect expression of human desired purpose that it seems like a worthy concept to explore elsewhere.

We've seen that in some cases, observing humans interacting in the real world provides such a clear indication of their natural purpose that no desire line is needed. Instead, watching the people is much like watching marching ants navigating an obstacle. Speeding vehicles approaching a speed camera provide an excellent example of these marching ants with their obstacle.

Taking a short trip into town I've come across a variety of desire lines all around us that could be used to inform design of anything from speed humps, to rising bollards.

In software terms, the desire lines concept matches very closely to aspects of web interfaces like search boxes, where users type in exactly what they want, as they think it should be expressed. Such information is gold dust to companies looking for competitive advantage.

It is not news that successful companies listen closely to their customers. It is however quite surprising that more companies do not actively seek to understand what drives their users, when there are desire lines left all over the place should they choose to look for them.

Companies like Apple, survive and carve ever deeper market niches. Apple users are not just customers – they are wildly loyal. Apple know about the principle which underlies the extended concept of desire lines. They don't refer to a concept of Normanian Natural Selection perhaps, but they understand design evolution.

Even when the consequences of natural human purpose, are very severe, there is no denying a desire line – it shows what people actually do in some etched form or another.

Normanian natural selection of design will have the last word in the raw commercial world, as Darwinian natural selection does in nature. Successful adaptions lead to commercial superiority and survival, failing to adapt will allow designs to lose ground and die out. Desire lines showing natural human purpose relating to a design are not so hard to see, yet few companies focus on them. Notably, successful companies do focus on them to stay ahead, like Apple, Microsoft and Amazon. Usually, market forces lead commercial competition and erode advantage of very successful companies on the very things they do well. Perhaps the lack of evidence for this is an indication that many companies still do not perceive clearly enough the commercial value of usability. Turning to look for some desire lines could be a good place to start – it is certainly a memorable concept!

References

1. Throgmorton, James A, Eckstein, Barbara: Desire Lines: The Chicago Area Transportation Study and the Paradox of Self in Post-War America. Published on-line (http://www.nottingham.ac.uk/3cities/throgeck.htm) with selected proceedings of the 3Cities Conference. Birmingham, England (2000).
2. Barlow Rogers, Elizabeth: Rebuilding Central Park: A Management and Restoration Plan. The MIT Press (1987)
3. Christopher Alexander, Murray Silverstein, Shlomo Angel, Sara Ishikawa, and Denny Abrams: The Oregon Experiment. Oxford University Press (1975.) ISBN 0-19-501824-9
4. Myhill, Carl: Get your product used in anger!: (before assuming you understand its requirements). Interactions, volume 10, issue 3 May & June 2003. ACM Press, New York, NY, USA (2003) (12-17)
5. Calderdale Council Website: (http://www.calderdale.gov.uk/roads-transport/highways/improvements4/loading.html) (2004)
6. Cambridge Evening News: Available in online news archive (http://www.cambridge-news.co.uk/archives/2001/08/09/lead5.html) (09/08/2001)
7. Speed camera plan 'may cause deaths'. BBC News: Available online (http://news.bbc.co.uk/1/hi/health/1976907.stm). (9/5/2002)
8. Chapanis, A. and Lindenbaum, L.E.: A reaction time study of four control-display linkages. Human Factors 1(4): 1-7. (1959)
9. Ray, R. D., and Ray, W. D.: An Analysis of Domestic Cooker Control Design. Ergonomics, 22(11), 1243- 1248. (1979).
10 Reynolds, Cath: Causes of fire deaths. Research Report No.72. ISBN 1 85893 778 7. Office of the Deputy Prime Minister. (1997)
11 The US 2000 Election and Voting Issues. Usability Professionals' Associaton. Available online http://www.upassoc.org/upa_projects/voting_and_usability/2000election.html. (2000)
12.Belam, Martin: Usability Aspects of BBCi Search Engine. UK UPA meeting, London (15th April 2003)
13.Belam, Martin: A Day In The Life Of BBCi Search. Online http://www.currybet.net/articles/day_in_the_life/index.shtml
14.Hill, W.C., Hollan, J. D., Wrobelwski, D. and McCandless, T.: Read wear and edit wear. In Proceedings of ACM Conference on Human Factors in Computing Systems, CHI '92: 3-9. (1992)
15.Norman, Don: The Psychology of Everyday Things. Basic Books, Inc, New York (1988)

Steering Law in an Environment of Spatially Coupled Style with Matters of Pointer Size and Trajectory Width

Satoshi Naito, Yoshifumi Kitamura, and Fumio Kishino

Osaka University, Graduate School of Information Science and Technology
2-1, Yamadaoka, Suita-shi, Osaka, Japan
kitamura@ist.osaka-u.ac.jp

Abstract. Steering law is an excellent performance model for trajectory-based tasks in GUIs. However, since the original law was proposed, it has been examined only in a graphical environment of spatially decoupled style. Moreover, pointer size has been limited to a small one, and the trajectory width of the trajectory has also been limited to a certain size. To solve this problem, in this paper we discuss the extension of the original steering law in order to apply the law to a wider range of environments. We prove the steering law in an environment of spatially coupled style. We explore three conditions of the pointer and trajectory: a sufficiently small pointer and a trajectory of certain width; a pointer of certain size and a narrow trajectory, and, a pointer of certain size and a trajectory of certain width. The experimental results show that the steering law is valid in an environment of spatially coupled style.

1 Introduction

A variety of new human interface systems using new devices have been proposed and are becoming widely used. In designing such systems, it is very important to clarify how they are superior to existing systems, to find lurking problems that may arise, and to develop ways to improve them. For these purposes, a whole range of methods have been proposed and used to evaluate these systems. Among them, a performance evaluation test has been widely employed to understand a system objectively and quantitatively. Performance parameters that can be measured quantitatively include the time needed by users to learn specific functions, speed of task performance, rate of errors by users, user retention of commands over time, and subjective user satisfaction[1]. However, if the task conditions or parameters (e.g., target size or target distance in a pointing task) are different, it is usually difficult to simply compare the performances. Therefore, theoretical quantitative performance models have been proposed and used, and these have provided guidelines toward designing new interface systems.

Fitts' law [2] is a well-known performance model for pointing tasks. However, recent progress in GUIs has produced variations of user interface systems that cannot always be covered by Fitts' law (for example, trajectory-based tasks).

M. Masoodian et al. (Eds.): APCHI 2004, LNCS 3101, pp. 305–316, 2004.

The steering law [3] has recently proposed to cover the performance model of trajectory-based tasks. Since this law was proposed, however, has been examined only in the context of a graphical environment of a spatially decoupled style, where the graphical space is logically corresponds to user' s operational space but does not collocated (for example, a GUI operated by a mouse). Moreover, the small size of the pointer has been limited, while the trajectory width has also been restricted. However, recent GUIs have produced variations of user interface systems such as ones using touch-panel displays or tablet PCs those having a graphical environment of a spatially coupled style, where the user' s operational space and graphical space are collocated, though these cannot always be covered by the law. It is therefore necessary to examine the validity of the steering law in a variety of environments in order to design and/or evaluate for future user interface systems.

In this paper, we discuss an expansion of the steering law's validity, and examine its validity in an environment of spatially coupled style. We also explore three conditions of the pointer and trajectory: (1) a small enough pointer and a trajectory of certain width: (2) a pointer of certain size and a sufficiently narrow trajectory, and (3) a pointer of a certain size and a trajectory of a certain width.

2   Previous Work

Theoretical models are important for investigating interactions between people and computers. The best known model is Fitts' law [2]. Commonly, Fitts' law is expressed in the following form:

$$T = a + b \times ID, \quad ID = \log_2(\frac{A}{W} + 1). \tag{1}$$

where T is the acquisition time, W is the target width, A is the target distance, a and b are empirically determined constants, and ID is the index of difficulty. The reciprocal of b is an index of performance used as a measure of interface systems. Fitts' law shows a model of speed/accuracy tradeoffs in pointing tasks, and since Fitts' law transforms the experimental measurements to an index of performance that is independent of the task parameters, it is possible to compare an experimental result of a task with others which are obtained from different tasks or experimental configurations. Various extensions of Fitts' law have also been presented [4,5,6].

Fitts' law is only suitable for pointing tasks and it cannot be used for the task of producing trajectories, such as in drawing and writing in human-computer interaction. To solve this problem the steering law was proposed as a performance model for trajectory-based tasks [3]. For the trajectory C in Figure 2, the steering law is expressed in the following form:

$$MT = a + b \times ID_C, \quad ID_C = \int_C \frac{ds}{W(s)}. \tag{2}$$

where MT is the task completion time for path C, ID is the index of difficulty, W(s) is the width of the path C at the point of abscissa s, and a and b are

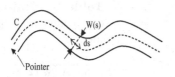
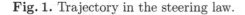

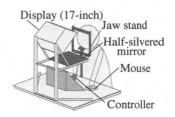

Fig. 1. Trajectory in the steering law.

Fig. 2. Experimental environment.

empirically determined constants. It is shown that the steering law is useful in environments with various control devices [7] and different movement scales [8]. The steering law is also proved in locomotion using a car-driving simulator [9]. In these studies, however, the steering law has been examined only in the context of a graphical environment of spatially decoupled style, and moreover, the size of the pointer has been limited to a small one, while the width of the trajectory has been limited to one with a certain width. Considering the recent spread of touch-panel displays, it is necessary to examine the validity of the steering law in the environment of spatially coupled style. In this style, a pointer the size of a certain real object is often used; therefore, it is necessary to examine the validity of the law in an environment with a pointer of a certain size. In the research employing a car-driving simulator [9], since the size of the car was fixed, tasks of the examination were not adequate. In case of the pointer of a certain size, a narrow trajectory can be considered, therefore, it is also necessary to examine the validity of the law against the relationship between the pointer size and the trajectory width.

3   A Sufficiently Small Pointer and a Trajectory of Certain Width

In this section, we examine the validity of the steering law in an environment of spatially coupled style with a sufficiently small pointer and a trajectory of a certain width.

3.1   Experimental Configuration (Experiment 1)

We conduct experiments in an environment of spatially coupled style with a sufficiently small pointer and a trajectory of a certain width, as illustrated in Figure 2. To generate a virtual environment and to control the experimental graphical environment, a graphics workstation (Silicon Graphics Inc., Onyx) is used. For displaying the virtual environment, a Developer Display 2B (Reachin, ReachIn Display) is used. A half-silvered mirror is placed between the screen and the workspace. The image-refreshing rate at 60 Hz is perceived by the subject as if it were below the half silvered mirror. A magnetic 6-DOF tracker (Polhemus Inc., Fastrak) is used as the controller, moved by the subject's right hand to

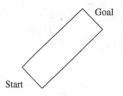

Fig. 3. linear trajectory

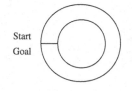

Fig. 4. circular trajectory

Table 1. Trajectory conditions in Experiment 1.

line	A	8, 12, 16, 24
(cm)	W	1, 4, 6
circle	A	30, 40, 50, 60
(cm)	W	1, 4, 6

track the position of the pointer at 60 Hz. Here, the control-display ratio is 1.The position of the subject's jaw is fixed on a jaw stand.

3.2   Task (Experiment 1)

In this experiment, a white-bounded trajectory and a circular light-blue pointer (radius = 0.2 cm) are presented to subjects. A mouse operated by the subject's left hand is used to control the task condition. When a subject clicks the left mouse button, a line appears at the center of the trajectory. At the same time, the color of the pointer and the centerline change to blue. When the blue pointer enters the trajectory, the colors of both the line and the pointer change to red, and when a subject successfully completes the task, the colors change to yellow. If the subject fails the task, their colors change to purple. This failed trial is performed again. If the subject clicks the left mouse button again when the colors are yellow, the color of the pointer returns to light blue, after which the centerline disappears. Two different trajectory shapes are tested: a linear trajectory and a circular one (Figs. 3 and 4). The subject is then re-quested to move the pointer as quickly and accurately as possible while staying on the presented trajectory. Table 1 lists the designs of the experimental tasks. Here, A is the length of the trajectory and W is the width of the trajectory, and A + W becomes the actual length of the trajectory in this experiment. The conditions are presented in random order in each session for each subject. Before the experiment, subjects prac-tice the tasks the same number of times as in the official session.

3.3   Results (Experiment 1)

Six subjects participated in the experiment and performed each condition four times. The regression analysis for the movement time (MT) and the index of diffi-culty (ID) on completed trials gave:

$$Line : MT = 0.159 + 0.061 \times ID \ (R^2 = 0.980)$$
$$Circle : MT = 0.301 + 0.128 \times ID \ (R^2 = 0.993)$$

The completion time and index of difficulty show a linear relationship in the environment of spatially coupled style with the pointer of sufficiently small size and a trajectory of a certain width as shown in Fig. 5. The results are discussed in Section 6.

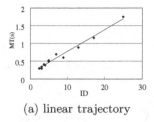

(a) linear trajectory

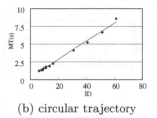

(b) circular trajectory

Fig. 5. Relationship between ID and MT in Experiment 1.

4 A Pointer of Certain Size and a Trajectory of Certain Width

In this section, we examine the steering law in the environment where a user moves the pointer of a certain size along the trajectory of a certain width. In this case, two different judgments can be considered for determining whether the subject fails the task: the pointer is determined to have deviated when the boundary of the pointer touches the border of the trajectory without closing the border, and the pointer is determined to have deviated when the pointer goes completely outside the trajectory's bounds. These are called the inscribed and circumscribed cases, respectively. Both cases are examined in the following experiments

4.1 Inscribed Case

Task Conversion
  First, we examine the inscribed case wherein the pointer is determined to have deviated when the boundary of the pointer touches the border of the trajectory without closing the border. Because the pointer has a certain size, we have to take care how to define the trajectory width. For that, we use a pointer of diameter D and a trajectory of W x A as illustrated in Fig. 6(a). At this time, if we consider a pointer whose diameter is small enough (negligible to zero) and a trajectory of (W-D) x (A+D) as shown in Fig. 6(b), the configuration shown in Fig. 6(a) is essentially the same as the one shown in Fig. 6(b). This is a way of considering the conversion of tasks in which a user moves the pointer of a certain size along the trajectory of a certain width; it is not, however, a method for comparing the results with the results from Experiment 1 described in Section 3. With this conversion, Eq. (3) can express the relationship between the movement time (MT) and the index of difficulty (ID). We examine whether the steering law is materialized by examining whether the expression 3 is right or not.

$$MT = a + b \times ID, \quad ID = \frac{A + D}{W - D} \tag{3}$$

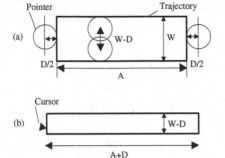

Table 2. Trajectory conditions in Experiment 2.

line	A	8, 12, 16, 24
(cm)	W-D(W, D)	1(2, 1), 4(6, 2), 5(6, 1)
circle	A	30, 40, 50, 60
(cm)	W-D(W, D)	3(4, 1), 4(6, 2), 5(6, 1)

Fig. 6. An equivalent transformation in Experiment 2.

Experimental Configuration (Experiment 2)

Experiment 2 uses a system almost identical to that in Experiment 1. The subject uses Fastrak as the controller on the operating stand to move the pointer of diameter D. Since the subject can understand the condition of the task from the pointer color, the line in the center of the trajectory is not displayed in this experiment. The shapes of trajectories are a linear trajectory and a circular one, just as in Experiment 1, as shown in Figs. 3 and 4. The task designs are listed in Table 2. These conditions are presented to the subjects in a random order, and subjects practice the tasks the same number of times as in the official session.

Results (Experiment 2)

Six subjects participated in the experiment and performed five trials under each condition. By changing two parameters, i.e., pointer size (D) and trajectory width (W), we examine three cases in this experiment. For the first case, only D is varied while W is constant. For the second case, only W is varied, and D is constant. For the third case, both D and W are varied. For the first case, where W is 6 cm, the regression analysis for the movement time (MT) and the index of difficulty (ID) on completed trials gave:

$$Line: MT = 0.013 + 0.071 \times ID \ (R^2 = 0.933)$$
$$Circle: MT = 0.186 + 0.077 \times ID \ (R^2 = 0.976)$$

Although the configuration of this experiment was relatively simple and the range of ID variation was smaller than in other experiments, the MT vs. ID showed a linear relationship with high correlation values (R^2). Therefore, we found that the steering law was valid in the first case.

Next, we examine the second case, where D is 1 cm. The regression analysis on completed trials gave:

$$Line: MT = 0.032 + 0.066 \times ID \ (R^2 = 0.993)$$
$$Circle: MT = 0.094 + 0.089 \times ID \ (R^2 = 0.992)$$

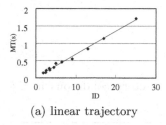

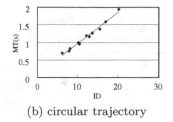

(a) linear trajectory   (b) circular trajectory

Fig. 7. Relationship between ID and MT in Experiment 2.

Both of these results on line and circle trajectories showed higher correlation values than 0.99. Therefore, we found that the steering law was valid in the second case. Finally, we examine all of the measured movement time. The regression analysis on completed trials gave:

$$Line : MT = 0.020 + 0.066 \times ID \ (R^2 = 0.994)$$
$$Circle : MT = 0.075 + 0.088 \times ID \ (R^2 = 0.983)$$

Both of these results on linear and circular trajectories show higher correlation values than 0.98.

From all of these experimental results shown in this subsection, we can conclude that the steering law was valid in an environment with the inscribed case where the pointer has a certain size and the trajectory a certain width. Furthermore, since the steering law was valid in all of the above three conditions, we can conclude that the influences of pointer size and trajectory width on the difficulty of the task are the same. Figures 7(a) and (b) show the results of Experiment 2.

4.2   Circumscribed Case

Task Conversion

Here we examine the circumscribed case, wherein the pointer is determined to have deviated when the pointer goes completely outside the trajectory. We use a pointer of diameter D and a trajectory of width and length W and A, respectively, as illustrated in Fig. 8(a). At this time, if we consider a pointer whose diameter is small enough (negligible to zero) and a trajectory which is (W+D) x (A+D) as shown in Fig. 8(b), the configuration shown in Fig. 8(a) is essentially equivalent to that in 8(b). Equation (4) can represent the relationship between the movement time (MT) and the index of difficulty (ID), and we examine the validity of the steering law in the circumscribed case by evaluating this equation.

$$MT = a + b \times ID, \quad ID = \frac{A + D}{W + D} \tag{4}$$

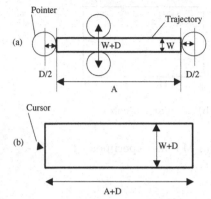

Fig. 8. An equivalent transformation in Experiment 3.

Table 3. Trajectory conditions in Experiment 3.

line	A	8, 12, 16, 24
(cm)	W+D(W, D)	1(0.5, 0.5), 1.5(0.5, 1), 2(1, 1)
circle	A	30, 40, 50, 60
(cm)	W+D(W, D)	2(1, 1), 3(1, 2), 4(2, 2)

Experimental Configuration (Experiment 3)

Experiment 3 employs the same system as in Experiment 2. Table 3 lists the task designs and all conditions are presented in random order. Subjects practice the tasks the same number of times as in the official session.

Results (Experiment 3)

Six subjects participated in this experiment and performed five trials under each condition. We examine three cases similar to Experiment 2. For the first case, where $W = 0.5$ cm for the linear trajectory and $W = 1$ cm for the circular one, the regression analysis on completed trials gave:

$$Line : MT = -0.107 + 0.049 \times ID \ (R^2 = 0.988)$$
$$Circle : MT = 0.050 + 0.082 \times ID \ (R^2 = 0.978)$$

The correlation values (R^2) between MT and ID are larger than 0.97, therefore, we found that the steering law was valid in the first case. Next, we examine the second case where $D = 1$ cm for the linear trajectory and $D = 2$ cm for the circular one. The regression analyzes on completed trials gave:

$$Line : MT = -0.012 + 0.040 \times ID \ (R^2 = 0.994)$$
$$Circle : MT = 0.316 + 0.063 \times ID \ (R^2 = 0.987)$$

The correlation values (R^2) between MT and ID are larger than 0.98; therefore, we found that the steering law is also valid in the second case. Finally, we examine the third case in which both D and W are varied. The regression analysis on completed trials gave:

$$Line : MT = -0.073 + 0.047 \times ID \ (R^2 = 0.986)$$
$$Circle : MT = 0.132 + 0.078 \times ID \ (R^2 = 0.981)$$

The results show larger correlation values than 0.98.

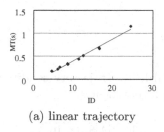

(a) linear trajectory

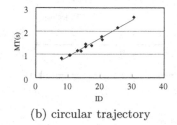

(b) circular trajectory

Fig. 9. Relationship between ID and MT in Experiment 3.

From all of these results, we can conclude that the steering law was valid in an environment with the circumscribed case where the pointer has a certain size and the trajectory a certain width. Furthermore, similarly to Experiment 1, since the steering law was valid in all of the above three conditions, we can conclude that the influences of pointer size and trajectory width on the difficulty of the task are the same. Figures 9(a) and (b) show the results of this experiment.

5   A Pointer of a Certain Size and a Narrow Trajectory

The steering law has already been examined above in a graphical environment in which the trajectory has a certain width. In this section, we examine the validity of the steering law in an environment where a user moves a pointer of certain size along a narrow trajectory.

5.1   Task Conversion

When we use a narrow trajectory in this experiment, we need to carefully define the trajectory width. Assume that we use a pointer of diameter D and a trajectory of length A, as illustrated in Fig. 10(a). At this time, if we consider sufficiently small pointer and a trajectory whose width and length are D and A+D, respectively, as shown in Fig. 10(b), the configuration shown in 10(a) is essentially equivalent to that in Fig. 10(b). Equation (5) can represent the relationship between the movement time (MT) and the index of difficulty (ID), and we examine the validity of the steering law by evaluating this equation.

$$MT = a + b \times ID, \quad ID = \frac{A + D}{D}. \tag{5}$$

5.2   Experimental Configuration (Experiment 4)

A similar experimental system to the previous experiments is used in this experiment. A subject moves a hemispherical piece of polystyrene containing a Fastrak

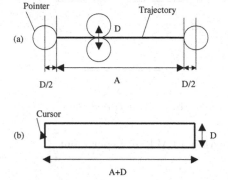

Table 4. Trajectory conditions in Experiment 4.

line	A	8, 12, 16, 24
(cm)	D	1, 4, 6
circle	A	30, 40, 50, 60
(cm)	D	1, 4, 6

Fig. 10. An equivalent transformation in Experiment 4.

as a controller. The size of the controller is same as that of the pointer. In this experiment a linear trajectory and a circular trajectory are used, and they are presented in green. Table 4 lists task designs, and all of these conditions are presented in random order to each subject. Subjects practice the tasks the same number of times as in the official session

5.3   Results (Experiment 4)

Six subjects participated in this experiment and performed four trials under each condition. The regression analysis on completed trials gave:

$$Line : MT = 0.173 + 0.064 \times ID \ (R^2 = 0.973)$$
$$Circle : MT = 0.566 + 0.151 \times ID \ (R^2 = 0.996)$$

The result show higher correlation values (R^2) than 0.97.

From this result, we found that the steering law was valid in an environment where a pointer of certain size is moved along a narrow trajectory. Figure 11 show the results of Experiment 4.

6   Discussion

6.1   The Size of Pointer and the Width of Trajectory

Results from the above experiments show that the steering law is valid in an environment with a circular pointer of a sufficiently small certain size. We proposed task conversions for each experiment; however, if we use a pointer with other shapes, we have to consider new task conversion according to the shape of the pointer. For example, if we use a rectangular pointer in which not all side lengths are the same, the task conversion described in this paper may not be

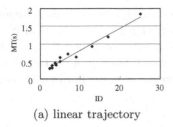

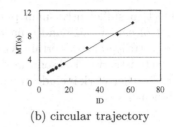

(a) linear trajectory   (b) circular trajectory

Fig. 11. Relationship between ID and MT in Experiment 4.

effective. For this problem, knowledge of Fitts' law for bivariate pointing [4,5] may be applicable to the steering law. However, further careful examination is required for this problem. Moreover, it might be interesting to consider the case in which the size of a pointer varies while a user moves it.

Although the width of the trajectory used in these experiments was simply constant throughout, it might be interesting to examine various trajectories such as a trajectory whose width is not constant and varies according to its position. Further-more, it might be more interesting to examine a case in which both the pointer size and trajectory width vary while a user moves the pointer.

6.2   Comparison of Index of Performance

We can compare index of performance, i.e., IP = 1/b, among parameters obtained from the experiments. The IP value obtained from both the linear and the circular trajectories in Experiment 3 was the largest among those of all the experiments. This means the configuration used in Experiment 3, i.e., an environment of spatially coupled style in which a user moves a pointer of certain size along a trajectory of certain width in the circumscribed case, achieved the best performance. Conversely a previous work [10] in which experiments were conducted on an environment of spatially decoupled style showed that the configuration equivalent to that in Experiment 2 with the inscribed case marked the largest IP. These differences suggest that the optimal condition of the pointer and the trajectory is different with respect to the spatially coupled style and the spatially decoupled style. Consequently, precise analysis and comparison of these differences will provide powerful information for designing and evaluating new user interface systems. In spatially decoupled style, there are variations in the configurations of the pointer and controller, and examining the most suitable condition for these configurations or tasks is promising as important future work for determining interface design.

7   Conclusion

In this paper, we proved that the steering law is valid in an environment of spatially coupled style by exploring the three conditions of the pointer and trajectory: (1) a sufficiently small pointer and a trajectory of certain width; (2) a pointer of certain size and a narrow trajectory; and, (3) a pointer of certain size and a trajectory of certain width. The knowledge obtained through these experiments is certainly useful in de-signing a whole variety of future interface systems. Further work includes a plan to examine the steering law in a 3D virtual environment.

Acknowledgments

A part of this research was supported by "The 21st Century Center of Excellence Pro-gram" of the Ministry of Education, Culture, Sports, Science and Technology, Japan and Grant-in-Aid for Scientific Research (B)(2) 13480104 from the Japan Society for the Promotion of Science.

References

1. B. Shneiderman, "Designing the user interface – strategies for effective human-computer interaction –," 3rd edition, Addison-Wesley, 1998.
2. P. M. Fitts, "The information capacity of the human motor system in controlling the amplitude of movement," Journal of Experimental Psychology, vol.47, no.6, pp.381–391, June 1954.
3. J. Accot and S. Zhai, "Beyond Fitts' law: models for trajectory-based HCI tasks," Conference on Human Factors in Computing Systems (Proc. of ACM CHI '97), pp.295–302, 1997.
4. I.S. MacKenzie and W. Buxton, "Extending Fitts' law to two-dimensional tasks," Conference on Human Factors in Computing Systems (Proc. of ACM CHI '92), pp.219–226, 1992.
5. J. Accot and S. Zhai, "Refining Fitts' law models for bivariate pointing," Conference on Human Factors in Computing Systems (Proc. of ACM CHI '03), pp.193–200, 2003.
6. C. Ware and K. Lowther, "Selection using one-eyed cursor in a fish tank VR environment," ACM Trans. Computer-Human Interaction, vol.4, pp.309–322, 1997.
7. J. Accot and S. Zhai, "Performance evaluation of input devices in trajectory-based tasks: an application of the steering law," Conference on Human Factors in Computing Systems (Proc. of ACM CHI '99), pp.466–472, 1999.
8. J. Accot and S. Zhai, "Scale effects in steering law tasks," Conference on Human Factors in Computing Systems (Proc. of ACM CHI '01), pp.1–8, 2001.
9. S. Zhai and R. Woltjer, "Human movement performance in relation to path constraint," Proc. of IEEE Virtual Reality 2003, pp.149–156, 2003.
10. S. Naito, Y. Kitamura and F. Kishino, "A study of steering law in 2D spatially-decoupled style," Proc. of Human Interface Symposium 2003, pp.217–220, 2003. (in Japanese).

Design of Information Visualization of Ubiquitous Environment for a Wearable Display

Makoto Obayashi[1], Hiroyuki Nishiyama[2], and Fumio Mizoguchi[2]

[1] Tokyo Metropolitan Industrial Technology Research Institute, Nishigaoka 3-13-10, Kitaku, Tokyo, Japan
obayashi.makoto@iri.metro.tokyo.jp
[2] Tokyo University of Science, Faculty of Science and Technology, Yamazaki 2641, Noda, Chiba, Japan
{nisiyama, mizo}@ia.noda.tus.ac.jp

Abstract. In this paper, we developed an information visualization system of the ubiquitous environment for a wearable computer using a small head-mount display. A wearable computer provides the user unlimited computer access in everyday places. The user of a wearable computer can acquire and process various information by hands-free operation. In this case, a tiny display communicates information from a wearable computer to the user. Downsizing a wearable computer's display is a result of the pursuit of portability. However, downsizing the display reduces the amount of information that can be displayed. Raising the resolution of a wearable display is sure that it can increase the amount of information displayed at once. However, information crowded onto the tiny display would be difficult to comprehend. Our information visualization system solves the above problems. It enables us to display the information of sensors equipped in an environment efficiently using a tiny display. We used a 12mm-square IIMD for our system. We also demonstrate the potential of our system by evaluating experimental results.

1 Introduction

A wearable computer can realize various services for its user with hands-free condition. Therefore it would enhance the user's perception and memory by sensing and processing phenomena that occur around the user, their physiology, and ecology information. It can record or manage a user's surrounding information and action history by providing a small display and small camera as a wearable devices[10]. However, the information a wearable computer obtains only relates to the user and the user's action. It can communicate environmental information to a user when used together with a ubiquitous environment represented by a "Smart Office"[2]. Also, there are merits in constructing systems, or the field of security, that are indicated with using a wearable computer in a ubiquitous environment[1]. Inspecting some situations in a ubiquitous environment by using a wearable computer has the advantages indicated below. (1) Service can be requested from the ubiquitous environment with hands-free operations. (2)

M. Masoodian et al. (Eds.): APCHI 2004, LNCS 3101, pp. 317–327, 2004.
© Springer-Verlag Berlin Heidelberg 2004

Ubiquitous environment information can be acquired regularly. Based on these advantages, a wearable computer enables a user to recognize their existence as a visitor to the environment, and a physical resource (the position of robot etc.), by catching changes of environmental information without choosing placement. Depending on environmental information captured, a wearable computer could also transmit various requests from any where to various kinds of physical apparatuses, which are scattered throughout the environment. In this instance, the computer needs to display to a user various kinds of events in the environment, physical devices, and condition of resources. It is important for an interface to connect the wearable computer with a user. Small keyboards, mice, and displays are generally used as user interfaces. An interface that mediates communication of information between a wearable computer and a user is required. Usually, portability is important for an interface of a wearable computer, but the computer should also be easy to use and possess adequate input-and-output operation. Various interfaces have been proposed and implemented[7][8], but the best device for presenting information to a user is a portable small display, considering the amount of information displayed per unit time. To achieve portability, the display of a wearable computer is implemented as a Head Mount Display (HMD) and a small display on wrist watch. Because of technical improvements in recent years, it is possible the display resolution will increase by leaps and bounds, and a vast amount of information will be displayed at one time on a small display. Therefore, it is capable of present information to users by displaying any information in a ubiquitous environment. Nonetheless, it is restricted if individual differences in vision capability are considered, and distinguishing features becomes difficult if the character, or picture of a character is below a certain fixed size. Therefore, even if it is possible to display huge amounts of environment information all at once, presenting the information is impossible when it is difficult to read. Another way to present information is to capturing and display only a limited part of the vast amount of information. Alignment zooming is another consideration for displaying specific information of a place of ubiquitous environment when complete information cannot be presented as observed. However, in this case, it is impossible to display requests simultaneously for the event, which is generated simultaneously in the distant place and devices. Furthermore, changes in the environment information generated by the display area can be overlooked.

In this research, we develop a system solve the above-mentioned problem, and present the user with ubiquitous environmental information efficiently. Also, the wearable display we use is a one-eye-type head-mounted display, 12mm square with resolution of 640x480. We have also developed a visualization system for zooming to a specific area as shown in Fig.1. Furthermore, we evaluate the system by experiment and consider its potential.

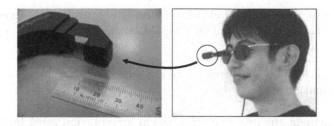

Fig. 1. The HMD for wearable computer used in our study

2   System Design

2.1   Visualizing Information of the Ubiquitous Environment

The information visualization system we developed is based on the premise that it is implemented in a wearable computer. Hence, it must not include complex operations for processing of acquired detailed information. Also, as described in the previous section, a large amount of environmental data should be depicted in the tiny display (Fig.1). Visualization technology enables various methods for visualizing large amounts of data. Linear zooming methods, such as Pad++[4], enable displaying arbitrary size change data indicated by the user. However, zooming with this method pushes a lot of data out of the display. Therefore, the Pad++ method is improper for environmental information visualization, because the user should watch all environmental information continuously. Fisheye[9] is another visual technology which enables nonlinear zooming. It is able to expand and display the area in which the user gazes, like a fish-eye lens. However, Fisheye does not visualize non-attention area. Therefore, it cannot provide visualization of a large amount of information data.

Considering the above problems, we adopted the Hyperbolic Tree visualization technology, and customized this method for ubiquitous environment visualization. Hyperbolic Tree of Xerox PARC is a WWW information visualization tool developed as an aid for WWW browsing. It employs a non-linear function to display an entire tree, which represents the structure of a web site using hyperbolic functions. Additionally, it has the smooth movement of mouse operation. The most significant advantage of this technique is that the hyperbolic transformation enables displaying a large amount of data in a specified area. Furthermore, the near data is displayed in large format, and far data is displayed in small format. As mentioned above, the method using hyperbolic geometry is an appropriate visualization technique for displaying a lot of data on one screen. However, because of the non-linear function, position relationships and links between nodes are distorted. This feature does not affect the user when web browsing,. because WWW information has no relationship with the real environment. In our study, however, the displayed nodes correspond to a specific sensor in the real environment. Therefore, distorted nodes inhibit the user's ability to intuitively grasp environmental information. Recognizing the above problems, we designed the wearable computer for information visualization of ubiquitous environment as follows:

1. Nodes that display real sensor data are projected using hyperbolic geometric transformation.

2. We implement the intuitive information presentation using linear converted nodes existing near the center of display.

3. We adopt an oval form screen for the drawing area in Hyperbolic Tree.

4. A zooming function enables zoom and reduction of the display area.

Items 1 and 2 above are contradictory. However, we try to solve this problem by using a novel technique in the visualization system. Item 3 means an effective 640x480 resolution HMD. In item 4, the view range based on the situation is displayed to a user. In this example, our visualization system prevents missing areas of environmental information.

2.2 Visualization Method of Node Status

Our visualization system is required for users to intuitively perceive the status of the real environment. The status of the real environment is represented by altering each node corresponding to a sensor.Many methods of representing numerous objects that include various information have been proposed by previous works. For example, KAGAMI[5] expresses the node that shows a web page in cone form. The page changes conic height and conic color according to the keyword in the contents and to the number of accesses. This is a very efficient method to provide an understanding of the intuitive web structure to a user. Since there is no concept of physical distance and position concerned with real world between two or more web pages, the developer can arrange node positions freely so that they do not overlap. However, since our visualization system represents node's status in the real world, the flexibility of node mapping layout is very limited. Moreover, different ways of representing information are required according to type and ability of sensors. Therefore, an original technique is required for efficient representation of sensor information. The node expression using the visualization system in this paper has the following features. (1) The basic shape of a node is a circle and cone form. (2) The node shape is transformed according to the status of sensors. (3) The drawing size of the node is determined according to the distance from the center of the display. (4) Node types and events are represented by animation of color changing.

We will describe these implementations in detail in the next section.

3 Implementation

3.1 Ubiquitous Environment

In this paper, we use the Information Media Center of Tokyo University of Science as the ubiquitous environment. The Information Media Center is constructed as a "Smart Office"[2] and consists of various sensors, information appliances, and robots. These are connected with each other via a network, and various applications are implemented using Smart Office functions[2].

Table 1. Sensors and Information Appliance in an area of the Smart Office

The kind of devices	number
Network Camera (pan-tilt camera & all direction camera)	9
Infrared sensor for detect robot position	37
Human infrared sensor	9
Mobile Robot	6
Manipulator	2
PC of each room	22

Four types of sensors are installed in our environment. These are infrared sensors for detecting humans and robots, laser sensors for detecting objects, and pan-tilt cameras for detecting moving objects. Moving objects, such as humans and service robots, can be recognized using these devices and sensors. LonWorksNetwork connects all sensors with each other, which are subsequently connected to a LAN with LonWorksNetwork via a special router. The sensor network in our environment enables us to acquire information from each sensor through a network. Mobile robots and arm robots in the environment enable us to provide various services based on commands from the user. Next, we describe the type and number of nodes in this environment. The experimental environment consists of the devices illustrated in the table.1. The visualization system for our wearable computer is designed to efficiently present information of the devices' activities to the user. In the next section, we describe the implementation of our visualization system in detail.

3.2 Implementation of the Visualize System

As described in Section 2, environmental information visualization for a wearable display adopts a non-linear transformation algorithm using hyperbolic geometry such as a Hyperbolic Tree[6] and KAGAMI[5]. It enables placing environmental information into a display. We also represent intuitive information by partially applying linear zooming to the gazing area. Next, we describe visualization algorithm in detail. The left illustration in Fig.2 depicts a situation of transferring

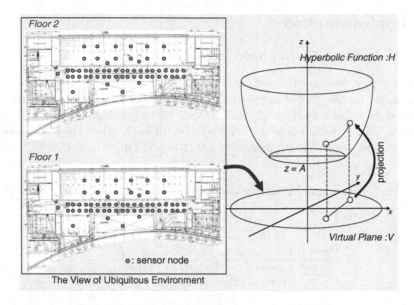

Fig. 2. Drawing position conversion of nodes using hyperbolic function (Step1): The information of environment is too large to draw all nodes of the sensor network into a tiny display.

environmental information to the display without conversion. Nodes representing sensor status and environment maps are displayed with real-world accuracy. However, if the environment information is too voluminous, it cannot be displayed in its entirety. Therefore, only partial information is displayed. Displaying all information in a small area requires extreme scaling down, and detailed information must be collapsed. Hence, we define the plane that draws the position of all nodes and environment accurately on a fixed scale as a virtual plane. The size of this virtual plane is assumed to be infinite.

Fig.2 (right) illustrates converting these node positions to visualization positions using hyperbolic coordinates. The converting equation is represented by equation 1.

$$\begin{cases} if(z \geq A) \\ \quad (x_{hi}, y_{hi}, z_{hi}) = (x_i, y_i, \sqrt{x_i^2 + y_i^2 + 1}) \\ else\ if(1 \leq z < A) \\ \quad x_{hi}^2 + y_{hi}^2 = r^2 \end{cases} \tag{1}$$

Here, x_i and y_i are node coordinates in the virtual plane V. The converted node's coordinates are x_{hi} y_{hi} and z_{hi}. Next, we calculate the hyperbolic coordinate of each node, and the line segment that connects it and $(0,0,-1)$. We then project the nodes to oval plane O_i. The oval plane and the coordinates of the projected node are represented as equations 2 and 3.

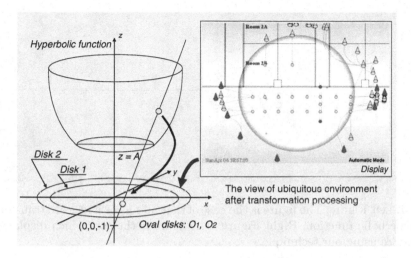

Fig. 3. Drawing position conversion of nodes using hyperbolic function (Step2): All nodes can be drawn in a tiny display using non-linear function. And a part of nodes near the center of display can be drawn according to real position using linear function.

$$\frac{x^2}{a^2} + y^2 < 1, z = 0, (a > 1) \tag{2}$$

$$(x_{pi}, y_{pi}, z_{pi}) = (\frac{ax_{hi}}{z_{hi}+1}, \frac{y_{hi}}{z_{hi}+1}, 0) \tag{3}$$

The point that our visualization method differ from the method of Hyperbolic Tree[6][3][5] is that cut the hyperbolic geometry at arbitrary point A ($A > 1$) on z-axis (Figs.2 and 3). The cutting plane is circular, expressed by $x^2 + y^2 = A^2 - 1$. Therefore, nodes located in the range of a diameter $\sqrt{A^2 - 1}$ from the center of the virtual plane, project to the oval plane without hyperbolic geometry conversion. This enables a partial display of nodes by linear zooming. Our visualization system utilizes several oval planes as illustrated in Fig.3. This reflects the difference in a display domain. That is, every domain of the real environment projects on a separate oval plane. It is possible to divide and display adjoining environment information and different environment information clearly. The transformed visualized environment information is illustrated in Fig.3(right). Also, several nodes located within a constant distance from the display center are drawn in the figure by linear zooming. Other nodes are located according to hyperbolic geometric conversion. Furthermore, this visualization method enables locating all nodes using an arbitrary zooming scale. Fig.?? shows the comparison of visualization technique between the former approach (left approach) and our approach (right approach).

The left image in Fig.5 illustrates a snapshot of nodes indicating event occurrence. An example of node display information is depicted to the right in

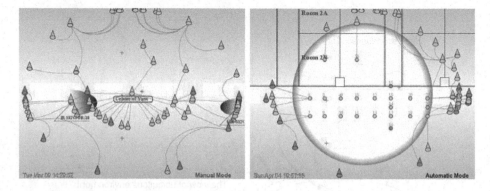

Fig. 4. Left Figure: The figure is the case of that all sensor nodes are transformed by hyperbolic function. Right Figure: The figure is the case which displayed all the nodes using our technique.

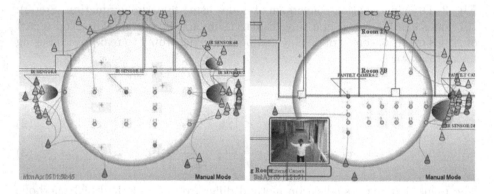

Fig. 5. Representation of status and event of nodes (Left Figure). Human detection by a pan-tilt camera (Right Figure).

Fig.5. The basic figure of a node is displayed as circular, and its diameter is inversely proportional to length from the center of display. In our system, nodes that exist far from the center of display are projected to the edge of oval plane according to hyperbolic geometry conversion. In addition, color gradation animation processing of a node drawing enables recognition of the specified node for the user. In the linear zooming area, representation of event occurrence is limited to color changing. This decreases the overlap of nodes in a linear area, and detects specified nodes in non-linear area.

4   Experiment and Discussion

In this section, we evaluate the applicability of our system through an experiment. We use the required time for detecting a specified event as a rating scale.

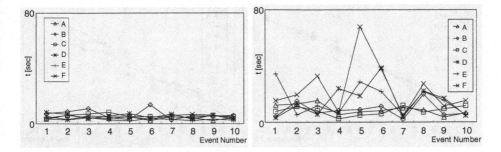

Fig. 6. Experiment Result 1: Time required for detecting the node that displays the event occurrence. Upper graph: The result for our visualization system. Lower graph: The result for normal drawing (without any visualization technique). The x-axis indicates the number of events. The y-axis indicates elapsed time.

We recruited six subjects and conducted experiments for every each person. The experiment is executed as follows. 1) Provide a test subject with the HMD and specify the event the subject should detect. 2) After a randomized time, we generate the event in the environment, without divulging the occurrence to the subject. 3) We record the time until a subject discovers the specified event, and terminate the experiment. In this experiment, we use another visualization method without any conversion for comparison. Next, we discuss the applicability of our visualization system for a wearable display based on the results of experiments.

Fig.6 indicates the time required to detect the event using the HMD. There are six data sets in this graph; the measured data corresponds to each subject. The top graph in Fig.6 illustrates the experiment result, which is measured using our visualization system. The bottom graph in Fig.6 depicts the experiment result measured without the visualization method. The two graphs clearly demonstrate the efficiency of our system. The result of our visualization system indicates that the measured times for detecting the specified event are nearly constant. This result indicates that all subjects are able to browse stably. However, the result of the experiment without visualization method (Fig.6 bottom) demonstrates a large variance in all subjects. This is due to the difficulty of instantaneous and intuitive perception of event detection in the environment. When the two graphs in Fig.6 are compared, the bottom graph has some data that has better performance than top graph. However, it is the case of that the event occurrence point is near the gazing area, then it is considered to be a accidental result. When the two graphs are compared overall, our system demonstrates better performance.

The graphs in Fig.7 illustrate measured experiment results for the same subjects. The time until detecting event information in the real environment is converted to a dimensionless number (divided by mean time T_m) and plotted. There are skill differences between the HMD and the interface operation between

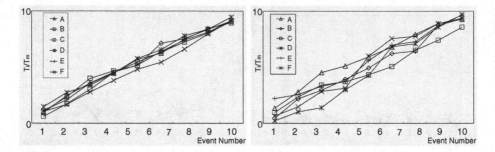

Fig. 7. Experiment Result 2: Time required for detecting the node that displays the event occurrence. Each plotted time required for the event number is the sum of previous times required. Upper graph: The result for our visualization system. Lower graph: The result for normal drawing (without any visualization technique). The x-axis represents the number of events. The y-axis represents the elapsed time divided by the average detection time of the node, of each subject.

subjects, resulting in major differences in the experiment data between subjects. Converting measured data to dimensionless number is intended to absorb the differences between subjects. The top graph in Fig.7 reveals the results of our visualization system. It illustrates that most plotted data appears on the same line. However, the bottom graph of Fig.7, demonstrates large differences between measured data. Therefore, these results suggest that our visualization system, which provides constant evaluation data, can provide intuitive information representation and usability to the user.

5   Conclusion

In this paper, we developed a visualization system to present information of the ubiquitous environment efficiently with a wearable computer. A small display is used for information presentation to a user fitted with a wearable computer. However, it is very difficult to display all the available information of the ubiquitous environment at one time for in such a small display area. In addition, it is possible that a user overlooks the change of important events and phenomena when displaying only a portion of the information. It is also possible to display large quantities of information on a small display at one time by using high-resolution hardware. However, with the increased amount of information in the display area it is impossible to distinguish individual information.

The ubiquitous information visualization system we developed solved this problem by using both nonlinear zooming and alignment zooming via hyperbolic conversion. We used a 12mm square and 640x480 resolution wearable display and displayed the users gazing area intelligibly, which enabled the display of all the environmental information. Therefore, a user can visualize all changes in environmental information while perusing information in the zoomed gazing area. Finally, we demonstrated these efficiencies through evaluation experiments using two or more subjects.

References

1. Bradley J.Rhodes, Nelson Minar and Josh Weaver, "Wearable Computing Meets Ubiquitous Computing: Reaping the best of both worlds," In Proceedings of ISWC'99, pp.141-149, IEEE Computer Society, 1999.
2. F.Mizoguchi, H.Nishiyama, H.Ohwada and H.Hiraishi, "Smart office robot collaboration based of a multi-agent programming," Artificial Intelligence, Vol.114, 1999.
3. Hayato Ohwada and Fumio Mizoguchi: Integrating Information Visualization and Retrieval for WWW Information Discovery, Theoretical Computer Science292, pp.547-571, 2003.
4. Hightower, R.R., Ring, L.T., Helfman, J.I., Bederson, B.B.,and Hollan, J.D., "Graphical Multiscale Web Histries: A Study of PadPrints," ACM Conference on Hypertext, 1998.
5. H.Hiraishi, F.Mizoguchi, "WWW Visualization Tools for Discovering Interesting Web Pages," Progress in Discovery Science, pp.650-660, 2002.
6. J.Lamping, R.Rao, P.Pirolli, "A Focus+Context Technique Based on Hyperbolic Geometory for Visualizing Large Hierachies," Proc.ACM CHI'95, 1995.
7. Kazushige Ouchi, Takuji Suzuki, Miwako Doi, "LifeMinder: A Wearable Healthcare Support System Using User's Context," ICDCS Workshops 2002: 791-792
8. Masaaki.Fukumoto, Yoshinobu.Tonomura, "Body Coupled FingeRing:Wireless Wearable Keyboard," SIGCHI97.
9. M.Sarkar, H.H.Brown, William York, "Graphical Fisheye Views of Graphs," *Human-Computer studies March '92*, 1992.
10. Nobuchika Sakata, Takeshi Kurata, Takekazu Kato, Masakatsu Kourogi, and Hideaki Kuzuoka: "WACL: Supporting Telecommunications Using Wearable Active Camera with Laser Pointer," In Proc. 7th IEEE International Symposium on Wearable Computers (ISWC2003), pp.53-56 (2003)

Perceiving Tools in 3D Sculpting

Jyrki Parviainen, Nina Sainio, and Roope Raisamo

Tampere Unit for Computer-Human Interaction (TAUCHI)
Department of Computer Sciences
FIN-33014 University of Tampere, Finland
{jypa, ns65332, rr}@cs.uta.fi
http://www.cs.uta.fi/hci/

Abstract. We introduce a 3D sculpting application and some 3D tools that help the user to understand and perceive the third dimension better on a 2D display. We call the new tools as perceiving tools. The tools are a perceiving box, a perceiving plane, a tool guide and an object guide. Other existing tools are carving and stuffing tools. The controlling in the application is done with two hands, and the goal has been to make it as natural as possible. This two-handed application makes use of a Magellan SpaceMouse, a six-degrees of freedom controller, and a basic wheel-mouse. The results of the evaluation showed that our sculpting program is easy to use and learn and that the perceiving tools help in the sculpting process.

1 Introduction

3D sculpting applications differ from well-known, traditional CAD programs in many ways. To use sculpting applications users do not need any mathematical skills or programming knowledge to be able to produce 3D models. The goal of 3D sculpting applications is to be highly intuitive to use so that the user could act as an artist who creates objects with his or her hands using tools that follow real-life metaphors. In addition, users do not have to seek the actions from the complex menus or palette systems: sculpting applications are based on direct manipulation interfaces. This means that every command can be done as an independent physical action, the actions are rapid and they complement each other. The actions can also be easily reversed. After all, the way of handling the modeled object in the 3D sculpting application resembles the actions of a living artist, who modifies and carves the real clay. The resulting object is not mathematically accurate, but it is suitable for the purpose of the sculpting program.

Sculpting applications are still not spread widely and there are no standards on how to create this kind of programs. Because of the two-dimensionality of the screen it is rather difficult to perceive the three-dimensional space in 3D sculpting programs if there are no spatial references. The human beings perceive the real 3D environments and depths naturally. But if we are in an abstract 3D environment it is quite difficult to understand the distances and especially the depth. The user needs a lot of extra information about the 3D space with a 2D computer screen.

M. Masoodian et al. (Eds.): APCHI 2004, LNCS 3101, pp. 328-337, 2004.
© Springer-Verlag Berlin Heidelberg 2004

Not only do the ways of presenting the state of the 3D environment vary, but there are also many kinds of control devices. Many different input devices have been used in sculpting applications, for example mice, keyboards, six-degrees of freedom devices (6DOF), different kinds of virtual controllers like 3D trackers, and SensAble PHANTOM [16] which produces helpful force feedback. Often regular users have become so accustomed only to a mouse and a keyboard as control devices that new control devices might at first increase the cognitive load before the devices become familiar to the user.

Control devices have been studied for years, but no ideal solution has been found for sculpting applications. Every device has its own strengths, but also its weaknesses. For example, Galyean and Hughes [7], Wang and Kaufman [18] and Perng *et al.* [14] used 3D trackers and Chen and Sun [5] used a PHANTOM.

In our research we have constructed a sculpting prototype that has a two-handed interface. So, the user can use naturally his or her both hands while sculpting the object. Using both hands is the most natural way of doing things in real life. In our application the left hand is used to rotate the object while the right hand is used to apply the sculpting tools. It is also possible to switch hands so that rotating is done by the right hand and sculpting by the left hand. The hands can be used both separately and simultaneously. At first the new setup of devices may cause some confusion, but rather quickly both hands are used naturally. It has been shown that adding the ability to use both hands increases the efficiency [3]. We have used a basic wheel-mouse and a Magellan SpaceMouse [1] as control devices. Magellan SpaceMouse is a six-degrees of freedom control device that is designed for this kind of purposes to handle 3D objects.

During the development of the application we created some tools that help the user to perceive the three-dimensionality and the depth better. We call them as perceiving tools: perceiving box, perceiving plane, tool guide and object guide.

Our aim has been to create a sculpting system that is easy to use with the devices we have used during this research. This kind of system does not need a 3D display or virtual controllers. 2D displays are so common that it is necessary to study how we can make such sculpting applications better. We had to pay attention to all above-mentioned restrictions and possibilities when designing new tools for this sculpting application.

Our initial results of using the program and the perceiving tools are promising. We had an evaluation, where the subjects were able to sculpt the given objects without major problems. They used perceiving tools voluntarily while sculpting different kinds of items like bowls, bears and chairs.

This research provides some aspects on developing the 3D sculpting application. In section 2 we have gathered previous work that has been a background for our prototype and research. The section 3 introduces the work we have done so far and some of the features of the prototype. Later in section 4 we present our user evaluation and results. The conclusions and future work is presented in section 5.

2 Previous Work

Our sculpting program is by no means the first of its kind. Parent [13] introduced the idea of 3D sculpting. With his program the user was able to make new objects from other objects by cutting and joining them together. Galyean and Hughes [7] developed the first 3D sculpting program that is based on volume sculpting. They developed it from the basis of a 2D program and extended it into three dimensions. Wang and Kaufman [18] also made this kind of program. They added a sawing tool into it. Bærentzen [4] introduced octree-based volume sculpting which allows greater resolution in sculpting. Octree data structure is more efficient in speed and memory issues. Raviv and Elber [15] introduced a program where the 3D grid is adaptive so the resolution can vary in different parts of the object.

Perng et al. [14] presented a program where the controlling was handled by virtual controller. Perng had also a modified Marching Cubes algorithm [11] that reduces the aliasing of objects. Ferley et al. [6] introduced a new tool, which allows using tool as a stamp printing its shape on the clay. This tool shape was also possible to design inside the application. Ferley et al. have also exploited stereo rendering to enhance the user's perception of the scene. Avila and Sobierajski [2] presented a haptic interaction method for volume visualization and modelling applications.

According to Shneiderman [17] direct manipulation interfaces should have rapid, complementary and reversible commands, present the objects visually with metaphors and show the results right away. Most of all, writing the commands should be replaced with pointing and selecting. The main benefits of direct manipulation interfaces are that they are quite natural, convenient and easy to use. Our application is also a direct manipulation application and it is based on principles Shneiderman created.

In a two-handed interface the user has two pointing devices at the same time. Our two-handed application is based on the research by Leganchuck et al. [10], Buxton and Myers [3], and Hinckley et al. [8]. Buxton and Myers [3] pointed out that two-handed control might be more efficient and understandable in many situations than only using a mouse and a keyboard. Leganchuk et al. [10] also noticed that using both hands in an application brings cognitive and manual advantages. Using both hands increases likewise the spatial reference in 3D applications [8].

In our application we use some perceiving tools to help the user to locate the sculpting tool on screen. Nielson and Olsen [12] have studied different kinds of position feedback methods to specifying a 3D point. They have used triad, full space and cube cursors to locate a tool in the 3D environment. Ferley et al. [6] have also pointed out how crucial the visual quality is for the perception of the position of the tool. Kjelldahl and Prime [9] studied how depth perception is affected by different presentation methods. They used different kinds of lighting, placement and distances of objects. Their results showed that placement and distance of objects are much more important factors on the depth estimates than the type of the rendering method.

3   Description of Our Sculpting Application

In the sculpting application the user modifies object, which can be thought to be like a piece of clay. The user can sculpt this "clay" with different shaped tools designed for sculpting. In our application (Fig. 1) it is possible to choose between carving and stuffing tools which can be either cubic or ball shaped. Behavior of this sculpting is much like real-life sculpting in the spirit of direct manipulation [17]. Using the program is rather easy, because users have some knowledge on real-life sculpting that they can use while sculpting with the computer.

The basis of the application is gathered from the work of Galyean and Hughes [7], Wang and Kaufman [18] and Perng *et al.* [14]. Our sculpting program is based on volume sculpting where the editable area is a 3D raster of voxels. These voxels are modified with the tools and surface of the object is built using the Marching cubes algorithm [11]. Volume graphics makes building complex and multi-layer objects possible. The resolution of the objects depends on the resolution of the 3D raster. The normal vector of each vertex has been estimated using a gradient vector that is linearly interpolated. These normal vectors are used for lighting the object correctly.

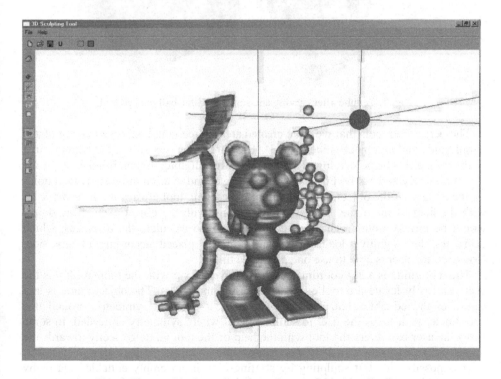

Fig. 1. The graphical user interface of our sculpting application.

3.1 Sculpting and Perceiving Tools

The program has tools for sculpting the object and tools that help the user to understand and perceive the 3D environment. According to Kjelldahl and Prime [9], humans use many different cues when estimating the depth, so it is important to construct these cues. Sculpting tools are stuffing and carving tools (Fig. 2) with two kinds of tool shapes, cubic and ball shapes. With these shapes the user can sculpt the object by adding clay into the object or by cutting pieces away from it. They both are based on mathematical formulas so the user can easily change their sizes. For example, the cubic shape can be changed as a plane or as a stick shape, because the user can alter the length of any edge of the cube.

Fig. 2. A cube after carving and stuffing with a ball-shaped tool.

The perceiving tools that we have created are a perceiving box, a perceiving plane, a tool guide and an object guide (Fig. 3). The perceiving box shows the editable area of the program. The perceiving plane is created for aligning the modified areas of the object correctly and easily. For instance, if the user had to align three equivalent holes on the surface of the object, he could align the carving tool always on the same level with the help of the plane. The plane goes along with the object even if the object would be turned around. The user does not have to calculate the distances, which decreases the cognitive load. The planes can be placed according to any side. However, the user is able to use one plane at a time.

The tool guide is a 3D coordinate, which moves along with the tool. With this the user can easily locate the tool even if it is inside the object. The object guide is in a centre of the editable area. The user can make the object symmetric around this coordinate, so it helps the user to sculpt objects where symmetry is needed. In some cases the user can direct the tool with the help of the tool guide correctly towards the object.

It is possible to start sculpting by stuffing clay in an empty editable area or by carving a piece of clay that fills the whole editable area. Any carved object can also be loaded as the starting piece. For example, it is much more appropriate to select a ball than a cubic piece if you are going to carve an apple.

There is a limited undo mechanism that helps in some cases. One of our leading principles is that the user would not need any undoes, because the user can reverse the actions by using the carving or stuffing tool as he or she would do in real life.

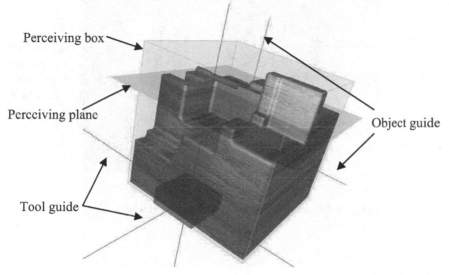

Perceiving box

Perceiving plane

Object guide

Tool guide

Fig. 3. Perceiving tools: perceiving box, perceiving plane, tool guide and object guide.

3.2 Controlling the Object and Tools

It is possible to control both the object and the tool with a single mouse. However, if the display and the mouse are 2D devices, this is not very intuitive. 2D environment and controllers do not allow natural interaction with 3D objects.

To make controlling more intuitive and modeless, it is possible to use both hands for controlling in our application. We ended up to this choice because using both hands increases efficiency and is a natural way of doing things for human beings, especially in direct manipulation interfaces [3]. We have chosen a Magellan SpaceMouse and a basic wheel-mouse as the controllers. One hand, usually the non-dominant hand, is used to rotate the objects with the Magellan SpaceMouse while the other hand is used to move the tool. It is possible to use both hands simultaneously. All the actions are shown immediately on the screen in real time.

The Magellan SpaceMouse and the wheel-mouse are shown in Figure 4. Buttons 1-8 in the Magellan SpaceMouse resize the tool while the user presses them. The motion controller rotates the object the same way as the user rotates the controller. Little buttons next to it in both sides move the perceiving plane.

When the right button is pressed down the wheel-mouse moves the sculpting tool. The left button is needed when the user stuffs or carves with the tool. So, if the user wants to do either action while moving the tool at the same time, he or she has to press both buttons down. The wheel is used for moving the tool in the z-axis.

Buttons 1-8 resize the tool   Action button   The button that moves
                                                          the tool in z-axis

Motion
controller   The button
                                                                    that activates
                                                                    the tool
                                                                    moving

The buttons
that move the
perceiving plane

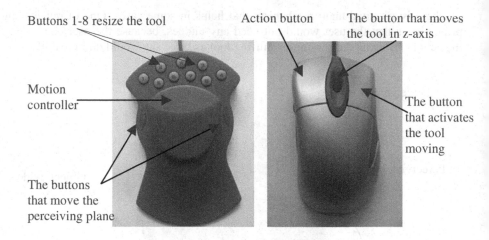

Fig. 4. Picture of Magellan SpaceMouse and wheel-mouse.

4   Evaluation

We have evaluated the application with 12 users, all under 30 year old. All of them
are quite experienced in computing, but their knowledge of 3D programs differed
from basics to comprehensive. None of them had heard about 3D sculpting programs
before, but two of the subjects were very accustomed to using the 3D CAD
applications like 3D Studio MAX and they consider themselves as artists or talented
in drawing.

The subjects were divided into two separate groups. There were six users in both
groups. The groups performed the same tasks but in different order. The evaluation
was focused on testing the potential use of the perceiving tools and the general
functionality of the prototype.

Every action the subjects made was written into the log that our application stored
automatically. We could see from the log, for example, how many times each tool
was selected and how long each task lasted.

The evaluation began with a five-minute introduction to the sculpting application
and its two-handed control. This stage was followed by a demonstration of the
program. After a short rehearsal with the interface the users started the evaluation.

Our evaluation tasks were divided in three different parts. In part one (tasks 1-3)
we gave pictures of starting and ending points. The subject was supposed to try to
sculpt an object from an initial form to the expected result form. They were not
allowed to use any perceiving tools at all at this stage. Part two (tasks 4-6) included
similar tasks than part one except that the user could use the perceiving tools while
doing the tasks.

Group 1 did part one at first and then part two. Group 2 did the tasks in the reverse
order. We wanted to diminish the effect of learning with this counterbalancing.

The first tasks were quite simple and we wanted to see how the users can understand our application and how the perceiving tools worked in use. For example, in task three the user should do a die without using any perceiving tools and later in task six a similar die with the given tools. The subjects were supposed to make as regular and good-looking a die as possible.

Part three (tasks 7-10) was the same for both groups. The subjects were shown only the expected result form. They had to decide how they began to sculpt – to carve or to stuff. They were also able to use the perceiving tools as much as they liked. We were interested in seeing how eagerly they use the tools developed and what kind of objects they could make with our prototype. Finally, we had a voluntary task for those who had patience, willingness and time to act as an artist. They were able to create creatures they wanted to.

Depending on how long the subject wanted to do the last task each evaluation lasted 45-60 minutes in total. The users could make comments during the evaluation, and each session was concluded with a short interview.

Perceiving the three-dimensional environment in 2D display and controlling and rotating both the object and the tools were rather easy for the subjects familiar with other 3D applications. The rest of the subjects learned quickly to use the program. The longer they sculpted the better they seemed to understand the environment and were able to create good-looking creatures.

The objects the users in Group 1 made improved when they carried out the tasks 4-6. The use of perceiving tools helped approximately 90% of the users to create more regular objects. With the users in Group 2 the differences were not so noticeable when comparing the objects. The subjects from Group 2 told us later that they had to concentrate on the controls so hard during the first few tasks that they had not attended to the perceiving tools as much as they would attended to if they could have done the tasks after learning to use the application better.

In general, the most important perceiving tool was the tool guide. Nine out of twelve subjects told that they were delighted when they knew where the tool was located even if it was inside the sculpted object. The object guide turned out to be useful when laying the object perpendicularly to the user. Three users told afterwards that they missed the opportunity to add unlimited amount of coordinates as separate guides.

The perceiving plane did not help the users much. However, users had lots of proposals to improve it. They suggested that it would be convenient to add many planes and some kind of feedback that tells when the tool touches it. Many of them said that perceiving tools are necessary but they still need to be developed.

All subjects used the perceiving box while carrying out the last five tasks. All completed the tasks by stuffing the clay in an empty editable area, even if five out of twelve subjects started the last tasks by carving. When starting with stuffing it is good to know the borders of the area and the perceiving box is excellent for that.

The most important results were the feedback and proposals the subjects gave us during the evaluation and later during the interview, where they could tell their opinions and thoughts about the application. For instance, eight subjects in one way or another suggested adding force feedback, which would help the use of the application.

In our subjects' opinion the application is usable, understandable and easy to use. Most of them learnt controlling immediately. The evaluation proved that our sculpting prototype is good enough for creating different kinds of 3D pieces, some of which can be seen in Figure 5.

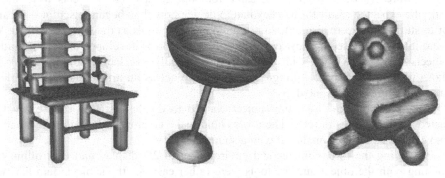

Fig. 5. Sculpted objects.

5   Conclusions and Future Work

In this paper, we have introduced a 3D sculpting application and some perceiving tools. We have identified many improvements that would help the user to perceive 3D environment. Adding perceiving planes limitlessly, rotating them freely and adding a visual feedback when the tool touches the plane would make the perceiving plane more usable and efficient.

One interesting improvement would be if the tool could move along the surface of the object. The solution would be to use force feedback. In addition, some kind of force feedback device like the PHANTOM would improve the spatial reference and would make the sculpting process closer to its real-world analogue.

The restrictions of the 2D display make the using of the 3D sculpting application more difficult than necessary. A stereo display or a 3D display would improve the visual feedback of the application and would display the object more naturally.

There are many improvements that are possible in the implementation of the sculpting process. In the future we are planning to use octrees to store 3D rasters of voxels that will make the program more efficient in speed and memory issues. In addition, improving marching cubes algorithm will reduce the aliasing of the edges of the objects. Using the unlimited editable area instead fixed-sized area would make sculpting less restricted.

In this version of our sculpting application there is only one object at the time, but in the future we are planning to make it possible to sculpt multiple objects at the same time. Then it would be possible to join different objects together or separate them and deform new objects.

Acknowledgments

This research was funded by the Academy of Finland (grant 104805). We also thank all the participants of the experiment for their valuable help.

References

1. 3Dconnexion, Magellan SpaceMouse, http://www.3dconnexion.com/spacemouseplus.htm
2. Avila, R., Sobierajski, L.: A Haptic Interaction Method for Volume Visualization. Visualization '96 Proceedings, IEEE (1996) 197-204
3. Buxton, W., Myers, B.: A Study in Two-Handed Input. Human Factors in Computer Systems CHI '86 Conference Proceedings, ACM Press (1986) 321-326
4. Bærentzen, A.,: Octree-Based Volume Sculpting. LBHT Proceedings of IEEE Visualization '98, IEEE (1998)
5. Chen, H., Sun, H.: Real-time Haptic Sculpting in Virtual Volume Space. Proceedings of the ACM Symposium on Virtual Reality Software and Technology, ACM Press (2002) 81-88
6. Ferley, E., Cani, M-P., Gascuel, J-D.: Practical Volumetric Sculpting. The Visual Computer 16(8) (2000) 211-221
7. Galyean, T., Hughes, J.: Sculpting: an Interactive Volumetric Modeling Technique. Computer Graphics 25 (4) (1991) 267-274
8. Hinckley, K., Pausch, R., Goble, J., Kassell, N.: A Survey of Design Issues in Spatial Input. Proceedings of the 7th Annual ACM Symposium on User Interface Software and Technology, ACM Press (1994) 213-222
9. Kjelldahl, L., Prime, M.: A Study on How Depth Perception is Affected by Different Presentation Methods of 3D Objects on a 2D Display. Computer Graphics 19(2) 1995 199-202
10. Leganchuk, A., Zhai, S., Buxton, W.: Manual and Cognitive Benefits of Two-Handed Input: An Experimental Study. ACM Transactions on Computer-Human Interaction 15 (4) (1998) 326-359
11. Lorensen, W., Cline, H.: Marching Cubes: A High Resolution 3D Surface Construction Algorithm. Computer Graphics 21(4) (1987) 163-169
12. Nielson, G., Olsen, D.: Direct Manipulation Techniques for 3D Objects Using 2D Locator Devices. Proceedings of the 1986 Workshop on Interactive 3D Graphics, ACM Press (1986) 175-182
13. Parent, R.: A System for Sculpting 3-D Data. Computer Graphics 11(2) (1977) 138-147
14. Perng, Kuo-Luen., Wang, Wei-The., Flanagan, Mary.: A Real-time 3D Virtual Sculpting Tool Based on Modified Marching Cubes. International Conference on Artificial Reality and Tele-Existence (ICAT) (2001) 64-72
15. Raviv, A., Elber, G.: Three Dimensional Freedom Sculpting Via Zero Sets of Scalar Trivariate Functions. Computer-Aided Design. 32 (8-9) (2000) 513-526
16. SensAble Technologies, PHANTOM haptic interface, http://www.sensable.com/products/phantom_ghost/papers.asp
17. Shneiderman, B.: The Future of Interactive Systems and the Emergence of Direct Manipulation. Behaviour and Information Technology 1 (1982) 237-256
18. Wang, S.W., Kaufman, A.E.: Volume Sculpting. Symposium on Interactive 3D Graphics Proceedings, ACM Press (1995) 151-156

A Tripartite Framework for Working Memory Processes

Peter J. Patsula

Nanyang Technological University
School of Communication and Information
31 Nanyang Link, Singapore 637718
usefo@patsula.com

Abstract. A key factor in understanding the usability of an interface is to understand the user's mental model. However, most mental model research tends to be more descriptive than predictive. The following work outlines a theoretical framework well supported by cognitive science and cognitive psychology research called Mental Model Imprinting (MMI). MMI attempts to explain *how* mental models are processed in working memory so designers are better able to predict user interactions and ascertain *why* certain design features are more effective than others. A study is currently being planned to test for positive correlations between MMI based design treatments and Web-based navigation menus.

1 Introduction

Despite the centrality of the mental model concept in human factors psychology, there is at present no formal framework which integrates mental model processes into a coherent whole which can then be used to predict user performance. Providing such a framework is the central aim of this research. A number of working memory (WM) researchers are leaning towards the assumption of a unified mental representation in WM as a basis for cognition. Baddeley [2] defines representations in the episodic buffer of WM as "current episodes." He speculates that a central executive controls operations and processing in WM and is responsible for binding information from a number of sources into current episodes. Cowan [9] prefers to define such representations as "scene coherence." A coherent scene is formed in the focus of attention and can have about four separate parts in awareness. Only one coherent scene can be held in WM at one time. In an effort to clarify past confusion surrounding the term mental model, Brewer [5] has proposed that researchers replace the term mental model with the term "episodic model." Brewer defines *Episodic models* as "the specific knowledge structures constructed to represent new situations out of more specific generic knowledge represented in local schemas" (p. 193). This definition agrees with a more recent conception by Cañas and Antolí [6] that mental models are dynamic representations created in WM by combining information stored in long-term memory (LTM) and characteristics extracted from the environment.

M. Masoodian et al. (Eds.): APCHI 2004, LNCS 3101, pp. 338-348, 2004.

2 Support for Three Working Memory Processing Systems

The idea of the mind functioning as a set of domain-specific subsystems or modules is well represented in the literature. Chomsky [8] proposed a universal grammar, where basic language structures and patterns were innate in all human beings. He found it useful to think of language and other faculties as "mental organs" with no clear lines between physical organs, perceptual systems, motor systems, and cognitive facilities. Fodor [13] expanded upon this idea proposing a functional taxonomy of domain specific computational mechanisms including perceptual subsidiary systems and what he referred to as domain specific input systems. He further speculated that these systems could be informationally encapsulated and neurologically hardwired. Though acknowledging nonmodular cognitive systems, the modular mind view assumes that the human brain is essentially made up of a number of highly-tuned domain-specific systems, analogous to specialized body organs like the liver or kidney, designed through evolutionary selection to solve specific problems that frequently confronted ancestral humans [4]. Hardwired mental modules evolved to facilitate rapid computation and learning within specific domains. Gardner [14] has further extended the concept of modularity with multiple intelligences theory. He makes a strong claim for several relatively autonomous intelligences, which he categorizes as linguistic, musical, logical-mathematical, spatial, bodily-kinesthetic, and personal.

More recently, it has been proposed that the mind is composed of two reasoning systems [12,25] referred to as System 1 and 2. System 1 is old in evolutionary terms and shared with other animals and operates with autonomous subsystems and more associative domain-specific knowledge input modules, while System 2 is more distinctly human and permits goal-directed abstract reasoning and hypothetical thinking. Both systems are supported by neuropsychological evidence. Using fMRI methodology, it was found that System 1 content-based semantically rich reasoning recruited a left hemisphere temporal system where as System 2 reasoning with abstract formal problems was associated with activation of a parietal system [16]. Goel and Dolan [17] found that System 2 processes can intervene or inhibit System 1 processes.

2.1 System 1

System 1 type processes are supported by illusory inference [18] and belief bias effect research [13], as well as, long-term working memory [11] and chess skills acquisition research [7]. Klein [19] has also extensively investigated how expert decision makers, such as fire fighters and medical doctors use feature-matching and pattern recognition between current situations and prior experiences to make rapid and accurate decisions in naturalistic environments. He calls this recognition-primed decision-making (RPD). RPD theory points to the acquisition over time of a system of domain-specific experiences and skills that decision-makers can access rapidly. In a similar vein, Tversky and Kahneman [28] have asserted that people rely on a limited number of heuristics, or rather "rules of thumb," to guide decision-making. Heuristics provide an efficient way of dealing with situations that might otherwise be too complex to manage in working memory. Extensive research on *availability*, which refers to "the ease with which instances or associations [can] be brought to mind" [27], has found that people employ the availability heuristic whenever they estimate frequency or probability by the ease with which they can remember an event or which examples come to mind. Entrenched biases caused by the salience of easily and frequently recalled examples, and examples with preferred associations, can impede and interfere with optimal performance. The "availability" of information also plays considerable importance in influencing the outputs of System 2 processes.

2.2 System 2

System 2 type reasoning processes have been traditionally the most frequently studied area of cognition. The existence of rule-based and abstract thinking is well supported [e.g., 12,25]. Working memory capacity research has also added significantly to understandings of reasoning system processes. Johnson-Laird [18] and Norman [23] agree that the mind has a limited ability to process information in WM, and that the fewer the mental models that need to be run in the head or called for, the better. Cognitive Load Theory [26] also maintains that WM can handle only a very limited number of novel interacting elements possibly no more than two or three.

2.3 System 3

In addition to System 1 and 2, it is now being proposed that a third system shares enough distinct processes and subsystems to be considered separate. System 3 consists of a collection of subsystems and processes that facilitate goal-orientated chunking. *Chunking* is a memory-related process in which several smaller units are combined or organized into larger units. Under Soar theory [22], all cognitive acts are some form of search task and chunking is "the pervasive architectural learning mechanism" [20, p. 35]. System 3 operates as a domain-general learning mechanism. However, it is also supported by Baddeley and Hitch's [3] phonological loop and visuospatial sketchpad buffers which facilitate maintenance of aural and visual inputs, thereby increasing WM capacity. This in turn facilitates perceptual chunking in System 1 and goal-orientated chunking in System 3. Goal-orientated chunking is very deliberate and under strategic control, whereas perceptual chunking is more automatic and continuous [15]. System 3 goal-orientated chunking and System 1 perceptual chunking help reduce cognitive load in System 2 and facilitate schema acquisition.

The processes in this third system can also be broken down into Rumelhart and Norman's [24] three modes of learning, where it is stated that "it is possible to learn through the gradual accretion of information, through the fine tuning of conceptualizations we already possess, or through the restructuring of existing knowledge" (p. 38). Though System 3 processes are distinct from System 1 and 2 processes, it is clear that there is a tradeoff between processing and storage [e.g., 3,9]. Levels of processing theory [10] assumes a strong connection between storage and processing through elaboration techniques that demand considerable attentional resources. Cognitive load theory [26] posits that "goal attainment and schema acquisition may be two largely unrelated and even incompatible processes" (p. 283) and that there indeed might be some kind of distinction or interfering factor between them.

3 MMI Theoretical Framework

Borrowing heavily from cognitive science, MMI proposes the existence of three non-unitary recognition, production, and chunking systems to describe and predict the mental model processes users go through as they encounter and respond interactively to new information. Controlled by the central executive, the processes within these systems are referred to as consistency, availability, and learnability processing, or more simply: System 1, 2, and 3. Consistency and availability processing systems resemble Evans [12] "System 1" and "System 2" dual-process accounts of reasoning, with MMI System 1 consisting of more domain-specific knowledge, skill, and LT-WM subsystems, and MMI System 2 consisting of more domain-general subsystems that permit abstract reasoning and the manipulation of information, constrained by WM capacity. System 3 can be considered a collection of subsystems dedicated to chunking, and more specifically, making associations in WM to reduce the load in System 2. System 3 also facilitates storage in LTM, and overtime, the development of domain-specific processing and learning mechanisms for System 1 and System 2.

3.1 Episodic Model Processing Sequence

To generate a *coherent* episodic model, the three processing systems of the MMI framework are accessed sequentially (see Fig. 1). A *coherent episodic model* is a mental representation of an event or problem situation perceived by the user to be sufficiently complete to facilitate the execution of a chosen interaction goal. At any point during the MMI processing sequence, if the user is satisfied with the functionality of their episodic model, they can proceed to goal execution. The processing sequence itself is a continuing iteration of recognition, production, and chunking processes. The sequence iterates until all desired interaction goals are executed. It has been conjectured that a full WM processing sequence from input to output, called a "cognitive cycle," takes a minimum of 200 msec [1]. This is equivalent to a maximum of about four or five decisions or goal formations or executions per second. In MMI, during episodic model generation, users may be able to refresh, change, update, and run their episodic model about four to five times a second. Baars and Franklin [1] have explained that "more than one cognitive cycle can proceed at any given time" (p. 167) and that because of overlapping and automaticity as many as twenty cycles might be running per second. However, consciousness imposes seriality on otherwise concurrent processes thus only one single cycle can be conscious at any given instant.

3.2 Associations Matrix

Cowan defines a *chunk* in WM as having strong intra-associations within a collection of items and weak inter-associations between items [9]. He also distinguishes between *pure STM capacity limit* expressed in chunks from *compound STM limits* obtained when the number of separately held chunks is unclear. He claims that Miller's "seven, plus or minus two" limit [21] should be more precisely defined as a "compound STM limit," in which support structures like Baddeley and Hitch's [3] phonological loop can

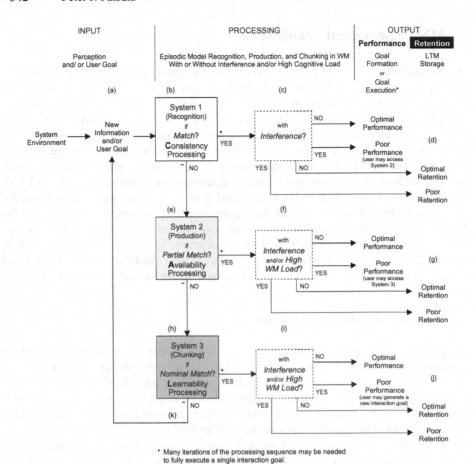

Fig. 1. Processing sequence for episodic models in working memory.

<u>Notes</u>: In S1 processing, there are *strong associations* between the episodic model created in WM and chunks stored in LTM, hence the episodic model may be immediately usable complete with built-in interaction goals. In S2 processing, there are *moderate associations* between the episodic model created in WM and chunks stored in LTM. System processing and several iterations of the sequence may be necessary to render the episodic model coherent. In S3 processing, there are *weak associations* between the episodic model created in WM and chunks stored in LTM. Substantial processing and iterations of the sequence will be necessary to generate a coherent episodic model.

(a) When a user encounters an information source, they automatically create an episodic model. At this point, the user may already have an interaction goal in mind. (b) If the new episodic model matches previously stored representations, the user processes it rapidly, and either creates a goal if they did not have one initially, or executes their initial goal. (c) If encountering interference, the user may access System 2 to process the increased load. (d) The user may store the interaction in episodic memory. (e) If the new episodic model partially matches stored representations, the user will attempt to process the missing parts using other easily available LTM chunks. (f) If encountering interference or high WM load, the user may access System 3 to chunk information with strong associations to reduce load. (g) The user may store some declarative and procedural memory chunks of the interaction. (h) If recognition of the new episodic model is low, the user will attempt to chunk new information with strong associations. (i) High load to the system will reduce performance. (j) The user may store some declarative, procedural, and structural memory chunks. (k) If unable to generate a coherent episodic model, the user may generate a different goal.

assist individuals in holding more items in STM. In extending these concepts to MMI, cognitive load can be classified according to strong, moderate, or weak associations between the episodic model and LTM, and strong, moderate, or weak associations within WM between new WM chunks, to yield six levels of associations (see Fig. 2).

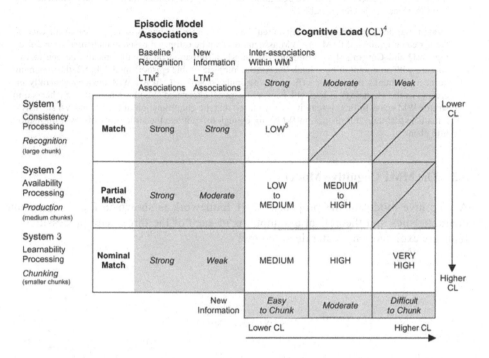

Fig. 2. Aggregate cognitive load for strong, moderate, and weak associations between information stored in LTM and the user's episodic model, and associations between new chunks created dynamically in WM.

[1] **Baseline Recognition** – When a user encounters new information, such as an interface navigation menu, a minimum amount of strong associations with information stored in LTM is needed to process basic inputs such as letters of the alphabet, font faces, and the meanings of words. This can be called *baseline recognition* and is generated automatically via *perceptual chunking*.

[2] **LTM Associations** – *LTM associations* are associations between the episodic model created in WM and long-term memory (LTM). If the new episodic model closely matches previously stored representations of similar information (i.e., strong LTM-associations), there is a low cognitive load. If the new episodic model does not match previously stored representations (i.e., moderate or weak LTM-associations), cognitive load increases.

[3] **Inter-Associations** – *Inter-associations* are associations between chunks in WM. For S1, inter-associations that make up the user's episodic mental model in WM will be strong. In S1, it is impossible to have models with moderate or weak inter-associations. In S2, new information extracted from the environment that is not familiar may be easy or moderately difficult to chunk. In S2, activated LTM chunks with strong or moderately strong inter-associations can be processed into a coherent episodic model. However, if inter-associations between activated LTM chunks or newly created WM chunks are weak, processing defaults to S3. In S3, new information that does not match previously stored representations and is furthermore difficult to chunk in WM will generate a very high cognitive load. On the other hand, if it is relatively easy to make new associations, the newly

chunked information will reduce cognitive load. *Intra-associations*, that is, associations within chunks, in all systems can be weakened by interference or distractions to attentional focus.

[4] **Cognitive Load** – Generally speaking, cognitive load is a measure of the demand that an information source makes on the information processing capacity of the human mind. The term is often used in the study of the effects of interface design on users. The term working memory load (WM load) and cognitive load are interchangeable.

[5] **System Capacity Limits** – It is conjectured that the number of chunks being processed for each of the six combinations of LTM and WM associations can be estimated based upon Miller's 7 ± 2 findings [21] and Cowan's 4 ± 1 findings [9]. In S1, information input will typically be one to two chunks, with an output of one chunk to create a complete usable episodic model. In S2, the maximum number of chunks that can be efficiently manipulated is 4 ± 1. In S3, WM capacity generally increases as the phonological loop (PL) and visuospatial sketchpad (VS) buffers facilitate rehearsal to stretch WM span. In this system, it is conjectured that the chief function of the PL and VS slave systems is to maintain information in WM long enough to facilitate the structuring of new information into chunks.

3.3   The MMI Cognitive Model

A cognitive model of the proposed MMI framework is shown in Fig. 3. Important characteristics and theoretical assumptions of each of the three main processing systems are explained in greater detail below:

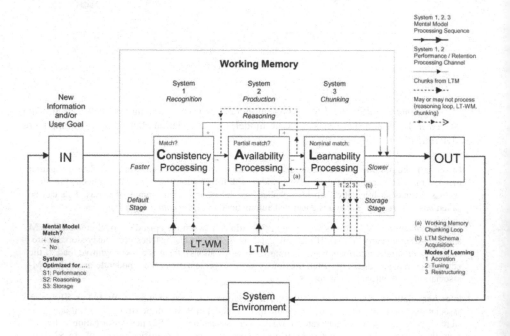

Fig. 3. Three central executive controlled non-unitary recognition, production, and chunking systems for processing episodic models in working memory.

System 1: Consistency Processing → Recognition. System 1 is the "default recognition stage of cognition" demanding limited attentional resources. It operates at a low WM load. *Consistency processing* is the process of reconstructing a single "familiar" episodic model in the user's WM of a recognizable event or problem situation through the activation of an existing "retained" episodic model. A *retained* episodic model is a stored representation of a similar event or problem situation, along with plausible goals, relevant cues, expectancies, and typical actions. Consistency processing is the most frequently used type of processing for everyday actions and decisions made under time pressure. Klein [10] defines this type of rapid decision making as recognition-primed decision making. Evans [7] would characterize this system as domain-specific and autonomous. Sloman [23] would characterize it as parallel associative-based processing responsible for intuition, imagination, and creativity.

System 2: Availability Processing → Production. If S1 fails to create an adequate "familiar" representation of an event or problem situation to enable the user to operate at a desired level of performance, S2 takes over to facilitate availability processing. System 2 is the "overriding production stage of cognition" that under executive control can direct attentional resources away from System 1 and inhibit System 3 if experiencing a high WM load. *Availability processing* is the process of updating a previously constructed "familiar" episodic model or building a new "functional" episodic model using other "retained" episodic models or LTM chunks, all of which can be easily "cued" or accessed, as well as more readily maintained and manipulated in WM. Availability processing is slower than consistency processing, frequently involves "recall" rather than "recognition," is limited by working memory capacity, and is the stage where most rule-based or abstract reasoning takes place. A *functional* episodic model is an incomplete representation of an event or problem situation but can usually be updated sufficiently to allow a user to operate at a desired level of performance. Evans [12] would characterize this system as central executive dominant with the capability to inhibit S1. Sloman [23] would characterize it as being sequential rather than parallel and responsible for deliberation, explanation, and analysis.

System 3: Learnability Processing → Chunking. If a novel situation or problem is encountered, in which both S1 and S2 fail to create a "familiar" or a "functional" episodic model, S3 takes over to facilitate learnability processing. System 3 is the "chunking stage of cognition" that demands a restricted goal-orientated attentional focus to form associations in WM. Strong goal-orientated associations in WM lead to better retention of episodic models and chunked information in WM. *Learnability processing* is the process of building a new "structured" episodic model that can be easily chunked in WM. Demanding more attentional resources and WM capacity, learnability processing is generally the slowest and most deliberate type of processing. System 3 is also the key system responsible for long-term working memory (LT-WM) skill acquisition, which when acquired becomes part of System 1 processes. In S3, learning by accretion is most likely to occur in conjunction with S1 processing, while learning by tuning is most likely to occur as a result of S2 processing. Learning by restructuring, that is, consistent chunking of new associations in the same domain over an extended period of time, as conjectured in the MMI framework, is most likely to occur as a result of iterative goal-orientated S3 processing.

4   Some Applications of the MMI Framework

Up to this point, developing the MMI framework has been primarily a creative and analytical task involving the synthesis of a great number of important relationships and processes as outlined in the cognitive psychology and cognitive science literature. Nevertheless, because of the depth and breadth of support for MMI, the scope of applications to human-computer interaction and other fields is promising. The key strength of MMI lies in its ability to predict *why* rather than merely describe *how*. Design heuristics typically arise out of extensive experience in the field, time-consuming trial-and-error testing, and/or expensive usability testing. With MMI, designers should be better able to predict design errors before they happen and rationalize these predictions, thereby increasing cost efficiency, as well as design confidence.

The MMI cognitive model can also be applied to Baddeley's research on the episodic buffer in working memory [2]. Baddeley and Hitch [3] originally proposed a three non-unitary component model of working memory consisting of a central executive, a phonological loop, and a visuospatial sketchpad. Recently, Baddeley [2] has updated this model with a fourth component: the episodic buffer. The *episodic buffer* is assumed to be "a limited-capacity temporary storage system that is capable of integrating information from a variety of sources. It is assumed to be controlled by the central executive, which is capable of retrieving information from the store in the form of conscious awareness, of reflecting on that information and, where necessary, manipulating and modifying it" (p. 420). It is now being tentatively suggested that the episodic buffer is fed by three processing systems controlled by the central executive.

5   Current and Future Work

Currently, the MMI framework is being applied to Web-based navigation menus to obtain qualitative and quantitative experimental evidence to verify performance and retention characteristics of each of the three proposed processing systems. One of the central hypotheses being tested is that strong inter-associations in working memory lead to better retention in long-term memory. A pilot study has been conducted to test a repeated measures experimental design that uses two-level navigation menus to facilitate or interfere with S1, S2, or S3 processing. Preliminary results from retention scores and think-aloud feedback are promising. In the future, relationships between chunking, working memory capacity, and retention, and *how* and to *what* extent the contents of episodic models can be manipulated by the central executive, will be examined more closely to provide further conceptual clarity to the MMI framework.

References

1. Baars, B. J., & Franklin, S. (2003). How conscious experience and working memory interact. *Trends in Cognitive Science, 7*, 166-172.

2. Baddeley, A. D. (2000). The Episodic Buffer: a New Component of Working Memory? *Trends in Cognitive Science, 4*(11), 417-423.

3. Baddeley, A. D., & Hitch, G. (1974). Working memory. In G. H. Bower (Ed.), *The psychology of learning and motivation*, Vol. 8 (pp. 47-89). New York: Academic Press.

4. Barkow, J. H., Cosmides, L. & Tooby, J. (1992) *The adapted mind: Evolutionary psychology and the generation of culture.* New York : Oxford University Press.

5. Brewer, W. F. (1987). Schemas versus mental models in human memory. In P. Morris (Ed.), *Modelling Cognition* (pp. 187-197). Chichester, UK: Wiley.

6. Cañas, J. J. & Antolí, A. (1998). The role of working memory in measuring mental models. In: T. R. G. Green, L. Bannon, C. P. Warren & J. Buckley (Eds.). *Proceedings of the Ninth European Conference on Cognitive Ergonomic–Cognition and Cooperation* (pp. 139-144).

7. Chase, W. G., & Simon, H. A. (1973). Perception in chess. *Cognitive Psychology, 4*, 55-81.

8. Chomsky, N. (1980). Rules and representations. *The Behavioral and Brain Sciences, 3*, 1-15.

9. Cowan, N. (2001). The magical number 4 in short-term memory: A reconsideration of mental storage capacity. *Behavioral and Brain Sciences, 24*(1), 87-186.

10. Craik, F. I. M., & Lockhart, R.S. (1972). Levels of processing. A framework for memory research. *Journal of Verbal Learning and Verbal Behaviour, 11*, 671-684.

11. Ericsson, K. A., & Kintsch, W. (1995). Long-term working memory. *Psychological Review, 102*, 211-245.

12. Evans, J. St. B. T. (2003). In two minds: dual-process accounts of reasoning. *Trends in Cognitive Science, 7*(10), 454-459.

13. Fodor, J. A. (1983). *The modularity of the mind.* Cambridge, Ma.: MIT Press.

14. Gardner, H. (1993). *Multiple intelligences: The theory in practice.* New York: Basic Books.

15. Gobet, F., Lane, P. C. R., Croker, S., Cheng, P. C-H., Jones, G., I Oliver, & Pine, J.M. (2001). Chunking mechanisms in human learning. *Trends in Cognitive Sciences, 5*(6), 236-243.

16. Goel, V. (2003). Evidence for dual neural pathways for syllogistic reasoning. *Psychologica,32*.

17. Goel, V., & Dolan, R. J. (2003). Explaining modulation of reasoning by belief. *Cognition, 87*, 11-22.

18. Johnson-Laird, P. N. (2001). Mental models and deduction. *Trends in Cognitive Science, 5*(10), 434-442.

19. Klein, G. A. (1998). *Sources of power: How people make decisions.* Cambridge, MA: MIT Press.

20. Lehman, J. F., Laird, J. E., & Rosenbloom, P. (1998). A gentle introduction to Soar: An architecture for human cognition. In D. Scarborough & S. Sternberg (Eds.), *An invitation to cognitive science*, Vol. 4, 2nd Ed., (pp. 212 –249). Cambridge, MA: MIT Press.

21. Miller, G. A. (1956). The magical number seven plus or minus two: Some limits on our capacity for processing information. *Psychological Review, 63*, 81-97.

22. Newell, A. (1990). *Unified theories of cognition.* Cambridge, MA: Harvard University Press.

23. Norman, D. A. (1983). Some observations on mental models. In D. Gentner & A. L. Stevens (Eds.), *Mental models* (pp. 7-14). Mahwah, NJ: Erlbaum.

24. Rumelhart, D. E., & Norman, D. A. (1978). Accretion, tuning and restructuring: Three modes of learning. In J. W. Cotton and R. L. Klatzky (Eds.), *Semantic factors in cognition* (pp. 37-53). Hillsdale, NJ: Erlbaum.

25. Sloman, S.A. (1996). The empirical case for two systems of reasoning. *Psychological Bulletin*, 119, 3-22. (In Gilovich, T., Griffin, D., & Kahneman, D. (2002). *Heuristics and biases: The psychology of intuitive judgment* (pp. 379-396). New York: Cambridge University Press.)

26. Sweller, J. (1988). Cognitive load during problem solving: Effects on learning. *Cognitive Science*, 12, 257-285.

27. Tversky, A., & Kahneman, D. (1973). Availability: A heuristic for judging frequency and probability. *Cognitive Psychology*, 5, 207-232.

28. Tversky, A., & Kahneman, D. (1974). Judgment under uncertainty: Heuristics and biases. *Science*, 185, 1124-1131.

Designing for Flow in a Complex Activity

Jon M. Pearce and Steve Howard

Interaction Design Group, Department of Information Systems, The University of Melbourne,
Australia, 3010
jonmp@unimelb.edu.au showard@unimelb.edu.au

Abstract. One component of a user's interaction with computer systems is
commonly referred to as 'flow'. Flow is an important consideration in
interactive system design as it encapsulates some of the affective aspects of
human behavior. The majority of current thinking conceptualises flow as a
desirable and somewhat enduring emotional state that a user may enter during
an activity. Analysis of data from 59 users engaged in an interactive online
learning task contradicts this prevailing view. We show firstly that flow, rather
than being enduring, is highly changeable during the term of an interaction.
This challenges both current theoretical models of flow, and the current
research methodology used to study the phenomenon. Secondly, we show that
flow arises from an engagement either with the interactive artefact or the task
being performed. This is an aspect of flow not well distinguished in other
studies. Finally, we present initial analysis that suggests flow can be
undesirable in some circumstances – that there may be competition between
task and artefact for the attention of the user. In response, we present a
'process' view of flow as a counterpoint to the existing 'state' based models.

1 Introduction

In studies researching the role of affect in human interaction with computers, the
related concepts of flow [1], motivation and play are frequently explored. These are
often grouped as 'affective factors' and used to complement the effectiveness,
efficiency and satisfaction aspects of user-experience [2].

In this paper we describe an experiment in which it was found useful to focus on
flow as a *process* rather than a *state*. In the context of an online interactive learning
system, we consider the manifestations of flow, how to measure flow and how to
design to maximize it. We present a visualization of flow as a process as well as some
of the experiences that users (in this case, students) describe when they have
experienced flow in this online learning context.

2 Flow

In 1975 Csikszentmihalyi coined the term 'flow' to refer to 'optimal experience'
events [1]. Flow describes a state of complete absorption or engagement in an activity
and has been studied in a wide range of disciplines including HCI, psychology,

M. Masoodian et al. (Eds.): APCHI 2004, LNCS 3101, pp. 349-358, 2004.
© Springer-Verlag Berlin Heidelberg 2004

information systems and education. For example: Web use and navigation [3]; Web marketing [4]; in everyday life [1, 5]; in group work [6]; technology use in information systems [7]; in HCI [8]; and in instructional design [9, 10]. This section gives a brief introduction to flow and the challenges encountered in measuring it.

2.1   Flow and Online Learning

Flow has been postulated by many as a desirable state to support learning [1, 4, 8, 11]. A 'flow activity' is one in which the mind becomes effortlessly focussed and engaged, rather than falling prey to distractions. Such an activity will usually comprise a clear set of goals, timely and appropriate feedback, and, most importantly, a perception of challenges that are well matched to the user's skills. As a result, a user might obtain a high degree of control over the activity and experience deep engagement or concentration. The activity will become enjoyable for its own sake and will often lead to a lack of awareness of the passage of time.

Many flow studies use retrospective interviews and surveys to observe participants over extended periods of time: days or weeks rather than minutes or hours. Such studies describe flow as a state attained during a particular activity: for example, when engrossed in a computer game or engaged in aspects of professional work. Draper [11], in contrast, proposes that a user may 'flick in and out' of flow from moment to moment. In being critical of Csikszentmihalyi's model of flow, he draws a distinction between flow during routine actions not requiring mental attention and flow requiring complete mental attention. It is during the latter that he postulates such rapid shifts might occur. Whilst he offers no evidence for these shifts, his postulation suggests that interviews and surveys may be instruments that are too blunt to observe flow in these situations.

In this study we were interested in monitoring flow during a short learning activity (40 minutes) in which deep engagement is essential. Whilst an educator might hope that participants maintain a high level of engagement throughout the entire activity, in reality we expected to see movements in and out of the flow state. Hence we designed an experiment to monitor flow attributes in a more fine-grained fashion and to observe users' movements amongst the flow states.

This study was carried out in an educational setting where the motives of control, concentration and enjoyment are important. However, many of the attributes of flow are desirable in the design of other computer-based system in which the aim is to engage the user and maintain that engagement.

2.2   Flow Models and Measurements

The research referenced earlier [1 to 10] presents several different techniques for measuring flow. One commonly-used technique is to survey participants, after an activity, to obtain Likert scale ratings for the affective measures of control, engagement and enjoyment [8, 12]. From these measures a score is derived that represents the overall degree of flow for the duration of the activity. This technique is used in our research as one measure of flow.

An alternative established technique, also used in this research, is to monitor the balance between the user's perceived challenge of an activity and their perception of their skills to carry out that activity. Flow theory predicts that a user will experience flow if their perception of the challenge of a task is balanced with, or slightly greater than, their perception of their skills to carry out the task. If these are out of balance, then the user may become anxious (challenge much greater than skills) or bored (challenge much less than skills). The perception of these challenges and skills has been described as *'theoretically, the most meaningful reference point for the presence or absence of flow'* [13] and has been established as a reliable measure of flow [14].

Often this representation of flow is presented on a 2-dimensional plot of challenge versus skills. The space on this plot can be partitioned into three, four, eight, or even sixteen 'channels', each channel representing an emotional state of the user. We have chosen to interpret our data using the 3-channel model shown in Figure 1 in accordance with Csikszentmihalyi's early work on flow [1]. This choice was made in recognition of the nature of learning, which offers the potential of flow even though the learner's skills may begin low and increase significantly during the activity. For example, a learner might begin a task with low skills and recognise that the challenge presented to her is low, yet commensurate with her skills. This low-challenge/low-skills situation could still induce a flow state. As the learning progresses, and the task increases in complexity, we might expect the learner to move up the flow channel to a region in which she is more highly challenged, but still commensurate with her (now improved) skills.

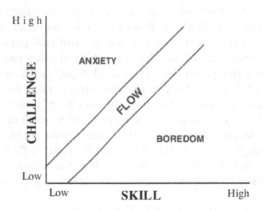

Fig. 1. Three-channel model of flow. We define the region where challenges and skills are balanced as 'flow'. An imbalance results in a state of 'anxiety' or 'boredom'.

3   An Experiment to Monitor Flow

The experiment described here aimed to identify flow patterns in an interactive online learning context, using two measurement techniques that focused on flow as a *process* and a *state*, respectively.

3.1 Experiment

Set-up. An experiment was conducted involving 59 first-year university students who worked through an online learning exercise in the domain area of physics. The exercise included interactive multimedia elements. Students worked in a computer lab comprising about 25 computers. They were first presented with an introductory screen requesting general background information about themselves followed by a pre-test to establish their prior knowledge of this area of physics (19 multiple-choice items). After an introductory screen, they worked through the sequence of seven physics learning pages, each containing explanatory text, a simulation of a cart moving along a track with related motion graphs, and navigation elements. Although each of the learning activities was a discrete Web page, they each used the same interactive simulation and progressed naturally from one to the next. Finally, students were presented with a post-survey, which gathered information about affective aspects of their experience (control, engagement and enjoyment), and a post-test which measured learning gains using the same question items as the pre-test.

In a follow-up study, eight students individually worked through a similar exercise whilst being monitored by video in a usability lab. They were interviewed after the session about their reaction to the various elements of flow that they experienced during the session.

For students in both studies their navigation and interaction with the simulation were recorded by Web server logs for later analysis. In the discussion that follows, any references to statistics or patterns of interaction relate to the initial cohort of 59 students; references to interview data relate to the group of eight interviewed later.

Flow measurement. **To obtain a fine-grained measure of flow throughout the exercise, we monitored the students' challenge and skill perceptions at the end of each of seven learning activities. This was achieved using two 5-point Likert scale items which asked the questions: "How challenging (or stimulating) did you find what you just did?" and "Were your skills appropriate for understanding it?". Response choices were from "too low" to "too high". The challenge-skill ratios derived from these data enabled us to categorize students into one the three states 'anxiety', 'boredom' or 'flow' after each activity in the exercise.**

For comparison, we also obtained a singular measure of flow from the post-survey at the end of the exercise. These data were analyzed using two similar models of flow reported by others that involved measures of control, engagement and enjoyment [6, 8].

3.2 Analysis

Data from the seven challenge-skill probes were used to plot each individual's 'flow path' through the learning exercise. The plot for one student is shown in Figure 2. Each square of the space represents one of the 25 possible states defined by the two five-point Likert scales measures of challenge and skill. The dotted 'flow-line' represents the ideal flow condition of challenge = skill.

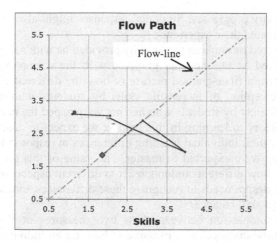

Fig. 2. Flow path for a student. The path commences on the 'flow-line' at the lower left and progresses initially upwards, in the end representing relatively high challenge but low skills.

This particular plot shows the 'flow-path', in challenge-skill space, of a student who performed very well on the exercise in terms of learning outcomes. It tells the story of her progress through the seven activities of the learning task. She began the task with relatively low skills and perceived the first activity to be relatively low challenge (bottom-left of path). The second activity she found more challenging but she also rated her skills as having increased to meet the challenge. The third activity presented less of a challenge and she still perceived her skills as increasing. The final two activities presented more challenge and she felt her skills were becoming increasingly less adequate for the requirements of the task.

This student's plot has some consistency with a flow model of learning: the student's perceived challenges and skills grew together through the first part of the learning exercise. However, for her, the final activities were difficult and she completed the activity sequence in a state of some anxiety.

Inspecting such plots for the cohort of 59 students does not show any clear pattern linking these diverse flow-paths to the post-survey flow measures. Students moved frequently between states during the exercise indicating that flow is a more complex concept than can be represented by a singular measure. Rather than relying on a single flow measure, or *state*, recorded at the end of the session, we need to regard flow as a *process* that changes throughout the activity. We developed a new visualization of this process in order to obtain a better understanding of what was occurring.

Flow as a *process* versus flow as a *state*. The experiment provided data on flow both from the students' reflections at the end of the learning activity, 'final-flow', as well as from data gathered throughout the activity. The question arises as to how these two different views of flow are related. The former provided us data on flow as a state, giving us insight into a student's retrospective view of what happened during the whole activity. A student might indicate an average high or low level of flow throughout the activity, but such a blunt instrument cannot describe the changing states as the activity progresses. Students' responses might also be biased by specific events that dominated their experience.

The data gathered throughout the activity provided us with a view of the twists and turns that occurred as the students grappled with the (complex) learning tasks. It enabled us to form a finer-grained picture of how the different challenges presented resulted in a perception of increasing skills by students who were coping, or in frustration and anxiety by students who had not yet grasped the necessary concepts. In applying flow theory to learning in this manner we expect to observe such variations as students show their individual learning differences in response to the materials and the concepts they were expected to master. The value of this process view is in the light it sheds on how different students react to different aspects of the activities, and how the activity design needs to recognize these differences and adapt to maintain an optimal challenge-skill balance.

To make a comparison between these two measures of flow we defined the quantity 'from-flow-distance' as a measure of how far an individual's challenge-skill ratio is from the flow-line (challenge/skill = 1) on the flow-path plot (see Figure 2). The expression for this quantity is derived from the geometry of the 5x5 challenge-skill space of the plot and is as follows:

$$from\text{-}flow\text{-}distance = 0.25 \; x \; (skill - challenge)$$

We calculated a value of from-flow-distance for each student for each of their seven activities as well an average value from their whole experience. We looked for a relationship between the flow recorded during the activity and the flow recorded at the end ('final-flow') in three ways. The first way was a visual examination of the flow-path plots looking for patterns of flow-like behavior correlating with final-flow ratings. We detected no discernable patterns that linked measures of flow recorded during the activity with the final reflective value that the students recorded through their questionnaires. Next we explored a statistical correlation between the from-flow-distances and the final-flow values for the cohort of students. This also showed no correlation between these two methods for measuring an overall value of flow.

Finally, we performed a statistical correlation between each student's seven activities' from-flow-distances and their final-flow value. In this third analysis we observed an interesting result. This is shown in Figure 3 as a plot of from-flow-distance versus final-flow for each of the seven pages of the exercise. Pages 2, 5, 7 and 8 resulted in correlations above the critical value (r_{crit} = 0.322, p<0.02).

The graph shows strong primacy and recency effects on pages 2 and 8 respectively (page 2 contained the first learning activity, page 8 the last activity). This suggests that the final-flow value measured by the survey may be dominated by the students' interactions on the first or final page of the activity. The spike on page 5 is interesting. The task on that page introduced a physics situation that many of the students found confronting, namely, that the cart was moving in one direction while it was accelerating in the opposite direction. This page also produced the highest average challenge score for all students. The suggestion here is that this particular challenging activity captured the students' interest in a way that influenced their final affective rating of the task as a whole.

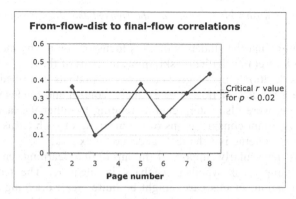

Fig. 3. Correlations of from-flow-dist to final-flow for the entire cohort for each page of the exercise.

The interesting outcome from the above analyses is the lack of a clear mapping between the students' responses during the exercise and their reflections at the end. Even students who indicated strong engagement, enjoyment and control in the final survey did not exhibit consistent flow patterns in their flow-paths. Students experienced a variety of ups and downs in their perceptions of challenges and skills that did not necessarily relate to their final-flow values. This suggests that we should not focus too strongly on a reflective measure of an extended 'flow experience' but rather should look at the process through which students pass during the exercise.

We have seen that the flow process can be a convoluted one and reflects the complexity of the interactions that the students undertook. However, due to the poor correlation with post-survey flow measures, this analysis also raised the interesting question of "what is being represented by this process?". To answer that question we interviewed several students about their experience during the exercise as discussed in the next section.

4   Distinguishing Task from Artefact

The post-interviews with the eight students aimed to explore the various elements that comprised a flow experience. We aimed to gain a richer understanding of how flow manifested itself in this online learning context as well as how this might relate to learning. In particular, we wanted to gain a better understanding of the challenge-skill plot information provided by the students' experiences during interaction with the learning environment.

It readily became apparent that a simple challenge-skill measure was not an adequate technique for indicating the complex behavior during a learning session. Many times during the interviews students made clear distinctions between when they were focusing on the task (in this case a *learning activity*) and when they were focusing on the technological artefact (a *screen-based simulation*). This distinction between task and artefact has rarely been acknowledged in the flow literature [15, 16]. It strongly influenced the students' interpretation of both challenge and skills as their minds moved between one and the other. This was strikingly put by one student:

"the simulation wasn't challenging but the concept that I got from the simulation was challenging."

Without knowing what the student's mind is focussing on at any moment, we cannot know how to interpret the challenge-skill plots in terms of flow.

Similar consideration must be given to how the students described their experience of some of the attributes of flow. For example, control and feedback, both essential elements of flow, were also interpreted as relating to either the task or the artefact. This leads to important considerations of the meaning of such terms when evaluating software involving interactive elements and a complex task.

Feedback is particularly important in an online learning environment. It is ambiguous to simply ask whether feedback is adequate. The feedback from the *artefact* (a simulation, in this case) might be quite clear: dragging and dropping an object on the screen might give clear feedback as to what had been achieved with the software. However, at the same time, feedback from the *task* might be quite confusing: the resulting output from the simulation might not assist the user in constructing the desired concepts.

Our conclusion from these experiments is that, whilst the system provided the same feedback to all students, those with better domain knowledge were able to interpret it more effectively than those with poorer knowledge. This is critical information for the design of engaging learning systems: the feedback essential for flow must take into account the individual's prior learning or domain knowledge. Whilst students could focus their minds on the artefact, or the task, or both, when the concepts were demanding it was the task that tended to dominate this concentration. Feedback is not simply an attribute of the software, but a consequence of the user's interaction with the system and how well its output fits their mental schema.

5   Implications for Design

Others have written about considering flow in Web design and the benefits of doing this are becoming more commonly accepted (see, for example, [17, 18]. The contribution from this research is to consider how the learning gained from understanding flow in an online interactive learning environment can be applied to the design of such an environment.

The general benefits of, and requirements for, flow are quite well understood. However, these are often considered for tasks that are either not well specified (e.g. 'using the Web') or are rather simple and confined (e.g. selecting a product from a list in an on-line shopping site). When the task itself is *complex* and the artefact also has a degree of complexity, then we may observe competition between task and artefact for the attention of the user.

The consequence of this is particularly important in designing for an appropriate level of *challenge* that will be perceived by the user. The challenges will vary from user to user but they should lead the user to focus on the *task,* not the artefact. This means that the artefact (Web page, simulation, etc.) must be sufficiently engaging without becoming a distraction to the user's attention. It should be transparent and allow the user to focus on the higher order task. This is hard to achieve since it relies on some knowledge of the user's skills both with the artefact and within the domain of the task. These are likely to vary considerably from user to user in a learning environment.

Similarly, the feedback presented to the user from the artefact should not distract the user from engaging with the task. The user needs to experience a sense of 'direct engagement' [19] when using the artefact so that challenges from the task can be addressed and explored. Through this the user needs to derive a sense of control over both artefact and task.

To measure how successful one has been in obtaining flow with a user in a learning context, a challenge-skill measure is useful but it needs to be carefully focused on the task. Whereas flow might be experienced by a user focusing on the artefact alone (having a fun time playing with a simulation, but learning little; we call this 'artefact flow'), our aim is to move the user's flow into the realm of the task and to engage her there ('task flow') and to focus her mind on learning about specific concepts, rather than merely playing with the software artefact. Flow could have a negative impact if it engages and distracts a student *away* from the learning task. Given the intrinsic enjoyment offered by many online activities, and the difficulty of many learning tasks, this can be a real danger.

6   Conclusion

Flow is an important consideration in designing for the Web in many contexts. The learning context presents challenges in terms of producing highly motivational materials in order to encourage students to use them and learn from them. In the research reported here we took a fine-grained approach to observing flow by monitoring challenge and skills throughout an activity and comparing this to other traditional measures of flow. This comparison suggested that flow is better viewed as a process rather than a state.

For flow to be a useful measure in this context, we need to ensure that we distinguish between measurements of 'task flow' and 'artefact flow'. Whilst the former has potential to enhance learning, the latter may actually distract the student from engaging with the concepts being presented.

The research prompts further questions about the relationship between flow and learning and the nature of an interactive environment that might encourage flow. These issues are currently being addressed by the researchers.

References

1.   Csikszentmihalyi, M., Beyond Boredom and Anxiety. 1975, San Francisco: Jossey-Bass Publishers.

2.   Bentley, T., L. Johnston, and K.v. Baggo. Affect: Physiological Responses During Computer Use. in 2003 Australasian Computer Human Interaction Conference, OzCHI 2003. 2003. University of Queensland.

3.   Chen, H. and M. Nilan. An Exploration of Web Users' Internal Experiences: Application of the Experience Sampling Method to the Web Environment. in WebNet 98 World Conference. 1998. Orlando, Florida.

4.   Novak, T.P., D.L. Hoffman, and Y.-F. Yung, Measuring the Flow Construct in Online Environments: A Structural Modeling Approach. Marketing Science, 2000. Winter.

5.   Csikszentmihalyi, M., Finding flow: the psychology of engagement with everyday life. 1st ed. MasterMinds. 1997, New York: Basic Books. ix, 181.

6.   Ghani, J.A., R. Supnick, and P. Rooney. The Experience of Flow in Computer-Mediated and in Face-to-Face Groups. in Proceedings of the Twelfth International Conference on Information Systems. 1991. New York.

7.   Agarwal, R. and E. Karahanna, Time flies when you're having fun: cognitive absorption and beliefs about information technology usage. MIS Quarterly, 2000. 24(4): p. 665 - 694.

8.   Webster, J., L.K. Trevino, and L. Ryan, The Dimensionality and Correlates of Flow in Human-Computer Interactions. Computers in Human Behavior, 1993. 9(4): p. 411-426.

9.   Chan, T.S. and T.C. Ahern, Targeting Motivation - Adapting Flow Theory to Instructional Design. Journal of Educational Computing Research, 1999. 21(2): p. 151-163.

10.   Konradt, U., R. Filip, and S. Hoffmann, Flow experience and positive affect during hypermedia learning. British Journal of Educational Technology, 2003. 34(1).

11.   Draper, S., Analysing fun as a candidate software requirement. http://www.psy.gla.ac.uk/~steve/fun.html. 2000.

12.   Ghani, J.A., Flow in human-computer interactions: test of a model, in Human Factors in Information Systems: Emerging Theoretical Bases, J. Carey, Editor. 1991, Ablex Publishing Corp.: New Jersey.

13.   Massimini, F. and M. Carli, The systematic assessment of flow in daily experience, in Optimal experience : psychological studies of flow in consciousness, M. Csikszentmihalyi and I.S. Csikszentmihalyi, Editors. 1988, Cambridge University Press: Cambridge ; New York. p. 266-287.

14.   Novak, T.P. and D.L. Hoffman, Measuring the Flow Experience Among Web Users. 1997, Paper presented at the Interval Research Corporation.

15.   Finneran, C. and P. Zhang, A Person-Artifact-Task (PAT) Model of Flow Antecedents in Computer-Mediated Environments. International Journal of Human-Computer Studies, Special Issue on HCI and MIS, 2003. 59(4): p. 397-402.

16.   Finneran, C.M. and P. Zhang. The challenges of studying flow within a computer-mediated environment. in Eighth Americas Conference on Information Systems. 2002.

17.   King, A.B., Speed up your site: Web site optimization. 2003: New Riders.

18.   Novak, T.P., D.L. Hoffman, and Y.F. Yung, Measuring the Customer Experience in Online Environments: A Structured Modelling Approach. 1999.

19.   Hutchins, E.L., J.D. Hollan, and D.A. Norman, Direct Manipulation Interfaces, in User Centered System Design, D.A. Norman and S.W. Draper, Editors. 1986, Lawrence Erlbaum: Hillsdale NJ. p. 87-124.

Enhancing Interactive Graph Manipulation Tools with Tactile Feedback

Jukka Raisamo and Roope Raisamo

Tampere Unit for Computer-Human Interaction (TAUCHI),
Department of Computer Sciences, Kanslerinrinne 1,
FIN-33014 University of Tampere
{jr, rr}@cs.uta.fi
http://www.cs.uta.fi/english/

Abstract. The sense of touch is important when interacting and exploring our physical surroundings. Haptic modality has also proved to be a promising feedback modality in user interfaces but there are still virtually no applications taking advantage of the versatile qualities of active touching, i.e. the active exploration of the virtual objects on the screen. Our research is focused on haptic interaction in a highly interactive desktop application.

A low-frequency tactile feedback mouse was applied to further enhance the directness and intuitiveness of the interactive graph manipulation tools. The overall positive results of our initial evaluation with the users support our design of the tactile effects.

1 Introduction

Since the conception of graphical user interfaces they have remained basically the same while the number of features in the software has been increasing dramatically. Without the assistance of new interaction techniques this ever-growing development is about to exceed the human cognitive limits.

In addition to the continuous visual feedback, sound feedback has been used to inform the user of the ongoing actions in the contemporary user interfaces [3]. However, even when combining both of these, human-computer interaction still stays far behind compared with the way the user communicates in the real world. The haptic modality has been proven to be a promising solution to broaden the bandwidth of human-computer interaction. For instance, Akamatsu *et al.* [2] compared the haptic, auditory and visual modalities in target selection tasks and found out that the effect of combined sensory feedback on positioning time was almost the same as for the most effective single condition that was the tactile feedback condition.

The goal of our current study is to construct interactive tools making use of the sense of touch to better connect the virtual and physical worlds. In this research, we chose to use a tactile feedback mouse instead of physical tools that would allow tangible interaction. The decision was made to maintain a high level of flexibility in the software without physical constraints related to real physical tools. As the domain for our research we have chosen a direct manipulation graph editor.

M. Masoodian et al. (Eds.): APCHI 2004, LNCS 3101, pp. 359-368, 2004.

When using a mouse in the standard graphical user interface, picking up and dragging the icon is moderately intuitive and can be easily associated with the real-life action of physically moving objects. The standard computer mouse, however, only provides passive haptic feedback on the accidental manner. When using a mouse, we obtain both visual and kinesthetic information about movement and position of the input device. The button clicks can be perceived as some sort of tactile and auditory feedback while the dragging always causes a light feel of passive force feedback. These outputs, however, cannot be controlled by the application.

The set of direct graph manipulation tools used as the basis of this study is suggested to fill the gap between interaction and efficiency in graph manipulation [12]. The tools are based on the concept of direct manipulation [13] and make it possible for the users to adjust the layout of the graph interactively and thereby maintain their mental map. These tools were used as the starting point in the work presented in this paper.

The main contribution of this paper is to present interactive graph manipulation tools enhanced with tactile feedback. We have constructed a graph drawing editor where we use a low-frequency tactile feedback mouse. It is also suggested that direct manipulation in desktop applications can be made more direct with tactile effects by adding physical properties in the objects to make them touchable. This way, it is possible to bring the desktop metaphors closer to their real life analogues and make the interface more intuitive to use. In this paper, we also present the results of an initial user evaluation where the concept was tested.

The rest of this paper is organized as follows. In Section 2, we take a look at haptics by giving a short introduction to the human sense of touch, research on haptic feedback with desktop computers and describe the low-frequency tactile feedback mouse. In Section 3, we describe our approach for adding tactile feedback effects in the direct graph manipulation tools of our domain of research. In Section 4, we discuss the results of an initial evaluation of the tactile tools. The results and some promising directions for further research are discussed in Section 5. Section 6 is the conclusion.

2 Haptics

Haptics is the science of applying the sense of touch to interact with computer applications. By using special devices users can both give input and receive output in the form of felt sensations in the hand or other parts of the body. As the research on haptics investigates the use of touch and haptic sensations as a means of communication, research on haptic interaction has turned out to be far from simple. Because of the requirement of physical contact, it is hard to generate artificial haptic feedback that corresponds to the real sensations. That is why most research done on haptic interaction uses the haptic modality in multimodal context to broaden the bandwidth of human-computer interaction.

In this section, we first discuss the human sense of touch. After that, an overview of previous work in design of haptic systems is given, and a low-frequency tactile feedback mouse is introduced.

2.1 Human Sense of Touch

Humans have adapted to use their diverse sensory system efficiently to gather information on their surroundings where the vision is considered as the most important sense followed by hearing [5]. However, these two senses do not allow the physical interaction with the concrete object that is being observed. Touch, on the contrary, is a mechanical sense that requires a physical contact with the object of interest and conveys more detailed information on its properties.

The sense of touch is closely related to the other somatosensory senses as well as the senses of pain and heat, and is thereby very difficult to isolate from them [5]. The main difference in touch compared with the proprioceptive (the knowledge of limb position) and kinesthetic (the knowledge of limb motion) senses is that the tactile sensations are perceived via skin. Thus, touch is a cutaneous sense as the tactile information is transmitted merely via the tactile receptors found in the skin.

We tend to use touch for various purposes in our everyday life, even in the situations where we do not recognize using it. Touch helps us, for example, to communicate with other people, to get information about the material and dynamic properties of an object, and to verify the current state of an ongoing operation. Touch can be either active exploration or passive sensing [5]. Active touching is more efficient when the physical dimensions and properties of an object are being identified, while passive touching is better in detecting the fine surface details of objects. This explains why we intrinsically tend to use different ways of touching depending on what we are looking for.

2.2 Haptic Feedback in Desktop Applications

In the desktop applications, the unique qualities of touch can be utilized by providing haptic feedback to make the virtual computer interface feel more concrete. The aim of the haptic research has usually been to provide an additional feedback channel that supports visual or auditory feedback. In addition to that, haptic feedback can also be used as a substitute for one or both of the visual and auditory feedback channels in, for example, systems designed for handicapped people [14].

Oakley et al. [11] propose that when designing haptic effects, special attention must be paid to the qualities and potential of the feedback device used – exceeding the limits of the device leads almost certainly to a failure. The haptic effects used in the application should also not disturb but rather support the intentions of the user [10]. This is why it is important to carefully design the touch effects to achieve good results compared with the non-haptic condition.

The major problem with the haptic devices used in the previous studies is that they are either special research prototypes or their prices are out of the scope of an average computer user. In addition to the studies carried out with more sophisticated haptic feedback also the use of force feedback in the desktop environment has been studied. For example, force feedback mouse was proven to improve the performance of combined steering and targeting tasks, and the authors suggested that the mouse has great potential when used in the desktop environment [4].

An interesting study is the comparison of the usability of a 2D force feedback mouse with a more advanced 3D haptic device in representing graphical data [15]. The study pointed out no significant differences between these two devices when the graphs were seen on the computer screen, but in the haptic-only condition the 3D device provided better performance. The study suggests that at least a low-quality force feedback device can be used effectively in two-dimensional interaction tasks together with visual feedback.

Some promising results have been achieved in the previous studies with different kinds of tactile mice but they have concentrated mostly in the single interaction events, for example in target selection [2], [8] or movement [1]. However, the use of tactile feedback in more complex and realistic patterns of interaction tasks has not been studied. Also, tactile feedback devices used in the previous studies have only provided static feedback or have just one type of effect which makes it impossible to take the full advantage of the benefits of tactile feedback.

2.3 Low-Frequency Tactile Feedback Mouse

Nowadays there is a group of commercial low-cost and low-frequency tactile feedback mice available on the market that take advantage of the TouchSense technology developed by Immersion Corporation [7]. The technology contains eleven different types of effects, ranging from simple tactile bumps and vibrations to more expressive dynamic force feedback effects but only four of them can be used with the iFeel tactile feedback mouse (Fig. 1) manufactured by Logitech Inc. [8] we used in our study.

Fig. 1. The iFeel tactile feedback mouse by Logitech Inc. [8]. This optical mouse has a special vibrating motor inside its body to produce the tactile sensations in the hand

The tactile feedback mouse (Fig. 1) generates the effects with a special motor inside the case of the mouse. These effects can be felt as vibrations and shakes on the mouse. Because of the low frequency of the effects produced, the mouse cannot efficiently imitate the characteristics and fine details of the real world. However, with this kind of device an additional feedback channel can be offered to the user to inform of events and indicate the states of the ongoing processes.

Immersion Corporation has released a set of applications that make it possible to add tactile features as a part of Windows desktop, Microsoft Office programs and games by using the sound card data [7]. The company also provides APIs for adding the TouchSense effects for both C++ and Java applications as well as web pages. With these extensions, the tactile mouse has a potential to improve the quality of human-computer interaction. The mouse does not, however, really let the user feel the interface in detail. Furthermore, these effects can be felt with the palm of the hand holding the mouse, not with the finger tips that are the most sensitive feeling the tactile sensations.

3 Tactile Effects in Interactive Graph Manipulation Tools

In this section, we present an approach for using tactile feedback effects in interactive graph manipulation tools making them more informative and intuitive to use. In our research, we have paid attention to three design factors: the effects should be informative without distracting the user, they must be dynamic in a reasonable degree, and they should correspond to the functions of the tools as closely as possible. The effects were implemented with Java, Immersion TouchSense SDK for Java [7] and Logitech iFeel tactile feedback mouse [8].

3.1 Graph Drawing Editor

The graph drawing editor used as a domain for our study consists of direct manipulation tools that are selected and used interactively to manipulate the drawing (an example shown in Fig. 2). The user can select an appropriate tool for each manipulation task and decide the order of applying each tool. The tools are suggested to cover most of the features required to adjust and manipulate different kinds of graphs, containing tools for linear and non-linear alignment, distribution, making clusters, as well as resizing and moving operations [12]. The current version of the editor has also interactive tools for cutting, copying and deleting the objects.

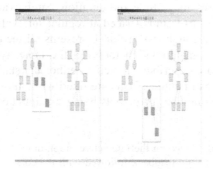

Fig. 2. The graph drawing editor used as the platform of our study. A group of objects is cut (on the left) and moved (on the right) with the direct manipulation tool called grabbing tool

Generally, each tool is visualized as a large tool-specific mouse cursor that is activated by pressing the left mouse button down and deactivated by releasing it. The sizes of the tool cursors can be adjusted whether the tools are active or inactive by dragging the mouse with the right mouse button pressed down. Also the orientation of most of the tools can be adjusted by dragging the mouse with the middle button.

The direct manipulation tools of the graph drawing editor are in practice an extension to the direct positioning, and they can be used to manipulate a number of objects simultaneously while the automatic features help the user to achieve the desired layout. Contrary to the traditional command-based alignment tools found in the most commercial graph drawing applications, the direct manipulation tools do not require a separate selection step of the objects to be aligned, but they affect all the objects touched with the tool. In this way, the tools can be used to manipulate only selected parts of the drawing, and they help the user to better maintain his or her mental map compared with the sudden changes that the automatic layout algorithms cause.

3.2 Effect Design

Excluding the computer gaming industry, haptic feedback has not really been utilized in widely used desktop applications. However, for example, Immersion [7] has released a plug-in to add tactile effects on Microsoft Office applications, but the effects provided are only simple static bumps and vibrations. There are also some applications that make it possible for the user to feel the perceivable properties of the objects, for example different colors and textures.

The basic starting point for the design of the tactile effects was to connect the functions of the tools and the interaction with the objects to similar phenomena in the physical world. We made a hypothesis that this approach suits for our domain of graph drawing editor where the physical laws and objects are evident. In our study, we also augment the traditional interaction methods by enhancing dragging and dropping of objects with tactile effects.

We have used two different kinds of effects, periodic and texture, which the tactile mouse is able to produce. The periodic effects consist of vibrations, the properties of which, such as waveform, magnitude and duration, can be varied. The texture effects are composed of a series of bumps spaced at regular intervals making the target feel like surfaces of different roughness. Table 1 presents all the different events that are recognized in the direct manipulation tools. In the table, types of tactile feedback effects for each event are described as well as either the static or dynamic nature of the effect. The properties of static effects are fixed while those of dynamic ones vary depending on either the number of objects being manipulated or the size of the tool cursor.

Table 1. The use of tactile effects in the interactive graph drawing tools. The event describes the moment of providing tactile feedback followed with the corresponding effect type and the nature of the effect

Event	Effect Type	Nature
Tool selection	Periodic	Static
Tool activation	Periodic	Static
Tool deactivation	Periodic	Static
Object selection	Periodic	Static
Tool dragging	Texture	Dynamic
Tool adjustment	Texture	Dynamic

In our application, all the static events have a unique effect that is supposed to describe the operation at a very low level and inform the user of certain actions. The effects for dynamic events, instead, convey more detailed information about the interactive task and objects involved. Each tool may provide several effects based on the events performed with the tool, for example, tool activation, dragging and adjusting the tool cursor, selecting objects with the tool and deactivating it.

The actions include selection, activation and deactivation of the tool as well as selecting and pointing the object. These effects are the same for each tool to keep the effects simple and to avoid having a large amount of different touch stimuli.

The gradient and magnitude of dragging the tool depends on the amount of objects currently manipulated with the tool. On the tool adjustment effect, the effect varies based on both the amount of objects currently manipulated with the tool and the size of the tool: as the length of the tool increases the magnitude of the effect decreases and vice versa. The different kinds of dynamic effects are played depending on whether the tool is being dragged and adjusted in an active or inactive state.

4 Initial Evaluation of the Tactile Manipulation Tools

We tested the set of direct manipulation tools in visual-tactile and visual-only modes with ten users. The users were between 24 and 35 years old, all of them having a strong background in computer science. Five of them have experience in graph drawing applications and four of them had tried earlier versions of the alignment stick. Nine of the users had used some haptic device including the game controllers and seven of them had some experiences of using tactile mice while only one of them uses such a mouse regularly.

A test sequence consisted of seven graph drawing tasks the level of which varied from easy to medium. The tasks included both object drawing and graph manipulation parts. Each user carried out the same tasks twice, once with both feedback modes. Before the test, the tools were briefly introduced to the user, and after it, the users were asked to fill in a questionnaire of 27 statements about their opinions on the tools and the use of tactile feedback using the Likert scale (1..5). The final outcome of each task was saved for further analysis. An average session lasted for 30 minutes from which the graph drawing tasks took an average of 24 minutes (the fastest completed the tasks in 20 and the slowest in 40 minutes).

The goal of the evaluation was to investigate the users' attitude towards tactile effects. Some averages and standard deviations of the statements are shown in Fig. 3 below. The two most agreed statements were related to noticing the tactile feedback (an average of 3.8) and whether the feedback was used in the tools in a right way (3.2). Furthermore, the users did not think that the tactile feedback effects stole their attention from carrying out the tasks (2.0) but they were very disagreeing in their opinions on the disturbance of the effects. Two of the least agreed statements were the discrimination of the tactile effects (1.7) and help in completing the tasks more efficiently (2.1).

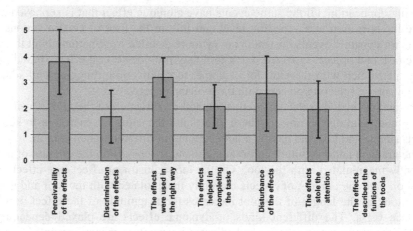

Fig. 3. The most interesting averages and standard deviations of the questionnaire

As this was only an initial evaluation, more rigorous testing is required before the benefits of the tactile feedback can be analyzed in more detail. Based on the observations made in the tests, we decided to remove the effect of activating the tools because the user got almost the same information by pressing the mouse button. It was also found that the effects must be further improved because the users were not able to distinguish effects representing different events (an average of 1.7) and did not think that the feedback described the functions of the tools (2.5). Overall, the users had quite positive opinion towards the tactile feedback.

5 Discussion

Previous studies with different kinds of tactile mice show that tactile and force feedback can improve the performance on single interaction events, for example in target selection [2], [8] or movement [1] as well as reduce the errors [11]. We suggest that direct manipulation tools can be made more real by enhancing them with haptic effects. This brings the tools closer to their real life analogues and in that way can make them more intuitive to use.

Even though three-dimensional haptic feedback is far more authentic in imitating the real world, also simpler two-dimensional tactile feedback has potential to do that. In our application, the tactile effects were used to give the user an additional feedback to the manipulation events and the properties of interaction tools and objects. Some constraints for the design process were due to the low-frequency tactile mouse. It was noticed that the possibilities of low frequency effects of the tactile mouse are mainly limited to inform the user of the different states and actions of the application – the intended dynamical nature of the effects could not be successfully achieved. This was mainly due to the limited capacity of the hardware inside the mouse. Force feedback could be used to produce feedback with a higher quality.

Based on our initial study, we found some issues that should be concerned in our future research when designing the tactile effects. First, the dynamic effects are important when trying to imitate the physical world, but sometimes they had to be forgotten because of the limits of the device. Second, the effects should be designed and used in the way that the user is able to feel the details essential to the successful interaction without confusing and disturbing the user.

Tactile feedback has potential to reduce the information overload and the cognitive load of the user. While force feedback makes it possible for the user not only to feel the output but also to have active feedback of the input, an interesting point of view would be combining the different qualities of tactile and force feedback devices by, for instance, using a force feedback device with the dominant hand and tactile feedback device with the non-dominant hand. In this way, the user would be able to sense an interesting and more authentic two-dimensional virtual world within a desktop application.

The functionality of tactile mouse is not as good as we would have preferred. Most of the problems related to haptic feedback were due to the device used, not haptic feedback as a concept. Thus, the users were not negative towards haptic feedback; they just would have liked to have it in a higher quality. Avoiding the unwanted feedback seems to be the most important design issue in haptic feedback; with additional feedback it is possible to make the user interface more natural and pleasant to use but also distract the user and cause frustration. This issue should be carefully considered when using the haptic feedback in applications.

6 Conclusions

In this paper we presented a way of using tactile feedback effects in a desktop application. The effects are used to further enhance the directness and intuitiveness of the direct graph manipulation tools. Based on the initial evaluation with ten users, the users could notice the effects and agreed on the way these effects were used. The main problems concerning the effects were related to the tactile feedback mouse used in our study, since it cannot produce high-quality feedback. However, the users were quite interested in the effects and thought that they were used properly in the application.

7 Acknowledgements

This research was funded by the Academy of Finland (grant 104805). We thank all the students and colleagues who have participated in the evaluation and development of this software in its many phases.

References

1. Akamatsu, M., and MacKenzie, S.: Movement Characteristics Using a Mouse With Tactile and Force Feedback. Int. J. HCS 45 (1996) 483-493
2. Akamatsu, M., MacKenzie, S., Hasbrouq, T.: A Comparison of Tactile, Auditory, and Visual Feedback in a Pointing Task Using a Mouse-Type Device. Ergonomics 38 (1995) 816-827
3. Brewster, S.A.: Non-speech auditory output. In: Jacko, J., Sears, A. (eds.): The Human-Computer Interaction Handbook. Lawrence Erlbaum Associates USA (2002) 220-239
4. Dennerlein, J.T., Martin, D.B., and Hasser, C.: Force-Feedback Improves Performance for Steering and Combined Steering-Targeting Tasks. Proc. CHI 2000, ACM Press (2000) 423-429
5. Goldstein, E.B.: Sensation & Perception. 5th ed. Brooks/Cole Publishing Company USA (1999)
6. Göbel, M., Luczak, H., Springer, J., Hedicke, V., and Rötting, M.: Tactile Feedback Applied to Computer Mice. Int. J. HCI 7 (1) (1995) 1-24
7. Immersion Corporation: http://www.immersion.com/
8. Logitech Incorporated: http://www.logitech.com/
9. Miller, T., and Zeleznik, R.: The Design of 3D Haptic Widgets. Proc. 1999 Symposium on Interactive 3D Graphics, ACM Press (1999) 97-102
10. Oakley, I., Adams, A., Brewster, S.A., and Gray, P.D.: Guidelines for the Design of Haptic Widgets. Proc. BCS HCI 2002, Springer (2002) 195-212
11. Oakley, I., McGee, M.R., Brewster, S.A., and Gray, P.D.: Putting the Feel in Look and Feel. Proc. CHI 2000, ACM Press (2000) 415-422
12. Raisamo, J., and Raisamo, R.: A Set of Intuitive and Interactive Tools for Graph Manipulation. Proc. APCHI 2002, Vol. 2, Science Press (2002) 754-764
13. Shneiderman, B.: The Future of Interactive Systems and the Emergency of Direct Manipulation. Behaviour and Information Technology 1 (1982) 237-256
14. Sjöström, C.: Non-Visual Haptic Interaction Design: Guidelines and Applications. Doctoral Dissertation, Certec, Lund Institute of Technology, September 2002.
15. Yu, W. and Brewster, S.: Comparing Two Haptic Interfaces for Multimodal Graph Rendering. Proc. Haptics 2002, IEEE Computer Society (2002) 3-9

HCI Practices and the Work of Information Architects

Toni Robertson and Cindy Hewlett

Faculty of Information Technology, University of Technology, Sydney,
PO Box 123 Broadway NSW 2007 Australia
{toni, chewlett}@it.uts.edu.au

Abstract. We interviewed 26 information architects about their work, their backgrounds and their perceptions of their roles as information architects. Our research aimed to identify and understand the work practices that define the position of information architect as well as the human-computer interaction and usability issues that are relevant to their work. Our findings show that the work practices of information architects are far broader than those included in the popular technology design literature. A major issue that emerged from the research was the ongoing struggle of information architects to bring user-centred design methods into the design and development processes used in their organisations. A thorough knowledge of human-computer interaction and usability principles increased the ability of individual information architects to influence design processes.

1 Introduction

Information Architect: 1) the individual who organises the patterns inherent in data, making the complex clear; 2) a person who creates the structure or map of information which allows others to find their personal paths to knowledge; 3) the emerging 21st century professional occupation addressing the needs of the age focused upon clarity, human understanding and the science of the organisation of information.
Richard Wurman, *Information Architects* (1996) p. 9

When I came up with the concept and the name information architecture in 1975, I thought everybody would join in and call themselves information architects. But nobody did—until now. Suddenly, it's become an ubiquitous term.
Richard Wurman, *InformationAnxiety2* (2001) p. 24

A few years ago the job title, *Information Architect,* began to appear in recruitment advertisements for information technology (IT) design positions, mostly within web design environments and/or projects. Round the same time it began to be included, both anecdotally and in the textbooks, as one of the jobs that human-computer interaction (HCI) and usability professionals might do. For example, it is not listed in Preece et al., *Human-Computer Interaction* (1994) but it is in the later book, *Interaction Design: beyond human computer interaction* (2002), where information architects are defined as "people who come up with ideas of how to plan and structure interactive products, especially websites" (p. 11). It is the sudden use of the term *information architect* as if it named some established and well understood role that

M. Masoodian et al. (Eds.): APCHI 2004, LNCS 3101, pp. 369-378, 2004.
© Springer-Verlag Berlin Heidelberg 2004

motivated the research reported in this paper. Who are the people who do this job? Where do they come from? What do they actually do? And where does the work they do fit within the wider technology design process? Our interest is to understand the phenomenon of information architects by understanding the commonalities and differences in their practices. In particular, we wanted to identify the HCI and usability issues that are relevant to the work of information architects and to understand how processes, broadly defined as user-centred, are being developed for, and applied to, the design of new and rapidly changing technology.

The research reported here is based on 26 intensive, loosely-structured, mostly workplace, but always work-based, interviews with people who are called and/or call themselves information architects. The first eight interviews were with known industry contacts and the other participants were recruited via a single call for participation posted on the listserv hosted by the Computer-Human Interaction Special Interest Group (CHISIG) of the Ergonomic Society of Australia. This is the Australian professional organisation for academics, researchers and practitioners in HCI and related fields. This call was in turn reposted by still unknown readers of the CHISIG listserv to a range of specialist information architecture (IA) lists and discussion groups. Most of our participants were working in Sydney and Melbourne in Australia, but five were based in Europe, one in Hong Kong and one from the US.

In the interviews we sought to identify the common issues affecting the work of information architects as well as those issues that were highly situated and domain specific in their affect on different individuals. The interviews lasted between 40 minutes and one hour. All interviews were fully transcribed. The interviews ranged over three main areas. The bulk of each focused on the actual work of information architects. Each participant was asked to situate their answers in their most recently completed project. This provided us with 26 examples of genuine work practice to represent what information architects actually do. We asked specific demographic questions about professional backgrounds, qualifications and ongoing professional development. Finally we asked how information architects viewed their own work and how they thought it was perceived by various others.

To our knowledge this is the only study to date of the work practices of information architects and the only study of any HCI or related practices that include mostly Australian practitioners. Our research is phenomenologically motivated [1] but because our space here is limited, we cannot give a full account of our findings nor engage in extended analysis. Our aim here is to provide a basic conceptual ordering and descriptive summary of the rich empirical data gathered in the interviews [8]. In the following section we summarise the demographic data from the study before discussing the range of work that the information architects themselves defined as part of their practices. From there, the participants view of their own work and its place within the broader design processes of their organisations is briefly examined. The paper concludes with a discussion of the benefits that a deep understanding of HCI and usability issues brings to the agency of information architects in their work practices.

2 Some Demographics

The ages of the participants ranged between approximately 25 to 45. Men and women were equally represented. Seven had worked as information architects or in closely related fields for more than five years, eight for between three and five years and the remaining eleven for three years or less. Only one participant had no university qualification. Three had no undergraduate degree but had gained, or were completing, post-graduate qualifications. Of those with undergraduate degrees, eight had first degrees in the humanities, eight in architecture/design (including one each from industrial design, graphic design and ergonomics); two had first degrees in mathematics, two in new media (digital design etc) and one in economics. None had undergraduate degrees in IT or information science. 15 had, or were completing, post-graduate qualifications; five in IT, three in new media and three had a specialist qualification in HCI. Two had postgraduate qualifications in education and two in the humanities.

None of our participants had studied information science despite its traditional contribution to information design as a discipline and its common claim to be the core discipline in the field of information architecture. We explicitly sought information architects from an information science background via the information science department at our university and through relevant professional organisations, but we were not successful. This could indicate that the claimed dominance of this discipline in the training of those who are called information architects is not reflected in the work place, at least in Australian technology design environments.

It is common for people who work in information technology design environments to come from other areas, and popular texts on information architecture emphasise its multi-disciplinarity (eg [7] especially chapter two). The professional backgrounds of our participants included: academia and research (five), web development (three), two each from HCI, instructional design, visual design, theatre, publishing and marketing; and one each from school teaching, fine arts, communication, industrial design, consulting and public relations. Despite the diversity of their backgrounds, some kind of design training and/or professional background was common to approximately half the participants. Given that information architects are such a recent phenomenon, the lack of specialist training is not surprising. But it means that there is no basic shared body of professional knowledge and skills that can be assumed for people working as information architects.

Most participants used mailing lists and specialist websites to sustain their professional development in information architecture and related areas. Round half attended industry conferences or short courses and almost all of these had attended at least one Nielsen/Norman short course in Sydney in the previous two years. A third of our participants regularly bought popular industry publications through Amazon.com and only five read academic research papers. Just over half the participants cited Garrett's ([2] [3]) definition of information architecture as the "structural design of the information space to facilitate intuitive access to content" and each of these were able to produce a copy of his 'elements of user experience' diagram [2]. Yet, as will be shown in the next section, the practices of the great majority of information architects we interviewed were far more varied than those Garrett described.

3 The Work of Information Architects

During their last project, half the participants had worked on the development of a specific website (or part), six on intranets (or part), two on extranets, three on specialist web-based applications and two had worked on projects that were not web-related. These projects were situated in a range of industry sectors including six from both government and ICT, five from finance, two each from retail, public utilities and entertainment, and one each from building/construction, real estate and the media. At the time these projects were completed twelve of our participants worked in the IT section of larger organisations, twelve were employed by smaller, specialist IT solution providers and two worked for dot.com companies. Ten of our participants were in recognised management roles.

In Table One (below) we provide a summary of the work each of the participants did in their last project. This table summarises a prior one developed from the initial interview transcripts by noting and then tabulating the activities specifically mentioned by each information architect. That table is far too big to reproduce here and we have included the summarised version in its place. The process of reducing the table to printable form was guided by our finding that all the kinds of work specifically mentioned fitted within the broad categories of Research, Focused Designing, Evaluation, Coordinating Internal and External Stakeholders and Management.

The top section of Table One maps the work practices of each participant (columns labelled **a** to **z**) to these broad categories of work (rows). Row order is not an indication of any sequence of work during the projects. The participants rarely described their work sequentially and any time relations between the various activities that were available from the data have been lost by the process of summarising it in this way. Those working in management positions have been grouped together on the right hand side of the table. The lower section of the table records whether the individual information architect indicated a familiarity with user-centred design methods as well as their experience in their current and related jobs.

We emphasise that these categories were not imposed on the data but emerged from the iterative analysis of interview transcriptions and then validated against additional transcriptions. To give our readers some understanding of the extent of reduction in this categorisation, Research includes user, process and domain research, research of any existing applications as well as any usage statistics. Focused Designing includes practices as varied as requirements development, defining scenarios and personas, developing sitemaps and navigational models, producing wireframe diagrams, interface design, interaction design and the design and development of prototypes for evaluation. Evaluation included heuristic evaluation, card sorting, various kinds of evaluation of different kinds of prototypes, user testing of various kinds, focus groups, informal feedback, implementation reviews and project process reviews. Coordinating internal and external stakeholders included working as the project's communication facilitator, liaising with content providers, liaising with external providers, preparing and delivering presentations and customer pitches as well as the range of activities usually covered by 'attending meetings'. Finally, Management work included defining the overall design process, managing that process, managing the project itself and/or the people working on it. Some grounding discussion of the work represented in Table One makes up the remainder of this section.

Table One. Summary of the work done by information architects in their last projects

	Non-managers																Managers									
	a	b	c	d	e	f	g	h	I	j	k	l	m	n	o	p	q	r	s	t	u	v	w	x	y	z
Research	X	U	X	X	U	X	U	X	X	U	U	U	X	U	X	*	X	U	X	U	U	X	X	U	U	*	*
Focused Designing	X	X	X	X	X	X	X	X	X	X	X	X	X	X	X	X	X	X	*	X	*	*	X	X	X	X
Evaluation		U	*U	U		*			X	*	*		*U		*U		*X	*U	U	X	*U	U	X	*		U
Coordinating Stakeholders	X	X	X	X	X	X	X	*	X	X	X	X	X	X	*	X	X	X	X	X	X	X	X	X	X	X
Management	*	*	*	r	*	*	r	*	*	*	*	*	*	*	*	r	P	P	P	P	P	R	P	E	E	P
User-Centred Design?	Y	N	Y	Y	Y	Y	Y	N	N	Y	Y	N	Y	Y	N	N	Y	Y	Y	Y	Y	Y	Y	Y	N	N
Years in Industry	7+	5+	3−	3+	3−	3−	3−	3+	3−	3−	3+	3+	7+	3+	3−	3−	9+	7+	5+	5+	3+	3−	7+	3+	3+	3+

Notes for reading this table.
A ***** indicates that the work was done on the project but not by the information architect.   **X** indicates the individual architect was involved in these work practices. **U** indicates users were also involved. ***U** means someone else did this work but users were involved.
A space in the Evaluation row means that no evaluation was done on the project.
In the Management row, **P** means the person managed the people and the process, **R** means they managed the process only, **E** means they managed the people only. **r** in the non-manager columns means that person managed the process but was not officially recognised.
In the User-centred Design row, **Y** means Yes, this information architect knew about user-centred design methods, **N** means No, they didn't.

3.1 Research

Information architects were as involved in various kinds of research about the developing product as they were in specific design processes. One of the participants specifically compared her work as an information architect to research work.

> *The ability to pose the question is the crucial thing. And then the ability to determine what an appropriate solution to that problem would be. And then the ability to define the methodology to get from there. Very similar to research, what you're doing at the moment. You're trying to pose the question: what should be actually focused on within all the confusion and messiness? (Interview b).*

When user research was done in a project, the information architects either did it alone, with specialist user experience modellers working under various job titles, or used the results from the work of these people. Most participants were also involved in both domain research and research into the use of any existing technology.

3.2 Focused Designing

We considered Information Architecture as the label for this category this did not specifically cover design work, such as scenario design, prototype development and interface and interaction design, which is common to information architects as well as those employed under other related job titles such as interaction designer, user experience modeller etc. This category is defined by the production of specialised design representations within each of the activities included in it. We eventually settled on Focused Designing, rather than just Designing because this study demonstrated that actual technology design practice includes the full range of work summarised in Table One and that the production of design representations is just one part of this practice.

Only half the participants were responsible for 'traditional' information architecture areas such as the production of navigation models and wireframe diagrams. But none worked only on these activities and none spent most of their time on this work. The information architect represented in column o is the only person whose work was restricted to processes categorised here as Focused Designing. She was the most junior information architect we interviewed and worked within a specialist provider company with a task-based organisational structure. But even her work also included interface and interaction design. Only three information architects were not directly involved in the focused designing but they were responsible for the management of their projects.

3.3 Evaluation

Our participants were less likely to be directly involved in the evaluation of the product (only seven of the 26). Our findings provide two explanations. The first is that some organisations either had people dedicated to usability evaluation in the design team or routinely outsourced those parts of the process to a specialist provider. The second is that in nine of the 26 projects (35 percent) no evaluation was done at all. Just over half the products that were evaluated involved users in that process (round 40 percent of the total). Relying on informal feedback throughout the design process was the most frequent evaluation method. We are aware that some in the HCI community would not consider informal feedback as evaluation at all but it is included in this category because the information architects in our study explicitly referred to informal feedback as one of the ways, sometimes the only way, their products were evaluated.

3.4 Coordinating Stakeholders

The centrality of the coordination of stakeholders to the work practices of information architects is one of the major findings of our study, confirming [6] and others' findings that the technology design process relies on the communication work done by designers to coordinate their work with the work of others. This is the activity that occupied most of the time of the information architects we interviewed and was regarded by almost all of them as defining of their work practice. Of the two information architects who were not involved in stakeholder coordination, one is the junior staff member referred to above and the other (column **h**) was building an already specified application to work on an existing web-site. He was a programmer on contract who had called himself an information architect (by ticking that box on an online cv generator) in order to get a job in web design work.

Most importantly, this coordination work is where the politics of the design process is played out and where usability gains are won and lost. Perhaps the most sobering theme to emerge from our interviews was the sense of technology design as some kind of struggle, or at least a competition. Participants described a range of projects where the final design was not shaped by any particular design method but instead by competition, from different parts of the organisation designing the technology and/or the client organisation, for control of the process, for control of budgets, for control of content and for control of how different parts of the organisation were represented within the product itself.

3.5 User-Centred Design Processes and Methods

18 (70 percent) of the information architects noted an understanding of, and experience in, developing design concepts using direct user involvement. Yet only twelve of the 26 projects included user research of some kind, only eight involved users in the product evaluations and just two involved users in both. Our findings confirm those of Vredenburg et al. from their extensive survey of user-centred design practices [9]. They wrote: "Some common characteristics of an ideal user-centred design process were not found to be used in practice, namely focusing on the total user experience, end-to-end user involvement in the development process, and tracking customer satisfaction" (p. 478). Eight (30 percent) of the participants either did not appear to be familiar with user-centred design processes, or while they may, in fact, have involved their users, they were unable to situate this involvement within the wider, established design methods for user involvement. An inspection of the Years in Industry row of Table One identifies seven of these participants as among the least experienced of the information architects. These information architects were also notable as having the least control over the design priorities in the products they were building relative to the other participants.

A third of the information architects explicitly noted that user involvement was the first item to be removed from the budget when things got tight. The resulting product design was based on assumptions about the user, not on genuine user participation. This applied even to those working within specialist service providers with established user-centred design processes who still faced unwillingness from clients to pay for user participation or to make potential users available to the design team. The information architect was expected to be able to represent the user in the design process. This meant an increasing reliance on discount usability methods and the use of information architects as user-representatives in the design process.

3.6 Information Architects as Managers

We have separated those in recognised management roles to make visible our finding that users were more likely to be explicitly involved in the design process when information architects were involved in management work. This was the case even when their management role was not officially recognised. Two managers did not express familiarity with user-centred design methods. One (column y) came from a product design background and was responsible only for people management within a specialist provider company that marketed itself on its user-focused design process. The other (column z) had chosen the title of information architect for strategic reasons and was rarely involved in the actual design of specific products. His main work was stakeholder co-ordination in a mid-size specialist IT service provider. Four of the managers had developed their own variations of user-centred processes that were being used, with various degrees of wider commitment, within their companies and one had been explicitly employed to demonstrate how user-centred methods might improve the quality of the organisations products. The importance of management clout and support to the involvement of users, and user-centred processes, in product development was one of the strongest issues that emerged from our analysis. Those working in management roles were also able to protect information architects within their teams and facilitate their work in the broader organisation.

4   Information Architects' Perceptions of Their Own Work

While the great majority of those interviewed were working in web design of one kind or another, the term information architect did not define a uniform and discrete role in the design and development process. Information architects did a variety of work and all participants saw their work as pivotal to the design process in their organisations. None of them gave definitions that were as tightly focused as those from the literature that have already been quoted in this paper [2] [3] [4] [10]. No one represented their work in terms of the production of site maps, wireframe diagrams or navigation models. Neither did they represent it in terms of meetings, research or the coordination of stakeholders. Instead they described a role that was defined by its fluidity, its place filling the gaps, holding both the process and the product together, reflecting a sense of ownership of, and responsibility for, a particular aspect of the final product. The part of the product most often claimed was 'its bones' and the corresponding relationship to the usability of the product.

It kind of defines that stuff that happens in between all that other stuff. I try and make things simpler for people to use (interview a).

So much of my job is about clarifying roles. Everybody says, "I don't know why I'm doing this, this is not my job to do, this is not my job to do" and it seems to be like this missing role and until you have somebody that comes in and says, "I'm an IA. Give that to me" (interview b).

Basically you work in between the rocks and the hard places (interview q).

I'm sort the meat in the sandwich (interview c).

A lot of I.A. is just a struggle for clarity (interview e).

I see it as a lynch pin between a lot of the other disciplines (interview f).

This role had no edges (laughs) (interview g).

Participants varied in their acceptance of the term information architect to describe their work. On the whole, those with the least experience were less likely to be reflective about the appropriateness of their title. These information architects were often the most recent graduates with qualifications in multimedia or new media design. Their professional experience had not included the period before information architect was used as a job title and they appeared to take for granted that it named what they did. Each participant with more than three years experience in the field said they had been called a range of titles in their careers but had done similar work (most frequently described as interaction design) in each. One participant commented that that the term was so associated with the dot.com boom that he wondered if it might disappear "along with the other excesses of that time" (interview m). Another commented:

I don't think that the role is necessary. I think that as a step in the design process, working out the information architecture and interaction design of the system is absolutely necessary, but the person that does that and performs that task doesn't necessarily have to be an information architect (interview x).

The slipperiness of the definition of the term did not appear to matter greatly to the information architects themselves. It was used strategically in some cases to cover a gap in the process, especially in relation to user involvement. It was used without reflection but also without apparent harm in others. But it always appeared to name some space, sub-process or role in the design process that needed a name.

5   Information Architects and HCI Practice

Those information architects able to reflect on and articulate their work practices displayed a real passion for the quality of the user experience of the final product and a desire to infuse the traditional software engineering approach with more user-centred approaches. What differed was the ease with which they managed to shape the usability of the final product within the other constraints of their organisations. Such organisational challenges are not unique to information architects but common to all those committed to user-centred design. The most successful and influential in our study were experienced professionals, usually working in management positions, who knew a great deal about HCI issues and usability principles.

Knowledge of HCI issues and usability principles emerged as one of the key elements that enabled participants to take more control over the design process used in their organisations. Those information architects most influential in their organisations were those who read research papers, who had research skills, who read beyond the popular titles on usability and web design and who worked actively within relevant professional associations. These information architects were more able to effectively argue for the value of user-centred processes within any kind of design process in any kind of organisation. At the same time they were sufficiently flexible in their own practices that they could select those user-centred processes and methods that were most likely to be successful. They were prepared to, and able to, undertake as many different design and evaluation methods as needed and had managed to find ways to make space for their users in even the most hostile environments: "We have a tendency to use guerrilla usability tactics" (interview s).

These information architects also played an active educative role, promoting the practice of information architecture within their work setting and to other industry practitioners. This took various forms; some tutored in HCI and related subjects at their local university; others spent time training work colleagues in analysis and design techniques they would use themselves; one even taught his colleagues and users how to use heuristics to evaluate the developing application. Sharing knowledge proved for some to be an effective way to promote a greater understanding and appreciation of the work that they did both with other members in their project team and those in the wider organisation.

Acknowledgements

We are most grateful to those information architects who participated in this research. We also thank Sam Harvey and Jenny Edwards for their contributions to this project.

References

1. Crotty, M.: The Foundations of Social Research. Allen & Unwin, Australia (1998)
2. Garrett, J.: The Elements of User Experience. Diagram retrieved January, 2004, from http://www.jjg.net/elements/ (2000)
3. Garrett, J.: The Elements of User Experience. New riders Publishing, USA (2002)
4. Preece, J., Rogers, Y. and Sharpe, W.: Interaction Design: beyond human-computer interaction. John Wiley, USA (2002)
5. Preece, J., Rogers, Y., Sharpe, W., Benyon, D., Holland, S. and Carey, T: Human-Computer Interaction. Addison-Wesley, UK (1994)
6. Robertson, T.: Embodied Actions in Time and Place: The Cooperative Design of a Multimedia, Educational Computer Game. Computer Supported Cooperative Work:, Vol 5, No 4.Kluwer Academic Publishers, Dordrecht The Netherlands (1996) 341-367
7. Rosenfeld, L. and Morville, P.: Information Architecture for the World Wide Web. O'Reilly, USA (1998)
8. Strauss, A. and Corbin.: J. Basics of Qualitative Research. Sage Publications, USA (1998)
9. Vredenburg, K., Mao, J., Smith, P. and Carey, T.: A Survey of User-Centred Design Practice. In CHI Letters, Vol. 4, No. 1, 471-478. ACM, USA (2002)
10. Wurman, R.: Information Architects, Graphic Press Corp, Switzerland (1996)

User Model of Navigation

Corina Sas

Computing Department, Lancaster University,
Lancaster, LA1 4YR, UK
corina.sas@comp.lancs.ac.uk

Abstract. This study proposes a user model of navigation in a Virtual Environment (VE), based on investigating the differences in movement patterns. Two methodologies enable accessing navigational rules and strategies employed by different groups of users: high versus low spatial users. These captured rules are summarised and hierarchically organised in a coherent structure which constitutes a basis for an efficient model of navigation. Implications of this model for designing navigable VEs are discussed.

1 Introduction

The need for understanding human spatial behaviour in both real and virtual worlds has been largely acknowledged. This is due to the prevalence and significance of this specific behaviour and to the high psychological distress associated with its failure.

The apparent gap between theoretical models of navigation and the design of VEs stems from limited interest in user modelling and insufficient accommodation of individual differences which impact on navigation. This gap impedes proper exploitation of current navigational models and theories of spatial cognition. This paper presents part of the work carried out for addressing this deficiency in the research literature. Therefore, consideration has been given to user model of navigation emerging from navigational rules employed by users.

The study of mental model of navigation, and of spatial behaviour which it supports, provides both theoretical and practical benefits. Such study could increase our understanding in the area of spatial cognition by validating or refining the current theories and models of navigation. Understanding user mental models enables also fruitful applications. Thus, some of the aspects embedded in user mental model can be formalised and used for running simulation of user behaviour. Once aspects of the user mental model have been embedded in system design, they can be used to increase user's understanding of how the system works, or in other words to assist users in the training process for learning to use the system.

In particular, studying mental models of navigation can be harnessed for training navigation in VE. Using VEs for training low spatial users or poor navigators can only be achieved through investigating user mental model of navigation and elaborating a user model of navigation. The latter, a simplified

M. Masoodian et al. (Eds.): APCHI 2004, LNCS 3101, pp. 379–388, 2004.

and schematic version of the former, encapsulates some rules and strategies which high spatial users or good navigators employ successfully in their navigation. Making these rules available to low spatial users could stay at the core of training.

This paper starts by introducing the concept of spatial mental models and their acquisition. A prototypical instantiation of these representations is captured by the construct of *cognitive maps*, whose features are briefly described. The subsequent section presents the study design, in terms of procedure, apparatus and sample. The following section focuses on user model of navigation, initially described in terms of low and high level navigational rules. These rules represent previous findings which are only summarised in this paper, without the description of the methodology for capturing them. The next section hierarchically integrates the identified rules into an efficient model of user navigation. The benefits of this model for designing VEs able to provide navigation assistance to low spatial users are discussed.

2   Spatial Mental Models

User modelling is a growing discipline in the field of Human Computer Interaction (HCI), extending itself in various areas which focus on the development of user adaptive systems. The major reason for this resides in the fact that these systems are and will continue to be used by heterogeneous user populations.

The distinction between *user mental model* and *user model* has been often drawn in HCI literature [2, 5, 14, 17]. The user mental model is developed by users during their interaction with the system, while a user model consists of knowledge that the system holds about user's mental model in order to improve the interaction [4].

The only way a system can adapt to successfully accommodate different groups of users is through the embodiment of the user model. A user model should relate to user mental model: it extracts the relevant features of user mental model which impact on system usability. In addition, these features should be addressed in the system design. Embedding the user model in the system means designing the system on the basis of a series of assumptions about user's knowledge, beliefs, intentions and behaviours. Thus, the user model is a simplified version of user mental model, which can be addressed by the system design.

In a broader sense, mental models are constructs which try to explain human understanding of objects and phenomena [9]. In her *Psychology of Mental Models*, Gentner [6] defines mental model as "a representation of some domain or situation that supports understanding, reasoning, and prediction". Simplistically, people carry small-scale models in their head which have correspondence to the external environment they represent. In the field of spatial cognition, such a mental model is usually related to the construct of spatial representation.

Hart and Moore [8] summarised several definitions of spatial representation, such as "symbolic and internalised mental reflection of spatial action" [16], "implicit action which is carried out in thought on the symbolized object" [10] or "internalised cognitive representation of space" [8].

A prototypical instantiation of these spatial representations is captured by the construct of *cognitive maps*. The concept of the cognitive map was coined by Tolman [23] who suggested that the goal-finding behaviour which rats seem to exhibit for food finding in a maze can be explained through the use of an "internal map-like representation of space". Cognitive maps define boundaries of places of interest, integrate separately learned routes into a configuration as a whole and allow an overview, the so-called bird's eye view [7]. As with any other types of representations cognitive maps are complex, highly selective, abstract and generalised representations which bear merely a functional analogy with the environment which inspired them [3].

The study of navigation in the area of HCI has developed mostly in the field of cognitive modelling, benefiting from inputs provided by both environmental psychology [16] and geography [12]. The most relevant models of navigation, focused particularly on spatial knowledge acquisition are outlined below.

Attempts to understand spatial behaviour in both real and artificial worlds were primarily concerned with highlighting the symbolic representation of spatial knowledge. Seminal in the field of studying the acquisition of spatial knowledge is the work carried out by Piaget and Inhelder [16] which led to a theory of development of the concept of space. They were the first to acknowledge the importance of moving in space and experiencing with objects through coordination and internalisation of actions for the development of early spatial representations. Piaget and Inhelder [16] showed that the child's initial understanding of space is topological, and is sensitive to simple qualitative relations like proximity, order, enclosure and continuity, whereas the Euclidean spatial relationships, for example angularity, parallelism and distance are understood later [11].

The Landmark-Route-Survey (LRS) model of cognitive mapping [21, 22] is one of the most widely accepted models designed to explain acquisition of spatial knowledge by adults, in the form of a developmental sequence. Landmark knowledge consists of information about discrete features in the environment, such as objects or places, identified and remembered because of their features: distinctiveness, location, personal significance assigned to them etc.

Once landmark knowledge has been acquired, individuals start developing information about possible spatial and temporal connections between specific environmental features, connections which represent route knowledge [1]. Golledge [7] defined route knowledge as the procedural knowledge required to navigate along a route or path between landmarks or distant locations. Route knowledge is limited to the knowledge of sequential locations without knowledge of general relations, which defines survey knowledge. Survey representations often show a hierarchical structure [24].

Survey knowledge represents the highest level of spatial knowledge, a map-like mental encoding which integrates both landmarks and route knowledge. Reaching this level enables an individual to make inferences about both landmarks and routes, based on a thorough understanding of the interrelationships between them.

Despite its large acceptance [25], this model of spatial knowledge acquisition received amendments for its simplistic view. Montello [13] proposed five stages. The first one consists of a mixture of landmarks and route knowledge (including metric knowledge) which increases in quantity, accuracy and completeness during the second stage. The third stage, which assumes the integration of discrete places into a hierarchical structure, represents a qualitatively different level. The fourth stage acknowledges the role of individual differences in spatial knowledge acquisition, while the last one emphasises the role of spatial language for topological knowledge, which exists independently of metric spatial knowledge.

Investigating the manner in which people understand the layout of an urban place, Lynch [12] identified a set of elements which describe the skeleton of a city: paths, edges, districts, nodes and landmarks. Paths are familiar major or minor routes used for travelling, such as streets, railroads, walkways etc. District or neighbourhood is an area which can be recognised as distinct on the basis of its internal homogeneity. Edges are boundaries dividing districts, while landmarks are external points of reference, such as physical objects which act as orientation aids. Nodes are strategic points, such as important crossroads, which differ from landmarks in their function: nodes are points of activity rather than physical objects.

Focusing on learning strategies which can be employed for learning a novel environment, Golledge [7] identified the following three: the active search and exploration according to a specific rules or heuristics, the prior familiarisation with secondary information sources about the environment, and the controlled navigation practices such as path integration, boundary following, sequenced neighbourhood search.

The benefits of each of these models for understanding spatial learning cannot be overestimated. They focus on behavioural aspects which provide a coherent background for further research. However, they provide only an overview of how the spatial learning process occurred in humans. Despite the fact that this process is seen in the larger framework of human action, usually tied to the spatial layout of the environment where the action occurs, these models also have limitations. They fail to provide insights into the understanding of how successful spatial learning occurs, in terms of those rules which would define efficient spatial behaviours. Usually successful spatial learning is simply seen as leading to a better, comprehensive and well-articulated cognitive map. Despite its significance, the inherently hidden character of any representation, and in particular cognitive maps, raises a complete new set of problems needing to be investigated (see Section 4).

3   Study Design

The experiments have been carried out within a desktop VE [15], which due to its tractable characteristics permitted recording of users' positions and headings at each moment in time. Adopting a physical world metaphor, the VE consists of a virtual multi-storey building where each one of the levels contains three rooms. Its projection has a rectangular shape of 16×27 virtual metres.

The sample consisted of 32 students: 19 males, 13 females; 19 novices (less than 2 years experience of playing computer games) and 13 experts (more than 12 years experience of playing computer games).

There is no predefined set of paths, such as halls or corridors which would limit the user choice of movements. The users can move freely in the space, freedom limited only by the walls and objects located within the spatial layout. Users can navigate in terms of moving forwards or backwards or rotating, through the use of the directional keys. They merely use the mouse for selecting a new floor on the panel located in the virtual lift.

The study involved three phases: familiarisation, exploration and performance measurement. Initially, users were allowed to become accustomed with the VE and to learn movement control. After this, they were asked to perform an exploration task. The exploration task within the virtual building lasted for approximately 25 minutes. After the completion of this task, during which participants acquired spatial knowledge related to the VE, they were tested. Users were placed on the third level and asked to find a particular room located on the ground floor of the virtual building. The time needed to accomplish this task acted as an indicator of the level of spatial knowledge acquired within the VE: the shorter the search time, the better the spatial knowledge. According to the time required for the search task, users have been identified as *low spatial users*, when they needed significantly longer time to find the library (Mean = 49 seconds), or *high spatial users* who found the library straight away (Mean = 7 seconds).

It appears that trajectories followed by low spatial users present a series of features which differentiate them from those followed by high spatial users. The former contain longer straight-line segments joined at sharp angles. They contain lots of turns and usually intersect themselves. Such trajectories look erratic suggesting that users are anxious to explore the space. In contrast, trajectories followed by high spatial users are smoother, usually circular, systematically covering larger areas and more landmarks [18, 19]. In order to formally describe these features, two methodologies were employed, as described in the following section.

4 Modelling Navigation

Spatial mental representations reflect the inherent complexity of human spatial behaviour. Such complexity contributes to the challenges and error-proneness which define spatial behaviour. These difficulties are even larger in the case of navigation in VEs [26]. Therefore, the understanding of human spatial behaviour, in both physical and virtual worlds, may have a tremendous practical impact.

At a theoretical level, the investigation of spatial mental models enriches the understanding of how humans perceive the space, make sense of space and exploit it. Apart from the theoretical contributions which such an understanding enables, the practical ones could lead to increased usability of VEs, as a result of identifying a set of guidelines meant to support efficient spatial behaviour.

The difficulties of investigating spatial mental models and the limitations of techniques developed for this purpose explain the lack of studies in this area. This work aims to address this gap, by focusing on investigating user spatial mental model. Such an investigation is based on a methodology involving machine learning techniques, that can overcome the limitations of traditional methods for eliciting mental models.

Given the complexity of and difficulties in capturing navigational rules, an inherent part of users' spatial mental model, several methods of analysing and interpreting data have been employed. Such a methodological approach enabled the identification of a larger set of rules which could not have been captured by the employment of just one method. Sections 4.1 and 4.2 concisely present these rules.

4.1   High-Level Navigational Rules

The first method employed for capturing rules consisted of a set of machine learning techniques. These techniques proved particularly useful in capturing some high level rules or navigational strategies. The findings suggest two efficient strategic rules which are summarised below.

The first efficient rule identifies specific areas, called *surveying zones*. Such zones are particularly appealing to high spatial users, but not to low spatial ones. What is interesting is that the attraction of these areas is not explained by the presence of some relevant landmarks, but quite contrarily, these zones are landmark free. Their attractiveness consists in their openness, which enables users to acquire a significantly larger view of their surroundings. Such observational behaviour provides users with valuable information about spatial layout and landmarks' configuration.

The second efficient rule presents an efficient way in which high spatial users conserve their resources. Moving in an indoor, unfamiliar VE which is cluttered with objects requires users to be selective and able to prioritise their visits to particular landmarks. This rule regards the movement pattern while none of the surrounding objects presents any interest for the user. In this case, the user moves along an *equilibrium path*, thus maintaining almost equal distance to each of the landmarks in his immediate vicinity. When one of the landmarks rises user's interest so that he/she decides to give it a closer look, this median path is not followed anymore and the user gravitates towards this particular landmark, with minimum energy expenditure.

The machine learning approach led also to the identification of one inefficient strategic rule. This rule is related to the difficulties encountered by low spatial users in passing through the sliding doors which separate each two adjacent rooms within the VE. These doors are designed to briefly open only when users are in their proximity, facing the doors almost at a right angle. Such door design puts unusual demands on users. This finding suggests how an inappropriate design can impede the performance on spatial tasks of low spatial users.

4.2   Low-Level Navigational Rules

The previous method for rule extraction has been complemented by a statistical analysis which led to low level spatial rules [20]. The findings suggest that low spatial users performed greater changes of heading compared to high spatial users. Looking at the distribution of these angles, it appeared that low spatial users performed significantly more rotations higher than 90° compared to high spatial users. High spatial users performed a significantly higher number of rotations (Mean = 12.07) on average per trajectory than low spatial users (Mean = 10.36), but significantly fewer consecutive rotations (Mean = 2.23), compared to low spatial users (Mean = 3.01).

High spatial users also performed significantly fewer consecutive translations (Mean = 1.60) than low spatial users (Mean = 1.80), and more translations per trajectory (Mean = 11.97) compared to low spatial users (Mean = 10.26). Findings suggest significant differences with respect to the average length of straight-line segments of trajectory performed by high spatial users (Mean = 2.94) as opposed to low spatial users (Mean = 3.82).

An important outcome suggests that low spatial users revisited significantly more times the same landmarks (Mean = 6.53), as opposed to high spatial users (Mean = 3.60). Without reaching significance, other findings suggest that high spatial users visited more rooms (Mean = 9) and more landmarks (Mean = 16.27) than low spatial users (Mean = 6.93) and respectively (Mean = 11.25). It appears that the area enclosed by the points of good trajectories is significantly larger than the area enclosed by the points of poor trajectories. Findings indicate that high spatial users move along the nearest landmarks significantly longer (Mean = 20.88 events), compared to low spatial users (Mean = 14.31 events), and significantly closer (Mean = 1.68 m) as opposed to low spatial users (Mean = 1.92 m).

The following section introduces the user model of navigation, elaborated based on these findings.

4.3   User Model of Navigation

Based on the previously identified navigational rules and strategies, a user model of navigation has been elaborated. Figure 1 depicts this model, where white arrows represent the flow of actions, and the black arrow represents a loop. The shadowed boxes present rules governing the behaviour outlined in the nearby boxes. Only efficient rules have been considered in the development of this model, since this model (and not the inefficient one) serves as a basis for adaptivity. Furthermore, the user model of navigation, based on the efficient rules extracting from the high spatial users' behaviour, is briefly described. From the original location where the user is automatically placed by the system, the user starts observing the environment through changing his/her heading. Besides acquiring valuable information about the spatial layout, such observations allow the user to identify the surveying zone, from where a better observation is enabled. Through performing a thorough observation while located in such surveying zone, user

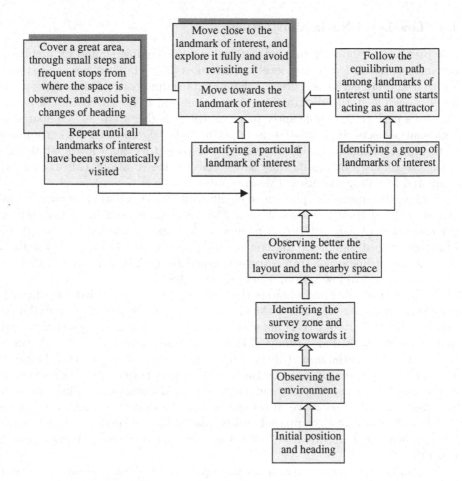

Fig. 1. User Model of Navigation

can identify a particular landmark of interest, or a group of landmarks sharing spatial proximity. In the first case, the user moves towards the landmark of interest and observes it closely, according to the efficient rules governing the behaviour around the landmarks. This decreases the need for later revisits. When the user is attracted by a group of landmarks, he/she follows the equilibrium path among them, until a landmark becomes a stronger attractor. At this moment, the median path is not followed anymore, and the user moves with minimum energy expenditure towards that particular landmark. Such a landmark is efficiently observed as described above. Once a landmark is explored like this, the user continues with the subsequent landmarks of interests, in a systematic order. In this recursive process, the user tries to cover the greatest possible area, given his limited resources. Along his route, a high spatial user carries out small steps and frequent stops which enable him to observe the space from numerous locations, while avoiding great changes of heading.

5   Conclusion

The findings outlined in this paper can provide a new approach to the design of adaptive VEs for navigation support. At the heart of this approach lies a user model of navigation, expressed in terms of navigational rules and strategies.

The basic idea is to help low spatial users to navigate more effectively in VEs by enabling their access to efficient spatial rules and strategies. These rules and strategies are determined by analysing the high spatial users' navigation patterns.

Such rules and strategies have a twofold purpose. On the one hand, they offer a deeper understanding of how high spatial users navigate in an unfamiliar indoor VE, thus offering an insight into their mental spatial model. On the other hand, such rules are merely simplifications which do not capture the full richness characterising user's spatial behaviour. However, they identify some relevant features which have the considerable advantage of being fully articulated, and therefore able to be used in the system design. This is important, particularly when the design of VE aims to assist low spatial users in their spatial tasks.

References

[1] G.L. Allen. The organization of route knowledge, new directions for child development. *Children's Conceptions of Spatial Relationships*, 15:31–39, 1982.

[2] D.R. Benyon and D.M. Murray. Applying user modelling to human–computer interaction design. *Artificial Intelligence Review*, 6:43–69, 1993.

[3] R.M. Downs and D. Stea. Cognitive maps and spatial behavior: Process and products. In R.M. Downs and D. Stea, editors, *Image and Environment*, pages 8–26. Aldine Publishing Company, Chicago, IL, 1973.

[4] T.W. Finin. GUMS—a general user modelling shell. In W. Wahlster and A. Kobsa, editors, *User Models in Dialog Systems*, pages 4–33. Springer-Verlag, Berlin, 1989.

[5] G. Fischer. User modeling in human–computer interaction. *User Modeling and User-Adapted Interaction*, 11(1-2):65–86, 2001.

[6] D. Gentner. Psychology of mental models. In N.J. Smelser and P.B. Bates, editors, *International Encyclopedia of the Social and Behavioral Sciences*, pages 9683–9687. Elsevier Science, Amsterdam, 2002.

[7] G.R. Golledge. Human cognitive maps and wayfinding. In G.R. Golledge, editor, *Wayfinding Behaviour*, pages 1–45. John Hopkins University Press, Baltimore, 1999.

[8] R.A. Hart and G.T. Moore. The development of spatial cognition: A review. In R.M. Downs and D. Stea, editors, *Image and Environment*, pages 246–288. Aldine Publishing Company, Chicago, IL, 1973.

[9] P.N. Johnson-Laird. Mental models of meaning. In A. Joshi, B. Webber, and I. Sag, editors, *Elements of Discourse Understanding*, pages 106–126. Cambridge University Press, Cambridge, 1981.

[10] M. Laurendau and A. Pinard. *The Development of the Concept of Space in the Child*. International Universities Press, New York, NY, 1970.

[11] T.R. Lee. Psychology of living space. In R.M. Downs and D. Stea, editors, *Image and Environment*, pages 87–108. Aldine Publishing Company, Chicago, IL, 1973.

[12] K. Lynch. *Image of the City*. MIT Press, Cambridge, MA, 1960.

[13] D.R. Montello. A new framework for understanding the acquisition of spatial knowledge in large-scale environments. In M.J. Eganhofer and R. Golledge, editors, *Spatial and Temporal Reasoning in Geographic Information Systems*, pages 143–154. Oxford University Press, Oxford, 1998.

[14] M.A. Norman. Some observations on mental models. In D. Gentner and A. Stevens, editors, *Mental Models*. Lawrence Erlbaum Associates, 1983.

[15] G.M.P. O'Hare, K. Sewell, A. Murphy, and T. Delahunty. An agent based approach to managing collaborative work within both a virtual environment and virtual community. In *Proceedings of the Workshop on Intelligent Agents for Computer Supported Co-Operative Work: Technologies & Risks*, 2000.

[16] J. Piaget and B. Inhelder. *The Child's Conception of Space*. W.W. Norton and Co. Inc., New York, NY, 1967.

[17] J.A. Preece. *Guide to Usability, Human Factors in Computing*. The Open University, Suffolk, 1993.

[18] C. Sas, G. O'Hare, and R. Reilly. Virtual environment trajectory analysis: A basis for navigational assistance and scene adaptivity. *Future Generation Computer Systems. Special Issue on "Interaction and Visualisation Techniques for Problem Solving Environments"*, 2004. In press.

[19] C. Sas, G.M.P. O'Hare, and R.G. Reilly. On-line trajectory classification. In *Lecture Notes in Computer Science 2659*, pages 1035–1044. Springer-Verlag, Berlin, 2003.

[20] C. Sas, G.M.P. O'Hare, and R.G. Reilly. A performance analysis of movement patterns. In *Lecture Notes in Computer Science 3038*, pages 984–991. Springer-Verlag, Berlin, 2004.

[21] A.W. Siegel and S.H. White. The development of spatial representations of large-scale environments. In H.W. Reese, editor, *Advances in Child Development and Behavior*, volume 10, pages 9–55. Academic Press, New York, NY, 1975.

[22] P.W. Thorndyke and B. Hayes-Roth. Differences in spatial knowledge acquired from maps and navigation. *Cognitive Psychology*, 14:560–589, 1982.

[23] E.C. Tolman. Coginitive map in man and animals. *Psychological Review*, 55:189–208, 1948.

[24] B. Tversky. Spatial mental models. In G.H. Bower, editor, *The Psychology of Learning and Motivation: Advances in Research and Theory*, volume 27, pages 109–145. Academic Press, New York, NY, 1991.

[25] B. Tversky. Cognitive maps, cognitive collages, and spatial mental models. In A.U. Frank and I. Campari, editors, *Spatial Information Theory: A Theoretical Basis for GIS, Proceedings COSIT'93*, volume 716 of *Lecture Notes in Computer Science*, pages 14–24. Springer-Verlag, Berlin, 1993.

[26] D. Waller. Individual differences in spatial learning from computer—simulated environments. *Journal of Experimental Psychology: Applied*, 8:307–321, 2000.

An Interface for Input the Object Region Using the Hand Chroma Key

Shuhei Sato, Etsuya Shibayama, and Shin Takahashi

Tokyo Institute of Technology, Dept. of information science,
2-12-1 Ohokayama Meguro-Ku, Tokyo 152-8550, Japan
{satou, etsuya, shin}@is.titech.ac.jp
http://www.is.titech.ac.jp/index-e.html

Abstract. We are developing the mobile system to identify wild flowers and grasses mainly from object images captured by a camera in the outdoor scene. In such systems, it is essential to inform the system an object region that the user interested in by some way. For example, if the captured image contains multiple leaves, the system can not determine which is the target leaf. In this paper, we propose interactive technique to inform the object region by placing hand behind the object. The system detects that situation, and extracts the object region automatically. Using this technique, a user can inform the system the object region in the interactive response time. Furthermore this input way is considered as natural because we often do this action to watch the object closely.

1 Introduction

We are developing the system to identify the wildflower mainly from it's flower and leaf images captured by a camera. The system consists of a handheld computer and a camera. (Fig. 1). The user interactively shoots the wildflower's flower part or leaf, and the system informs the user the wildflower's information, e.g. the flower's name.

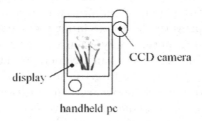

Fig. 1. The mobile system components

In such systems, it is necessary to extract the object region, e.g. flower region, from the shot image to remove the influence of background. For instance, the

M. Masoodian et al. (Eds.): APCHI 2004, LNCS 3101, pp. 389–398, 2004.

flower color information must be obtained from the image of the flower region. However, it is difficult to obtain such regions fully automatically. For example it is difficult to segment a leaf from the other similar leaves shown in Fig. 2. The contour of the leaf in the center of the image seems to be difficult to identify even for a human. It is difficult for the system to extract the contour by image processing robustly from the limited information that the object is in the center.

Fig. 2. An obscure leaf

Fig. 3. a leaf on a hand

In this paper, we propose a method to specify the region of interest in the field with a mobile PC by placing a hand behind the object like in Fig. 3. In the field, the color of the image captured by camera is changes a lot even the same scene under various illumination.

Though the leaf in Fig. 3 is the same as the leaf in Fig. 2, the contour of the leaf is more conspicuous than that in Fig. 2. Using this method, the system can extract the object region semi-automatically in the interactive response time and the user can specify the object region expressly.

2   Interface for Input Object Regions Using a Hand

We propose a method that the user places a hand behind the object to input the region of the object. The region with background of a hand is the object region. The system captures images continuously and if the system detects an object is on a hand, the region of the object is automatically extracted. The user does not need to press the button to input the region. Putting an object on the palm of the hand is a natural way when we watch the object closely. This system needs no input device other than a camera essentially. Consequently the user can concentrate in putting the target in a frame of a camera.

Detecting the hand region is necessary before extracting the object region. The skin color extraction technique is effective because the skin color is distributed in the small portion of the whole color space. However our system is used at outdoor situation under various illumination and the distribution of skin color varies substantially. Consequently skin color model should be created dynamically to adapt to various illumination.

Our system has the calibration interface easy to input skin color model's parameters. If the user shoots a hand to fill the image with it like Fig. 4, the system detects this action automatically, and uses the distribution of the image to calculate parameters of the skin color model.

It is necessary to use automatic exposure control with a camera to adapt various brightness. However, it does not necessarily work well, and in that situation the color of the object is lost because of overexposure or underexposure like Fig. 5. Usually, overexposure occurs when the object is placed against dark background. Using our input method, overexposure or underexposure is reduced comparatively because the skin reflectance is near the 18%. The normal automatic exposure producing an average 18% reflectance image. Fig. 6 shows that overexposure of the leaf is suppressed by placing a hand at the back of the leaf.

Fig. 4. An image for calibaration   **Fig. 5.** A leaf is overexposured   **Fig. 6.** A leaf is exposured sufficeintly

The color of the object changes according to illumination condition. For example, the object is tinged with red by the setting sun. This change has a negative impact on the object recognition system. The automatic white balance can suppress this change of color and produce normalized colored images under standard white light. However the automatic white balance is not perfect, the object color can not be normalized depending on the input image. Using our method, the object region and the skin region are both detected in the same image. If we know the color of the skin in white light, we can suppress the change of color of the object based on the color of the skin.

2.1 Comparison with Other Region Input Interfaces

Pen or Touchpad There are many works that input regions with a pen or a touchpad. For instance, to use the method of F. Zanoguera et al.[8], a user can input the region, only by drawing a line on the target region roughly. It is suitable way in front of a desk. However this action needs user's both hands to use in mobile systems. The user must specify the line with a pen or a finger, and the user must hold the display by the other hand. There is often a case that the user must use his hand to clear the obstructive weeds to shoot the object. For instance, leaves occlude the target flower or the target flower is moving because of the wind. In such a case, the user can not shoot a target picture and specify the region with a pen at the same time. Our interface needs only one hand and the other hand can be used for clearing the obstructive weeds.

Using Camera with Distance Information There are systems that can produce the distance from a camera to the pixels' resource point. For instance, it can be computed by using two cameras. Using these systems, the object region can be obtained robustly in the situation that background objects are far from camera compared to the object. But when many leaves are overlapped each other, the system may not detect the object region with distance information. In such situation, our system can extract the object region, by picking the target leaf and put it on the hand. This method is not suitable for the system using distance information, because the hand and the leaf is too close.

3   Implementation

In this section, we describe the implementation of the region input method. It is necessary to detect the hand region at first in order to recognize the object region with background of a hand. We detects a hand region by using color information utilizing the human skin colors cluster in the color space [4].

3.1   Skin Color Model

We used three dimensional gaussian distribution in HSV color space as a model for a skin color distribution[1]. We uses HSV color space because it is relatively insensitive to the change of the brightness component. It is also known that the skin color extraction in HSV color space is more effective than in RGB color space[3]. A color vector captured by a camera is described in RGB color space, should be transformed to HSV color space at first. This process can be done at high speed with a transformation table. The parameters of this model are a mean vector and a covariance matrix. We describe how to get these parameters of skin distribution in next subsection.

3.2   Acquisition of Skin Color Model Parameters

We prepare the interface that the user can input skin color model parameters very easily. The system can detect skin color regions under various illumination. The system calculates a mean vector and a covariance matrix of the color vector of all the pixels in each images captured at every frame. If the values in the covariance matrix are all less than thresholds then it is considered that the image is filled by almost a single colored object like Fig. 4. We use the mean vector and the covariance matrix at that time as parameters for the skin color distribution. Notice that a single colored object does not need to be a hand. It is not a problem because it usually does not happen without the user's intention. It is rather convenient because single colored objects can replace a hand as background if the user wants.

3.3   Skin Color Extraction

Using gaussian color filter[1], the system calculates a probability of skin image from the captured image in each frame. Gaussian color filter is expressed as the formula (1).

$$c^i = e^{(X_i - \hat{X})^T \sum^{-1} (X_i - \hat{X})} \tag{1}$$

X_i denotes the color vector of i'th pixel in the image. c^i denotes the dissimilarity from the skin color correspond to i'th pixel. $\hat{X}$ denotes the skin color mean vector and $\sum^{-1}$ denotes the inverse of skin color covariance matrix. The original image is shown at Fig. 7. The result image is shown at Fig. 8. The brightness of the image represents the dissimilarity from the skin color. Consequently the hand region is emerged as a darker region.

Fig. 7. An original image   **Fig. 8.** Dissimilarity image of the skin

Before applying gaussian color filter, we apply moving average filter to original images to degrade an influence of noise.

3.4   Identification of the Object Region

The object region is surrounded by the region with the color of skin. First, skin colored region is calculated by thresholding the dissimilarity of skin image. Then, dilate filter and successive erode filter is applied to remove noise and narrow regions between adjacent two fingers shown at Fig. 8. Finally, we identify connected components in the image, and the hole of the largest region is regarded as the input image. Small holes under the threshold are ignored as noise. For example, in Fig. 9, suppose white connected pixels as a skin region, B2 and B4 are regarded as the object region, if B2 and B4 are larger than the threshold. Notice that W4 is not included in the input region. The W4 is regarded as the hole of the object.

4   Evaluation

4.1   Processing Time

We measure the processing time with two machines, a mobile PC SONY PCG-GT1(TM5600, 600MHz) with a incorporated camera, and a desktop PC (Pentium III 600E, 600MHz) with a camera IO-DATA USB-CCD.

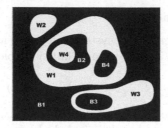

Fig. 9. regions

Table 1 shows the average number of frames processed per second. The number in parentheses is the number of frames to calculate that average. There is a tendency that the amount of the processing task if the system detects the region is larger than that of not detected. For example if the system does not detects the object region the skin colored region may be not detected and an area of the skin colored region is not calculated. On the other hand the object region is detected then an area of the skin colored region is calculated certainly. The first row represents the frame rate while the system detects the input region. The second row represents the frame rate while the system does not detect the input region. The third row shows the average of all frames. For example, with PCG-GT1, the input region is detected in 573 frames per 1440 frames.

From the average frame rate of the all frames, the interactive response time is achieved with both PCs. The difference between the average rate of frames while the system can detect the region and that of not detected is sufficiently small. Consequently, the processing speed is considered as stable.

Table 1. frame rate

	TM5600	P3 600E
frames that the input region detects	6.8 fps (265)	16.2 fps (573)
frames that the input region are not detects	8.4 fps (735)	17.0 fps (867)
all frames	7.9(1000)	16.7(1440)

4.2   Precision and Input Time

We performed an experiment that a user inputs the regions of 15 leaves and flowers using "SONY PC-GT1". The experiment was done at about 16:00 in August. It was fine weather. From Fig. 10 to Fig. 15 shows examples of the detected regions. Which are represented as closed white lines. Fig. 10, 11 and 12 shows the examples that succeeded to detect intended regions. Fig. 13, 14 and 15 are examples that failed to input intended regions.

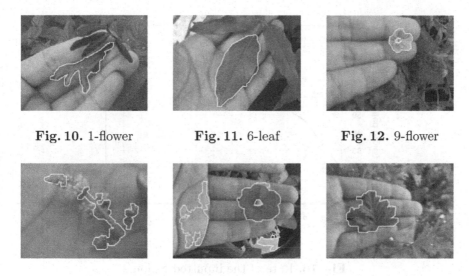

Fig. 10. 1-flower   **Fig. 11.** 6-leaf   **Fig. 12.** 9-flower

Fig. 13. 3-flower   **Fig. 14.** 8-flower   **Fig. 15.** 10-leaf

The detected regions in Fig. 13 do not match the real shape of the flower. The flower part is so small that color of the flower is weakened by applying moving average filter to suppress noise components. If we use a camera that can produce images with lower noise, this kind of flowers can be extracted. In Fig. 14 unintended region is detected. This region can be input by moving the object close to a camera. The unintended region is detected because the skin color distribution is changed from the time the user input the skin color by the automatic exposure control. To avoid this situation, more applicable skin color model is against the change of brightness of images needed. The region in Fig. 15 is almost correct but the outline of the shape is not accurate. The shadow of the leaf on the hand is not recognized as the skin, because the skin can not to be expressed by the gaussian color model sufficiently. The more expressive model for the skin color is needed to detect this kind of shapes accurately.

Fig. 16 shows the rate of regions that can be detected by the system precisely as time elapses form the beginning. The timing starts when the object region is captured in a frame of a camera completely. The graph shows that 20% of regions can be input in 2 seconds. The experiment is done with 15 kinds of region, 3 kinds of region can be input in 2 second. This result indicate that this interface has capability to input the object region very fast. As time elapses the number of regions that can be detected increases because the user tries to input the correct region in various ways. For example, the user may reinput the skin color parameters described at Section 2, or move a target close to the camera. In the case shown in Fig. 14, the user can understand that the unintended region will be removed if the user move a target close to the camera. About 70% of regions can be input in 14 seconds. This result indicates that most kinds of region can be input in acceptable time.

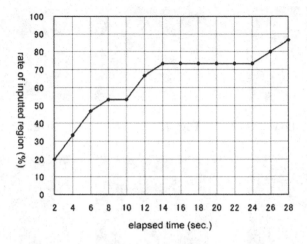

Fig. 16. Rate of the inputted region

5 Related Works

S. Walherr et. al developed the system that extracts skin regions to make a robot that understands arm gestures[1]. Our system uses the gaussian color filter described in the paper. However it uses static skin color model which is not suitable for outdoor use, we added the interface to change skin color model's parameters easily.

S.Ahmad[6]'s system tracks hands on the desk to recognizing gestures. The system divides the input image into small rectangles, and match the histogram of each rectangle and the skin color histogram prepared beforehand. The rectangles whose histograms are similar to the skin color histogram are recognized as skin color regions. In this way, more robust skin extraction can be possible than pixel wise extraction of the skin, the resolution of the skin color image will be smaller than that of the input image. In our system, the shape of the hand region is more important than their system, because the hole of the hand region is used as the target object shape.

L.Sigal[3] at. el tracks skin color regions in movies encoded with MPEG-2. The system changes color model to utilize the location of the skin colored region in the image assumed not to change a lot. Using this technique, the hand region can be tracked robustly, but the skin color at the first frame probably have to be ordinary color of the skin illuminated by almost white light. Therefore this technique does not have sufficient ability to detect the skin region under unusual illuminations, like red light in the sunset. Our system equipped the interface to input the skin color parameters easily then any color distributions that can be represented as Gaussian can be input as skin color distributions. Consequently the skin region under unusual illuminations can be detected.

Madirakshi Das at. el developed the system that classifies images of flower patents based on colors of the flowers[7]. The system is not supposed the background color of the flower unlike our system. First, the system removes the region regarded as background iteratively and regard the conspicuous region remained as the flower region. But this technique is valid if the color used for the background is different color from the flower color. The flower patent images satisfies this condition. But this technique is not suitable to input a leaf region clustered with the other leaves. Because a leaf and the other leaf have almost the same color. Consequently, even using this technique, it is necessary to place a hand behind the object in order to make conspicuous the object contour.

6   Future Works

Improving Precision Descrived at previous section, gaussian distribution is too simple to model skin color distribution of even a specific people sufficiently. More applicable skin color model against the change of brightness of the skin is also needed. We are developing a more robust skin extract technique.

Enhancement of Kinds of the Region That Can Be Input In our method it is impossible to input the region larger than a hand. It's region cannot be specified by placing a hand behind the target object.

Implementation of the Flower Recognition System In this paper, we described the region input method for the flower recognition system. Using this method, we can input flower regions or leaf regions. Now we can match the regions with that in the database of flowers. To implement the whole system we have to select the region matching algorithm suitable for and the inference engine that returns the species incorporating the result of the matching a flower and a leaf and the other information, such as the season.

7   Conclusion

We proposed the object region input method that the user places a hand in back of the object. The system detects this automatically so that the user can input the target region without any other input devices. Consequently the user can concentrate in putting the target in a frame of a camera. This action is considered as natural, because this action is shown when one watch the object closely. This interface is suitable for the system that used in the outdoor scene such as the system that identifies the flower species.

References

1. S. WALDHERR, S. THRUN, R. ROMERO, and D. MARGARITIS. Template-Based Recognition of Pose and Motion Gestures On a Mobile Robot, In Proc. of AAAI, pp. 977-982, 1998.

2. Yu-Hua (Irene) Gu, and T.Tjahjadi. Corner-Based Feature Extraction for Object Retrieval, In Proc. of ICIP. pp.119-123, 1999
3. L. Sigal, S. Sclaroff, and V, Athitsos. Estimation and Prediction of Evolving Color Distributions for Skin Segmentation Under Varying Illumination, In Proc. of CVPR, 2000.
4. J. Yang, W. Lu, and A. Waibel. Skin-color Modeling and Adaptation, In Proc. of ACCV'98, Vol. II, 1998, pp.687-694.
5. B. D. Zarit, B. J. Super, and F K. H.Quek. Comparison of Five Color Models in Skin Pixel Classification., ICCV'99 International Workshop on Recognition, Analysis, and Tracking of Faces and Gestures in Real-Time Systems, pp58-63, 1999
6. S. Ahmad. A Usable Real-Time 3D Hand Tracker. Conference Record of the Asilomar Conference on Signals, Systems and Computers. pp. 1257-1261, 1994
7. Madirakshi Das, R. Manmatha, and E. M. Riseman. Indexing Flower Patnet Images Using Domain Knowledge, IEEE Inteligent Systems, pp. 24-33, 1999
8. F. Zanoguera, B. Marcotegui and F.Meyer. A Toolbox for Interactive Segmentation Based on Nested Partitions. ICIP, pp. 21-25, 1999
9. Intel Open Source Computer Vision Library, http://www.intel.com/research/mrl /research/opencv/

Menu-Selection-Based Japanese Input Method with Consonants for Pen-Based Computers

Daisuke Sato, Buntarou Shizuki, Motoki Miura, and Jiro Tanaka

Department of Computer Science, Graduate School of Systems & Information Engineering,
University of Tsukuba
{daisuke, shizuki, miuramo, jiro}@iplab.is.tsukuba.ac.jp
http://www.iplab.is.tsukuba.ac.jp

Abstract. We have developed a menu-selection-based Japanese input method for a pen device. To obtain user-input kanji-form text rapidly, the system requires sequence of consonant. Following this, the user selects kanji-form candidates inferred by the system. In some situations, consonant sequences can trigger an explosion of kanji-form candidates. Therefore, we have implemented a method for reducing candidates through vowel fixing. The user can input consonants, and select kanji-form candidates fluidly, using FlowMenu.

1 Introduction

Computers that are operated with a pen, such as PDAs and TabletPCs, have recently become popular. Large displays with a touch-sensitive panel are available as electronic whiteboards for seminars and meetings.

Presently, these computers use, primarily, a software keyboard for character input. However, there are two problems in using a software keyboard with a pen:

1. The user must move the pen between scattered interfaces, such as a menu bar and the software keyboard. The larger the display is, the more severe the problem becomes.
2. Tap operations with a pen put a heavy strain on the user, since the user must manipulate the pen.

Another popular character input method is that of an on-line character recognition system. Unfortunately, the recognition accuracy is low with respect to Japanese, due to the large number of Japanese characters to be recognized. Furthermore, current character recognition systems are implemented in a window like a software keyboard. Therefore, this system inherits the problems of a software keyboard.

If the problem of Japanese input using a pen can be solved, pen-based computers will become more efficient. We describe a new and efficient Japanese input method called "Popie", which solves these problems. The Popie system is based on Flow-Menu[1], which has a doughnut-shaped interface and has been developed for pen devices. FlowMenu inputs characters using Quikwriting[2], selects menus with a single interface, and integrates all operations fluidly. Unfortunately, FlowMenu does not support inputting non-alphabet characters, such as Japanese or Chinese characters.

M. Masoodian et al. (Eds.): APCHI 2004, LNCS 3101, pp. 399-408, 2004.

This problem occurs when working in languages such as Chinese or Korean, with a large number of characters. We can apply the Popie method to languages in order to solve this problem.

2 Japanese Input Using FlowMenu

2.1 Japanese Input Method

In this section, we briefly explain the method used to input Japanese text on desktop computers. Japanese text consists of *kanji* and *kana*. *Kanji* are Chinese characters, and *kana* are character in a phonetic alphabet. We input words using a sequence of phonemes by means of *kana*. Then, the input system shows possible candidates for the Japanese text that correspond to the input. The Japanese text input finishes when a candidate is selected.

Most *kana* characters are composed of a consonant and a vowel. In total, *kana* consists of 15 consonants, five vowels and the symbol 'X' (Table. 1). An additional five consonants (G, Z, D, B, and P) can be represented using another consonant (K, S, T, and H) and a second symbol '*'. In general, a *kana* word is typed as a sequence of consonants, vowels, and symbols.

For example, to input "日本語", which means "Japanese"), the corresponding *kana* sequence "にほんご", is typed in, which reads as "Ni Ho N Go".

Table 1. *Kana*: corresponding to consonants, vowels, and the symbol X

Vowels	φ(A)	K	S	T	N	H	M	Y	R	W	G (K*)	Z (S*)	D (T*)	B (H*)	P (H**)	X	XY	-
a	あ	か	さ	た	な	は	ま	や	ら	わ	が	ざ	だ	ば	ぱ	ぁ	や	
i	い	き	し	ち	に	ひ	み		り		ぎ	じ	ぢ	び	ぴ	ぃ		
u	う	く	す	つ	ぬ	ふ	む	ゆ	る		ぐ	ず	づ	ぶ	ぷ	ぅ	ゅ	
e	え	け	せ	て	ね	へ	め		れ		げ	ぜ	で	べ	ぺ	ぇ		
o	お	こ	そ	と	の	ほ	も	よ	ろ	を	ご	ぞ	ど	ぼ	ぽ	ぉ	ょ	
φ				ん														ー

2.2 FlowMenu

FlowMenu has a doughnut-shaped interface, creating a radial menu, which consists of eight octants and a central area called rest area.

Fig. 1 presents an example of operation that duplicates an object and moves the object using FlowMenu.

First, the user taps and holds the pen on the target object (a). Then, the FlowMenu is shown (b). Next the user moves the pen from the rest area into the "edit" octant (c). The "edit" sub menu appears, and the user moves the pen into the "duplicate" octant (in this case, the user does not need to move the pen) (d). When the pen returns to the rest

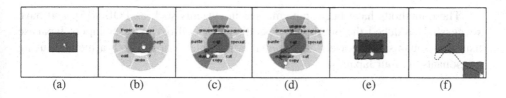

| (a) | (b) | (c) | (d) | (e) | (f) |

Fig. 1. Example of a FlowMenu operation: duplicate an object, then move the object

area, the object is duplicated (e). Finally, the user can move the duplicated object (f). In this way, FlowMenu provides a series of operations with a single stroke.

One of the advantages of FlowMenu is that it is "eyes-free." If the user memorizes locations of the FlowMenu items, the user can select a menu item quickly, by means of a gesture. In the example shown in Fig. 1, if the user memorizes the object she/he wants to duplicate by moving the pen into the lower left octant and returning it to the rest area, the user can perform a duplication without looking at the menu item.

2.3 Input Japanese Using Consonants Only

As previously noted, we generally use both consonants and vowels to input Japanese. Some methods that require only ten consonants and a symbol have been developed[3][4]. To input "にほんご" ("Ni Ho N Go") using such a method, one inputs "NHWK*". In this method, 'ん' and '一' are input using 'W'. 'G' is replaced with 'K' and the symbol '*'.

Our Popie system uses a consonants method to input Japanese. We think that reducing operations the number of operations required to input characters is important, because an operation using a pen takes longer than one using a keyboard.

Consonant methods for inputting Japanese have a problem: the number of candidates can explode. This problem can be partially solved by sorting candidates using frequency statistics, based on newspaper articles. Such methods are effective in reducing the number of operations required to input Japanese, including candidate selection. Nevertheless, two problems remain:

1. If the result of candidate sorting is irrelevant, the rank of the target word of the user is lower, so the cost of the select operation is higher.
2. The user can only input known words that are contained in the learning corpus.

We solved these problems by allowing the user to select a vowel with a simple operation when necessary.

Moreover, we adopted completion and inference to reduce the number of operations. With completion, the system estimates the best candidate before the input is complete. For example, the system shows "日本語" ("NHWK") when "NH" is input. With inference, the system guesses the next word from the last word input. For example, the system shows "入力", which means "input", when "日本語", which means "Japanese", is input.

These methods have been implemented in systems such as POBox[5], and have successfully reduced the number of operations. In POBox, the user inputs Japanese using consonants and vowels, however, it is possible to apply such a method, using consonants to input Japanese.

3   Popie

We have developed a Japanese input system called Popie, which uses consonants to input Japanese. We have also solved the two above-mentioned problems when using computers with a pen.

Popie requires a sequence of consonant keys "AKSTNHMYRW". "あいうえお" has no consonant, we use 'A' as an expedient consonant. In addition, 'ん' and 'ー' are input using 'W'. Moreover, our method can input "Ni Ho N Go" as "NHWK" without using the symbol '*'. Since the Popie interface is on FlowMenu, the operation consists of a continuous stroke.

3.1   Popie Interface

Fig. 2 shows the Popie interface. The interface consists of three parts: the input & selection, user input and candidate display parts. The user conducts all the operations of Popie in the input & selection part. Popie shows candidates that correspond to the user input in the candidates display part. The input of consonants is shown in the user input part.

When the user inputs "NHWK", the system shows "日本語", which means "Japanese" and reads "Ni Ho N Go", "日本が", which means "Japan is" and reads "Ni Ho N Ga", "日本画", which means "Japanese-style painting" and reads "Ni Ho N Ga", and so on (see Fig. 2).

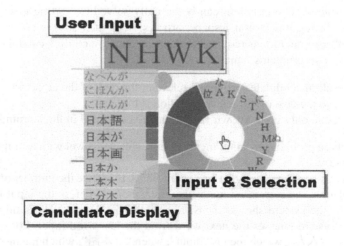

Fig. 2. Popie Interface: The user wants to input "日本語".

3.2   Narrowing Down Candidates Using Vowels

As we have already noted, the problem of the explosion in the number of candidates using a consonants method to input Japanese has been improved. Nevertheless, two problems remain: selecting lower-rank candidates and inputting unknown words.

Our solution is to select a vowel using a simple operation when necessary. Table 2 indicates the number of candidates when the user inputs N consonants and selects M vowels from the beginning of the consonants sequence. This table was made from Popie's dictionary, which consists of the dictionary of the Japanese input method system SKK[6] and word frequency data from newspaper articles (see Section 3.6). If the sorted candidates do not help the user, the user must select the target word from among many candidates, as seen in the case of M=0 in Table 2.

Our method solves this problem by selecting vowels that correspond to the sequence of consonants, from the beginning. Vowel selecting can reduce the number of candidates. For example, if the rank of "日本語" is lower when the user inputs the sequence of consonants "NHWK" to input "日本語" ("にほんご", "Ni Ho N Go"), then the user selects vowel 'i' corresponding to 'に' ('Ni'), and the input becomes "に HWK". Selecting the vowel that correspond to the beginning of the consonant sequence reduces the number of candidates, as seen from the case of M=1 in the table.

Selecting all the vowels corresponding to the consonants also solves the problem of inputting unknown words.

Table 2. The number of candidates in Popie's dictionary when the user inputs N consonants and selects M vowels from the beginning of the consonant sequence

Consonants N		Fixed Vowels M				
		0	1	2	3	4
1	Average	194.10	23.40			
	SD	162.07	28.17			
2	Average	129.42	20.05	4.99		
	SD	122.68	24.74	10.54		
3	Average	34.63	7.26	3.04	1.95	
	SD	40.78	11.46	5.21	3.23	
4	Average	8.06	3.10	2.19	1.60	1.46
	SD	12.67	4.21	3.06	1.66	1.39

3.3   Input Consonants and Candidate Selection

This section presents the example of inputting "日本語" in Popie in Fig. 3. When the target word is "日本語" ("Ni Ho N Go"), the user inputs "NHWK" and selects "日本語" from the candidates shown by Popie.

First, the user moves the pen from the rest area (a) to the octant labeled "STN", (b). Then, she/he moves to the octant labeled 'N' (c), returns to the rest area (d), and 'N' is

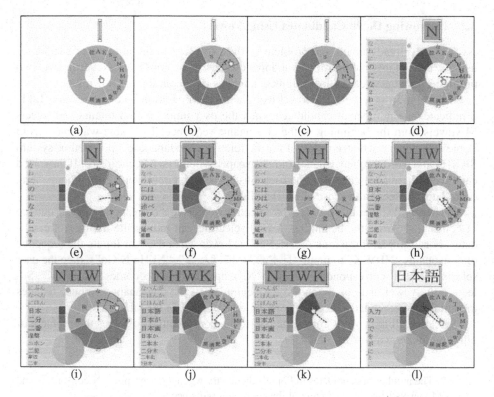

Fig. 3. The operation of inputting "NHWK" and selecting "日本語"

input. Next, she/he moves the pen to the octant labeled "HMY", then to octant 'H' (e), then back to the rest area, and 'H' is input (f).

'W' and 'K' are input in a similar manner (g, h, i, and j). Finally, the user moves the pen from the rest area to the octant corresponding to "日本語", then back to the rest area, and "日本語" is selected. This series of operations involves a continuous stroke.

If the target word does not appear in the top three, candidates, the user can select any candidate by selecting the up or down arrow (k) to scroll the list.

3.4 Vowel Selection

This section presents an example that involves selecting a vowel using Popie in Fig. 4. The user has already input "NHWK" (a), and the user wants to select the vowel 'i' corresponding to 'に' ('Ni'). First, the user moves the pen from the rest area to the octant labeled "STN" (b), then crosses over this octant with across 'に' (c) and vowel 'i' is selected. The user returns the pen to the rest area and continues operation (d). The vowels "aiueo" are placed at the outer edge of the octant, from north to south in a clockwise manner.

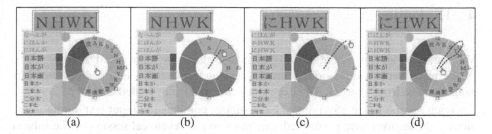

(a)   (b)   (c)   (d)

Fig. 4. The operation involved in selecting vowel 'i', which corresponds to 'に'("Ni")

3.5   Consonants Key Configuration

In Popie, the main menu has eight items, and each sub menus has eight items. Therefore, the user can input 64 keys. Table 3 shows the key configuration in Popie. The main menu is oriented in a longitudinal direction, and sub menus are placed in a transversal direction. In the sub menu, frequently used keys are placed closest to the parent main menu item. In fact, frequently used keys appear in the diagonal element or the adjacent element in Table 3.

Table 3. Key configuration for Popie

		Sub							
		N	NE	E	SE	S	SW	W	NW
Main	N	A	K						
	NE	S	T	N					
	E		H	M	Y				
	SE			R	W	Space	Return	Tab	
	S				Symbol	Delete	Undo	Redo	
	SW	Scroll				Scroll			
	W	Upper				Lower	Candidate Select		
	NW								

3.6   Dictionary

The dictionary in Popie consists of three dictionaries: word frequency, co-occurrence, and user dictionaries. The co-occurrence dictionary is used to infer the word following the last word selected.

We used text data from the CD Mainichi Newspapers 2001[7] published by Mainichi-Newspaper Co., as the corpus of the dictionary. The text data was analyzed by Chasen[8]. In addition, the word frequency dictionary was augmented using SKK's dictionary[6].

4 Evaluation

We conducted an experiment with six users to evaluate the input speed of Popie. None of the participants had previously used a computer operated with a pen device. They ranged in age from 18 to 21. The experiment was run using TabletPC (Fig. 5).

Each session lasted 15 minutes. Each subject continued to input text during a session; eight sessions were performed (one practice and seven real sessions). The subject completed one or two sessions per day, with sufficient time between sessions. Text examples were made from a corpus different from the corpus used for the system's dictionary. Each text consisted of 15 to 45 characters. Although the learning function was on, no two texts were exactly alike.

4.1 Results of the Experiment

Fig. 6 shows the results of the experiment and indicates the speed of input using Popie. The horizontal axis shows the sessions, and the vertical axis shows the number of characters input per minute(cpm).

The first session was a practice session, so it is not plotted on the graph. In the second session, the input speed ranged 9 to 14 cpm, and averaged 11.9 cpm. By the last session, input speed ranged from 19 to 29 cpm, and averaged 24.7 cpm.

In a pilot study, the speed of character input using the character recognition tool supplied with WindowsXP TabletPC Edition averaged 18 cpm. The subject was one of the authors, and the procedure used was the same as in the experiment. This result is thought to reveal a general trend, because each individual's writing ability is alike.

Therefore, we believe that Popie is a practicable method for inputting Japanese.

Fig. 5. TabletPC

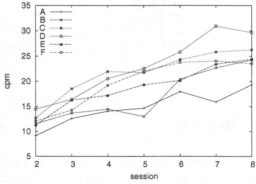

Fig. 6. Input speed of Popie

5 Discussion

Currently, the Popie interface uses the simple kana order ("AKSTNHMYRW") for the consonants key layout. Since layout optimization is often discussed, we examined the key layout in Popie. Nevertheless, we hypothesized that key layout has little influence on the input speed, because the pen is located in the rest area after inputting each consonant.

We examined the layout optimization of ten keys placed on the numbered circle in Fig. 7. In order to discuss key layout optimization, data on the frequency of key use and the input cost of each key are required. In addition, it is also necessary to consider the input of N consecutive keys, because the frequency in the use of consecutive keys changes with each value of N. We calculated the cost for the cases N=1 and N=2.

In this optimization, the input cost was thought of as the input time. Moreover, if the movement speed of the pen is constant, the input time is proportional to the distance, the pen moves, so we use the distance data as the input cost. The frequency of key use was computed from CD Mainichi Newspapers 2001[7], and we considered the following three costs.

1. The distance cost, consisting of r, the distance from the rest area to one octant, and a, the distance between two adjacent octants. (see Fig. 7)
2. The distance cost was computed from the strokes in the experiment, shown as stroke s in Fig. 7.
3. The time cost was computed from the experimental data. Since this cost includes the factor wontedness, we used the average relative time, which is based on the average time per stroke in each session for each user.

The result of the key layout optimization is shown in Table 4. With an optimized key layout, the user can input, at most, 5.5% faster, confirming our hypothesis. We believe that using the familiar *kana* order for the key layout is more important than a 5.5% improvement in input speed.

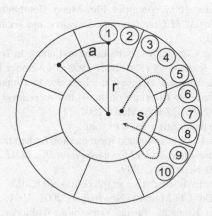

Fig. 7. The numbered circles for the layout, distance (r, a), and stroke s

Table 4. The solution for the optimized key layout and the rate to the current layout for N consecutive keys, and the cost of each

N	Kind of cost	Solution 1 2 3 4 5 6 7 8 9 10										Rate (%)
1	Using r and a	T	W	R	A	N	H	S	Y	M	K	96.98
	Distance for a stroke	T	R	W	S	Y	N	K	H	M	A	97.58
	Time for a stroke	T	K	W	S	H	Y	N	M	R	A	99.17
2	Using r and a	T	W	R	S	Y	M	K	H	N	A	94.58
	Distance for a stroke	A	W	H	T	Y	N	S	M	R	K	95.12
	Time for a stroke	T	W	A	S	R	Y	N	M	H	K	98.86

6   Conclusion

We discussed Popie, a method of inputting Japanese for pen-based computers. The user inputs Japanese on the FlowMenu by inputting consonants and selecting candidates shown by the system. Thanks to FlowMenu, the user can input consonants rapidly. Thus, the problems of pen movement between scattered interfaces and numerous tap operation have been solved.

In addition, we implemented a way to select a vowel corresponding to a consonant, in order to solve the problems of selecting lower-rank candidates and inputting unknown words. We showed that the input speed of Popie is higher than that of character recognition. Moreover, we verified that optimization of the consonant key layout was inefficient.

We are planning to evaluate Popie's performance on a large display, and to apply Popie to other languages.

References

1. François Guimbretière and Terry Winograd. FlowMenu: Combining command, text, and data entry. In *Proceedings of ACM User Interface Software and Technology 2000 (UIST 2000)*, pp. 213–216, May 2000.
2. Ken Perlin. Quikwriting: Continuous stylus-based text entry. In *Technical Note of ACM User Interface Software and Technology 1998 (UIST 1998)*, November 1998.
3. K. Tanaka-Ishii, Y.Inutsuka, and M.Takeichi. Japanese text input system with digits –can japanese text be estimated only from consonants?-. In *Proceedings of Human Language Technology Conference 2001 (HLT 2001)*, March 2001.
4. T9. T9 text input home page. http://www.t9.com.
5. Toshiyuki Masui. POBox: An efficient text input method for handheld and ubiquitous computers. In *Proceedings of the International Symposium on Handheld and Ubiquitous Computing (HUC'99)*, pp. 289–300, September 1999.
6. SKK Openlab. SKK. http://openlab.ring.gr.jp/skk/index-j.html.
7. Mainichi Newspapers Co. CD-Mainichi Newspapers 2001, 2001.
8. Yuji Matsumoto, Akira Kitauchi, Tatsuo Yamashita, Yoshitaka Hirano, Hiroshi Matsuda, Kazuma Takaoka, and Masayuki Asahara. *Japanese Morphological Analysis System ChaSen version 2.2.1*, December 2000.

Framework for Interpreting Handwritten Strokes Using Grammars

Buntarou Shizuki, Kazuhisa Iizuka, and Jiro Tanaka

Institute of Information Sciences and Electronics, University of Tsukuba
1-1-1 Tennoudai, Tsukuba, Ibaraki 305-8573, Japan
{shizuki,iizuka,jiro}@iplab.is.tsukuba.ac.jp

Abstract. To support the rapid development of pen-based structured diagram editors, we propose a framework for describing such editors. The framework uses grammar to describe the context, *i.e.*, the positional relationship between handwritten strokes and other objects, which can be used to interpret ambiguous results of pattern matching, and to describe the syntax of the target diagrams. We implemented the framework by extending our visual system, which supports the rapid prototyping of structured diagram editors.

1 Introduction

Diagrams are used frequently. Examples used in UML software design include class diagrams, sequence diagrams, and statecharts. Other examples are diagrams that represent data structures, such as binary trees, stacks, and lists. Organization charts are widely used in daily life. Consequently, it would be convenient if there were a system that would allow users to sketch such diagrams on tablet computers and electronic whiteboards using a stylus. The system would then interpret the handwritten strokes to recognize the structure of the diagrams, and then make them neater or transform them into other styles.

One big problem with developing such systems is the ambiguity that is inherent in handwritten strokes. Often, a single stroke cannot be interpreted from its shape alone. However, the context of where a stroke is drawn can eliminate some choices, and sometimes eliminate the ambiguity. For example, assume that we are editing a binary tree. In this context, if a linear stroke is made within a circular stroke, we might recognize the circular stroke as a circle, whereas the linear stroke might be either the letter "l" or the number "1".

Diagram editors that can analyze *handwriting* must be able to perform the following two functions:

Recognize handwritten strokes: The editor must recognize a given handwritten stroke using both the shape of the stroke and its context.

Parse the relationships between strokes: A *spatial parser* parses the relationships between recognized strokes that have been input in a random, unordered fashion. The parser recognizes the structure of strokes and then performs follow-up actions based on its interpretation of the results.

M. Masoodian et al. (Eds.): APCHI 2004, LNCS 3101, pp. 409–419, 2004.

Fig. 1. A binary tree editor generated from its description

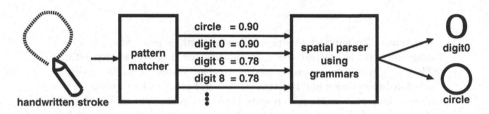

Fig. 2. The interpretation of handwritten strokes depending on the context

To help the systematic development of spatial parsers, *spatial parser generators* have been proposed, such as SPARGEN[1], VLCC[2], and Penguins[3]. A spatial parser generator generates the parser automatically from the specifications of the target diagram. A *grammar* is used to describe these specifications. However, no framework to assist in the systematic development of both of these functions has been proposed.

To provide developers with the means to develop structured diagram editors with these two functions, we propose a framework that recognizes ambiguous handwritten strokes that are drawn as parts of structured diagrams. The framework adopts an approach that uses grammar to describe: 1) the syntax of the target domain, and 2) how handwritten strokes should be interpreted. The spatial parser then selects appropriate candidates from several possible candidates from a pattern matcher using the grammatical description given by the developer. We have implemented the proposed framework. Fig. 1 shows a structured diagram editor for editing binary trees that was produced using our framework.

2 The Interpretation of Handwritten Strokes Using Grammar

Fig. 2 illustrates the proposed framework for interpreting handwritten strokes using grammar. The pattern matcher performs its pattern-matching algorithm for each handwritten stroke every time a stroke is drawn. The matcher then produces an n-best list for each stroke. The spatial parser then parses the stroke with other existing strokes and objects to find plausible choices in the n-best list according to a given grammatical description. When the parser can select one

Fig. 3. An example of a diagram: a binary tree

choice, then the stroke has been recognized. When the parsing fails, the parser leaves the stroke on the canvas for future analysis.

For example, consider a diagram editor for binary trees. When the circular stroke illustrated in Fig. 2 is drawn on the canvas, the pattern matcher produces an n-best list of probabilities, which includes 0.90 for a circle, 0.90 for the digit 0, 0.78 for the digit 6, 0.78 for the digit 8, and so forth. The spatial parser will select the digit 0 if a stroke is drawn within a circle, since the stroke can be considered the label of a node. If the stroke is drawn around some text, the parser will select a circle pattern.

Note that the framework uses both the shape of the stroke and its context, *i.e.*, the positional relationships involving the handwritten strokes and other objects, to recognize a given handwritten stroke. This recognition enables the selection of one choice from multiple choices, even if the choices have the same or lower probabilities than others, such as the digit 0 and the circle in Fig. 2.

Below, Section 2.1 describes the grammar that we use in this paper, with a description of a sample structured diagram editor. Section 2.2 introduces a special token that enables the developer to describe rules for recognizing a handwritten stroke depending on its context.

2.1   Describing Structured Diagram Editors Using Grammar

We use a grammar that is based on CMGs[4]. In this grammar, a rule has the form:

$$P ::= P_1, \cdots, P_n \text{ where } C \text{ with } Attr \text{ and } Action$$

This means that the non-terminal symbol P can be composed of the multiset of symbols $P_i(i = 1, \cdots, n)$ when the attributes of all of the symbols satisfy constraint C. The attributes of P are assigned in *Attr*. It also executes *Action* after performing the application. Note that *Action* is our extension of the original CMGs for convenience.

The two rules listed below are the specifications for binary trees (see Fig. 3), and they are used as examples to provide explanations in the remainder of this paper.

```
# Rule 1
Node::=C:Circle,T:Text where (
   close(C.mid,T.mid)
) {
```

Table 1. The attributes of a gesture token

name	value
pattern	n-best list from the pattern matcher
start	x-y coordinates of the starting point
end	x-y coordinates of the ending point
bound	bounding box of the handwritten stroke
length	length of the handwritten stroke
time	turnaround time for inputting the stroke

```
    cp = C.mid;
    r  = C.radius;
} { }

# Rule 2
Node::=N1:Node,N2:Node,N3:Node,L1:Line,L2:Line where (
    inCircle(L1.start,N1.cp,N1.r) && inCircle(L1.end,N2.cp,N2.r) &&
    inCircle(L2.start,N3.cp,N3.r) && inCircle(L2.end,N2.cp,N2.r)
) {
    cp = N2.cp;
    r  = N2.r;
} { }
```

The first rule indicates that a node consists of a circle and some text. The midpoints of the circle and text should be close together. `close(P1,P2)` is the user-defined function that tests whether the distance between P1 and P2 is within a given threshold. If so, the circle and text are reduced to a node. The attribute cp of the node is defined as specifying the *connection point*. This connection point is the point at which an edge might be connected within a tolerable error r, which is defined by the midpoint and radius of the circle. cp and r are for later use. This rule does not specify any action.

The second rule defines the composition of the nodes. It specifies a composite node consisting of three nodes, N1, N2, and N3, and two lines, L1 and L2. L1 must start near the connection point N1 and end near N2. The condition is checked by calling the user-defined function `inCircle(P,C,R)`. The function tests whether a given point P lies within a circle with center point C and radius R. Similarly, L2 should start near the connection point N3 and end near that of N2. The connection point for the composite node itself is assigned as the connection point of N2.

By providing the spatial parser generator with these two rules, `close()`, and `inCircle()`, a structured diagram editor specialized for editing binary trees can be developed.

2.2   A Handwritten Stroke as Token

Now, we introduce *gesture tokens* to enable grammar descriptions that refer to handwritten strokes. A gesture token is instantiated for each handwritten stroke every time a stroke is drawn. Each token holds an n-best list that the pattern matcher produces. In addition, the token holds information that is derived directly from the stroke, such as the bounding box, the stroke, and the coordinates of the starting point. Table 1 shows the attributes that a gesture token holds. Attribute `pattern` is the n-best list and the others are derived from the stroke.

Gesture tokens can be referred to in the same ways as other kinds of tokens that correspond to graphical objects such as circles and lines. This enables the developer to specify what should happen when a handwritten stroke is drawn, based on the shape of the stroke and the positional relationship between the stroke and other objects, such as graphical objects that are already drawn on the canvas and even other handwritten strokes.

2.3 Rules Using Gesture Tokens

To explain how gesture tokens can be used in grammatical descriptions and how handwritten strokes can be processed, this section presents a simple rule that is described using a gesture token. This rule transforms a handwritten stroke into a circle, as illustrated in Fig. 4, if the pattern matcher determines that the probability that the stroke has a circular shape exceeds 0.5.

```
_CreateCircle::=G:Gesture where (
   findGesture(G,"circle",0.5)
) {} {
   createCircle(G.bound);
   delete(G);
}
```

Fig. 4. The transformation of a circular stroke into a graphical object

This rule indicates that _CreateCircle consists of a gesture token G. G should be circular. The user-defined findGesture(G,N,P) checks this condition. The function tests whether a given gesture token, G, has a candidate named N whose probability exceeds P. When this constraint holds, the rule creates a circle that is inscribed within the bounding box of the stroke using createCircle(B), where B is the bounding box of the circle being created.

Note that the rule deletes the handwritten stroke using delete(G). As a result, the corresponding handwritten stroke disappears from the canvas. Simultaneously, the non-terminal symbol _CreateCircle disappears, since its criteria are no longer satisfied. This scheme systematically deletes unnecessary handwritten strokes (G in this rule) and pseudo-tokens (_CreateCircle in this rule) that are introduced for the description of rules.

3 Context-Dependent Interpretation

When the user draws a handwritten stroke on a structured diagram editor, the context of the stroke can be classified into the following three categories:

(1) Syntax for the target diagram that the structured diagram editor supports

(2a) Existing tokens around the handwritten stroke that are already recognized as parts of the target diagram

(2b) Existing gesture tokens around the handwritten stroke that are not yet recognized as parts of the target diagram

Since category (1) is the precondition of a structured diagram editor, all the rules assume the context of category (1). A rule that assumes only the context of category (1) can be described by placing only a gesture token as the rule's multiset of symbols P_i. An example of a rule in this category is the rule described in Section 2.3, which creates a circle that forms a binary tree. This rule assumes only the syntax of binary trees. A rule that assumes the context of categories (1) and (2a) should use tokens other than gesture tokens. A rule that assumes the context of categories (1) and (2b) should use two or more gesture tokens. The next two subsections describe examples of these two kinds of rules.

3.1   Interpretation Depending on Existing Tokens

A rule for recognizing handwritten strokes depending on the existing tokens of the target diagrams uses tokens of the syntax other than gesture tokens. As an example of such rules, we show the rule for recognizing a linear handwritten stroke drawn between two nodes like Fig. 5 as an edge between the two nodes on a binary tree editor.

```
_CreateEdge::=G:Gesture,
    N1:Node,N2:Node where (
  findGesture(G,"line",0.3) &&
  inCircle(G.start,N1.cp,N1.r) &&
  inCircle(G.end,N2.cp,N2.r)
) {} {
  createLine(N1.cp,N2.cp);
  delete(G);
}
```

Fig. 5. The interpretation of a linear stroke between two nodes

This rule holds that `_CreateEdge` consists of a gesture token and two nodes. The shape of the gesture token should be linear. The probability of the pattern should exceed 0.3. The stroke should run from the connection point (see Section 2.1) of one node to the connection point of another. This condition is checked by calling the user-defined function `inCircle()`. If these conditions hold, a line object is created between the connection points of the two nodes. Finally, the gesture token is deleted. The line object that this rule creates is then processed using the second rule described in Section 2.1. As a result, a composite node consisting of the three nodes appears on the canvas.

Note that this rule requires very low probabilities, *e.g.*, 0.3 is the threshold for recognizing a linear handwritten stroke between two nodes as an edge. This means that ambiguous strokes sketched roughly by the user can be recognized. This powerful recognition is achieved by referring to the context.

3.2   Interpretation Depending on Existing Gesture Tokens

A rule for recognizing handwritten strokes depending on other handwritten strokes uses two or more gesture tokens. As an example of such a rule, we show a rule for recognizing two handwritten strokes, a circular stroke and a stroke inside the circular stroke, as a circle and a text label that form a node of a binary tree, as depicted in Fig. 6.

```
_CreateNode::=G1:Gesture,
    G2:Gesture where (
  findGesture(G1,"circle",0.5) &&
  insideOf(G2.bound,G1.bound)
) {} {
  C = createCircle(G1.bound);
  createText(getString(G2),C.mid);
  delete(G1);
  delete(G2);
}
```

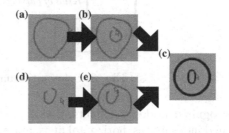

Fig. 6. The interpretation of a circular stroke and a stroke written inside the circular stroke

This rule claims that if two gesture tokens G1 and G2 exist, and G2 is inside G1, an inscribed circle in the bounding box of G1 is created. Moreover, new text is placed at the center of the circle. Function getString(G) is used to obtain the text string. It returns a string that corresponds to the textual pattern with the highest score out of the textual patterns in the n-best list of G.

Note that this rule enables the user to draw the two strokes in any order. For example, when the user draws the circular stroke first (Fig. 6a), and then the inner stroke (Fig. 6b), the rule transforms the two strokes in the manner depicted in Fig. 6c. The same result is obtained when the user draws the inner stroke (Fig. 6d) and then the circular stroke (Fig. 6e). Therefore, the proposed framework can provide the user with natural recognition.

4   Another Example

This section shows another example of a structured diagram editor that is defined in this framework. Fig. 7 illustrates a network diagram editor that is defined using nine rules. The user can handwrite a network node, a network segment, and a connector that connects the network node with the network segment.

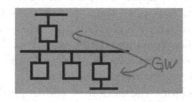

Fig. 7. Another example: a network diagram editor

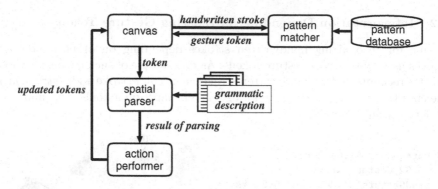

Fig. 8. Schematic diagram of the system

Recognized nodes, segments, and connectors are automatically connected and tidied into squares, horizontal lines, and vertical lines, respectively. Since the constraint solver maintains all connections and alignments, all objects connected to a dragged object are automatically moved for maintaining the structure. Therefore, the user can drag objects while maintaining the syntax of the diagram.

Note that the user can handwrite such an annotation using free strokes such as the "GW" with two arrows shown in Fig. 7, since the framework leaves all handwritten strokes that are not recognized by the given rules.

5   Implementation

Fig. 8 is a system structure that implements the proposed framework. The figure illustrates the components and the flow of data between the components. Below is a description of how each of the components performs:

Canvas feeds the raw data of a handwritten stroke into the pattern matcher, *i.e.*, the coordinates of the sampled points, and receives a gesture token. Moreover, when the state of the canvas changes, *i.e.*, new tokens are created, existing tokens are deleted, or the attributes of the existing tokens are changed, the canvas requests that the spatial parser parse them.

Pattern matcher tries to match a stroke with the patterns registered in the pattern database. The matcher returns the n-best list of the match and the raw data of the stroke as a gesture token.

Spatial parser searches for applicable rules in the grammatical description. If the parser finds one, it applies the rule and asks the action performer to perform the rule's action, if any. If the parser cannot find any applicable rule, the gesture token remains on the canvas for future use. This mechanism enables the recognition of handwritten strokes that depend on other handwritten strokes, as described in Section 3.2.

Action performer executes the action of the applied rule and updates the state of the canvas, if necessary.

We implemented the proposed framework using this system structure. Currently, we have implemented the pattern matcher using the recognizer distributed as a part of SATIN[5]. We used Tcl/Tk, C, and Java for the implementation.

6 Related Work

Several frameworks have been proposed for processing a handwritten stroke depending on its context.

Electronic Cocktail Napkin[6] supports the recognition of the configuration of handwritten strokes in a drawing. The recognizer parses handwritten strokes depending on the context, with user-defined production rules. Therefore, the target application domain is similar to ours. However, the system only allows several built-in gestures. In our framework, the developer can define new gestures by describing rules.

Artkit[7] is a toolkit that supports the implementation of interactions using handwritten input. The toolkit supports handwritten input using *sensitive regions*. A sensitive region has a set of acceptable shapes of handwritten input and algorithms for processing the drawn input. In Translucent Patches[8], the notion of patches corresponds to the context. Each patch defines how handwritten strokes should be processed and displayed. Strokes drawn within the region that a patch covers are processed using the patch. Flatland[9] is an electronic whiteboard system. A context is defined as a *behavior* that defines how strokes are processed and displayed. A handwritten stroke drawn by the user is added to a *segment*, which can have a behavior. This means that the recognition of new strokes is determined by the behavior. Plugging another behavior into the segment can change the recognition of a stroke. The system provides several behaviors. Unlike these systems, our proposed framework has the capacity to define context as a grammatical description.

DiaGen[10] and Electronic Cocktail Napkin provide *syntax-directed editing*, which enables the user to reshape a diagram, while maintaining the syntax of the diagram. This framework can also support syntax-directed editing. We use a constraint solver for this end. Rules can request the spatial parser to maintain the conditions while objects are dragged, once objects are parsed to form a non-terminal symbol. Currently, we use SkyBlue[11] as the constraint solver.

Our implementation can also realize the beautification described in [12] using the capabilities of the constraint solver in *Action*. For example, we can align two leaf nodes to make a composite node on a binary tree editor. This beautification requires only the addition of a command in the *Action* of the second rule in Section 2.1, which constrains the y coordinates of N1 and N2 to be the same.

7 Discussion

About recognition The proposed framework does not exclude existing algorithms for recognition and interfaces for resolving ambiguity in handwritten strokes. By incorporating such algorithms and interfaces, it is possible to achieve higher precision in recognition. One example is the incorporation of the n-best list interface for higher precision in character recognition. Then, the developer can define a rule that activates the n-best list interface on nodes of binary trees. The interface will show the possible recognition of the text, asking the user to indicate an intended choice. When the user selects the choice from the list, recognition of the text is fixed.

About description The framework enables a developer to define powerful rules for recognizing handwritten strokes by utilizing a parsing algorithm that is derived from CMGs. Moreover, the developer can describe both rules for recognition and rules defining the syntax of a diagram in one specification language. However, our current implementation forces the developer to embed some "magic numbers" directly in the grammatical description, such as 0.5 in the rule described in Section 2.3, to define the threshold for recognition. Since such parameters are dependent on the pattern database, the developer may have to re-tune the parameters in the rules when new patterns are registered in the pattern database. We are now investigating how to separate such numeric parameters from the grammatical description to allow developers to tune parameters more easily.

8   Summary

We proposed a framework to support the rapid development of pen-based structured diagram editors that support the recognition of a handwritten stroke depending on its context. The framework uses CMGs to describe the context or positional relationships of handwritten strokes and other objects, which in turn can be used to interpret the ambiguous results of pattern matching and to describe the syntax of target diagrams.

References

1. Golin, E.J., Magliery, T.: A compiler generator for visual languages. IEEE VL'93 (1993), 314–321
2. Costagliola, G., Tortora, G., Orefice, S., Lucia, A.D.: Automatic generation of visual programming environments. Computer **28** (1995) 56–66
3. Chok, S.S., Marriott, K.: Automatic construction of intelligent diagram editors. ACM UIST'98 (1998) 185–194
4. Marriott, K.: Constraint multiset grammars. IEEE VL'94 (1994) 118–125
5. Hong, J.I., Landay, J.A.: SATIN: a toolkit for informal ink-based applications. ACM UIST'00 (2000) 63–72
6. Gross, M.D., Do, E.Y.L.: Ambiguous intentions: a paper-like interface for creative design. ACM UIST'96 (1996) 183–192
7. Henry, T.R., Hudson, S.E., Newell, G.L.: Integrating gesture and snapping into a user interface toolkit. ACM UIST'90 (1990) 112–122
8. Kramer, A.: Translucent patches. JVLC **7** (1996) 57–77
9. Igarashi, T., Edwards, W.K., LaMarca, A., Mynatt, E.D.: An architecture for pen-based interaction on electronic whiteboards. AVI 2000 (2000) 68–75

10. Minas, M., Viehstaedt, G.: DiaGen: A generator for diagram editors providing direct manipulation and execution of diagrams. IEEE VL'95 (1995) 203–210
11. Sannella, M.: SkyBlue: a multi-way local propagation constraint solver for user interface construction. ACM UIST'94 (1994) 137–146
12. Chok, S.S., Marriott, K., Paton, T.: Constraint-based diagram beautification. IEEE VL'99 (1999) 12–19

A Rapidly Adaptive Collaborative Ubiquitous Computing Environment to Allow Passive Detection of Marked Objects

Hannah Slay[1], Bruce Thomas[1], Rudi Vernik[1,2], Wayne Piekarski[1]

[1] e-World Lab, School of Computer and Information Science, University of South Australia, Mawson Lakes, SA 5095, Australia
{Hannah.Slay, Bruce.Thomas, Rudi.Vernik, Wayne.Piekarski}@unisa.edu.au

[2] Defence Science Technology Organisation, PO Box 1500, Edinburgh, SA 5111, Australia
Rudi.Vernik@dsto.defence.gov.au

Abstract. This paper presents a tool to support the rapid and adaptive deployment of a collaborative, ubiquitous computing environment. A key tool for the configuration and deployment of this environment is a calibration tool to quickly and efficiently calculate the positions of cameras in a dynamic environment. This tool has been incorporated into our current Passive Detection Framework. The paper describes the context where our rapidly adaptive collaborative ubiquitous computing environment would be deployed. The results of a study to test the accuracy of the calibration tool are also presented. This study found that the calibration tool can calculate the position of cameras to within 25 mm for all lighting conditions examined.

1. Introduction

Ubiquitous computing was coined by Weiser [1] in his seminal paper "The Computer of the 21st Century" where he described the notion of computing being woven into the backdrop of natural human interactions. One of the key steps in the move towards these computing environments is a shift from the use of traditional workstations as a primary computing interface, towards environmental or workspace interfaces. In these environments the traditional input devices of mice and keyboards will be replaced with more human-centric approaches.

We are applying the rapidly adaptive collaborative ubiquitous computing environment to allow passive detection of marked object technology to the intense collaborative domain, in particular the Augmented Synchronised Planning Spaces (AUSPLANS) project. AUSPLANS is a defence domain project that focuses on distributed synchronised planning in organisations through the rapid augmentation and enablement of physical workspaces using emerging ubiquitous computing and human interaction technologies. Two key aims of AUSPLANS are to create cost effective infrastructure to augment and enable physical spaces and to create components to have a short set up time and be adaptable to

M. Masoodian et al. (Eds.): APCHI 2004, LNCS 3101, pp. 420–430, 2004.
© Springer-Verlag Berlin Heidelberg 2004

suit changing user and team needs. Our tracking infrastructure provides a cost effective tracking platform that can be used to augment traditional meeting room environments. The application Calibrate Collaborative Environment (CalibrateCE) allows the tracking infrastructure to be quickly and easily reconfigured to suit the changing requirements of users in a collaborative, ubiquitous computing environment.

We foresee the research detailed in this paper to be applicable to any intense collaboration environment where users must work collaboratively to complete time critical tasks. In organizations such as the civil disaster relief departments, there are periods of high levels of activity. Rigid and fixed infrastructure may not be the most appropriate form for such intense collaborative environments. The shape of the environment may need to change depending on the number of collaborators. The location of the environment may not be known before the emergency, and the environment may have to be placed close to the emergency. In such environments, large, multi user, ubiquitous computing workspaces may need to be employed. The ability to replicate these environments is critical for such situations.

This paper presents a tool that we have created to support the rapid and adaptive deployment of a collaborative, ubiquitous computing environment. Central to making these systems rapidly adaptive is the ability to calibrate the resources available in such an environment for use with tracking of marked objects in that workspace. CalibrateCE allows users to calculate the six degrees of freedom (6DOF) pose (translation and orientation) of cameras in an environment. It uses cameras with image based pattern recognition to calculate the 6DOF pose of a camera relative to a fixed point in the environment. Once the poses of the cameras are known, the framework can be used to determine the real time physical world pose of objects such as laptops, furniture, computer input devices affixed with markers in the environment [2]. Given the known location of calibration points in a physical coordinate system, and a trained marker, the calibration process takes approximately one minute and a half for each calibration point (where a calibration point is a known position relative to the coordinate system). The user must simply place the trained marker on a calibration point, enter the x,y,z position of the marker on a computer, then start the calibration application on the computer to which the camera to be calibrated is attached.

1.1.   Universal Interaction and Control in Multi Display Environments

This research is included in an overarching project focusing on universal interaction and control in multi display environments. These environments are likely to offer a variety of display and interaction modalities, each of which is best suited to specific classes of application. Gesture based interaction, for example may be more suited to an object manipulation application than a word processing application. This project aims to investigate appropriate interaction devices to control and manipulate information across a large range of display devices, applications and tasks in the context of command and control centres [3]. In particular, this project investigates the use of information visualization in such environments [4]. A key component we require in interacting with multiple displays in a collaborative environment is a tracker. This tracker can be used to calculate the position of devices, people and information in the environment.

Consider the scenario where a tidal wave hits low level parts of a small island country. A joint planning group would be formed to determine the actions to be taken to assist the residents and return order to the country. A hall at a local school is transformed into temporary headquarters for the group. Laptops, projectors and other personal computing devices are taken to the hall to create both large public displays and private display areas. Cameras are attached to ceilings to track the information flow (physical documents) as well as position of mobile devices in the environment. CalibrateCE is used to rapidly calibrate the work environment so the information can be tracked.

1.2. Passive Detection Framework

The Passive Detection Framework (PDF) [2] was created as an infrastructure for physical meeting rooms that can be used to rapidly augment the space and transform it into a tracked environment. The user can track an object in the environment by attaching a marker card (or fiducial marker) to the object and moving the card around the workspace. The pose of the marker card is calculated using an image based recognition library called ARToolkit [5]. Once the pose is determined, it is placed on a shared location. These tasks are carried out passively on dedicated machines so that a wide range of devices (PDAs, tablet PCs, laptops, and traditional workstations) can utilise the infrastructure without draining the resources of the device. Cameras are mounted on the ceiling to provide the most complete view of the workspace, whilst still being discrete.

Fig. 1. Current LiveSpaces configuration. The camera and marker used in experiment are highlighted.

Unlike many tracking techniques, an advantage of the PDF is that the hardware components of the framework can be easily reconfigured to suit the requirements of the users of the workspace. Cameras can be repositioned in the environment using simple clamping mechanisms to attach to ceilings, desks etc, and computers can be relocated. For example, the default position of the cameras may be to spread them out over the entire meeting room, to provide the largest tracked volume possible. However, if a small group were to use the room they may want to reposition the cameras to give a more complete coverage of a section of the workspace. To do this however, a mechanism must be created to allow users to quickly and efficiently calculate the pose of the cameras in the real world. CalibrateCE was created to allow users to perform this task.

Figure 1 shows the current configuration of the PDF in our environment at e-World Lab. All cameras are roof mounted using a simple clamping mechanism. This allows cameras to be moved both along the surface of the roof and moved further from / closer to the roof surface. Several of the cameras mounted in the e-World Lab can be seen in this image. There are two key steps in the process of transforming a traditional work area to a tracked working volume. Firstly the pose of cameras in the room must be calculated. Secondly using this information, the pose of marker cards can be calculated in physical world coordinates. In previous research [2], we have detailed the method in which we performed the latter of these two steps. This paper aims to describe the former step, workspace calibration.

1.3.   Outline of Paper

This remainder of this paper is divided into four sections. Section 1 reviews existing research into the area of next generation work environments. This is then followed by a detailed description of CalibrateCE and its role in our adaptive collaborative ubiquitous computing environment. Section 3 section details an experiment performed to determine the accuracy of a workspace after calibration has been performed with CalibrateCE along with an analysis of the results. The final section contains conclusions and future directions for this research.

2.   Related Work

Several organisations and groups have been investigating the use of ubiquitous computing for future work environments. This research has two main focuses: embedding computational facilities into everyday furniture and appliances [6, 7], and creating interactive environments in which the environment can be controlled by a computer [8, 9]. We are concerned with the latter category, in particular the research being carried out by Stanford University's Interactive Workspaces (iWork) project, Massachusetts Institute of Technology's (MIT) Project Oxygen, and the University of South Australia's LiveSpaces project.

The key goal of Stanford University's iWork project is to create system infrastructure that provides fluid means of adjusting the environment in which users are working. Instead of automatically adjusting the environment of a workspace for the user (as is provided by Project Oxygen), iWork provides the user with the ability to smoothly and cleanly control their own environment[9].

The primary goal of Project Oxygen is to create a room that is able to react to users' behaviour. This is attempted by combining robotics, camera recognition, speech recognition and agent based architecture to provide intrinsic computational assistance to users in a workspace. This computation is designed to be available without the user of the computation having to shift their mode of thinking or interaction with people [8]. Project Oxygen has been investigating tracking the movement of people in the workspaces using a combination of vision based tracking[10, 11], and more hardware oriented systems such as pressure sensitive floor tiles[8]. We are not only interested in tracking the movement of users in a room, but in tracking the movement / placement of devices in the workspace.

LiveSpaces is the overarching project within e-World lab at the University of South Australia that is addressing how physical spaces such as meeting rooms can be augmented with a range of display technologies, personal information appliances, speech and natural language interfaces, interaction devices and contextual sensors to provide for future interactive/intelligent workspaces. Research is being undertaken to address how these future workspaces can be rapidly configured, adapted, and used to support a range of cooperative work activities in areas such as military command environments, large-scale software enterprises, and health systems [12]. AUSPLANS is an example of a LiveSpace as a military command environment.

For working indoors, a number of tracking technologies have been developed such as: the first mechanical tracker by Sutherland, ultrasonic trackers by InterSense, magnetic trackers by Ascension and Polhemus, and optical trackers such as the Hi Ball. These systems all rely on infrastructure to provide a reference and produce very robust and accurate results. The main limitation of most of these systems is that they do not expand over wide areas, as the infrastructure to deploy has limited range or is prohibitive in cost. Newman et al [13] describe the use of proprietary ultrasonic technology called Bats that can be used to cover large building spaces. The hybrid tracking technique described in Piekarski et al [14] operates using a number of input sources. Orientation tracking is performed continuously 3 DOF orientation sensor and indoor position tracking is performed using a fiducial marker system based on AR-ToolKit. The VIS-Tracker by Foxlin and Naimark [15] demonstrates the possibility of using dense fiducial markers over large indoor areas using small portable hardware. This system requires four or more markers to be within the camera's field of view for a 6DOF solution, compared to the single marker required by ARToolkit. The systems described by Newman, Piekarski, and Foxlin all require specialised hardware for each object to be tracked. Once the infrastructure of the PDF has been installed, each object only requires a new paper fiducial marker to be tracked. Each camera can track approximately twenty markers. Kato and Billinghurst's ARToolKit [5] produces reasonable results with the use of fiducial markers, and as mentioned is the underlaying tracking technology used for the PDF and CalibrateCE. This tracking does not drift over time and produces reasonably accurate results.

3. CalibrateCE

CalibrateCE is an application that allows users to quickly and easily create a tracked volume within their work environment, and then to easily reconfigure the infrastructure components (computers, hubs, cameras) to suit their changing requirements. In order to do this, CalibrateCE allows users to efficiently calibrate the features of their work environment (camera poses, room attributes) and store this data in a shared location for use by other applications at a later time. This data is accurate until a camera is moved in the work environment, at which point the workspace must be recalibrated. The output of CalibrateCE is used by the PDF to calculate the position of the markers in the physical world.

We calculate the physical world pose of the camera by calculating the pose of the camera with respect to the known location of a fiducial marker, and then factor in the pose of the marker in the physical world. Figure 2 shows the transformation of the camera in physical world coordinates. Arrows on axes show the positive direction of each dimension. To calculate the 3x4 transformation matrix C, the inverse of the transformation between the marker and the camera T, must be multiplied by the rotation in coordinate systems between the marker and the physical world R, and then multiplied by the transformation between the marker and the origin of the physical coordinate system M.

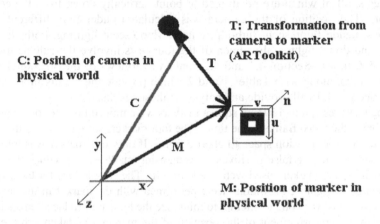

Fig. 2. Transformation of Camera in Physical World

CalibrateCE uses the PDFs distributed system consisting of two components: node computers and a combiner computer. Cameras are attached to the node computers and an ARToolkit based application [5] is executed per camera attached to the computer. The application calculates the transformation of the marker in the camera coordinate system and sends this 3x4 transformation matrix to the combiner computer. This calculation is performed and sent in a UDP packet 500 times to attempt to overcome factors such as uneven lighting. The combiner computer receives the UDP packets and calculates an average pose for each camera using the quaternion form of each rotation matrix. Having a distributed architecture makes CalibrateCE easy to extend to either track a larger volume or to provide a more complete coverage of the currently tracked volume. In both cases, an extra node computer can be added to the framework.

The output of CalibrateCE is a XML file containing user defined fields (such as a name for the environment), and an element for each computer that sent UDP packets to the combiner. Each computer element has sub-elements that detail the node number and pose of each camera. This XML file is placed in a shared location for use by other applications, such as PDF.

4. Experimental Results

This section provides an overview of an experiment we have undertaken to determine the accuracy to which the CalibrateCE application can calculate the pose of a fixed camera in an environment. The work environment that the experiment was performed in has two separate lighting systems, fluorescent lights and halogen down lights. The fluorescent lights are divided into two sections, one section runs around the perimeter of the ceiling, and the other runs in the middle of the ceiling. We refer to these as the outside and inside fluorescent lighting systems respectively. The inside fluorescent lighting system contains one quarter as many lights as the outside fluorescent lighting system. The halogen down lights are a group of 5 small directional lights, all of which are positioned to point vertically down from the ceiling to the floor. The position of the camera was calculated under four different lighting conditions: inside fluorescent lighting, outside fluorescent lighting, both fluorescent lighting, and down lights only. Each of the four tests involve the calculation of the position 500 times. Section 4.1 and 4.2 contain overviews of the positional and orientation results, along with Tables 1 and 2 which provide the results in a condensed format. Section 4.3 will provide an analysis of these results.

During these tests, four 150 mm square markers were trained but only one marker was ever visible in the video frame at one time. The four markers were trained so the program would have a large decision space to choose from. If only one marker was trained, this would result in multiple false positives in recognising markers. To reduce the effect of uneven lighting, all markers used were made of felt. The calculations for the position of the camera in all lighting conditions were performed with the marker in the same place for each test. This was done to attempt to minimize the human introduced errors in calculations (only one measurement of the position of the marker was taken and the marker remained in the same position throughout the execution of the experiment). The distance between the camera and the marker was 1645 mm.

4.1. Positional Results

Table 1 shows results obtained after performing the configuration under each of the four lighting conditions. Shown are the minimum, maximum, mean and standard deviation calculated over the 500 iterations for each lighting condition. All measurements are taken in room coordinates, where the centre of the transformation matrix space was in the corner of the room. The measured position of the camera is 3320, 2080, 1680 (x, y, z respectively). The minimum and maximum values for x, y and z were calculated separately. They therefore show the range of values calculated for each of the dimensions.

If we consider the top half of Table 1 (results for tests where all lights are on, and where only the outside lights are on), we can see that the fluctuations between minimum and maximum values are approximately 100 mm. However, if we compare these values to those obtained where the lighting was low and inconsistent (in the tests where only the inside lights or only the down lights were used), we can see that the fluctuations between minimum and maximum values have now risen to values of approximately 300 mm. However, by considering the mean values for each of the lighting conditions, we can see that the distance between the measured position and the mean positions are within 25mm of each other for all lighting conditions. We consider this error to be acceptable.

Table 1. Calculated positions of camera under four lighting conditions.

All	x (mm)	y (mm)	z (mm)	Out	x (mm)	y (mm)	z (mm)
Min	3270.41	2044.57	1618.69	Min	3264.09	2048.36	1612.73
Max	3315.53	2109.1	1737.79	Max	3313.26	2091.73	1756.15
Mean	3300.45	2065.77	1682.33	Mean	3299.18	2067.32	1687.74
St Dev	4.66	8.47	22.46	St Dev	4.48	7.96	24.98
Inside	x (mm)	y (mm)	z (mm)	**Down**	x (mm)	y (mm)	z (mm)
Min	3233.61	2037.01	1601.09	Min	3235.13	2032.62	1574.46
Max	3322.8	2207.35	1910.27	Max	3335.16	2201.51	1897.43
Mean	3300.74	2066.51	1686.61	Mean	3306.01	2062.15	1682.19
St Dev	5.91	11.34	27.59	St Dev	6.77	11.88	31.57

4.2.   Orientation Results

Because the cameras can be rotated around three axes, we have found it difficult to measure the actual orientation of the cameras in the physical world. Instead of comparing the measured and calculated orientation of each camera, the accuracy of the orientation results will be discussed by comparing all results from all lighting conditions..

Table 2. Calculated Orientation of camera under four lighting conditions. The three values shown are Euler angles[1]. All measurements in degrees.

All	heading	bank	attitude	Out	heading	bank	Attitude
Min	-79.115	-89.993	-26.864	Min	-79.227	-89.981	-27.106
Max	-77.524	-85.376	-25.860	Max	-77.399	-85.127	-25.963
Mean	-78.219	-87.984	-26.399	Mean	-78.308	-88.206	-26.419
Std Dev	0.284	0.907	0.178	Std Dev	0.306	1.010	0.166
Inside	heading	bank	attitude	**Down**	heading	bank	Attitude
Min	-79.036	-89.992	-26.871	Min	-79.473	-89.966	-26.921
Max	-67.965	-70.427	-19.124	Max	-68.171	-69.869	-19.228
Mean	-78.270	-88.068	-26.375	Mean	-78.246	-87.808	-26.283
Std Dev	0.561	1.302	0.386	Std Dev	0.589	1.418	0.383

Table 2 shows the minimum, maximum, mean and standard deviation calculated over the 500 iterations for each of the four lighting conditions. The minimum and maximum values were calculated by comparing the heading, bank and attitude values separately.

---

[1] Euler angles were calculated using formulae described by Martin Baker in http://www.euclideanspace.com/maths/geometry/rotations/conversions/matrixToEuler/index.htm

They therefore represent the range of values that each of the Euler angles took under each of the lighting conditions.

Before analysis was performed on the data shown in Table 2, outliers were removed. Six outliers were removed from data produced in the lighting situation where all lights were on, and where only the outside lights were on. 12 outliers were removed from the inside lighting tests, and 18 were removed from the down lights test. These outliers occurred only in the calculation of the bank, irrespective of the lighting condition being used. By comparing the mean values for each of the lighting conditions, we can see that the largest fluctuation can be found in the mean bank value 0.081 radians (4.64 degrees) compared to a fluctuation of 0.002 radians (0.11 degrees) in heading and attitude.

4.3.   Analysis

When considering the accuracy of the position of the cameras, we noticed that the x and y values are always more accurate than the z value in all lighting conditions. When the lighting conditions become uneven (in the cases where only the inside fluorescent lights or the down lights are used), the range that the x, y, and z values take becomes large. As an example, consider the range of values z takes in the case where all lights are used (a range of 119 mm), compared with the lighting condition where only the down lights are used (a range of 322 mm). Not surprisingly, the results we obtained when consistent lighting was used are comparable to those obtained in a study under similar conditions by Malbezin, Piekarski and Thomas [16].

For each of the lighting conditions, we discovered a number of outliers in the bank angle. Surprisingly there are no outliers for the heading or the attitude. The outliers found were all approximately 180 degrees away from the mean value. When the lighting conditions become more uneven, we found that the number of outliers increases. When only down lights were used, the number of outliers was triple those found in conditions of even lighting (all lights on, outside fluorescent lights on). We believe that poor lighting causes false detections, resulting in the outliers.

We also believe that part of the jitter in positional values can be attributed to the jitter in orientation. Because of the lever arm affect, a jitter of 1 degree at a distance of 1.645m will result in a movement of 28 mm.

5.   Conclusions and Future Work

In this paper we have described tools that can be used to help rapidly configure a workspace to allow passive detection of marked objects. Fiducial markers are attached to objects such as laptops, furniture, or any other object to be tracked and their physical world pose can be calculated in real time. The application described in this paper, CalibrateCE, has become an integral part of the Passive Detection Framework as it allows users to quickly and efficiently recalibrate some of the features of the environment after the workspace has been reconfigured.

An experiment to determine the accuracy of CalibrateCE was also presented in this paper. We have shown that the accuracy of the calibration is not dependent on the lighting condition under which the calibration takes place. This is due primarily to the number of iterations undertaken in the calibration process, and the ability for the accurate results to cancel out any outliers.

The rapid deployment of the collaborative ubiquitous computing environment described in this paper may be achieved through the utilization of mobile computing and specialized equipment. The node and combiner computers are replaced by notebook computers. The firewire cameras are no longer placed on the ceiling of the room, but on extendible aluminum tripods. The placement of cameras via the tripods is determined for the best coverage of the tracking region. The firewire hubs and cables are very portable. All these components would easily fit into a padded suitcase. We have not built this portable system, but there are no technology challenges to the construction of such a system.

6. References

1. Weiser, M., *The computer for the 21st century*. Scientific American, 1991. **265**(3): p. 66-75.
2. Slay, H., R. Vernik, and B. Thomas. *Using ARToolkit for Passive Tracking and Presentation in Ubiquitous Workspaces*. in *Second International IEEE ARToolkit Workshop*. 2003. Waseda University, Japan.
3. Slay, H. and B. Thomas. *An Interaction Model for Universal Interaction and Control in Multi Display Environments*. in *International Symposium on Information and Communication Technologies*. 2003. Trinity College Dublin, Ireland.
4. Slay, H., et al. *Interaction Modes for Augmented Reality Visualisation*. in *Australian Symposium on Information Visualisation*. 2001. Sydney, Australia.
5. Kato, H. and M. Billinghurst. *Marker Tracking and HMD Calibration for a Video-based Augmented Reality Conferencing System*. in *2nd IEEE and ACM International Workshop on Augmented Reality*. 1999. San Francisco USA.
6. Streitz, N.A., J. Geißler, and T. Holmer. *Roomware for Cooperative Buildings: Integrated Design of Architectural Spaces and Information Spaces*. in *Cooperative Buildings – Integrating Information, Organization and Architecture. Proceedings of the First International Workshop on Cooperative Buildings (CoBuild'98),*. 1998. Darmstadt, Germany.
7. Grønbæk, K., P.G. Krogh, and M. Kyng. *Intelligent Buildings and pervasive computing - research perspectives and discussions*. in *Proc. of Conference on Architectural Research and Information Technology*. 2001. Arhus.
8. Brooks, R.A., et al. *The Intelligent Room Project*. in *Second International Conference on Cognitive Technology Humanizing the Information Age*. 1997. Los Alamitos, CA, USA.: IEEE Computing Society.
9. Johanson, B., A. Fox, and T. Winograd, *The Interactive Workspaces Project: Experiences with Ubiquitous Computing Rooms*. IEEE Pervasive Computing, 2002. **1**(2): p. 67-74.
10. Morency, L.-P., et al. *Fast stereo-based head tracking for interactive environments*. in *Proceedings Fifth IEEE International Conference on Automatic Face Gesture Recognition, 20-21 May 2002*. 2002. Washington, DC, USA: IEEE.
11. Pentland, A., *Looking at people: sensing for ubiquitous and wearable computing*. IEEE Transactions on Pattern Analysis and Machine Intelligence, 2000. **22**(1): p. 107-19.
12. Vernik, R., T. Blackburn, and D. Bright. *Extending Interactive Intelligent Workspace Architectures with Enterprise Services*. in *Evolve: Enterprise Information Integration*. 2003. Sydney, Australia.

13. Newman, J., D. Ingram, and A. Hopper. *Augmented Reality in a Wide Area Sentient Environment.* in *International Symposium on Augmented Reality.* 2001. New York, USA.
14. Piekarski, W., et al. *Hybrid Indoor and Outdoor Tracking for Mobile 3D Mixed Reality.* in *The Second IEEE and ACM International Symposium on Mixed and Augmented Reality.* 2003. Tokyo, Japan.
15. Foxlin, E. and N. Leonid. *VIS-Tracker: A Wearable Vision-Inertial Self-Tracker.* in *IEEE Virtual Reality.* 2003. Los Angeles, USA.
16. Malbezin, P., W. Piekarski, and B. Thomas. *Measuring ARTootKit accuracy in long distance tracking experiments.* in *Augmented Reality Toolkit, The First IEEE International Workshop.* 2002.

The Misrepresentation of Use in Technology Demonstrations

Wally Smith

Department of Information Systems, The University of Melbourne,
VIC 3010, Australia

Abstract. Demonstrations are ubiquitous in the world of information systems development, but it is not clear what role they play. It is contended that demonstrations are an informal attempt to examine issues of usefulness and usability, insofar as they bring together the technology, the user, genuine tasks and the organizational context. This raises the question, How well are new technologies and their use represented in demonstrations? An interview study with experienced demonstrators and audiences is reported and investigated in terms of Goffman's frame analysis. Demonstrations are interpreted as a kind of theatrical performance in which the situation of use is acted out. Various types of potential misrepresentation are identified in the study, including simulated and exaggerated functionality, serendipitous interaction paths and the manipulation of demonstrator credibility. It is argued that these distortions may mask the importance of human-computer interaction.

1 Introduction

A fundamental way of learning about new technology is for one person or group to see it demonstrated by another. Demonstrations are universal in the world of information systems, but surprisingly they receive scant if any attention in standard accounts of systems analysis and design, such as [4], [14]. A demonstration is defined here as an occasion when one party shows another party a piece of information technology in action as evidence to support claims about it. It might be a developer showing application components to colleagues, a team presenting new versions to their managers, or a company presenting its product to a potential customer. The questions raised here are: What is actually represented in a demonstration? How is it represented? and, What is the scope for misrepresentation? The focus of the investigation is on commercial systems development.

Demonstrations in a commercial context, it is contended, are moments when developers and user organizations attempt to communicate about the broad issues of usefulness and usability; these being central concerns of HCI research that are often neglected in other phases of development. The basis of this assertion is that demonstrations attempt, successfully or otherwise, to examine the interaction between elements: a piece of technology, a user, a task and aspects of organizational context. In this way, they contrast with the abstraction of much development effort, and may be regarded as a latent concession to the importance of context and realness raised by

M. Masoodian et al. (Eds.): APCHI 2004, LNCS 3101, pp. 431-440, 2004.

approaches to HCI, such as technomethodology [5]. As will be seen, however, the demonstration as a full 'dress rehearsal' can be misleading and may paper over the cracks of systems that have shortcomings. They may serve to mask issues of usefulness and usability and consequently to downplay the significance of HCI.

A secondary point of interest, is that HCI researchers themselves make great use of demonstrations for presenting innovative development and associated theories. In an analysis of the Digitial Libraries Initiative in the United States, Gross [9] makes the point that some innovative technologies exist only in demonstration form. Although the study here concerns commercial systems, it might also be the starting point for questions about what is actually communicated through research-based demonstrations.

To investigate the questions posed here, an interview study is reported here of experienced demonstrators and audiences. The interpretation takes a social perspective using Goffman's frame analysis, which concerns how people construct nested levels of understanding about what is 'really going on' in a situation. From this, demonstrations are interpreted as a kind of theatre in which a use scenario is acted out. The following sections explore the basis of demonstrations further and explain Goffman's frame analysis. After this, the study is reported with most space given to describing the types of misrepresentation that can occur.

1.1   What Are Demonstrations for?

A simple view of demonstrations is that they merely show functions of a new technology to customers, users, managers or colleagues. This view overlooks three important aspects.

First, and most central to this paper, demonstrations are social interactions in which one party attempts to *persuade* another party of the efficacy of their technology. The demonstrator must bring the critical element of persuasiveness where it is lacking in the technology itself (see [6]). As with social impression management [11], it is likely that the subtleties of demonstrating play a significant role in the way the technology is perceived. Is it possible that the techniques of presenting the 'self' in a positive light [7], transfer to the presentation of the machine? By using an analogy with theatre, the account here is inspired partly by Brenda Laurel's expression of design: 'In an important sense, a piece of software is a collaborative exercise of the imagination of the creators of a program and people who use it.' [10] (p9.) An effective demonstrator is charged with continuing this collaboration into the eleventh hour when the software is before the user. They must bridge the gap between technology and the social context of its use; a familiar goal to the HCI practitioner, e.g. [1]. As will be explored in this paper, the closing of the social-technical gap may be illusory and may not outlive the demonstration. In a similar way, Brown and Duguid describe how a technology can develop problems when the 'invisible hands' of support are removed [2].

Second, heightening the relevance of the social aspect, much of what is communicated in a demonstration is highly implicit. Although it provides a real instance of an interaction between user and machine, it often leaves open for interpretation precisely what aspects of use are being exemplified.

Third, demonstrations require an extreme form of inductive reasoning. What is witnessed is a very limited and carefully selected history of events concerning one particular interaction sequence. From this, more general conclusions about functionality and use are invited. But what validity do they have? Certainly, explicit claims are made and implications readily drawn, but the boundary conditions of the claimed functionality are likely to be very fuzzy.

1.2   Concepts of Frame Analysis

Goffman's frame analysis offers a way to understand social interactions in which shared make-believe or deceit may occur [8]. A frame defines the rules and expectations imposed on a situation that guide the actions and expectations of participants. Goffman provided a detailed theoretical framework of how situations are transformed when they are framed and re-framed as participants' beliefs change in response to the hypothetical question of 'What is it that's going on here?' Taking a relevant example (from [8] p.159), a door-to-door salesperson transforms a basic behaviour of vacuum-cleaning by performing a sales demonstration. The type of transformation in this case is called *keying*; meaning both parties are aware of the frame and know that the salesperson is not 'really' vacuum-cleaning. Suppose further, that the salesperson is not genuine and is actually gaining access to the watcher's house to steal. Or suppose instead, that the host has no intention of purchasing the vacuum-cleaner but allows the demonstration to proceed for some free cleaning. In either case, the situation has been transformed again. But now the transformations are instances of *fabrication*; meaning that one party is not aware that a new frame has been imposed on the situation. The tricked party is said to be *contained* in the frame and unable to see its edge. Fabrications are not always *exploitative*, as in these cases of illicit access and free-cleaning. Some can be *benign*, such as if the customer let the demonstration proceed only because refusal seemed offensive. These scenarios illustrate how parties can independently and jointly create complex structures of nested frames of collusion and deception.

2   The Study of Demonstrations

There are clearly many different types of demonstration, depending on when they are carried out in the development process and what other stages are used such as Requests For Proposals and requirements checklists. Space precludes a full account of this aspect, and for simplicity demonstrations are treated as homogenous events. The emphasis was placed on large demonstrations which feed directly into decisions about whether to adopt a new technology or not.

This paper reports the preliminary analysis of 8 structured interviews with experienced IT practitioners (see Table 1). Stringent criteria were applied in the selection of interviewees. They had 10 or more years of experience in IT and related industries;

Table 1. Demonstration cases examined in the study

case 1 Demonstrator, MD ERP RESELLER
Managing Director of medium-size ERP software reseller with customization. Example: showing how an invoice can be prepared to a required accounting standard, from data in an existing state.
case 2 Demonstrator, CEO START-UP
CEO of a small start-up company showing an innovative internet product. Example: showing how users can browse and access websites.
case 3 Demonstrator, SOFTWARE MANAGER
Software Manager (for user interface functions) in large software house. Example: showing how a user can configure the information displayed about a manufacturing process to suit task needs.
case 4 Demonstrator, DIRECTOR OF PRESALES
Director of Presales Support for a large multinational software vendor. Example: showing how users can process a batch of data about telephone calls to produce invoices; showing how payment plans can be configured.
case 5 - Audience, REGIONAL IT MANAGER
Regional IT Manager of a large transport company evaluating technology for a call centre, including various IT components. Example: showing how different technologies can work together; showing how a call is logged.
case 6 - Audience, SENIOR TECHNICAL SUPPORT
Senior Technical support in a utilities company evaluating executive information system software. Example: showing how a user can plot data in a way suitable for senior managers.
case 7 - Audience, USABILITY CONSULTANT
Consultant on usability project to evaluate software for a bank. Example: showing how user enters data and receives output for a counter transaction.
case 8 - Audience, IT STRATEGY CONSULTANT
Consultant on technology strategy to government department. Example: showing how a user can compare prices from different suppliers and make a purchase.

many had 20 or more years. They had experience as both demonstrators and audiences in various situations. To facilitate a candid account, all were no longer working in the position that was the focus of the interview.

The interviews followed a structured process in which each interviewee was invited to think of a familiar scenario that involved demonstration. They gave a general description of the situation and were asked probing questions about: the process that was followed, the design of demonstrations, the skill of the demonstrator, the level of understanding achieved, and the faithfulness of the way technology and its use was represented. Interviewees were encouraged to link their observations to other scenarios where appropriate. The cases investigated covered demonstrations held in Australia, Germany, UK and Israel.

Interviews were recorded and transcribed and subjected to a microanalysis of content following Strauss and Corbin, [13]. The analysis did not strictly adhere to grounded theory approach, because Goffman's frame analysis was used as an organizing framework. However, the interview texts were analysed by open-coding and organized into categories. The chief observations that emerged from these categories are now reported in the following sections.

3 Demonstrations as Theatre

The main contention of this paper is that technology demonstrations are structurally analogous to theatre (e.g., [3]) and that it is useful to view them as such. In each demonstration a story of a user interacting with to-be implemented system is acted out by the demonstrator team usually with a narrative commentary. In frame analysis, this *use scenario* becomes the first frame - the primary or original behaviour which, during the demonstration, is transformed and re-transformed. The theatrical representation of the use scenario occurs as a keying transformation into a *technical frame,* meaning all parties know that the illustrated behaviour (for example, preparing an invoice) is not being done for real, but rather is simulated for the purpose of evaluation. In the *social frame*, a further transformation of the situation occurs in which the real aim of the event is a not technical display, but rather to develop confidence in the relationship between parties. What is at stake here is the credibility of the demonstrator as really believing in their solution and in being able to deliver it. Finally, the situation may be transformed again into a *misrepresentation frame* if the technology is either misrepresented by the demonstrator or thought to be misrepresented by the demonstratee. The focus of this paper is on the fourth frame of misrepresentation, with the other frames providing a necessary context. Justification of the full frame analysis will be reported elsewhere.

Views expressed on the importance of demonstrations further reflect a theatrical form. All interviewees regarded demonstrations as universal and important; and for some, of utmost importance. But this was punctured by severe qualifications. Demonstrations were described as 'just a show', 'a comforter', 'just to reassure', 'over-rated' by the customer, 'fairly glossy and just showing the best points'. Some were regarded as just 'going through the process' while others were given with the mundane purpose of simply showing that system exists.

Demonstrations adopt a theatrical form because the circumstances of presentation are necessarily artificial relative the use scenario being represented. There are two basic sources of artificiality. The first is that the reconstruction of organizational and task context is limited. Demonstrators strive for realism, usually having carried out an analysis of the organization's tasks and collected real data for display. However, the analysis and data can seldom be fully representative of the true work situation including such things as process exceptions, idiosyncratic understandings of process, and data anomalies. The second source of artificiality is that the demonstration platform is usually very different from the to-be-implemented system. A portable platform is normally used, with performance consequences. The software is very often a different version from the one the customer will use; possibly a current version, a pre-release or special demonstrator version. Both pre-release and demonstrations versions are highly vulnerable to bugs and crashes.

The study probed the degree of scripting used. All interviewees reported that successful demonstrations were very carefully prepared and that the performance of the demonstrator was critical for success. Reports on the degree of scripting varied, with most describing highly scripted and choreographed segments but with the freedom to move between segments as determined by the audience interest. Where the technology was unstable or the demonstrator less familiar, greater scripting was needed. The implication of these observations is that demonstrators tried to meet the contradictory aims of providing a carefully crafted demonstration while appearing as though their behaviour was merely a natural interaction sequence, always open to audience direction. Attempts to force a structure against audience wishes would be seen as evasive. Just as in drama, the effective demonstrator must aim for the audience to 'suspend disbelief' in the artificiality of presentation, so that the story of use can be consumed.

4   Types of Potential Misrepresentation

Different responses were received to the direct question: Does the demonstrator present a fair view of the system including both positive and negative aspects? In one view this question was ridiculed:
   'No, of course not ... don't be silly, I'd never sell it ... We would highlight efficiencies, and underplay its deficiencies' CEO START-UP
   'you wouldn't highlight the negative aspects' MD ERP RE-SELLER
   In another view, an important qualification was expressed that demonstrators may exaggerate and omit reference to problems, but typically they do not present untruths which would damage the relationship:
   'where they're bigger and where failure for them would be as much as a problem for them as it is for the customer, they don't want the demo to be misrepresenting anything ... they want it to be a clear honest representation' REGIONAL IT MANAGER.
   However, it was acknowledged by all interviewees that optimism, exaggeration and omission could create a significantly distorted understanding, whether intentional or not. In the following sub-sections, different types of misrepresentation are identified and illustrated.

4.1   Simulating Functionality

The interviews contained a few reports of functionality being simulated by presenting prepared screenshots as if they were generated live during the demonstration. Sometimes this was declared to the audience but sometimes it was not. When is it was not declared, it was described as benign fabrication if it was 'only showing what the real system would do', or that it was only used because the system couldn't be ready in time for the demonstration. In other cases it was reported as exploitative fabrication:
   '... and a lot of people out there will often pretend they've got software they haven't got ... they'll put data in .. and say this has computed this here ... when in fact it has-

n't they've just typed it in , knocked up a screen with data in ... they pretend they've got functionality and it doesn't exist' MD ERP RE-SELLER

4.2   Blurring the Boundary of Current Functionality

The most frequently described potential for misrepresentation was simply exaggerating the scope of currently implemented functionality, and its application to the situation of use. Blurring occurs between what is currently implemented, what modifications are needed to meet a particular need, and the practicality of making those modifications. This is illustrated by the description of a gifted colleague:

'... he almost made people believe that the stuff was in the software that he was showing them ... people would match what he was doing with what was in the software ... he would say things like 'and at this point XYZ , it's not there now' and he was so convincing that people would believe him' SOFTWARE MANAGER

A similar blurring was also described for systems sold as packages of modules. Here, confusion was sometimes exploited over whether particular tasks could be carried out with particular modules, or whether in fact further modules were needed.

4.3   Disguising Undesirable Events

Frequent references were made to disguising unfavourable events. A general principle was that difficult interaction sequences were highly practiced by the demonstrator so that their difficulty or awkwardness for typical users was disguised:

... if the product is actually very difficult to use, they will have memorised how to use it and be very quick with the mouse or the keyboard, and also talk in a very reassuring ... way while they're doing it ... USABILITY CONSULTANT

A second technique was talking fluidly to cover long pauses in the computer's response. A third example was a case of having multiple versions of the software running simultaneously so that a crash in one could be concealed by continuing the demonstrations seamlessly with another.

4.4   Serendipitous Interaction Paths

One way in which a technology is sometimes subtley misrepresented is through the phenomenon described here as the serendipitous interaction path. This is where the demonstrator navigates within a software environment taking a carefully planned route through areas that are more favourable to present. Favourable areas are those that work effectively or show data that is appealing in format or content. Unfavourable areas include, functions that are not yet working, or where the data is confusing or conflicting with organizational outlook. The deception is for the demonstrator to navigate through favourable areas under a carefully choreographed interactive sequence presented *as if* it is an impromptu interaction path. The unstated implication is that unvisited areas of the system, are as impressive as the visited ones.

One reported example concerned an internet interface in which the user selects an item in one menu (choosing between Life Style, Finance, Banking, Television & Sport), and then a further item in a sub-menu where, in the case of Banking for example, the user selects a link to a particular Bank. However, in this situation only some of the links would work, while others were known to crash. This could be tacitly misrepresented through a serendipitous path:

'that was the trick with the XXX ... was because you had a certain number of links on the front page, you demonstrate those links, you'd gloss over the fact that you didn't go to any other site ... or if you did, say to them 'anyone want to go to a site, give me a sector' ... and if they said banking, you'd fire up Bank X, you wouldn't fire up Bank Y which went crmmmph! every time you did it ... we wouldn't necessarily tell that not all banks would open and if they did <ask>, we had an answer for that : that 'we would work with the bank to change their site ' CEO START-UP

Another example illustrates how precise a serendipitous path can be:

'... I'm talking about major things that actually every time you clicked on a screen, the system crashes ... and you'd have to re-boot it all from scratch ... so you were absolutely walking on egg shells ... in fact in the end we'd have specific people who could demonstrate that ... and I would say to them 'look you have to do it because ... you know it so well' DIRECTOR OF PRESALES

As with other types of misrepresentation, the serendipitous path is regarded as benign fabrication in certain situations:

' but you don't tell them that this is the only way ... you don't tell them, you don't need to ... in that context ... you've told them its under development' SOFTWARE MANAGER

4.5   Manipulating Demonstrator Credibility

Audiences typically expect to be persuaded and do not want a purely technical exhibition. However, a reverse of this situation can arise where the audience is potentially suspicious that a sales pitch does not reflect technological reality. Here a manipulation may occur of the apparent perspective of the demonstrator away from sales towards a technical stance which may be taken to be more authentic:

'... there were a couple of sales people present and a technical presales guy ... the marketing people wear the crisp suits and good hair cuts ... and the presales guy is scruffy, and gets up there and talks quickly and ums and ahs, but in doing that he's actually just as smooth as the sales guy' SOFTWARE MANAGER

In one report a demonstrator resorted to a small deception of the audience to preserve a correct view of their credibility:

'I used to work with a salesman who I thought was tremendous, and he would always say 'No' to one question - and I'd say to him afterwards, 'We could do that' - and he said 'We've been saying 'yes' for the last two hours, if you don't say No they won't believe the Yes's' MD ERP RE-SELLER

4.6   Audience Disingenuousness

The last phenomenon of misrepresentation reported here is perpetrated by the audience. If unimpressed by the demonstration the audience may indicate so directly through their comments and questions. However, it was also reported that they might instead resort to a fabrication themselves, by not indicating their negative appraisal and thereby containing the demonstrator in a false frame of success:

   'you can honestly walk out the room thinking that was just the best demo - and in fact they said ... it wasn't what we're looking for at all - and you're thinking its absolutely what you're looking for - they don't flag it up to you at all' ERP RE-SELLER

5   Summary and Conclusions

An interview study with experienced demonstrators and audiences has been reported and six basic types of potential misrepresentation have been identified. In some situations, these misrepresentations may be unethical and may constitute exploitative fabrication in the terms of Goffman's frame analysis [8]. However, the interview study suggests that misrepresentation may also occur as benign fabrication, meaning it is done in secret but for the audience's benefit. Or it may be part of a keyed frame, meaning all parties know of the make-believe. The occurrence of misrepresentation, exploitative or benign, is linked to the theatrical form taken by demonstrations. Demonstrations, it has been argued, are necessarily theatrical because they attempt, in principle, to show a future implementation of a technology with a user performing realistic tasks within an organizational context. As Goffman argued, a situation once transformed by a particular frame is vulnerable to further re-framing. In the case of demonstrations, the theatrical frame of a make-believe scenario of use, leaves the situation vulnerable to further reframing, including an evaluation of the credibility of presenters, and the potential misrepresentation of the total system.

The types of misrepresentation described here become important for HCI when we consider what it is that is being misrepresented. At one level, most of the phenomena reported can be seen as simply technical: misrepresenting what functionality is present and what is not. However, this level of misrepresentation *in itself* is possibly of least significance, because purely technical shortcoming are typically later corrected using functionality checklists and more rigorous testing, or are quickly learned in communities of customers and users. What is more significant is that the technical level of misrepresentation allows for a more subtle manipulation of the understanding of usability and usefulness. That is, the audience members of a well crafted demonstration apparently witness a story of a user in their own organization performing significant tasks effectively with ease, and without conflict with existing processes and modes of working. The veridicality of this story may rest on lower level technical illusions, however slight, brought about by *simulating functionality*, *blurring the boundary of current functionality*, *disguising undesirable events* and using *serendipitous interaction paths*. While these techniques might often be benign and regarded as exercising a reasonable dramatic licence, they may underpin a deceptive drama of a real use situation. Similarly, by *manipulating demonstrator credibility*, an audience's capacity to judge the significance of the story presented for usability and usefulness may be undermined. On the other side, *audience disingenuousness* may prevent an open expression of problems with the perceived level of usability and usefulness. Whether or not the demonstrators or audience are aware of these misrepresentations, or whether or not they constitute benign or exploitative fabrication, they are likely to mask the importance of HCI issues, and potentially mislead efforts to understand whether new technologies can support and enrich organizational activity.

References

1. Ackerman, M.S. The intellectual challenge of CSCW: the gap between social requirements and technical feasibility. Human-Computer Interaction, 15. (2000)
2. Brown, J. S. and P. Duguid The Social Life of Information. Boston Mass., Harvard Business School Press. (2000).
3. Chatman, S. Story and Discourse: Narrative structure in fiction and film. New York, Cornell University Press. (1978).
4. Dennis, A. and Wixon, B. Systems Analysis & Design. Wiley. (2000).
5. Dourish, P. Where the Action Is: the foundations of embodied interaction. Cambridge, Mass., MIT Press. (2001).
6. Fogg, B.J. Persuasive Technology: using computers to change what we think and do. San Francisco, Morgan-Kaufmann. (2003).
7. Goffman, E. The Presentation of Self in Everyday Life. New York, Doubleday. (1959).
8. Goffman, E. Frame Analysis: An essay on the organization of experience. New York, Harper & Row. (1974).
9. Gross, B.M. Demonstrations of Information Systems Research. (Unpublished research paper, University of Illinois, Urbana-Champaign.)
10. Laurel, B. Computers As Theatre. Reading, Mass., Addison-Wesley. (1991).
11. Leary, M. R. Self-Presentation: impression management and interpersonal behaviour. Boulder, Colorado, Westview Press. (1996).
12. Norman, D. The Psychology of Everyday Things. New York: Basic Books. (1988)
13. Strauss, A. & Corbin, J. Basics of Qualitative Research: Techniques and Procedures for Devel oping Grounded Theory. (Second Ed). Thousand Oaks, Calif.: Sage. (1998)
14. Whitten, J. Bentley, L. & Dittman, K. Systems Analysis & Design Methods. McGraw-Hill. (2001).

An Implementation for Capturing Clickable Moving Objects

Toshiharu Sugawara[1], Satoshi Kurihara[2], Shigemi Aoyagi[1],
Koji Sato[3], and Toshihiro Takada[1]

[1] NTT Communication Science Laboratories,
2-4 Hikaridai, Seika-cho, Soraku-gun, Kyoto 619-0237 Japan
{sugawara,aoyagi,takada}@entia.org
[2] NTT Network Innovation Laboratories,
3-9-11 Midori-cho, Musashino, Tokyo 180-8585 Japan
kurihara@entia.org
[3] NTT Cyberspace Laboratories,
1-1 Hikari-no-oka, Yokosuka, Kanagawa 239-0847 Japan
koji@entia.org

Abstract. This paper discusses a method for identifying clickable objects/regions in still and moving images when they are being captured. A number of methods and languages have recently been proposed for adding point-and-click interactivity to objects in moving pictures as well as still images. When these pictures are displayed in Internet environments or broadcast on digital TV channels, users can follow links specified by URLs (e.g., for buying items online or getting detailed information about a particular item) by clicking on these objects. However, it is not easy to specify clickable areas of objects in a video because their position is liable to change from one frame to the next. To cope with this problem, our method allows content creators to capture moving (and still) images with information related to objects that appear in these images including the coordinates of the clickable areas of these objects in the captured images. This is achieved by capturing the images at various infrared wavelengths simultaneously. This is also applicable to multi-target motion capture.

1 Introduction

Still images are often embedded in web pages published on the World Wide Web (WWW). These images are sometimes made wholly or partly interactive (clickable) so that users are redirected to related information according to predetermined URLs when they click on the active regions of these images. Similar interactive facilities have also been developed for moving images delivered via digital TV broadcasts or across the Internet, whereby users can click on specific regions or specific objects in the moving images to display information related to the clicked object (normally specified by a URL) or to generate some kind of event (e.g., launching a certain computer program), such as ATVEF [2], Cnew [9], SMIL [8] and MPEG-7 [6].

For both types of image (still and moving), the active regions with which hyperlinks are associated are defined as virtual regions within the digital pictures (such as in picture

M. Masoodian et al. (Eds.): APCHI 2004, LNCS 3101, pp. 441–450, 2004.
© Springer-Verlag Berlin Heidelberg 2004

coordinates) rather than by recognizing the actual objects in the images. Since it is the objects themselves that convey meaning, rather than their pictorial representations[4], it is better to have some way of establishing links directly from the real-world objects to their related information when capturing still or moving images.

Additionally it is not easy to specify the regions of objects in an image. Objects in an image cannot accurately be recognized by computer, so instead a human has to identify the objects in the image, specify the regions they occupy, and associate each of these regions with links such as URLs. However the objects may move around in the frames of moving pictures.

In this paper, we propose a method whereby, when capturing objects with a digital (video) camera, the regions in which the objects to be made clickable appear are also stored along with collateral information related to the objects such as link destination URLs and the time/locations at which the images were produced. These object regions and collateral information are acquired simultaneously with the original image. Then when the images are displayed (in a web browser for example), the displaying system can also obtain information such as the areas of the clickable objects and their link destination URLs. Studies aimed at implementing similar capabilities include augmented reality (AR) [3], where digital data such as text and images is overlaid on the real world (e.g., [7]). In AR, a computer is used to superimpose information and virtual object representations on the user's view of the real world in order to provide annotations or for entertainment. This is normally achieved by placing identification tags or devices at locations where annotations are required, and then working out where to display the annotations based on knowledge about the IDs and positions of these tags or devices.

On the other hand, the technique proposed in this paper aims to produce images in which the used tags or devices of this sort are invisible or too small to see. We also focus on identifying regions within a captured movie rather than specific locations in space. Of course, it would be perfectly feasible to use this technique to embed annotations into the generated video and collateral information, but we will not deal with such applications in this paper. Instead, we will concentrate on producing of video content that appears to be free of artificial tags and the like while extracting the regions of objects to be made clickable. This requirement is important to create natural TV programs such as drama. In this way we aim to allow point-and-click interactivity to be added to video content.

2   Capturing and Clicking on Real Objects

2.1   Problems to Be Addressed

Some of the authors of this paper have proposed the concept (and the system) Cmew (Continuous media with the Web) as a means of allowing links to originate from video images (which were always "leaves" of URL link graphs) [9]. In Cmew, link information is embedded in the private2 packet region of the MPEG system stream and delivered simultaneously with the images, thereby allowing links to be inherited from one

---

[4] There are some exceptions, such as photographs. An old family snapshot, for example, can be regarded as an object in its own right.

frame of a moving image to another. It also allows this link information to be shared within specific groups and communities by using proxy or annotation servers in which link data is dynamically embedded into the video streams [4].

However, it is not easy to create video images of this sort, (not just in Cmew but in general) because the objects associated with these links are liable to occupy different positions at different times, so the regions have to be specified in each frame manually. In Cmew, for example, it is tried to tackle this problem by incorporating a simple image recognition algorithm to track the movement of objects in subsequent frames once their clickable regions have been specified in one frame. However, current image recognition techniques are either too ineffective to track objects with sufficient accuracy, or take a very long time to perform recognition with high precision. Automatic object tracking is therefore avoided in schemes such as VHM [5], where the clickable regions are instead specified manually at key frames in the video and approximated by linear interpolation in the intervening frames. However, this approach requires a great deal of careful editing by humans because objects do not always move linearly.

2.2   Capturing Real-World Objects and Clicking on Objects in Images

The motive of this research is to lighten this workload by automatically finding the clickable regions in an image at the time of capture, instead of specifying them afterward with an authoring tool. Furthermore - if possible and where necessary - we aim to acquire the URLs associated with these regions in a similar manner. This sort of model is also useful for still images. In the conventional workflow, the region of an object in a video sequence is defined by reading the video into a PC, specifying the region with special editor software (sometimes involving guesswork), and then producing a so-called image map in which the link destination URL is defined. On the other hand, in the workflow of our proposed scheme an image map can be created at the time the image is captured without having to worry about changes in camera angle or object size.

We think that the regions of clickable objects in video images are only specified by coordinates for part of the video data, and thus constitute little more than abstractions (or representations) of objects (or entities) in the real world. In this study, we work from the viewpoint that the URLs to be associated with these clickable regions connect to information related to the actual read-world objects depicted in the video. For the first approach from this viewpoint, we want to generate clickable images by just taking pictures/videos of real-world objects.

Our proposed method for the capture, recording, conversion, and playback of video data is outlined below. When capturing a certain object, its position in the captured video (i.e., its rough outline coordinates) and its collateral information (whatever is necessary and available) are simultaneously extracted and stored. The video data and collateral information are then pre-converted into the required format. The protocols and specifications used for embedding this information into the video signal are beyond the scope of this paper, but an appropriate protocol specification, such as MEPG-7, SMIL, VHM, and Cmew, will be used depending on the applications.

When a video file is played back, the file containing related information (information file, hereafter) is read in simultaneously (if necessary) and this information is reflected in the behavior of the displaying system. For example, when a still image is pasted into a web page as an image map, or when a clickable moving image is played back, the information file transcoded into the formation of the appropriate protocol specification contains sets of coordinates specifying the clickable areas, and the destination URLs of each link. It is also possible for the collateral information to be varied with time and position during capture, so that the contents of the associated URL can ultimately be made to depend on the time at which the video was captured.

3   Proposal of a Specific Implementation Scheme

3.1   Using Wavelength Differences – The Basic Idea

This section describes a scheme for achieving our research goal. In this scheme, the clickable regions are specified by infrared light sources with specific wavelengths.

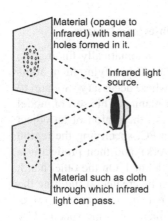

Fig. 1. Installation of light sources.

To specify the clickable regions, light sources that are small enough so as not to be noticeable in the captured images can be directly embedded in the objects. Alternatively, the light sources can be fitted behind a group of small holes (about 0.1 mm) formed in the object, or placed directly behind materials such as cloth that allow infrared light to pass through to some degree (Fig.1). A number of light sources are provided in each object so as to delineate the boundary of its region.

To extract the positions of these light sources, we used an image-capturing device consisting of an ordinary CCD camera with a number of additional infrared CCD cameras aligned to the same optical axis. In the following example, there were three additional cameras, making a total of 4 CCDs in the image-capturing device. The infrared cameras were fitted with infrared pass filters that only admitted light over a limited range of wavelengths.

The principle of this set-up is as follows. As Fig. 2 shows, the infrared pass filters fitted to the CCD cameras have a fairly wide pass band (in Fig. 2 about 30 nm either side of the central wavelength). On the other hand, the light sources are made so as to produce light over a smaller range of wavelengths. These were either lasers or LEDs/halogen bulbs covered with infrared narrow-bandpass filters. In Fig. 2, this pass band extends for 5-10 nm either side of the central wavelength. The characteristics of an actual filter used in our examples are shown in this figure. If the CCD filters have central wavelengths of 800, 850, and 900 nm, and the light sources have central wavelengths of 800, 825, 850, 875, and 900 nm, then it is possible to distinguish up to five objects. Each light source is visible to only one or two of the infrared CCDs. Any light sources that are visible to all three infrared CCDs can be assumed to be natural light and are excluded.

Once the points have been distinguished in this way, points of the same type are collected together and their outlines are determined. Each outline corresponds to the

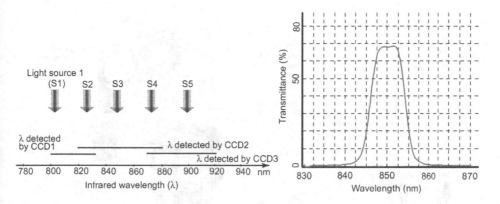

Fig. 2. Relationship between the light source wavelengths and the wavelengths detected by the CCDs.

clickable region of each object. Meanwhile, it is assumed that collateral information is separately extracted at the place of capture by an infrared communication link (e.g., at a wavelength of 940 nm that cannot be captured by the three CCDs) or by a wireless link such as Bluetooth (see the example of Section 3.5). In practice, the collateral information of the objects is read out by combining this information with the wavelength of the corresponding light source[5].

3.2 Components and Devices

(1) Light sources: For the infrared light sources, we made two types of miniature light source (Fig. 3). One consists of a high-luminance LED (approx. 15 mW) covered with a circular infrared narrow bandpass filter (approx. 1 mm thick), with the surrounding regions blacked out (with black paper). This device has a diameter of 6 mm and is about 5 mm thick. The other type was made by tapping a laser light source with several optical fibers (the output power of each fiber is class 1). When necessary, they are equipped with diffusers made of a material such as Teflon tape, thin cloth or paper to the output of the light sources. Although these diffusers are not nec-

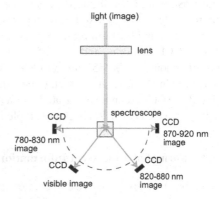

Fig. 4. Example of four-CCD cameras.

essary when the light sources are fitted behind materials such as cloth, when the light is emitted directly they are essential to ensure that it is visible from all viewing angles. (They can also help to disguise the light-source devices. Note that in Fig. 3 the wave-

---

[5] It is not always necessary to gain the information about the object at the time of capture. For example, when such information is provided at the link destination URL or when the video is subsequently placed in an online environment, this correspondence can also be made by using the time and location at which the object was captured to access an appropriate database. Other collateral information related to the objects can also be obtained later based on the wavelength

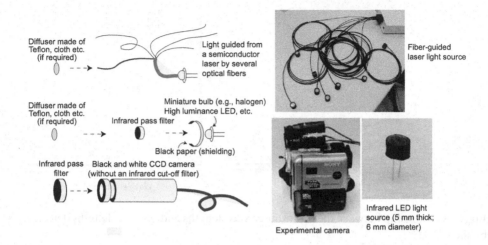

Fig. 3. Light sources and the image-capturing CCD camera.

lengths of light that pass the filter vary depending on the angles of incidence. So an LED that has a lens to narrow the angle of irradiation is more appropriate.

(2) Cameras and video acquisition devices: Our example image-capturing device acquires four video images - one visible image and three infrared images. The CCDs for the infrared video images are covered with filters that pass a slightly wider range of wavelengths than the light sources (Fig. 3). The infrared images are used to determine the positions of the light sources in each frame; with three infrared CCDs it should be possible to distinguish between points produced by five different light sources - the 800-, 850-, and 900-nm light sources whose central frequencies match those of the infrared CCD cameras, and the 825- and 875-nm light sources picked up by two CCDs simultaneously (800/850 nm and 850/900 nm respectively). The video outputs are all acquired in DV format. Note that the camera shown in Fig. 3 is experimental; we think that these CCDs can be integrated into a single piece of equipment like a normal camera with three CCDs for RGB. An example is shown in Fig. 4.

3.3 Format of Collateral Information

Because there are only five detectable infrared wavelengths, it is necessary to determine collateral information such as URLs in a position-dependent manner to some extent. For this purpose, when infrared communication is used for example, it is possible to exploit the directional nature of the infrared communication by placing the infrared transmitter close to the imaged object. So a communication link can be established whenever the camera is turned towards the object so that the collateral information can be received by the camera's infrared communication receiver while the images are being captured. With Bluetooth communication on the other hand, the communication link can be established when the camera is near the object.

At present, it is assumed that collateral information is sent in the form shown in Fig. 5. Figure 5 (a) corresponds to the case where all the necessary information is acquired in this environment (and stored in the information file), and Fig. 5 (b) corresponds to the case where only an ID is extracted from the wavelength of the infrared image and then URLs and programs are resolved by accessing a database (they are resolved, for example, when the video is viewed on a browser or when the video data is converted into a suitable format).

(a)
```
<object>
    <name>string</name>
    <url>url string</url>
    <lambda>wavelength</lambda>
    <time>date-time string</time>
    <location>location</location>
    <java>java script</java>
</object>
```

(b)
```
<object>
    <id>id</id>
    <lambda>wavelength</lambda>
    <time>date-time string</time>
    <name>string</name>
</object>
```

Fig. 5. Format of colateral information related to the captured objects. The bold items mean mandatory data while others are optional.

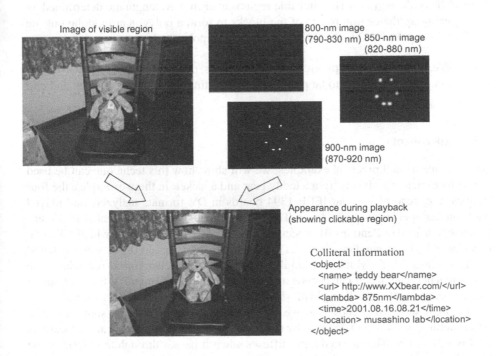

Fig. 6. Teddy bear example.

3.4   Extracting and Playing Back Clickable Regions

To extract the clickable regions from the infrared video image, the following algorithm is applied to each frame (720 x 480 pixels). Since our experimental camera uses four different CCDs, we first had to approximately determine the offsets of each video image and the common valid region (calibration).

(S1) (**Filtering**) Extract the bright points (brightness > B for a constant B > 0) from the three infrared pictures (black and white) and delete the rest.

(S2) (**Chunking**) In each wavelength region, extract the contiguous areas of bright pixels (this area is called a block hereafter). If any of the blocks found at each wavelength share any pixels with blocks found at the other two wavelengths, they are flagged for deletion in all three wavelengths.

(S3) (**Elimination of unnatural blocks**) If a block with no deletion flag is found to be especially non-circular, or if it covers an extremely small or large region, the block is flagged for deletion. If this flagged block shared any pixels with a block found at either of the other two wavelengths (not both, as it would already have been deleted), then the other block is also flagged for deletion.

(S4) (**Determination of wavelengths and center points**) The remaining circular blocks that have not been flagged for deletion are divided into wavelengths of 800, 825, 850, 875, and 900 nm according to the wavelengths at which they were imaged, and their central coordinates are determined.

(S5) (**Clickable regions**) The clickable regions at each wavelength are determined by joining up the central points of the blocks to form a polygon around the outside of these points. (This should result in a convex polygon.)

In practice, when using non-progressive video images, due to the characteristics of their signals, this processing has to be performed by splitting the images into even and odd lines.

3.5   Experiments

As experiments and practical examples, we will show how this technique can be used to produce clickable objects from a teddy bear and a jacket. In these examples, the four images were read in via four IEEE 1394 boards in DV format, analyzed, and played back on our special purpose player. These experiments were implemented in a computer with a 1 GHz Pentium III processor and 512 MB of memory in which XFree86 (version 3.3.6), Gnome (version 1.2.1) and libraw1394 (version 0.9.0) were installed on Vine Linux 2.1.5 (which is a family of RedHat Linux customized for a Japanese environment). The player can decode and display the image from a DV file at about 15 frames per second; with clickable playback, the speed was 14 frames per second.

Figure 6 shows the teddy bear we used for this experiment. Light sources with a wavelength of 875 nm and powered by two AA batteries were implanted at six locations in this stuffed toy. The infrared light diffuses when it passes through the fabric of the toy. These light sources could only be seen by the 850- and 900-nm CCD cameras. The clickable region extracted from the composite of these camera outputs is superimposed on the figure. The data received as collateral information is also shown in Fig. 6. This example assumed a case where this technique is used to market products depicted in a video so the clickable region's destination URL is the home page of the company manufacturing the toy. The originating source of collateral information could either be directly embedded in the stuffed toy (in which case the toy's collateral information does not change as the toy is moved), or installed in the vicinity of the toy (in which case the collateral information does change as it is moved).

In the jacket example (Fig. 7), 850 nm light sources were embedded at 12 locations in the front and back of the garment. These light sources were situated and wired up between the outer fabric and inner lining, and were powered by two 3 V lithium cells. For this example, we assumed that such a garment might be worn by an actor in a video production, allowing users to click on him when he appears in the video. Collateral information in this example should be acquired not in a location-dependent manner but in a scene-dependent manner.

Fig. 7. Jacket example.

4 Future Issues

In this paper, we discussed how image maps can be captured using infrared light. However, there are still a number of issues that need to be investigated. For example, the infrared light sources are susceptible to interference from sunlight (even light from a north-facing window can contain strong infrared components). When a view is wholly or partly illuminated by sunlight, it can become relatively difficult to detect the infrared light sources due to the effects of the camera's white balance. It is also harder to detect the light sources when there are incandescent light bulbs or reflections of these bulbs behind the infrared light sources. It is therefore important to take these constraints into consideration when installing the light sources.

Problems may also arise due to there being only five types of light source. At present, we are using a location- or scene-dependent method for the acquisition of collateral information (which is arguably adequate in its own right), but if the initial requirements are relaxed slightly, then a substantial increase can be achieved by combining this with other methods (See, e.g., reference [1]). It may also be a good idea to operate the infrared sources in the direction of the camera only when taking pictures.

The technology described in this paper can be used for various other applications besides those mentioned in the previous section. For example, it could be used to capture museums exhibits. When the captured video (picture) is subsequently played back (displayed), it could be used to obtain a description of the item via the Web. If light devices cannot be embedded or attached to objects (such as showpieces in museums), this system can recognize the regions by irradiate a number of lazer lights to their boundary and captureing the reflected lights. If real-time capturing and playback is possible, then it should even be possible to obtain a description of the article on the spot. It may also be possible to develop forms of entertainment based on this technology, such as adventure games that combine the real world with a virtual world where invisible objects can be used.

Current PCs are fast enough to implement our scheme as a realtime system. We are implementing the system that can take moving pictures with some clickable objects and deliver them via network.

Moreover, this technology may also be useful for motion capture although not directly related to making objects clickable; if light sources with characteristic wavelengths are attached to several people, it should be possible to track their individual movements simultaneously in a realtime manner. This would allow multi-target motion capture to be performed much more easily than with conventional approaches. Of course it is probably unnecessary to disguise the light sources for motion capture applications.

5   Conclusion

This paper proposed a model in which real objects are captured by a special digital (video) camera. This technique makes it possible to capture and record clickable regions of objects and other collateral information related to these objects such as link URLs and capture times simultaneously with the video footage of these objects. As a means of implementing this model, a method in which different wavelengths of infrared light are used to identify and track the clickable regions of objects was discussed. We described two experiments that show that this method accurately can generate clickable regions of objects. When video captured by this scheme is displayed in a browser or a player, the clickable regions, link destination URLs, and other related information can be obtained from information embedded in the video data.

References

1. Aoki, H. and Matsushita S. Balloon Tag: (In)visible Marker Which Tells Who's Who. *Proceedings of the 4th Int. Sym. on Wearable Computers (ISWC'00)*, pages 181 – 182, 2000.
2. ATVEF. http://www.atvef.com/, 1999.
3. Azuma, R. T. A Survey of Augmented Reality. *Presence: Teleoperators and Virtual Environments*, 6(4), pp. 355 - 385, 1997.
4. Hirotsu, T. *et al.* Cmew/U — a multimedia web annotation sharing system. *Proceedings of the IEEE Region 10 Conference (TENCON '99)*, pages 356-359, 1999.
5. Igarashi, S., Kushima, K. and Sakata, T. A multimedia database system VHM and its application. *Proceedings of 14th IFIP World Computer Congress*, 1996.
6. MPEG-7. http://www.mpeg-industry.com/ , 2002.
7. Rekimoto, J. and Ayatsuka, Y. Cybercode: Designing augmented reality environments with visual tags. *Proceedings of DARE2000*, 2000.
8. SMIL. http://www.w3.org/audiovideo/ , 2001.
9. Takada, T. et al.   Cmew: Integrating continuous media with the web. *Proceedings of the 3rd Annual Multimedia Technology and Applications Conference (MTAC '98)*, pages 136–140, 1998.

A Prototyping Framework
for Mobile Text Entry Research

Sanju Sunny, Yow Kin Choong

School of Computer Engineering,
Nanyang Technological University, Singapore 639798
{PA5758266, askcyow}@ntu.edu.sg

Abstract. The mobile phone has become the most widely used communication medium in the world, making our lives simpler by delivering services into our palms. Texting - using a mobile phone to send a text message - has become a form of mass communication. The effectiveness of many computing systems can be proven with objective tests and quantifiable results. Text entry methods on mobile phones however, interface directly and intimately with the end user. Developing a high-fidelity (typically, highly interactive) prototype for a new mobile text entry system is not an easy task. This paper describes the conceptualization, design and development of a prototyping framework for text entry research on mobile devices. The primary goal of the framework is to help text entry researchers produce high-fidelity working prototypes of their concept. It aims to ease development effort and maximize reusability of code.

1 Introduction

The effectiveness of many computing systems can be proven with objective tests and quantifiable results. Text entry methods however interface directly and intimately with the end user. Subjective satisfaction is also important because if users do not like the newer technologies of text entry, they are less likely to buy a phone, which offers that technology. Users like to stick with things that are more familiar to them, that are available on older phones and that they already know how to use. Introducing new methods of data entry often causes apprehension and mistrust before the users actually use the technology. An empirical evaluation with users is therefore, paramount to the viability of new methods of text data entry [1]. Designing new text entry methods for computing systems is a labor intensive process. It is also expensive, since a working prototype must be built, and then tested with real users [2].

1.1 Motivation

Developing a high-fidelity (typically, highly interactive) prototype for mobile applications is not an easy task. Often, the text entry researcher may need the help of a mobile application developer in converting new text entry algorithms into a working

M. Masoodian et al. (Eds.): APCHI 2004, LNCS 3101, pp. 451–460, 2004.

prototype that is sufficiently complete for user testing. The problem is compounded if the researcher wishes to test custom key layouts or opts for an entirely new device design. In the past, applications for mobile devices were designed to work within the constraints of the target device. There is an increasing trend, primarily in the mobile phone market, to tailor device designs for important applications like SMS (The Nokia 6800[1] allows the user to flip open the phone cover to reveal a full size keyboard to ease text entry).

While rapid prototyping and presentation tools like Macromedia Director are useful for explaining a system to users, useful testing requires a working prototype that is a close match to the final system. In an ideal world a prototype would be completely separate from the final product. However in the fast paced environment that is software development, it is an economic necessity to reuse components of the software prototype [3].

The current crop of phone simulators serves only as an application development aid and does not address the requirements for usability testing or quick prototyping. They are also highly manufacturer and device specific. Prototyping a new text entry method by developing it on an actual phone or phone simulator is akin to premature optimization.

Recent years have seen many text entry methods being designed. However, each of these projects typically spent substantial effort developing their own prototypes for presentation and user testing. A better technique would be to develop for a well-designed generic framework (or even interface existing code to the framework) to rapidly prepare a realistic prototype which can then be tested with target users using a variety of usability testing methods.

2   The Prototyping Framework

The Prototyping Framework is an object-oriented application framework implemented in Java targeted at researchers in the field of mobile text entry. Its primary goal is to help developers create high-fidelity prototypes of their text entry concept rapidly and with minimal effort. It achieves this goal with a set of core classes, an intuitive programming model and a configuration system.

2.1 Domain Analysis

Frameworks are targeted at specific domains and therefore, the development process starts with domain analysis. It involves studying as many systems as is practical from the target domain. Systems are analyzed to identify areas of specificity and generality. This is similar to the popular refactoring technique for classes albeit from a macroscopic perspective. Recurring patterns in the systems under study indicate possible candidates for refactoring into the framework. Areas that are specific to particular system are candidates for 'pluggable' implementations in the framework. Current text

---

[1] http://www.nokia.com/nokia/0,8764,4486,00.html

entry methods were analyzed with these goals in mind. A brief overview of recurring patterns identified is outlined in the next section.

The MultiTap method is currently the main text input method for mobile phones. In this approach, the user presses each key one or more times to specify the input character. For example, the number key 2 is pressed once for the character 'A', twice for 'B', and three times for 'C'. MultiTap typically requires more key presses than most other methods. However, there is no ambiguity and all text typed by the user is immediately *committed* to the data model.

The T9[1] input method uses a dictionary as the basis for disambiguation. The method is based on the same key layout as MultiTap, but each key is pressed only once. For example, to enter "the", the user enters the key sequence 8-4-3-0. The 0-key, for SPACE, delimits words and terminates disambiguation of the preceding keys. Naturally, linguistic disambiguation is not perfect, since multiple words may have the same key sequence. While T9 reduces character level ambiguity, it introduces word level ambiguity. In these cases, T9 gives the most common word as a default. To select an alternate word, the user presses a special NEXT function key. For example, the key sequence 6-6 gives "on" by default. If another word was intended, the user presses NEXT to view the next possible word. In this case, "no" appears. If there are more alternatives, NEXT is pressed repeatedly until the intended word appears. Pressing 0 accepts the word and inserts a SPACE character. During this phase, the user is in *composition* mode which is reflected in the display using visual cues like text color inversion. Pressing 0 accepts the word and inserts a SPACE character. The text is now said to be *committed*.

EziText[2] is similar to T9 in that it uses a dictionary based disambiguation system. However, EziText improves on T9 by providing candidates for completing the current word that the user is entering. Users do not need to tap multiple times to reach letters because EziText predicts words before all letters are pressed. Possible completions for the user's input are displayed at the bottom of the screen and the best completion is displayed inline ahead of the *composing* fragment of text. The predicted text, with its visual cues is called *lookahead* text.

2.2 Text Processing in the Framework

At the heart of the framework is the text processing system. Text processing is the gist of any modern text entry method. It is therefore the most variable aspect across applications as identified in the case studies. The TextManager class provides the facade to access this system. A hook is provided in the form of the TextProcessor class. Client applications using the framework are expected to write their custom implementations to accommodate their specific text processing algorithms. If a custom implementation is specified by the project, the TextManager routes all text processing events through the custom TextProcessor.

---

[1] www.tegic.com

[2] www.zicorp.com/ezitext.htm

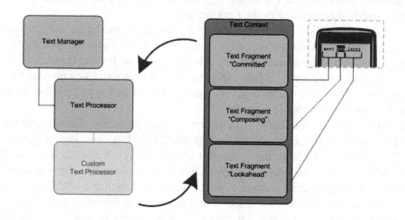

Fig. 1. Text processing in the framework

The concept of *committed, composed* and *lookahead* text fragments were introduced in the domain analysis. These are discussed in further detail in this section. In the MultiTap system, lack of ambiguity means that all text entered by the user is directly committed to the model. In the T9 system, the disambiguation algorithm does not always provide the word intended by the user. The user is in composing mode until he confirms a chunk of text, in which case it is committed. Many devices also let users type text in Chinese, Japanese, or Korean, languages that use thousands of different characters, on a regular-sized keyboard. The text is typed in a form that can be handled by regular-sized keyboards and then converted into the form that is really intended. Typically a sequence of several characters needs to be typed and then converted in one chunk, and conversion may have to be retried because there may be several possible translations.

While this "composition" process is going on, the text logically belongs to the text processing model, but still needs to be displayed to the user. Modern conventions dictate that the text be displayed in the context of the document that it will eventually belong to, albeit in a style that indicates that the text still needs to be converted or confirmed by the input method. This is called *on-the-spot editing*. Some systems provide a separate window to display the text. Such systems are said to use *root-window editing* [4].

State of the art methods like EziText add another type of fragment, the *lookahead*. Using the current context, they make predictions as to what the user intends to type in the future. This fragment also requires unique visual cues to distinguish itself clearly to the user.

Extrapolating from the previous discussion, we can argue that future methods might require additional fragment types or might drop current types. This is clearly yet another area in the framework that should be opened up for application specific customization. The framework handles these aspects using the `TextFragment` and `TextContext` classes. A `TextFragment` encapsulates a string of text. It is also associated with a visual style. A `TextContext` is an ordered list of named `TextFragments`. An application, on startup, registers its fragment types and associated visual styles with the `TextManager`. This information is stored in a `TextContext` which is then passed to the text processing engine each time a text event is encountered. The `TextContext` holds all relevant information about text entered by the user so far and provides the `TextProcessor` with sufficient context with which to make informed text processing decisions (eg: for prefix based prediction).

2.3 Core Framework Design

The core classes of the framework are outlined in Figure 2. The *Facade* design pattern [5] is used extensively in the framework to hide complexity. The functionality provided by the framework is accessed through a set of `Manager` classes. For example, the `KPManager` class hides the intricacies of keyboard management behind easy to use methods. The managerial classes also use the *Singleton* pattern [5] to ensure that only one instance of the class can be instantiated in the framework scope. The framework is designed to be used by developers and hence an overview of the key classes is provided.

`DeviceManager` : This class is responsible for the entire visible UI presented by the framework. It uses instances of `KPManager`, `ScreenManager` and `TextManager` to handle the dynamic aspects of the framework. These aspects include receiving, filtering and forwarding user input, managing the screen display and processing text.

`ProjectManager` : Every application that makes use of the framework is required to create a project file describing the application specific configuration of the framework. Typical configuration data includes information about custom classes that are designed to replace certain aspects of the framework and a layout file that defines the visual look of the device.

`KPManager` : This class abstract low level details of keyboard handling and keybinding. The physical keyboard is remapped using the configuration data supplied by the application. The framework also includes printable templates for labeling remapped keyboards. Raw keyboard input is filtered and processed into high level framework objects (eg: `KPButton`) before being passed on to the framework for event handling. It also handles the requirement for button timeout techniques identified during the domain analysis.

`ScreenManager`: The `ScreenManager` handles text display using the `Screen` and `ScreenDocument` classes. This design is based on the Model-View-Controller architecture.

The initial version of the framework uses two XML configuration files.
`Project.prj` : This file contains information about the a project. This includes type information, location of custom classes that need to be dynamically loaded and the path to the layout file.

`Layout.xml` : Each project requires a layout file that describes the layout of the mobile device in terms of dimensional information and custom attributes if any. This information is used by the `DeviceManager` to render the device UI. An important feature of the framework is its ability to support custom attributes for the input buttons defined in the layout.

Usability testing is expected to be a major application for the framework. Therefore, special considerations have been made in the visual design of the framework. For example, the framework renders to a full screen window (with no embellishments) and the device UI is embedded in the center. This is to avoid distracting visual clutter and to help the user to focus on the task at hand. The buttons also support visual feedback on key events.

2.4 Application Development Using the Framework

A good method for testing the applicability of a framework to its task domain is to develop applications using it. With this goal in mind, two text entry methods, Multi-Tap and T9, were developed and integrated into the framework. This section outlines the key steps a developer has to follow to configure and use the framework with his application.

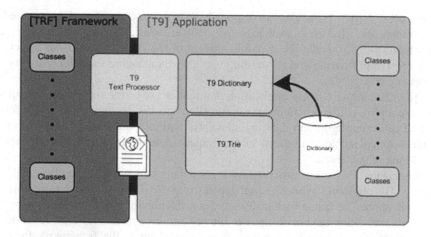

Fig. 2. An implementation of the T9 system integrated with the framework

1. Product Design
The developer has a choice of using one of the standard device designs provided by the framework. However, the framework is in its element when handling innovative product design. The static image of the product is segmented into logical sections like buttons, screen etc.

2. Layout and Attributes
The layout of the device's component elements are defined using an XML configuration file (layout.xml). At this point, any custom attributes required by the text proc-

essing engine are also specified. The T9 implementation uses a modified Trie data structure to store the word dictionary. Searching this data structure in an efficient manner requires the application to obtain a special 'id' from the currently pressed button. To configure the framework to support this requirement, a custom button class is written with an accessor method for this id. The button element in the lay-out.xml is given the id attribute. The `DeviceManager` upon detecting the new attribute uses reflection to introspect the custom button class to detect the correct accessor method and makes the button id available to the text processing engine for application specific processing. The T9 implementation is shown in Figure 2.

3. Code Integration
A custom `TextProcessor` class is written and linked to the framework using the project file. This class registers with the framework the fragment types it intends to use along with their associated visual styles.

The framework can now be launched and once pointed to the project file, the proto-type is configured, rendered and ready for testing.

2.5 Preliminary Evaluation

An analysis of current research projects in mobile text entry show a wasteful trend. Most such projects have innovative ideas for improving text entry. However, they make minimal changes to the basic user interaction strategy. The innovation typically lies in the language model and backend algorithms. Understanding this environment, we can see that there is a need for a framework to conceptualize and prototype the text entry system. This is to allow researchers to focus on their core contribution without spending costly time and effort on building systems to prototype their idea. We have not been able to identify any similar frameworks in the field and hence a comparative evaluation is not possible. It is hypothesized that the lack of similar framework is due to individual projects not being able to spend substantial effort on generalizing and implementing a reusable framework when a specific application would serve their immediate needs.

It is a well-known fact that framework development is an iterative process. Tradi-tional software development also requires iterations but iterations are more important and explicit when designing frameworks. The underlying reason, according to Bosch et.al, is that frameworks primarily deal with abstractions, and that abstractions are very difficult to evaluate [6]. Therefore, the abstractions need to be made concrete in the form of test applications before they can be evaluated. Due to time constraints, application development using the framework was limited to three similar applica-tions (by similarity, we refer to the method of integration with the framework and not the actual applications themselves, which are quite different), namely implementa-tions of MultiTap, T9 and Glyph (a new text entry system currently under develop-ment). While this does not afford enough information to evaluate the design thor-oughly, a basic evaluation is still possible.

Froehlich et.al has identified several desirable features of a framework [7]. The framework is evaluated on the basis of these and other relevant criteria.

Degree of Reuse

Listing 1 shows the minimum amount for code required to implement a MultiTap system using the prototyping framework. The code saving and reduction in programming effort are obvious as the framework code performs the majority of the extraneous work required to configure and display the device interface and interact with the user. The programmer is free to focus solely on the task of developing the text entry algorithm.

The framework is aimed at rapid prototyping and user testing. Once the efficacy of a text entry method has been verified through the prototype, the text entry algorithms must be, in all likelihood, rewritten and optimized for the actual mobile device. However, a fair amount of conceptual reuse can be expected even in this process.

Listing 1. Minimum code required to implement MultiTap using the framework

```
// Perform one-time setup
public void initialize( TextManager textMngr )
{
// Create fragment types
SimpleAttributeSet committedStyle = new SimpleAttributeSet();
StyleConstants.setForeground( committedStyle, Color.BLACK );

SimpleAttributeSet composingStyle = new SimpleAttributeSet();
StyleConstants.setForeground( composingStyle, Color.WHITE );
StyleConstants.setBackground( composingStyle, Color.BLACK );

// Register fragment types
textMngr.addFragmentType( 0, "committed", committedStyle );
textMngr.addFragmentType( 1, "composing", composingStyle );
}


// Hook method for text event processing
public TextContext processText( TextContext inputContext, KPButton button )
{
// Check for MultiTap timeout
if( button.isTimerReset() )
{
String prevComposing = inputContext.get( "composing" ).getFragment();
inputContext.get( "committed" ).appendFragment( prevCompos-ing );
inputContext.get( "composing" ).setFragment( button.getCurrentChar() );
}
else
{
inputContext.get( "composing" ).setFragment( button.getCurrentChar() );
}
return null;
}
```

Ease of Use

Ease of use refers to an application developer's ability to use the framework. The programming model adopted for the framework is intuitive providing the developer with high level abstractions for textual context and user input. For example, the TextContext class logically abstracts the data displayed in the interface into clearly demarcated and easily modifiable TextFragments.

Extensibility and Flexibility

A framework is extensible if new components can be added with ease. Flexibility is the ability to use the framework in many contexts. Core classes of the framework can be replaced with application specific polymorphic variants to add additional functionality However, in its current stage of development, swapping the core classes require the client programmer to be familiar with the design of the backend interactions.

There is also a heavy dependence on the Java Swing API implying that developers are limited to the generic functionality provided by the Swing classes. This dependence can be minimized by developing a set of classes to manage the visual look of TextFragments.

The framework is flexible enough to be integrated with most text entry systems. However, truly innovative systems which require special and substantial changes to the interaction model will require the developer to extend and customize the framework. The framework is still in its infancy and additional applications need to be developed using it to iron out rigidities and add features that are required.

Cohesion and Coupling

A class is cohesive if it has a well defined purpose and all its members are implemented in such a way as to achieve this purpose. Classes in the prototyping framework exhibit a high degree of cohesion. An example is the KPButton class whose sole purpose is to abstract a keypad button along with its associated functionality. Its methods, like startTimer(), work towards achieving that purpose.

Coupling refers to the linkages between classes and should be minimized. In the case of framework, coupling is unavoidable in certain cases like in design of the core classes and within individual packages. Bi-directional associations between classes have been avoided where possible.

3 Conclusion

The prototyping framework is an object-oriented framework for text entry research on mobile devices. The architecture of the framework is founded on solid design fundamentals. Case studies of current text entry methods were studied and the findings incorporated into the framework design. Two text entry methods were developed using the framework. The framework was found to be sufficiently adaptable to these tasks and there was a notable decrease in development effort when using the framework.

A key limitation of the framework is the relatively narrow domain of its applicability. In its current form, it does not cater to more complex input methods (eg:chording) and is restricted by the input capabilities of the standard mouse and keyboard. A comparative evaluation is planned to ascertain quantitative improvements in development time over rapid prototyping technologies like Macromedia Director. The framework is expected to be most useful for small to medium projects either to be used directly or integrated with existing algorithms. It also provides a well designed codebase for projects to develop their own specific prototyping frameworks.

Framework development is an iterative process. This has been stressed repeatedly in the report and in literature. The framework is still in its formative stages. The authors are currently using the framework for prototyping an advanced predictive text entry system. It will take many applications and continuous refinement in the design before the framework matures and its rigidities are identified and removed.

Many statistical models have been proposed for evaluation of text entry performance. These include the KSPC (Key Strokes Per Character) [8] metric and variations of Fitt's Law [9]. Integrating these methods into the framework and automating their tabulation is an important enhancement that is planned for the future.

It is hoped that the framework will provide a boost to text entry researchers by helping them move from conceptualization to prototype with minimal effort. An early version of the framework is targeted for public release in the first quarter of 2004.

References

1. Zachary Friedman, Sarani Mukherji, Gary K. Roeum and Richesh Ruchir. Data Input Into Mobile phones: T9 or Keypad?. SHORE 2001 (2001)
   http://www.otal.umd.edu/SHORE2001/mobilePhone/index.html
2. M. Silfverberg, I. S. MacKenzie, and P. Korhonen. Predicting text entry speed on mobile phones. Proceedings of the ACM Conference on Human Factors in Computing Systems - CHI 2000, pp. 9-16. New York: ACM (2000)
3. J. Purtilo, A. Larson and J. Clark. A methodology for prototyping-in-the-large. Proceedings of the 13th international conference on Software engineering, Austin, Texas, pp. 2-12 (1991)
4. Sun MicroSystems. Input Method Framework : Design Specification Version 1.0 (1998)
5. Erich Gamma, Richard Helm, Ralph Johnson, John Vlissides. Design Patterns: Elements of Reusable Object-Oriented Software. Addison-Wesley Professional Computing Series (1994)
6. Jan Bosch, Peter Molin, Michael Mattsson, PerOlof Bengtsson. Object-Oriented Frameworks–Problems & Experiences. Department of Computer Science and Business Administration, University of Karlskrona/Ronneby (1999)
7. Garry Froehlich, H. James Hoover, Ling Liu, Paul Sorensen. Hooking into Object-Oriented Application Frameworks. Department of Computer Science, University of Alberta, Edmonton, AB. T6G 2H1 (1997)
8. I. S. MacKenzie. KSPC (keystrokes per character) as a characteristic of text entry techniques. Proceedings of the Fourth International Symposium on Human-Computer Interaction with Mobile Devices, pp. 195-210. Heidelberg, Germany: Springer-Verlag (2002)
9. Fitts, P.M. The information capacity of the human motor system in controlling the amplitude of movement. Journal of experimental Psychology. 47, 381-381 (1954)

The Effect of Color Coding
for the Characters on Computer Keyboards
for Multilingual Input Using Modeless Methods

Kuo-Hao Eric Tang[1], Li-Chen Tsai[2]

[1] Department of Industrial Engineering, Feng Chia University, Taichung, 407, Taiwan
khtang@fcu.edu.tw
[2] Office of Computing, Feng Chia University, Taichung, 407, Taiwan
lctsai@fcu.edu.tw

Abstract. When using computer keyboard in a multilingual environment, due to different languages and input methods, it requires switching back and forth between input modes. Although computer keyboard design has been discussed in numerous literatures, however, the colors of characters printed on the keys used for multiple input method has not been investigated. Along with the introduction of the intelligent "modeless" input method, the color-coding of the characters used on keyboard and how it impacts the performance need to be evaluated. A series of three experiments using Chinese and English as input text were conducted and the results show that keyboards with color-coding improved the performances, especially when typing text mixed with English and Chinese. The use of modeless input method also outperformed the traditional approach. And the color-coding particularly improved the performance of modeless input method for mixed input text. The results are discussed with motor program theory.

1 Introduction

Although innovative input methods for computers such as gesture or voice recognition are increasingly popular, keyboards are still the most popular input devices up to this date [5]. Within English-speaking countries, a standard "QWERTY" keyboard is sufficient for most of documents. However, for non-English countries such as China, Japan, Korea, Taiwan, Arabia and many others, a keyboard with only English Characters is not enough. For these countries, more than one set of coding system is required on the keyboards (Fig. 1 shows some examples).

It is straightforward to assign each set of code a different color to help users to identify them as numerous studies have indicated that redundant color coding is one of the most powerful coding systems in terms of discrimination and searching speed (e.g. [3], [7], [12]). However, mostly due to cost concern, many of these multi-coded keyboards are manufactured in monochrome instead of color design. Although there are also numerous studies regarding keyboard design (e.g., [4], [10]), this color coding issue was seldom been discussed.

M. Masoodian et al. (Eds.): APCHI 2004, LNCS 3101, pp. 461–470, 2004.

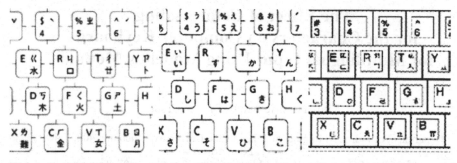

Fig. 1. Partial keyboard layouts from Chinese, Japanese, and Korean keyboards (from left to right) showing multiple characters printed on a single key for multilingual input

When using these multi-coded keyboards in a multilingual environment, due to different languages and input methods, it requires switching back and forth between input modes. This mode switch may cause some inconveniences. First, for non-touch typists, during input processes, those users need to search the correct keys. According to information theory ([6], [1]), the searching time will increase as the number of stimulus (in this case, the number of characters on the keyboard) increases. Since users may need to search more than one coding system for multilingual input, the searching time may be longer. For example, the most popular Chinese input method in Taiwan is a phoneme-based method, Mandarin Phonetic Symbols (MPS), which has 37 phonemes. When input a document with mixed English and Chinese, this user may need to search from not only 26 letters but from a set of codes combining 26 letters and 37 phonemes.

The second inconvenience is that even for the most experienced users, it is still easy for them to forget mode switch when changing input language. To this end, Microsoft Research China has invented an inline input user interface for Asian languages called Modeless Input User Interface ([2], [11]), which allows users smoothly enter English and Chinese text without constantly switching between input language modes.

For most routine users, even they are non-touch typists; they are still familiar with the coding system to some extend so that they can quickly reach to a given key. According to motor program theory ([8], [9]), such users may need to mentally "load" the coding system layout on the keyboard before start typing. For multilingual input case, using switching from MPS to English as an example, a user may either simultaneously "load" MPS and English characters layouts in the user's mind, or the user may "unload" the MPS layout first and then "load" English character layout for continuing typing.

Although traditional approach with mode switch is an annoying UI problem, the hot key required for switching modes may provide an extra cue for users to mentally load and unload these motor programs. For example, when a user presses "shift-ctrl" to switch from inputting Chinese to English, this action may provide a mental cue that facilitating shifting this user's searching focus from 37 phonemes to 26 letters and vice versa. Thus, with innovative modeless input method, users may be lack of this mental cue.

This study is to investigate the effects of using color coding on computer keyboards in a multilingual environment in an effort to improve the potential shortcomings caused by multilingual input and modeless input method. Particularly, the effects of using color coding to modeless input are addressed.

2   Method

A series of three experiments were conducted in this study. The first experiment compared the searching time of each single character individually, either use monochrome or color keyboard. The timing of appearance of each character was controlled by a program and the intervals were all equal. The purpose of this experiment was simply to provide a baseline for comparison of the searching time for monochrome and color keyboards under different coding systems. The second experiment observed the relationship between preceding and following characters, particularly from different coding systems (e.g., an English letter followed by an MPS phoneme). Since the purpose of this experiment was to observe the relationship between characters and coding systems, the users were asked to type prompted characters continuously. The third experiment mimicked a real typing environment and used whole words/sentences as input text to investigate the differences between color-coded and monochrome keyboards on modeless input and traditional input methods.

All three experiments were conducted on PC's with 17 inch LCD monitors and the testing environment was developed by using Microsoft VB.

2.1   Experiment I

Twenty-four paid volunteers from the Engineering School of Feng-Chia University that were familiar with English and MPS input methods but were non-touch typists served as participants. A 2X3 within-subjects design compared two types of keyboards, monochrome and color, and three different input text styles, namely, English only, Chinese only and Mixed. The sequences of the six combined sessions were counter balanced across 24 participants. The dependent variable was response time measured in milliseconds.

There were 260 trials during English only session with each English letter randomly appeared 10 times. The interval time between two trials was 3 seconds and a prompt was provided 200 ms before the letter appeared on the screen. The participants were asked to press the corresponding key as fast as possible. There were 370 trials during Chinese only session since there are 37 MPS phonemes. And for the Mixed session, due to time constraint, each character from English letters and MPS phonemes randomly appeared five times which summed up 315 trials for this session. The rest of the experimental procedures for Chinese only and Mixed sessions were the same as English only session.

2.2 Experiment II

All the participants, experimental design, and procedures were the same as Experiment I except for the experimental task. In Experiment I, the appearance time of each character was controlled by program with a fixed interval time of 3 seconds. In this experiment, however, the next character would appear on screen for a participant as soon as he or she finished the previous input. In other words, the participants were asked to finished all character inputs continuously followed the prompts on the screen as soon as possible.

2.3 Experiment III

Sixteen paid volunteers from the Engineering School of Feng-Chia University served as participants. A 2X4 within-subjects design compared two types of keyboards, monochrome and color, and four different input text styles, namely, English only, Chinese only and Mixed input text using modeless input method, and Mixed input text using traditional "mode switch" approach in a relatively real input situation. The Mixed using traditional "mode switch" approach required a participant to press "shift-ctrl" hot keys to switch language modes while the Mixed using modeless input method automatically distinguished a participant's input strings. The sequences of the eight combined sessions were also counter balanced across 16 participants.

The experimental tasks in Experiment III were copy tasks where a participant copied a document displayed on the screen. The documents were composed of words and sentences instead of characters as used in Experiment I and II. Both copy tasks in English only and Chinese only sessions were designed requiring 520 key presses to finish the input respectively. For Mixed session, the materials required 260 key presses from English letters and 260 key presses from MPS phonemes. The dependent variable thus was time to finishing inputting a document measured in milliseconds.

3   Results

3.1   Experiment I

A within-subject ANOVA analysis revealed two significant main effects: Keyboard style, $F(1, 23)=6.50$, $p<0.05$ and Text style, $F(2, 46)=16.05$, $p<0.001$. Table 1 lists the mean response time taken to complete a trial for the different levels of these two main effects and their standard deviations. It can be shown from Table 1 that color coded keyboard outperformed monochrome one as expected. A Tukey HSD test with $\alpha=0.05$ on Text style factor revealed that participants required more time to respond a character from Mixed style than Chinese only style, while English only took the least time. The results meet the expectation according to information theory. Although the two-way interaction term was not significant, a priori contrast tests revealed that color keyboard had most significant improvement on response time for the Mixed style than Chinese only or English only styles ($\alpha=0.05$) as shown on Fig. 2.

Table 1. Results from Experiment I: Mean searching time (ms) for different levels of the two main effects, with standard deviations in parentheses

Factors	Levels		
Keyboard style	Monochrome		Color
	1054 (160)		1014 (150)
Text style	English only	Chinese only	Mixed
	963 (116)	1058 (177)	1081(147)

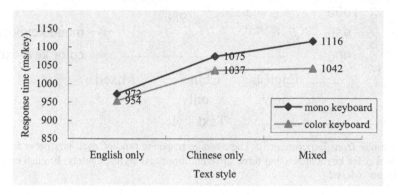

Fig. 2. Results from Experiment I: The average response time of each key press for monochrome and color keyboards using three different input text styles, namely, English only, Chinese only, and Mixed

3.2   Experiment II

A within-subject ANOVA analysis revealed two significant main effects: Keyboard style, $F(1, 23)=12.74$, $p<0.005$ and Text style, $F(2, 46)=16.07$, $p<0.001$. Table 2 lists the mean response time taken to complete a trial for the different levels of these two main effects and their standard deviations, showing a similar trend as in Experiment I. A Tukey HSD test with $\alpha=0.05$ on Text style factor also revealed the same trend as in Experiment I. The response times, however, were generally longer than those in Experiment I, presumably due to interferences between input characters.

Table 2. Results from Experiment II: Mean searching time (ms) for different levels of the two main effects, with standard deviations in parentheses

Factors	Levels		
Keyboard style	Monochrome		Color
	1052(188)		1009(136)
Text style	English only	Chinese only	Mixed
	977(137)	1016(158)	1098(176)

The two-way interaction term was significant, $F(2, 46)=16.07$, $p<0.001$. Both Tukey HSD and Duncan tests with $\alpha=0.05$ revealed that the response time for the Mixed text using monochrome keyboard session was longer than the rest of sessions as shown on Fig. 3.

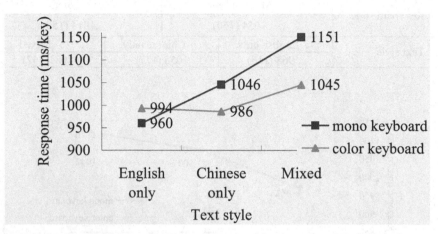

Fig. 3. Results from Experiment II: The average response time of each key press for monochrome and color keyboards using three different input text styles, namely, English only, Chinese only, and Mixed

Since the purpose of this experiment was to observe the relationship between characters and coding systems, we further investigated the relationship between preceding and following characters during continuous input process, particularly from different coding systems. Each pair of consecutive input characters from Mixed session was analyzed. For an MPS phoneme input case, if the preceding input character is another MPS phoneme, this pair is defined as CC and if the preceding input character is an English letter, then this pair is defined as EC. For example, if the input sequence is "K-A-ㄅ-ㄛ", the response time to "ㄅ" is an MPS phoneme input case and the preceding character is an English letter, thus the response time to "ㄅ" is an EC case. With the same fashion, the response time to "ㄛ" is a CC case. Thus, for an English letter input case, if the preceding input character is another MPS phoneme, this pair is defined as CE and if the preceding input character is an English letter, then this pair is defined as EE.

With this newly defined factor, characters in different input sequence, along with the keyboard style, a within-subject ANOVA analysis revealed that both main effects were significant: Keyboard style, $F(1, 23)=10.27$, $p<0.01$; Input sequence, $F(3, 69)=11.37$, $p<0.001$. Both Tukey HSD and Duncan tests with $\alpha=0.05$ revealed that the response times for the four different input sequences were significantly different. The two way interaction term was also significant, $F(3, 69)=5.84$, $p<0.01$. It can be shown from Fig. 4 that when preceding characters were from different coding systems (i.e., EC and CE), the response times were longer than those when the preceding characters were from the same coding system.

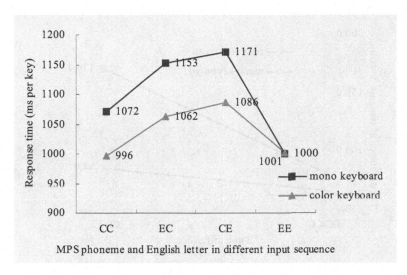

Fig. 4. Results from Experiment II: To further investigate the relationship between preceding and following characters, particularly from different coding systems, each pair of input characters from Mixed session was analyzed. For an MPS phoneme input case, the preceding input character can be another MPS phoneme (CC) or an English letter (EC), and for an English letter input case, the preceding input character can be an MPS phoneme (CE) or another English letter (EE)

Further analysis on the results from Fig. 4, we can observe how the input sequences affect response times. It seems a user requires some "mental overhead" to switch from one coding system to another. This overhead can be shown as (EC-CC) for an MPS phoneme input case and (CE-EE) for an English letter input case and is shown on Fig. 5. This finding is consistent with the motor program theory as described in Introduction and the results may suggest that a user switches between MPS and English characters layouts instead of loading both simultaneously. Fig. 5 also suggests that in general, a color keyboard can reduce this overhead and it seems that an English letter input case requires more such overhead than an MPS phoneme input case, and a color keyboard is particularly useful for an English letter input case than an MPS phoneme input case.

3.3 Experiment III

For a whole document input task performed in Experiment III, a within-subject ANOVA analysis on completion time also revealed two significant main effects: Keyboard style, $F(1, 15)=45.87$, $p<0.001$; and Text style, $F(3, 45)=3.60$, $p<0.05$. The results suggest that color keyboards consistently outperformed monochrome ones throughout all types of input text as shown in Fig. 6. The two way interaction term was also significant, $F(3, 45)=4.575$, $p<0.01$. According to our discussion in the Introduction section, we hypothesized that hot key required for switching input modes may provide an extra cue for users to mentally load and unload motor programs of keyboard ayouts. A planned *a priori* contrast test revealed that the benefit of using

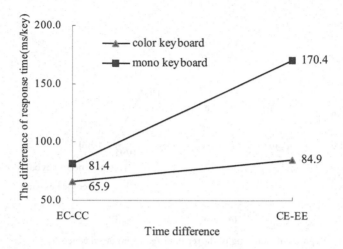

Fig. 5. Results from Experiment II: It can be shown that the response times were longer when the coding system of preceding characters were different from current input ones (i.e., CE and EC cases), and these overheads shown as EC-CC and CE-EE were significantly affected by the color coding of keyboards.

color keyboard for Mixed using modeless input method was greater than Mixed using traditional "mode switch" approach ($\alpha=0.01$). This finding is consistent to our hypothesis and can also be shown by the trend on Fig. 6.

4   Discussion

The results from the three experiments suggest that keyboards with color-coding improve keyboard input performance, especially when typing text mixed with English and Chinese. The results from the first experiment provide a baseline for comparison between color-coded keyboards and monochrome keyboards, and again prove that redundant color coding is useful in discrimination and searching task. Based on these findings, the results from the second experiment suggest the existence of "mental overhead" in switching input language. This finding also provides evidence supporting motor program theory, and it may also suggest that instead of loading both coding system layout simultaneously, a user will load and unload corresponding coding system layout when switching an input language. The last experiment further validates the benefit of color-coded keyboard in a real input situation, and also provides evidence supporting the using hot key as "mental cue" for switching input language.

Since the only difference between Mixed using modeless input method and Mixed using traditional "mode switch" approach is a set of hot key, the time difference shown on Fig. 6 can caused by only two reason: 1. the extra time required for pressing that set of hot key, and 2. the change to the loading time for motor program. By looking into raw data again, it can be recalculated that the reason "mode switch" approach has longer time than modeless input is due to the extra key press for hot keys. However, on the other hand, the planned *a priori* contrast test also suggests that color keyboard helps improving modeless case than mode switch case. We have predicted that without the hot key as mental cue, modeless input may need a longer time for loading and unloading motor programs. The current results may suggest that color coding plays a role similar to "mental cue" to expedite the loading motor program processes so that it impact color keyboard more than monochrome one.

Overall, the study suggests that color coding for keyboard, although as minor as it may seem, indeed improves the typing performance for non-touch typists.

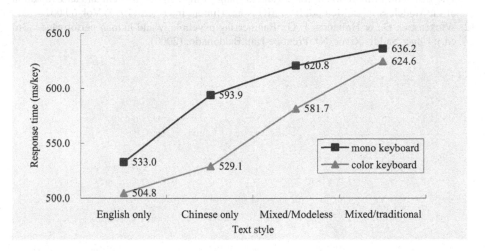

Fig. 6. Results from Experiment III: The mean response times for four different types of input text styles, namely English only, Chinese only, Mixed using modeless input method, and Mixed using traditional "mode switch" approach in a relatively real input situation with two types of keyboard

References

1. Bertelson, P.: Serial choice reaction-time as a function of response versus signal-and-response repetition. Nature. (1965) Vol. 206 217–218.
2. Chen, Z., and Lee, K.F.: A new statistical approach to Chinese pinyin input. ACL-2000. The 38th Annual Meeting of the Association for Computational Linguistics, Hong Kong, 3-6 October 2000 (2000).
3. Christ, R. E.: Review and analysis of color-coding research for visual displays. Human Factors. (1975) Vol. 17 542-570.
4. Ferguson, D. and Duncan, J.: Keyboard design and operating posture. Ergonomics. (1974) Vol. 17 731-744.
5. Hargreaves, W. R.: Why an alternative keyboard? Think productivity! Occupational Health & Safety. (2002) Vol. 71(4) 70-75.
6. Hyman, R.: Stimulus information as a determinant of reaction time. J. exp. Psychol. 45 (1953) 188-196.

7. Kanarick, A. F. and Petersen, R. C.: Redundant color coding and keeping-track perform-
    ance. Human Factors. (1971) Vol. 13 183-188.
8. Schmidt, R.: A schema theory of discrete motor skill learning. Psychological Review.
    (1975) Vol. 82 225-260.
9. Schmidt, R.: More on motor programs and the schema concept. In J. Kelso (ed.): Human
    motor behavior: An introduction. Hillsdale, NJ, Lawrence Erlbaum Associates (1982) 189-
    235.
10. Sears A, Zha Y.: Data entry for mobile devices using soft keyboards: Understanding the
    effects of keyboard size and user tasks. International Journal of Human-Computer interac-
    tion. (2003) Vol. 16(2) 163-184..
11. Suzumegano, F., Amano, J.I., Maruyama, Y., Hayakawa, E., Namiki, M., Takahashi, N. :
    The Evaluation Environment for a Kana to Kanji Transliteration System and an Evaluation
    of the Modeless Input Method. IPSJ SIG Notes Human Interface. (1995) Vol. 60 002.
12. Wickens, C. D., & Hollands, 1. G.: Engineering psychology and human performance (3rd
    ed.): Upper Saddle River, NJ, Prentice-Hall.Baldonado. (2000).

Extended Godzilla: Free-Form 3D-Object Design by Sketching and Modifying Seven Primitives at Single 2D-3D Seamless Display

Shun'ichi Tano[1], Yoichiro Komatsu[2], Mitsuru Iwata[1]

[1]University of Electro-Communications
Chofu, Tokyo 182-8585, Japan
{tano, iwata}@is.uec.ac.jp
[2]Honda R&D Co., Ltd.,
Haga-machi, Haga-gun, Tochigi 321-3393, Japan
bandit@tlab.is.uec.ac.jp

Abstract. We previously developed a prototype system called "Godzilla" that supports creative design, specifically by car-exterior designers. Godzilla provides an environment in which designers can draw concept image on a 2D pad (a tablet with an LCD), and when they hold the image in midair, the shape of the 2D sketch is automatically recognized and appears as a 3D sketch displayed on a 3D pad (stereovision TVs). Designers can sketch, modify, and view their drawings from different viewpoints in either two or three dimensions. The 3D images are not displayed as beautiful CG images, but as 3D sketches that consist of many 3D cursive lines produced by mimicking the designer's pen touch. Although Godzilla was successfully used on a trial basis at an automobile manufacturer, it has serious drawbacks: (1) the designable shapes are limited to those of cars, (2) the 2D and 3D view areas are separated, and (3) the equipment is expensive. We have now extended Godzilla to overcome these drawbacks: (1) free form design is possible using a combination of seven primitives, (2) presentation is seamless between the 2D and 3D spaces, and (3) off-the-shelf equipment is used. We devised a recognition technique that uses a topology matrix and implemented a user interface for transforming and manipulating the recognized primitives. Two preliminary experiments demonstrated the effectiveness of the system.

1 Introduction

The role of computers is rapidly changing: the computer has become a kind of artifact that we have developed to expand our creativity and intelligence. For example, car-exterior designers now use 3D modeling software from the earliest stages of the design process. While conventional 3D design systems enable beautiful, realistic, artistic images to be produced, they are not useful for conceptual design. It has gradually become obvious that these systems have a serious drawback—instead of promoting creative work, they often discourage it or inhibit active thinking.

Extended 3D design support systems are now needed to enable designers to sketch 3D images freely in 2D and 3D spaces. In this paper, we describe a design environ-

M. Masoodian et al. (Eds.): APCHI 2004, LNCS 3101, pp. 471-480, 2004.
© Springer-Verlag Berlin Heidelberg 2004

ment called "Extended Godzilla" that enables designers to create free-form 3D-object designs by sketching and modifying seven primitives on a single 2D-3D seamless display.

2   Related Work and Problems

Many 3D design systems have been proposed. Some have a 3D input device and a 2D display [5-8]. Others have 3D input and output [2,3,9]. In this section, we will briefly review our previous work as a typical example of a 3D design support system and then summarize the problems.

2.1   "Godzilla" [2,3]

We have been studying systems that will support creative and intelligent work based on the real-virtual-intelligent concept [1]. They range from systems for knowledge workers to ones for car-exterior designers [2-4]. The system reported here is an extension of our previous "Godzilla" system, which provides car-exterior designers with a natural, seamless interface between 2D and 3D images.

As illustrated in Figure 1, the designer first draws a concept image on the 2D pad (a tablet with an LCD). The designer then holds the image in midair, and the shape of the 2D sketch is automatically recognized and appears as a 3D image on the 3D pad (stereovision TVs). By holding and rotating the 3D image, the designer can view it from different viewpoints. When the designer grasps the image and places it onto the 2D pad, it appears on the 2D pad as a 2D sketch. The system displays the hand-drawn sketch all the time, even in the 3D space. It can automatically recognize the 3D shape of a 2D image and transform between the 2D and 3D sketches with different viewpoints while preserving the designer's pen touch.

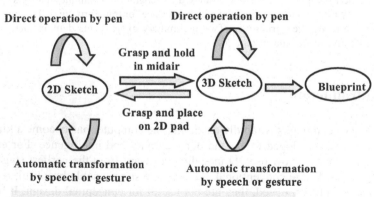

Figure 1. Design Flow in Godzilla System

As shown in Figure 2, the current Godzilla system consists of
- Two 3D pads (18-inch LCD stereo-vision TVs with a head-tracking unit)
- Four 2D pads (14-inch LCD pen pads)

- A pen with a 3D location sensor (magnetic field)
- A headset (for voice commands)

3D pad

(Stereo vision TVs)

3D pen

Designer

2D pad
(Tablet)

Figure 2. Prototype of Godzilla System

2.2 Related Work and Problems

Work in this area can be categorized as follows:
- automatic transformation from handwritten sketches to 3D images [2,3,10],
- reconstruction of 3D image from cross-sections [11,12], and
- generation of 3D image from predefined gestures [13-15].

We have analyzed the work done so far and have identified three fundamental problems.

(1) Limited Forms

The range of forms systems can handle is severely restricted. For example, Godzilla [2,3] can handle only car-like forms, and Teddy can handle only round forms, such as stuffed animals. While this restriction is inevitable from the technical point of view, designers regard it as the most serious drawback of current systems since it restricts their creativity.

(2) Unnatural Display of 3D Images

In some systems, 3D images are displayed on a conventional 2D monitor. In more advanced systems, they are displayed on a stereoscopic monitor. No system, however, provides a single display on which designers draw a sketch and then view it in 2D and 3D. It is quite unnatural.

(3) Expensive Equipment

The 3D design systems have been built using expensive equipment: 3D TVs with a head tracker, 3D magnetic sensors, and so on.

3 Our Approach

Our previous "Godzilla" system had the same set of problems summarized above. To overcome them, we have extended the system specifically to address these problems.

3.1   Free Form Design Using a Combination of Seven Primitives

It is obviously impossible to recognize a 2D sketch of a 3D form without any knowledge of the sketched form since a 2D sketch cannot retain all of the shape information. However, limiting the range of forms restricts the designer's creativeness. To enable free-form design, we developed a design approach than enables the designer to draw primitive forms and then combine and modify them. With this approach, the system need only recognize the primitive shapes; the designer can create any 3D form by combining and modifying the primitives. The approach is sound from both the system's and designer's points of view.

Our system has seven primitives, as shown in Figure 3. They can be roughly categorized into primitives with flat surfaces and primitives with curved surfaces.

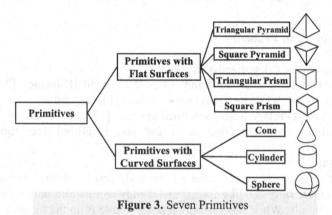

Figure 3. Seven Primitives

A typical design flow is now as shown in Figure 4. First the designer sketches the primitive shapes, and the system recognizes them. The designer then combines and modifies the primitives or views and checks the shapes in 3D space.

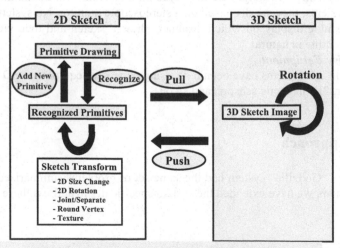

Figure 4. Design Flow in Extended Godzilla System

3.2 Natural Seamless 2D-3D Display

To provide a natural display, the display unit should support three display modes concurrently, as shown in Figure 5.

In our previous system (see the photo in Figure 2), we used two types of display units. A 2D-3D mixed display capability is also required, which means that the two types had to be merged and that the integrated unit had to support continuous transition between 2D and 3D. To meet these requirements, we used an LCD monitor with polarized light screens (a "micro-pole filter") and polarized glass.

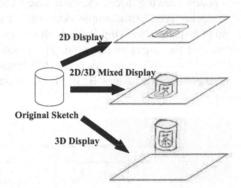

Figure 5. Three Display Modes

3.3 Less Expensive Equipment

A 3D design environment that can be used by many designers to get rich inspiration for their creativity must have a reasonable cost. Extended Godzilla is built using off-the-shelf components—an LCD monitor, polarized light screens, and polarized glass for mixed 2D-3D display. For the 3D location sensor, we use a simple 3D locator comprised of acceleration sensors. All of the components are easy to buy at a reasonable price. A photo of the current system is shown in Figure 6.

Figure 6. "Extended Godzilla" System

4 Extended Godzilla: System Recognition Engine and Interface

The most important features of Extended Godzilla are the engine for 2D image recognition and the user interface.

4.1 Sketch Recognition Engine

To enable our system to recognize 2D sketches composed of seven primitives of any size, at any orientation, and at any viewing direction, we devised a topology matrix to represent the structure of the primitives. An example sketch (of a cube) with a specific size and orientation and at a specific viewing angle is shown on the left in Figure 7. The symbols A, B... represent the edges of the cube. The topology matrix of the cube is shown on the right. A "1" means a connection; a "-1" means a disconnection. For example, edge A has connections with edges B, E, D, and F and disconnections with edges C, G, H, and I.

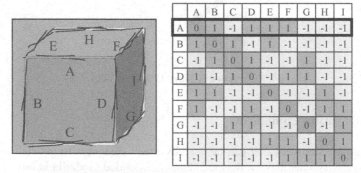

Figure 7. Example Sketch and Corresponding Topology

The topology matrices are automatically generated based on the definitions of the seven primitives. Each primitive can have many topology matrices because the projected images of each primitive differ with the viewing angle. The system thus has many topology matrices. We call the pre-calculated topology matrices as the models.

The recognition process has two stages. In the first, the eigenvalues of the topology matrix for the sketched image are calculated and compared with those of the models. An example is shown in Figure 8. The left side shows the formalized rendering and topology matrix corresponding to the designer's sketch; the right side shows two potential models. The recognition engine tries to identify a model matrix that has eigenvalues similar to those of the sketch matrix. Then, in the second stage, the recognition engine enumerates the correspondences between the edges in the sketch matrix and each model matrix. In the example shown in Figure 8, the recognition engine determines that the formalized rendering of the sketch matches model 1 (in the first stage) and then that edge A in the sketch matches edge D in model 1 (in the second stage).

Although calculating the eigenvalues is not inexpensive, calculating the model eigenvalues can be done before the recognition, and handling vectors of actual values is much easier than handling topological structures.

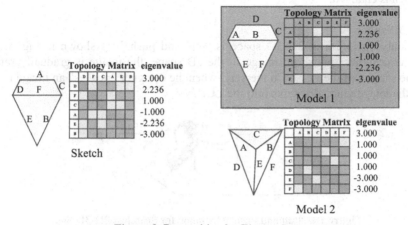

Figure 8. Recognition by Eigenvalues

4.2 User Interface

There are three spaces (2D, 3D, and 2D-3D), and the system has a user interface for each one.

(1) 2D space

The basic operations in the 2D space are drawing and deleting lines; there are three special operations for primitives.

Join and Separate: The designer can join primitives and separate joined primitives.

Round vertex: The designer can round the vertex of primitives by drawing a rounded line on the surface, as shown in Figure 9.

Draw texture: The designer can draw a line only on a surface, which enables sketching on a curved surface.

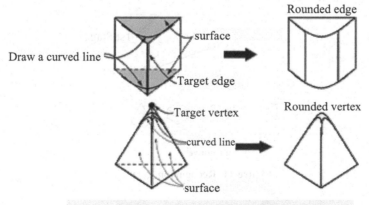

Figure 9. Modification: "Round Vertex"

(2) 3D space

The only operation in 3D space is "rotation." The orientation of an image shown in 3D (i.e., above the LCD surface) changes smoothly and continuously as the direction of the pen is changed.

(3) 2D-3D space

The only operation in 2D-3D space is "pull and push." As shown in Figure 10, when the designer "pulls" an image in the 2D space, the image is gradually raised from the surface of the LCD. Conversely, when the designer "pushes" an image in 3D space, the image gradually sinks into the LCD.

Figure 10. "Pull and Push" Operation for Seamless 2D-3D Space

5   Evaluation

For a preliminary evaluation, we conducted two informal experiments. In the first experiment, we asked 11 participants to sketch each of the seven primitives five times and then evaluated the recognition rate. As shown in Figure 11, although all the recognition rates in the first stage were high (>90%), those in the second stage for the square pyramid and prism were low. This is because the sketches of these shapes at the popular angle tended to produce many candidates.

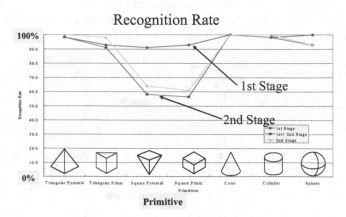

Figure 11. Recognition Rate

In the second experiment, we asked the same participants to sketch a die, a camera, an airplane, and anything else they liked. Figure 12 shows the total number of primitives used to draw these objects. While the participants used the sphere and square prism the most, they used all the primitives effectively. Two representative sketches are shown in Figure 13; since the sketches had a 3D structure, the images could be viewed from any angle.

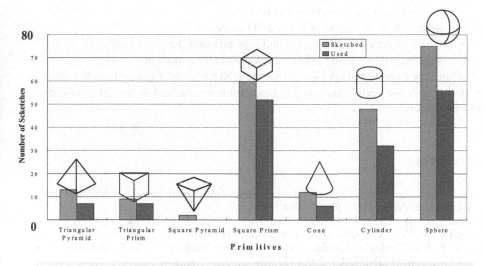

Figure 12. Number of Primitives Sketched and Used

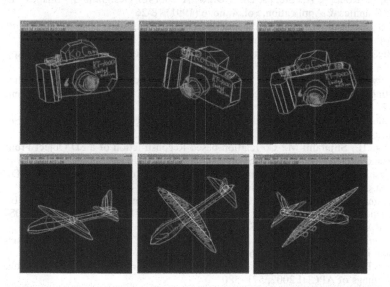

Figure 13. Example Sketches

6 Summary

We have developed a design environment called "Extended Godzilla" that enables designers to create free-form 3D objects by sketching and modifying seven primitives in a 2D-3D seamless display. Extended Godzilla features

- free form design using a combination of seven primitives,
- recognition using a topology matrix,
- seamless presentation in 2D and 3D space,
- a user interface for operating and manipulating the primitives, and
- implementation using low-cost off-the-shelf equipment.

Preliminary experiments demonstrated the effectiveness of the system. We are now improving both the performance of the recognition engine and the usability of the join and round operations.

References

1. Tano, S. et al.: Design Concept Based on Real-Virtual-Intelligent User Interface and its Architecture, Proc. of HCI-97, 901-904
2. Tano, S.: Design Concept to Promote Both Reflective and Experimental Cognition for Creative Design Work, CHI-2003, Extended Abstract, 1014-1015
3. Tano, S. et al.: Godzilla: Seamless 2D and 3D Sketch Environment for Reflective and Creative Design Work, INERACT-2003, 131-136
4. Tano, S., Sugimoto, T.: Natural Hand Writing in Unstable 3D Space with Artificial Surface, CHI-2001 Extended Abstract, 353-354
5. Sachs, E., Roberts, A., Stoops, D.: 3-Draw: A Tool for Designing 3D Shapes, IEEE Computer Graphics & Application, vol. 4, no. 6 (1991) 18-26
6. Han, S., Medioni, G.: 3Dsketch: Modeling By Digitizing with a Smart 3D Pen, Proceeding of Fifth ACM International Conference on Multimedia (1997) 41-49
7. Massie, T.A.: Tangible Goal for 3D Modeling, IEEE Computer Graphics and Applications, vol. 18, no. 3 (1998) 62-65
8. Gregory, A., Ehmann, S., Lin, M.: inTouch: Interactive Multiresolution Modeling and 3D Painting with a Haptic Interface, Proceedings of IEEE Virtual Reality Conference (2000) 45-52
9. Schkolne, S., Pruett, M., Schroder, C.: Surface Drawing: Creating Organic 3D Shapes with the Hand and Tangible Tools, CHI-2001, 261-268
10. Lipson, H., Shpitalni M.: Correlation-based Reconstruction of a 3D Object From a Single Freehand Sketch, AAAI Spring Symposium on Sketch Understanding (2002) 99-104
11. Igarashi, T., Matsuoka S., Tanaka, H.: Teddy, A Sketching Interface for 3D Freeform Design, ACM SIG-GRAPH'99, Los Angels (1999) 409-416
12. Grossman T., Balakrishnan, R., Kurtenbach, G., Fitzmaurice, G., Khan, A., Buxton, B.: Interaction Techniques for 3D Modeling on Large Displays, 2001 SYMPOSIUM ON INTERACTIVE 3D GRAPHICS, 17-23
13. Zeleznik, R.C., Herndon, K.P., Hughes, J.F.: SKETCH: An Interface for Sketching 3D Scenes, in Proc. of SIGRAPH 96, 163-170
14. Qin, S.F., Wright, D.K., Jordanov, I.N.: A Sketching Interface for 3D Conceptual Design, Proceedings of APCHI 2002, 571-580
15. Igarashi, T., Hughes, J.F.: A Suggestive Interface for 3D Drawing, 14th Annual Symposium on User Interface Software and Technology, ACM UIST'01, 173-181

Quantitative Analysis of Human Behavior and Implied User Interface in 3D Sketching

Shun'ichi Tano[1], Toshiko Matsumoto[2], Mitsuru Iwata[1]

[1]University of Electro-Communications
Chofu, Tokyo 182-8585, Japan
{tano, iwata}@is.uec.ac.jp
[2]Hitachi, Ltd.
Yoshida-cyo, Totsuka, Yokohama 244-0817, Japan
toshiko@tlab.is.uec.ac.jp

Abstract. Designers normally create three-dimensional images on paper. As a natural extension of this, we are developing a design support system that will enable people to draw 3D lines in 3D space directly. However, we first need to better understand how people behave when sketching in three-dimensional space and then design a user interface that supports natural 3D sketching. This paper describes the experiment we conducted to quantitatively analyze the diverse aspects of this behavior. The experiment clarified the characteristics of 3D drawing, particularly the effect of the drawing location, the perception of depth, the sense of balance, the direct/indirect input method, and the preferred drawing direction. We propose improving the user interface by using the metaphor of "shadow" and the metaphor of "hand mirror" to promote the user's awareness of errors and/or by using "adaptive rotation" to improve the user's comfort when sketching.

1 Introduction

The role of computers is rapidly changing—the computer has become a kind of artifact that we have developed to expand our creativity and intelligence. For example, car-exterior designers now use 3D modeling software from the earliest stages of the design process. Although most conventional 3D design systems enable us to produce beautiful, realistic, artistic images, they are not useful for conceptual design. A need is thus growing for extended 3D design support systems that will enable people to draw 3D lines in 3D space directly.

2 Related Work

We have been studying systems that will truly support creative and intelligent work that are based on the RVI (real-virtual-intelligent) concept [1]. They range from systems for knowledge workers to ones for car-exterior designers. The study reported here builds on our previous work.

M. Masoodian et al. (Eds.): APCHI 2004, LNCS 3101, pp. 481–490, 2004.

2.1 Godzilla [2,3]

The "Godzilla" system provides car-exterior designers with a natural, seamless interface between 2D and 3D images. As shown by the photo in Fig. 1, our current Godzilla system consists of
- *Two 3D pads* (18-inch LCD stereo-vision TVs each with a head-tracking unit)
- *Four 2D pads* (14-inch LCD pen pads)
- *A pen with a 3D location sensor* (magnetic field)
- *A headset* (for voice commands)

Figure 1. Prototype of Godzilla System

Figure 2 shows the typical design flow. First, the designer sketches the concept image on one of 2D pads. The designer then holds the sketch on the pad in midair; the shape of the 2D sketch is automatically recognized and appears as a 3D sketch on one of 3D pads. While holding and rotating the 3D-image, the designer can look at it from different viewpoints. When the designer grasps the image and places it onto one of 2D pads, it appears as a 2D sketch. Note that the system displays the hand-drawn sketch at all times, even in the 3D space, and that it can automatically recognize the 3D shape of a 2D image and transform between the 2D and 3D sketches with different viewpoints while preserving the designer's pen touch.

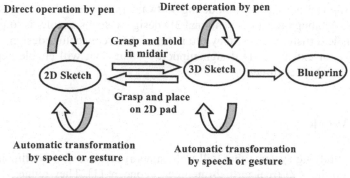

Figure 2. Design Flow in Godzilla System

2.2 3D Drawing with Artificial Surface[4]

Testing of the Godzilla prototype revealed four points in particular.
- Sketching in 3D really fascinated all users. It may be a new media.
- 3D space is very unstable, so it is almost impossible to sketch in 3D space.
- There is too much freedom when sketching in 3D.
- Perceiving the depth in a 3D image is difficult.

We devised four types of force fields, which are generated using the PHANToM™ arm-link mechanism, to cope with these problems.

(a) *Uniform force field:* Uniform inertia is produced in the drawing area, giving designers the feeling of "drawing in jelly."

(b) *Automatic surface generation:* An artificial surface is automatically generated that matches the drawing. When many lines are judged to be on the same plane, a force field is created to shape the plane.

(c) *User-defined surface:* The user can indicate the need for a surface by gesturing.

(d) *Use of 3D rulers:* We designed several virtual 3D rulers: a sphere, a rod with a straight dent for drawing straight lines in 3D, a French curve, and so on. The surface is artificially generated at the position of a 3D sensor, so they are easily fixed in 3D.

3 Problems and Goal

Many 3D design systems have been proposed. Some use a 3D input device and a 2D display [5-8]. Some use 3D input and output [9]. There have also been many reports on the problems with 3D drawing: difficulty of depth perception, poor sense of balance, instability of drawing in midair, and so on [10]. As described above, we have also encountered these difficulties and have worked on ways to overcome theme. However, our findings and those of others largely depended on subjective observation—there is a lack of quantitative data.

To be able to design a user interface that truly supports natural 3D sketching, we need to fully understand how people behave when sketching in three dimensions. We have thus conducted an experiment to gather quantitative data on 3D sketching in a variety of drawing environments for a variety of tasks.

4 Experiment

We built an environment in which the participants in our experiment could sketch 3D images in 3D space directly. The participants were asked to sketch several types of 3D shapes, and we qualitatively analyzed the shapes they sketched.

4.1 Environment

We built a natural and diverse 3D drawing environment with the following components.

  (1) Display: We used a Sanyo 3D TV with a head tracker so that the participants did not have to wear special equipment, such as liquid crystal shutter glasses.

  (2) Input devices: We used two types of input devices: a 3D magnetic sensor pen (FASTRAK®) and an arm-link mechanism (PHANToM™). When the participant used the 3D pen, a line appeared at the pen point. When the participant used the arm-link mechanism, a line appeared at some distance from the participant's hand. The former can thus be seen as a direct input device and the latter as an indirect input device.

  (3) Canvas rotator: For comfortable sketching, the direction of the canvas must be freely adjustable. We used a special device we call a "canvas rotator" to enable the participant to freely change the direction of the canvas in 3D space. The rotator was implemented using the 3D magnetic sensor.

4.2 Tasks

The participants were asked to draw specific shapes at specific locations. The terminology used for the locations and directions is illustrated in Figure 3.

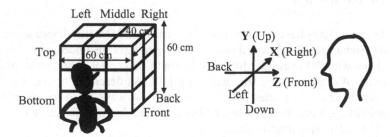

Figure 3. Terminology for Drawing Locations and Directions

  (1) Shapes
  The participants were asked to sketch four shapes:
    - 3 lines perpendicularly intersecting each other, with each line 5 or 10 cm long,
    - a cube 5 x 5 x 5 cm,
    - an arbitrary shape copied from a wire pattern, and
    - a free shape (any shape the participant wanted to draw).
  (2) Locations
  The participants were asked to draw each shape at specific locations:
    - immediately in front of the participant and
    - at the 18 locations shown on the left in Figure 3.

4.3 Procedure

The 11 participants (who were all right-handed) were asked to perform tasks that combined different environmental features, shapes, and locations; for example,
- Display: on
- Input device: arm-link mechanism
- Canvas rotator: no
- Shape: cube
- Location: Immediately in front of participant.

5 Preliminary Results

We are still analyzing the results, so this is only a preliminary report of the results.

5.1 Effect of Visual Feedback

We compared the accuracy of the three lines perpendicularly intersecting each other for "with" and "without" visual feedback (i.e., 3D display on or off). The accuracy was evaluated based on the errors in the lengths, the errors in the angles, and the deviations from the target line.

With visual feedback, the average error in length was 1.2 cm; without feedback, it was 2.1 cm. This is statistically significant ($p < 0.05$, Wilcoxon Signed Rank Test).

With visual feedback, the average error in the Z-direction angle was 6.2°; without feedback, it was 19.9°. This is also statistically significant ($p < 0.05$, Wilcoxon Signed Rank Test).

The result is important because it quantitatively shows that the visual feedback is effective even when the target shapes are very simple. In the following subsection, the effect will be precisely analyzed.

5.2 Effect of Location

We compared the accuracy of the three lines drawn at the 18 locations. As shown in Figures 4 and 5, the lines drawn in the X direction (i.e., the lines drawn from right to left) can be roughly categorized into the two lines shown in Figure 4. When drawn in the front or right-back areas, the lines tended to tilt backward and upward. When drawn in the other locations, i.e. top-middle or left-back, the lines tended to tilt downward and backward.

The tendency of the lines drawn in the Z direction (i.e., drawn from front to back) can be roughly categorized into the two lines shown in Figure 5. When drawn in the left area, the lines tended to tilt upward and to the right. When drawn in the right area, they tended to tilt upward and to the left.

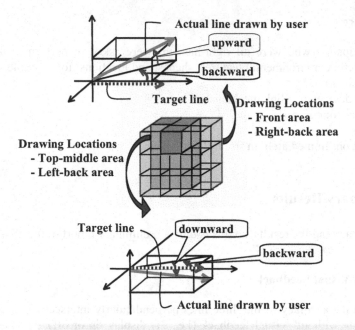

Figure 4. Tendencies of Lines Drawn in X Direction

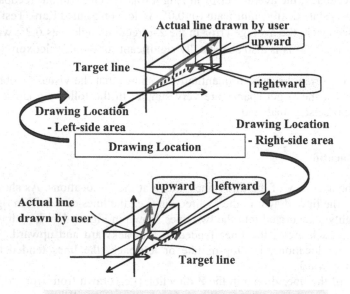

Figure 5. Tendencies of Lines Drawn in Z Direction

The result shows that the effect of the visual feedback is not enough to compensate the errors.

5.3 Effect of Rotation

To analyze the effect of rotation, we focused on the first lines drawn immediately after the participant rotated the canvas (the 3D space). We assumed the first lines represented the preferred direction. In other words, the participants probably feel the first lines are easy to draw. We therefore recorded the directions of the first lines drawn and categorized them using the k-means clustering method. As shown in Figure 6, "downward" and "rightward" were overwhelmingly the preferred directions. This corresponds with our intuition.

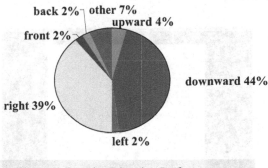

Figure 6. Drawing Direction Preferences

5.4 Effect of Direct/Indirect Input Device

To estimate the effect of the input device, for each device we compared the accuracy of the three lines, of the cube, and of the arbitrary shape. The accuracy of the first two was evaluated by the error in length, error in angle and deviation from target line. That of the last one was evaluated based on a checklist.

The indirect input method was more accurate based on many evaluation criteria, including the errors in length and angle. Both were statistically significant ($p < 0.05$, Wilcoxon Signed Rank Test).

According to the subjective evaluation, the preference of the direct/indirect input device depends on users or tasks. But interestingly, according to the qualitative analysis on the drawing error, the indirect input device is always better than the direct method.

6 Implied User Interface

Our experiment has shown that sketching in 3D space is difficult, particularly because the senses of depth and balance are poor. It also qualitatively demonstrated that the characteristics of drawing in 3D space are not simple. They are affected by many factors (drawing position, drawing direction, and so on).

Our analysis indicates that a user interface is needed to compensate for the difficulties in drawing in 3D space. At this point, we have two opposing approaches: indirect and direct assistance.

6.1 Indirect Assistance: Awareness of Error

For indirect assistance, the interface should enhance the user's awareness of errors. We found that using the metaphor of "shadow" and the metaphor of "hand mirror" are effective in achieving this, as illustrated in Figure 7. Note that the shadow and mirror are also 3D images.

Figure 7. Use of "Shadow" and "Hand Mirror" for Indirect Assistance (Stereoscopic Image)

6.2 Direct Assistance: Adaptive Rotation

It gradually became clear that the participants could draw the exact line they wanted in a particular direction, which we call the "preferred direction" (see Figure 6). For example, they could draw downward lines more comfortably. For example, we can represent the degree of preference for "downward" on a graph, as shown in Figure 8. We can then calculate the preference for all directions by summing up graphs for all directions. Eventually the results can be represented as a sphere, the surface of which represents the preference value. Using this "preference sphere," we can rotate the 3D space to maximize the preference of the direction for the lines that the users want to draw or modify. It maximizes the user's comfort when sketching.

In a preliminary test of direct assistance using this "adaptive rotation," 6 of the 11 participants showed a measurable reduction in the drawing error (Figure 9).

7 Conclusion

We have investigated the characteristics of sketching in 3D space, particularly the effect of visual feedback, of the location, and of the input method, as well as the preferred drawing direction. Note that these diverse characteristics were quantitatively and statistically evaluated. Our analysis showed that direct and/or indirect assistance is needed to offset the difficulties of sketching in 3D space. Using our prototype system, users have been able to make beautiful sketches.

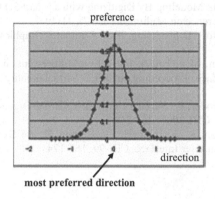

Figure 8. Preference for Downward Drawing Direction

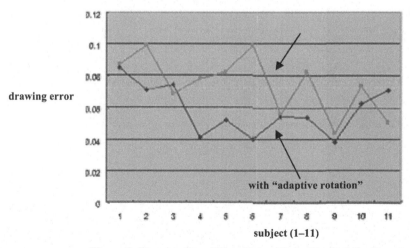

Figure 9. Drawing Error When Using "Adaptive Rotation"

References

1. Tano, S. et al. Design Concept Based on Real-Virtual-Intelligent User Interface and its Architecture, Proc. of HCI-97, 901-904.
2. Tano,S. Design Concept to Promote Both Reflective and Experimental Cognition for Creative Design Work, CHI-2003, Extended Abstract, 1014-1015.

3. Tano, S. et al. Godzilla: Seamless 2D and 3D Sketch Environment for Reflective and Creative Design Work, INERACT-2003, 131-136.
4. Tano, S., Sugimoto, T., Natural Hand Writing in Unstable 3D Space with Artificial Surface, CHI-2001 Extended Abstract, 353-354.
5. Sachs, E., Roberts, A., Stoops, D. 3-Draw: A Tool for Designing 3D Shapes, IEEE Computer Graphics & Application, vol.4, no.6(1991), 18-26.
6. Han, S., Medioni, G. 3Dsketch: Modeling By Digitizing with a Smart 3D Pen, Proceeding of fifth ACM international conference on Multimedia(1997), 41-49.
7. Massie, T. A Tangible Goal for 3D Modeling, IEEE Computer Graphics and Applications, vol.18, no.3(1998), 62-65.
8. Gregory, A., Ehmann, S., Lin, M. inTouch: Interactive Multiresolution Modeling and 3D Painting with a Haptic Interface, Proceedings of IEEE Virtual Reality Conference(2000), 45-52.
9. Schkolne, S. Pruett, M., Schroder, C. Surface Drawing: Creating Organic 3D Shapes with the Hand and Tangible Tools, CHI-2001, 261-268.
10. Fitzmaurice, G., Balakrishnan, R., Kurtenbach, G., Buxton, B. An Exploration into Supporting Artwork Orientation in User Interface, CHI-99, 167-174.

What Are You Looking At?
Newest Findings from an
Empirical Study of Group Awareness

Minh Hong Tran[1], Gitesh K. Raikundalia[2,1], and Yun Yang[1]

[1] CICEC – Centre for Internet Computing and E-Commerce
School of Information Technology, Swinburne University of Technology
PO Box 218, Hawthorn, Melbourne, Australia 3122.
{mtran, yyang}@it.swin.edu.au
[2] Internet Technologies & Applications Research Lab (ITArl)
School of Computer Science & Mathematics, Victoria University
PO Box 14428, Melbourne City MC, Australia 8001.
Gitesh.Raikundalia@vu.edu.au

Abstract. *Real-time, distributed, collaborative writing systems* are useful tools allowing a group of distributed authors to work on a document simultaneously. A very important factor in achieving effective and efficient collaborative writing is the incorporation of *group awareness* (GA). GA conveniently provides comprehensive knowledge about the status of a document and activities other authors perform upon the document. However, far more work needs to be carried out in determining exactly what *awareness elements* (awareness information, such as where users are viewing within a document versus where they are working on a document) are required in collaborative writing. This involves empirically determining which elements are more important than others for support.

The authors report results and findings of an empirical, laboratory-based study of GA elements. These findings are completely novel since no other empirical study of GA elements has been done. The findings guide designers in developing relevant mechanisms supporting GA.

1 Introduction

Real-time distributed collaborative writing systems (RDCWS) facilitate the task of joint authorship in a distributed environment. Various RDCWS have been produced over the years, such as GROVE [1], SASSE [2] and ShrEdit [3]. However, only a small number of such tools are widely used in the real world. A major reason for this lack of usage is that existing RDCWS have not yet been able to match the diversity and richness of interaction, which is provided in face-to-face interaction.

One example of the use of a RDCWS is in synchronous composition of essays. Collaborative essays may be used in teaching, such as in learning about negotiation of meaning (see [4]). However, in a workplace situation, a RDCWS may not necessarily be used to write an entire document in one sitting. Participants may use email or workflow to write parts of a document in an asynchronous manner, whilst writing

M. Masoodian et al. (Eds.): APCHI 2004, LNCS 3101, pp. 491–500, 2004.

other parts together synchronously. Participants may have an initial meeting to agree and work on the structure and content of the document together at the same time, leaving participants to finish the document separately at different times. On the other hand, medical researcher colleagues of one of the paper's authors work on a document at different times, only to come together *at the end of the process* to finalise the document. These medical researchers find greater efficiency in finalising the document together at the same time rather attempting to finalise it separately at different times.

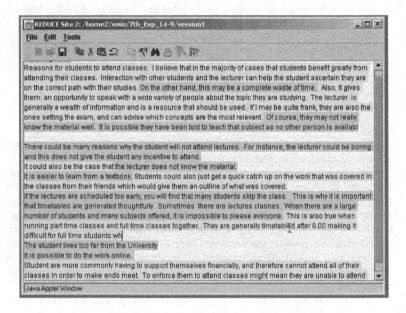

Fig. 1. REDUCE collaborative editor

Figure 1 shows *REDUCE*—Real-time Distributed Unconstrained Cooperative Editor [5]—used in our research. The Figure shows the tool being used by two users in writing a document. The two colours represent the text entered by each user. To be extremely brief for space reasons, the reader can understand REDUCE as simply being like a collaborative form of Microsoft Word or other word processor.

Perceiving and understanding the activities and intentions of other members of a collaborating ensemble is a basic requirement for human interaction. In face-to-face interaction, people find it naturally easy to maintain a sense of awareness about whoever else is present in a workspace, what others' responsibilities are, what others are doing and where they are located. However, when group members are geographically distributed, supporting spontaneous interaction is much more difficult due to various reasons such as limited capabilities of input and output devices, restricted views or weak communication [6]. To support distributed collaborative writing most effectively and efficiently, RDCWS must provide *group awareness* (GA) ([6, 7]).

GA is defined as "an understanding of the activities of others, which provides a context for your own activity" [3]. GA plays an essential and integral role in cooperative work by simplifying communication, supporting coordination [1], managing coupling, assisting "anticipation" [6] and supporting "convention" [7]. In collaborative writing, GA provides users with sufficient knowledge about the status of a document itself and past, current or future activities other users perform upon the document.

Gutwin and Greenberg [6] have proposed various *awareness elements*. Awareness elements represent fundamental awareness information required in supporting group awareness. Examples of awareness elements include knowing others users' current actions or knowing others' working areas in a document.

It is highly important to study such elements as they indicate what information is required in providing group awareness. This information reflects how group awareness is supported during collaboration, and therefore what types of functionality *awareness mechanisms* can provide. Awareness mechanisms in the literature include those such as *radar views* [8] or *distortion-oriented views* [9]. Radar views, for instance, provide a "birds-eye" (overall) view of a document. Thus, the element of knowing others users' current actions means that some sort of novel mechanism requires development to show whether all other users are either currently pulling down a scrollbar or entering text into the document or pulling down a menu, etc.

The objectives of this research are to:

- investigate what awareness information is important in supporting group awareness, and
- differentiate the importance of different awareness information (e.g., Is it more important to know past actions carried out by users or to know current actions being carried out?)

Although Gutwin and Greenberg [6] have proposed a set of awareness elements in their conceptual framework for workspace awareness, they have not experimented with these elements. Thus, they have not published empirical results related to the two objectives above. Hence, the novel contribution of this paper is to present experimental results for awareness elements and provide findings for awareness support based upon these results. These findings can therefore be used to develop new and more effective mechanisms beyond the current limited set available for supporting group awareness. The results reflect which awareness information is more important in designing mechanisms compared to other awareness information.

2 Related Work

As indicated in the last section, the closest work related to the authors is that of Gutwin and Greenberg who proposed awareness elements. These researchers have yet to provide empirical results for their awareness elements.

Apart from fundamental awareness information, the awareness mechanisms that represent this information are worth noting. The current set of mechanisms includes the most well-known ones of telepointers [10], radar views [8], multi-user scrollbars [2] and distortion-oriented views ([9]). For example, telepointers provide information about other users' presence and their activities, and radar views convey information about other users' locations in the workspace. Systems can also incorporate audio and video facilities for supporting communication [11].

3 Research Methodology

The research involved conducting laboratory-based usability experiments to determine the importance of different awareness information. REDUCE was selected as the editor for experiments because it has been adopted by the prestigious ACM SIGGROUP (Special Interest Group on Supporting Group Work) as a demonstration collaborative editor for trial worldwide and it provides almost no GA support, allowing determination of awareness information from scratch.

The usability experiment involved ten pairs of subjects, excluding the pilot pair, working on three writing tasks, including *creative writing* (CW) (e.g., writing short essays from scratch), *technical document preparation* (DP) (e.g., writing research papers) and *brainstorming* (BS) (e.g., generating ideas about a topic). An example of a BS task is for participants to write a document answering the question, "Why do or do not university students attend lectures?". The document formed will then encapsulate problems with student attendance and may possibly contain solutions to this problem. An example of a CW task (like ones used at [4]) is an essay written in answer to, "To what extent do you agree/disagree with this statement? Parents are the best teachers". These three categories were used for two main reasons. First, these categories represent a wide range of collaborative writing tasks. Second, the categories require different styles of collaboration. For instance, DP involves greater structure than the other two types of writing. The types of awareness information that are needed in different contexts of collaborative writing are found by using these varied tasks.

Table 1. Experimental task allocation

| | | \multicolumn{10}{c|}{Experiments} | | | | | | | | | |
		0	1	2	3	4	5	6	7	8	9
Verbal. first	CW	⊠									⊠
	DP			⊠			⊠				
	BS								⊠		
Silence first	CW				⊠		⊠				
	DP							⊠			
	BS		⊠			⊠					

Key:
CW: creative writing task
DP: technical document preparation task
BS: brainstorming task

Subjects performed collaborative tasks in pairs. In each pair, subjects were located in two visually-isolated subject rooms and participated in a two-and-a-half hour session, which included half-an-hour of training in REDUCE and the following activities.

Experiment (1 hour): Each pair performed two writing tasks of the same category, one task *with* verbal communication for thirty minutes and another task *without* verbal communication for thirty minutes. Five pairs started with verbal communication first (verbal first) and five pairs started without verbal communication first (silence first), as shown in Table 1. Conducting the experiments with and without support of verbal communication allowed identification of problems users had and the workarounds users resorted to when verbalisation was absent.

Questionnaire and interview (1 hour): Subjects filled in a questionnaire, which included nineteen five-point questions (ranging from 1-"not at all important" to 5-"very important") and seventeen open-ended questions[1]. Subjects also took part in an interview to discuss awareness information and awareness mechanisms they needed when performing tasks. The five-point scale questions allowed users to rank the importance of different awareness information. The open-ended questions allowed free responses and gave the subjects the freedom to suggest and comment on various awareness support mechanisms. This paper, however, focuses on the results of analysing the five-point scale questions.

The ten pairs were allocated to perform the three tasks such: 4 pairs worked on CW, 3 pairs worked on DP and 3 pairs worked on BS (Table 1).

The usability laboratory includes two subject rooms and one control-and-observation room. For each subject room, there is a one-way glass window between the observation room and the subject room. Apart from an observer making notes of observations, Hypercam [12] was used to capture entire sessions as movie files for analysis later. A drop-down blind over the window between the two subject rooms allows the two subject rooms to be separated visually. The laboratory contains auditory equipment allowing: verbal communication via intercom devices between the observation room and the two subject rooms, or between the two subject rooms.

4 Results of Awareness Study

This section presents the results of analysing the five-point scale questions. The results were useful in differentiating the importance and necessity of different awareness elements. The five-point scale questions were analysed to:

- calculate the mean, median and standard deviation of each five-point scale question
- construct the distribution of responses for each question

It should be noted that *each question represents one awareness element*. Thus the importance of an awareness element is determined by the mean of the corresponding question. The higher a mean is, the more important that awareness element is.

Table 2 shows awareness elements sorted by the values of their means. The top four most important awareness elements rated by subjects were **being able to comment on what other users have done** (4.53), **knowing actions other users are currently taking** (4.50), **having a communication tool** (4.50), and **knowing where other users are currently working** (4.50). Interestingly, these four elements were equally rated "very important" by 55% of the responses (as seen in Figure 2).

The distribution of responses to each element is examined. Figure 2 illustrates overwhelmingly the importance of the ability to comment on other authors' work. No responses indicated it was unimportant to comment on what other authors have done, nor were there respondents who were doubtful about this issue. Merely 5% of the respondents were not sure whether it was important to know other authors' current

---

[1] Due to space reasons, the questionnaire could not be included in an Appendix. However, the five-point scale questions from it are found in Table 2. The open-ended questions are not relevant to this paper.

actions, or to have a communication tool (when they do not have the support of verbal communication) or to know other authors' working areas in a document.

Table 2. Scores of Awareness Elements

Awareness elements	Mean	Me-dian	Std Dev
15. Being able to comment on what other users have done	4.53	5	0.51
10. Knowing what actions other users are currently taking	4.50	5	0.61
19. In the case of nonverbal communication, having a communication tool that supports communication between users	4.50	5	0.61
7. Knowing parts of a document on which other users are currently working	4.50	5	0.61
2. Knowing tasks for which other users are responsible	4.35	4	0.75
14. Knowing if other users know what I have been doing	4.25	4	0.72
1. Knowing who is in the workspace	4.15	4	0.81
16. Knowing if other users are satisfied with what I have done	4.10	4	0.64
8. Knowing parts of a document at which other users are currently looking	3.95	4	0.83
13. Knowing to what extent a portion of a document has been completed	3.85	4	0.88
17. Having voice communication	3.80	4	1.11
9. Knowing what actions other users are going to take in the future	3.75	4	1.07
11. Seeing the position of other users' cursors	3.70	4	0.80
12. Knowing to what extent you have completed your work compared to the extent others have completed their work	3.50	3	0.76
6. Being able to view the list of past actions carried out by a specific user	3.40	4	1.14
3. Knowing how much time has elapsed since other users have used REDUCE	3.40	4	1.23
18. Having video communication	3.25	3	0.97
5. Knowing how long other users have been in the workspace	2.40	2	1.19
4. Knowing where other users are geographically located	1.68	1	0.95

Two of these elements concern communication. This reflects the importance of awareness mechanisms allowing suitable communication amongst users in order to author a document effectively. The results also show that knowing whatever the other users are doing currently in the task—be it entering text into the document, reading help on the tool, etc.—is one of the most important things that a user wants to know about other users. Knowing exactly the parts of a document where other users are working is also highly important.

4.1 Knowing Tasks for Which Other Users Are Responsible

Almost all subjects found this an important issue, of which about half consider support for knowledge of others' responsibilities to be extremely important (Figure 3).

Yet awareness mechanisms hardly address this form of awareness. In all of the experiments, the subjects spent a certain amount of time discussing their strategy to complete a writing task, and more importantly, assigning responsibilities to each subject. Hence, ignorance of others users' responsibilities is unhelpful in collaboration and thus new tools that conveniently present these responsibilities are required.

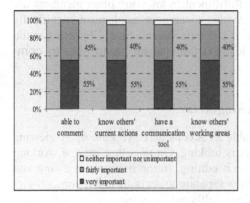

Fig. 2. Four most important awareness elements

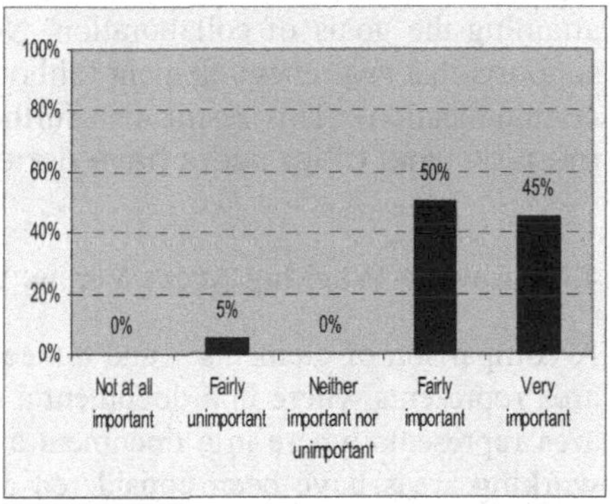

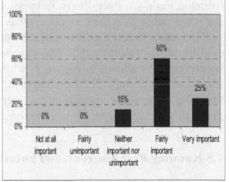

Fig. 3. Knowing tasks for which others are responsible

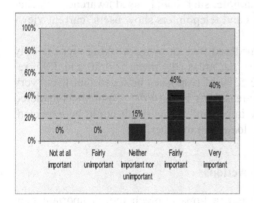

Fig. 4. Knowing if other users know what I have been doing

Fig. 5. Knowing if others are satisfied with what I have done

4.2 Knowing if Other Users Know What I Have Been Doing

The far majority of subjects' responses fell within the range from "fairly important" to "very important" (Figure 4). This result indicates that encouraging confidence in user *A* regarding the understanding of user *A*'s contribution by other users assists collaboration. Therefore, a mechanism continually tracking the contributions of users can be used to provide assuredness to any user that the other users are collaborating effectively with that user.

4.3 Knowing if Other Users Are Satisfied with What I Have Done

As shown in Figure 5, most respondents believed it to be at least reasonably important to know whether other users are satisfied with what I have done. A positive result here is unsurprising as it would be expected that since a group desires to achieve synergy, then members would experience fulfillment in knowing other members are attaining the goals of collaboration. No existing awareness mechanism specifically supports this awareness element (although it can be achieved simply by using audio communication). This result also further justifies the element being able to comment on what other users have done.

4.4 Knowing Working Areas Versus Viewing Areas

A comparison of elements 7 and 8 (see Table 2) is considered (Figure 6). A viewing area represents where in a document a user is looking. On the other hand, a working area represents where in a document a user is editing. In the literature, viewing and working areas have been considered as two separate aspects of conveying activity (e.g., [13]). In real-time collaborative writing, although viewing and working areas are usually the same, in certain cases they can indeed be different. Unfortunately, none of the existing, implemented awareness mechanisms distinguish between a user's viewing and working areas. For example, such widely used awareness mechanisms as multi-user scrollbars, radar views and telepointers show users' current viewing areas rather than their working areas.

This study found that the subjects considered that knowing working areas is only slightly more important than knowing viewing areas (the mean is 4.50 and 3.95, respectively). As shown in Figure 6, while 55% of responses believed that it is "very important" to know other users' working areas, only 15% of the responses considered knowing other users viewing areas "very important". This result could be expected, given that users are after all *working* on a document together.

4.5 Knowing Past, Current, and Future Actions

From Figure 7, knowing other users' current actions is much more important than knowing their past or future actions. Overall, knowing users' future actions is slightly more important than knowing their past actions, however, this difference is not significant.

5 An Effective Co-authoring Session

From the results covered, it is now possible to gain an idea of what awareness is required for an effective, efficient and fulfilling session of collaborative writing. In summarising the results, a fruitful session involves the following use of awareness, although the use is not an exhaustive coverage of all awareness required for such a session.

The session involves effective communication amongst participants to achieve successful authoring of the document. This means both real-time discussion as well as asynchronous remarks given by users to one another. If more than textual communication is required, users feel they can collaborate effectively mostly with voice communication.

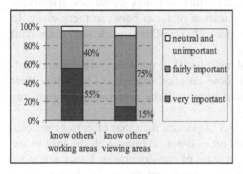

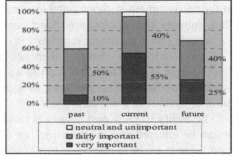

Fig. 6. Working areas versus viewing areas

Fig. 7. Knowing past, current and future actions

Users need to be clear on what other users will contribute to the document as well as exactly what parts other users are working on during the session. Users feel the need to have access to the various actions that others are carrying out currently with the tool. That is, users wish to be highly knowledgeable of what others are doing in the session.

Users want to know if other users are aware of what they have been doing with the document. This helps them to be reassured that other users are interested in or keeping track of what they have been doing. If user A knows other users are keeping track of what they are doing, one can infer that user A would feel much less need to communicate to others about what they are doing, which would improve the efficiency of collaboration.

Along with this previous awareness element, user A also wishes to know that other users are satisfied with the current state of their contribution to the document. This would suggest the user derives fulfillment and confidence in making their contribution to the document. This is understandable given that authoring is meant to be a collaboration, that synergy is required in working together and that members rely on one another's contribution to author the document successfully.

6 Conclusion

This paper has presented the results of an experimental study of group awareness in real-time distributed collaborative writing. To the best of the authors' knowledge, this is the first empirical study that has attempted to differentiate the importance of different awareness elements. The results yield a number of noteworthy insights.

The results suggest that knowing where others are working in a document, compared to where they are viewing, is worth further investigation. Current mechanisms such as telepointers, multi-user scrollbars or radar views, do not achieve this. Hence, new mechanisms that address where users are working, and separate this from where they are viewing, may indeed be very useful.

The awareness elements with the highest and second-highest means and medians include the ability to comment on what others have done and to confer via a communication tool. These results reinforce that users truly felt they could not effectively author a document without suitable communication of ideas between themselves. In fact, subjects strongly believed their own comments on others' work were important for working on a document together.

Users like to know that the others are taking interest in what they are doing or following their work. They also wish to know how satisfied other users are about their work, which is relevant feedback in a group situation where members rely on one another to achieve a common goal.

The ability to view past actions is much less important than that of current actions. It can be inferred that keeping track of what other users' actions with the tool in the past were is of little relevance to the current state of the document. Users are more interested in what others have contributed, as a whole, so far to the document (as discussed in the last paragraph).

References

1. Ellis, C., Gibbs, S., Rein, G.: Groupware: Some Issues and Experiences. Communications of the ACM. 34(1) (1991) 39–58
2. Baecker, R., Nastos, D., Posner, I., Mawby, K.: The User-centred Iterative Design of Collaborative Writing Software. In: Proceedings of InterCHI '93. (1993) 399-405
3. Dourish, P., Bellotti, V.: Awareness and Coordination in Shared Workspaces. In: Proceedings of the ACM Conference on Computer Supported Cooperative Work (1992) 107–114
4. Irvin, L.L.: http://www.accd.edu/sac/english/lirvin/ExercisesNCTE.htm
5. Yang, Y., Sun, C., Zhang, Y., Jia, X.: Real-time Cooperative Editing on the Internet. IEEE Internet Computing. 4(1) (2000) 18–25
6. Gutwin, C., Greenberg, S.: A Descriptive Framework of Workspace Awareness for Real-Time Groupware. Computer Supported Cooperative Work. 11(3-4) (2002) 411–446
7. Grudin, J.: Groupware and Social Dynamics: Eight Challenges for Developers. Communications of the ACM, 37(1) (1994) 92–105
8. Gutwin, C., Roseman, M., Greenberg, S.: A Usability Study of Awareness Widgets in a Shared Workspace Groupware System. In: Proceedings of ACM Conference on Computer Supported Cooperative Work.. Boston, Massachusetts, 16–20 Nov. (1996) 258–267
9. Greenberg, S., Gutwin, C., Cockburn, A.: Using Distortion-oriented Displays to Support Workspace Awareness. In *Proceedings of the HCI'96* (1996) 229–314
10. Greenberg, S., Gutwin, C., Roseman, M.: Semantic Telepointers for Groupware. In *Proceedings of Sixth Australian Conference on Computer–Human Interaction* (1996) 54–61
11. Bly, S., Harrison, S., Irwin, S.: Media Spaces: Bringing people together in a video, audio and computing environment. Communications of the ACM. 36(1) (1993) 28–47
12. Hyperionics Technology, LLC.: Hyperionics. http://www.hyperionics.com/
13. Benford, S., Bowers, J., Fahlén, L., Greenhalgh, C., Snowdon, D.: User Embodiment in Collaborative Virtual Environments. In: Proceedings of the ACM Conference on Computer-Human Interaction (1995) 242–249

Cultural Usability in the Globalisation of News Portal

Tina Wai Chi Tsui[1], John Paynter[2]

University of Auckland
[1] wtsu009@ec.auckland.ac.nz
[2] j.paynter@auckland.ac.nz

Abstract. The paper aims to identify areas of web usability in the News Portal industry that may be culturally specific so that web designers would target these areas when designing web sites. It also explores the current state of globalising these web sites in terms of catering for languages of users. Findings indicates that cultural preferences are shown to exist in terms of the number of animations used in the web page, the graphical density and length of the web page, navigation menu display, colour and family, male and female related images. In addition, it was found that majority of the web sites from the sample does not cater for language of different users.

1 Introduction

The number of web sites are expected to reach 200 million by 2005 (Palmer, 2002), so creating websites that effectively responding to user needs is *"critical"* in order to obtain competitive advantage. Having an effective international E-Commerce strategy is thus a necessity. Many web usability models, frameworks and guidelines have been developed to measure the level of usability and guide developers and managers to create effective web sites; only well-designed sites will acquire and maintain custom (Nielsen & Norman, 2000; Lais, 2002). Since the reach of the web is global, it is almost certain that there will be complexities associated with determining what is a usable web site due to differences in individual preferences, the diversity of language, culture and religion that may impact the measurement of usability components (Becker, 2002).

Culture affects the aesthetics preferences users have for web sites as well as other usability components. However, web site design generally remains locally customised and lacks consideration for the cultures of other nations. Thus web sites are limiting their ability to reach to the users around the world. Users place more value on web experience, as opposed to the technology behind the web sites. Thus the study of culture is important, especially when the diversity creates barriers for web sites to attract audiences. Site designers often do not pay enough attention to this issue. Unless other cultures are considered, the ability of web sites to effectively reach the users multinationally is limited. Thus culture and usability are merged into a single entity "Cultural usability" or "Culturability". How these cultural preferences may affect the degree of a web interface design is thus the core of this study.

M. Masoodian et al. (Eds.): APCHI 2004, LNCS 3101, pp. 501-510, 2004.

While proclaiming that premature standards would lead to failure (Marcus, Cowan & Smith, 1989) due to the complexity of culture, the main objective of this research is to understand the role of culture in web interface design. We explore how culture varies in preferences and how such variations could be used in designing web interfaces. The value of this research is not restricted to academics and web developers. It is hoped that the issues that emerge here will aid web developers and E-Businesses in raising the awareness of the importance of culture in web interface design as part of an effective international E-Business strategy.

2 Literature Review

2.1 Culture Defined

Hofstede (1991, cited in Simons 2001) defines culture as the pattern of thinking, feeling and behaviour that individuals learnt during a lifetime. It is the *"collective programming of the mind"* that distinguishes members of one group from another. Cultural studies are important especially in globalisation of E-businesses. The operation of cultures differs; what is liked by one culture will be disliked by another. Recognising cultural differences is the first step to identify potential opportunities for businesses wanting a multinational presence (Scheider & Barsoux, 2003). While culture exists between groups of people, organisation, districts and across countries, we focus on culture at the *international level*, the differences or similarities of culture on an international perspective.

While it is informative to study countries individually, it is difficult and infeasible to develop web sites that dynamically adjust to the culture of each country. A useful way of exploring cultural similarities in the world is to study culture in clusters. Robbins & Stylianau (2003) group countries into six clusters based on their similarities. China was not included in any cluster, but with an online population of 46 million[1], studying the cultural preferences for this country would seem prudent. Thus China has been added as a separate cluster. Figure 1 provides an illustration of country clusters. It will be the basis on which web sites in this research will be grouped and evaluated.

2.2 Cultural Usability

As the web site is the instrument that E-businesses use to interact and communicate visually with users it is important that it is designed to facilitate usability. Usability is defined as "the extent to which a product can be used by specified users to achieve specified goals with effectiveness, efficiency and satisfaction in a specified context of

---

[1] http://www.nua.ie/surveys/how_many_online/index.html

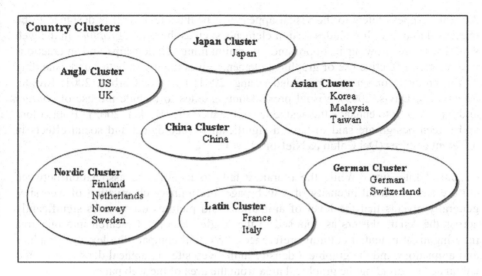

Figure 1 – Country Clusters

use" (ISO 9241-11: Guidance on Usability, 1998)[2].   One must develop a web site that closely matches user needs and requirements. When users interact with an interface, how they use the system and how they perceive where certain things is located are influenced by their culture (Shneiderman, 1998). Thus culture and usability should not be separated. Understanding how culture influences these areas could help create a cultural usability measurement. Cultural preferences exist that effect user satisfaction, performance and quality expectation of web sites (Badre, 2000; Tsikriktsis, 2002; Simon 2001). The basic principle behind this research is that issues of culture and usability remain cannot be separated in web interface design.

Following a literature review and initial web site observations, four areas of usability are identified: Graphical Intensity, Object Arrangement, Appeal and Language Variety as will as their components.

Language Variety - *Language* plays an important culture-specific variable in web design (Kukukska-Hulme, 2000; Hillier, 2003; Badre, 2000). A web site is virtually inaccessible when users do not understand its content. Without a common language, shared meaning could not exist and true communication would not take place (Schiffman, Bednall, Cowley, O'Cass, Watson & Kanuk, 2001, p382; Becker, 2002).

Object Arrangement - The *placement of web objects* and the *alignment of text* have been suggested to be culturally specific (Kang, 2001; Kang & Corbitt, 2001; Badre, 2000). Navigation menu and advertisement placement are also included in this category to be tested for cultural variation.

---

[2] http://www.usabilitynet.org/tools/r_international.htm

Appeal - Appeal refers to the visual appearance of the site, how it is designed to be presented to users. It includes design elements such as the use of *graphics* in the web site. These are growing in importance in maintaining relationships and interactions with users. Effective use of graphical elements gives the user a better understanding of the products or services provided (Kang, 2001; Kang & Corbitt, 2001; Eroglu, Machleit & Davis, 2003). Visual presentation extends to include the use of *colours* and *page layout* to enhance the aesthetics of the web site (Becker, 2002). Both colour and screen design are said to have a significant psychological and social effects in different cultures (Del Galdo & Nielson, 1996).

Graphical Intensity - While the literature fails to identify the association between culture and graphical intensity of a web page, preliminary observation of web sites generally reveals that the level of animations and pictures used varies significantly across the Asian clusters as opposed to the Anglo clusters. Research into this area may highlight potential cultural preferences. We will compare the level of graphics and animations and the graphical density in the web site. Graphical density is a ratio calculated by dividing the graphical area from the area of the web page.

Figure 2 illustrates the conceptual framework of cultural usability that will be applied to the newspaper/news portal context. The model shows the four areas that are associated with cultural usability as identified in the literature ant their respective constituents. By identifying the areas and variables in the model, we will investigate whether there are cultural preferences.

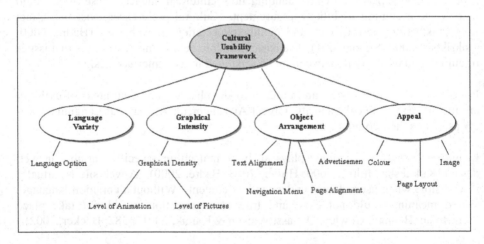

Figure 2 – Conceptual Model

Does culture impact web site design? This raises the question of whether these identified cultural influences are an accurate outlook on reality. Our aim is to identify the *culturally specific variables* that are apparent in developing a global web interface as well as providing an insight into how E-Businesses address the language barrier issue. Figure 3 provides an illustration of the research questions.

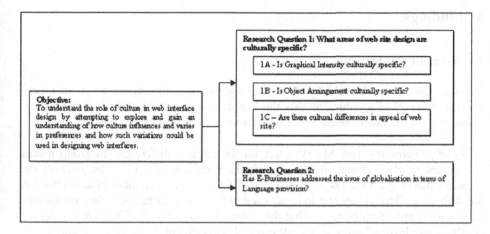

Figure 3 – Research Questions

3   Methodology

Content analysis was chosen for this research with the aim to explore any current cultural variation in a global context. Human coding is used for this research. A codebook and coding form were created and documented for use in analysing web sites. Two coders were used to enhance reliability of the results.

Judgment sampling was used to identify the sample for data analysis. Businesses included in this study were selected from Alexa.com's[3] top 100 sites sorted by each language. The most frequently visited sites represent user preferences, since usability relates to web sites retention of users. Each sample was assigned to an appropriate country cluster using Hofstede's framework. Having a sample that is large enough to deem generalisable to the population is important for social science. The sample size of 103 sites used for content analysis is deemed appropriate (Hair, Anderson, Tatham & Black, 1998[4]).

ANOVA was used to test whether significant differences exist between variables in the graphical intensity aspect of the web interface design. This statistical method was used as the variables satisfy the assumptions of this test. Graphical representation were used for all other design aspect of the web site as we cannot satisfy the random sampling assumption of a chi-square test and we could not obtain a software package that allowed us to conduct cluster analysis using both ordinal and nominal variables.

---

[3] http://www.alexa.com
[4] Page 12

4 Findings

4.1 Graphical Intensity

Level of Graphics - The ANOVA test for the cultural differences in group means against the level of graphics reveals the F statistics of 1.293 is less than the critical value of ± 2.198. There are no cultural differences in the number of pictures used.

Level of Animation - The ANOVA test for the cultural differences in group means against the level of animation used reveals the F statistic of 7.177. This exceeds the critical value of ± 2.198. There are cultural differences in the number of animations in the web sites. The Tukey method was used to test group differences that are statistically significant. Results reveal that the China cluster (a mean of 3.38) has a significantly higher level of animation to all other clusters except Asian (2.71), compared to Anglo (2.00), Nordic (2.35), German (2.00), Latin (2.32) and Japan (2.00). Sites in the China cluster have an intense use of animations.

Graphical Density - The ANOVA test for the cultural differences in group means against the graphical density reveals the F statistic of 3.600 exceeds the critical value of ± 2.198. There are cultural differences in the graphical density of the web sites. Turkey test reveals that Japan has significantly lower graphical intensity (1.22) than other clusters except countries from the Anglo cluster. The other clusters have higher graphical density, Nordic (2.43), German (2.31), Latin (2.16), Asian (2.21) and China (2.23). This represents low graphical usage by sites in the Japanese cluster.
China has a significant high usage for Animation, but exhibits no apparent difference in graphical density compared to other clusters. We explore this issue further and test the variable that makes up the formula for Graphical density to see if we could explain this apparent contrdiction. The page length across clusters was tested.

Page Length - The ANOVA test for the cultural differences in group means against the length of web page reveals the F statistic of 2.612 is greater than the critical value of ± 2.198. There are cultural differences in length of web page across cultures. Turkey test reveals that there are differences in terms of page length between the Latin (mean 2.68) and Asian (2.64) clusters against the China cluster (3.62).

4.2 Object Arrangement

Text Alignment – Web sites in all of the countries from the Anglo, Nordic, German, Latin and Japan clusters display text horizontally. A minority of the web sites from the Asian cluster displays text both horizontally and vertically (14%), while the majority still aligns text horizontally (86%). Half (54%) of the sample web site from the China cluster aligns text both horizontally and vertically and 46% horizontally.

Navigation Placement - Results reveal that the Anglo, Nordic and Latin clusters appear to have no significant differences in terms of the preferences for navigation arrangement. 44% of the web sites from the Anglo cluster use vertical menus, 33% use horizontal and only 11% use both. Similar patterns are obtained for web sites from the Nordic cluster where 43% use vertical menus, 30% horizontal and 26% both. Latin cluster also shows no significant preferences with 21% using vertical menu, 37% horizontal and 42% both. Significant preferences can be observed for all other clusters. 62% of web site from the German cluster use vertical menus and only 31% horizontal and 8% both. This indicates preferences for vertical menu display. For web sites from the Asian cluster, 71% use horizontal menus, 7% vertical and 14% both. Similar patterns are observed with web sites from Japan. 67% use horizontal menus, 22% vertical and 11% both. China displayed significant preferences for horizontal menus with all of the web sites from the cluster showing this arrangement.

Advertisement Placement - Results reveal that there appears to be no prominent preferences in terms of advertisement placement for the Anglo, German, Japan and China clusters. Advertisement placement preference for the right side of the web page can be observed for the Nordic (57%), Latin (75%) and Asian (64%) clusters.

In the main web sites shun utilising pop up advertising methods. The clusters avoid them: Anglo (100%), Nordic (78%), German (92%), Latin (84%) and Japanese (89%). Web sites from the Asian and China clusters show no discernment in this.

Page Alignment - Results indicated that while there is no strong single preference regarding the page alignment for the Latin and Asian clusters, significant preferences can be observed for Anglo, Nordic, Japan and China clusters. 78% of the web sites from the Anglo cluster, 61% from the Nordic cluster and 69% from the German cluster show preferences for left web page alignment. 56% of the web sites from the Japanese cluster show preferences for centre alignment of web page and 54% of the web site from the Chinese cluster show preferences for using the whole web page.

4.3 Appeal

Colour - Results indicate that while there is no strong colour preference for the Nordic and Latin cluster, significant preferences in colour choice were identified for all other clusters. 78% of the web sites from the Anglo cluster strong preferences in using the colour blue. 67% of the web site from the Japan cluster shows strong preferences in using white. Although, 54% of the web sites from the China cluster show strong preference in predominantly utilising the colour red, this percentage is not significant.

Image - The results for each image category can be summarised as follows: There are no preferences for using flag, animal or festival related images; usage level for all clusters are below 30%. Results for iconic images indicates that over 50% of the web sites from the Anglo (56%), Nordic (70%), German (62%), Latin (58%), Asian (64%) and Japan (78%) clusters use icon images on their web page. However, the use of iconic images is less for the web sites from China (46%). Results for family related images reveals that more web sites from both Nordic (61%) and China (69%) clusters tend to use pictures that are family related, as opposed to web sites from Anglo (14%), Japan (14%) and German (38%) clusters. There is no observable preference in terms of using family related pictures for the Latin (47%) and Asian (43%) cluster web sites. There is no observable preference in terms of using male pictures for clusters: Anglo (56%), Nordic (48%), German (54%), Latin (58%), Asian (43%) and China (54%). However, web sites from Japan show low (11%) preference. Web sites from China (77%), Nordic (65%), German (62%) clusters contain female images. There is no observable preference for using female pictures for the Latin (53%) and Asian (50%) clusters, and only a 22% of Japanese web sites do so.

Page display - Web sites from all clusters: Anglo (78%), Nordic (74%), German (62%), Latin (68%), Asian 93%, Japan 78% and China (92%) have asymmetric pages.

4.4 Language Provision

67% of the web sites from the Anglo cluster, 74% of the web sites from the Nordic cluster, 77% of the web sites from the German cluster and 79% of the web sites from the Latin cluster do not cater for languages other than that used in the country. While only 50% of the web sites from the Asian cluster offer other language options, 67% of the web sites from Japan and 54% of the web sites from China offer other languages.

5 Conclusion

Cultural differences are shown to exist in terms of the number of animations used in the web page, the graphical density and length of the web page, but there are no cultural differences in terms of the number of graphics used. Thus web developers should concentrate on these four elements when designing the web page for a specific country. This could mean increasing the use of animation and page length if targeting audiences from China and less animation when targeting those in Japan. Other than the navigation menu, object alignment of text, page and advertising placement are shown to have no cultural differences. Thus web developers should focus on menu display aspect of object arrangement. For German audiences, web developers could consider using vertical navigation menus as opposed to horizontal and the opposite applies if China, Asian or Japan audiences are the target audience. All clusters prefer asymmetric page layout. However, colour, family, male and female images exhibited cultural preferences. There was no preference for the usage of other images: icon, flag, animal and festival, among the clusters. Thus web developers could consider using blue colouring when targeting countries from the Anglo clusters but use white colours for Japanese audiences. Web developers might choose not to utilise male images in a Japanese web interface, not to use female images when targeting Japanese or audiences from the Anglo clusters and not to use family related images for Anglo, Japan and German audiences. Conversely, web developers may want to utilise female images when designing web interfaces targeting China, Nordic and German audiences and use family related images when targeting China, and Nordic audiences. The majority of the E-Businesses have not addressed the issue of globalisation in terms of language provision.   Only Japan has addressed language barriers.   E-Businesses should take into account the preferences identified in this research and the lack of language provision and translate them into practical cultural usability guidelines to design web sites that cater for the needs of their different audiences.

Culture affects the user expectations of web site quality.   Different cultures have differing degrees of perception and satisfaction about a given web site.   It is clear that we cannot just have one interface to cater for global audiences; web interfaces need to be culturally dimensional and capable of rapid change.

The study is exploratory in nature and focus only on cultural differences at the international level and examines only the news portal industry.   Although there are limitations to this research, the findings are still very useful for web developers and E-Businesses showing design elements that are culturally sensitive and those that are not.   The research had made a significant finding in cultural usability and initiated a need to focus on developing a set of web interfaces for different cultures.   This study generates a set of generic guidelines that web developers and E-Businesses can follow.   It also clarifies some of the design issues that lead to cultural preferences and provides direction for web developers and E-Businesses to follow in the very competitive Internet market highlighting factors that can be employed as an effective globalisation strategy.

References

1. Badrc, A.N., (2000), "The Effects of Cross Cultural Interface Design Orientation on World Wide Web User Performance", *GVU Technical Report Number: GIT-GVU-01-03*, Available: http://www.cc.gatech.edu/gvu/reports/2001/abstracts/01-03.html.
2. Becker, S.A., (2002), "An Exploratory study on Web Usability and the Internalization of US E-Business", *Journal of Electronic Commerce Research (3:4)*, 2002.
3. Del Galdo. E. & Nielson, J., (1996) "International User Interfaces", Katherine Schowalter, USA, 123-177.
4. Eroglu, S.A., Machleit, K.A., & Davis, L.M., (2003), "Empirical Testing of a Model of Online Store Atmospherics and Shopper Responses", *Psychology & Marketing (20:2)*, pp.139–150, February 2003.
5. Hair, J.F., Anderson, R.E. Tatham, R.L., Black, W.C. (1998). Multivariate Data Analysis 5th Edition. Prentice-Hall International.
6. Hillier, M., (2003), "The Role of Culture Context in Multilingual Website Usability", *Electronic Commerce and Applications*, Vol 2, 2003.
7. Kalin, S, (1997), "The Importance of being multiculturally correct", Computerworld, (31:40), pp. G16.
8. Kang, K.S., (2001), "Cultural Issues of User Interface Design in Implementing Web based Electronic Business", *Proceedings of OZCHI 2001*. Faculty of Information Technology, University of Technology.

9. Kang, K.S., & Corbitt, B. (2001), "Effectiveness of Graphical Components in Website E-commerce Application – A Cultural Perspective", *The Electronic Journal on Information Systems in Developing Countries*.

10. Kukulska-Hulme, A. (2000), "Communication with users: insights from second language acquisition", *Interaction with Computers*, 12, November.

11. Marcus, A., Cowan, W.B., & Smith, 1989, "Colour in User Interface Design: Functionality and Aesthetics", *CHI Proceedings*, May 1989.

12. Nielsen, J., (1999), "Web Usability: Past, Present, and Future". Available at: http://webword.com/interviews/nielsen.html.

13. Nielsen, J., & Norman, D.A., (2000), "Web site usability: Usability on the web isn't a luxuary", Informationweek online, Jan 2000. Available at: http://www.informationweek.com/773/web.htm

14. Palmer, J.W., (2002), "Website Usability, Design, and Performance Metrics", *Information Systems Research* (13:2), June 2002.

15. Robbins, S.S., & Stylianou, A.C., (2003), "Global Corporate website: an Empirical investigation of content and design", *Information & Management*, 40.

16. Schiffman, L., Bednall, D., Cowley, E., O'Cass, A., Watson, J., & Kanuk, L. Consumer Behaviour, 2nd Ed, Prentice Hall.

17. Schneider, S.C. & Barsoux, J.L., (2003), "Managing Across Cultures", 2nd Edition, Pearson Education Limited, England.

18. Shneiderman, B. (1998). Designing the user interface. Strategies for effective human-computer interaction. 3d ed. Addison-Wesley.

19. Simon, S.J., (2001), "The Impact of Culture and Gender on Websites: An Empirical Study", *The Database for Advances in Information Systems* (32:1), Winter 2001.

20. Tsikriksis, N., (2002), "Does Culture Influence Website Quality Expectations? An Empirical Study", *Journal of Service Research*, (5:2), Nov 2002.

Collecting, Organizing, and Managing Non-contextualised Data by Using MVML to Develop a Human-Computer Interface

Michael Verhaart[1], John Jamieson[1], and Dr. Kinshuk[2]

[1] Eastern Institute of Technology, Hawke's Bay
mverhaart@eit.ac.nz, jjamieson@eit.ac.nz
[2] Massey University New Zealand kinshuk@massey.ac.nz

Abstract. One aspect of information technology increasingly being researched is organizing and managing the huge repository of data and information available. This is particularly relevant in the context of the explosion in Internet use. As knowledge is gathered from the Internet the ability to retain and recall the knowledge is becoming more and more difficult and complex. Computer based techniques are often used to store and manage this data. Managing the data typically takes two forms; firstly cross-referencing to the original source as in a bibliography or reference list, or secondly collected by an individual, such as purchasing a book, creating a hard copy of a web page, and so forth. With the Internet, web based tools and techniques are frequently employed to manage this information. This may be by maintaining a list of links as in a portal to actual web content, by using the available web search engines, or saving the content into a personal electronic knowledge space. This paper will look at the ways this knowledge could be collected and the smallest unit required to organize small pieces of data. The ability to map this into an electronic medium is then explored, and a prototype meta-data schema is then discussed. Finally, the Human-Computer Interface will be discussed that could enable the data to be organized in a variety of ways based on the meta-data schema.

Methods keywords: XML, multimedia meta language.

1 Introduction

In an educational context researching, organizing and distributing information and knowledge are fundamental processes. In this setting vast amounts of information are often read, recorded and categorized. As well, prior work is merged, organized and placed into the relevant context. It is in this context that the paper will look at knowledge collection. The ability to reuse portions of content is a major area of research and development at the present time. Many Institutions, both academic (for example, DLNET from Campus Alberta and University of Mauritius Learning Objects Repository) and commercial (for example, Cartridges in Blackboard [1]) are setting up repositories that store and

M. Masoodian et al. (Eds.): APCHI 2004, LNCS 3101, pp. 511–520, 2004.

manage chunks of pedagogical information, under the heading of "Learning Objects". One noticeable design structure is the looseness of the definition of what constitutes a learning object. The Learning Technology Standards Committee (LTSC) of the Institute of Electrical and Electronics Engineers (IEEE) defines a learning object as, "any entity, digital or non-digital, which can be used, re-used or referenced during technology-supported learning" [6]. Others, such as DLNET introduce pedagogy into the definition and define it as, " a structured, standalone resource that encapsulates high quality information in a manner that facilitates learning and pedagogy. It has a stated objective and a designated audience" [2]. These definitions are very broad and include, not only, the computer-based components, but also people, places, things and ideas [13]. Unfortunately the flexibility of the Learning Object definition also restricts its usefulness, especially when trying to allow for automatic structuring of domain content. The model proposed in this paper refines this definition and clarifies a distinction between the learning object and the resources attached to the learning object. The Resource Definition Framework (RDF) as specified by W3C defines a structure that can be used to describe resources, but requires that a vocabulary is developed for a specific set of users. This paper will consider such a resource definition model and present a meta-data schema that will assist in the use and reuse of resources whether for learning objects or media objects required for other purposes.

1.1   The Sniplet, a Contextualized Piece of Information

Verhaart [12] developed a learning management system that managed a type of learning object called "Sniplets", where the sniplet was defined as **a piece of knowledge or information that could be represented by one overhead transparency.** Figure 1 illustrates the basic architecture.

The Sniplet includes content descriptors such as Creator id, Backbone taxonomy id, title, description, summary, multimedia id and bibliographic id, and had supporting entities including: a backbone taxonomy [5], where the sniplet is placed in a structure created by experts in the domain; a multimedia entity where associated elements such as graphics, animation, sound, video, slideshows, documents can be defined; a bibliographic entity where any books, articles, papers that were used can be acknowledged.

This sniplet, or group of sniplets could be used by existing learning object meta-data repositories and with the addition of an xml definition file, could programmatically transform the sniplet into a web page. The major drawback would be that the sniplet would then be frozen in time and lose its dynamic nature. This could possibly be solved by using a hyperlink to the original resource, however access issues could be a mitigating factor here.

1.2   Developing a Resource Definition

As the sniplet library grew there evolved a need for a better way of organizing and retrieving attached objects. Images were to be displayed "on-screen" and

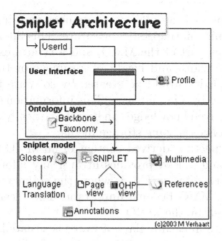

Fig. 1. Sniplet Architecture

made suitable for printing. So two images were created, and the appropriate image was used relative to the context. Meta-data was also required for image captioning. This concept has evolved into a need to describe media objects in a consistent way that allows for the multiple output requirements. Hence a model that would allow multiple representations of the same media object was developed. How we gather and collect knowledge and information, and the way it varies depending on context required further investigation. This paper looks at the current state of media objects both physical such as a book or a person, and electronic, such as a multimedia file (image, sound and video) and any current standards that are available to manage their meta-data. An XML based vocabulary is then proposed, that allows multiple representations of a wide variety of media elements. This is followed by a discussion on how different technologies can be used to automatically generate suitable outputs to mobile agents, adaptive technologies and different output or content delivery devices.

2   Capturing Knowledge

The resources attached to a learning object require information and knowledge useful and usable in a variety of contexts. In order to facilitate discussion on the resources, this paper will refer to a resource as a multimedia object (MMO). The MMO contains all information related to the resource, and may be made up of several files, including both derived and the unwritten knowledge that needs to be annotated [4]. In a general context, files such as audio, a graphical image or a video are the typical MMO's under consideration. The actual definition for the MMO becomes more definitive as the paper progresses. To begin, there are two points of view that will be considered. Firstly what the computer "sees" and secondly what the human user sees when either of them works with a MMO.

The viewpoint of a computer is an abstract statement pertaining to the use and manipulation of electronic information by software. This information is the derived knowledge that forms part of the MMO, and a typical example of this derived knowledge would be width and height of an image or the duration of a video segment. This knowledge would be created by software to be used by software and is seldom created by a human user. This information exists in many forms and structures. The derived knowledge can be automatically captured from the MMO that has an existence on some storage media.

From a human user perspective, derived content of an MMO is not enough to successfully describe it, and indeed provides little if any information about actual content or context of the object. This is where the actual context and the "scene" depicted within the MMO become important. The "scene" is what is happening or what is depicted by the MMO.

Consider 2a and 2b, where in each a glass of water is situated on a table. A typical description of the image would be "glass of water". The context of the scene describes more in depth knowledge about the scene. The "glass of water" scene context could contain the type of glass, type of table, time of day, season, lighting, just to name a few. A vocabulary is required to describe this scene in such a way that it is understandable by the computer.

Fig. 2. Two Images of "a glass of water".

3   The Multiple Forms of Data and Information

Resources can exist in a variety of forms, and include; implicit or physical elements (such as books, people, and objects), and electronic objects (such as multimedia (text, images, animation, sound and video) and collections (learning objects, presentation objects e.g. PowerPoint slides).

Implicit resources will require human annotated knowledge and in most cases do not have derived knowledge meta-data, whereas electronic resources have many common meta-data attributes and media dependant properties. Various standards exist that describe how the MMO's should look and their relative behavior when manipulated or used by software. These standards allow for software interoperability and MMO interchange. For example, one common Internet standard is the Multipurpose Internet Mail Extensions or MIME standard (http://www.iana.org). This standard uses the filename extension of an MMO file to determine how software will behave for a specific MMO. Typical mime definitions are:

```
image/jpeg jpg jpeg jpe
image/gif gif
application/octet-stream    bin exe com class
```

4   Media Vocabulary Markup Language (MVML)

To illustrate how the MMO is constructed, an image of a cartoon as shown in figure 3 will be discussed.

Fig. 3. Copyright cartoon

The image resource can be made up of several associated files

- Different images depending on the final output device. For example, a full sized image suitable for printing, and a reduced sized image for computer screen display.
- A sound file that describes the image that could be used in a presentation.

In order to manage the multiple files a meta-file needs to be created that uses a meta-vocabulary to describe the components. A Media Vocabulary Markup

Language (MVML) is being developed to allow for an electronic representation of the various media elements. In order to be useful, each resource object has an associated MVML file that contains the meta-data describing both the derived and contextual information associated with the file. As the object could be made up of many files the MVML file will contain a manifest of associated files, with their properties included. This will allow the object to be correctly displayed on various output devices, such as Computer Screen, Printer, PDA and even voice based systems.

For the image in figure 3, a simplified example of an MVML file structure is listed in figure 4.

```
<?xml version="1.0"?>
<mvml>
  <object>
    <file>
      <src>cCopyright.gif</src>
      <width>375</width><height>392</height>
      <type>IMG</type>
    </file>
    <half>
      <src>cCopyright^.gif</src>
      <width>289</width><height>239</height>
      <type>IMG</type>
    </half>
    <audio>
      <src>cCopyright.wav</src>
      <kbytelength>86</kbytelength>
      <type>SND</type>
    </audio>
  </object>
  <content>
    <longdesc>Cartoon of a fraudster holding a bank note saying "But they don't have a
copyright Notice on them anywhere ||"</longdesc>
    <alt>But they don't have a copyright notice on them anywhere ||</alt>
    <caption>Copyright</caption>
  </content>
  <info>
    <creator>Michael Verhaart</creator>
    <copyright>(c)1998. M Verhaart. All Rights Reserved</copyright>
  </info>
</mvml>
```

Fig. 4. MVML file for ccopyright.gif

It should be noted that this is a simplified example, and W3C RDF definitions are being incorporated into the language.

From the above example, information that may seem repetitive or irrelevant can be portrayed, however it gives the software something to work with and understand. Software would "know" what is happening in the "scene" of an image. Another strong supporting advantage is to do with video and audio files. These specific multimedia files can contain a rather large amount of derived knowledge but no knowledge of the auditory or visual content. This is where the mvml presents an important function.

For example, an audio file is 5 minutes long and recorded in stereo with no compression presenting a file of nearly 200MB. All derived content can be determined from the physical file, but what is the actual audio content all about? The MVML can describe a song, artist, genre, etc. Then the context of the song could state that the song was recorded from a live concert on a specific date and not recorded in a studio. As a second example, if an MVML file is attached to photographic, sound and video images from a digital camera then developing generic software to manage the MMO can be developed.

4.1 Multimedia Object (MMO:MVML) and Human/Computer Interfaces

Figure 5 illustrates a MMO:MVML framework and how a human or computer would interact with the system.

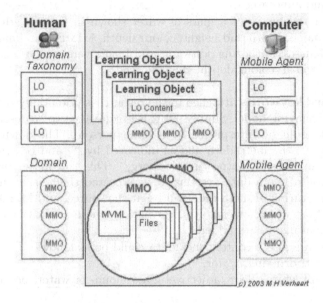

Fig. 5. MMO:MVML electronic repository, human and computer interfaces

The center column represents an electronic repository of Learning objects (LO) and/or MMOs. An MMO is made up of an mvml file and associated files, while a learning object can be made up of the learning object content and related MMO's. Note that individual MMO's could be used by multiple Learning objects. A human can interact with the repository either via a domain taxonomy that provides a structure to the repository, or using a search on the MMOs. The computer-assisted generation of content is probably the most significant benefit of the mvml structure. If a repository is structured in a consistent and uniform way, other systems could access the resources and produce meaningful results. For example, if a course was being developed on house building and an image of framing in a wooden house was required, electronic agents could search through servers that have mvml compliant resources and would produce accurate results plus if context and content meta-data were present, associated knowledge. Indeed it should be possible for much of the content to be automatically generated.

4.2   Vocabulary

Figure 4 shows a simplified XML vocabulary that has been prototyped to illustrate concept. Development is under way to use the W3C RDF framework, the Dublin Core definitions and those from the Publishing Requirements for Industry Standard Metadata [9] to enable interoperability between the various meta-data systems. It is envisioned that the mvml file would be split into two sections, derived and annotated.

If we reconsider the image of a glass of water shown in figure 2, **derived data** is the image name, width and height, colour depth, MIME type image/gif, file size, date of changes, authoring software, and image version. For example, <derived> height, width, colour depth, etc</derived>

The **context** and **keywords** attached to the resource is potentially the most beneficial part of the mvml model. Simply put this is equivalent to "a description of the object that could be interpreted by a blind person". The downside is the necessity to create the meta-data and as indicated by [8] and contributors in the IFETS Forum website (http://ifets.ieee.org/). This is a major problem in terms of adoption of meta-data systems. It is expected that, using internet technologies, the capturing of meta-data will be at the source, and MMO's will have mechanisms that will allow for synchronization where a MMO has been copied and additional meta-data added.

Using the glass in figure 2 context metadata could be as follows;
Keywords: Cooking, drinking, water.
Context: A <u>half full</u> [state] <u>clear</u> [adjective] <u>glass</u> [noun] of <u>water</u> [noun] on a <u>table</u> [situation].
Context could contain;

- A **situation**, glass of water on a table, this could also include the time of day, environment, and so forth.
- A **state** for a glass empty, half full, full.
- An **interpretation**, a glass of water, still life abstraction, purity, etc.
- A comment that describes the **mood**, for example a soothing piece of music.

Using a picture of flowers (deliberately not shown), keyword and context metadata could be as follows; **Keywords**: Bouquet, painting, plant. **Context**: A <u>bouquet</u> [state] of <u>red</u> [adjective] <u>roses</u> [noun] in a <u>vase</u> [situation].

This example is incomplete since the given context is too simplistic to derive a suitable mental picture. The context could include type of vase, surface it is standing on, condition of the roses, the arrangement of the bouquet,etc.

5   The System Interface

As an MMO will have a standard and structured vocabulary, MVML meta-data will allow standard interfaces to be developed that could be used to allow for the sharing of objects, either by maintaining a link to a repository or maintaining a "personal" repository. Textual or graphical interfaces such as "Kartoo" (http://www.kartoo.com) can be built utilizing the MVML meta-data, and could also be easily transformed into a variety of alternative interfaces (such as an audio based interface). From a human perspective, mvml repositories allow for Boolean or Natural Language Processing (NLP) searching based on keywords or context, and the construction of context specific resources in a structured and consistent format. From a computer perspective, an index of MVML repositories can be maintained. These could be searched by mobile (electronic) agents where a criterion is specified. For example, tell me about Drinking water, would search through both the keyword and context information to produce a summary. If the search was changed to "Give me a history of Drinking water" dates would also be included and the agent would return the MMOs or LO's in date order. The MMO could produce the data using the MVML metadata for the appropriate device, PDA, voice or PC screen. The output would be adapted to the appropriate user interface.

6   Conclusion

This paper discusses the development of a Multimedia object (MMO) that uses a markup vocabulary, MVML, to define a collection of related resource objects suitable for use by adaptive technologies. Further, the MMO:MVML model can be used as a knowledge manager, as context can be added as meta-data to any resource object. This will further allow context searching that is a goal of the Semantic Web.

In short the MVML provides for:

- Uniform structure to derived knowledge.
- Device input and output independence.
- Self documenting vocabulary.
- Context enabled multimedia elements.
- Versatility in usability.
- Software independence.

Foremost considerations in developing the MVML structure are, is it simple to generate, and are there real advantages that will encourage its adoption? In the first case using XML standards to define the structure and incorporating universal standards such as the Dublin Core and RDF will allow for simple generation and transportability among various systems, and as system interfaces are developed that manage MMO:MVML's many advantages could be realized.

Development of the MVML Specification is work in progress and can be found at http://is-research.massey.ac.nz/verhaart/

References

1. Blackboard Course Cartridges (http://cartridges.blackboard.com)
2. Brief Introduction to Learning Objects in DLNET (2002). Retrieved 15 June, 2002, from *http://www.dlnet.vt.edu/working_docs/reports/ARI_LO_Def.pdf*
3. Campus Alberta Repository of Educational Objects (2003). Retrieved March 9, 2003, from *http://careo.ucalgary.ca/cgi-bin/WebObjects/Repository.woa?theme=careo*
4. Charles F Goldfarb and Paul Prescod (2002) *XML Handbook 4th Edition.* , Prentice Hall NJ 07458, ISBN 0-13-065198-2, pg 653
5. Guarino,N and Welty, C. (2002, Feb) Evaluating Ontological Decisions with OntoClean. *Communications of the ACM*, Vol 45. No 2. pp 61-65
6. IEEE Learning Technology Standards Committee (1999) Learning Object Metadata. Retrieved June 15, 2002, from *http://ltsc.ieee.org/doc/wg12/LOM3.6.html*
7. IFETS Forum website (http://ifets.ieee.org/)
8. Phillips, Lee Anne (2000) *Using XML: Special Edition.* , Que. ISBN 0-7897-1996-7, pg 494
9. PRISM: Publishing Requirements for Industry Standard Metadata Version 1.2h (2003). Retrieved November 21, 2003 from *http://prismstandard.org/*
10. RDF Vocabulary Description Language 1.0: RDF Schema (Work-in-progress) (2002). Retrieved May 31,2002 from *http://www.w3.org/TR/2002/WD-rdf-schema-20020430/*
11. University of Mauritius Learning Objects Repository (2003). Retrieved October 1, 2003, from *http://vcampus.uom.ac.mu/lor/index.php?menu=1*
12. Verhaart M., Kinshuk (2003). An Extensible Content Management System using Database and Internet Technology. In D. Lassner, C. McNaught (Eds.), *EdMedia 2003 Conference Proceedings*, Norfolk, USA: AACE, 152-155 (ISBN 380094-48-7)
13. Wiley, David (2000) Connecting learning objects to instructional design theory: A definition, a metaphor, and a taxonomy. Retrieved April 27, 2003, from *http://reusability.org/read/chapters/wiley.doc*

Common Industry Format: Meeting Educational Objectives and Student Needs?

Karola von Baggo, Lorraine Johnston, Oliver Burmeister, and
Todd Bentley

Swinburne Computer-Human Interaction Laboratory, Swinburne University of Technology,
Hawthorn, Victoria 3165 Australia
{kvonbaggo, ljohnston, oburmeister, tbentley}@swin.edu.au

Abstract. The Common Industry Format (CIF) provides an industry standard
for the reporting of usability test results. The ongoing success of the CIF will in
part be determined by the support of future IT professionals. The work reported
in this paper describes our experience in adapting and using the CIF in an introductory Human-Computer Interaction course at an Australian University. It
also examined subsequent student perceptions about the usefulness and ease of
use of a CIF-style template, and the degree to which students were able to generate CIF-compliant reports. It was found that few modifications to the template were required to meet the educational objectives of the course. Overall,
students were neutral as to whether the CIF was a useful or easy to use device,
but were able to generate moderately compliant reports. Comments from students indicated that more formal training in the CIF might be useful.

1 Introduction

The National Institute of Standards and Technology (NIST) proposed that a common
standard (to be known as the Common Industry Format) be used to report user-based
evaluations of software. NIST envisages that:

> "The overall purpose of the Common Industry Format (CIF) for Usability Test Re-
> ports is to promote incorporation of usability as part of procurement decision-
> making for interactive products. It provides a common format for human factors
> engineers and usability professionals in supplier companies to report the methods
> and results of usability tests to consumer organizations." [1].

A key factor in the success of the CIF will be industry acceptance of the format as
a reliable source of consumer information. Some work has already been done in this
area (e.g., Boeing and Oracle [2]). However, if the standard is to be successful it will
also need the support of future managers, software developers and the Human-
Computer Interaction (HCI) profession. One way of achieving this is to include it as
part of the training of the professional body. A positive experience with the CIF in
undergraduate academic courses should enhance its future acceptance in the industry.
In addition, future IT professionals will be better placed to make informed interpretations of CIF reports and if the need arises, better prepared to generate their own CIF

M. Masoodian et al. (Eds.): APCHI 2004, LNCS 3101, pp. 521-530, 2004.

reports. Therefore, it is important to consider how the CIF can be incorporated into an academic teaching environment.

Initially, we were concerned about the degree to which we would have to explicitly support student learning of the CIF. Teaching time is valuable, and ideally we hoped that the material produced by NIST about the contents of the CIF (i.e., the template and guidelines) would stand alone (along with appropriate instruction about usability testing). Thus, we wished to determine what, if any, additional support might be required to assist students' use of the CIF. We did this by exploring student perceptions of the CIF (particularly whether they found it easy or difficult to use) and their ability to write CIF-compliant reports. The former being important as even if students were able to generate a CIF-compliant report, a negative experience would not assist in gaining acceptance for the CIF. An additional aim was to explore whether students whose first language is not English faced problems in using the CIF. Given the global nature of the software industry, it is important to ensure that people with a wide range of English skills are able to use the CIF effectively.

The study described here used the CIF as the basis of a reporting template for two assignments in an introductory HCI subject at an Australian university. In the initial phase of the study, it was necessary to modify a draft version of the CIF to meet the educational objectives. In the second phase, surveys were performed to determine students' attitudes towards using the CIF. In the final phase student reports were examined to determine their level of conformity with the CIF guidelines.

2 The CIF

At the time this study was conducted the CIF was a draft proposal to standardise the manner in which user-based evaluations are reported. As of December 2001, it has become an ANSI standard (ANSI/NCITS 354-2001), and is being proposed as an international standard for reporting on usability testing. NIST provides the CIF in three forms: a detailed description, a template and a checklist. The detailed format provides short examples, explanations and elaboration on key points. The template format consists of the main section headers and brief descriptions of what is required for each section. The checklist is similar to the template but in a checklist format rather than document format.

Our aim in introducing the CIF to introductory HCI students was to provide them with a report writing format that (a) has industry support and therefore will be of value to them when they complete the course, (b) is replicable, and (c) provides students with a better understanding of the process of usability testing. The CIF standard appears to fulfil these requirements in that it provides well-motivated standardised guidelines that promise industry support. In addition, the structure of the report not only provides guidelines about how to write a usability report, it also ensures that practitioners think about important issues such as participant selection and context of use.

2.1 The CIF in an Educational Context

In an educational environment the aim is to expose students to a variety of evaluation techniques. The students in our course were required to (a) conduct and write a report on the heuristic evaluation of a website, and (b) conduct and write a report on a user-based evaluation of their modified version of the original website. We envisaged that students could use the CIF as the basis of their reports. However, the CIF is specifically designed around summative user-based evaluations, which posed a problem. We considered using a completely different format for the heuristic evaluation. However, it was decided that a modified version of the CIF was preferable. We realised that problems might arise in attempting to make the CIF fit a task it was not designed for, but it was argued that this potential problem was outweighed by the benefits to the students of maintaining some level of consistency. Thus, we developed a version of the CIF that accommodated a heuristic approach. In addition, minor modifications were made to both versions to match other educational aims of the course. The following section describes in detail how the CIF was modified for the needs of our course.

2.2 Customizing the CIF

Two modified versions of the CIF template were used (see Table 1), one specific to heuristic testing and the other maintaining the user-based testing focus. An important aim of the course is to demonstrate the iterative nature of software development and evaluation. Therefore, discussion sections were added to both versions of the template.

The heuristic evaluation template required relatively major changes to the results sections of the CIF, and several minor changes to the wording of sections (i.e., participant to expert). This was to ensure it fitted with an evaluation procedure based on Nielsen's 10 usability heuristics [2]. The user-based template did not differ significantly from the original CIF layout, except for changes to the basic format outlined above. Table 1 lists the modifications made. In addition to the templates, students also had access to an unedited copy of the CIF guidelines, a CIF check list and the NIST sample report, "DiaryMate". However, we cannot be sure as to the extent students made reference to any of these documents apart from the template itself.

Table 1. Summary of modifications made (Legend: H = Modifications made to CIF for heuristic testing; U = Modifications made to the CIF for user based testing)

Section in CIF	Report	Modifications
Title Page	-	Unchanged
Executive Summary	H, U	Results were described verbally at a high level, rather than detailed statistics
Introduction		
Full Product description	-	Unchanged
Test Objectives	U	Required the description and justification of usability goals

Table 2. Continued.

Section in CIF	Report	Modifications
Method		
Participants	H	Changed to 'Expert Reviewers' Relevant details in this section were still collected.
Tasks	-	Unchanged
Test Facility	-	Unchanged
Participant Task Instructions	H	Removed
Results	H	Summary of the results from heuristic evaluation. All subsections were removed
Data Analysis	U	The need to describe statistical tests performed was removed
Presentation of Results	-	Unchanged
Discussion	H, U	Section added to allow students to discuss and make recommendations based upon results.
Future Work	H	Section added to allow students to describe intended changes to their prototype

3 Student Perceptions of the CIF

The second phase of the study involved assessing student perceptions of how easy the CIF was to use and the degree to which they felt it was useful to them. The following section describes the method used to survey student perceptions.

3.1 Method

3.1.1 Participants
Undergraduate and graduate students undertaking an Introduction to Human-Computer-Interaction subject at an Australian university were the participants in this study. There were 173 students enrolled in the course at the end of semester. The students were surveyed twice. 103 of the 173 completed the survey after completing the heuristic report and 77 after completing the usability report. The section on Procedure discusses the low return rate for Survey 2. The median age of participants in both surveys was 23, with a range of 19-50.

3.1.2 Materials
To assess the student's perception about the usefulness and ease of use of the CIF, we developed a survey using our own scales. It contained four main sections: *Demographics*, *Experience and Motivation*, *Attitudes Towards the CIF*, and a *Comments* section.
Section 1: Demographics: The aim of this section was to obtain demographic information from the participants. Respondents were asked to report their age, gender, the country they were born in, their number of years in Australia and the language spoken at home when growing up. The last three questions were important to help distin-

guish between students with English as a first language (EFL) and those with English as a second language (ESL).

Section 2: Experience and motivation: The aim of this section was to gauge the pre-existing skills of participants and their aspirations towards further work in HCI. These questions were designed to provide an indication of their level of motivation towards doing well in HCI (i.e., *I would like to work in the usability area in the future*). They also determined the level of involvement in using the CIF during the course of their project (i.e., *My contribution to the project required extensive use of the CIF*). Questions relating to the students self-rated proficiency in English were included to establish whether the ESL group were less confident of their English skills than their EFL counterparts (e.g., *I speak English well*).

Section 3: Attitudes towards CIF: This section contained three scales: *Usefulness, Ease of Use* and *Skill Acquisition*. There were six Usefulness questions related to the usefulness of the CIF in report writing (e.g., *The CIF helped me understand what is required to conduct a usability study*). There were eight questions about the Ease of Use of the CIF template related to its understandability, clarity and consistency (e.g., *I feel that someone with limited usability experience would have no trouble using CIF*). In both Section 2 and 3 Participants were asked to respond to each of the statements on a five-point scale from "Definitely Agree" (5) to "Definitely Disagree" (1).

Section 4: Open-ended comments: An open ended question was also provided at the end of the questionnaire to elicit any further comments that the participant had pertaining to the CIF (i.e., *Is there anything else you would like to tell us about your experiences using CIFs?*).

3.1.3 Procedure
Both surveys were administered during a tutorial. The person administering the survey was not involved with the teaching or assessment of the students. The tutor left the room until all surveys had been collected. The survey was administered immediately after the first (heuristic evaluation) report was submitted in mid-semester and again after the final (user-based evaluation) report was submitted. The latter was an optional review tutorial. Many students took the option not to attend. For this reason, participant numbers in Survey 2 were not as great as in Survey 1.

3.2 Results

Student responses to the survey were entered into a database. To assess the internal consistency of the Usefulness and Ease of Use scales the Cronbach alpha coefficients were calculated. These were within the acceptable range for the Usefulness scale ($\alpha = 0.7695$) and for the Ease of Use scale ($\alpha = 0.7006$). These results indicated that a summation of scores within the two scales was justified and this was subsequently done.

3.2.1 Participant Experience and Motivation
The level of agreement with the statement "I would like to work in the usability area in the future" was used to gauge the respondent's level of motivation for using the

CIF. The mean response was only just above the neutral level ($M = 3.25$) indicating that as a group the students were ambivalent about furthering their knowledge of usability. Figure 1 shows that there appears to be a drop in motivation from Survey 1 to Survey 2. However, an independent t-test indicated this difference was not significant ($t(177) = 1.747, p > .05$). The overall low level of motivation probably reflects the fact that our HCI is a compulsory subject in degrees that have a heavy programming bias.

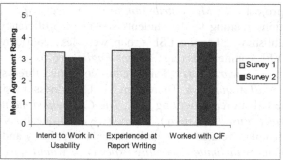

Fig. 1. Mean Agreement Ratings for Usability Work Intention, Experience in Report Writing and Work with CIF as a function of Survey.

Figure 1 also shows the mean agreement rating in Survey 1 and 2 for statements relating to their experience in report writing and their personal involvement with the CIF. Respondents rated their experience at report writing as just less than the Agree value ($M = 3.46$), indicating that they did not feel experienced in report writing. Their rating of involvement in using the CIF was also quite low ($M = 3.78$). This may reflect the fact that the assignments were group based and use of the CIF may have been delegated to one or two members of the team.

3.2.2 Participant Language Skills
In both surveys, students were asked to indicate what language they spoke when growing up. Students who nominated a language other than English were classified as English as a Second Language (ESL) group. The remaining students were classified as the English as a First Language (EFL) Group. Cronbach alpha reliability coefficients were calculated across the three self-rated English skills measures (speaking, writing and reading). The alpha value was high ($\alpha = 0.917$) indicating that a summation of scores over the two scales was justified. This was subsequently done and the two language groups were compared on their mean self-rated English skills.

Table 2 shows the mean self-rated English Skills for the ESL and EFL groups in Survey 1 and 2. A two-way non-repeated Analysis of Variance (ANOVA) (Survey x Language Group) indicated that there was a significant difference between the self-rated English skills for ESL and EFL groups ($F(1,175) = 102.37, p < 05$). The ESL group rated themselves as significantly less skilled in English than the EFL group, and there was no significant difference between the overall self-rated English Skills across Survey 1 and 2 ($F < 1$). There was no interaction between Survey and Language groups on self-rated English skills ($F < 1$). These results showed that the ESL and EFL groups were clearly differentiated by their English skills.

Table 3. Mean self-rated English Skills (SD in parentheses) and number of students as a function of Survey and Language Group[1]

	ESL	EFL
Survey 1	3.80 (.79), n = 59	4.87 (.36), n = 43
Survey 2	3.86 (.75), n = 47	4.81 (.42), n = 30

3.2.3 Student Perception of the CIF

The overall mean Usefulness rating was 3.71. Thus, as a group, the students agreed that the CIF was useful to some extent. Figure 2 shows the mean Usefulness Rating for the ESL and EFL groups in Survey 1 and 2. A two-way non-repeated ANOVA (Survey x Language Group) indicated that there was a significant difference between the two survey groups ($F(1,176) = 4.90, p < .05$). Overall, students rated the CIF as more useful in Survey 2 ($M = 3.80$) than in Survey 1 ($M = 3.61$). There was no significant effect of language group on the students' perception of the usefulness of the CIF ($F(1,176) = 2.60, p > 05$). There was no interaction between Survey and Language Group on perceived usefulness ($F < 1$).

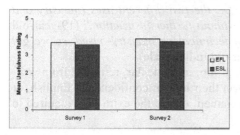

Fig. 2. Mean usefulness rating as a function of Survey and Language Group

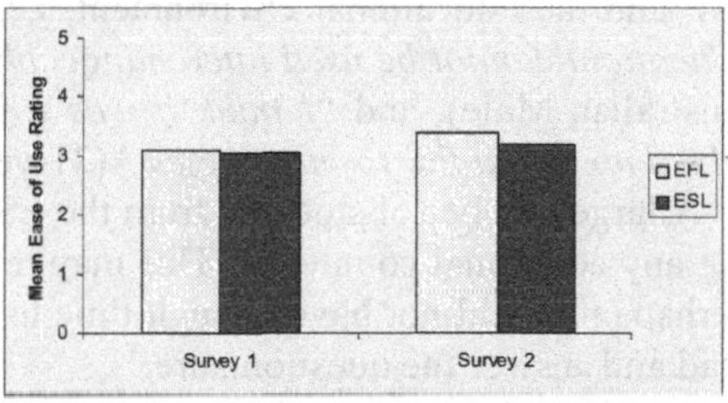

Fig. 3. Mean ease of use rating as a function of Survey and Language Group

The overall mean Ease of Use rating was 3.17 indicating that in general the students did not perceive the CIF to be particularly easy or difficult to use. Figure 3 shows the mean Ease of Use Rating for the ESL and EFL groups in Survey 1 and 2. A two-way non-repeated ANOVA (Survey x Language Group) indicated that, there was a significant difference between the two survey groups ($F(1,176) = 7.18, p < 01$). Overall students rated the CIF as slightly easier to use in Survey 2 ($M = 3.27$) than in Survey 1 ($M = 3.07$). Once again, this may be because the students felt more familiar with the CIF, having used it previously for their first report. There was a marginal effect of language group on the student's perception of how easy the CIF was to use ($F(1,176) = 2.75, p < 10$). The ESL students rated the CIF as being slightly less easy to use ($M = 3.10$) than the EFL students ($M = 3.22$). Thus, although the ESL students found the CIF useful, they tended to rate it as less easy to use than the EFL students.

---

[1] One student did not complete the English skills questions. However, their demographic data clearly indicated an ESL background and they are included in all other analyses.

There was no interaction between survey and language group on perceived usefulness ($F < 1$).

3.2.4 Comments Data

The comments data suggested that the CIF was relatively well received by some students. For example, a 28-year-old Japanese male wrote that the CIF was "*Very good, if only every subject has some standard format like CIF*" and a 22-year-old Swedish female wrote that "*It is good to use the CIF at university, to get familiar with it at an early stage before using it in a professional environment.*" However, some students did appear to have difficulties with its ease of use. For example, a 22-year-old Australian female indicated that "*A standard format is useful but this format is difficult to use.*" A number of students appeared to have difficulty with the terminology, e.g., "*It would be helpful if the English used was just a little more understandable*" (20-year-old Australian male) and "*...the section on data interpretation was very unclear.*" (21-year-old Australian male) and felt more instruction in its use would be beneficial, e.g., "*There should be more explanation on how to use the CIF*" (23 year old Thai male).

Two students felt that there was a conflict between the industry-based nature of the CIF and the educational environment, i.e., "*... the two different uses (industry and education) cannot be used interchangeably without further instruction.*" (19-year-old Australian Male), and "*I think it was a bit technical or industry-based, so we got mixed up with a few terminologies.*" (21-year-old Indian male).

A large number of students from the ESL group, in particular, refrained from writing any additional comments. This may reflect their lack of confidence in English, or perhaps they did not have enough time to comment due to the extra time required to read and answer the questionnaire.

4 Student Assessment Data

The final phase of the study involved examining the reports generated by the students using the CIF template. During marking, the tutors were asked to record the degree to which students completed each section in accordance with the CIF requirements. The sections were defined as in Table 1. If the student included all of the required material listed for each section of the template (regardless of quality and quantity), they scored 1 for that section. If they had none, or only part of the requirements, they were scored a 0 for that section. A value representing the percent of sections fully completed was calculated for each assignment. The assignments were completed in groups of 4-5.

The mean percent of sections fully completed for students in the first assignment was 55.8% ($SD = 25.6$, $n = 39$). In the second assignment it was 55.6% ($SD = 26.7$, $n = 38$). Students did not improve between the first and second reports. Unfortunately, we were unable to find equivalent data to compare this performance against. However, the overall quality of the work presented by students was good. The mean percentage grade for Assignment 1and 2 were 73.5% ($SD = 20.5$) and 77.5% ($SD = 12.37$), respectively. Informal feedback from tutors teaching the subject indicated that the quality of the reports seemed better than in previous semesters (all tutors had tutored the subject for at least one previous semester). All tutors agreed that the students had the most difficulty with the results section, particularly the data analysis section.

5 Discussion

Overall, the students did not perceive the modified CIF template particularly useful or easy to use. They found the CIF more useful for their user-based evaluation (second report) than for their heuristic evaluation (first report). However, this effect may simply be due to experience with the template. The students also found the CIF easier to use for the second report. Again, this may be due to their increased familiarity with the style of the format. It is likely that their knowledge of the CIF and its requirements was also increased due to the feedback that they received on their first report. In addition, students may have found the user-based version easier to understand and more useful because the CIF is specifically designed to support user-based usability testing.

There was no significant difference in the perception of usefulness of the CIF between EFL and ESL students. It would appear that neither language group perceived the CIF as particularly useful to them. However, the ESL found the CIF slightly less easy to use. One would expect the ratings of usefulness to be independent of English skills, as both groups should realise the value of the document. However the ease of use of a document can depend on these skills. Interestingly though, several EFL students did comment on the complexity of the CIF, indicating that the usability of the CIF itself could be improved. Comments from students indicated that more formal training in the CIF may be useful. It is suggested therefore, that class time needs to be devoted to explaining the requirements of the CIF, particularly in relation to the results section. This would also assist the ESL students who appeared to have difficulty interpreting the terminology used in the template.

6 Conclusion

Overall the students appeared to be under-whelmed by the introduction of the CIF into the curriculum. They did not perceive it as particularly useful or easy to use. However, they appeared to have a much better idea of the assessment requirements despite their less than enthusiastic reception of the tool. The fact that non-native speakers of English found using the CIF slightly more difficult suggests they need more help to understand what is required. We postulate that this is more an issue of training than of greater difficulty in use.

In conclusion, it was found that the CIF could be modified for the reporting of an alternate evaluation paradigm (namely heuristic evaluation), and that minor modifications were required to the template to fully meet the educational aims of the course. We remain committed to using our modified version of the CIF. However, in the future more consideration will be given as to how we introduce it to the students. This includes providing a greater amount of class time and additional documentation to assist in explaining its requirements. Hopefully, improvements in this aspect will also increase student perception of the usefulness and ease of use of the CIF that they will carry with them into their professional lives.

Acknowledgement

The authors acknowledge a grant of $1,000 from the Teaching and Learning Committee of the School of Information Technology at Swinburne University of Technology. This money was used for data entry related to the two surveys undertaken.

References

1.   NIST (1999) The IUSR Project: Industry Usability Report, White Paper, *National Institute of Standards and Technology*,
     http://www.itl.nist.gov/iaui/vvrg/iusr/documents/WhitePaper.html, Accessed 13/06/03.
2.   Morse, Emile (2002) Usability Reporting Document proves to be useful to industry developers, *National Institute of Standards and Technology*,
     http://www.itl.nist.gov/iad/highlights/2002/CIF.html. Accessed 13/6/03.
3.   Nielsen, J. (1994), Enhancing the explanatory power of usability heuristics. *Proc. ACM CHI'94 Conference,* Boston, MA, April 24-28, 152-158.
4.   NIST (2001) Common Industry Format for Usability Test Reports (version 1.1) *National Institute of Standards and Technology,* http://www.itl.nist.gov/iaui/vvrg/iusr/index.html, Accessed 30/4/02.

Accessibility: A Tool for Usability Evaluation

Daniel Woo and Joji Mori

School of Computer Science & Engineering, The University of New South Wales,
UNSW Sydney NSW 2052, Australia

Abstract. Infrastructure intended to support accessibility can be employed to provide useful information for the usability evaluation of graphical user interfaces. In this paper, we discuss how software infrastructure designed to augment assistive technologies for disabled users can be used to provide event information relevant to usability analysis. The problem is that extracting information about the interaction is difficult and there is no standard method for extracting complete event logs describing the interaction. Approaches to extract usability interactions so far have been ad-hoc, and on the whole quite complex to incorporate into logging systems. Encouraging support for accessibility generates a valuable, high-level channel of information for user interface evaluation and provides benefits to reach the broader user community.

Introduction to Usability Event Logging

It is important for usability analysts to understand what the user is doing when interacting with a system. If we are testing an application, we can observe users interacting with the application, ask the user to think aloud whilst using the system [1], take notes and use video and audio to record the session. We can complement these techniques with logs of events that are automatically generated by the software system.

Event logging is the process of generating time-stamped, window event information that can be analysed to measure user interaction. Useful results can be deduced from the time-stamped interaction logs, including the frequency of use of specific functions, where users spent most of their time, and the order in which users completed tasks. Log information can be derived directly from the low-level window operations or can be programmatically generated.

Quantitative methods that predict expected completion times like GOMS and Fitt's law [2] can be verified against the real usage data. With this information, inferences can be made about the usability of certain aspects of the interface. Perhaps on average, users accessed help more times than the developers would have expected. Or the time spent performing specific tasks was too long. Using the aggregated results over a number of users, logged event data can be used to validate statistical hypotheses, especially when comparing different interfaces to determine the more efficient software system.

M. Masoodian et al. (Eds.): APCHI 2004, LNCS 3101, pp. 531–539, 2004.
© Springer-Verlag Berlin Heidelberg 2004

Difficulties with Usability Event Logging

A major problem with event logging is that it is difficult to extract useful data. Hilbert [3] proposes a method where logging operations are inserted into the source code of an application, which is then sent to a server over the Internet for analysis. However, only applications for which source code is available can be analysed and developers must be encouraged to add meaningful information relevant for usability evaluation, in contrast to adding code-related debug information. Another way is to have intimate knowledge of the windowing system and write tools to be able to monitor the low level events [4]. A recent implementation for monitoring how people use multiple applications to complete a task has been based on the Common Object Model (COM) for Microsoft Windows based systems [5]. This technique requires that applications under test contain an embedded COM object to supply usability information. For web interfaces, the methods typically include monitoring web usage logs, creating alternative web browsers to extract more useful data about the interaction [6] or embedding commands within the pages to generate logs. The problem with these approaches is that significant work is required from developers to create complete and useful user interaction logs. Specialized knowledge of the window event manager is a requirement to extract usability data.

The primary reason usability logging is so difficult is because there is limited support from the operating system to supply meaningful information that is useful to the usability specialist. Thus the developer needs to come up with ad-hoc approaches to extract comprehensive usability data. The challenge is how to unify the process of generating useful logs across all applications on a particular operating system. The solution we propose is by leveraging technologies aimed to provide accessibility functionality. It will be shown that the high-level descriptions of interaction applicable to usability evaluation are available using technologies designed to provide services for accessibility. Accessibility APIs[1] provide a structured method for describing the visual appearance of the applications interface and usability analysts can use this information in the evaluation process, providing an additional channel of information to reconstruct the interaction.

Accessibility

With recent legislation changes [7], supporting accessibility is an essential requirement for software application vendors. This means that software applications should communicate seamlessly with 3rd party assistive technologies in addition to conventional input/output devices. The role of the application developer should be to concentrate on the core business of the software application whereas the assistive technology developer aims to provide alternative input/output technologies that enable impaired people to interact with the user interface. Major operating system providers have pro-

---

[1] API stands for Application Programmer's Interface and is a toolkit available to developers to be able to achieve certain tasks, in this case accessible applications.

vided software infrastructure that standardizes the way that user interface widgets are exposed to assistive software developers.

It was common for assistive developers to utilise undocumented or unsupported programming workarounds to make their technologies work. With the Accessibility APIs, such workarounds are unnecessary. If the application developers adopt standard user interface controls then little or no programming effort is required to make an application to work seamlessly with other accessibility technologies.

In the past, applications were developed specifically for the needs of disabled users (eg. Intellitalk [8]) and off-the-shelf or generic GUI applications were cumbersome or impossible to use with out appropriate assistive middleware. As a result of the assistive infrastructure support, any software application that adheres to the accessibility requirements can be used in conjunction with an appropriate assistive application.

Privacy is an issue that needs to be addressed with any logging of user events. This is still true for Accessibility APIs. Usernames and passwords need to be hidden from any assistive applications. The user must also be aware that they are being monitored and understand what information is being collected. In a controlled usability environment, this is possible because the user can be informed of the specifics of the test, but for other scenarios such as remote logging via the Internet, it may be an intrusion into someone's privacy to have their interactions logged.

Accessibility APIs

Overall, the features provided by the Accessibility APIs offer three different functions:

- A structured representation of the visual interface that describes the type of control, a name and location
- A notification mechanism that is triggered by changes to any of the visual controls
- An ability to interact with controls by sending events that simulate user interaction

The structured representation of the visual interface can be represented as a hierarchy of user interface objects and can be made available upon request to assistive application. At any point in time, a "snapshot" of the screen contents can be generated, revealing the active applications, the windows that are open, the user interface elements displayed within windows, the positions and sizes of the elements and the values of each of the elements. In addition, the front most application and user interface element that has the keyboard focus is also known.

On Mac OS X[2], the structured representation of an application is shown in Figure 1, the application contains a single window and within the window are several user interface objects. The Accessibility API provides a simple hierarchy, identifying each control and its current value.

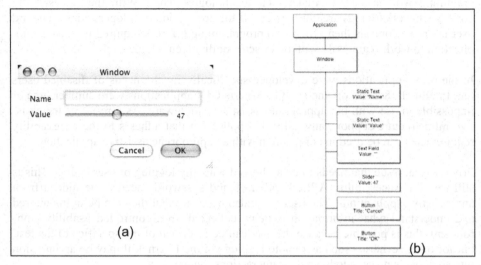

Figure 1. (a) Visual appearance of a window,
(b) Corresponding accessibility hierarchy

Changes in the user interface are important for accessibility applications to notify users that visual elements have been updated. Usually, the assistive application is sent notifications if the values of elements change, for example, the value of an updated text field, or possibly a button title changing. For a screen reader application, blind users could be notified of the current status of a progress bar.

Finally, the Accessibility APIs provide a way to programmatically control user interface elements in place of conventional mouse or keyboard control. Examples include selecting or clicking buttons, modifying text, or changing parameters with slider controls. This function allows an assistive application to remap inputs from a disabled user who could be using an alternative input device into specific events meaningful to the application.

Most major operating systems have incorporated some level of accessibility support. Table 1 provides a short description of features provided by different platforms.

---

[2] Current work is based around Mac OS X Accessibility functionality introduced in Mac OS X 10.2

Table 1 - Accessibility APIs on different platforms

Platform	API description
Apple	Mac OS X's Accessibility API [9]. Developers creating simple applications are by default adhering to the Accessibility API by using the standard GUI controls.
Microsoft	Microsoft Active Accessibility SDK [10]. Developers must explicitly set the interactive objects and what actions each object can perform.
Linux	Each windowing environment on Linux requires it's own API [11]
Java	The Java Accessibility API [12] means any Java application can be made accessible. Good for cross platform accessibility.

Comparison of Usability Evaluation and Accessibility APIs

The usability evaluator is interested in understanding what actions a user performed when confronted with a particular screen representation. Typically they are not focused on software code issues and would not be comfortable reading through tomes of time stamped event descriptions partially described with hexadecimal.

System event logs can be generated from a running software application but contain low-level information intended for software developers. By using system event logs in a usability session, a quantitative account depicting the entire user interaction can be stored and later analysed. If the system event logs are generated from low-level window manager events then the data will most likely contain too much detail for the typical usability test. Event logs typically contain machine specific data that offers little or no high-level information, for instance, clicking a specific button may be represented as a mouse down event at a particular screen location, with no reference to the actual button that was pressed.

Accessibility APIs provide a detailed representation of all user interface elements active at any particular point in time. There is sufficient detail to enable an assistive application to describe the appearance of all active applications. Unlike system event logs, the name of the user interface element and its relationship to the parent window and any child views contained within the element can also be derived. The information is more appropriate to the needs of the usability evaluator since it conveys events in terminology relevant to user interface design, not low-level system events.

The accessibility API outputs alone are not directly interpretable by the naïve reader, but with the appropriate tools can be converted into a simplified description of the user actions.

Usability testing can take advantage of accessibility functionality by logging the information provided through the accessibility APIs. At any point in time, the usability tester can get a representation of all the applications and the states of all the windows and controls as long as they conform to the accessibility protocols. Notifications of interface state changes can also be logged so that the usability tester knows specifically when the changes in the interface occurred. This information reveals useful information about the interaction that can be analysed.

Features Missing for Usability Logging

Accessibility APIs on different platforms have subtle differences in their implementations and thus, different logs will be extracted from each platform. There are also subtle issues that have been met with using accessibility for usability logging. Mac OS X doesn't provide a notification of buttons being selected through accessibility. The assumption is made that the interface will change based on the button click. Sometimes this is not the case, so in terms of usability logging, this is a feature that is missing. To extract this information, monitoring window events for mouse down occurrences along with accessibility achieves a more complete log of the interaction.

The Java accessibility API has been described to have problems with windows not notifying that they are being displayed [13]. Accessibility API developers need to understand the needs of usability analysts so that usability logging can benefit from APIs. If the concerns that are met, then a unified way of usability logging over operating systems is possible.

Incorporating Usability Logging Through Accessibility

Every application that is accessible can then be logged for usability. In most cases, the developer only has to include the standard suite of controls to provide accessibility support. This is because standard user interface controls such as buttons, text fields, sliders and other standard window objects usually adhere to the requirements of the Accessibility APIs. The developer only needs to be aware of the requirements of the Accessibility API if custom controls are created. For each custom control, attributes such as size, position, and value need to be specified and the events that the control can respond to must be defined.

It is a win-win situation for developers to use the accessibility APIs for application development. There is growing pressure on developers to make accessible software [7], so the incentive to develop for accessibility means that as a consequence, high-level usability data can be generated with negligible effort on the developers part. Likewise, those developers interested generating usability logging data can use accessibility aware controls to generate the log information, and indirectly can make their application accessible.

Example

To illustrate the type of information that can be derived from accessibility, Figure 2 shows a sequence of screen shots of user interaction with the Speech Preferences panel in Mac OS X. Figure 3 provides a trace of mouse clicks to illustrate the order of the tasks. This is an example of an application for which the source code is not available to the usability analyst and is based on work described in [14]. Accessibility provides a high-level description of a control, reporting the name, state or value. An additional application was used to monitor and record the accessibility information.
The example in Figure 3 is a sequence of the following steps: (a) Turn on the Text under the mouse check box; (b) Adjust the pause time before speech is spoken with the slider; (c) Change the text to speech voice from Victoria to, (d) Trinoids; (e) Turn off Speak the Phrase check box; (f) Turn off speaking highlight text with a keystroke. The final state of the interface is shown in (g). Time of the event is also presented in this diagram.

Discussion

We predict that Accessibility APIs will need to be adopted beyond computer systems and support should be provided on mobile technologies and other portable consumer devices. By combining accessibility with usability logging on mobile devices, usability testing of mobile technologies will be simplified.

Combining usability logs and other time-based data with video data is another research area we are working on ([14], [15]) Multimedia technologies can store, synchronize and playback usability information in a suitable form for usability analysts. More research into standardizing the representation of user interface events is required. We have described in detail the information that can be obtained through by using accessibility for usability testing, but not a format for how this data should be represented.

Conclusion

This paper has presented a way of extracting high-level usability event logging information using the Mac OS X Accessibility APIs. The concepts should work on other operating systems that provide accessibility functionality. For simple applications that use standard widgets, an application may already be completely accessible, and hence can produce high-level usability descriptions of the interaction with the help of an additional monitoring application.

Rather than having a developer implement ad-hoc techniques for extracting low-level system events, encourage and educate the developer to support accessibility. In return, the accessible application can be instrumented to provide high-level usability information, satisfying two goals: making an application accessible to serve a broader audience and helping to quantify user interaction.

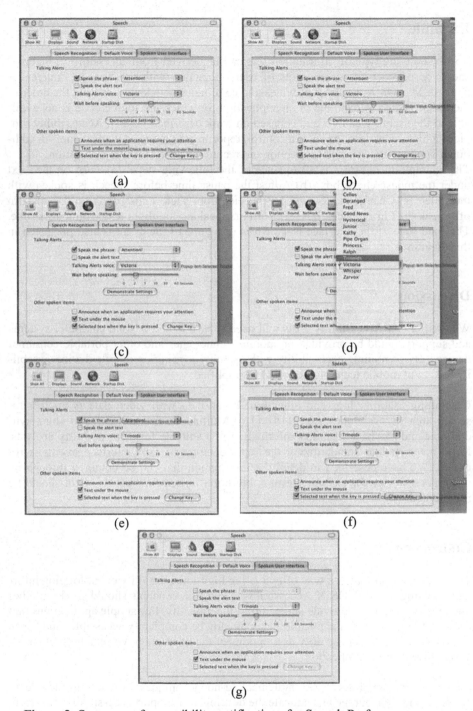

Figure 2. Sequence of accessibility notifications for Speech Preferences

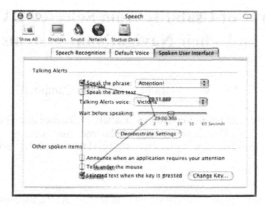

Figure 3. Mouse click events corresponding to changes in control value

References

[1] Nielsen, J., Usability Engineering, Morgan Kaufmann, San Diego (1993)

[2] Raskin, J., Chapter 4: Quantification, The Humane Interface: New Directions for Designing Interactive Systems, Addison-Wesley, Reading MA (2000) 71-97

[3] Hilbert, D., Redmiles, D., An Approach to Large-Scale Collection of Application Usage Data Over the Internet. In Proceedings of the 1998 International Conference on Software Engineering. IEEE Computer Society Press, April 1998.

[4] Chen, J., Providing Intrinsic Support for User Interface Monitoring, Proceedings of INTERACT '90 (1990)

[5] Fenstermacher, K., Ginsberg, M., A Lightweight Framework for Cross-Application User Monitoring, IEEE Computer Magazine, Vol. 35, Issue 3 (March 2002) 51-59

[6] Hong, J., Heer, J., Waterson, S., Landay, J., WebQuilt: A Proxy-based Approach to Remote Web Usability Testing, ACM Transactions on Information Systems, Vol. 19, Issue 3 (July 2001) 263-285

[7] Section 508, http://www.section508.gov/ [accessed 16th January, 2004]

[8] IntelliTalk, http://www.intellitools.com/products/intellitalk/home.php [accessed 16th January, 2004]

[9] Accessibility Documentation, http://developer.apple.com/documentation/Accessibility/Accessibility.html [accessed 16th January, 2004]

[10] Microsoft Active Accessibility, http://msdn.microsoft.com/library/default.asp?url=/nhp/default.asp?contentid=28000 544 [accessed 16th January, 2004]

[11] Current Work on Linux Accessibility, http://trace.wisc.edu/linux/current.html [accessed 16th January, 2004]

[12] Desktop Java Accessibility, http://java.sun.com/products/jfc/accessibility/index.jsp [accessed 16th January, 2004]

[13] Alexandersson, B., Event Logging in Usability testing, Masters Thesis, Chalmers University of Technology, Goteborg Sweden 2002

[14] Mori, J., Improving Data Management in Usability Tests, Masters Thesis, University of New South Wales, Sydney, Australia, March 2004.

[15] Mori, J. and Woo, D., COAR: An Objective-C Framework for Usability Data Collection, Proceedings of the AUC Academic and Developers Conference, Adelaide, Australia, September, 2003.

The Degree of Usability from Selected DVD Menus and Their Navigational Systems

Guy Wood-Bradley, Malcolm Campbell

School of Information Technology, Faculty of Science and Technology,
Deakin University, Melbourne, Australia
guywb@deakin.edu.au, malcolmc@deakin.edu.au

Abstract. The purpose of this research is to investigate the usability of DVD interfaces via their menus and navigation, inspired by Donald Norman who has had a pivotal role in user-centred design and usability. The paper encompasses theoretical aspects of interactivity, usability and DVD technology. A usability test was administered with the DVDs chosen. The results from the usability test were the main focus in this research. Such results were supportive of Norman's claims, as participants experienced varying degrees of usability issues. Furthermore, the findings were used to develop a set of guidelines and recommendations designers could follow. If these were adhered to, it would have significantly alleviated the difficulty the participants had in interacting with the DVDs.

1.0 Introduction

The Digital Versatile Disk[1] (DVD) and associated DVD technology is still relatively new compared with Compact Disk (CD) technology and provides a more interactive experience for the user. The primary purpose of DVD technology is to deliver movies and other video programs whereas CD technology was created to deliver high quality digital sound to consumers. This technology has become pervasive in today's society and replaces the older medium, VHS (or video tapes) by providing superior quality in home entertainment. The key to this new technology is the incorporation of a menu system that is pivotal in providing high levels of interactivity. In addition, the menu directs users to the range of content available on the DVD. A typical menu screen from a DVD is illustrated in Figure 1.1 and shows most of the common features available on DVDs.

As with all technology, the ease of which users can interact and utilise the product (such as Figure 1.1) is an issue of primary concern. It is important that this technology encompass usability principles and guidelines. Failure to fully understand how users interact with the product will result in a poor design that is unable to achieve user goals in the most efficient and effective way possible. Furthermore, the development

---

[1] This is a common definition, however, in some places it is referred to as "Digital Video Disk". The medium is more typically referred to as simply "DVD"

M. Masoodian et al. (Eds.): APCHI 2004, LNCS 3101, pp. 540-549, 2004.
© Springer-Verlag Berlin Heidelberg 2004

and publication of guidelines supports this importance and allows developers to produce products that are consistent yet distinctive.

Figure 1.1: An example of a DVD movie menu (Gregg, 2000)

Comments by Donald Norman have emphasised the lack of guidelines developed for DVDs compared to websites. Norman (2002) states "it is time to take DVD design as seriously as we do web design". Newer technology such as interactive television appears to have well developed design guidelines, however, DVDs being the older technology appear to have fewer guidelines in place.

DVD menus and the onscreen visual elements that tell the user what they have currently selected should be easily recognisable and not confusing. This aids the user in easily accessing the areas they wish to use on the DVD. It is not considered good design practice if users become lost or confused in achieving their goals. The structure of websites and DVD menus are similar in that both can become very complex. Such complexity needs to be counteracted by ensuring the user is always aware of where they are in relation to their goal.

1.1 HCI and DVD Concerns

DVDs despite their popularity they have a fundamental flaw in that the menus and navigational systems have been poorly designed and developed. This may be evident by struggling to select a particular scene or becoming confused and agitated over where particular content is located. Such problems could result from any combination of design choices such as colours and typefaces. Furthermore, criticism from one of the leaders in user-centred design and usability, Donald Norman openly stated his disapproval with the usability of DVD menus and navigation. In describing the menu structure, Norman (2002) emphasises that they are "getting more and more baroque, less and less usable, less pleasurable, [and] less effective". This can be seen when comparing simplistic DVD menus produced when its full capacity had not been discovered to those produced today. The sophistication in the menus has increased significantly over time. Consequently Norman calls for more regulation and guidance into this new and more interactive medium to help promote its usability. In addition Norman also published a series of short guidelines to help strengthen his case towards the medium in his essay titled "DVD Menu Design: The Failures of Web Design Recreated Yet Again" (Norman, 2002). Furthermore the same issues are dealt with through the World Wide Web Consortium's (W3C's) accessibility guidelines (Consortium, 1999) and the Nielsen Norman group's report (Coyne, 2001). It is these concerns that motivate an investigation into the efficiency or lack thereof, of DVD menus. For example, Figure 1.2 is relatively simple in design, however, viewers are forced to watch small cut-scenes after selecting an option off the 'Main Menu'. In addition, no visual cues are provided on the 'Scene Selection' screens to efficiently navigate the user to their desired scene choice. By failing to provide any real guidance and relying on past experience is a significant assumption made by the designers. Essentially this research is concerned with that investigation and exploring the problems of menu and navigational structures and the provision of guidelines.

1.2 DVD Menus

DVD features include, for example, the ability to view subtitles, modify audio settings and select and play specific scenes. The placement of these features within a DVD menu and interaction is indicative of a hierarchical menu structure and navigation. An example of a typical DVD menu is presented below in Figure 1.2.

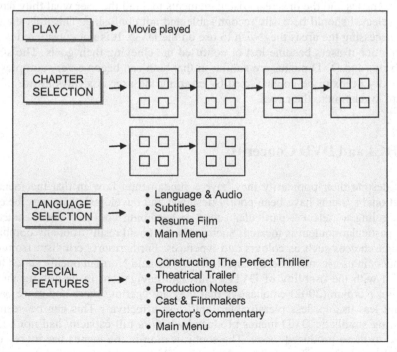

Figure 1.2: An example of a fully expanded DVD movie menu based on Figure 1.1 (Gregg, 2000)

"One of the fundamental rules of interface design is that you give immediate feedback to user actions" (De Lancie, 2001 p.4). In DVD menus this should be demonstrated through one or two different states with the first showing the button being selected followed by another showing that it has been triggered. Some design choices can be made with more fancier shadows and glows, for example it may take one to two seconds whereas basic predetermined or built-in highlights may take under a quarter of a second. Furthermore pointers such as arrows and dots are presented well onscreen and in four colours.

2.0 Study Methodology and Results

A usability study was administered with twenty participants being both male and female university students who responded to the call for participants with varying degrees of DVD experience. The study included a survey questionnaire that was completed prior to interacting with the interfaces and related to their background and experience with DVDs. In addition, the usability study required each participant to interact with four different DVD menus and focused on how successfully they achieved the task goal. This was measured by the number of times the cursor was moved, how many non-relevant sections were accessed and the number of attempts it took to successfully execute the task for DVDs 1 through 3. In DVD 4, participants were only measured in terms of the number of times the cursor was moved and the number of non-relevant sections that were accessed. This was due to the DVD being a 'bonus disc' and containing a different set of content compared to typical movie discs. The researcher guided the participants through the test by asking them to perform specific tasks with their actions recorded. The duration of each task was also recorded for each DVD. A heuristic evaluation was also executed by the researcher based on the DVDs used within the usability study to determine if it revealed similar or the same concerns the participants raised.

The participants who were involved in the usability test were required to complete three separate tasks using the four DVDs selected (see Figures 2.1 to 2.4 for their respective 'Main Menus'). Each DVD was unique in design style, layout and the types and functionality of the navigation. The tasks for DVDs 1 through 3 involved the participant accessing a specific scene, switching the English subtitles on and returning to the 'Main Menu' from a specific location within the DVD. DVD 4, however, focused on asking participants to access three unique sections. Furthermore, the results obtained showed clearly that the participants were learning how to interact with the interface. From the four DVDs used in the study, however, only Task 1 from DVD 4 (see Table 2.2) was a true reflection of the problems users may have in interacting with DVDs. The participants moved the cursor well above what were optimally required and experienced significant levels of frustration and anxiety. Each DVD, however, presented its own individual usability issues and was rated by the researcher in terms of its level of content and aesthetic appeal.

Figure 2.1: 'Main Menu' of
DVD 1 (Roth, 2001)

Figure 2.2: 'Main Menu' of
DVD 2 (Requa, 2001)

Figure 2.3: 'Main Menu' of
DVD 3 (Kloves, 2002)

Figure 2.4: 'Main Menu' of
DVD 4 (Kloves, 2002)

The results presented below in Tables 2.1 and 2.2 show the average totals of the data collected related to cursor moves. In this instance, the allowable range was between 1 and 10 cursor moves. This data highlights in various points the trend of participants moving the cursor excessively and rarely completing the tasks inline with the minimum number of moves.

Average number of cursor moves made within the allowable range			
	DVD 1	DVD 2	DVD 3
	Average	Average	Average
Task 1: Select & Play a Scene	6.9	6.3	6.9
Minimum number of moves to complete task:	5	4	6
Task 2: Switching the subtitles on	2.3	6.6	6.1
Minimum number of moves to complete task:	2	2	2
Task 3: Returning to the 'Main Menu'	8	4.4	4.6
Minimum number of moves to complete task:	5	3	2

Table 2.1: Average number of cursor moves made within the allowable range

Average number of cursor moves made within the allowable range	
DVD 4	
	Average
Task 1: Accessing the "Production Sketches"	>10
Minimum number of moves to complete task:	4
Task 2: Accessing the HP Game Credits	8.5
Minimum number of moves to complete task:	4
Task 3: Accessing "The Forbidden Forest Challenge" activity	6.6
Minimum number of moves to complete task:	4

Table 2.2: Average number of cursor moves made within the allowable range

2.1 DVD Usability Issues Identified from the Study

All DVDs selected presented usability issues as participants were not able to perform the tasks within the prescribed number of optimum cursor moves at any given time. This was determined by analysing all possible pathways to complete a specific task with the optimum being the least number of cursor moves to complete a given task. A positive correlation was seen to exist between the frequency of cursor movements and the time taken to complete the task. Designers appear to have misjudged the way in which users would logically complete the task. This misjudgement is indicative of poor design and lack of consideration of user cognitive processes.

2.1.1 DVD 1 Results

The 'Main Menu' screen forced users to interact with the menu in a linear approach. For example, it does not allow the cursor to move to the right from 'Play' to select the 'Chapter Selection' option. Significant errors were made on the 'Chapter Selection' screen as participants tried to move the cursor to lower levels by moving it to the right-hand side of the screen. As the cursor did not automatically move down to the level directly below, it resulted in the participants becoming confused. Consequently, further cursor moves were recorded and contributed to the 80 per cent of participants who moved the cursor above the optimum number. A similar issue with the scene block at the bottom of the screen allowed participants to only move left and right if there was a scene group placed immediately before or after the group that is currently highlighted. This inflexibility resulted in the cursor moving additional times as the participants became frustrated as they were forced to rethink their pathway in attaining the task goal.

2.1.2 DVD 2 Results

A key issue that participants encountered was the colour contrast between the green highlight and the green background when the two are combined with some of the on-screen elements. Participants also squinted at the screen as they were unable to locate the cursor and relied on purposely moving the cursor to identify it on-screen. These actions resulted in unnecessary moves being made. In the second task, for example, participants averaged 6.6 cursor moves to switch the subtitles on. This figure is substantially higher from the 2 cursor moves required to optimally complete the task. Furthermore, the pathways chosen were either logical or systematic in nature, that is, either selecting each scene in numerical order or moving the cursor horizontally to the end of the first row of scenes and then downwards to the scene groups,

2.1.3 DVD 3 Results

Most participants were not aware of the non-linear interactivity techniques incorporated into DVD 3 similarly to that of DVD 2, for example, being able to push left on the remote control to go from 'Play Movie' to 'Language' (see Figure 2.5). This was characterised by the lack of shortcuts taken on screens such as the 'Main Menu' thus increasing the number of unnecessary cursor moves. Participants through lack of experience or knowledge that such movement is permissible would move the cursor along the scene boxes in scene order and then from the beginning of the scene block, or took more direct paths such as selecting scene 1, scene 3 and then selecting the appropriate scene block. Although these processes represent clear thinking and logic, they can be shortened thus reducing the number of cursor moves. For this to occur, however, the participant must be aware of the DVDs non-linear interactivity or "three-dimensional" qualities. Figure 2.5 below provides an example as to how the participants altogether executed the third task for this DVD.

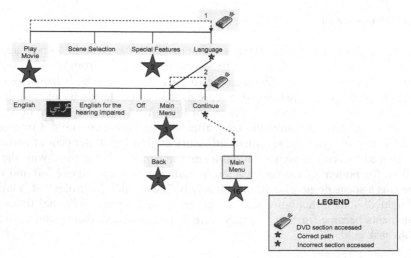

Figure 2.5: A graphical summary of participant interaction in completing Task 3 from DVD 3

2.1.4 DVD 4 Results

It became apparent that some participants believed that "Additional Scenes" was the only section on the DVD as it was selected by default after the DVD had loaded. One participant even attempted to complete all three tasks with DVD 4 utilising the additional scenes only. As no clues were present suggesting that other menu items did exist, signifies both poor visibility and affordance in terms of the menu design; participants were forced to explore and access numerous sections in order to establish a mental model of the DVD. Such exploration resulted in excessive moves of the cursor as participants struggled to complete the tasks set as efficiently as possible.

The transition sequences caused some annoyances for the participants due to their length of time in addition to already being frustrated at the difficulty experienced in trying to complete the tasks successfully. Task completion was also made more difficult with the participants being confident as to the section the required content was located in, yet the answer did not present itself clearly on the screen. This was typified in the second task in which participants were asked to access the Harry Potter game credits. Participants had come across the menu heading "Game Preview" throughout their exploration, however, after accessing it, still did not know where the game credits were located. Many did not realise the task was complete when they selected the arrow icon as it was assumed the section would close and return directly to the 'Main Menu'.

3.0 Summary

Participants often failed to take advantage of the non-linear benefits in the design of some DVDs and can be likened to the functionality of linear and non-linear interfaces. This allows the user to interact with a DVD in a matrix-like fashion and not be forced in moving the cursor via unnecessarily long pathways. Conversely participants became frustrated at the menus not being coded to allow for efficient interaction, such as permitting the cursor to automatically jump to lower areas on the screen.

The tasks the participants were asked to perform were clear in structure. However, the options presented on the 'Main Menu' only provided clues; the way the tasks were completed relied on the sole judgement of each participant. The methodology chosen was not full-proof either as the manual recording of participant actions could have lead to the researcher failing to observe critical usability flaws in the DVD menus.

The evolution of DVDs has seen advances in both the level and sophistication of graphical content and capabilities. Early DVDs were very simple in design compared to current DVDs in which high levels of graphical content with more unique and creative design, menus, navigation and interaction that are now becoming commonplace.

3.1 Conclusion and Recommendations

To a certain extent the DVD menus conformed to common HCI and usability principles, however, this was haphazard in its inclusion. Very few participants were able to complete the tasks in the minimum amount of steps this is indicative of poor usability. On reflection of the participant's performance and the heuristic evaluation, there is substantial room for improvement. Finally, as discussed in the next section, a series of guidelines were produced as a result of the research, to assist in the usability of DVD menus and navigational systems.

The following guidelines are proposed for future research to increase the level of usability in DVD menus and navigational structures:

Make It Clear and Simple and Resist Extravagance

1. Ensure the DVDs theme, for example, a movie is identifiable within the menu. Users will then feel like they are a part of the environment or fantasy and enjoy interacting with the menu.

2. Show off DVD technology and its ability to be highly interactive, just include flexible menus. Do not force users into having to follow inefficient steps as this will only encourage frustration.

3. Be aware of the size your DVD menus should be. A user squinting at a television screen or computer monitor is a significant usability flaw.

4. There are some projects that require a DVD to be produced that encourages the user to freely explore its content. Do not fall into a trap of aimlessly placing content on to a DVD and forcing users to adopt a 'process of elimination' technique to just arrive at the desired content.

User Orientation

5. Keep the navigation simple – arrows, squares, circles and other basic shapes work best. Watch out for clashes with other colours though as users may not be able to see the pointer.

6. Animate the navigational pointer – one colour, for example, to show that the current item is highlighted and a different one to show it has just been selected. This keeps users in the know.

7. If using a transition sequence between one screen to the next, ensure users can skip it if they wish. The enjoyment may wear off sooner rather than later. Let the user control the DVD and not vice versa.

8. Your menu items must be highly visible. Do not expect that a user will conveniently stumble across it. The labels given to the menu headings and navigational controls must be clear. They must tell the user where it will lead to or specifically what function it will perform.

Websites Can Be Tested for Usability and So Should DVDs

9. It is highly advisable you get some users involved either while the menu is being designed or on a fully working prototype. The advantages website usability testing can provide are widely documented. DVDs should also be released with the same care and attention to detail to make them as easy to use as possible.

Menus That Work Best

10. Weigh up and consider the menu and navigational system based on the DVDs purpose. Different DVDs with different purposes all call for varying menus. Consistency still remains the key. Investigate your target users, their levels of experience and the content it needs to contain.

The application of these guidelines within the DVDs used within the study would have produced significantly different results; participants would not have experienced the same level of difficulty in completing the required tasks. Such guidelines were not devised to remove the uniqueness from each DVD menu, but rather ensure consistency and ease of use in interacting with the medium.

References

Consortium, WWW. 1999, *Web Content Accessibility Guidelines 1.0*,
    Available: [http://www.w3.org/TR/WAI-WEBCONTENT/] (11/6/03).

Coyne, K. P. and Nielsen, J. 2001, *How to Conduct Usability Evaluations for
    Accessibility: Methodology Guidelines for Testing Websites and Intranets With Users
    Who Use Assistive Technology*, Nielsen Norman Group

De Lancie, P. 2001, *Post Linear: Menu Design for DVD*,
    Available: [http://www.dvdmadeeasy.com/] (19/3/03)

Gregg, C. 2000, 'What Lies Beneath', ed. Zemeckis, R., Fox Home Entertainment. (DVD)

Kloves, S. 2002, 'Harry Potter and the Chamber of Secrets', ed. Columbus, C.,
    Warner Home Video. (DVD)

Norman, D. 2002, *DVD Menu Design: The Failures of Web Design Recreated Yet Again*,
    Available: [http://jnd.org/dn.mss/DVDmenus.html] (26/1/03).

Requa, J. and Figarra, G. 2001, 'Cats & Dogs', ed. Guterman, L.,
    Roadshow Home Entertainment. (DVD)

Roth, B. 2001, 'Heartbreakers', Buena Vista Home Entertainment. (DVD)

Taylor, J. 2003, *DVD Frequently Asked Questions (and Answers)*, Available:
    [http://dvddemystified.com/dvdfaq.html] (29/9/03)

OPR-LENS: Operation-Lens System for Supporting a Manipulation of Information Appliances

Takumi Yamaguchi[1,2], Haruya Shiba[2], and Kazunori Shimamura[1]

[1] Kochi University of Technology, 185 Miyanokuchi, Tosayamada, Kami-gun, Kochi
782-8502, Japan
{076020z@gs.,shimamura.kazunori@}kochi-tech.ac.jp
[2] Kochi National College of Technology, 200-1 Monobe, Nankoku, Kochi 783-8508,
Japan
{yama,shiba}@ee.kochi-ct.ac.jp

Abstract. This paper describes how to mount a new pointing device by which users, who have an existing metaphor for using information appliances, can effectively apply that including Personal Computer (PC). We propose the system wearing the operation lens support, which is called "OPR-LENS (Operation-Lens)". The OPR-LENS system is composed of the OPR-LENS module and the OPR-LENS device, and mounted on the server and the viewer software connected via TCP/IP, respectively. The OPR-LENS device forms a temple block suitable for a palm operation. Users' manipulation can be effectively supported by the effect of the spherical lens with the partial GUI image. This research investigates the evaluation of the OPR-LENS system through mounting a prototype system and implementing the performance evaluation experiment. In addition, the application example when applying to the existing metaphor such as information appliances was shown in this paper.

1 Introduction

As Information technology (IT) has developed, attractive usage of information resources also has become prevalent in all areas of people's lives. The number of PC novice users is increasing rapidly. Also, the use field is greatly expanding to the whole real life as an information appliance such as mobile environments and information appliances.

The GUI on PCs is based on a WIMP (Window/Icon/Menu/Pointing device) interface. Therefore, it is not designed as an interface for utilizing in the real world. However, the operation procedure of information appliances and information kiosks take over the operation procedure of the PC's GUI. Because it is necessary to allocate the functions of the information appliance in the limited button and display by mounting on built-in type Operating System (OS) on the information appliance. Besides, the information appliance needs to be selected and operated it by users. As the computer and the network environment have become popular at each home, various home appliances are organically connected

M. Masoodian et al. (Eds.): APCHI 2004, LNCS 3101, pp. 550–559, 2004.

on the network. Consequently, the information appliance is made to high performance and more multifunctional. Under such these environments, the interface that can be readily used by the gesture and the voice without giving priority to efficiency is requested [4,5,6,8,10].

Recently, the operation desire of elderly peoples regarding the information appliance such as PC is rising highly[7]. As for PC novice users and aged people, the part of a human interface by ways of a pointing operation differs greatly among individuals. Especially, even if they can recognize the whole GUI image, it is often too difficult for them to identify its details. The size of the character and the figure should be enlarged in order to support the sight. In comparison with comparatively big operations of the bodily movement such as the hand, arms, and necks, it is difficult to operate with detailed work to use the finger and the tip of a finger, and besides, the operation time is long.

We establish the system and interaction actively operated according to users' own intention while utilizing the characteristics of an existing WIMP interface. We propose the OPR-LENS system wearing the operation lens support without altering an original GUI layout[1].

This paper describes how to mount a new pointing device in a temple block shape operated by the patting movement while emphasizing the gazed region. We investigated the evaluation of OPR-LENS system through mounting a prototype system and implementing the performance evaluation experiment.

The OPR-LENS system aims to support the sight and the manipulation of the information appliance while reducing the new remembrance. Also, our goal is a realization of the easy user interface that is not pushy and a leisurely manipulation.

2   OPR-LENS System

As shown in Figure 1, the entire system is composed of the OPR-LENS module on the information appliance, which has been automatically connected on the network via IP, and the OPR-LENS device on the pointing device. By operating the OPR-LENS device, users select one of information appliances.

By mounting on the telecommunication and the supporting application, the user's various operations can be supported with the appliance on the OPR-LENS device. Support for the emphasis of the gazed region is one of the supporting applications of the OPR-LENS device. The operation of the appliance is enlarged in order to suit users' action on the OPR-LENS device. Also, the operation requirement requested from the OS, which is mounted on the appliance, moderates. In a word, our system realizes both sight supports and pointing manipulations through the collaboration between the information appliance and the OPR-LENS system. The key concept of the OPR-LENS system is the following three points.

– Supporting the visual cognition and operation by synchronizing with visual effects.

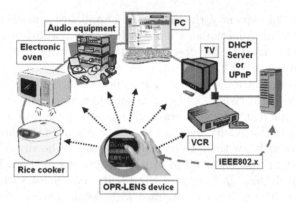

Fig. 1. Basic concept of OPR-LENS system.

– Pointing device suitable smooth operations.
– A unified interface of a variety of appliance operations.

The OPR-LENS module has the image taking out function, the image transfer function and automatic retrieval function of the target appliance. The OPR-LENS device forms the shape of a temple block. Moreover, it has the nonlinear magnification function of captured images from the OPR-LENS module, and besides, it has the same function as a general mouse. The OPR-LENS module and the OPR-LENS device are based on TCP/IP protocol.

The method of forwarding the taken out image from the OPR-LENS module applies to alter the image size captured from the OPR-LENS module according to user's magnification ratio[1].

Thus, this OPR-LENS system may not depend on the construction and the distance of a physical connection, and it is easy to apply it to other usage. When the GUI is hard for a user to see, our system enables him to confirm the details at hand. When it is not necessary to see the details at hand, the user operates our system while looking at the PC screen.

We propose the OPR-LENS system that we notice the characteristic of the body. We also select the OPR-LENS system having comfortable shape for aged users. As a consequence, the movement of the entire palm operates its system.

2.1 OPR-LENS Device

The size of the OPR-LENS device is that of child's head. The spherical part of the OPR-LENS device combines the capsule and the operation part. Moreover, the sensor mechanism as the mouse operation is installed. The hardware of the OPR-LENS device consists of the dome structure putting a transparent hemisphere on the thin-film transistor liquid crystal display (TFT-LCD).

The operation detection of the hand designed the mechanism that the hemisphere inclines at a stroking direction a little. Through moving the pointer in

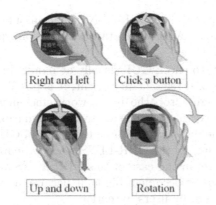

Right and left   Click a button

Up and down   Rotation

Fig. 2. Pointing operation of OPR-LENS device.

the inclining direction, the OPR-LENS device was configured with the positional detection method using optics in proportion to the inclination of the operation part of its device. To detect the rotation operation, the optical rotary encoder was built into the OPR-LENS device.

The expansion and emphasis function of the gazed region have been realized by implementing nonlinear magnification [2] processing to GUI's display on the TFT-LCD.

2.2   Operation Method

The operation method of the OPR-LENS device as shown in Figure 2 consists of the following procedures. First, the partial image of GUI taken out of the OPR-LENS module is expanded nonlinear in the vicinity of the top of the transparent dome. Then, the user handles like stroking it with his hand. Finally, by moving the objective operation function to the vicinity of the top of the OPR-LENS device, the user can operate the device while checking the operation visually at hand. Thus, the OPR-LENS device is different from the interaction with a mouse and a track pad, etc.

Figure 2 describes the operation method of the OPR-LENS device about a necessary operation as an operation device of the information appliance such as PC. Figure 2 shows a right and left operation, the operation of the vertical direction, the click operation and the rotation operation.

The cursor movement of the right and left or the vertical movement operates by which the hemisphere is slightly inclined from side to side and up and down at the fulcrum a center axis on a hemisphere when the hemisphere is pressed for under.

The click operation operates by pressing a hemisphere. The double-clicking operation operates by pressing the click operation twice.

The drug operation operates by keeping pressing it. The drag and drop operation operates by operating movement while pressing a hemisphere, and releasing pressing it at the end point. The OPR-LENS device mounted the same function as the one-button mouse. Also, the rotation operation operates by rotating a hemisphere by the hand.

On the other hand, to check GUI visually at hand, this device accompanies the movement of the gazed region. As a result, it is possible that the movement of the gazed region might drop the user's work efficiency and also make him feel tired. However, our target user leads to the stagnation and mistake of the operation caused by the difficulty to watch the detail of GUI. That is, only when the user looks at the image of the OPR-LENS device, the movement of the gazed region occurs. Therefore, in the case of this OPR-LENS system, the movement of the gazed region doesn't become a big fault because a gazed direction for the operation could be chosen by users' intention.

2.3   Prototype System

The OPR-LENS device was mounted on a laptop PC. Figure 3 shows the OPR-LENS device made as a prototype. It has a structure wearing a transparent hemisphere on the TFT-LCD of PC like the dome. The diameter of the hemisphere is 15cm. The operation detection mechanism of the hand was constructed under the TFT panel.

The size of the displayed images, which was drawn by the OPR-LENS device, was set to 256 256 pixels. The number of displayed colors was set to 24bit True Color. The performance of PC used for a coordinated experiment of the OPR-LENS module and the OPR-LENS device is shown below. In the case of the OPR-LENS module, the performance of PC is Intel Pentium2-450MHz. In the case of the OPR-LENS device, the performance of PC is Intel Mobile Celeron-600MHz. IEEE802.11b of wireless LAN was used for the communication interface of the OPR-LENS module and the OPR-LENS device.

Software was mounted on a server, and a viewer on TCP/IP. The sending and receiving processes between the OPR-LENS module and the OPR-LENS device mounted on an original protocol over TCP/IP. Mounted software is an application program designed to work within ".NET Framework 1.1". Also, we have chosen to apply the Joint Photographic Experts Group (JPEG) format. The cursor on OPR-LENS module has been synchronized with moving the cursor on OPR-LENS device. The displayed image on the OPR-LENS device has been changed according to the movement of the focus area on the OPR-LENS module, too.

In this system, the system performance, which includes drawing performance, communication performance and JPEG encoding performance, has been realized an enough reaction rate less than 30ms where the user did not feel pressured.

When the image data received from the OPR-LENS module is expanded on the OPR-LENS device, one of the geometric transformations is processed. The expansion style is switched in the toggle by pushing a specific key on the keyboard.

Fig. 3. Prototype of OPR-LENS device on PCs.

3   Evaluation

There is little width of the movement of manipulations on the OPR-LENS device because the OPR-LENS device operates the device to stroke it by the palm. Thus, it is operated in the similar condition to 2-D pointing of the indirect instructing device. The operation time to manipulate the target object with a prototype device was measured. The measurement results analyzed using a presumption formula [12] enhancing Fitts' law to the 2-D space.

Experimental icons arranged on the PC display that mounted the OPR-LENS module. The elapsed time from a central icon to other icons on the PC display measured with the experimental software for the measurement. We explained the operating procedure to the subjects beforehand that they experiment. They experimented on the following conditions after their several-time practices.

(a) In case of using a general optical mouse,
(b) In case of using OPR-LENS device with spherical nonlinear expansions,

The subjects are in their twenties who are experienced to manipulate the PC, and besides, the subjects are in their fifties and in their seventies who are not experienced to manipulate PCs in their daily life.

Figure 4 shows the comparison of operation time caused by using OPR-LENS device and a general mouse. The nonlinear expansion used the expansion like a sphere mapping.

Relative operation time increases with the rise of the age. The contribution rate R^2 value indicates a highly value to use the OPR-LENS device than to use the general mouse. Also, it has shown a similar tendency at any age. Consequently, the steady manipulation of the OPR-LENS device is available without depending on the user's various operations.

As unreserved advices in the subjective evaluation, there were some of following comments. First, it is useful for operating the menus. Second, it is not

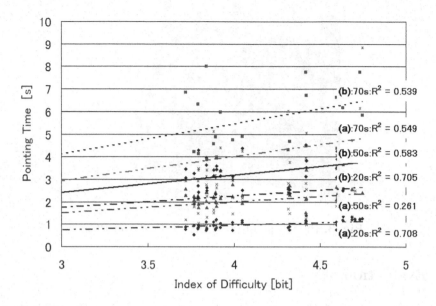

Fig. 4. Relationship between ID and pointing time; (a)in case of using a general optical mouse, (b)in case of using OPR-LENS device with spherical nonlinear expansions.

useful for viewing the photographs. Finally, it is difficult to consecutively handle a detailed operation for PCs. We will study the applied fields and the further tasks while drawing upon these advices.

4   Application to Home Electric Appliances

In the case of the remote control operation via multifunctional remote control, it is necessary to learn making the button of the remote control correspond to the function of the information appliance. This problem is reduced by the following techniques.

In the case of the information appliance for which GUI is not so necessary, it is necessary to leverage the existing metaphor of an original appliance. First of all, the photograph, which is used the front panel of the information appliance to resemble a desktop on the GUI, is saved on the OPR-LENS module. The buttons and volume controls add the events such as "Push", "Move" and "Rotation" corresponding to an existing operation action.

Figure 5 indicates the applying example to the audio equipments. When the OPR-LENS device obtains the list of the information appliance to participate in the network by using the Universal Plug and Play (UPnP) or the Dynamic Host Configuration Protocol (DHCP), the list of that is displayed on the OPR-LENS device. If the user selected the audio equipment by his/her own intention, the OPR-LENS device displays the photograph of the front panel of the audio

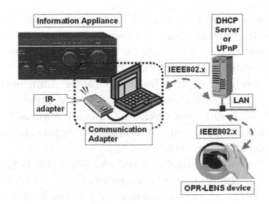

Fig. 5. Examples of advanced operation using OPR-LENS system.

equipment. When the user moves the image of the button or volume-control to the center of the OPR-LENS device, the part of that can be operated according to the added events by handling the OPR-LENS device. For example, the event as "Rotation" realizes through recognizing the rotation mechanism on the OPR-LENS device.

We will describe at another chance how to mount on the attachment of the OPR-LENS module on home electric appliances.

5   Related Work

As for the comparison between our OPR-LENS system and related work, we describe three technical regions, which are the gesture input interface, the real world interface, and the display interface.

In the case of gesture input interface, there are a lot of approaches operated by mounting on the type of a glove and the sensor of finger, while Ubi-Finger [5] is a compact interface installing to the forefinger. Ubi-Finger focuses on a mobile environment and information appliances, and makes the number of sensors to a minimum. It is an interesting method to select the target appliance by pointing it and using a simple gesture. Our method also utilizes some simple movements of the physical actions, and can operate the GUI while supporting the visual cognition. The OPR-LENS system can make the operation form of information appliances to correspond to the same operation on the OPR-LENS device.

Numazaki [3] has proposed a visual interface configured the Motion Processor and the extraction of the attention area of tangible objects. However, our device has the feature mounting on the movement and the rotation of the hand's operations while displaying the PC's GUI.

In the case of the real world interface, there are ToolStone [11] and Attachable Controller [9]. ToolStone is a rectangular solid device to manipulate on the tablet device. This device can be controlled the moved operation on horizontal plane and the rotation on central axis caused by the movement of the whole input device. Our study is different from ToolStone because our device is suited a mouse operation and other operation by the natural action of user's hands. Consequently, it operates like the gesture rather than operating its device.

Attachable Controller has the functions of the information presentation caused by attaching the sensor and the computer control to the information appliances in the real world. Our device is different approach from Attachable Controller, because we are focusing on adding the input, the manipulation and the display of the OPR-LENS device.

Finally, in the case of the display interface, i-ball [13] is the display device, which projects the image onto the transparency sphere like the crystal ball, and browses the content of the information resources by the wrapping action of the hands. Also, it is one of the user interfaces utilizing an intuitive operation for the information appliances, and it is a passive information terminal. The projected image is displayed through the display under the transparency sphere. This sphere has the configuration of overlapping two hemispheres. It is very interesting viewpoint, which the user wants to operate and the method of information presentations has an innovative approach.

As for the spherical display, it is difficult to realize linearly display caused by optical characteristics of the refraction and the reflection. So, i-ball has achieved the immersive perception by obtaining subjective view that the user looks into in the sphere.

However, out study is different from i-ball, because our device is composed of the operated device respect to natural posture of the hands, while users operate the target object in daily life with objective view.

6   Conclusions and Further Work

In this paper, we described how to mount a new pointing device by which PC users, who have difficulty in capturing GUI images, can effectively access the information appliances on PC. We investigated the evaluation of the OPR-LENS system through mounting a prototype system and the performance evaluation experiment. We proposed the OPR-LENS device of temple block shape operated by the patting movement while emphasizing the gazed region. The OPR-LENS device is composed of the viewer software and hardware where the data between OPR-LENS module and OPR-LENS device are exchanged.

- Prototype of system of OPR-LENS device has been mounted.
- Evaluation of pointing tasks by three different age groups has been investigated regarding OPR-LENS device.

  As a result,

- Relative pointing time increases. However, in case of using the OPR-LENS device, the contribution rate of linear regressions is higher than that rate in case of using a general mouse.
- Pointing time shows a similar tendency at any age.

Consequently, the steady manipulation of the OPR-LENS device is available without depending on the user's various operations. In addition, the application example when applying to the existing metaphor such as information appliances was shown in this paper.

In the future, we would like to further investigate the coexistence of both the visibility and the pointing operation, as well as the subjective evaluations of the operation of temple block shape.

References

1. Yamaguchi, T. and Shimamura, K.: A proposal of a palm-pointing device using lens-effect with partially capturing of PC's GUI. Proceedings of APSITT2003, (2003) 25-30
2. Keahey, T. A., Robertson, E. L.: Techniques for non-linear magnification transformations. IEEE Symposium on Information Visualization, (1996) 38-45
3. Numazaki, S., Morishita, A., Umeki, N., Ishikawa, M., Doi, M.: A kinetic and 3D image input device. Proceedings of CHI'98, (1998) 237-238
4. Segan, J., Kumar, S.: Simplifying human-computer intraction by using hand gestures. Comm. ACM, vol.43, no.7, (2000) 102-109
5. Tsukada, K., Yasumura, M.: Ubi-Finger: Gesture Input Device for Mobile Use. Proceedings of APCHI 2002, vol. 1, (2002) 388-400
6. Weiser, M.: The Computer for 21th Century. Scientific American, vol.265, no.3, (1991) 66-75
7. Nielsen//NetRatings, "The survey of Internet access time during month," http://www.netratings.co.jp/, (2003) (in Japanese)
8. Fukuchi, K., Rekimoto, J.: Interaction Techniques for SmartSkin. ACM UIST2002 demonstration, (2002)
9. Iga, S., Itoh, E., Higuchi, F., Yasumura, M.: Attachable Computer: Augmentation of Electric Household Appliances by Fit-up Computer. Proceedings of APCHI'98, (1998) 51-56
10. Siio, I., Masui, T., Fukuchi, K.: Real-world Interaction using the FieldMouse. Proceedings of the ACM Symposium on User Interface Software and Technology (UIST'99), (1999) 113-119
11. Rekimoto, J., Sciammarella, E.: ToolStone: Effective Use of the Physical Manipulation Vocabularies of Input Devices. Proceedings of UIST 2000, (2000)
12. MacKenzie, I.S.: A note on the information-theoretic basis for Fitts' law. Motor Behavior, Vol.21, (1989) 323-330
13. Ikeda, H., Naemura, T., Harashima, H., Ishikawa, J.: i-ball: Interactive Information Display like a Crystal Ball. Conference Abstracts and Applications of ACM SIGGRAPH 2001, (2001) 122

A Novel Locomotion Interface with Independent Planar and Footpad Devices for Virtual Walking

Jungwon Yoon and Jeha Ryu

Human-Machine-Computer Interface Laboratory, Department of Mechatronics,
Kwangju Institute of Science and Technology, Bukgu, Kwangju 500-712, Korea
{garden, ryu}@kjist.ac.kr

Abstract. This paper describes a novel locomotion interface that can generate infinite floor for various surfaces. This interface allows users to participate in a life-like walking experience within virtual environments, which include various terrains such as slopes and stairs. The interface is composed of two three-DOF (X, Y, Yaw) planar devices and two three-DOF (Pitch, Roll, and Z) footpads. The planar devices are driven by AC servomotor for generating fast motions, while the footpad devices are driven by pneumatic actuators for continuous support of human weight. For sensing system, a motion tracker is attached to the human foot in order to track the foot positions, and the combination of planar forces from the planar device and the vertical forces of the footpad device gives the gravity reaction forces (GRF), which is important to recognize the walking condition. For control implementation, even though the human is walking continuously, the human body should be confined in certain area to walk on an infinite floor. Thus, the walking control algorithm is suggested to satisfy above conditions keeping the safety of the walker. For preliminary experimental evaluation of the interface device, the walking interface is proven for a general human to walk naturally without disturbing human body. This interface can be applied to various areas such as VR navigations, rehabilitation, vocational training, and military exercises.

1. Introduction

Walking is the most natural way to move in everyday life. A locomotion interface (LI) is an input-output device to simulate walking interactions with virtual environments without restricting human mobility in a confined space such as a room [1]. LI can make a person participate actively in virtual environments and feel real spatial sense by generating appropriate ground surfaces to human feet. Also, LI can be used in several application fields such as walking rehabilitation, virtual design, training, and exercises. For patients who have the fear about real environments, the task specific training with virtual environments by using LI may be very helpful to reduce the fear for real life walking. Also, for the purpose of design, a designer can walk through architectural building, airplane, and ship with the use of the LI. Moreover, it can be applied to train fire fighter or army personals, which are very difficult to do in real situations. For entertainment purpose, it can be used to winter sports such as ski

M. Masoodian et al. (Eds.): APCHI 2004, LNCS 3101, pp. 560-569, 2004.
© Springer-Verlag Berlin Heidelberg 2004

and skates as well as general exercise such as promenade. More possible applications using locomotion interfaces are well summarized in [1].

Several different types of locomotion interfaces have been proposed. The devices can be classified into four types: treadmills, pedaling devices (such as bicycles or unicycles), sliding device, and programmable foot platforms comprising active three degree-of-freedom (DOF) platforms for each foot. The traditional locomotion devices like treadmill [1-3] in general have limitations for generating different ground surfaces and diverse training trajectories. Pedaling devices [4] cannot generate motions for natural human walking due to their limited motion. Sliding machines [5] can simulate only passive human walking on planar surfaces. Only programmable foot platforms can simulate uneven omni-directional surfaces that are required for locomotive interactions in diverse virtual environments with active motions and forces. The Sarcos Biport [6] employed three-axis hydraulic serial-drive platforms for each foot. The device can simulate translational motions of the articulated arm in 3D space but cannot simulate slope since the device has no rotation motions. Roston [7] proposed a "Whole Body Display" that has three-DOF motions. They utilized 3-DOF parallel device which are driven by sliders. To generate desirable workspace, their system is too large to be located inside indoor a laboratory environment. Iwata [8] developed the "Gait Master" which consists of two three-DOF (x, y, and z) Gough-Stewart Platforms and a turntable. Even though the Gait Master utilized high rigidity and multi-DOF motion of a parallel device, the available stride distance is only 30cm, which is not large enough to allow natural walking. Schmidt [9] suggested a robotic walking simulator for neurological rehabilitation with three- DOF motions of sagittal plane at each foot. However, their experimental results are not reported. Except for mechanical locomotion device, Slater el al. [10] proposed locomotion sensing in VEs by "walking in place". Their device was just used to recognize the gesture of walking using a position sensor and a neural network.

Even though programmable foot platform devices can ideally simulate foot trajectories for natural walking, the previous devices cannot satisfy simultaneously enough workspace for natural walking distance and good force capability to support various ground terrains such as omni-directional level, slope and stair surfaces, which are important to experience diverse walking environments. Therefore, in order to simulate natural walking over various surfaces, a new mechanical structure should be suggested and designed based on the more thorough gait analysis. We propose a new LI called the "K-Walker" that can simulate various surfaces and natural walking distance. It is composed of two three-DOF (X, Y, Yaw) planar devices and two three-DOF (Pitch, Roll, and Z) footpads. The separation of planar and spatial motions can achieve sufficiently large workspace for general walking and force capability enough to support the user's full weight. Therefore, K-Walker can satisfy most of natural walking conditions.

This paper describes the ongoing development of new LI in our laboratory. The following section explains the system overview of the K-Walker. Mechanical design and sensing systems are briefly explained. Section 3 presents the control algorithm of the new K-walker to satisfy walking on infinite floor. Section 4 shows some experimental results of the control algorithm and preliminary evaluation of the interface. Conclusions and future research items are summarized in Section 5.

2. System Overview of K-walker

2.1 Overview

Normal gait is defined as series of rhythmical alternating movements of the limb and trunk [11]. Gait cycle is activity that occurs between heel strike of one extremity and the subsequent heel strike on the same side. Gait cycle is composed of stance and swing. The entire period during which the foot is on the ground is the stance phase. On the other hand, during the swing period, the foot steps forward without contacting any objects. Stance phase accounts for approximately 60 percent of a single gait cycle, while swing phase accounts for approximately 40 percent. During walking cycle, the swing requires sufficient workspace, while the stance requires sufficient force-bearing capability and the ground reaction force to support human weight should be generated only during the stance phase. Therefore, independent devices for each phase of motion may be a better design solution than a combined device such as the Gait Master [8] which can not generate sufficient step length and can not simulate the slope surfaces. Unlike the Gait Master, by separating the planar and the footpad devices, the load capability of the footpad device will not be reduced, even though the planar device becomes more distant from its home position.

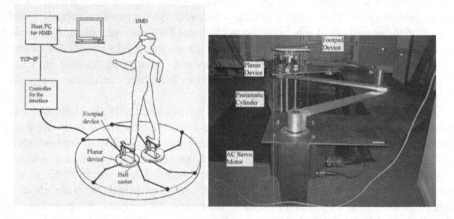

Figure 1. The Novel Walking Interface

From the thorough understating of the human gait, Figure 1 shows the structure of the suggested locomotion interface. Ball casters are inserted between the planar device and the large base rotation plate to reduce significantly the friction between the planar device supporting a human weight and the base plate. Therefore, the planar device can generate fast and high rigidity motions with relatively small motors. Figure 1 also shows a system for interactions with virtual environments using the suggested VWM. The user standing on K-Walker can walk and interact with the virtual environment by wearing a Head Mount Display (HMD), or watching big display screen.

The major characteristics of the suggested VWM can be summarized as follows:
- Mechanism designed for separate planar motion (x, y, and yaw) by a planar device and spatial motion (z, pitch, roll) by a footpad device;
- Wide workspace for natural human walking and force capability sufficient to support the user's weight;
- Presentation of uneven, omni-directional surfaces

2.2 Mechanical Design

a. Planar device

The planar device with a three DOF parallel mechanism is composed of three limbs which have three serial revolute joints with the actuated first revolute joint. Since the actuators can be fixed on the base, the weight of the mobile equipment can be reduced. In addition, revolute joints have no mechanical limits, which significantly maximizes the workspace. The planar device driven by AC servomotors is designed to generate sufficient breaking forces to prevent sliding when the foot contacts the ground and then put back the limb in the original position to allow continuous walking. In addition, interference between two planar devices can be avoided by locating the configuration of the device asymmetrically and by use of link offsets in the vertical direction. All links of the planar device are made of light aluminum frames in order to reduce link inertia. Rotary motors are directly connected to lower bars without reduction gears. This direct drive can achieve low friction and high bandwidth and eliminate backlash so that the device can achieve fast motions. This construction is possible due to the fact that all motors are fixed at the common base, which allows use of high power motors without increasing moving inertia. In addition, in order to reduce joint frictions, ball bearings are inserted at every revolute joint.

b. Footpad device

During the stance phase, the footpad device should generate various surfaces such as even plane, stairs, and slope surfaces to allow navigation in diverse virtual environments. Therefore, the footpad device is composed of three active prismatic joints that can generate pitch, roll, and heaving motions. Even though the heaving motion of the foot trajectory during general walking is within 5cm, the footpad device should generate larger heaving motion for surfaces like stairs. In addition, since the trajectory of the gravity reaction force by the human weight varies from heel to toe during stance phase, the footpad device should support the reaction force at any contact point of the footpad device. Computer simulations showed that the device can satisfy normal gait requirements; the heaving motion is maximum 20cm, the maximum payload is over 1000N, and the maximum pitch rotation angle is over 30°, respectively. The platform of the footpad device is made up of a lightweight aluminum material. This material was chosen because it doesn't affect magnetic tracker and contributes very little to the device's weight.

2.3 Sensing System Design for K-walker

a. Position

The position and orientation of a human foot can be measured using a Polhemus 3D magnetic tracker (FASTRACK). The magnetic tracker generally suffers from magnetic noise caused by metals in the motion platforms. However, since the platforms of the footpad device are made of aluminum, the magnetic noises are not so severe to measure the posture of the human foot. The tracker-sampling rate was set to 30Hz. Magnetic tracker is tightly connected to the shoe as shown in Figure 2, so that it should precisely trace the foot motion without delay.

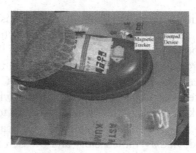

Figure 2. Magnetic tracker attached to the shoe

b. Force estimation

To apply this interface into lower limb rehabilitations, the force of human foot during walking should be measured. If we assume that the joint friction is negligible, the planar force vector F_{planar} exerted on the platform of the planar device when one foot contacts the ground after swing phase can be obtained by

$$F_{planar} = (J_{planar}{}^T)^{-1} \tau_a - J_{planar}{}^T (m\ddot{\theta} - b\dot{\theta}) \qquad (1)$$

where τ_a is motor torque, J_{planar} is Jacobian matrix of the planar device, θ is the Cartesian coordinate of the planar device, m is the mass matrix, and b is viscosity matrix. Note that τ_a can be estimated by motor input current, mass and nonlinear viscosity matrices can be precisely computed by equations of motion, and finally $\dot{\theta}$ and $\ddot{\theta}$ can be estimated by joint angle measurement. In the meantime, vertical forces on the footpad device can be estimated by pressure sensors in the cylinder:

$$F_{pneu} = \{A_l P_{li} - A_u P_{ui}\} \ (i = 1,2,3,4)$$

$$F_z = (J_{footpad}{}^T)^{-1} F_{pneu} \qquad (2)$$

where A_l and A_u are the lower and upper side areas of the double acting cylinder piston, P_l and P_u are measured lower and upper pressures, and , $J_{footpad}$ is Jacobian matrix of the footpad device. If we get vertical force values from pneumatic cylinders and get horizontal forces from planar device, the gravity reaction forces (GRF) can be obtained to recognize the walking condition. The GRF gives important information of the typical gait pattern. Thus, the GRF from the walking interface can be applied to the lower limb rehabilitation to check the walking conditions of the patients.

3. Control

For the planar device, we used a 8-axis motor controller which is connected through PCI slot to the Pentium IV-3.5G PC which performs walking control algorithm with a C program, in which kinematics and dynamics, communication, and feedback position control are performed at the rate of 1kHz. For the footpad device, double-acting low-friction cylinder actuators are used. They have linear potentiometer transducer inside the cylinder. The device outputs 6 air pressures that drive the eight double-acting cylinders. Each of these pressures is controlled by proportional pneumatic valves. Seeking to maximize bandwidth, the interface's valves were specially chosen for their low response time and high airflow, which are less than 10 ms (100 Hz) and 350 Nl/min, respectively. The pressures in each of the 12 air compartments are read by pressure sensors. These pressure values are used to feedback control and sensing of the force. The D/A card outputs a control signal for each of the 6 pressure valves.

The control algorithm should be designed to keep the position of the human at the neutral position of the K-Walker during walking. In order to achieve this goal, the principal of the cancellations is suggested: The K-walker will follow the magnetic tracker attached to the foot during swing phase, while the device will move back during stance phase when human foot is contact with ground. The transition phase between swing phase and stance phase are detected by using threshold of the ground height. When the human foot height is smaller than ground height, it is considered that the human foot is contact with the ground; thus, the device will be moving back. On the other hand, when the human foot height is larger than ground height, it is considered that the human foot is moving forward without contact with the ground, thus, the device will follow the human foot trajectory. The algorithm to implement this walking scenario is shown in Figure 3.

Figure 3 shows in detail that if the z coordinate, z_{track}, of the foot tracker is higher than ground height, $H_{threshold}$, the gait cycle is recognized as swing phase and the back-and-forward direction (y_{track}) of the motion tracker is inserted to the command input for motion control of the planar device. On the other hand, if the z_{track} is lower than $H_{threshold}$, the gait cycle is recognized as the stance phase and the planar device is moving back.

In order to put back the limb in the original position with human walking speed, the following algorithm is suggested:

$$\text{If } y_m \geq 0, V_{commnad} = -V_{track}$$

$$\text{Else, } V_{commnad} = -V_{track}(y_{max} + y_m)/y_{max}$$

where y_{max} and V_{track} is the maximum distance and the average speed during swing phase for back-and-forth direction, $V_{commnad}$ is the control velocity input of the interface device, and y_m is the measured back-and-forth distance of the interface device. When $y_m \geq 0$, average speed V_{track} during the swing phase is inserted to command input. On the other hand, when $y_m < 0$, the command speed $V_{command}$ is decreasing with respect to the platform coordinate y_m. It is observed that with this algorithm, the unstable motion of the interface device due to large inertia was deleted. This walking control algorithm, therefore, will sustain continuous walking with the device.

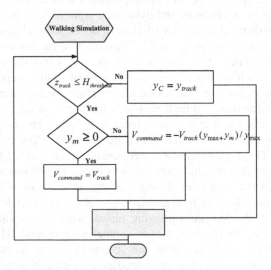

Figure 3. Walking control algorithm

4. Walking Experiments and Evaluation

To implement the real walking simulation with the proposed interface device, the safety of a user should be guaranteed all the time. Therefore, we let a user wear a harness, which can support totally human weight above 100kg and have shock absorber. In addition, the balance bar is constructed for a user to keep balance of his/her body during walking above the interface device. The balance bar is moved by the hand of the human walker. Currently, only one platform for the right foot is constructed and the other platform is under construction. Even though two platforms are not simultaneously operating, the walking experiments are possible since during all gait cycle the left and right lower limb motions are same except the phase of two limbs.

Figure 4. Harness and balance bar for safe walking with the interface

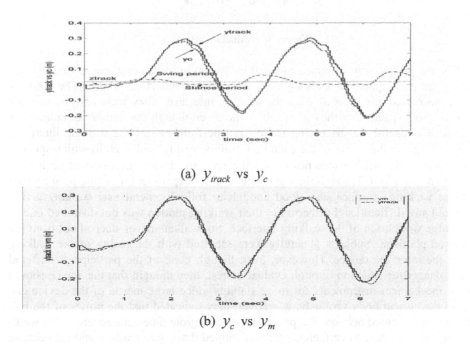

(a) y_{track} vs y_c

(b) y_c vs y_m

Figure 5. Walking test for plane level

Figure 5 shows real experimental results of human walking using the K-walker with the walking control algorithm. Figure 5(a) shows the tracker value z_{track} of heave motion, the y_{track} of back-and-forth motion, and the command input y_c for back-and-forth motion. The swing phase is recognized when z_{track} is higher than ground, and the interface device tracks the magnetic tracker attached to the shoes on which person wears, while the interface device is moving back with walking control algorithm satisfactorily during stance phase. Figure 5 (b) show that the interface device is tracking well the trajectory of the command input. This results shows that the control of the interface is well operating enough to follow human walking speed. It should be noted that the ratio of stance and swing phase during general walking with the K-walker was very similar to normal gait cycle. Therefore, we can guess that the natural walking can be achievable by using the new interface device.

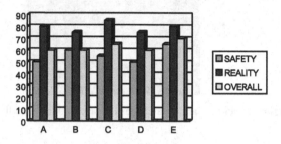

Figure 6. Evaluation results

For the preliminary interface evaluation, five subjects among our laboratory students are participated in walking with the designed interface device. The subjects were instructed how to walk over the walking interface. They were allowed to walk with normal speeds that they generally walk. Even though the number of subjects is small, it is useful for discussing the overall performance of the walking interface. Figure 6 shows the scores of the each item (safety, reality, and overall) with respect to subjects A...E. After interactions with the walking device, they scored each item between 0 and 100. Through the observation of the experiment, tracking performance of the walking interface was good enough to follow general user walking action without any difficulties. Furthermore, their walking motion was not disturbed due to the large workspace of the walking interface. So, walkers never steeped out from the footpad platform. Subjects generally were satisfied with the reality of the walking with the interface device. However, even though none of the participants suffered from dangerous situation through evaluation test, they thought that the device should have mechanical instruments for more stability since large inertia of the device can harm the human body seriously. Moreover, they indicated that the noises of the ball caster implemented between the planar device and ground become severe as the walking speed increases. Nevertheless, they mentioned that it was realistic enough because it incited them to walk by using their whole body. Obviously, there were a few limitations in the system compared to the real walking such as the noises of the mechanical operations, the limited speed of the walking, and wearing safety harness. However, it provided a framework to make it possible for the walker to enjoy natural walking with full immersion and realism using the K-Walker interface.

5. Conclusions

This paper presented a novel locomotion interface that can simulate natural walking and omni-directional various terrains. This interface is composed of independent planar, and footpad devices and can generate infinite surface for continuous working in a confined area. This structure allows the support of human weight and sufficient workspace for natural walking (step: max 1m, load capability: max 100kg). For real experiment with the walking interface, the natural walking can be achievable by using the walking control algorithm. The walking control algorithm operates differently for each gait phase. During the swing phase, the walking interface is following human foot, while the device is moving back during the stance phase. For safety, a handle guide is implemented at the center position of the interface for walker to keep balance of the human body, and the walker should wear harness to protect the physical damage for any unexpected accidents by malfunctions of controller, sensor, and actuators. For preliminary evaluation test, the responses of subjects are positive in that the natural walking is possible using the proposed walking interface. Future research will develop the haptic effects for various surface conditions, and evaluation with two platforms.

References

[1] R.R. Christensen, J. M. Hollerbach, Y. Xu, & S. G. Meek, "Inertial-Force Feedback for the Treadport Locomotion Interface," *Presence*, Vol. 9, No. 1, pp. 1-14, 2000.
[2] R. Darken, W. Cockayne, D. Carmein. "The Omni-Directional Treadmill: A Locomotion Device for Virtual Words," *Proc. of User Interface Software Technology (UIST 97)*, pp.213-222, 1997.
[3] H. Iwata, "Walking About Virtual Environment on an Infinite Floor," *Proc. of IEEE Virtual Reality 99*, pp. 286-293, 1999.
[4] D.C. Brogan, R.A. Metoyer, and J. K. Hodgins, "Dynamically Simulated Characters in Virtual Environments," *SIGGRAPH Visual Proc.*, pp.216, 1997.
[5] H. Iwata and T. Fuji, "Virtual Perambulator: A Novel Interface Device for Locomotion in Virtual Environments," *Proc. of IEEE 1996 Virtual Reality Annual Int'l Symp.*, pp.60-65, 1996.
[6] http://www.sarcos.com/interpic_virtualinter.html
[7] G. P. Roston and T. Peurach, "A Whole Body Kinesthetic Display Device for Virtual Reality Applications," *Proc. of IEEE Int'l Conf. on Robotics and Automation*, pp. 3006-3011, 1997.
[8] H. Iwata, The GaitMaster: Locomotion Interface for Uneven Virtual Surface, *Proc. of 4th VRSJ Annual Conf.*, 1999, 345-348.
[9] H.Schmidt, D. Sorowka, S. Hesse, & R. Bernhardt, Design of a Robotic Walking Simulator for Neurological Rehabilitation, *IEEE/RSJ Int. Conf. On Intelligent Robots and Systems*, pp. 1487-1492, 2002.
[10] M. Slater et al., "Taking Steps: The influence of a Walking Metaphor on Presence in Virtual Reality," *ACM Trans. On Computer Human Interaction*, Vol. 2, No. 3, pp.201-219, 1995.
[11] J. Perry, Gait Analysis: Normal and Pathological Function (Thorofare, N. J. :Slack Inc., 1992).

Designing Intelligent Environments – User Perceptions on Information Sharing

Craig Chatfield[1], Jonna Häkkilä

Griffith University, Australia
c.chatfield@griffith.edu.au, jonna@avaruusmies.com

Abstract. This study examines user's opinions on personal information exchange with an Intelligent Environment providing information for HCI design for acceptable and usable application development. It found that users are more comfortable with their information being exchanged if it is clear what the information is being used for, and who will have access to it. 83% of all subjects wanted control over the exchange of their information, and a third would be more likely to share information with a service provider if they had a good global reputation and if the user could request that their information could be deleted. The biggest influence on a user's information sharing preferences was found to be the existence of a prior relationship with the information recipient.

1 Introduction

During recent years, developments in technology have lead to introduction of Intellgent Environments (IEs), which are ubiquitous computing environments that interactively provide services based on context information such as user characteristics and environmental data. In addition to the technical challenges, intelligent environments set new demands for application design in user acceptance and privacy issues. Users unwillingness to trust ubiquitous computing systems is seen as the major impediment to the acceptance of these systems [1]. Intelligent environments infringe on user privacy, but the effects can be minimized with effective system design and implementation. Privacy design is affected by personal privacy, economics and social acceptance [2]. In order to enhance the design and usability of future intelligent environments, it is important to understand users' perceptions and ideas about privacy and trust.

Smart meeting rooms, virtual cafés, context sensitive applications and some m-commerce applications [3] are examples of IEs where sharing and transmitting information about the users can be a critical part of the system. In order to develop acceptable applications, designers have to consider users' perceptions of their privacy and find ways to ensure it. The question of trust becomes relevant when user has to define who is allowed to access his/her personal information. Trust has been investigated with e-commerce and online communication via internet, e.g. Friedman et al. [4]. However, with these kinds of applications, the user is usually controlling the data

---

[1] The author would like to acknowledge the support of the Smart Internet Technology CRC.

M. Masoodian et al. (Eds.): APCHI 2004, LNCS 3101, pp. 570–574, 2004.

flow and aware of the other parties involved with the situation. This is not often the case with intelligent environments, and the information sharing and data exchange can occur without the user's knowledge. Thus, knowledge about people's perceptions of information access rights is crucial. The discussion on the topic has raised several approaches, which introduce a usage of pseudonym or alias when information sharing takes place. As an example, Lederer, Dey and Mankoff [5] have suggested *Faces* approach, where users could select a different *face*, a virtual skin or mask, for use in different situations. Further research into information sharing within mobile computing suggests that who is making the request is much more important than the situation in which the request is made [6].

Our study provides user data of people's perceptions of privacy and trust. The research questionnaire used in the study was related to mobile phone usage, as they are familiar to all our respondents. The questionnaire included questions regarding mobile phone usage, information sharing and user perceived trust.

2 Survey and Results

The survey was conducted among Australian university students participating in information technology courses. The focus group consists of active mobile phone users. 119 participants between 17 and 40, predominately in their 20's, filled out a written questionnaire. 115 of the participants reported to have a mobile phone, which results 97% ownership rate. No respondents reported sharing a phone with someone, e.g. a family member. The multiple choice based questionnaire was designed to measure user privacy opinions on mobile communications and information sharing within intelligent environments.

2.1 Influences on Information Sharing

Participants' were first questioned on sharing information with a service provider. Table 1 describes characteristics that would make the users comfortable with sharing their information. Table 2 describes the influences identified by the users as affecting what information they would be willing share. As participants were advised to select one or more options for both questions, the sum of results exceeds 100%.

Table 1. Influences on participants' comfort for information sharing

Would you feel more comfortable disclosing information if you could clearly see:	n = 119
What the information will be used for	52 %
Who will have access to the information	47 %
All information you provided was recorded anonymously	29 %
Where the information was being stored	26 %
How information is being gathered	23 %
How long the information will be stored before being erased	21 %
None	13 %

Table 2. Information sharing likeliness for different influence factors

When would you be more likely to share information with a service provider?	n = 119
Could request your information be deleted	33 %
The service provider had a good reputation globally	32 %
All information you provided was recorded anonymously	29 %
The service provider has a clear, easily accessibly privacy policy	25 %
If you considered the service rendered to be especially valuable	19 %
None of the answers	19 %
The service provider was recommended to you by your friends	8 %

The questionnaire next inquired about users' desire to control the information shared with their environment or an external person. The question described a scenario where information could be automatically shared between the user's phone and the environment, a case common to IEs and ubiquitous computing research:

> *Each time someone wants to access your information, they have to send an information-sharing request to the database. Each request is considered separately in order to decide if the information request is answered or not. Would you prefer requests for information to be handled by:*
>> *a. Default settings on your mobile phone*
>> *b. Individually approving each exchange*
>> *c. Combination of the two*

Only 17% of the respondents chose to automate the information exchange with the environment. 38% indicated they wanted complete control, while 45% selected a combination of the two.

2.2   Information Sharing Preferences

The final question of the survey was an exploratory research question, seeking to identify whom users would be most likely to share information with. The goal of this question was to contribute to the direction of future research on user information sharing preferences, and automated information sharing systems.

The information that was available to share was as follows: *Name, Alias, Contact Details, Primary* and *Secondary Email Addresses, Interests,* the users *Approximate* and *Actual Location* and their *Current Activity.* The different user types to share information with are described in Table 3. Being an exploratory question, the authors sought to identify which of the different user types caused the subjects to share more information. To determine this, each selection was considered separately in relation to the subject's responses to other user types, as people clearly had individual strategies in information sharing. For example, we expected that within close social groups users would share all their information with their family and almost everything with all the other groups, whereas other participants would share only their name with everyone else. Thus, we chose to determine the relative change in information shared to determine which groups were identified the most.

The first four user categories in Table 3 were used as positive reference values: *family members, friends, associates* and *employers. A stranger that provides you with no personal information* was used as a negative reference. The aim was to indicate which of the other categories could be used to influence personal information sharing systems, and how these groups behaved in comparison to the reference groups. Therefore the authors sought to identify which of the last eight categories in Table 3 influenced the respondents the most. A category was considered to have influenced the user if they indicated they would share more information with them, than with a stranger that shared no personal information. More information was considered in this case to be another piece of primary information *(Name, Contact Details, Primary Email* or *Actual Location)*, or two pieces of secondary information *(Alias, Secondary Email, Interests, Approximate Location* or *Current Activity)*.

Of the 119 respondents, 22 left the question blank, indicating they would either share no information with the environment, or that they didn't wish to answer the question. The results in Table 3 are calculated for the 97 remaining participants.

Table 3. Different User Types and results for allowing information sharing

User Types	n = 97
Someone you met previously at a social function / party	59%
Someone you met previously at a business function	57%
Services you have subscribed to (e.g. Auto Club, Directions providers, etc)	57%
Stranger who is a friend of a good friend	40%
A stranger, or organisation, with a good reputation (e.g. Red Cross, Amnesty)	40%
Stranger that provides you with most/all of their information	31%
Stranger that is nearby (e.g. in the same room)	29%
Nearby Information Providers (e.g. Information Booths, Advertisers)	24%

3 Discussion and Conclusions

The results of this questionnaire have implications for the design of information sharing systems in IEs and mobile computing. The high percentage of users (83%) wanting control over the exchange of their information could indicate a level of distrust with automating the exchange of sensitive information. With intelligent and context-aware systems, the potentially uncontrolled transmission of the user's data to the system infrastructure has already risen concerns [7]. Our results support the view that users want to stay in control over the information they share, and are concerned about their privacy and personal information exchange.

The factors most influencing users' opinions about information sharing, i.e. *what the information will be used for* and *who will access the information,* see Table 1, were quite expected results. A third of the respondents also indicated they would be more likely to share information with a service provider if they had a good global reputation and if the user could request that the information could be deleted. However, the relatively high frequencies that *nothing* would make user more likely to share information with a service provider (13%) can be seen as indications of the general mistrust to information sharing systems. This was reflected in the second question, where one fifth of the subjects indicated that none of the mentioned attributes would have made them more likely to share information with a service provider.

This study also found that an existing relationship between the users of an Intelligent Environment is the biggest influence on user information sharing. This took place both for individuals (a person who had been met) and organizations (service which the user had subscribed to). These results are consistent with Zheng et al's [8] research into user trust. The authors therefore suggest that a user model should identify whether a prior relationship exists before any information exchange. The importance of the prior relationship is seen also from the results concerning organizational parties, as users were more willing to share information with the services they had subscribed than e.g. services nearby. This result also suggests that reputation is also important when no prior relationship exists. This supports Goecks and Mynatt's [9] findings that trust and reputation are essential components of any intelligent environment.

A third party's willingness to share information, or their proximity seems to have very little influence on a users desire to provide them with information. This could perhaps be because in these cases, there is no expectation of a future relationship. An established relationship would suggest that one would exist in the future.

The results cannot be regarded as absolute measures as users may behave differently in real life usage situation than what they assume in interviews. However, we believe that the results give indication of the trends for user perceived privacy and information sharing. Further research is required to determine the extent of the influence, and to determine the influence these findings should have upon the user models and user information sharing preferences.

References

1. Langheinrich, M. *Privacy by Design - Principles of Privacy-Aware Ubiquitous Systems*. in *Ubicomp*. 2001.
2. Langheinrich, M. *Privacy Invasions in Ubiquitous Computing*. in *Ubicomp Privacy Workshop*. 2002. Göteborg, Sweden.
3. Sun, J., *Information Requirement Elicitation in Mobile Commerce*. Communications of the ACM, 2000. **Vol 43**(No.12): p. pp. 45-47.
4. Friedman, B., P.H. Kahn, and D.C. Howe, *Trust Online*. Communications of the ACM, 2000. **Vol. 43**(No. 12): p. pp. 34-40.
5. Lederer, S., A.K. Dey, and J. Mankoff, *A Conceptual Model and a Metaphor of Everyday Privacy in Ubiquitous Computing Environments*. 2002, University of California.
6. Lederer, S., J. Mankoff, and A.K. Dey, *Who Wants to Know What When? Privacy Preference Determinants in Ubiquitous Computing*. 2003.
7. Barkhuus, L. and A.K. Dey. *Is Context-Aware Computing Taking Control Away from the User? Three Levels of Interactivity Examined*. in *UbiComp*. 2003.
8. Zheng, J., et al., *Trust without Touch: Jumpstarting long-distance trust with initial social activities*. Letters of CHI, 2002. **Vol 4**(Iss 1): p. pp. 141-146.
9. Goecks, J. and E. Mynatt. *Enabling Privacy Management in Ubiquitous Computing Environments through Trust and Reputation Systems*. in *Computer-Supported Cooperative Work*. 2002.

Sony EyeToy™: Developing Mental Models for 3-D Interaction in a 2-D Gaming Environment

Geanbry Demming

Amberlight Partners, Ltd, 3 Waterhouse Sq, 142 Holborn
London, SW15 6EL, UK
gigi@amber-light.co.uk

Abstract. The Sony EyeToy™ is a webcam attachment for the Playstation2 (PS2) gaming console. The EyeToy™ places a user's mirror image on a television screen while it detects their movements in order for them to manipulate objects and characters within a game. Although EyeToy™ is immediately popular due to the novelty of interaction, users often have trouble forming a mental model of how to manipulate their own image in a 2-dimensional (2-D) 3rd person gaming scenario. Multiplayer testing sessions were carried out to explore the impact that a game's theme and a user's age and previous gaming experience would have on how users initially cope with this form of gaming interaction. A lack of tangible feedback and unrealistic game scenarios were the main hindrances to users reconciling the fact that they were in a 3-dimensional (3-D) space but had to behave as 2-D characters.

1 Introduction

Commercial gaming has seen a trend in the increasing demand for games that require physical interaction, mainly musical in nature. Users are looking more and more to full body movement to entertain themselves in the commercial world of video games. "Dance Dance[sic] Revolution" is a highly popular arcade game that's spawned an increase of dancemat purchases for home entertainment (Mixed Reality Lab). There is even an increasing amount of tournaments dedicated to dancing games (Diniz-Sanches, 2004). Users can also become virtual musicians by shaking maracas or playing with digital turntables (Walker, 2003). As removed as these games may seem from traditional handheld-controller gaming, they still rely on tactile interaction.

The EyeToy™ is a product developed by Sony Computer Entertainment Europe (SCEE) for the Playstation 2 games consoles. The EyeToy™ webcam attaches to the USB port of a PS2 gaming console. Users stand in front of the camera and see their inverted image (as if looking in a mirror) on screen. The camera then detects any movement, allowing users to manipulate various screen elements – effectively putting users in the game by having their movements dictate play. Considering the lack of

M. Masoodian et al. (Eds.): APCHI 2004, LNCS 3101, pp. 575–582, 2004.
© Springer-Verlag Berlin Heidelberg 2004

commercial access users have had to this form of interaction[1] until recently, this research was conducted to investigate the usability and general appeal of EyeToy™ and the games within the "EyeToy™: Play" package.

1.1 Nature of Interaction

Computer supported collaborative play (CSCP) is defined as "computer technology that enhance[s] physical exertion, social interaction, and entertainment in sport and play" (Ishii et al in Mandryk & Maranan, 2002). While EyeToy™ descriptively fits in the CSCP paradigm, the games readily associated with CSCP (e.g. PingPongPlus or The Pirates) require tactile manipulation of artefacts to promote physical gameplay (Mandryk & Maranan, 2002). Therefore, EyeToy™ presents an opportunity to define use cases, barriers to task completion, and determiners of a pleasurable experience that previous gaming research may not be able to account for.

With EyeToy™, whatever existing mental models about physical movement users adapt for gameplay can be complicated by the fact that, in several games, characters respond in a 3-D manner. For example, in the game "Kung Foo", if a player hits a character, one of the programmed visual effects is having the character fly towards them and hit the screen. Users could simply flick a finger to their side to elicit this same type of behavioural feedback from a character. However, users could easily mistake a swift forward striking motion as the cause of a character behaving in this manner. Somewhat misleadingly, the game does not actually provide an analogous 3-D response to users 3-D actions.

Intuitive interaction is also hindered by the fact that there is no tangible feedback for EyeToy™. For more traditional games in which users' input is mediated through handheld controls, or a dancemat, users can more readily associate their tactile interaction with the feedback on the screen (Diniz-Sanches, 2004). With EyeToy™, however, the visual and aural feedback users receive is not an absolute indicator by which they can determine the exact timing and 3-D location of their input controls (i.e. body parts). The exact path from cause to effect is further camouflaged when taking into consideration interference from other moving objects and persons visible to the camera, or the lack of contrast between the user's skin/clothing colour and their background. Both instances make it difficult for the camera to detect movement and subsequently cause confusion amongst users as to why the game is not behaving in the way they anticipated.

1.2 Games Themes

The set of 12 games known as "EyeToy™: Play" was used for testing. The games range both in theme and the nature of the movement that they require. All the games in the Play package can be divided across 2 high-level categories in terms of their

---

[1] Logitech offered similar software with some of their webcams but gameplay and interaction is extremely limited compared to EyeToy™.

objectives: Realistic and Abstract.   Realistic games easily map onto real world scenarios or actions popularised by television or films (e.g. Kung Foo or Boxing Chump). Abstract games are those that bare no relationship to a real world scenario or situation (e.g. UFO Juggler). Realistic games allow for users to access inherent mental models of movements in order to emulate realistic scenarios. For abstract games, users were initially less sure of how to behave or move without the aid of a tutorial or help.

There also appears to be an unintentional correlation between game themes and the nature of the movement required for *intended* gameplay [for games that do not require precision hand movements, it is easy to cheat simply by standing within 1 meter of the camera while waving arms frantically]. Realistic games most often require fast long movements with the arms. Abstract games most often require precision hand placement. Given the limited number of games available for testing, it is hard to say if this trend is significant. It is addressed for the purpose of investigating the impact the type of movement required might have on users' ability to intuitively engage in gameplay. Table 1 describes how each game fits into a matrix of game themes and the movement required for intended

Table 1. The 12 Play games classified in terms of **gameplay**.theme and type of movement required for successful gameplay.

Games theme	Long quick motions	Short quick motions	Precision hand placement
Realistic	Kung Foo, Boxing, Wishi Washi, Keep Ups	Plate Spinners	
Abstract	Beat Freak, Slap Stream	Ghost catcher, UFO Juggler	Rocket Rumble, Mirror Time, Boogie down, Slap Stream

2 Method

Testing was aimed at 3 objectives: 1) scoping initial reactions towards the technology and general appeal of EyeToy™ 2) determining users mental models for navigation and gameplay 3) determining to what extent the factors that contribute to a pleasurable experience with EyeToy™ differ, if at all, from those for traditional console games.

Several assumptions were made in order to formulate a viable framework for testing. While players generally play computer games on their own (Mandryk & Maranan, 2002), EyeToy™ best affords social gameplay – even though the multiplayer mode is designed for asynchronous inter-player gameplay. Therefore, groups of 4 users were recruited for multiplayer testing sessions. Four was determined as an ideal number: a) to foster a highly sociable environment and b) to accommodate what would customarily be the absolute maximum number of players normally allowed for co-located multi-player console games. Finally, each session was held at the home of one of the users taking part in the session. All participants within a session were also acquainted with one another to promote a comfortable social environment for testing.

2.1 User Groups

Children and teenagers were SCEE's assumed target audience, due to the look and feel of the games to be tested. However, groups for testing were extended to incorporate adults to see what appeal EyeToy™ might have for them. The final groups were: Children aged 5 – 10; Children aged 11 – 14; Family of 4; University Students (aged 18 – 25); Young professional men (aged 24 – 28). Aside from the young professional men each group had an equal male-female ratio and all groups contained 4 participants. Young professionals was delineated as a same sex group based on fact that even though 46% of console purchases are by women, women only account for 28% of regular games players (Hafer, GamesFirst.com).

Users were also recruited on the basis of their previous console gaming experience ranging from novice (play console games at *most* once a month) to 'hard-core' gamers (play at least 3 times a week and across various gaming genres). The definition for novice and hard-core gamers was decided in conjunction with SCEE. Finally, to capture novice feedback and requirements, all users had no previous experience playing with EyeToy™.

2.1 Session Agenda

Each testing session lasted for approximately 90 minutes. The majority of each session (approx. 60mins) was devoted to users interacting with EyeToy™ with little to no interference from the facilitator. Users were given an 'out of the box' scenario. Their foreknowledge about the nature of interaction was limited to understanding that they will see themselves on the television and they can use their various body parts to play the game. Users were then left to their own devices to navigate through the menu structure and to play games both of their choosing and those chosen by the facilitator. The facilitator noted comments and behavioural signs of frustration and positive responses.

3 Reactions to Technology

The novelty of interaction was well-received by all participants – regardless of their statistical background. There is not enough conclusive evidence to suggest gender has an effect on users understanding of the nature of interaction, despite males' inherent advantage over females when it comes to spatial manipulation (Kimura, 2001).

However, age and previous gaming experience appear to be the two main contributors to how readily users understand the nature of interaction needed to play EyeToy™ games.

Users who have difficulty with EyeToy™ appear to experience a conflict between seeing themselves on screen, yet having to ultimately play in a 3rd person scenario. In other words, they become the avatar they have to manipulate, but not by means of traditional analogue control mechanisms.

3.1 Impact of Age

Most of the children (aged 5-14) saw EyeToy™ almost as a touch screen interface. The more negative feedback children would receive from the game, the more they approached the screen, until they were actually touching it. This suggests they may have been trying to resort to the more familiar tactile interaction they are accustomed to with traditional video games or most other interfaces they encounter – i.e. they feel if they apply physical pressure to a mechanism of control they will see a response on screen.

Furthermore, for children, seeing their image on screen was often incidental. All their attention was devoted to using the characters and elements in the games as spatial cues about where to place their hands in a 3-D space, not knowing they needed to manipulate their image in a 2-D plane. Therefore, they concentrated solely on where the characters were being generated from, rather than the relationship between their image on the screen and the characters. At times only the top of their heads would be visible on screen, and yet they would still exhibit extreme concentration while enthusiastically trying to bat away characters.

3.2 Impact of Previous Gaming Experience

Those users with more previous console gaming experience performed overwhelmingly better at games than their novice counterparts. It may not be surprising that those with more extensive gaming experience would be better at gameplay due to their relatively sharpened skills in hand-eye coordination. However, the concept of their relationship to the characters on screen should still be fairly abstract as they are accustomed to an avatar performing on their behalf not manipulating their own image in real-time. Nevertheless, they tended to pick up on the proper use of EyeToy™ more readily than their novice counterparts. One suggestion is that hardcore gamers are used to seeking out gaming cues to frame interaction – they may more readily notice the positioning outlines players are supposed to stand in or the fact that their head accidentally selected a button.

3.3 Impact of Games

Table 2 reflects the popularity of the 12 games, across all users, within the context of their demarcation in Table 1.   There was very little variation between user groups when it came to gaming preference. Kung Foo and Boxing Chump were unanimously listed as the 2 most popular games. Some games with mixed popularity, such as Beat Freak, did not elicit a strong positive or negative response from users in terms of

Table 2. Game popularity based on game theme. 1 = highly popular; 2 = mixed popularity; 3 = unpopular.

Games theme	Long quick motions	Short quick motions	Precision hand placement
Realistic	1	3	
Abstract	2	3	2

preference. For other games, which received a mixed response, some users really enjoyed a particular game while others disliked it (e.g. Slap Stream).

Users' preference in terms of movement had more to do with physical fatigue than how intuitive it was to engage in game play. In contrast, their preference in game themes actually had an impact on how readily they came to understand the nature of interaction needed for successful gameplay.

Users performed best on the games Kung Foo, Boxing Chump and Wishi Washi (objective is to clean as many windows as possible) simply by emulating the motions they would expect to execute in a comparable real world situation. There is not enough evidence, however, to discount the fact that the direction and timing of characters' behaviour in these games did not affect users' level of understanding about intended gameplay. For example, in Boxing Chump, users are encouraged to fight in a 2-D plane due to the positioning of the robot they are sparring with and the visual feedback for successful blows. The robot never falters to the left or the right, but always doubles over in a way that suggests it is being hit in the stomach, directly from the front. Hence, users are given cues that punching directly at the robot, and not to its side, is the best way to defeat him.

3.4 Bridging the 2D/3D Divide

A user's statistical background (e.g. age and previous gaming experience) cannot be ignored when it comes to how they will cope with trying to form a mental model for 2-D interaction in a 3-D world. However, in terms of future development of games that will sit on this type of interaction, the findings of this study point to 2 key requirements to promote the successful acquisition of mental models for gameplay by novice users:

1. Develop games around real world and practical scenarios
2. Do not provide visual cues that appear to respond as a 3-D analogue to users' movements

The first requirement allows novice users to bring to the game pre-existing mental models of movement and use them to their advantage for gameplay. The second requirement acts as a guidepost for interaction, albeit retroactively at first, by illustrating how best to get a reaction from characters and other gaming elements. The second requirement also opens the door for games with more abstract themes by easing users into developing a mental model of 2-D movement.

4 Future Research

For users that have trouble with the relationship of their image to the characters on the screen, it would be of interest to see if creating an avatar that responded directly to users' movements would work to reconcile the conceptual rift between their 3-D environment and the game's 2-D world. The integration of EyeToy™ with other accessories is also an area of interest. Children had the hardest time grasping the concept of interaction needed, potentially due to the lack of tangible feedback. The fact that the most highly quoted suggestions from children were the integration of a dancemat for dancing games and a number of fighting accessories for combative games lends credence to this argument.

Also of interest is exploring various themes for EyeToy™ games and their subsequent effect on users' understanding of intended gameplay. Many users expressed an interest in having more games relating to sports themes or an exercise video based around EyeToy™ technology. Games with these themes have an inherent set of rules and movements that are implicit to most users, which could allow for a more intuitive interaction. Finally, continued investigation is needed for the visual and aural feedback users receive to drive gameplay. Continuing with the aforementioned example of the sparring robot in Boxing Chump, its responsive behaviour was analogous to the type of movement the user needs to employ to consistently score points. This could explain why users preferred and performed better on this game. However, in order to isolate this type of feedback as having a significant impact on how users come to understand intended 2-D interaction, further testing needs to be carried out.

5 Conclusion

The nature of interaction mediated by the EyeToy™ has opened up numerous opportunities for growth in the gaming industry in terms of broadening the appeal of games and subsequently the gaming market. Its appeal is also strengthened by providing domestic access to games that aid in alleviating the sedimentary lifestyle that is often associated with long-term game use and its subsequent effect on the health and social interaction of gamers – especially children. Optimising game design to make for a more intuitive and compelling interaction should then be a priority to promote more sociable and healthy gameplay.

References

1. Diniz-Sanches, J. EyeToy:Groove. *Edge 132* (2004), 103.
2. Hafer, M. GamesFirst.com
    http://www.gamesfirst.com/articles/monica/womenwant/womenwant.htm
3. Kimura, D. Biological constraints on parity between men and women. *Psynopsis* 23,1 (2001), 3.
4. Mandryk, R. and Maranan, D. False prophets: Exploring Hybrid Board/Video games. *Proc. CHI*
    2002, Interactive Poster: Fun, 640-641.
5. Mixed Reality Research Lab – Research – Human Pacman.
    http://mixedreality.nus.edu.sg/research-HP-inform.htm
6. Walker, I. (2003). Gamerswave.com. http://www.gamerswave.com/musicspecial.htm

Face and Body Gesture Analysis for Multimodal HCI

Hatice Gunes, Massimo Piccardi, Tony Jan

Computer Vision Group, Faculty of Information Technology
University of Technology, Sydney (UTS), Australia
{haticeg, massimo, jant}@it.uts.edu.au

Abstract Humans use their faces, hands and body as an integral part of their communication with others. For the computer to interact intelligently with human users, computers should be able to recognize emotions, by analyzing the human's affective state, physiology and behavior. Multimodal interfaces allow humans to interact with machines through multiple modalities such as speech, facial expression, gesture, and gaze. In this paper, we present an overview of research conducted on face and body gesture analysis and recognition. In order to make human-computer interfaces truly natural, we need to develop technology that tracks human movement, body behavior and facial expression, and interprets these movements in an affective way. Accordingly, in this paper we present a vision-based framework that combines face and body gesture for multimodal HCI.

1 Introduction

In many HCI applications, for the computer to interact intelligently with human users, computers should be able to recognize emotions, by analyzing the human's affective state, physiology and behavior [23].

Non-verbal behavior plays an important role in human communications. According to Mehrabian [4], 93% of our communication is nonverbal and humans display their emotions most expressively through facial expressions and body gestures. Considering the effect of the message as a whole, spoken words of a message contribute only for 7%, the vocal part contributes 38%, while facial expression of the speaker contributes 55% to the effect of the spoken message [4]. Hence, understanding human emotions through nonverbal means is one of the necessary skills for computers to interact intelligently with their human counterparts. Furthermore, recent advances in image analysis and machine learning open up the possibility of automatic recognition of face and body gestures for affective human-machine communication [2,7].

This paper analyzes various existing systems and technologies used for automatic face and body gesture recognition and discusses the possibility of a multi-modal system that combines face and body signals to analyze the human emotion and behavior. The rationale for this attempt of combining face and body gesture for a better understanding of human non-verbal behavior is the recent interest and advances in multi-modal interfaces [24]. Pantic and Rothkrantz in [1] clearly state the importance of a multimodal affect analyzer for research in emotion recognition. The

M. Masoodian et al. (Eds.): APCHI 2004, LNCS 3101, pp. 583-588, 2004.
© Springer-Verlag Berlin Heidelberg 2004

modalities considered are visual, auditory and tactile, where visual mainly stands for facial actions analysis. The interpretation of other visual cues such as body language (natural/spontaneous gestures) is not explicitly addressed in [1]. However, we think that this is an important component of affective communication and this will be a major goal in this paper. Moreover, an automated system that senses, processes, and interprets the combined modes of facial expression and body gesture has great potential in various research and application areas [1-3] including human-computer interaction and pervasive perceptual man-machine interfaces [23,24].

The paper is organized as follows. Section 2 and 3 cover previous work done on automatic facial expression and gesture analysis, respectively. Section 4 presents the possible efforts toward multimodal analyzers of human affective state. Section 5 presents our approach on combining face and body gesture for multimodal HCI and finally, Section 6 gives the conclusion.

2   Facial Expression

Facial expression measurement provides an indicator of emotion activity and is presently used in a variety of areas from behavioral research to HCI. Research in psychology has indicated that at least six emotions are universally associated with distinct facial expressions: happiness, sadness, surprise, fear, anger, and disgust [5,6]. Several other emotions, and many combinations of emotions have been studied but remain unconfirmed as universally distinguishable.

Facial Expression Recognition

Within the past decade, analysis of human facial expression has attracted great interest in the machine vision and artificial intelligence communities. Systems that automatically analyze the facial expressions can generally be classified into two categories: (1) systems that recognize prototypic facial expressions (happy, sad etc.); (2) systems that recognize facial actions (frown, eyebrow raise etc.).

(1) Systems that Recognize Prototypic Facial Expressions: There has been a significant amount of research on creating systems that recognize a small set of prototypic emotional expressions from static images or image sequences. This focus follows from the work of Ekman [5]. Bassili suggested that motion in the image of a face would allow emotions to be identified even with minimal information about the spatial arrangement of features [6]. Thus, facial expression recognition from image sequences can be based on categorizing prototypic facial expressions by tracking facial features and measuring the amount of facial movement; various approaches have been explored [9, 10].

(2) Systems that Recognize Facial Actions: Although prototypic expressions are natural, they occur infrequently in everyday life and provide an incomplete description of facial expressions. To capture the subtlety of human emotion and paralinguistic communication, automated recognition of fine-grained changes in facial expression is needed [11]. Ekman and Friesen developed the Facial Action Coding System (FACS) for describing facial expressions by action units (AUs) [5]. The system is based on the enumeration of all "action units" of a face that cause facial

movements. Out of the 44 AUs defined, 30 are anatomically related to the contractions of specific facial muscles: 12 for the upper face, and 18 for the lower face. AUs can be classified either individually or in combination. Vision-based systems attempting to recognize action units (AUs) are motivated by FACS [5]. Some of them have used optical flow across the entire face or facial feature measurements [9, 14]. Tian and Kanade used facial features to recognize 16 AUs and their combination by describing the shape of facial features by multistate templates [7]. Donato *et al.* compared optical flow, principal component analysis, independent component analysis, local feature analysis, and Gabor wavelet representation to recognize 6 single upper face AUs and 6 single lower face AUs [8]. Pantic and Rothkrantz developed a facial gesture recognition system from both frontal and profile image sequences [12]. Kapoor and Picard used pupil detection from infrared sensitive cameras for recognizing upper AUs [13].

3 Gesture

Gesture is "the use of motions of the limbs or body as a mean of expression; communicate an intention or feeling" [14]. Gestures include body movements (e.g., palm-down, shoulder-shrug) and postures (e.g., angular distance), and most often occur in conjunction with speech. It has been shown that when speech is ambiguous or in a noisy environment, listeners rely on the gestural cues [3]. Thus, gestures serve an important communicative function in face-to-face communication [3, 16]. The majority of hand gestures produced by speakers are connected to speech. Kendon has situated these hand gestures along a "gesture continuum" [14], defining five different kinds of gestures: (1)*Gesticulation–* spontaneous movements of the hands and arms that accompany speech; (2)*Language-like gestures–* gesticulation that is integrated into the vocal expression, replacing a particular spoken word; (3)*Pantomimes–* gestures that represent objects or actions, with or without accompanying speech; (4)*Emblems–* familiar gestures such as thumbs up (often culturally specific); (5)*Sign languages–* The well defined linguistic systems, such as Australian Sign Language.

Gesture Recognition

According to Turk [17], most research to date in computer science, focuses on emblems and sign languages in Kendon's continuum, where gestures tend to be less ambiguous, more learned and more culture-specific. However, the concept of gesture is still not well defined, and depends on the context of the particular interaction (static/dynamic). Currently, most computer vision systems for recognizing gestures have similar components [17]. Human position and movement is sensed using cameras and computer vision techniques. In the preprocessing stage images are normalized, enhanced, or transformed. Gestures are modeled by using various representation techniques [18, 19]. Features are extracted and gestures analyzed with motion analysis, segmentation, contour representation etc. [17-19]. In the final stage, gesture recognition and classification is performed.

4 Multimodal HCI

Multimodal systems provide the possibility of combining different modalities (i.e. speech, facial expression, gesture, and gaze) that occur together to function in a more efficient and reliable way in various human-computer interaction applications [1], [24]. Studies showed that these interfaces support more effective human-computer interaction [24]. Currently, there are very few multi-modal systems introduced attempting to analyze combinations of communication means for *human affective state analysis* [20-22]. These are systems mostly combining auditory and visual information by processing facial expression and vocal cues for affective emotion recognition. According to a recent survey by Pantic and Rothkrantz in [1], the work presented by Picard *et al.* [23] is the only work combining different modalities for automatic analysis of *affective physiological signals*. See [1] and [24] for further review of the recent attempts at combining different modalities in HCI.

5 Proposed Framework

Face and body gestures are two of the several channels of nonverbal communication that occur together. Messages can be expressed through face and gesture in many ways. For example, an emotion such as sadness can be communicated through the facial expression and lowered head and shoulder position. Thus, various nonverbal channels can be combined for construction of computer systems that can *affectively* communicate with humans.

We propose a vision-based framework that uses computer vision and machine learning techniques to recognize face and body gesture for a multimodal HCI interface. To our best knowledge there has been no attempt to combine face and body gesture for nonverbal behavior recognition. For our multimodal analyzer we will use a human model including the face (eyes, eyebrows, nose, lips and chin) and the upper body (trunk, two arms and two hands) performing face and body actions (i.e. raising eyebrows, crossing arms etc.). Hence, multi-modality will be achieved by combining facial expression and body language. Proposed system framework is shown in Fig.1.

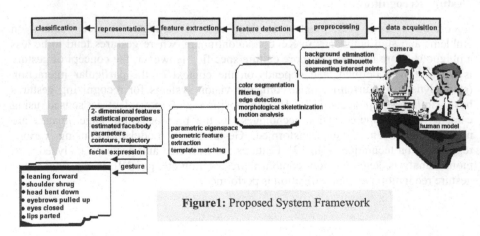

Figure1: Proposed System Framework

Due to being a new research area, there exist problems to be solved and issues to be considered in order to develop a robust multimodal analyzer of face and body gesture. In a multimodal system, the basic problem to be solved is to fuse information from different modalities [1]. Fusion could be (a) done early or late in the interpretation process; (b) some mode could be principal and other auxiliary. Another potential issue to consider in our work is that gesture analysis is even more context-dependent than facial action analysis. For this reason, we clearly want to treat face and body information separately. Another issue to consider is that detection of gesture actions could be technically more challenging than facial actions. There is a greater intrinsic visual complexity; facial features never occlude each other and they are not deformable, instead, limbs are subject to occlusions and deformations. However, the use of gesture actions could be an auxiliary mode to be used only when expressions from the remaining modes are classified as ambiguous.

6 Conclusion

This paper presented a vision-based framework that recognizes face and body gesture for multimodal HCI by firstly presenting various approaches and previous work in automatic facial expression/action analysis, gesture recognition and multimodal interfaces. "The advent of multimodal interfaces based on recognition of human speech, gaze, gesture, and other natural behavior represents only the beginning of a progression toward computational interfaces capable of human-like sensory perception" [24]. However, due to being a fairly new research area, there still exist problems to be solved and issues to be considered [1,24].

References

[1] M. Pantic and L.J.M. Rothkrantz, 'Towards an Affect-Sensitive Multimodal Human-Computer Interaction '. In: *Proceedings of the IEEE*, vol. 91, no. 9, pp. 1370-1390, September 2003

[2] M. Pantic and L.J.M. Rothkrantz,, "Automatic analysis of facial expressions: the state of the art", *IEEE PAMI*, pp. 1424-1445, Vol: 22, Issue: 12, Dec 2000

[3] J. Cassell. A framework for gesture generation and interpretation. In R. Cipolla and A. Pentland, editors, *Computer vision in human-machine interaction*. Cambridge University Press, 2000.

[4] A. Mehrabian, "Communication without words," *Psychol. Today*, vol. 2, no. 4, pp. 53–56, 1968.

[5] P. Ekman and W. V. Friesen. *The Facial Action Coding System*. Consulting Psychologists Press, San Francisco, CA, 1978.

[6] J. N. Bassili. Facial motion in the perception of faces and of emotional expression , *Experimental Psychology*, 4:373–379, 1978.

[7] Y. Tian, T. Kanade, and J. F. Cohn. Recognizing action units for facial expression analysis. *IEEE PAMI*, 23(2), February 2001.

[8] G. Donato, M. Bartlett, J. Hager, P. Ekman, and T. Sejnowski. Classifying facial actions. *IEEE PAMI*, 21(10):974–989, October 1999.

[9] I. Essa and A. Pentland. Coding, analysis, interpretation and recognition of facial expressions, *IEEE PAMI*, 7:757–763, July 1997.

[10] K. Mase. Recognition of facial expressions for optical flow. IEICE Transactions, Special Issue on Computer Vision and its Applications, E 74(10), 1991.

[11] Joseph C. Hager and Paul Ekman, Essential Behavioral Science of the Face and Gesture that Computer Scientists Need to Know, 1995

[12] M. Pantic, I. Patras and L.J.M. Rothkrantz, 'Facial action recognition in face profile image sequences ', in *Proc. IEEE Int'l Conf. on Multimedia and Expo*, vol. 1, pp. 37-40, Lausanne, Switzerland, August 2002

[13] A. Kapoor and R. W. Picard. Real-time, fully automatic upper facial feature tracking, In Proc. of FG, May 2002.

[14] A. Kendon. How gestures can become like words. In F. Poyatos, editor, *Cross-cultural perspectives in nonverbal communication*, New York, 1988. C.J. Hogrefe.

[16] D. McNeill, (1985). So you think gestures are nonverbal? *Psychological Review, 92*, 350-371.

[17] M. Turk, "Gesture Recognition," in *Handbook of Virtual Environments : Design, Implementation, and Applications*, K. Stanney, Ed.: Lawrence Erlbaum Associates, Inc.(Draft version), 2001.

[18] H. Ohno and M. Yamamoto, Gesture Recognition using Character Recognition Techniques on Two-Dimensional Eigenspace, Proc. of ICCV 1999, pp. 151-156

[19] P. Peixoto, J. Gonçalves, H. Araújo, Real-Time Gesture Recognition System Based on Contour Signatures", *ICPR'2002*, Quebec City, Canada, August 11-15, 2002

[20] L. S. Chen and T. S. Huang, "Emotional expressions in audiovisual human computer interaction," in *Proc. ICME*, 2000, pp. 423–426.

[21] L. C. De Silva and P. C. Ng, "Bimodal emotion recognition," in *Proc. FG*, 2000, pp. 332–335.

[22] Y. Yoshitomi, S. Kim, T. Kawano, and T. Kitazoe, "Effect of sensor fusion for recognition of emotional states using voice, face image and thermal image of face," in *Proc. ROMAN*, 2000, pp. 178–183.

[23] R. W. Picard, E. Vyzas, and J. Healey, "Toward machine emotional intelligence: Analysis of affective physiological state," *IEEE PAMI.*, vol. 23, pp. 1175–1191, Oct. 2001.

[24] J.L. Franagan,T.S. Huang, "Scanning the issue special issue on human-computer multimodal interface", In Proceedings of the IEEE*, Vol: 91, no: 9, pp. 1267- 1271, Sept. 2003

Ambulance Dispatch Complexity and Dispatcher Decision Strategies: Implications for Interface Design

Jared Hayes[1], Antoni Moore[1], George Benwell[1], and B.L. William Wong[2]

[1]Department of Information Science
University of Otago, Dunedin, New Zealand
[2]Interaction Design Centre, School of Computing Science
Middlesex University, London

Abstract. The domain of ambulance command and control is complex due to dispatchers being required to make potentially hazardous decisions, often based on uncertain data, received from distributed sources in an environment that is extremely dynamic. These complexities were established after observing and interviewing fourteen ambulance command and control dispatchers located in two communications centres in New Zealand. In addition to the identification of complexities, the interviews resulted in the formulation of decision strategies utilised by the dispatchers when working in the communication centres. This research has implications for display design and provides avenues of research regarding how best to display the decision-making data required by ambulance dispatchers to overcome the complexities they encounter.

1   Introduction

Many operators of sociotechnical systems (e.g. ambulance command and control, power station control, chemical process control) face complexities that are unique to that particular system. Often the operators of such systems develop strategies for overcoming the complexities that are present in the environment. This paper discusses the complexities associated with dispatch decisions in the domain of ambulance command and control, and the decision strategies that these dispatchers use to continually perform the dispatch task effectively. By understanding these complexities and the strategies used by dispatchers, we are able to determine the effect that complexity has on the nature of the dispatch task and how complexity can change the interaction between people, technology and work. Using this knowledge the interfaces between the dispatchers and the system can be designed to minimize the effects of the complexities and support the decision-making strategies of the dispatchers. This should subsequently improve the performance of dispatchers during routine and abnormal tasks.

2   Ambulance Command and Control

The two communications centres studied during this research are located in New Zealand. The Southern centre handles approximately 20,000 emergency calls per year

M. Masoodian et al. (Eds.): APCHI 2004, LNCS 3101, pp. 589-593, 2004.

and is responsible for the command and control of ambulances covering an area of 54,000 square kilometers. The usually resident population of this area is 273,500.

The second communication centre studied is located in the North Island of New Zealand. The approximately 30,000 square kilometres area this centre is responsible for has a usually resident population in excess of 1.2 million and handles over 100,000 incidents per year.

Whilst the two communications centres have a number of contrasting features, (e.g. workload, computer systems) the primary goal of operators in both centres is similar. That is to dispatch the appropriate resources to emergency incidents as quickly as possible whilst managing other incidents that may be occurring simultaneously. In a large proportion of incidents this involves dispatching the closest vehicle, as this will often be the quickest to arrive at the scene. However there are a number of characteristics of these two dispatch environments that contribute to the complexity of this task. These are discussed in later sections.

3   Methodology

3.1   Data Collection

The data that forms the basis of this paper was collected using a Cognitive Task Analysis technique called the Critical Decision Method (CDM) [1-3]. The CDM is a retrospective interview technique that required the fourteen dispatchers (six Southern and eight Northern) to recall a memorable incident involving the allocation of a significant number of resources. The purpose of this was to elicit information from the dispatchers regarding their decision strategies when handling demanding incidents.

CDM interviews are one-on-one in nature and utilise three information gathering sweeps [1]. The first sweep identifies the key decision points along a timeline. The second sweep probes deeper into each of the decision points and leads to a more detailed and meaningful account of the incident. The final sweep is a 'what-if' sweep, which in the case of these interviews involved asking questions such as 'what if there had been two ambulances on station?' or 'what other options were available to you?' These questions helped identify potential areas of difficulty for the dispatchers and potential differences in dispatch strategies.

3.2   Data Analysis

The data gathered from the CDM was analysed using an Emergent Themes Analysis (ETA) [6, 7]. This process involved the coding and initial identification of broad themes that occurred across all interviews. These initial themes were then dissected into smaller sub-themes. For example the broad theme of 'assessment' could be dissected into the smaller sub themes: assessment of incidents and assessment of resources. Each of the sub-themes were analysed further to identify each decision activity, the cues dispatchers used, their considerations when performing these activities, the knowledge requirements of the dispatchers, possible errors and the source of the information used by dispatchers. Following this the data for each sub theme was summarised into meaningful sentences outlining the strategies used by dispatchers when dispatching ambulances.

4   Ambulance Dispatch Complexity

Rasmussen and Lind, Vicente, and Woods discuss the characteristics of environments that contribute to the complexity of problem solving [4, 5, 8]. Woods suggests that characteristics such as dynamism, many interacting parts, uncertainty, and risk contribute to the complexity of the world and thus the complexity of problem solving tasks. These characteristics are all evident in the ambulance dispatch world.

Worlds that are high in dynamism mean problem solving tasks occur over time and at indiscriminate intervals. Also in such worlds there are time pressures, overlapping tasks and a constant need to maintain a high level of performance to achieve goals that can be constantly changing. These are challenges faced by dispatchers as it is impossible to predict when the next incident is going to occur and when one does, all of the information regarding this incident may not be readily available. This is combined with the dispatchers having to cope with many overlapping incidents, the pressure to make timely dispatch decisions and a requirement to continually maintain a high level of performance.

A number of highly interacting parts is also a feature of the dispatch environment. Not only is a successful response to an incident dependent on the decision making of the dispatchers but it is also reliant on other factors such as the accurate recording of call details. A failure at any point in the system can have serious consequences such as an ambulance being sent to the wrong address.

The requirement for dispatchers to make decisions based on uncertain data is also a common occurrence. The source of this uncertain data can range from callers not being able to provide accurate data on a patient's condition to the location of resources when they are transiting between points. Often it is left to the dispatcher to call on past experiences to determine the appropriate response to an incident.

The final feature of the dispatch environment that contributes to the complexity of problem solving is risk. In a risky environment a major incident can happen at any time and there is risk involved with making wrong decisions. This is true of the ambulance dispatch environment. Therefore dispatchers have to weigh up every decision that they make against being able to deal with any number of 'what if' scenarios.

As mentioned in the previous section the Northern centre has a greater workload and one of the consequences of this is that it rates higher on the dimensions of complexity discussed in this section.

5   Decision Strategies

As mentioned, dispatch decision strategies were developed for each of the two centres. The strategies ranged from those used by the dispatchers to determine the validity of calls, to those employed by the dispatchers when distributing available resources around their areas to provide the most appropriate levels of coverage. When the strategies are separated into the broad phases of the ambulance dispatch process (e.g. call taking, incident assessment, resources assessment/allocation and management) and compared across the centres there are many similarities between the strategies. The strategies below are examples of strategies used by the Northern and Southern centres respectively to determine the most appropriate resource to allocate to an incident when multiple resources are available.

> Northern: Dispatchers try to match the severity of an incident with the skills of a particular ambulance crew. For a priority one call when there are multiple choices of vehicles to send, dispatchers will normally send the vehicles with a crew that will best match the requirements at the scene. However dispatchers are obliged to balance the workload of the crews and this often dictates the dispatch decisions.

> Southern: If multiple choices are available to respond to an incident, the dispatchers try to match the severity of the incident with the skills of the available ambulance crews. For example if a patient has serious chest pains a dispatcher is likely to send a more qualified ambulance crew so that they are able to provide more advanced medical care. However when choosing which resource to allocate to an incident the dispatchers must also consider the immediate workload of ambulance crews as they have an obligation to balance the workload amongst the crews.

In both instances the dispatchers base their decisions on similar criteria and so it could follow that the consequence for interface design may be that similar interfaces could be used for the two centres to aid the decision making process. However given the greater level of complexity in the Northern centre the interface requirements of this centre are different.

6   Implications for Interface Design

It is hoped that the outcomes of this research will influence future interface designs in a number of ways. First the identification of the decision strategies used by the dispatchers provides interface designers with a high level overview of the information that the dispatchers use to make their decisions and gives insight into the format that this information should be in. By presenting the information required by the dispatchers in a format that complements their decision making this should subsequently reduce their cognitive load and improve their decision making during normal and abnormal dispatch situations. An example of a shortcoming in the current interface used in the dispatch centres is that there is no indication of the location of vehicles when they are in transit. This information is essential for the dispatchers and therefore they must rely on their own experiences and mental pictures to determine the likely location of these vehicles or call each vehicle individually via radio. Secondly the identification of the complexities inherent in the ambulance dispatch environment is useful for predicting areas where improved display designs may result in improved dispatcher performance. Perhaps the areas where the greatest improvements could be made involve reducing the effects of the dynamism in the environment and the uncertainty associated with the data dispatchers often have to base their decisions on. Two possible solutions to these issues are interfaces that provide the dispatchers with an indication of the accuracy of the data they are using and incorporating checklists into the displays to ensure all of the steps essential to the successful handling of an incident are not overlooked by the dispatchers as they swap between different incidents.

7   Conclusion

An understanding of the decision strategies used by the dispatchers provides insights regarding the information required by the dispatchers when they are making dispatch decisions and the format that this information should be presented in. This coupled with an evaluation of the complexity present in a particular domain is useful for determining the requirements of system interfaces and specific areas to be addressed that could possibly improve dispatch performance. Future work will involve the development and testing of prototype displays. It is envisaged that these displays will not only complement the decision-making processes of the dispatchers but also help to negate the effects of the complexities that contribute to the difficulty of ambulance dispatch.

References

[1]   Hoffman, R.R., Crandall, B., and Shadbolt, N. (1998). *Use of the Critical Decision Method to Elicit Expert Knowledge: A Case Study in the Methodology of Cognitive Task Analysis*. Human Factors. **40**(2): 254-276.

[2]   Klein, G., Calderwood, R., and Macgregor, D. (1989). *Critical Decision Method for Eliciting Knowledge*. IEEE Transactions on Systems, Man and Cybernetics. **19**(3): 462-472.

[3]   Klein, G., Kaempf, G.L., Wolf, S., Thordsen, M., and Miller, T. (1997). *Applying Decision Requirements to User-Centered Design*. International Journal Of Human-Computer Studies. **46**(1): 1-15.

[4]   Rasmussen, J. and Lind, M., (1981). *Coping with Complexity*. in *European Conference on Human Decision and Manual Control*. Delft, The Netherlands.

[5]   Vicente, K.J., (1999). *Cognitive Work Analysis: toward safe, productive & healthy computer-based work*. Mahwah, N.J.; London: Lawrence Erlbaum Associates.

[6]   Wong, B.L.W., (2004). *Data Analysis for the Critical Decision Method*, in D. Diaper and N. Stanton (Eds.), *Task Analysis for Human-Computer Interaction*. Mahwah, NJ: Lawrence Erlbaum Associates. 327-346.

[7]   Wong, B.L.W. and Blandford, A., (2002). *Analysing Ambulance Dispatcher Decision Making: Trialing Emergent Themes Analysis*. in *HF2002, Human Factors Conference "Design for the whole person - integrating physical, cognitive and social aspects"*. Melbourne, Australia: A joint conference of the Ergonomics Society of Australia (ESA) and the Computer Human Interaction Special Interest Group (CHISIG).

[8]   Woods, D.D., (1988). *Coping with Complexity: the Psychology of Human Behavior in Complex Systems*, in L.P. Goodstein, H.B. Andersen, and S.E. Olsen (Eds.), *Tasks, Errors and Mental Models: A Festschrift to celebrate the 60th birthday of Professor Jens Rasmussen*. London: Taylor & Francis. 128-148.

Supporting Group Learning Using a Digital Whiteboard

Raymond Kemp, Elizabeth Kemp, and Thevalojinie Mohanarajah

Institute of Information Sciences and Technology,
Massey University, Palmerston North, New Zealand
r.kemp@massey.ac.nz, e.kemp@massey.ac.nz,
tmohanarajah@yahoo.co.uk

Abstract: Three important ways in which student learning can be facilitated are: getting them to work in groups, ensuring they can communicate face-to-face, and by using a computer. The question arises, can we do all three at the same time? One answer is to use a digital whiteboard. This device allows a group of users to share a workspace in an orderly fashion, and the computer driving the board can be programmed to support the students' learning. We describe some of our research where we have observed groups using whiteboards (both digital and non-digital) and our work towards producing a computer system to help and guide learners in this kind of setting.

1 Introduction

In this paper, three aspects of learning will be considered and combined. There is much research supporting the view that students learn effectively in a group setting particularly when they work collaboratively on a project. Also, there is evidence to suggest that communication between individuals is most effective and direct when they are in the same location rather than when they are communicating by email, telephone or using other electronic links.

Following on from these observations, the question arises, can we maintain group learning in a face-to-face situation and, at the same time, use the computer to facilitate such interaction? One answer is to use a digital whiteboard. This device allows a group of users to share a workspace in an orderly fashion, but the computer driving the board can be programmed to support the students' learning. We describe some of our work where we have observed groups using whiteboards (both digital and non-digital) with a view to producing a computer system to help and guide learners in this kind of setting.

2 Background

Given that, when possible, we would like group interaction to be face-to-face, where does the computer come in? There is much evidence to show that computers can support and encourage learning, but when there is a group gathered around the computer, logistical problems can occur. How can everyone get equal access to the mouse or keyboard? How can everyone even see the screen or feel a sense of ownership of the work being done, or the artefact being produced?

M. Masoodian et al. (Eds.): APCHI 2004, LNCS 3101, pp. 594-598, 2004.

This is where the digital whiteboard can help. It provides a much larger screen area which groups of four or five learners can comfortably share. Eden et al [1], observing the students working with the SMART Board, noted that it appeared to be "inside people's personal space". Although computers have come a long way in the last 30 years they are still, for the most part, seen as 'the box in the corner', rather like a television. Such an attitude encourages passivity and discourages active learning. Research into such devices as wearable computers [5] and digital toys [3] helps us break away from this mindset as does work on digital whiteboards for group learning.

3 Experiments

Our overall aims in these experiments were to compare the digital whiteboard with an ordinary whiteboard, and to see how the performance of a group of learners using a digital whiteboard could be enhanced by providing appropriate software.

3.1 Pilot Study Using a Digital Whiteboard

In order to get some indication of what additional features might be provided when using a digital whiteboard, we conducted a preliminary experiment where a group of three university students were asked to use a SMART Board to produce a *use case diagram* for a system design scenario. The subjects had all previously been introduced to this method of analysing a system, but were by no means experts.

Since the aim was not just to solve the problem but to engage each subject in the process so they could all learn, it was important to try to ensure everyone became involved. This means trying to stimulate collaboration [2]. Also, contributions should be focussed and distinguishable. Consequently, we required each subject to use a different coloured pen and we also asked them to use appropriate sentence openers (SOs) when making comments [4].

The behaviour of the subjects during the problem solving session was closely observed, as was their usage of the digital whiteboard. Lastly, subjects were debriefed in a semi-structured post-experiment interview. The main conclusions from our analysis are shown below:

- Subjects felt there were too many SOs and that they were difficult to remember.
- Participation was very uneven between the members of the team.
- Subjects were confused about who had contributed what.
- They often preferred to develop their own ideas separately before contributing to the group solution.

3.2 Non-interactive Whiteboard Versus Digital Whiteboard

We wished to check whether there appeared to be any benefit to having a large touch-sensitive computer screen for a work area compared to using a non-interactive board of a similar size. There were various issues that needed to be addressed as a result of the pilot experiment before we conducted the second one and we considered each of the problems noted at the end of the previous section. Conversation with the students suggested that the SOs were useful but that there were too many, so we reduced the number and made their usage optional.

In our second experiment, we had two groups each containing four subjects. Again, each group had to solve a problem involving the construction of a use case diagram. This time, we had one group using a digital whiteboard and the other using an ordinary one of a similar size. Both groups were carefully observed during the experiment and then had to fill in a questionnaire containing 22 questions. The main findings from the analysis of this data were:

- The digital whiteboard was easy to work with – the features for saving personal pages, moving items around the board, calling back saved pages and saving parts of diagrams were found particularly useful.
- Space in the ordinary whiteboard was limited and there was some congestion – subjects wished to keep personal ideas and information and either had to write it down on separate pieces of notepaper, or increase the clutter on the board.
- Some subjects found the SOs useful but even those that liked them thought there were too many.
- The use of different coloured pens was found confusing – this is probably at least partly due to a distracting feature of SMART Board. The colour that appears on the board does not depend upon the colour of the pen used for writing but on the colour of the last tray that a pen was taken from.
- All the participants agreed that non-verbal cues (gestures, body language, facial expressions etc) were an important component in their communication.

There were a few technical problems with the use of the SMART Board but, even so, the response from the team using it was much more positive than that from the other team.

3.3   Modified Digital Whiteboard Scheme

Encouraged by the way in which our subjects had embraced the digital whiteboard technology, we looked at ways of improving the software support to enhance learning. We wanted to retain all of the features that subjects liked, but also improve on ones that were less desirable, and also include new ways of facilitating student interaction.

The first problematic feature we needed to consider was the SOs. Although there were some difficulties, most subjects did appreciate having their discussion focussed, particularly those for whom English was not a first language. However, the large number of possible SOs used in the first two experiments appeared to inhibit discussion. What we wanted was a way of focussing and registering contributions that were made on the board without constraining the dialogue.

We, therefore, experimented with replacing the sentence openers with 'contribution types'. Most of these relate to the specific stage that the team has reached. "Let's write down the facts", for example, would be appropriate to add to a screen where the main assumptions are being collected together. We have experimented with colour-coding these stages and the comments associated with them. Thus, comments relating to the initial assumption stage are coded in blue, those relating to intermediate results are in green and those relating to the final results, are red.

We considered how we might track individual contributions. Having multiple pens did not work very well as mentioned earlier, partly due to problems with SMART Board and so we now require users to identify themselves to the system when they take over from someone else, by changing the name on the 'current contributor' list, rather than using different pen colours.

A personal workspace was also found to be desirable so this is created automatically for each student and can be accessed as required. Information can be cut and pasted or dragged across between personal workspaces and the team pages.

Figures 1 and 2 show screen shots from the modified version of our teaching system. Figure 1 shows the basic organization including pull-up menus at the bottom for students to select verbal or written contributions and also to select the name of the contributor. In Figure 2, the current contributor, Tania wishes to add a fact to what the group knows about the system and so selects the appropriate pull-up menu option. The colour of the screen will turn to a pale blue, and Tania can then enter information.

The evaluation of this system was carried out by an advanced researcher who found it intuitive, robust and helpful in problem solving. A full evaluation of this version, with subject groups has yet to be completed.

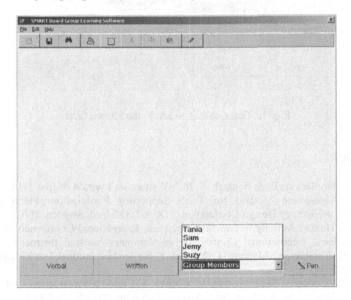

Fig. 1. Choosing contributor name

4 Conclusions and Further Work

Our aims are to assess the feasibility of collaborative learning using a digital whiteboard and investigate ways in which the process can be facilitated. Our first two experiments indicated that students sharing a digital whiteboard did, indeed, find the process productive. Based on the response of students, we made some significant changes to the system, and we have carried out some preliminary tests on this new version.

Future plans include the testing of a scheme where students in remote locations communicate via digital whiteboards, reproducing aspects of face to face communication by the use of digital cameras.

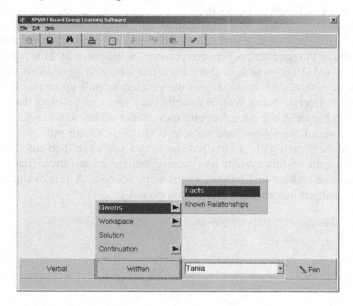

Fig. 2. Tania wishes to add to the known facts

References

1. Eden, H., Hornecker, E. & Scharff, E. In MY situation I would dislike THAAAT! - Role Play as Assessment Method for Tools Supporting Participatory Planning, Seventh Biennial Participatory Design Conference (PDC '02) (Malmö, Sweden, 2002).
2. Lewis, R. Human Activity in Learning Societies, International Conference on Computers in Education / International Conference on Computer-Assisted Instruction 2000 (eds. Young, S. S., Greer, J., Maurer, H. & Chee, Y. S.) 36-45 (National Tsing Hua University, Taipei, 2000).
3. Luckin, R., Connolly, D., Plowman, L. & Airey, S. Children's interactions with interactive toy technology. Journal of Computer Assisted Learning 19, 165-176 (2003).
4. Soller, A. L. Supporting social interaction in an intelligent collaborative learning system. International Journal of Artificial Intelligence in Education 12, 40-62 (2001).
5. Thomas, B. H. Using augmented reality to support collaboration in an outdoor environment, Systems, Social and Internationalization Design Aspects of Human-Computer Interaction (eds. Smith, M. J. & Salvendy, G.) 743-747 (Lawrence Erlbaum Associates, London, 2001).

Verifying the Field of View Afforded to the Pilot due to Cockpit Design, Stature, and Aerodrome Design Parameters

Eugene Aik Min Khoo and Kee Yong Lim

Center for Human Factors & Ergonomics
School of Mechanical and Production Engineering
Nanyang Technological University
50 Nanyang Avenue, Singapore 639798

Abstract. This paper examined the contribution of various design parameters towards the pilot's forward field of view (FFOV). This study was based upon the SQ006 crash at Chiang Kai Shek Airport, Taipei, Taiwan on 31 Oct 2000. A 3-dimensional scale model was created to simulate certain design features experienced on the night of the accident. A simulation of the Boeing 747-400 taxiing towards Runway 05R was constructed to visualize the FFOV afforded. Conclusions and implications of the specifications of the design parameters studied will be reviewed.

1. Introduction

The period of time before a passenger aircraft takes-off, presents the pilot one of the most stressful part of the task. This is due to the various tasks to be performed, ranging from aircraft safety checks to communication with ground control, while steering the aircraft to the designated runway for take-off.

Taxiing and navigation towards the runway would require the pilot or co-pilot to compare features outside with a map. Checking the congruence of these sources of information with the desired state, is required to maintain situation awareness at each aircraft location. Such situational awareness is particularly vital during low visibility.

The FOV is vital to the performance of these tasks. In this respect, the cockpit position of the Boeing 747-400 is the highest among commonly used passenger aircraft. This presents an elevated angle of disparity and substantial proximal obscurity (e.g. by the nose cone) of the world outside. While the design of the aerodrome is standardized by the International Civil Aviation Organization (ICAO) Annex 14 [3], not all international airports adhere to these stipulations. Where discrepancies prevail, the cost of such omissions could potentially lead to an accident. This paper examines the interplay of three design parameters and the impact on the FOV of the pilot in the case of SQ006 crash, where a confluence of such inadequacies, poor visibility and weather conditions, led the pilot to take off from the wrong runway.

M. Masoodian et al. (Eds.): APCHI 2004, LNCS 3101, pp. 599-603, 2004.
© Springer-Verlag Berlin Heidelberg 2004

2. Materials and Method

This project used AutoCAD 2002 to construct a model of the Boeing 747-400, and Discreet 3D Studio MAX 5 for the 3 dimensional rendering and simulation. The 3D environment of the aerodrome leading to runway 05L and 05R was modeled to scale, according to the Chiang Kai Shek Airport in Taipei, Taiwan (see Figure 1). Data on the latter were extracted from Taiwan's Air Safety Council's (ASC) Aircraft Accident Report [1].

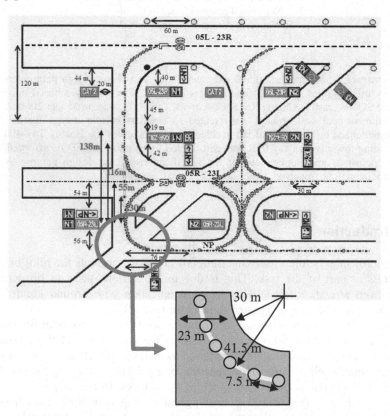

Fig. 1. Aerodrome dimensions assumed for the simulation

The separation between center lights were taken as 30 m for straight routes and at a denser 7.5 m for curved routes, while the edge lights were spaced at 60 m intervals from the threshold of the runway. Both center lights and edge lights used in the simulation were set to a high intensity and omni directional (in reality it would be bi-directional). This is due to the limitation of the software to project directionally. Moreover, creating a bi-directional light would require increased complexity to replicate the azimuth that the light projects out to.

In this project, the dimensions of the Boeing 747-400 Domestic [2] were assumed. Its dimensions were scaled according to a no-load condition for the purpose of achieving maximum possible height. This would lead to maximum possible obscurity of the runway due to the cockpit design and aircraft nose cone. At this level, any added weight would lower the point of view, allowing for a better FOV.

It was assumed that the centre of the pilot was 0.53m from the center of the plane and that his seated eye height is 1.01 m. To simulate the pilot's vision, 3 light sources were used to replicate the 210° the human eye would be capable of seeing. However, the simulation software restricted these light sources from being placed together. This was because the Boeing 747-400 3D-model was rendered from polygons. Where the polygon plane was parallel to the light beam, no shadow would be projected. This was overcome by extending the light source behind the pilot's seated eye position, with the ray still passing through the same position the eye. The 3D rendering also assumed that the pilot made a perfect centerline turn. Follow-up research on this project should investigate the impact of over- and under-steering.

3. Results and Discussion

Figure 2 shows the simulated Boeing 747-400 taxiing towards Runway 05R. Light sources were used to simulate the field of view of the pilot. Here, yellow light was used to represent the Captain's vision, and the blue light was used to represent the co-pilot's vision. The green light represents what both pilots were able to see. The combination of the cast shadows, created by the various light sources, demarcates the limitation of the pilot's field of vision, as obscured by the airplane.

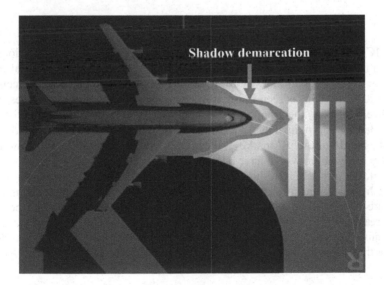

Fig. 2. Simulated Field of View

Figure 3 shows the location of the airplane after completing its turn from N1 into Runway 05R. It can be seen that the airplane obscures the "R" in the runway designation 05R painted on the tarmac. This result may be anticipated because the airplane's turning radius is 45 m. As the centerline radius is 41.5 m, some inherent obscuring of the runway designation would be expected.

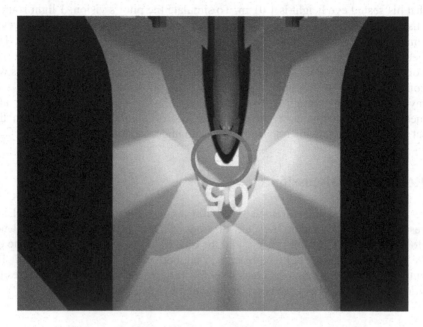

Fig. 3. Obscured "R" of 05R

The ICAO Annex 14 stipulates that the runway designation must be located at least 48 m from the threshold. Thus, at Chiang Kai Shek Airport, the base of the "R" of 05R would be about 54 m away from the threshold. This is just after the centerline turns into Runway 05R as seen in Figure 1. Note that the simulation assumes that the front wheel follows the centerline, which has a curvature radius of 41.5 m. Compounded by approximately 28 m of obscuring by the nose cone and allowing for 9 m for the height of the 'R' marking, it can be deduced that upon completing the turn, the runway designation would have been obscured.

In Figure 4, the airplane is at the location shown in Figure 2. It can be seen that only the green lights turning towards Runway 05R are visible. The center lights leading straight are not visible (in the actual case the interceding are found to be dim or faulty), creating the illusion that there is no taxiway ahead (the one that leads to the correct runway). This is aggravated further by the absence of a straight leading centerline that should have been painted on the tarmac as required by ICAO Annex 14.

4. Conclusion

In conclusion, the simulation was found to be useful for visualising the limited field of view afforded to the pilot. Recommendations concerning the adequacy of the existing aerodrome design may then be made in respect of each introduction of new models of aircraft. Preliminary findings for an aerodrome design uncovered by such a simulation, may then be subjected to closer scrutiny. In the case of Chiang Kai Shek airport and ICAO Annex 14, it was found that existing specifications of the runway designation, might not be adequate to accommodate visibility requirements for an unloaded Boeing 747-400.

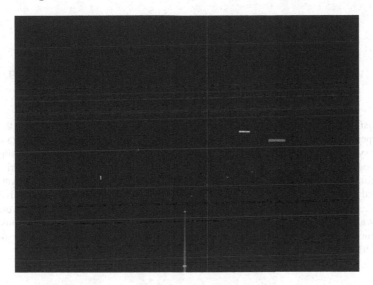

Fig. 4. View from the cockpit along taxiway N1

5. Acknowledgements

The authors would like to acknowledge the contributions of Mr. David Chan and Mr. Ong Kai Wei towards this project.

6. References

1. Aviation Safety Council, SQ006 Aircraft Accident Report, Taipei, Taiwan, Republic of China (2001)
2. Boeing Commercial Airplanes, 747-400 Airplane Characteristics for Airport Planning, Seattle, Washington, USA (2002)
3. International Civil Aviation Organization, Aerodromes Annex 14, Volume 1 to the Convention on International Civil Aviation, Montreal, Quebec, Canada (1999)

Creative Information Seeking and Interface Design

Shu-Shing Lee, Yin-Leng Theng, Dion Hoe-Lian Goh, and
Schubert Shou-Boon Foo

Division of Information Studies
School of Communication and Information
Nanyang Technological University
Singapore 637718
{ps7918592b, tyltheng, ashlgoh, assfoo}@ntu.edu.sg

Abstract. Inspired by Weisberg's argument that everyone is creative, this paper highlights a model of information seeking capturing users' creative traits by synthesizing established models in information seeking and creativity. Using Google, a pilot study was conducted to understand subjects' creative information seeking process. Claims Analysis and Interaction Framework were used to elicit design features that might have supported subjects' creative, "serendipitous" information seeking. This paper presents novel, initial work towards eliciting conceptual design features for users' creative, "serendipitous" information seeking behaviors. It concludes with a discussion on creativity and interface design for information retrieval systems.

1 Introduction

Most information retrieval (IR) systems are designed to judge precision and recall based on a match between index and query terms. This mode of operation is the 'best-match' principle [1]. However, precision and recall are limited, as they do not consider the contextual nature of human judgment [3]. Measures of precision and recall should consider that relevance is influenced by the intentions and knowledge states of users [3]. Hence, one way of addressing users' needs in IR systems may be to consider users' creative process in information seeking during interface design.

This paper presents novel, initial work towards a model for supporting users' creative, "serendipitous" information seeking behaviors. This model is inspired by Weisberg's [15] argument that everyone has creative traits. Hence, it can be logically inferred that every information seeker is creative, and the extent of a person's creativity influences his/her information seeking behavior. Creativity can be defined from many perspectives. For example, creativity may be "natural" based on one's creative traits or creativity may be "nurtured" which is due to domain knowledge and information seeking skills. Here, we are concerned with "nurtured" creativity.

The proposed model differs from traditional information seeking models [e.g., 7] as it focuses on how "creative" features in an IR environment, for example, providing collaboration features and contacts of experts [e.g. 11], may support information seeking. These features aim to support users' information seeking behavior, hence

M. Masoodian et al. (Eds.): APCHI 2004, LNCS 3101, pp. 604–609, 2004.
© Springer-Verlag Berlin Heidelberg 2004

possibly addressing users' needs and increasing the quality of search results in terms of relevance and user satisfaction.

It is hoped that this model may possibly lead to new and improved ways of developing interfaces for supporting IR and users' needs.

2   Creative Information Seeking Model

To provide context for understanding findings presented later, we briefly describe the proposed six stages for creative information seeking [10]:

- Stage 1: Preparation for starting information seeking. The information seeker recognizes a knowledge gap. This triggers his/her information seeking behavior.
- Stage 2: Chaining information sources. Here, he/she is tracking related materials to understand the breadth of the topic. This helps him/her select a topic to focus.
- Stage 3: Browsing and searching. At this stage, he/she is searching and browsing information on the selected topic.
- Stage 4: Incubation for differentiating purposes. The information seeker is filtering information and establishing linkages among filtered information.
- Stage 5: Monitoring and extracting for illumination. Here, he/she is monitoring developments in the selected topic and pulling out relevant materials from sources. This helps him/her achieve a personal understanding and produce an idea
- Stage 6: Verification of information sources. Here, he/she is concerned with verifying information used to produce the idea.

3   Pilot Study

As a first step to understand the proposed model of information seeking, a pilot study was conducted using 4 subjects to carry out a preliminary investigation to ascertain the qualities of a typical interface, Google in this instance, to understand the subjects' information seeking process and to elicit "creative" design features in the interface to support it through the use of Carroll's Claims Analysis (CA) [4] and Abowd and Beales' Interaction Framework (IF) [6].

Subjects
Subject A is a 2nd year PhD student. Subjects B and C are 1st year and 2nd year Masters students respectively. Subject D is a 2nd year undergraduate student. Subjects A and C have 5-6 years of experience and Subjects B and D have 3-4 years of experience using search engines. Subjects were selected based on their experience with search engines.

Methodology
Subjects were given 30 minutes to complete an open-ended information seeking task using Google. The task was chosen based on work in [2] and had two parts. Part A required subjects to find all inventions by Leonardo Da Vinci (LDV). The purpose was to prompt their information seeking process. Part B required subjects to select an

invention and describe the invention in detail, how it was created and its significance to the world. The purpose was to enable users to express their natural information seeking behavior. A form was constructed for subjects to note their answers.

As subjects performed their tasks, they were asked to think aloud. The think aloud method requires little expertise to perform but can provide useful insights into problems with an interface and how the system is actually used [6]. As subjects thought aloud, their actions were recorded by a video camera. The video data was later transcribed, including speech and descriptions of interaction between subjects and Google's search interface. These video transcripts were used to derive subjects' summaries of interactions.

After subjects completed their tasks, an interview was conducted. Questions corresponding to proposed stages in creative information seeking and questions to prompt CA [4] were asked. CA was used to elicit subjects' feedback on features that could have supported their creativity. These questions provided a better understanding of subjects' information seeking behaviors. Each interview lasted about 45 minutes and was later transcribed for analysis.

4   Findings and Analysis

CA and IF were used to analyze interview transcripts and summaries of interactions respectively to propose design features to support creative information seeking. CA is an appropriate technique as it makes use of positive and negative claims in system-user interaction to elicit design features. IF is another appropriate technique as it provides an understanding of subjects' needs through their system-user interactions.

We coded summary of interactions, proposed in [13], using the four categories in IF [6]: user action (UA), user evaluation (UE), system display (SD), and system response (SR) to elicit supportive design features. The following shows the coding for an extract of Subject C's summary of interactions. The code "(SD)" was used to elicit design features for creative information seeking.

> Subject C began his information seeking process by using the query, "Leonardo Da Vinci inventions" (UA, SD)... He used the highlighted keywords (SD, SR) and descriptions (SD, SR) to find relevant sources to access

For example, the above transcript was coded 3 times with "(SD)", suggesting the presence of the following supportive design features: providing search box and fields; ranking results; and providing highlighted keywords and descriptions in results list. Similarly, all other subjects' interactions coded with "(SD)" code were taken to suggest design features to support subjects' creative information seeking behaviors.

The interview included modified questions from CA and questions to clarify subjects' information seeking behavior. These were also used to elicit design features. We coded the interview transcripts using: positive experiences "(+)" and negative experiences "(-)". The following extract of Subject C's interview transcript demonstrates how coding was done. We made the assumption: areas in interview transcript coded with "(+)" suggested design features available in Google and areas coded with "(-)" suggested design features unavailable in Google. Using this coding, three other features were inferred from Subject C's interactions: highlighting query keywords in contents; ranking results; and providing description of each result. All interview transcripts were coded similarly to arrive at available and non-available design features for creative information seeking in Google.

> ...normally I also use the Google toolbar...it allows you to highlight the words on that page (-)...the system ordered the links and put the descriptions (+) so that's how useful it was...

Next, extracts of subjects' summary of interactions and interview transcripts were organized to correspond to proposed stages in creative information seeking. Using this organization and their respective schemes of coding, an aggregated list of available and non-available design features for each proposed stage was derived. The coding "(+)" and "(SD)" elicited design features available in Google while the coding "(-)" and "(SD)" elicited design features non-available in Google. Figure 1 illustrates some proposed design features available in Google. Table 1 illustrates a list of proposed design features "non-available" in Google. In the table, proposed Stages 1-6 are depicted as S1-S6.

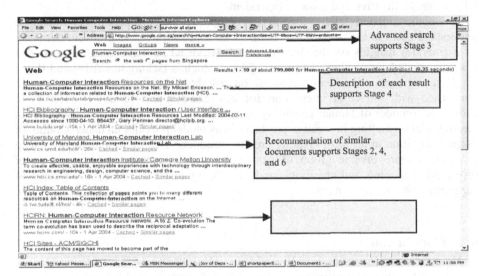

Figure 1. Some supportive design features available in Google

Table 1. Supportive design features non-available in Google

Supportive Design Features Non-Available in Google	S1	S2	S3	S4	S5	S6
Highlight keywords in contents of documents				✓	✓	
Provide a structured organization of contents				✓	✓	
Provide a variety of accessible sources	✓	✓	✓	✓	✓	✓
Provide contacts of experts	✓	✓	✓	✓	✓	✓
Provide collaborative features	✓	✓	✓	✓	✓	✓
Provide links to other search engines						✓
Provide recommendations to related sources		✓	✓			✓

5   Discussion

Related works in creativity usually address users' creative traits and provide an environment for the creative process to take place [e.g., 14]. Shneiderman [11] proposes eight ways to improve software to support human creative processes. These works provide insights on the types of design features and guidelines to interface design that support creativity. However, in our work, we are concerned with developing an IR environment with "creative" features that supports users' information seeking behavior.

Modern user interfaces do not explicitly support users' creative process that requires experimentation, exploration of variations, and continual evaluation of one's progress. Instead, a linear progression through tasks is imposed, providing a poor fit for creative pursuits [12]. Our work attempts to address this limitation by developing an IR interface that closely supports users' creative information seeking behavior which may be iterative and context dependent.

In another related study, Dervin [5] proposes a sense-making approach to understand users in the design of systems. This approach may be useful in our work as it provides insights on the decisions users make while completing tasks so that features elicited are responsive to users' needs, which is lacking in CA [4] and IF [6] as these methods elicit features based on insights from system-user interaction, concerned with model of interaction for task completion. Hoorn [9] attempts to formulate a model of human capability to combine familiar objects and concepts in unusual ways, resulting in creative products. This model provides an understanding of human cognition in terms of creating creative products. This understanding may help to elicit a more diverse group of design features to support various aspects of information seeking and creativity, and may result in new and improved ways of supporting IR and users' needs.

6   Conclusion

In our earlier work, we propose a creative information seeking model [10] by synthesizing established models in information seeking [e.g. 7] and creativity [e.g. 9].

Findings suggested that Google provides features that could support creative information seeking but it does not provide an integrated environment. Hence, more can be done to possibly strengthen Google's support by incorporating other features highlighted in our pilot study.

As this work is preliminary and on-going, more needs to be done to refine and test stages in creative information seeking before they can emerge as stages and principles for designing better IR systems to support users' creative information seeking behaviors.

References

1. Belkin, N.J., Oddy, R. N. and Brooks, H., ASK for Information Retrieval: Part I. Background and Theory. *Journal of Documentation*, 1982. **38**(2): p.61-71.
2. Blandford, A., Stelmaszewska, H. and Bryan-Kinns, N., Use of Multiple Digital Libraries: A Case Study, *Proc JCDL* 2001. p. 179-188.
3. Case, D. O. (2002). *Looking for Information: A Survey of Research on Information Seeking, Needs, and Behavior*. California, USA: Elsevier Science.
4. Carroll, J. (2000). *Making Use: Scenario-Based Design of Human-Computer Interactions*. The MIT Press.
5. Dervin, B., Sense-Making Theory and Practice: An Overview of User Interests in Knowledge Seeking and Use. *Journal of Knowledge Management*, 1998. **2**(2), p. 36 – 46.
6. Dix, A., Finlay, J., Abowd, G, and Beale, R. (1998). *Human-Computer Interaction*. London, England: Prentice Hall.
7. Ellis, D., Cox, D. and Hall, K., A Comparison of Information Seeking Patterns of Researchers in the Physical and Social Sciences. *Journal of Documentation,* 1993. **49**(4), p. 356-369.
8. Hoorn, J. (2002). A Model for Information Technologies That Can Be Creative. *Creativity and Cognition 2002*, p. 186 – 191.
9. Rhodes, M., An Analysis of Creativity. *Phi Delta Kappan*, 1961. **42**(7): p.305-310.
10. Lee, S. S., Theng, Y. L. & Goh, D. H. -L. (2003). *Creative Information Seeking Part I: A conceptual framework*. Manuscript accepted for publication.
11. Shneiderman, B. (2002). Creativity Support Tools: A Tutorial Overview. *Creativity and Cognition 2002*, p. 1- 2.
12. Terry, M. and Mynatt, E. (2002). Recognising Creative Needs in User Interface Design. *Creativity and Cognition 2002*, p. 38 - 44.
13. Theng Y. L., Information Therapy, *Proc ICADL* 2002. p.452-464.
14. Vass, M., Carroll, J. and Shafer, C. (2002). Supporting Creativity in Problem Solving Environments. *Creativity and Cognition 2002*, p. 51-37.
15. Weisberg, R. W. (1993). *Creativity Beyond the Myth of Genius*. New York: W.H. Freeman and Company.

Connecting the User View with the System View of Requirements

Ralph R. Miller[1] and Scott P. Overmyer[2]

[1] Computer Sciences Corporation, 304 West Route 38,
Moorestown, New Jersey, 08057, USA
rmiller@csc.com
[2] Massey University, Private Bag 102 904, NSMC, Auckland, New Zealand
s.p.overmyer@massey.ac.nz

Abstract. In a pilot study, professional information technologists from both commercial and academic institutions showed that representing the requirements for a simple television remote control device could be done accurately and completely using separate languages that are for 1) user interface specification, and 2) system specification, and, 3) with natural language. That individuals can create 3 separate, but equivalent representations is important because, with the aid of an underlying meta-representation, it allows system stakeholders to view software requirements in whatever way best represents their particular area of concern, while maintaining internal consistency between views.

1 Introduction

Imagine a tool that has, as its underlying representation, a part of the same internally consistent language in which data flow diagrams, object models, and entity-relationship diagrams are also represented. Thus, as user interface requirements and design emerge, they are automatically registered and integrated with other existing system views under development. Such a tool would allow concurrent work in all design and development disciplines to take advantage of a number of different but consistent views of requirements while facilitating incremental validation and consistency checking of new requirements.

We are currently working toward enhancing an existing requirements meta-language so that multiple views can be represented in a common repository, facilitating cross-contributory activity between all players in a software development effort. To illustrate the validity of this notion of concurrent consistent views of requirements for a user interface, we sought to determine if user interface requirements could be accurately and consistently represented across views. We asked volunteers to represent the requirements for an existing device (i.e., the Zenith "ZEN400", a universal home media remote control) in different languages. In effect we asked the volunteers to "reverse engineer" the ZEN400 user interface requirements. By using an existing device rather than some representation of the requirements for a device, issues of interpretation and understanding were considerably diminished.

M. Masoodian et al. (Eds.): APCHI 2004, LNCS 3101, pp. 610-614, 2004.

2 Background

Studies have looked at different aspects of the efficacy of different requirements representations and their use. For example, in a series of trials over several years, it was found, using undergraduate systems analysts, that when requirements understanding is tested, that the object-oriented design (OOD) and DFD representations outperform the natural language representations [1]. However, the students have consistently shown a higher "descriptive" understanding of the requirements when working from a natural language representation. Popular graphical methods for representing requirements were found to be inconclusive due to multiple possible interpretations. It was suggested that ontological clarity can only come from a narrowing of possible interpretations of a model, implying that it is possible to create a model that can have only one interpretation [2], possibly via using one paradigm throughout development [3].

Others suggest that only formally defined requirements languages can create unequivocal representations of requirements. For example Greenspan et al [4] proposed a Requirements Modeling Language to bring "semantic clarity" to requirements representation. However, even those who advocate formal methods admit that all requirements representations begin with a discourse using natural language [5]. Others [6, 7] have reported on techniques to formalize natural language using semantic analysis and structured natural language elicitation techniques.

Previously we demonstrated [8, 9] that all elements and relationships of the User Interface Markup Language (UIML) [11] could be represented in the Requirements Element Language (REL) [10] and that they are compatible. We further showed that all elements and relationships of the REL could be represented in the eXtensible Markup Language (XML). The strategy of using the XML as an intermediary between the REL and the UIML makes it also possible to connect together any XML-consistent language with the REL. The authors of the REL [10] did not intend for it to be a primary language for practitioners to use directly. Rather the language was meant to be a "meta-language", hidden from view and acting as a bridge between commonly used system representation techniques (e.g., ERD, DFD, UML, FSM, JSD, etc). As a next step, we have sought to demonstrate that equivalent representations of requirements for an interactive system could be constructed using both the REL and the UIML languages. That step is the subject of this current report. We expect that if the user view can be accurately represented in a system view using REL constructs, requirements information entered via the UIML inform or contribute to other views of the system that are represented in the REL. Since we are using semi-formal representations, we chose expert judgment as the best way to demonstrate semantic equivalence.

3 Approach

Having shown that the UIML and the REL are cross-compatible, we needed to show that representing the requirements for a user interface can be equivalent in all three languages (REL, UIML, natural language). Here we report on a demonstration that these languages can equally well represent the user interface requirements for a common home entertainment general purpose remote control device (the ZEN400).

We recruited six information technology (IT) professionals as volunteers for our study. Our volunteers were from a large information technology company (CSC), an IT PhD student and an IT academic. The average amount of time spent by volunteers in completing all work for the study was on the order of 12-13 hours.

The volunteers were split into three groups. Each group represented the requirements for the ZEN400 using one of three representations; REL, UIML, or natural language. For each language volunteers were given four Projects to perform. In the first Project, they learned use of the personal timing tool. In the second Project, they learned about the ZEN400 from which they would be creating the requirements of the user interface. In the third Project they learned the particular language they would be using and then created an initial skeletal representation of the device's user interface requirements. In the fourth Project they completed their requirements representation. After completing their requirements representation, the volunteers conducted walkthroughs of their representations to find and correct errors. They stopped after three walkthroughs or until they found no more errors. Volunteers used a tool from the University of Hawaii to time their performance on the projects [12]. In addition, they completed questionnaires. These probed the volunteers' knowledge of the project, project materials, and the language they were using.

In order to evaluate the representations created by the volunteers, three experts were also recruited to evaluate the work products of the volunteers. These experts were a professor of information technology, one of the current authors, and an expert in developing large-scale software systems. Each expert judged the work of the volunteers in one language. The expert reviewers reviewed each of the representations for errors of omission (EOO), errors of commission (EOC), and errors of overspecification (EOS). Errors of over-specification were those in which a duplicate or unnecessary requirement was introduced into the specification. As well, experts were asked to judge the apparent correctness of the representations and the value of the materials provided for the volunteers.

4   Results

Each volunteer is coded in terms of the representation language used (e.g., U1 = UIML volunteer #1). Overall, the volunteers who created REL representations of the user interface requirements for the ZEN400 spent the most time, while the volunteers who used natural language averaged less time. Between the most and least amount of overall time spent, the spread was almost 4:1. The major difference in effort expended by the volunteers is found in the Create category while the time spent in the other categories was roughly similar. In comparing the total errors, it appeared that two of the six volunteers did not complete "successful" requirements representations.

Figure 1 shows the cumulative errors found for each of the six volunteers' representations. If the totals for volunteers U2 and R1 are excluded, there were around 10-20 errors in the other representations. This was consistent across all three requirements representation languages studied. Based upon the remarks of the expert reviewers, we term the representations by volunteers U2 and R1 as "unsuccessful" while the rest are termed as "successful".

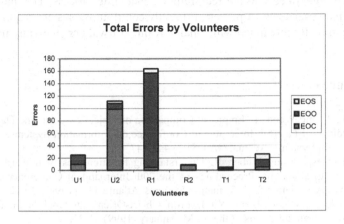

Fig. 1. Errors Found By Reviewers and Volunteers per Language

5 Discussion

We wanted to know if our modification to REL were sufficient to permit expert users to construct equivalent requirements representations, in this case "as-built" descriptions, using the 2 notations of interest plus natural language. Despite the small number of volunteers who were able to complete this study, we think that several interesting observations can be made. First, we found that, in terms of errors introduced and roughly in terms of the time spent, all three languages studied are equally expressive in representing the requirements for a user interface of an existing device. We had expected there to be an obvious trend in errors from the "easiest" language to learn (i.e., our own natural language) to the "hardest" to learn (i.e., the code-like UIML). This expectation was in keeping with results reported by other researchers [1]. However, this was not the case. On the contrary, we found that semantically rich and cognitively complex graphical languages can be as effective as natural language in representing the user view. If, as many researchers claim, natural language specification is inherently ambiguous, then a clear superiority of REL and/or UIML should emerge in subsequent, larger studies.

In summary, we have found that professional IT experts can use rather complex and abstract notations to represent requirements typically associated with the "user view". We suspect, however, that the "average" end user would not be able to accomplish this task at all. Our results also support the notion that this meta-notation should remain just that - "meta", and an intermediate representation should be created to link the meta-notation to a more usable representation for the use of non-technical stakeholders (e.g., REL linked user interface prototypes).

The semantic links between user interface objects -> UIML -> REL are nearly in place. Since state transition-based rapid prototyping tools have existed for over 20 years, and state charts are already supported within REL [14], we look forward to rapid prototypes being built that generate system requirements representations that are completely integrated into the requirements modeling process. This has the potential to make the "user view" a powerful directly contributory system requirements representation, directly integrated with "mainstream" software engineering models.

References

1. Gemino, A. and Wand, Y. Empirical Comparison of Object-Oriented and Dataflow Models, Proceedings of the 18th International Conference on Information Systems, Association for Information Systems, Atlanta, GA (1997) 446-447.
2. Burton-Jones, A. and Weber, R. Understanding Relationships with Attributes in Entity-Relationship Diagrams, Proceedings of the 20th International Conference on Information Systems", Association for Information Systems, Atlanta, GA (1999) 214 228.
3. Mylopoulos, J., Chung, L. and Yu, E. From Object-Oriented to Goal-Oriented Requirements Analysis, Communications of the ACM, January (1999) 31-37.
4. Greenspan, S., Mylopoulos, J. and Borgida, A. On Formal Requirements Modeling Languages: RML Re visited, Proceedings of the 16th International Conference on Software Engineering", IEEE Computer Society Press, Los Alamitos, CA, (1994) 135-147.
5. Van Lamsweerde, A. Formal Specification: A Roadmap, Proceedings of the Conference on the Future of Software Engineering", ACM Press, New York, (2000) 147-159.
6. Leite, J.C.S. do Prado and Gilvaz, A.P.P. Requirements Elicitation Driven by Interviews: The Use of Viewpoints, Proceedings of the 8th Workshop on Software Specification and Design (1996) 85-94.
7. Rayson, P., Garside, R., and Sawyer, P. Assisting requirements engineering with semantic document analysis. In Proceedings of RIAO 2000 (Recherche d'Informations Assistie par Ordinateur, Computer-Assisted Information Retrieval) International Conference, Collge de France, Paris, France, C.I.D., Paris, (2000) 1363 – 1371.
8. Miller, R. and Overmyer, S.P., "Deriving the 'User-View' from Analysis and Design Models of Requirements", Proceedings of AWRE 2001, Sydney, Australia (2001) 61-69.
9. Miller, Ralph R., "Learning and Using Requirements Representation Notations by Information Technology Professionals", unpublished PhD thesis, Drexel University, Philadelphia, PA, November (2002).
10. Davis, A.M. Jordan, K and Nakajima, T. Elements Underlying the Specification of Requirements, Annals of Software Engineering (3) (1997) 63-100.
11. Abrams, M., Phanouriou, C., Williams, S.M. and Shuster, J.E. UIML: An Appliance-Independent XML User Interface 8th Language, Hypertext and Hupermedia: International World Wide Web Conference, Toronto, Canada, retrieved March 24, 2000 from http://www8.org.
12. http://csdl.ics.hawaii.edu
13. Parnas, D.L. and Weiss, D.M. ActiveDesign Reviews: Principles and Practices", Proceedings of the 8th International Conference on Software Engineering, IEEE Computer Society Press, Los Alamitos, CA (1985) 132136.
14. Overmyer, S.P. and Campbell, H.E., Jr. "Rapid Prototyping -An approach to user interface design", Paper presented at the 28th Annual Meeting of the Human Factors Society, San Antonio, TX (1984).

Recourse for Guiding Didactical Creators in the Development of Accessible e-Learning Material[1]

Valeria Mirabella, Stephen Kimani, Tiziana Catarci

University of Rome *La Sapienza*, Dipartimento di Informatica e Sistemistica
Via Salaria 113, 00198 Rome, Italy
{mirabell, kimani, catarci}@dis.uniroma1.it

Abstract. Most of the existing efforts for supporting the preparation and delivery of accessible e-learning materials propose guidelines that prevalently address technical accessibility issues. However, little or no consideration is given to the didactical creators in the learning material preparation. The existing guidelines also usually provide generic indications on alternative forms of didactical content to enable equivalent access of the content. However, the sole provision of equivalent forms does not guarantee effective access. While this paper acknowledges the role of the existing guidelines, it proposes that the didactical domain creators be provided with a non-technical recourse that can enable them to contribute to or participate in the development process of accessible e-learning content aiming at guaranteeing an effective learning experience.

1 Introduction

Though the talk about accessibility has become commonplace, never in history has there been as much confusion about accessibility as in our times. Many design companies and organizations are engaged more in paying it lip service than paying attention to it. While establishments often adopt accessibility for various reasons, it is important to keep in mind that accessibility has to primarily do with the provision of equal opportunities for accessing resources for people with special needs. It has been previously observed, "As long as companies and government agencies view accessibility as solely a matter of complying with regulations and technical specifications, rather than a way to support the work practices and customer needs of people with disabilities, equal opportunity will remain a travesty." [1]. There exist various guidelines, standards, and techniques [2, 3, 4, 5, 6] for facilitating accessibility with respect to aspects such as hardware, software, and the Web.

Traditionally, learning material has been developed for a very specific purpose e.g., for a particular course unit. Technical developments have demonstrated various beneficial possibilities e.g., customizability, reusability, and flexibility of learning material. Such benefits can be realized through the use of learning objects. A learning

---

[1] This work is supported by the VICE 'Comunità virtuali per la formazione' subproject of the CNR/MIUR project

M. Masoodian et al. (Eds.): APCHI 2004, LNCS 3101, pp. 615–619, 2004.

object (LO) is defined as "any entity -digital or non-digital- that may be used for learning, education or training" [7]. Very few efforts exist that aim at facilitating the creation and delivery of accessible learning objects and content. The few existing efforts include [8, 9, 10]. The process of creating and delivering e-learning content can benefit a lot from inputs from various arenas of expertise e.g., technical expertise and domain/subject knowledge. Most efforts for supporting the preparation and delivery of accessible e-learning material, such as the ones mentioned earlier, propose guidelines that are devoted prevalently to technical accessibility aspects, such as the format of learning materials. Those guidelines also usually provide high-level/generic indications on alternative forms of didactical content to enable equivalent access of the content. However, the sole presence of the equivalent forms is no panacea for effective access e.g., an alternative form may be of low quality leading to discrepancies in the overall quality of the learning material, and therefore may have a serious impact on learning effectiveness. One approach to address such limitations could be to provide didactical experts[2] with non-technical guidance for choosing the alternative content, thereby potentially improving the learning experience. While this paper does acknowledge the place and role of the technical experts in the realization of e-learning material, it recommends the provision of a relevant non-technical avenue that can enable specific domain experts to effectively participate in the preparation and delivery of accessible learning objects.

The rest of the paper is organized as follows: Section 2 analyzes various proposals for dealing with accessibility in the field of e-learning. In Section 3, we describe our approach for enabling domain experts get involved in the development of accessible e-learning content. Section 4 points out future work and also wraps up the paper.

2 Addressing Accessibility Issues in e-Learning

In [8] the IMS Global Learning Consortium presents the 'best' practices for producing accessible software applications and accessible content for online distributed learning. In the Learner Information Packaging (LIP) specification [11], IMS proposes indications for aspects such as on the accessibility for information model, and the XML schema binding. The Learning Federation proposes the accessibility specifications [9] for guiding the creation, delivery, and usage of accessible learning content. A set of measurements and requirements to achieve the compliance with the guidelines are also provided.

---

[2] In this paper, a didactical expert/creator is an individual who has knowledge about the subject/domain of the learning material such as the instructor, teacher or tutor

3 Involving the Domain Expert in the Development of e-Learning Content

We propose the provision of a relevant avenue that can enable specific domain experts to appropriately participate in the preparation and delivery of accessible learning material. Our approach is intended to help didactical experts to choose good sets and styles of additional didactical content. We propose a set of non-technical guidelines that can guide didactical experts in the preparation of accessible e-learning content. As for now, the approach provides an avenue for translating visual critical content to textual content. Critical content is didactical e-learning content that can affect accessibility. We have chosen to start by considering textual format since *"it can be the most flexible way to present content"* [8]. We first introduce a conceptual model for representing LOs and propose a set of critical resource type. Then we provide an example of guidelines for one of the critical content described.

3.1 The Conceptual Model and Critical Learning Resource Type

The proposed LO conceptual model, which is shown in Figure 1, aims at separating the structure of the LO from the content. We assume that every didactical content has a principal representation (i.e. the visual representation for a graph) and one or more alternative representations (i.e. the textual or audio translation for the same graph).

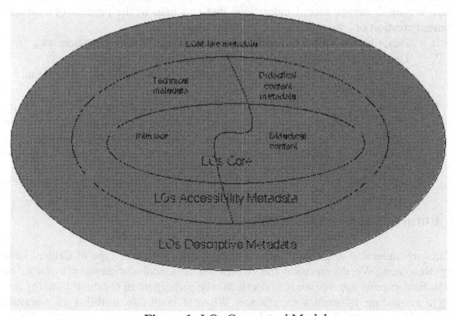

Figure 1: LOs Conceptual Model

Critical learning resource types are typical didactical content of e-learning module that can affect accessibility. The IEEE Learning Object Metadata (LOM) [7] is one of the most comprehensive scheme developed for the description of learning objects. We start with an investigation of only the elements from the LOM list that are both critical from an accessibility perspective and that are format independent. We consider the following elements from the LOM proposal to be format dependent: exercise, simulation, questionnaire, exam, experiment, problem statement, and self assessment. Moreover, we consider a slide to be non-digital content with respect to the LOM definition. Since our approach so far translates visual content to text, we do not consider text to be a critical content. Therefore, we consider six types of typical didactical content from the LOM model: diagram, figure, graph, index, table and lecture. We also consider the following resource type from the CPB/WGBH National Center for Accessible Media (NCAM): multimedia, scientific and mathematics expressions. We do not consider forms because they seem to have accessibility issues related more with the format than with the semantic meaning; we also assume consider textbooks to be in textual form. We do not consider interactivity because it is not a content

3.2 The Equivalent Form for the Didactical Content: A Line Graph Example

The alternative form is essentially the equivalent description of the didactical content by the didactical expert. It involves a textual translation of the non-visual content. To make the translation as effective as possible, specific guidelines will be proposed. Here are some non-technical indications that can help in the process of alternative content creation of a line graph:
1. Describe what the line graph is created for (i.e. its didactical purpose).
2. Describe the meaning and the range of the axes.
3. If the graph is a well-known geometrical figure, indicate the name and the position in relation with the axes.
4. If the graph is not a geometrical figure describe the structure of the curve. Explain where the curve is positioned (north-west) and the size in relation with the overall dimension of the axes. Point out the most relevant point such as the starting and ending points, intersection, tangency, inflexion and so on. Indicate their positions in relation with the axes.

4 Future Work and Conclusions

Plans are underway to provide didactical guidelines for every type of Critical Learning Resource. We do envision the realization of a tool/environment that can help didactical experts appropriately and effectively participate in (or contribute to) creating a rewarding e-learning experience. When it comes to usability in e-learning, learnability is one of the crucial usability measures [12]. In fact in the same reference, Michael Feldstein quotes Don Norman as having said that in e-learning "usability is not the major issue; learnability is." We are investigating how we can employ various usability methods during the entire development process of the anticipated tool.

In this paper we have proposed the provision of non-technical guidelines that can help didactical experts in choosing good sets and styles of additional didactical content in the preparation of accessible e-learning content. We have characterized a set of types of content that can affect the accessibility of learning. Inline with the foregoing, the paper has presented an example of such guidelines for one of the critical contents.

References

1. Nielsen J., Beyond Accessibility: Treating Users with Disabilities as People, Alertbox, November 11 2001, http://www.useit.com/alertbox/20011111.html
2. Theofanos M. F., Redish J.: Bridging the gap: between accessibility and usability Volume 10, Bridging the gap, Issue 6 2003, ACM Press New York, USA.
3. Web Content Accessibility Guidelines 1.0, W3C Recommendations. http://www.w3.org/TR/WAI-WEBCONTENT/.
4. Techniques for Web Content Accessibility Guidelines 1.0, W3C Note http://www.w3.org/TR/WAI-WEBCONTENT-TECHS/.
5. Authoring Tool Accessibility Guidelines 1.0 W3C Recommendation http://www.w3.org/TR/ATAG10/
6. Web Content Accessibility Guidelines 2.0, Working Draft, W3C Recommendations http://www.w3.org/TR/WCAG20/#overview-design-principles
7. IEEE LTSC Learning Object Meta-data LOM_1484_12_1_v1_Final_Draft http://ltsc.ieee.org/wg12/files/
8. IMS Guidelines for Developing Accessible Learning Applications, Version 1.0, White Paper, 2002. http://www.imsproject.org/accessibility/
9. The Learning Federation http://www.thelearningfederation.edu.au/repo
10 CPB/WGBH National Center for Accessible Media (NCAM) http://ncam.wgbh.org/cdrom/guideline/
11 IMS Learner Information Package Accessibility for LIP Information Model. Version 1.0 Public Draft. http://www.imsproject.org/accessibility/acclipv1p0pd/imsacclip_infov1p0pd.html
12 Feldstein M., What Is "Usable" e-Learning?, eLearn Magazine, http://www.elearnmag.org

DIANE^{nx}: Modelling Exploration in the Web Context

Aaron Mullane and Sandrine Balbo

Department of Information Systems, The University of Melbourne, Australia
{a.mullane@pgrad.}{Sandrine@}unimelb.edu.au

Abstract. The process of exploring is an important aspect of a user's general understanding of the environment they are navigating through in computational systems. The research outlined in this paper briefly presents an empirical study of user exploratory behaviour within the web context. It outlines the development of an exploratory grid obtained from this study and its use in forming the DIANE^{nx} task model, enabling user interface and web designers to model users' exploration.

1 Introduction

A task model generally represents diagrammatically actions performed by the user. The research discussed in this paper was developed due to a lack of research in applying and modelling, using task models, exploratory concepts of a user's exploration within the web context. The research question under observation is *"How can a task model be extended to capture navigational exploration in the web context?"*

The research conducted and presented in this paper, outlines the developed DIANE^{nx} task formalism. The formalism allows designers at the evaluation stage of a website to model a user's task exploration based on the exploratory behaviour observed, including the use of navigation and psychological navigating methods, such as landmark, routes and maps, which play an important role in navigating in the physical and computational world [3] [5].

The modelling provides designers with the ability of understanding the exploration process throughout the defined task and the possible deviations that occur from the intended task. The paper briefly outlines the empirical study taken to gather a better understanding of exploratory behaviour and the development of the exploratory grid, which considers the use of navigating methods. Based on the concepts obtained, this paper then presents the DIANE^{nx} (^{nx} = navigational exploration) task model, and highlights its main operations built upon the existing DIANE+ formalism [6].

2 The Exploratory Grid

The empirical study performed consisted of an experimental approach and helped us refine exploration in the web context [4]. The experiment involved participants exploring web sites. The participants (9 in total) were asked to complete two tasks for

M. Masoodian et al. (Eds.): APCHI 2004, LNCS 3101, pp. 620-624, 2004.
© Springer-Verlag Berlin Heidelberg 2004

each site including a five-minute exploration stage before the tasks began [4]. The results from this initial study resulted in the development of the exploratory grid and are summarised in figure 1.

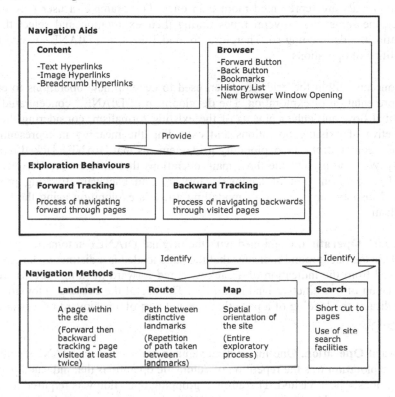

Fig 1. The exploratory grid and the relationship between its components.

The exploratory grid identifies and categorises two exploration behaviours, four navigation methods, and the use of navigational aids. It forms the foundation of a user's exploratory behaviour whilst focusing on the use of navigating methods.

3   Need for a New Formalism: DIANE^{nx}

Balbo *et al.* reviewed existing task modelling formalisms, providing a set of criteria and guidelines based on aspects for using task models in a given context [1]. Considering the abilities of various models and the context in which the exploratory task model will be used, the DIANE+ formalism was chosen for its very powerful, formal representation of a task, rich graphics notations and high usability for modelling and communication [6]. The DIANE+ formalism was analysed against the exploratory grid. This indicated where DIANE+ lacked in its ability to model task exploration. The following two issues arose when modelling forward and backward tracking behaviours using DIANE+.

Linear Representation. Large navigational tasks will produce a long linear model.

Page and Navigation Aid Repetition. Previously visited pages and the selection of navigation aids are represented more than once. For example, a user may navigate through the same page several times during their exploration and select the same navigational aids in doing so. Therefore, to model this using DIANE+ would require a repetition of operations.

The concepts within the grid were then used to develop new operations to enhance the representation of exploration. The development of DIANE^{nx} concentrated on the sequential flow and enhancements of the existing formalism, considering the visual perspective of existing operations and extending the meaning in representing the various elements from the exploratory grid, elements that DIANE+ lacked representing [4]. We now present the three main operations that differentiate DIANE^{nx} from DIANE+: representation of landmark, forward and backward tracking processes. Figure 2 displays an example of modelling a user's exploration using the DIANE^{nx} formalism.

Landmark Operation. Combined with the original DIANE+ automatic operation, a triangle in the background indicates that the page loaded is a distinctive landmark and is formed from the indication of a backward and forward tracking process, after the re-visitation of a distinctive landmark page. The use of the existing automatic operation indicates the loading of a page that was not part of a backward or forward tracking process.

Backward Operation. One major disadvantage that existed in DIANE+'s ability to model exploration was the repetition of automatic operations that indicated pages that had previously been visited. Therefore, a grouping operation was required to eradiate the redundancy of multiple appearances of the same page due to the backward and forward tracking process. The backward tracking process feeds the development of the backward operation. The majority of backward tracking through pages was initiated through the use of the browser's back button. The use of going backwards using navigational aids present in the contents of the page were unique and introduced complexity in the development and application of the operation. Therefore, they were not considered part of the backward operation and are represented by the page jump operation. The operation represents the exploratory behaviour of using the browser components, back button, and new window closure. It is applied as a container, whereby holding all operations that were explored forward from the page before the user explored back. This operation therefore indicates the existence of a landmark page, if the page was visited multiple times.

Forward Operation. The forward operation was developed from the forward tracking element in the criteria. The operation captures the use of the forward browser button and eradicates the modelling of multiple operations of a revisited page. The use of an operation visually enhances the sequential process of task exploration modelling.

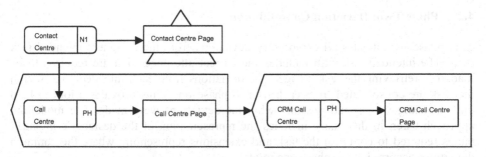

Fig. 2. Representation of a user's exploration of a given scenario using DIANE^nx. First symbol, *'contact centre'*, indicates the selection of a hyperlink (extended DIANE+ interaction operation) *'contact centre'* was selected in the specified navigation sub-section (determined by the modeller) in the page, *N1* (e.g main menu *n*avigation *1*). The resulting symbol to the left, *'contact centre page'*, represents the page loaded (landmark operation) after the selection. The 'T' arrow symbol (section link), below the first, indicates the use of a pre-defined sub-section of navigation has changed, in this example to *PH* (e.g *p*age contact *h*yperlink). The outer surrounding rectangles of the remaining symbols indicate the initialisation of the backward operation after the loading of each surrounded page. The examples sequential page loading process is: (1) *Contact Centre page*, (2) *Call Centre page*, (3) *back to Contact Centre page*, (4) *CRM Call Centre page*, (5) *back to CRM Call Centre page*.

4   Two-Phase Modelling Process

In addition to the exploratory grid and its use in the development of the DIANE^nx formalism, a two-phase modelling process was developed to enhance the development of the model.

The creation of the exploratory task model is split into two phases: the modelling of individual explorations and the deviation consolidation. This two phase process is inspired from the contextual design process proposed by Beyer and Holtzblatt [2]. Our approach focuses on providing the designer with a method for understanding exploration of a single user and then to highlight primary deviations of multiple users.

4.1   Phase One: Individual Exploration

The individual exploration phase models a single user's task exploration using the exploratory task model. This provides the designer with the ability of capturing multiple models of the same task, each performed by individual users. Therefore, the designer can analyse the exploratory deviations from the intended task path, including the navigational aids selected, and the exploration behaviours applied.

4.2 Phase Two: Deviation Consolidation

This phase consolidates all exploratory deviations from the designers intended task path. The intended task path includes the correct site pages that are required to be loaded in retrieving the task's page. The deviations from each intended page within the task are consolidated from each user in phase one. This provides a tool to help understanding where, and possibly why, the deviations were made. The modelling approach taken in this phase includes the representation of the designer's intended pages required to complete the task and extensions representing where the common deviations occurred in the phase one models.

5 Conclusion

This research has examined and built upon the application of exploratory behaviour and the use of navigating methods in the web context. These results drove the development of the exploratory grid, the $DIANE^{nx}$ task model and the two-phase modelling process.

Although it should be noted that the usability and readability of the $DIANE^{nx}$ formalism, in comparison to the DIANE+ formalism, is yet to be performed. As it stands, $DIANE^{nx}$ gave us an opportunity to think about defining web exploration and how to model it. This lead us to the development of a task model formalism that incorporates aspects of navigational exploration in the web context. Moreover, the added two phase process provides the potential to understand why deviations are occurring from common tasks within the site. We foresee that $DIANE^{nx}$ could also be used to provide more effective and efficient navigational structures that cater for exploration.

References

1. Balbo, S., Ozkan, N., Paris, C: Choosing the right task modelling notation: A taxonomy. The Handbook of Task Analysis for Human-Computer Interaction, D. Diaper and N. Stanton (Eds.), Lawrence Erlbaum Associates (LEA) (2003)
2. Beyer, H., Holtzblatt, K: Contextual Design: A Customer-Centered Approach to Systems Designs, Morgan Kaufmann (1997)
3. Boling, E.: Wayfinding. Indiana University Accessed: 15/01/04. http://www.indiana.edu/~iirg/iirgarticles/NAVIGATION/wayfinding.html
4. Mullane, A: DIANEnx: Modelling Navigational Exploration in the Web Context. Honours Dissertation. Department of Information Systems, University of Melbourne, Australia (2003). http://www.dis.unimelb.edu.au/staff/sandrine/PDF/AaronM_HonsThesis_2003.pdf
5. Whitaker, LA.: Human Navigation, in C Forsythe, E Grose and J Ratner (eds), Human Factors and Web Development, Lawrence Erlbaum Associates (1997) 63-70
6. Tarby, J., Barthet, M.: The DIANE+ Method, International Workshop of Computer-Aided Design of User Interfaces, June 5-7, Facultés Universitaires Notre-Dame de la Paix (1996)

Factors Influencing User Selection of WWW Sitemaps

Chris J. Pilgrim[1], Gitte Lindgaard[2] and Ying K. Leung[3]

[1] School of Information Technology, Swinburne University of Technology, Melbourne,
Australia
cpilgrim@swin.edu.au
[2] Human-Oriented Technology Laboratory, Carleton University, Ottawa, Canada
[3] Department of ICT, Institute of Vocational Education, Tsing Yi, Hong Kong

Abstract. One challenge confronting web site designers is to provide effective navigational support. Supplemental navigation tools such as sitemaps are frequently included on web sites to support navigation. However, there is a lack of empirically based guidelines for designers of such tools. This paper reports an empirical investigation into the factors influencing the decision by users to select sitemaps or search tools. The study establishes a relationship between goal specificity and user selection of sitemap and search tools providing a basis for the design of further investigations into the usability and design of such tools.

1   Introduction

Browse around the World Wide Web for a few minutes and you will inevitably come across a link called 'Sitemap'. Links entitled 'Sitemap' may be found on approximately 50% of commercial web sites [1, 2] which would translate into millions of dollars of design, development, storage and maintenance costs each year. Given this pervasive presence of sitemaps on the WWW it could be assumed that there would be well-established guidelines for the design of sitemap interfaces underpinned by rigorous empirical research and usability studies. It is therefore surprising that the limited guidelines that do exist are either based on extrapolation of navigation research into pre-web hypertext systems or on empirical studies that use methods and measures that may not take into account the particular nature of sitemap tools.

A common assumption in both the application of previous empirical studies is that sitemaps are selected by users who wish to search for something specific. Such studies use fact-finding tasks and measures of completion times and task success in their design. This assumption may be appropriate for evaluating the usability of search tools which are designed for users with a specific information need. However, it may not be suitable for other navigation tools. Users have a variety of goals, needs and motivations when interacting with web sites hence task must be a consideration in any study that examines usability of tools such as search tools and sitemaps.

The objective of this study was to investigate empirically the relationship between user goals and the use of supplemental navigation tools such as search tools and

M. Masoodian et al. (Eds.): APCHI 2004, LNCS 3101, pp. 625–630, 2004.

sitemaps, and thereby contributing to the design of future usability studies into the development of design guidelines.

2   Goals Types and Sitemaps

There are a variety of approaches to the classification of goal types. A popular classification method is based on complexity. Shneiderman [3] suggests that the complexity of information goals vary between specific fact-finding, where the outcome can be achieved by visiting a single node in the information space, and extended-fact finding where several nodes are visited to accomplish a goal through aggregation or comparison.

Another method of classifying goals is based on specificity [4, 5]. Previous research by the current authors [6] has proposed a classification of goal types as lying along a continuum based on the level of 'goal specificity' and ranging from tightly defined closed goals to more general open goals. Closed goals have a discrete answer, or set of answers, and once achieved will result in closure of the need. At the other end of the continuum are open goals which do not have a finite answer and hence will not have a specific point of closure where the information need is satisfied. Examples of open goals would include achieving a general overview of the site's purpose and contents, or an understanding of meta-information about the site such as its general size and structure.

Clear and informative site maps help users gain overview knowledge of web sites and hence are most likely to be a tool that supports users undertaking tasks of low goal specificity. In comparison, search tools provide users with the ability to locate pages in a site that contain matches to specific text. Hence these tools will support tasks of high goal specificity.

It is interesting to note that many previous empirical studies examining navigational tools have not considered goal specificity as a factor relying primarily on search-oriented tasks in their experimental design [7, 8, 9]. Further, such studies have only reported measures of completion times and task success, which are suitable for evaluating tools chosen when a user attempts to find a specific piece of information on a web site. Due to their discrete nature, these measures are unsuitable for measuring use and performance of open task types.

This present study will determine whether goal specificity influences the selection of different types of supplemental navigation tools thereby establishing its importance as a factor in empirical studies. It is hypothesized that (1) Users of web sites selecting sitemaps are more likely to be undertaking open tasks than closed tasks and (2) Users of web sites selecting search tools are more likely to be undertaking closed tasks than open tasks. Also investigated is the effect of goal specificity on overall navigation tool use (both search and sitemap tools) given that the alternative to using a navigation tool is to simply browse from page to page to complete the task.

3   Method

Fifty students from Swinburne University of Technology participated in the experiment. A repeated measures design was used in which participants each completed eight tasks on eight large government and commercial web sites. Two tasks, one open and one closed, were designed for each web site, amounting to a total of 16 tasks. For example the open tasks included "Use this site to find out what it is about and how it is organised" and "You need to describe this web site to someone after your visit". Closed tasks were more site specific such as "What does TASSAB stand for?" and "Who developed the GRASSLinks system?" Each participant completed four closed tasks and four open tasks with the order of the task types counterbalanced. Tasks were performed on a purpose-built web browser that logged all interactions to a central database including URL visited, system time, subject number and task. After 3 minutes that browser closed automatically and returned to a task control interface which allowed the participant to select the next task.

4   Results

To investigate the first hypothesis linking use of sitemaps to open tasks we calculated the number of times each participant chose to use a sitemap for each task they completed. Here we report the number of participants who chose a sitemap 0, 1, 2, 3 or 4 times for each of the task types. The analysis includes both overall use, that is immediate and eventual selection of a tool, and immediate sitemap use, that is, when participants did not go to another page before selecting the sitemap.

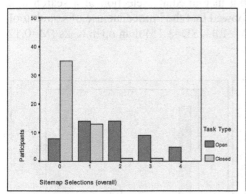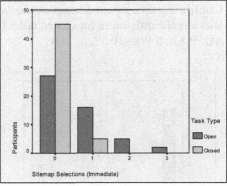

Fig. 1. Sitemap Use (Overall Use)   **Fig. 2.** Sitemap Use (Immediate Use)

Figure 1 reports the number of times each participant selected a sitemap for the four open and four closed tasks. A visual inspection of the results indicates that participants used sitemaps more for open tasks than closed tasks. The results show that 42 subjects used a sitemap at least once for their four open tasks compared with 15 subjects who used a sitemap at least once whilst undertaking closed tasks. Of the

200 closed tasks performed in total, a sitemap was selected only 18 times. By contrast, of the 200 open tasks a sitemap was selected 89 times in total. A paired-samples t-test found that sitemaps were used significant more for open tasks (M=1.78, SD=1.22) than closed tasks (M=0.36, SD=0.63), t(49)=7.49, p<.001.

A further analysis of sitemap use is reported in Figure 2 which examines immediate selection of sitemaps. Whilst the total number of sitemap selections for open tasks amounted to 32 times out of a possible 200 open tasks, 23 participants selected a sitemap immediately upon entering a web site. When compared with only five participants who selected a sitemap immediately when completing a closed task this is a clear indication that users who select sitemaps are more likely to be undertaking an open task than a closed task. A paired-samples t-test found that the immediate use of sitemaps was significantly more for open tasks (M=0.64, SD=0.83) than closed tasks (M=0.10, SD=0.30), t(49)=4.31, p<.001.

Considering both the analysis of overall and immediate sitemap selections it is clear that the users' goal specificity when selecting a sitemap is more likely to be open than closed in nature.

Figure 3 reports the number of times each participant selected a search tool for the four open and four closed tasks. It is clear from the results that when undertaking a closed task most participants used a search tool. In fact, 47 participants used a search tool for closed tasks at least once, whilst when undertaking open tasks only 10 participants used a search tool and only then for only one task. A paired-samples t-test found a statistically significant difference in the use search tools between open tasks (M=0.20, SD=0.40) to closed tasks (M=2.90, SD=1.17), t(49)=-16.39, p<.001 suggesting a strong relationship between goal specificity and tool selection, particularly search tools and closed tasks. Figure 4 shows that only six participants immediately chose to use a search tool for one of their four open tasks. The strength of the relationship between closed tasks and the selection of search tools is clear when we see 32.5% of all closed tasks resulting in immediate selection of a search tool. Confirming this, a paired-samples t-test showed that the immediate use of search tools was significantly more for closed tasks (M=1.84, SD=1.15) than open tasks (M=0.12, SD=0.33), t(49)=-10.32, p<.001.

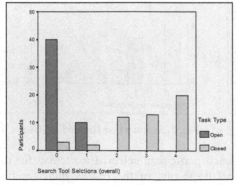

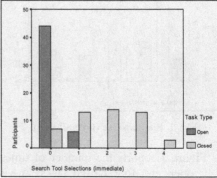

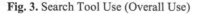

Fig. 3. Search Tool Use (Overall Use)   **Fig. 4.** Search Tool Use (Immediate Use)

Another option for participants undertaking the experiment was to not use either tool but instead simply browse from page to page whilst undertaking the task. It was found that 49.5% of open tasks resulted in browsing only compared with 17.5% of closed tasks. A paired-samples t-test found a statistically significant difference from open tasks (M=49.5, SD=30.1) to closed tasks (M=17.5, SD=27.3), t(49)=7.57, p<.001. This indicates a strong use of navigation tools when completing closed tasks (predominately search tools) whilst navigation tools are used for approximately half of the open tasks with the others choosing to browse from page to page in order to complete the task.

5   Discussion and Conclusion

The results indicate that use of sitemaps is relatively low, with subjects opening the sitemap immediately upon entering the site in slightly less than 10% of all tasks, and in just over 25% of the tasks when including immediate and eventual use. By contrast, a search was issued immediately in nearly 25% of all open and closed tasks, and overall use in nearly 40% of the tasks. These findings are in line with those of [10] who report an empirical study that suggests that people simply do not use sitemaps. Thus, whilst the use of sitemaps is relatively low when compared with that of search tools, it is relatively high when considering only those situations when a user is undertaking a task of low goal specificity, i.e. when considering overall usage of sitemaps, including both immediate and eventual use for the 200 open tasks, participants use the sitemaps in 44.5% of the tasks.

As predicted, the results confirm that users conducting a closed task in which they are looking for a specific answer to a specific question are more likely to select a search tool. Such a strong mapping is likely to be a result of the consistency in search tool design: users know what a search tool will do for them, when to use it and how to use it. It appears that the same cannot be claimed for sitemaps. The findings suggest that users who wish to obtain a general overview of a site or who are interested in meta-information about a particular web site, are more likely to browse the site rather than choosing to use a navigation tool. If a navigation tool is selected under those circumstances, it is significantly more likely to be a sitemap than a search tool, and it is more likely that users will browse around the site before selecting the sitemap. The results support the hypothesis that goal specificity influences the selection of different types of supplemental navigation tools. Given these findings, empirical studies into the design of supplemental navigation tools for web sites should consider task as a key factor.

Several immediate implications for the design of sitemap interfaces arise from this study. The acknowledgment that sitemaps must primarily support users with low goal specificity who are after general overview information about a site provides interface designers with guidance regarding the level of detail that users should be exposed to in a sitemap. For example, sitemaps, particularly those that are automatically created by tools, are notorious for displaying the complete site structure, resulting in an extremely complex view. These complex representations do little to help the user get any type of overview of the site and may introduce navigation problems themselves. Sitemap designers may consider either a basic overview design or, alternatively, employ visualisation techniques such as fisheye lenses or bifocal displays to manage complexity by providing global and detailed views.

One of the limitations to this study is that the experimental tasks were based on extremes of the goal specificity continuum. Other task classification methods could be considered. Further work is required to generate appropriate design guidelines for sitemaps and to investigate the feasibility of visualization techniques to reduce interface complexity. There is also a need for future work on the development of empirical techniques to evaluate and measure user performance and satisfaction when undertaking open tasks as traditional measure of completion times and task success are unsuitable.

References

1. Nielsen, J. Sitemap Usability, Alertbox, www.useit.com/alertbox/20020106.html (2002)
2. Bernard, M. Using a sitemap as a navigation tool. Usability News, 1.1. http://psychology.wichita.edu/surl/usabilitynews/1w/Sitemaps.htm, (1999)
3. Shneiderman, B. Designing Information-Abundant Web Sites: Issues and Recommendations, Int. J. Human-Computer Studies 47(1) (1997) 5-30.
4. Cove, J. F. Walsh B. C. Online Text Retrieval Via Browsing. Information Processing and Management 24(1) (1988) 31-37.
5. Carmel, E., Crawford, S., Chen, H. Browsing in Hypertext: A Cognitive Study. IEEE Transactions on Systems, Man and Cybernetics, 22(5) (1992) 865-84
6. Pilgrim, C. J. Leung, Y. K. Lindgaard, G. An Exploratory Study of WWW Browsing Strategies. Proceedings of APCHI 2002, Beijing, China, (2002)
7. McDonald, S. & Stevenson, R. J. Navigation in hyperspace: An evaluation of the effects of navigational tools and subject matter expertise on browsing and information retrieval in hypertext. Interacting with Computers, 10, (1998) 129-142
8. Danielson, D. R. Web Navigation and the Behavioral Effects of Constantly Visible Site Maps. Interacting with Computers 14, (2002) 601-618
9. Hornbæk, K. and Frøkjær, E. Do Thematic Maps Improve Information Retrieval? Proceedings of INTERACT '99, Edinburgh, Scotland, (1999)
10. Stover, A., Pernice Coyne, K. & Nielsen, J. Designing Usable Site Maps for Websites. Nielsen Norman Group, Fremont, CA. (2002)

ViewPoint: A Zoomable User Interface for Integrating Expressive Systems

Darryl Singh, Mitra Nataraj, Rick Mugridge

Department of Computer Science, University of Auckland, New Zealand
{dsin038, mnat010}@ec.auckland.ac.nz, r.mugridge@auckland.ac.nz

Abstract. Naked Object applications are Expressive – a desirable quality not present in traditional software systems. However, these applications can generate a large number of windows leading to a cluttered desktop. In order to rectify this problem we have used a Zoomable User Interface (ZUI), which provides the user with an infinite amount of space. A system titled ViewPoint was developed to effectively integrate Naked Objects with a Zoomable environment. The finished system enhances Naked Objects by making full use of ZUI capabilities. ViewPoint also introduces various generic context awareness and navigation mechanisms to optimise the use of ZUIs.

1 Introduction and Background

Traditional user interfaces are characterised by predefined scripts, wizards, and dialogue boxes, which force users to interact with the core functionality of the system in a set of predetermined ways. Expressive systems aim to allow users to order their interactions with a system as they wish, so that they can become "problem-solvers instead of process followers" [1].

The Naked Objects framework allows developers to create expressive systems, by exposing the business objects of the system directly to the user through an auto-generated user interface [2]. Users can directly manipulate the core objects instead of accessing them through an intermediate representation.

The classes in a Naked Object application are graphically represented as icons. Class icons can be dragged and dropped onto the desktop to instantiate an object. An instantiated object is represented by a form, where the fields represent attributes, and methods are accessed using a right-click pop-up menu. Additionally, associations between objects can be formed using drag-and-drop gestures.

As every instantiated object is represented in its own window, the desktop is prone to becoming cluttered and confusing. The problem of insufficient screen space is prevalent in all traditional desktop applications. However, we specifically wish to enhance the user interface for Naked Objects because of their expressive qualities [1].

One such enhancement was the creation of First-Class Viewers for Naked Objects, which included Tables, Trees, Containers and Map viewers. We have developed Iduna – a Java Swing interface for Naked Objects. Iduna allows for the dynamic construction of various viewers at runtime [3]. For example, users can construct

M. Masoodian et al. (Eds.): APCHI 2004, LNCS 3101, pp. 631–635, 2004.
© Springer-Verlag Berlin Heidelberg 2004

composites that are made up of subsets of fields of Naked Objects. However, these extensions amplify the screen space problems considerably as users are given the freedom to create various views of Naked Objects, which result in additional windows on the desktop.

We investigate the use of a Zoomable User Interface (ZUI) as a solution to the limited screen space problem. The ZUI provides the user with an infinite amount of 2D space to display graphical objects. The user navigates around this area by panning and zooming a virtual camera. Jazz is a Java Toolkit for creating ZUIs, which uses a hierarchical scene graph as its underlying structure [4]. Our system, ViewPoint, uses Jazz to create a ZUI for Naked Object applications and thus provides a zoomable environment for expressive systems.

2 ViewPoint: Merging Naked Objects with a Zoomable Environment

The infinite space provided by the ZUI allows users to keep any number of instantiated objects open. We found that the ZUI not only solved screen space issues related to Naked Objects, but gave other benefits.

For instance, Semantic zooming is a powerful feature of ZUIs, where objects can be rendered at increasing levels of detail as the users zooms in. In most ZUI applications, the levels of detail are "hard coded" by system designers who decide, on behalf of the user, what degree of detail is to be displayed at every level of camera magnification. Users have no control over what they see upon zooming into an object, which undermines the expressive system paradigm. As customized interfaces of numerous applications can be developed within ViewPoint, it is impossible to generically predefine appropriate levels of detail.

Instead of predetermined levels of detail, we introduce the concept of user-defined semantic zooming in ViewPoint. A user is able to dynamically specify their own levels of detail and when each of these levels should displayed with respect to camera magnification. Using the compose functionality of Iduna, the user can determine the fields of a Naked Object that are to appear at each level of magnification.

In Jazz, camera actions are animated to provide continual feedback in terms of navigation. This is an important feature, as abrupt changes in the user interface can be confusing for the user and create cognitive burden [5]. Consequently, we have animated all allowable actions within Naked Objects so that every aspect of ViewPoint provides continual feedback.

3 Navigation and Context Awareness in ViewPoint

While the ZUI enhances the use of Naked Objects, there are problems associated with ZUIs themselves which deter Naked Objects from being used effectively.

Successful navigation is a major issue in ZUIs. Users are forced to use tedious panning and zooming gestures in order to move between various areas. We have implemented JazzViewers, which allow the user to simultaneously access different parts of the ZUI. Each JazzViewer has its own pane and independent camera that looks into the same underlying scene graph. The JazzViewers have unique colored backgrounds to distinguish the different cameras, as shown by the four large panes in Fig. 1.

Naked Object applications are heavily reliant on drag-and-drop gestures, which are impossible over large changes in location and scale. JazzViewers address this problem by allowing for physically distant objects to be shown simultaneously on screen, allowing for Naked Objects to be dragged from one JazzViewer onto another.

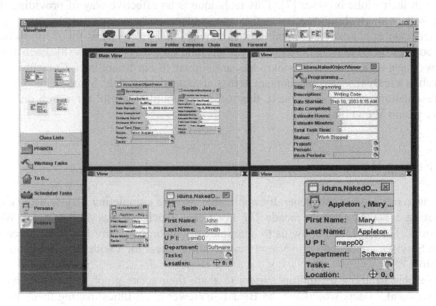

Figure 1. ViewPoint: JazzViewers, BirdsEyeViewer and SnapShotList.

The SnapShotList, shown in the top right hand corner of Fig. 1, was developed in order to aid navigation. Users can save any area of the ZUI which they wish to return to at a later stage. A SnapShot acts as a static camera over the saved space.

Due to the vast and seamless space available through a ZUI, users do not have sufficient contextual information regarding their current location. The BirdsEyeViewer was developed as a context awareness mechanism. It is a specialized view over the same underlying scene graph with its own camera at a zoomed out position. The position of each JazzViewer camera is shown in the BirdsEyeViewer as a coloured rectangle, as shown in the left-most pane of Fig. 1.

Changes to the location and zoom of a JazzViewer's camera are reflected in the BirdsEyeViewer, as the corresponding coloured rectangle also moves or scales accordingly. If a camera from one JazzViewer is moved into a space where another camera is focused, their colours superimpose on each other, indicating that two Jazz-Viewers are viewing the same area.

4 Related Work

Pook et al has identified insufficient contextual information as one of the difficulties of using a ZUI [6]. In order to address this issue, a context layer is drawn transparently over the current area of focus. While this approach avoids the screen real estate that is dedicated to the BirdsEyeViewer, contextual information is not as readily available for the user as it must be explicitly requested for.

Cockburn et al explore speed-dependant automatic zooming, where the zoom-level is changed automatically according to scrolling speeds which they demonstrate through their globe browser [7]. This technique is an effective way of providing the user with contextual information as they navigate.

Bederson et al have developed various navigational mechanisms for ZUIs, including content-based search, bookmarks, portals, and directory browsers [8]. Each Jazz-Viewer acts as a portal and bookmarks are similar to our SnapShots. Content-based search is a textual search mechanism across all objects in a ZUI. Since Naked Object representations heavily utilise text, this technique could be useful for search-oriented users within ViewPoint.

5 Future Work

To make our work more generally applicable, we are completing a system for constructing a Naked Objects facade for JavaBeans (such as JavaMail) and for Web Services. This will then allow us to automatically incorporate any JavaBean-based or Web Services application into ViewPoint, to allow integration with other applications within a ZUI.

We plan to allow for multiple users to share their scene graph in a collaborative environment. Users would see the BirdsEyeViewer at all times making them aware of their camera position relative to others. If more than one individual occupies the same space, camera colours will superimpose forming a useful co-ordination mechanism.

Currently, the scene graph is not saved between sessions. We wish to include persistence so that the user can return to the same consistent space and continue working. Techniques, such as the rental system of Java Spaces, will need to manage garbage collection.

If the objects in a scene graph in Jazz were modeled with Naked Objects, it would make the scene graph available reflectively. This would make it possible for users to visually construct one scene graph that is rendered as Naked Objects in a separate scene graph. For example, this could allow a user to build groups of objects that can be transformed as a whole group.

6 Conclusions

We have created ViewPoint, a ZUI for Naked Object applications. We have introduced the user-defined semantic zooming and incorporated animation to provide continual feedback to the user. We have also developed several generic navigational techniques for ZUIs. Users are given contextual information through the BirdsEyeViewer. They are able to efficiently access physically different parts of the ZUI using JazzViewers and SnapShots. Usability testing will be required to establish whether users are more proactive and empowered using ViewPoint than the desktop. While refinements are necessary to extend ViewPoint, it is the first step in merging expressive systems and zoomable environments.

References

1. Pawson, R., *Expressive Systems: A manifesto for radical business software*, CSC Research Services, UK, 2000.
2. Pawson, R., and Matthews, R., *Naked Objects*, Wiley, 2002.
3. Mugridge, R., Nataraj, M., Singh, D., "Emerging User Interfaces through First-Class Viewers", *4th Annual Conference of the ACM Special Interest Group on Computer Human Interaction*, CHINZ, Dunedin, July 2003, pp75--80.
4. Bederson, B.B., Meyer, J., Good, L., "Jazz: An Extensible Zoomable User Interface Graphics Toolkit in Java", *HCIL-2000-13*, CS-TR-4137, UMIACS-TR-2000-30, 2000.
5. Chang, B., and Ungar, D., "Animation: From Cartoons to User Interface", *UIST1993*, pp. 45--55, 1993.
6. Pook, S, Lecolinet, E., Vaysseix, G., Barillot, E., "Context and interaction in zoomable user interfaces", *Proceedings of the Working Conference on Advanced Visual Interfaces*, Palermo, Italy, 2000, pp 227--231.)
7. Cockburn, A., Looser, J., Savage, J., "Around the World in Seconds with Speed-Dependent Automatic Zooming", Human-Computer Interaction Lab Department of Computer Science University of Canterbury Christchurch, New Zealand, www.cosc.canterbury.ac.nz/~andy/sdaz.mov.
8. Bederson, B., Hollan, J. "Pad++: A Zooming Graphical Interface for Exploring Alternate Interface Physics", *Journal of Visual Languages and Computing*, 7, pp 3--32, March 1996.
9. S. Jul and G. W. Furnas, "Critical zones in desert fog: Aids to multiscale navigation", *UIST '98*, ACM Press, 1998, pp 97--106.
10. Hornbaek, K., Bederson, B. B., and Plaisant, C. "Navigation Patterns and Usability of Zoomable User Interfaces With and Without an Overview", *ACM Transactions on Computer-Human Interaction*, 2003, 9(4), pp 362--389.
11. Pook, S., "Interaction and Context in Zoomable User Interfaces". Doctoral thesis, École Nationale Supérieure des Télécommunications, Paris, France, 2001.

Passing on Good Practice: Interface Design for Older Users

Mary Zajicek

Department of Computing, School of Technology, Oxford Brookes University, Wheatley Campus, Oxford OX33 1HX
mzajicek@brookes.ac.uk

Abstract. There exists a pressing need for the fruits of research into interface design for older adults to be made available to the wider design community. Older people form a special user group as a result of age related capability changes, who cannot easily participate in User Centred Design activities. Interface designers must take this into account. This paper introduces patterns as a solution for passing on successful design for older adults

1. Introduction

Researchers present their work in published papers and prove from the results of experiments that their interface design helps older people to perform a particular function and is successful in certain respects. There exists a sizeable pool of knowledge in this area. However it is difficult for new designers of systems for older people to access, as the knowledge is buried within research papers.

This paper discusses the challenges involved in designing for older people and in particular why standard interface design techniques that depend on a relatively homogeneous user group, and effective user participation, are not appropriate. It is argued that guidelines do not supply sufficient information to a would-be designer and that the more structured approach afforded by the use of patterns provides more accessible design knowledge. A sample pattern for speech systems for older adults is presented.

2. Special Design Issues for Older Adults

The effects of ageing are manifest at different rates relative to one another for each individual. This pattern of capabilities varies widely between individuals, and as people grow older, the variability increases [5]. This presents a fundamental problem for the designers of interfaces to computing systems. The 'typical user' of standard systems is assumed to have abilities which are broadly similar for everybody. User-Centred Design the standard approach for human computer interface design, tends to rely upon homogeneous groups for user testing in order to focus on design decisions.

M. Masoodian et al. (Eds.): APCHI 2004, LNCS 3101, pp. 636-640, 2004.
© Springer-Verlag Berlin Heidelberg 2004

The interface development tools and methods we currently use are less effective in meeting the needs of diverse user groups or addressing the dynamic nature of diversity. Additionally the cultural and experiential gap between designers and older people can be especially large when developing new technology [2] and this can severely limit their ability to contribute actively to a discussion about their requirements.

Lines and Hone [4] found that older people participating in focus groups are inclined to 'wander' from the topic under discussion, providing unrelated anecdotes and chatting amongst themselves. They reported that it was difficult to keep the participants' attention focused on the task and felt that smaller numbers in sessions were preferable, allowing everybody time to contribute and those who appeared nervous to be drawn into the discussion more easily by the moderators.

Interface design for older people is therefore more complex than for standard groups, where optimum interface design is more difficult using standard user centred design techniques. It is therefore particularly important that instances of design that work well for older people, should be carefully documented and passed on for other designers to use.

3. Passing on Good Practice

HCI design knowledge is traditionally encapsulated in design guidelines in the form of simple statements that provide the interface designer with a diluted version of the information provided by the original experimental work. The W3C, Web Access Initiative, Web Authoring Guidelines (Web Authoring Guidelines, 1999) developed for Web designers to help them create more accessible Web pages for non-standard users, are accompanied by the reasons for the guidelines, in order to make the Web designer more aware of who she or he is excluding by not following the guidelines. Interestingly however in order to reduce the complexity of their formal guidelines the Web Access Initiative have created a set of ten Quick Tips to be used as a quick checklist for accessibility. So the Quick Tips are actually a set of simpler guidelines derived from the more detailed guidelines because they were too complex for new designers to apply. The ambivalent approach demonstrated by the Web Access Initiative exemplifies the dilemma inherent in the use of guidelines.

This paper puts forward as an alternative design patterns [1] which were formally defined at the CHI 2003 workshop 'Perspectives on HCI Patterns: Concepts using the Pattern Language Markup Language (PLML) [3].

A robust set of design patterns will enable interface designers to access best practice and help them to create sympathetic and successful designs. Importantly the patterns will reflect the experience of older people through experimentation and observation, which the designers themselves are lacking. Their use will nurture good design and provide a framework for analysis and discussion.

4. A Sample Pattern for Speech Systems for Older People

The interface design pattern described here in PLML form sets out a successful dialogue construct for handling input errors.

(7) Error Recovery Loop Pattern in PLML Form (7-CM-SPST-OP-MPZ)

Pattern ID: 7-ERL-SPST-OP-MPZ

Pattern Name: Error Recovery Loop

Problem: Errors and error recovery represent the primary usability problem for speech systems. Standard menu driven systems often start with a long set of instructions in a bid to avoid errors happening. Older users are not able to remember these messages, which also slow down the dialogue, rendering them useless.

Context: This approach is most useful in dialogues which are used mostly by experienced users who are unlikely to require any instruction and will if they use the dialogue successfully never have to listen to an error recovery message. Use in speech systems for older adults where errors in data input are likely to occur.

Forces: F23 Errors and error recovery represent the primary usability problem for speech systems.
F48 Standard menu driven systems often start with a long set of instructions in a bid to avoid errors happening.
F13 Older people find difficulty in remembering long speech output messages
F14 Older people are confused by long messages and remember more information
F50 Long instructions slow down the dialogue, rendering it useless for older people.
F52 Providing different levels of error recovery ensures support for each user at their own level
F53 Error Recovery Loop does not delay those who make few errors.
BUT
F54 Error Recovery Loop allows users to make errors before it instructs them which might irritate some users.

Solution: The pattern described here directs designers to embed instructions in an error recovery loop: in effect to wait for the error to happen and then try to recover it. Count how many times an erroneous data input occurs and on each count invoke an increasingly detailed error recovery message. In the examples below Example (1) simply gives instructions for efficient input, but the more detailed Example (2) provides information about which might help the user work better with the system.

Synopsis: Error Recovery Loop provides increasing levels of information as more errors occur.

Evidence: The Error Recovery Loop pattern was successfully applied in the VABS (Zajicek et al, 2003).

Example: (1)   "Your name has not been recognized. Please speak slowly and clearly into the telephone.
(2)   "The system is trying to match your name against the names it holds in the database. Please try to speak your name in the same way that you did when you registered for the Voice activated Booking System.

Rationale: Because older people cannot remember lengthy preliminary spoken instructions about data input, it is best to let them try to input data and if it goes wrong invoke an error recovery message. This form of error recovery does not prepare the user in advance for possible errors, as they have to create the error before it is invoked.

Confidence:` 50% (used successfully in one system – the VABS)

Literature: Zajicek M., Wales, R., Lee, A., 2003, Towards VoiceXML Dialogue Design for Older Adults, In Palanque P., Johnson P., O'Neill E (eds) *Design for Society.* Proceedings of HCI 2003

Related Patterns: This pattern is a member of the Pattern Group (3) – **'Reducing Input Errors patterns'** consisting of three patterns that offer different solutions to reduce the errors associated with speech data input.
(3) Default Input Message Pattern (3-DIM-SPO-OP-MPZ)
(7) Error Recovery Loop Pattern (7-CM-SPST-OP-MPZ)
(8) Partitioned Input Message in PLML Form (8-PIM-SPST-OP-MPZ)
Pattern **(4) Context Sensitive Help Message Pattern** (4-CSHM-SPO-OP-MPZ) can be used as part of pattern **(7) Error Recovery Loop Pattern** (7-CM-SPST-OP-MPZ)

Author: Mary Zajicek

Creation Date: 7th January 2004

Revision Number: 3

Last Modified: 24th March 2004

We see that each pattern has its own unique identifying code. It also includes a description of the problem that it seeks to solve, the context in which it would be used and the way in which it can be achieved with examples. Forces refer to existing circumstances that force the need for the pattern. This pattern is one of a complete pattern set [7]

5. Conclusions

The pattern put forward in this paper is for speech systems, but the argument for building patterns hold equally well for all interface design for older people.
The very existence of a set of patterns will have the effect of sensitizing interface designers to the design considerations expressed in the patterns, and enable them to consult a body of good practice. For example patterns, in the domain of speech interaction for older people, should encourage designers to think in terms of the functionality of output messages, and should clarify their perception of the components of the dialogue and the part they play in its overall construction. Interface designers will then be able to draw upon a rich and fertile information base that will help them to design successful systems for older people, thus enabling the older adult community to be well served with usable designs.

References

[1] Alexander, C., 1979, The Timeless Way of Building, Oxford University Press

[2] Eisma R., Dickinson A., Goodman .J, Mival O., Syme A., Tiwari L., 2003, Mutual Inspiration in the Development of New Technology for Older People. Proc. Include 2003 conference, London

[3] Fincher, S., 2003, CHI 2003 Workshop Report, Interfaces No. 56, Journal of the BCS HCI Group.

[4] Lines , L., Hone, K., 2002, Research Methods for Older Adults, Presented at the workshop 'A new research agenda for older adults' at HCI 2002

[5] Myatt, E. D., Essa, I., Rogers, W, 2000, Increasing the opportunities for ageing in place. In Proceedings of the ACM Conference on Universal Usability, Washington DC, ACM Press, New York (2000) 39-44.

[6] Web Authoring Guidelines, 1999, http://www.w3.org/TR/WCAG10/, (last accessed 27.12.3)

[7] Zajicek, M., 2004, Patterns for Speech Dialogues for Older Adults, http://cms.brookes.ac.uk/computing/speech/index.php?id=61 (last accessed 27.3.4)

Interfaces That Adapt like Humans

Samuel Alexander, Abdolhossein Sarrafzadeh

Institute of Information and Mathematical Sciences, Massey
University, Private Bag 102 904, NSMC, New Zealand
{S.T.Alexander, H.A.Sarrafzadeh}@massey.ac.nz
+64 9 414-0800 ext.{9257, 9549}

Abstract. Whenever people talk to each other, non-verbal behaviour plays a
very important role in regulating their interaction. However, almost all human-
computer interactions take place using a keyboard or mouse – computers are
completely oblivious to the non-verbal behaviour of their users. This paper
outlines the plan for an interface that aims to adapt like a human to the non-
verbal behaviour of users. An Intelligent Tutoring System (ITS) for counting
and addition is being implemented in conjunction with the New Zealand
Numeracy Project. The system's interface will detect the student's non-verbal
behaviour using in-house image processing software, enabling it to adapt to the
student's non-verbal behaviour in similar ways to a human tutor. We have
conducted a video study of how human tutors interpret the non-verbal
behaviour of students, which has laid the foundation for this research.

Keywords. Affective computing, non-verbal behaviour, adaptation

1 Introduction

Non-verbal behaviour plays a very important role in interpersonal communication. It
almost goes without saying that humans can interpret the non-verbal behaviour (e.g.
facial expressions, gestures and vocal inflections) of others, which enables them to
adapt their own behaviour. This is what allows humans to be kind and considerate, to
be aware of the needs of others, to guess what others are thinking – to have
meaningful, constructive relationships. In fact, the inability to respond to the non-
verbal behaviour of others has serious implications for interacting with others, of
which autism is a sobering example.

However, the ability to respond to non-verbal behaviour is exactly what modern
"autistic" computers do not have. Almost all human-computer interactions take place
using a keyboard or mouse – computers are completely oblivious to the non-verbal
signals of their users. Many researchers now feel strongly that human-computer
interactions could be significantly enhanced and enriched if computers could adapt
appropriately to users as they perceive these signals (e.g. [10], [9]).

This paper proposes an interface that will enable a computer to adapt to the non-
verbal behaviour of users. In particular, an Intelligent Tutoring System (ITS) for
counting and addition is being developed in conjunction with the New Zealand
Numeracy Project. The system will use non-verbal behaviour to help identify the

M. Masoodian et al. (Eds.): APCHI 2004, LNCS 3101, pp. 641–645, 2004.

cognitive ability of students based on an existing nine-stage model used by the New Zealand Numeracy Project [8], and thus to help adapt its tutoring. We have studied Numeracy Project video clips of how human tutors do exactly that, and these results will be used in the design of the system. The system will detect the non-verbal behaviour of students using in-house image processing software.

2   Related Work

This research falls loosely within the relatively new field of *affective computing* [10], which broadly defined concerns artificial systems that recognise or exhibit emotions.

It is not an easy task to find examples of interfaces that adapt to recognised affect or non-verbal behaviour in users, and harder still to find such interfaces that have actually found a useful application. Some of the most recent work in affective interfaces is by Lisetti et al. [5], who propose a multimodal interface for tele-health that will provide health-care providers with affective state information about their patients. So far as ITSs are concerned, Kort et al. [4] propose to build a Learning Companion, which will initially use eye-gaze as an input of affective state. Litman and Forbes [6] propose an ITS that adapts to the emotions revealed by the acoustic and prosodic elements of a student's speech.

Many groups (e.g. [7]) are certainly working towards affect-sensitive interfaces, but most are still at the stage of recognising affect with an acceptable accuracy.

3   How Do Human Tutors Interpret Non-verbal Behaviour?

The current research is being undertaken in conjunction with the New Zealand Numeracy Project, a non-profit government organisation that works to improve the teaching of maths in New Zealand schools.

The New Zealand Numeracy Project divides students into nine stages, based on their ability to use increasingly complicated strategies to solve number problems [8]. The nine stages are shown in Fig. 1, although only the first seven of these are relevant to counting and addition, and thus the current research. Tutors use these stages to assess the progress of individual students. This then allows the tutors to adapt their tutoring to individual students because they know at what level to pitch their instruction.

We studied video clips of human tutors to determine how they assess the Numeracy Project strategy stage of students. We found that several non-verbal behaviours are significant indicators for human tutors to classify students into the correct strategy stage [1]. In total, there were five factors in determining the strategy stage of students from their observable behaviour: the accuracy of answers, the student's delay-time in answering, and three non-verbal behaviours – counting on fingers, eye gaze and movements, and subvocalisation. These five factors were consistently interpreted by human tutors to assess the strategy stage of each student.

Strategy Stages

	Stage & Behavioural Indicator
0	**Emergent** The student has no reliable strategy to count an unstructured collection of items.
1	**One to One Counting** The student has a reliable strategy to count an unstructured collection of items.
2	**Counting from One on Materials** The student's most advanced strategy is counting from one on materials to solve addition problems.
3	**Counting from One by Imaging** The student's most advanced strategy is counting from one without the use of materials to solve addition problems.
4	**Advanced Counting** The student's the most advanced strategy is counting-on, or counting-back to solve addition or subtraction tasks.
5	**Early Additive Part-Whole Thinking** The student shows any Part-Whole strategy to solve addition or subtraction problems mentally by reasoning the answer from basic facts and/or place value knowledge.
6	**Advanced Additive Part-Whole Thinking** The student is able to use at least two different mental strategies to solve addition or subtraction problems with multi-digit numbers.
7	**Advanced Multiplicative Part-Whole** The student is able to use at least two different mental strategies to solve multiplication and division problems with whole numbers.
8	**Advanced Proportional Part-Whole** The student uses at least two different strategies to solve problems that involve equivalence with and between fractions, ratios and proportions.

Fig. 1. The nine strategy stages in the New Zealand Numeracy Project

4   Detecting Non-verbal Behaviour of Students

The results of the video study imply that the ITS for counting and addition should be able to detect each of the significant non-verbal behaviours that were identified in the video study: counting on fingers, eye gaze and movements, and subvocalisation. This research will use in-house image processing software to detect these behaviours.

A major branch of image processing is automated facial expression analysis. Using a simple web-cam, automated facial expression analysis systems identify the motion of muscles in the face by comparing several images of a given subject, or by using neural networks to learn the appearance of particular muscular contractions [9]. This builds on the classic work of Ekman and Friesen, who developed the Facial Action Coding System for describing the movement of muscles in the face [2]. An affective state can be inferred from analysing the facial actions that are detected.

A state-of-the-art automated facial expression analysis system has been developed in-house at Massey University in Auckland, New Zealand – Fig. 2 shows a screenshot of the system's output [3]. The system is yet to be extensively tested, but informal tests have shown that the system is capable of accurately identifying seven affective states: surprise, happiness, sadness, puzzlement, disgust, and anger, plus a neutral state. Hardware is currently being customised for real time operation.

Eye gaze/movements and subvocalisation also fall under the automated facial expression analysis umbrella, so the expression analysis system can be adapted to detect each of these behaviours. Similar techniques employed by automated facial expression analysis can also be used to automatically detect gestures, such as a student counting on his/her fingers. Therefore we are currently developing an image processing system that will be capable of detecting each of the non-verbal behaviours that were identified in the video study of human tutors.

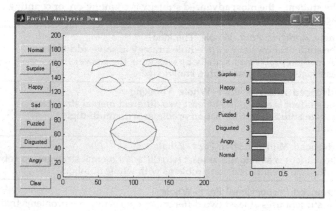

Fig. 2. A screenshot taken from the in-house facial expression analysis system

5   Current Research

The video study of human tutors identified five indicators of a student's strategy stage according to the New Zealand Numeracy Project: the accuracy of answers, the student's delay-time in answering, and three non-verbal behaviours – counting on fingers, eye gaze and movements, and subvocalisation.

An ITS for counting and addition is being developed that will consider each of these factors to artificially assess the strategy stage of students. Clearly the accuracy of answers and answer delay-times are easily identified; the three non-verbal behaviours will be detected using in-house image processing software. Once the system has assessed the strategy stage of the student, it will be able to adapt its tutoring by pitching its instruction at precisely the right level. The system will be able to present tutoring material that will push the student on to the next stage.

The ITS for counting and addition will be the test bed for a new interface that will enrich the interaction between human and computer far beyond what is possible through keyboard and mouse alone. Users will actively interact with the system using a keyboard and mouse, but will also passively interact with the system through the web-cam - the system will actually be aware of the user's non-verbal behaviour.

There are many ways in which this new generation of interface could improve our interaction with computers. For example, pre-emptive help facilities could react to perceived confusion, artificial agents could stimulate motivation if they sense a lack of interest, or provide encouragement if they sense frustration. As the image processing technology continues to improve, computers should be able to adapt to users in a much more appropriate, efficient and sensitive manner.

References

1. Alexander, S.T.V., Sarrafzadeh, A., Hughes, P., Fan C.: How do Human Tutors of Counting and Addition Interpret Non-verbal Behaviour? Submitted to ITS'04 (2004)

2. Ekman, P., Friesen, W.V.: Facial Action Coding System. Consulting Psychologists Press (1978)

3. Fan, C., Johnson, M., Messom, C., Sarrafzadeh, A.: Machine Vision for an Intelligent Tutor. Proceedings of the International Conference on Computational Intelligence, Robotics and Autonomous Systems, Singapore (2003)

4. Kort, B., Reilly, R., Picard, R.W.: An Affective Model of Interplay Between Emotions and Learning: Reengineering Educational Pedagogy - Building a Learning Companion. IEEE International Conference on Advanced Learning Technologies (2001) 43-48

5. Lisetti, C.L., Nasoz, F., Lerouge, C., Ozyer, O., Alvarez, K.: Developing Multimodal Intelligent Affective Interfaces for Tele-Home Health Care. International Journal of Human-Computer Studies (2003) 59 (1-2) 245-255.

6. Litman, D., Forbes, K.: Recognizing Emotions from Student Speech in Tutoring Dialogues. In Proceedings of the IEEE Automatic Speech Recognition and Understanding Workshop (ASRU), St. Thomas, Virgin Islands (2003)

7. Nasoz, F., Lisetti, C.L., Alvarez, K., Finelstein, N.: Emotional Recognition from Physiological Signals for User Modeling of Affect. In Proceedings of the 3rd Workshop on Affective and Attitude User Modeling, Pittsburgh (2003)

8. New Zealand Ministry of Education: Book 1, The Number Framework. Numeracy Professional Development Projects. Wellington: Ministry of Education (2003)

9. Pantic, M., Rothkrantz, L.J.M.: Toward an affect-sensitive multimodal human-computer interaction. Proceedings of the IEEE (2003) 91(9) 1370-1390

10. Picard, R.W.: Affective Computing. Cambridge, Mass., MIT Press (1997)

Designers Search Strategies Influenced by the Interaction with Information Retrieval Systems (IRS): Within the Early Stages of the Design Process

Caroline Francis

School of Design and Built Environment, Faculty of Built Environment and Engineering
Queensland University of Technology Brisbane QLD 4000, Australia
c.francis@qut.edu.au

Abstract. As Industrial Designers handle information within the early stages of the design process they are influenced by the information viewed and the Information Retrieval Systems (IRS) that they utilise. The purpose of this research is to investigate the influences that Information Retrieval Systems such as Search Engines, the Internet and Academic Databases have on Industrial Designers' searching strategies. The study involves the observation of designers transforming early design language into query 'keyword' language for the operation of IRS's and how this transition causes a design direction shift.

1 Introduction

The Information Age has provided Industrial designers with invaluable Information Retrieval Systems (IRS). These systems manage and retrieve information that can aid designers to make informative design decisions. However, as there are various IRS's that vary in their information quality designers need to be aware of advanced searching strategies to insure successful search results.

2 The Design Process

Industrial design is a process of innovation within products or systems for the improvement of usage by people. Design projects require knowledge of manufacturing, technology, social trends and users and every project varies and requires knowledge in different fields. As designers face multiple and varying design problems in every new project, they must have access to a vast amount of information in order to inform them in making just decisions when creating products or systems that they may know little about. Many methods are available in order to gather information for designers for example user observations. However the majority of information sourced is from tools such as repositories known as Information Retrieval Systems.

The design process has identified phases that structure the overall progression and development from when the design problem is introduced to the designer through to

M. Masoodian et al. (Eds.): APCHI 2004, LNCS 3101, pp. 646–650, 2004.
© Springer-Verlag Berlin Heidelberg 2004

the final design solution. The activity that the individual designer experiences throughout the design progression has been identified through many theories however there is two main paradigms that have influenced design activity. Simon [1] has highlighted design as a process of *rational problem solving* and Schon [2] a *reflection-in-action*. Both design methodologies consider the design processes and designers thinking, and together, they combine to provide a comprehension of the design practice. They offer an insight into how designers work either through rational decisions or reflective conversations.

Communication is crucial for designers to exchange, present or question concepts and decisions. Communication requires a language which in the case of industrial designers, need not be restricted to verbal dialect. *Design language* consists of sketching, writing, story-telling, brainstorming, description through body movement and through discussion. These methods of communication begin at an abstract level where designers are expanding their thinking to move beyond the here and now. Searching through this information space and gathering other forms of data enables designers *searching strategies* to remain broad and unhindered.

3 Searching Strategies

Searching strategies or information management behaviours are the activities that occur when designers are searching through knowledge. According to Baya and Leifer [3] these behaviours can be classified under the headings of 'Generate, Access and Analyse'. 'Information generated from an unidentified source such as writing, drawing/sketching or talking can alter the information space; this action is known as the *Generate* action. Within or outside the information space, information can be gathered through reading, listening and observing which constitutes the action of *Access*. The representation or form of information can change through the action *Analyse* where the information value has altered.' (ibid) The use of Information Retrieval Systems require all three activities as they require generation of keywords for query searches (Generate), reading of information results (Access), and sifting and recording data (Analyse). As the designer jumps from one activity to another the designers thought process is being refined to specific information in order to gain relevant results. The results of the research study later discussed demonstrate this activity.

4 Language

Language enables Industrial Designers to communicate with each other and also with the tools utilised within the design process such as Information Retrieval Systems. Although, when crossing over domains, the communicator or inquisitor is required to translate the language into terms understood by the receiver in which this case the receiver is a computational device.

4.1 Early Design Language

Throughout the early stages of the design process Industrial designers are encouraged to maintain an abstract mindset when understanding the design problem so as to expand the possibilities when searching and generating initial ideas. For example, there are more possibilities for a designer to generate concepts from a design description such as a 'non-motorised transport device' than a specific design description such as 'Scooter'. The former is an example of early design language in which designers adopt to expand their thought processes beyond the existing solutions to the current problem. The latter is defined as an existing design that has four small wheels, a platform to stand on and a collapsible control stick that aids in balance and moveability when in use.

If a designer, in the midst of conceptualising new innovative ideas, focuses on existing designs or products, how will he or she move beyond into the unknown? Therefore, industrial designers are required to break out of the general though process of identifying existing solutions for a design problem and go further by thinking primitively about what is the fundamental aspects of the designs purpose. To achieve this objective, one must simplify descriptives and adopt an abstract language.

4.2 Information Retrieval Systems Language

Designers first must define the design problem through initially categorising the problem into several areas of interest based on their exploration through their brainstorming and sketching. When they bring this knowledge to IRS's they must then translate their design language into specific keywords. This is due to the operational programming which requires queries to be specific titles and keywords (such as 'bicycle rack') instead of concepts (like 'storage unit for human powered transport devices'). Entering into the search engines query line a concept sentence such as this will certainly retrieve information dealing with bicycle racks yet little information on other topics (for example rollerblade storage systems) will be recovered. This research suggests that this is because the field may be saturated with one main topic and the other topics are lost within the haystack of results. Godby and Reighart [4] suggest that all users of IRS's are affected by this process as their study shows that the search terminology differs to that of the terminology found in published articles. This demonstrates that operators of IRS's translate their language accordingly to suit particular domains.

Although IRS's classify data under categories in order to store and retrieve information when required, designers have to classify their early design language into specific keywords and sentences in order to successfully retrieve relevant information. This activity will be referred to as the CLASS activity, the process of Converting Language from Abstract to Specific Searching.

5 Research Study

Several experiments were set up to test the CLASS activity by observing (expert and student) Industrial Designers Searching Strategies whilst utilising IRS's.

5.1 Methodology

Through a Co-Discovery method, the designers were asked to explore a given design brief dealing with public storage areas for non-motorised transport devices. The studies attempted to simulate an industrial design problem that encouraged the participants to explore advanced searching techniques to retrieve information dealing with alternative storage methods.

The question designed to guide this research is: how does classification systems impact on individual designers search strategies within the problem definition stage of the industrial design process?

5.2 Pilot Study Findings

Seven pilot studies were undertaken utilising video analysis to record and observe Industrial Designers utilising IRS's while progressing through the given design project. The results show that Industrial designers searching strategies are affected by the use of IRS's that operate on keywords or natural language queries. The keywords generated from searching through sketches, initial brainstorming and other methods is seen to be broader and contains more scope for further ideation, however after the designers begin to utilise IRS, the keywords entered into such systems are significantly different to those previously generated. The keywords transform into specific keywords which are required to operate the IRS's. This causes the designers thought process to focus on obvious solutions to the design process as the searching strategies are restricted to specific keywords.

To expand the experiment further to ensure that it was not only designers that were influenced by such systems, a Reference Librarian was asked to take part alongside an Industrial Design professional. Kumar [5] suggests that reference librarians are not experts in all fields (i.e. Industrial Design), however are experts in quality information retrieval.

The results showed that reference librarians with the knowledge of advanced operational skills for Information Retrieval Systems were also swayed in topic direction however did show more reflection on the searching progression and found more quality based information.

5.3 Further Study

Further studies are being undertaken with the combination and comparison of the searching strategies of an Industrial Design expert from industry with an Information Retrieval Systems librarian expert from an academic background. By doing so, this enables the isolation of operational problems that Industrial designers may have with IRS's and therefore the study can focus primarily on the searching strategies. This study will then be able to demonstrate whether the combination of industrial design knowledge with IRS knowledge aids in reducing the CLASS activity when compared to the studies with industrial designer participants only.

This research attempts to provide a better understanding of individual designers searching strategies within the early stages of the industrial design process. In addition to this, this study will demonstrate whether design language and searching strategies are altered under the influences of Information Retrieval Systems.

6 Conclusion

At present, the findings indicate that Industrial Designers searching strategies are influenced by Information Retrieval Systems and that existing information systems hinder the early stage of the design process. Recommendations include the further investigation into the designer/information retrieval system interaction to justify a move towards developing Information Retrieval System's founded on professional design jargon and terminology specific to the Industrial Design field.

This research supports the recommendations made by Winograd and Flores [6] who proposes the development of future systems which would 'allow us to interact as though we are in a conversation with another person who shares our background'. Systems that would query the user in return to enable a clarification on searching direction in comparison to learnt advanced searching techniques. Reflective systems would cater for the design activity of searching and retrieving quality based information and would be a beneficial aid to abstract thinking when conceptualising.

References

1. Simon, H. A.: The Sciences of the Artificial. Cambridge, MIT Press. (1998)
2. Schon, D. A.: The Reflective Practitioner. London, Arena, Ashgate Publishing Ltd. (1983)
3. Baya, V., Leifer, L.J.: Understanding Information Management in Conceptual Design. Research in Design Thinking II: Analysing Design Activity, West Sussex, England, John Wiley & Sons (1994)
4. Kumar, K.: Theory of Classification. Delhi, Vikas Publishing House (1979)
5. Godby, C. J., Reighart, R.: Terminology Identification in a Collection of Web Resources Journal of Internet Cataloging 4(1/2) (2001).
6. Winograd, T., Flores, F.: Understanding Computers and Cognition - A new foundation for design, USA, Addison-Wesley Publishing Company Inc. (1987).

Personal Digital Document Management

Sarah Henderson

Department of Information Systems and Operations Management, University of Auckland
Auckland, New Zealand
s.henderson@auckland.ac.nz

Abstract. Knowledge workers today have a lot of digital documents to manage, and most employ some sort of organizational system or scheme to help them. Most commonly used software provides the ability to create a hierarchical organization, but the appropriateness of this structure for personal digital document management has not been established. This research aims to understand how people currently organize their documents, identify the strengths and weaknesses of current systems and explore the usefulness of other information structures. This will provide insight into how personal digital document management systems can be made more usable.

1 Introduction

Personal digital document management is the process of acquiring, storing, managing, retrieving and using digital documents. It is personal in the sense that the documents are owned by the user and is under their direct control, not that they necessarily contain information about the user [6]. Information overload is making document management increasingly difficult. Farhoomand and Drury found that the two most common definitions of information overload were "an excessive volume of information" (reported by 79% of respondents) and "difficulty or impossibility of managing it" (reported by 62%) [4].

One large part of managing documents involves organizing them so that they can later be easily retrieved. Most current software provides a facility to organize documents in a hierarchical set of folders. This organization scheme was adopted over 40 years ago to provide efficient access to files on disk. Although hierarchies are a very powerful and natural organizing scheme, there is no clear reason why these systems must use hierarchies, nor is there evidence that they are necessarily the best option for document management.

Understanding how the current hierarchical model supports users in organizing documents, and more crucially, where it doesn't, is important to being able to develop more usable systems that better support personal document management.

M. Masoodian et al. (Eds.): APCHI 2004, LNCS 3101, pp. 651-655, 2004.
© Springer-Verlag Berlin Heidelberg 2004

2 Previous Research

Previous work has included studies of how people manage and use paper documents [8, 12], email [3, 9, 13] and files [1]. Findings included identifying two main types of structuring approaches: 'neat' and 'messy' [7, 8], as well as the use of information for reminding people of tasks or events. The two studies of files revealed that many people did not create any kind of digital organizational structure at all [1], and that people used their knowledge of the locations of files to retrieve them again in preference to searching for files.

Technology has changed significantly since some of these findings were published. For example, in the two studies of files that were published in 1995, some of the participants were limited to file and folder names of 8 characters in length (plus a 3 character extension), and many did not have access to a hard drive to store information. Also, the command line interfaces used by some participants did not allow visualization or direct manipulation of information structures. The features offered by current document management software are significantly different from software 8 years ago; hence user interaction with this software is likely to have changed. How current software supports personal document management still needs to be investigated.

Other researchers have created experimental prototypes to explore alternative systems of organizing personal information such as documents. These include primarily logical/topical [2], temporal [5] and spatial metaphors [10, 11]. Many of these researchers appear to operate from the premise that the current predominantly hierarchical system of organization is inadequate for document management, and propose a (sometimes radically) different alternative organizational scheme. Unfortunately, there is not enough information about how people currently use the hierarchical model, and where and how it is inadequate. Additionally, little attention has been given to the fact that current systems do provide some (albeit limited) ability to organize spatially (on the desktop and within folders), temporally (sorting by date last modified/accessed) and logically/topically (through folder and file names). How people actually use these features is not currently known.

3 Research Aims

The aim of this research is to understand how to build more usable software for personal digital document management. The specific objectives of this research are:

- Identify where current document management software is adequate and where it is inadequate.
- Understand how people organize their personal digital documents with current software, particularly how spatial, temporal and logical/topical facilities are used.

4 Methodology

This research uses a number of different methodological techniques in order to provide rich data about the phenomenon of document management. These include semi-structured interviews, observation, and automated data gathering using a software tool that takes a snapshot of the file system. The participants are staff at the University of Auckland Business School, which uses the Microsoft Windows operating system. Twenty participants in total will be included in the study, ten academic and ten administrative staff.

Interviews. The semi-structured interviews ask the participants basic demographic information and then the participants are asked to give a tour of their file systems and email. File System Snapshot software is run during the interviews. These interviews will be fully transcribed and analyzed. This will be used to understand how people structure their file systems, and how these structures have evolved over time. These techniques should provide a thorough understanding of the subjective aspects and rationale for people's current organizations.

File System Snapshot. This software collects information about the folder structures and file names in the file system, and the folder structures used in the email system. It also stores the structure of Internet Bookmarks, My Favorites and captures a screenshot of the Desktop. Software to analyze this data is being written as part of this research. The information gathered will provide an objective empirical description of how people currently organize information, which can be compared and contrasted with the subjective description gained from the interviews.

Document Use Monitoring. Software will be installed on the participants' computers that will track their document management activities over an extended period of time (1-5 days). This will record all document open and close events, document creation, deletion, renaming, copying and moving. The information gathered will provide objective data about how people use their documents over time. It is anticipated that this monitoring will occur with 4 or 5 participants only.

5 Pilot Study Results

A pilot study has been conducted with 4 administrative participants, involving an interview and file system snapshot. The interview data has been transcribed and coded (with the assistance of QSR NVivo qualitative analysis software).

The most troublesome problem reported by the participants was managing different versions of documents (reported as a significant problem by three participants) Two reported trouble identifying where the most recent version of a document is (whether in the email system or the file system, and in which folder). Three had systems in place for tracking multiple versions of documents using conventions based on file name, folder name or folder location.

The data collected by the file system snapshot software has been analyzed to reveal basic statistics about the file structures used by each participant, as shown in Table 1. Only folders nominated by the participant as document directories were included in this analysis (for instance, the Windows and Program Files directories were always excluded).

Table 1. File System Snapshot summary data. This shows some basic statistics about the file systems of the pilot participants

Metric	A	B	C	D
Years Experience	3	3	3	10
Files	4,395	44,196	3,793	1,545
Folders	426	7200	854	211
Files per Folder	10.3	6.2	4.5	7.3
Maximum Depth	6	16	11	8
Average Depth	2.6	5.9	6.2	3.8
Duplication (same name)	6.3%	80.1%	14.1%	14.5%

What these statistics show is firstly, the variation in the size of the collections managed by these participants, and also some very different patterns of use. For example, participant A has a relatively high number of files per folder and a shallow hierarchy, indicating a classic 'non-filer' who tends not to spend much time on organizing files, and relies more on search to locate them. In contrast Participant C has a low number of files per folder and tends towards deeper hierarchies, indicating a 'frequent filer' who stays organized and uses the hierarchy to locate documents.

The duplication figure counts the proportion of files that have the exact same name as another file. This is likely to understate the true duplication figure, as a copy of a file with a different version number would not be counted as a duplicate. The relative magnitudes of the duplication figures correlate well with the severity of the version management problem as reported by the participants.

6 Discussion

Much of the version management problem centers on the difference between files and documents. The participants are attempting to manage documents, using an interface that supports the management of files. As far as the user is concerned, a document is a structured set of information, to which changes and events occur over time. A user might talk about a status report that went through five drafts, was edited once by the boss and sent to a client. However this is actually represented as six separate files in the file system plus two in the email system, with no relationship between any of them (except perhaps a similar file name, but that is up to the user). An interface that recognizes and manages documents (rather than files) could help overcome the version management problems reported by these participants.

7   Future Work

Additional interviews and file system snapshots are planned with both academic and non-academic participants. In addition, some participants will have their document use over time monitored. More comprehensive analysis of the file system snapshot data will also be carried out, including age profiles of files.

References

1.   D. K. Barreau and B. A. Nardi: Finding and Reminding: File Organization from the Desktop. SIGCHI Bulletin, 27 (3). (1995) 39-43.
2.   P. Dourish, W. K. Edwards, A. LaMarca and M. Salisbury: Presto: An Experimental Architecture for Fluid Interactive Document Spaces. ACM Transactions on Computer-Human Interaction, 6 (2). (1999) 133-161.
3.   N. Ducheneaut and V. Bellotti: E-mail as Habitat: An Exploration of Embedded Personal Information Management. Interactions, 8 (5). (2001) 30-38.
4.   A. F. Farhoomand and D. H. Drury: Managerial Information Overload. Communications of the ACM, 45 (10). (2002) 127-131.
5.   E. Freeman and D. Gelernter: Lifestreams: A Storage Model for Personal Data. SIGMOD Bulletin, 25 (1). (1996) 80-86.
6.   M. Lansdale: The psychology of personal information management. Applied Ergonomics, 19 (1). (1988) 55-66.
7.   W. E. Mackay: More than just a communication system: diversity in the use of electronic mail. In CSCW'88 Conference on Computer-Supported Cooperative Work, Portland, Oregon, USA. (1988) 344-353.
8.   T. W. Malone: How do people organize their desks? Implications for the design of office information systems. ACM Transactions on Office Information Systems, 1 (1). (1983) 99-112.
9.   J. McKay and P. Marshall: The dual imperatives of action research. Information Technology and People, 14 (1). (2001) 46-59.
10.   J. Rekimoto: Time Machine Computing: A time-centric approach for the information environment. In UIST'99 Symposium on User Interface Software and Technology, Asheville, North Carolina, USA. (1999) 45-54.
11.   G. G. Robertson, M. Czerwinski, K. Larson, D. C. Robbins, D. Thiel and M. van Dantzich: Data Mountain: Using Spatial Memory for Document Management. In UIST'98 Symposium on User Interface Software and Technology, San Francisco, California, USA. (1998) 153-162.
12.   S. Whittaker and J. Hirschberg: The Character, Value, and Management of Personal Paper Archives. ACM Transactions on Computer-Human Interaction, 8 (2). (2001) 150-170.
13.   S. Whittaker and C. Sidner: Email Overload: exploring personal information management of email. In CHI'96 Conference on Human Factors in Computing Systems, Vancouver, Canada. (1996) 276-283.

A Study of the Impact of Collaborative Tools on the Effectiveness of Clinical Pathology Conferences

Bridget Kane[1], Saturnino Luz[2]

[1] Histopathology Department, Central Pathology Laboratory
St James's Hospital, Dublin 8, Ireland,
kaneb@tcd.ie
[2] Computer Science Department, Trinity College Dublin 2, Ireland,
luzs@cs.tcd.ie

Abstract. Multidisciplinary conferences in hospitals are becoming an everyday part of health service delivery and being recommended as a mechanism for ensuring quality patient care and management. This paper reports preliminary findings of an ethnographic study of Clinical Pathology Conferences with Respiratory teams. Educational, patient management and organizational objectives of the conference are identified. The findings so far suggest that collaborative technologies have the potential to improve the effectiveness of clinical conference activity. Time, location and missing artefacts are identified as being issues as well as the coordination of the series of events associated with patient investigative and assessment procedures. The implications of recording data and interactions at the conference are also being investigated.

1 Background

A Clinical Pathology Conference (CPC) is a meeting between the pathologists and clinicians to discuss the pathology in patients of interest. The CPC originated in the teaching institutions as an educational forum. Developments in medicine such as sub-specialisation, the volume and pressure of work and the development of clinical practice guidelines have resulted in the CPC fulfilling a much wider role. Today the CPC has important organizational and patient management objectives, as well as maintaining its educational function.

Different forms of the CPC will be found in various institutions, and even within the same institution. For this study, the CPC with the respiratory teams, also called the Respiratory Conference (RC), was chosen because it has been part of the standard practice of the respiratory teams at St James's hospital since the 1970s. As well as representing a meeting with a well established practice it has demonstrated its role as a patient management, research and audit tool [1] [2].

M. Masoodian et al. (Eds.): APCHI 2004, LNCS 3101, pp. 656-660, 2004.
© Springer-Verlag Berlin Heidelberg 2004

1.1 Patient Investigation and Management

The investigation of disease in a patient involves a number of independent and separate procedures, performed by different specialists. For respiratory disease, the patient undergoes pulmonary function testing, radiological imaging and bronchoscopy procedure where the lung is visualised and samples taken for histopathology, cytology and microbiology.

When all the tests are completed on each patient the results are presented and discussed at the Respiratory Conference (RC). The diagnosis is agreed and the best course of treatment / management of the patient identified. Throughout the investigative / assessment process the patient is under the care of a designated Consultant Respiratory Physician / Surgeon. This Consultant has ultimate responsibility for the management of the patient in his/her care.

2 Study Method

The idea for this study came from involvement in the RC, between 1983 and 1995 as medical scientist attendee, presenting the results of patient cytology investigations. While the researcher knew a small number of the RC participants in 2002/2003, most were new attendees and developments were evident.

An ethnographic approach was adopted involving participant observation, discussions with respiratory conference participants and the study of artefacts. Observations during the respiratory conference, work undertaken by participants and their collaborative practices were considered. The approach aimed to be reasonable, courteous and unthreatening. At the outset efforts were made to ensure the confidence, support and trust of participants. This involved talking to participants in a one-to-one setting and explaining my history and involvement with the conference in the past.

Research on CSCW and common information spaces (CIS) was reviewed [3,4].

A questionnaire was used to provide an indication of participant's attitudes and use of technology.

3 Findings

Medical diagnosis is an intellectually complex task and the product of complex social processes involving individuals who vary in status and expertise [5] [6]. Complex group processes are involved as well as individual activity. The investigative tasks, conducted independently of one another, are discussed at the respiratory conference and a decision made on the most appropriate course of action for the patient. Policy on the investigation and management of disease may also be discussed and policy developed as a result of discussions at the conference. The RC is the end task of a series of work processes necessitated in lung cancer diagnosis and assessment.

The items of information that are essential to this process are: -
- The case history
- The working clinical diagnosis

- The radiology results
- The laboratory results
- Results of various other diagnostic procedures that may be relevant e.g. ECG, EEG, pulmonary function etc.

Most of these items of information have to be laboriously gathered by hand making a CPC a very time consuming process for a considerable number of people. In addition it is not uncommon for some of the items to have been mislaid, lost or erroneously filed rendering the decision making process inadequate.

All histopathology findings and selected cytology results are displayed on a monitor, using a camera attachment to a microscope. Radiological images are displayed on a light box or overhead projector. (The overhead projector allows magnification of images.) The information used is largely available in digital form (e.g. radiology, results of diagnostic procedures, histopathology /cytology images etc.) with certain notable exceptions such as the clinical data. Most of the items of information are stored electronically on stand-alone programmes.

Currently the interactions among the individuals involved, namely patient, doctor and paramedical staff, and the group processes are generally unsupported by technology. There is no formal record of the discussion or the data items used at the CPC meeting.

The role of computers at present is confined to the systems in use within the different sections of the hospital: the patient administrative system, the laboratory information system, and radiology system. (The hospital does not yet have a PACS system.) Pulmonary function tests are recorded electronically and held within the instrument. Videos are sometimes taken at bronchoscopy and held on tape/ DVD by members of the respiratory team. Sometimes a Polaroid photograph may be taken at bronchoscopy, or at the out-patient clinic.

It is a period of rapid developments in the field of health service delivery and management. The respiratory teams at St James's provide a professional consultative service to outlying hospitals. Specialist centres and multidisciplinary teams are being promoted as the way forward in the development of quality service to patients [7]. Planned development in the health services relies heavily on strong commitment to teamwork and effective working of multidisciplinary teams [8].

Clinical Practice Guidelines (CPGs) are being continually developed and refined. For lung cancer diagnosis and management, like other areas of medicine, there is rapid proliferation of new medical knowledge [9] [10]. There is also enormous pressure on healthcare workers to deliver the highest quality service with limited resources.

State-of-the art management of lung cancer requires input from, and participation by, a number of specialties. Optimal care is therefore dependant on a coordinated series of events from identification of the patient with possible lung disease, to diagnosis, to evaluation of potential treatment options, to actual management, and finally to palliative care (if necessitated). Currently, this coordination is achieved in the multi-disciplinary forum of the RC. Joint conferences and virtual networks have been identified to provide possible solutions to the issues in multi-disciplinary care, and as 'laudable goals worth pursuing' [11]. It is recognized that development of multi-disciplinary and interfunctional cooperation will require organizational structures that emphasise lateral interservice planning and service delivery [12].

The RC developed from a teaching and educational role. It now serves important hospital and patient management objectives and can be regarded as an organizational quality assurance mechanism [13]. The RC is a lateral process in the hospital that coordinates the multidisciplinary tasks and the hierarchical investigative processes.

4 Challenges and On-Going Research

While most experts agree that collaborative systems supported by ubiquitous technologies could play an important role in supporting medical decision-making processes, little research has been done on concrete forms of support and their potential impact on service delivery. This project is investigating the use of collaborative technologies to support Clinical Pathology Conferences in the domain of lung cancer patient diagnosis and management. The project is also exploring aspects that are likely to benefit from the enhanced facilities for recording data and interactions taking place at CPCs. These include the teaching and educational roles of the meeting, as well as its hospital and patient management objectives as an organizational quality assurance mechanism.

The health care system is way behind in the implementation of IT systems compared with modern industry [14]. The study is investigating the organizational and sociological causes if this observation. Part of the problem is believed to be that traditional computer systems have not supported the mobile, multidisciplinary and team working found in hospitals [15] [16]. The collaborative technologies have been generally overlooked in the healthcare domain, yet they have the potential to be usefully applied in clinical settings. With the emergence of ubiquitous computing systems, mobile applications and maturing in the area of CSCW this situation is likely to change.

The on-going maintenance of confidence and trust with participants will be challenging. Participants are enthusiastic at present but some may have already anticipated the outcome of the research and may be disappointed if they find that others do not share their view. Already issues of role redefinition for the RC have been raised. One participant expressed frustration that sometimes cases that are not of great academic interest have to be discussed. Time is a major issue and the time taken in preparation for conference and spent at conferences is felt by many to be too much and not 'part of their main work'.

Some reservations have been expressed about the potential for increasing patient litigation against medical professionals. For example, if a patient felt their case was not properly dealt with / given enough time. However, so far this fear has been counterbalanced by the belief that formalising the conference and documenting its role and objectives will offer protection against potential patient litigation or offer support to participants who might find themselves under investigation for malpractice.

References

1. McLoughlin, P., F. Mulcahy, D.S. O Briain, B. Kane, E. Mulvihill, and J.S. Prichard, Lung Pathology in HIV Positive patients. Irish Medical Journal, 1990. 83(3): p. 109 - 111.
2. MacLeod, D., B. Kane, D. Kidney, J. Murphy, D.S. O Briain, F. Jackson, B. Mulvihill, F. Mulcahy, L. Clancy, and J.S. Prichard, A Clinicopathological study of 79 bronchoscopies in HIV positive patients. Irish Medical Journal, 1993. 86(5): p. 167 - 169.
3. Bossen, C. The Parameters of Common Information Spaces: the heterogeneity of Cooperative Work at a Hospital Ward. in CSCW '02. 2002. New Orleans, Louisiana, USA: ACM.
4. Preece, J., Y. Rogers, and H. Sharp, Interaction Design beyond human-computer interaction. First ed. 2002, New York: John Wiley &Sons.
5. Cicourel, A.V., The integration of distributed knowledge in collaborative medical diagnosis, in Intellectual Teamwork: Social and Technological Foundations of Cooperative Work, J. Galegher, R.E. Kraut, and C. Egido, Editors. 1990, Lawrence Erlbaum Associates, Publishers: Hillsdale, New Jersey.
6. Ginsberg, R.J., Lung Cancer. First ed. American Cancer Society. Vol. 1. 2002, Hamilton London: BC Decker Inc.
7. Hanly, D., Report of the National Task Force on Medical Staffing. 2003, Department of Health and Children: Dublin.
8. Leathard, A., ed. Interprofessional Collaboration: from policy to practice in Health and Social Care. First ed. 2003, Brunner-Routledge: Hove and New York.
9. Coiera, E., Guide to Health Informatics. Second ed. 2003, London: Arnold.
10. Alshawi, S., F. Missi, and T. Eldabi, Healthcare information management: the integration of patients' data. Logistics Information Management, 2003. 16(3/4): p. 286 - 295.
11. Alberts, W.M., G. Bepler, T. Hazelton, J.C. Ruckdeschel, and J.H. Williams, Practice Organization. Chest, 2003. 123(1 Supplement): p. 332S - 337S.
12. Coghlan, D. and E. McAuliffe, Changing Healthcare Organizations. First ed. 2003, Dublin: Blackhall Publishing.
13. Hatch, M.J., Organization Theory: Modern, Symbolic and Postmodern Perspectives. First ed. 1997, New York: Oxford University Press.
14. Garsten, C. and H. Wulff, Eds. New Technologies at Work. First ed. 2003, Berg: Oxford, New York.
15. Heathfield, H., D. Pitty, and R. Hanka, Evaluating information technology in health care: barriers and challenges. British Medical Journal, 1998. 316: p. 1959 - 1961.
16. van der Meijden, M.J., H.J. Tange, J. Troost, and A. Hasman, Determinants of Success of Inpatient Clinical Information Systems: A Literature Review. Journal of the American Medical Informatics Association, 2003. 10(3): p. 235 - 243.

Physical Computing – Representations of Human Movement in Human-Computer Interaction

Astrid Twenebowa Larssen

Faculty of Information Technology, University of Technology, Sydney,
PO Box 123, Broadway NSW 2007, AUSTRALIA
atalarss@it.uts.edu.au

Abstract. Interactions between humans and computers are becoming increasingly physical. Technology is embedded in the environment around us and is now hosted by the human body. This research explores characteristics of human-computer interaction when the human body and its movements become input for interaction and interface control.

1 Context of Research

Interaction between humans and computers depends on humans communicating intentions to the computer, using input devices, in such a way that the computer can interpret them. This is coupled with the use of output devices to provide relevant information from the computer in a form that is perceivable by humans. The interaction is structured by various protocols [12]. This research investigates the characteristics of human-computer interaction when the human body and its movements are themselves the input for interaction.

The input-output interaction loop between humans and technology is a sequence, all stages of which need to be at least partially successful to enable the interaction. These stages are:

1. People communicate their intentions to technology;
2. The computer receives, interprets, and acts on this information (the intentions);
3. The computer represents its relevant workings and results to an output device; and
4. People perceive these representations, and act accordingly.

The use of the human body and its movements for input for interaction and interface control presents challenges to all stages. For example:

1. Research to extend input options has focused on extending the capabilities of the current devices by developing new devices and related techniques for the manipulation of objects [4, 11], including multimodal input [10], and the use of physiological data [1].

2. *Computer vision, motion capture and recognition*, and *image processing* are all fields that explore approaches and techniques for the computer to receive and interpret human intentions.

3. Currently, feedback on movement is mainly limited to changing visual cues [5, 6], or tactile feedback, which incorporates the sense of touch in the interaction [14].

M. Masoodian et al. (Eds.): APCHI 2004, LNCS 3101, pp. 661–665, 2004.

Auditory feedback is mainly used as an extension of visual feedback, and is less frequently used on its own.

4. Different understandings of human action, including cognition have demonstrated that human perception is structured both by human physical and cognitive abilities [13, 15, 16, 17, 18].

The input-output interaction loop describes the actions of humans and the actions of the computer. The interaction between the two is only captured in the synthesis of the two working together.

For an understanding of the place of the body in the world and subsequently to technology, we look to Merleau-Ponty's phenomenology [8]. His account of the *"lived experience of the embodied subject, as the basis of both our experiences in our world and our agency in our actions within it..."* [13], can inform technology design through its analysis of the body's role in perception. According to Merleau-Ponty, perception is active, embodied, and always generative of meaning.

Mine et al. proposed a design framework based on *proprioception* [9]. They describe three forms of "body-relative" interaction techniques:

- Direct manipulation - ways to use body sense to help control manipulation;
- Physical mnemonics - ways to store/recall information relative to the body; and
- Gestural actions - ways to use body-relative actions to issue commands.

In the implementation of this framework Mine et al. developed and tested interaction techniques such as "head butt zoom" and "over-the-shoulder deletion". Ängeslevä et al. proposed a similar interface design concept, "Body Mnemonics", which explores embodied interfaces by using a combination of the physical space and the body of the user as an interface [2].

Mine's and Ängeslevä's design frameworks for immersive virtual environments and portable devices, respectively, are relevant for this research as they consider the body a key part of the interaction, *"...most existing theories in human-computer interaction (HCI) treat the body as a machine executing commands of a disembodied logical mind."* [16]. However, the body creeps up on HCI in several ways:

- The make up (shape, size etc.) of the physical body determines what kinds of physical interactions are possible [16];
- The physical skills of a person determine what interactions actually will take place [16];
- The body gives meaning to the interactions. The premise of experiencing a virtual reality rests on our having had the experience of a physical body [17]; and
- The structure of the body and bodily experiences form the background and colour the meaning given to the experiences [16].

2 Research Design

Using these theoretical foundations, the focus of my research is to investigate characteristics of human-computer interaction when movements of the human body become the input device for interaction and interface control. The outcomes sought are to develop:

- an understanding of the techniques currently used;
- an evaluation of the effectiveness of these techniques;

- new interface and interaction design principles which can extend existing user-centred design guidelines; and
- new evaluation methods that can extend existing user-centred design methods.

It is envisaged that a *kinaesthetic* understanding of the movements of the human body will lead to more appropriate frameworks for interaction design. The extension of *input options* to include the human body as host technology [18], and for the human body and its movements to become input for interaction and interface control, needs an *understanding of how best to represent and characterise the human movements that the computer has to register*. Further developments of *output devices* rely on our understanding of how people *perceive* representations of their movements.

The research will be undertaken in three distinct parts; each step will be used to refine the research questions, and to determine the appropriate setting for further studies. The first phase aims to identify the techniques used by current systems to represent and characterise movement of the human body. It is an observational study of computer games that use the human body and its movements as input. Computer games were chosen for the study, as they are easily accessible, existing systems. The second phase is an in-depth study to evaluate the findings and issues from phase one for generalisability and extendability to human/computer interactions other than games. This could involve the development of a prototype and evaluation of this prototype in a laboratory or in a real use situation and/or further investigation of findings from the first phase. The third phase is dependent on the two preceding phases; more concrete statements will be made about this phase by the time of the doctoral consortium. However, it is envisaged that this study will test the design principles that have been developed, by either a build and/or evaluation of phase two.

3 Progress to Date

The first study was carried out to gain an understanding of the techniques used by current technology to represent movement of the human body, as well as to explore ways of documenting and analysing the bodily actions taking place. Video, demographics and interview data were gathered from eight people playing immersive computer games. The methods used were adapted from participant observation and game usability evaluation.

Four female and four male participants were recruited from staff and students at the University of Technology, Sydney. The participants were invited to play two games using the SONY Playstation2® with the Eyetoy™. The two games, *Beat Freak* and *Kung Foo*, were selected by the researchers, because they required a range of user movements while being fairly easy to learn.

Beat Freak requires the player to move their hands over a speaker in one of the four corners of the screen at the same time as a CD flies across the speaker. The CDs fly out from the centre of the screen and reach the centre of the speaker in time with the music. In Kung Foo the player needs to intersect with little Wonton henchmen to prevent them from reaching the middle of the screen. The Wonton henchmen appear randomly from both vertical edges of the screen. Extra points are gained by breaking wooden boards, and slapping Wonton himself.

After a warm-up session of light moves and stretches, the participants were introduced to the game via its *Help* feature. Each then played both games twice on the "easy" level and once on the "medium" level. The participants were filmed from two angles. One view captured the participants' projection on the screen; the other view captured the participants' full body whilst playing. Data on demographics and previous experience with the games was collected prior to playing. The participants were interviewed about their experience with the game, and asked usability related questions in a post briefing sessions.

Interaction with the Eyetoy™ games, Beat Freak and Kung Foo, produced a range of movements, primarily movements of the torso and arms. An examination of both games including menu selection identified the following movements: reach, punch, slap/swat, wave, slash, and flick.

The movements were performed either as a:

- *Command* in the selection of game choices and settings;
- *Reflex response* by hitting either a:
- stationary object;
- moving object by coinciding with target location; or
- moving object as soon as the object appears.

These movements were analysed using *Labanotation*, a notation used to describe bodily action developed by dance/movement theoretician Rudolf Laban [7]. When transcribed, it became evident that each game has its own set of basic movements that will enable game play. Laban's *Effort-Shape* dimensions of *space, time, weight* and *flow*, described in terms of *light – firm* (space); *direct – flexible* (time); *slow – fast* (weight); *bound – free* (flow), revealed that each participant played with individual styles and characteristics. The Effort-Shape dimensions provided detailed qualitative description of these individual/distinctive movements. It remains to be discovered whether any of these styles are more effective for game play. The Eyetoy™ interface is tolerant of movements with different characteristics, provided that the movement takes place within range of the sensor.

Further analysis will include developing a taxonomy of movements and actions for the Eyetoy™ interface, an analysis according to the *sensible, sensable, desirable framework* [3], and investigation of how the body reciprocates the different game events, such as navigating, choosing, waiting, and playing. The results of these analyses will be presented at the Doctoral Consortium.

The next phase of this research will evaluate the findings from the first study for generalisability and extendability to human/computer interactions other than games.

References

1. Allanson, J., 2002, 'Electrophysiologically Interactive Computer Systems', *IEEE Computer Magazine*, pp. 60-65.
2. Ängeslevä, J., O'Modhrain, S. & Hughes, S., 2003, 'Body Mnemonics', in *Physical Interaction Workshop at Mobile HCI 03*, Udine, Italy. [Online. Available: http://www.medien.informatik.uni-muenchen.de/en/events/pi03/papers/angesleva.pdf, Accessed: 16. Dec., 2003].

3. Benford, S., Schnadelbach, H., Koleva, B., Gaver, B., Schmidt, A., Boucher, A., Steed, A., Anastasi, R., Greenhalgh, C., Rodden T., and Gellersen, H., 2003, *Sensible, sensable and desirable: a framework for designing physical interfaces*, [Online. Available: http://machen.mrl.nott.ac.uk/PublicationStore/2003-benford.pdf, Accessed: 5. Nov, 2003].

4. Bowman, D., Hodges, L., 1999, "Formalizing the Design, Evaluation, and Application of Interaction Techniques for Immersive Virtual Environments", *Journal of Visual Languages and Computing*, vol. 10, no. 1, pp. 37-53.

5. Couvillion, W., Lopez, R., Ling, J., 2002, "Navigation by Walking Around: Using the Pressure Mat to Move in Virtual Worlds" in *Medicine Meets Virtual Reality 02/10*, eds. Westwood, J.d., Hoffman, H.M., Robb, R.A., Stredney, D., pp. 103 – 109, IOS Press, Amsterdam.

6. Harris, L. R., Jenkin, M.R., Zikovitz, D., Redlick, F., Jaekl, P.,Jasiobedzka, U.T., Jenkin, H.L., Allison, R.S., 2002, "Simulating Self-Motion I: Cues for Perception of Motion", *Virtual Reality*, vol. 6, pp. 75-85.

7. Hutchinson, A., 1970, Labanotation or Kinetography Laban: The System of Analyzing and Recording Movement, 3rd revised and expanded edn, Theatre Arts Books, New York.

8. Merleau-Ponty, M., 1962, *Phenomenology of Perception*, trans. C. Smith, Routledge, London.

9. Mine, M. R., Brooks Jr., F. P. & Sequin, C., 1997, 'Moving Objects in Space: Exploiting Proprioception in Virtual-Environment Interaction', in *Proceedings of the 24th annual Conference on Computer Graphics and Interactive Techniques*, ACM Press/Addison-Wesley, pp. 19-26.

10. Oviatt, S., Coulston, R., Tomko, S., Xiao, B., Lunsford, R., Wesson, M. & Carmichael, L., 2003, 'Attention and Integration: Toward a Theory of Organized Multimodal Integration Patterns During Human-Computer Interaction', in *Proceedings of the 5th international conference on Multimodal interfaces*, Vancouver, British Columbia, Canada, pp. 44-51.

11. Poupyrev, I., Weghorst, S., Billinghurst, M., Ichikawa, T., 1997, "A framework and testbed for studying manipulation techniques for immersive VR". *Proceedings of VRST 1997*, pp. 21-28.

12. Preece, J., Rogers Y., Sharp H., Benyon D., Holland S., & Carey T., 1994, *Human-Computer Interaction*, Addison-Wesley, Harlow, England.

13. Robertson, T., 2002, 'The Public Availability of Actions and Artefacts', *Computer Supported Cooperative Work*, vol. 11, pp. 299-316.

14. Stanney, K. M. ed., 2002, *Handbook of Virtual Environments: Design, Implementation, and Applications*, Lawrence Erlbaum Associates, Mahwah.

15. Suchman, L., 1987, *Plans and Situated Action: The Problem of Human-Machine Communication*, Cambridge University Press, Cambridge.

16. Svanæs, D., 2000, *Understanding Interactivity: Steps to a Phenomenology of Human-Computer Interaction*, (thesis), Norwegian University of Science and Technology, Trondheim.

17. Vasseleu, C. J, 1998, *Textures of Light: Vision and Touch in Irgaray, Levinas and Merleu-Ponty*, Routledge, London.

18. Viseu, A., 2003, 'Simulation and Augmentation: Issues of Wearable Computers', *Ethics and Information Technology*, vol. 5, pp. 17-26.

Creative Interface Design for Information Seeking

Shu-Shing Lee

Division of Information Studies
School of Communication and Information
Nanyang Technological University
Singapore 637718
{ps7918592b}@ntu.edu.sg

Abstract. Inspired by Weisberg's argument that everyone is creative, and exists in varying degrees, this PhD proposal aims to investigate the relationship between creativity and information seeking, and explores implications for interface design with design features that might support users' information seeking behaviours. A holistic model of creativity was proposed synthesizing established models in creativity. Based on the model, five approaches investigating relationships between creativity and information seeking were highlighted. Initial work carried out attempted to understand users' information seeking behaviours to elicit supportive features. Discussion of on-going work is also presented to indicate approaches proposed to design, implement, and evaluate a prototype with design features to support information seeking.

1 Background and Motivation

Traditional approaches to solving precision and recall problems seem inadequate in addressing users' needs and intentions as they assume that users are competent information seekers and can specify their needs in queries, and that words used to describe documents are similar between indexers and users [5]. Hence, this PhD research proposes a novel way to address limitations in traditional information retrieval (IR) systems by incorporating design features in an IR interface to support users' information seeking behaviours.

This investigation is inspired by Weisberg's argument that creativity exists in everyone and is a result of ordinary thinking [14], and *creativity varies in people and may have a relationship with information seeking*. It can, hence, be logically inferred that every information seeker is creative, and the extent of a person's creativity influences his/her information seeking behaviour. Creativity can be defined from many perspectives. For example, creativity may be "natural" based on one's creative traits or creativity may be "nurtured" which is due to domain knowledge and information seeking skills. Here, we are concerned with "nurtured" creativity.

The proposed model differs from traditional information seeking models [e.g., 7] as it focuses on how design features in an IR environment, for example, providing collaboration features and contacts of experts [e.g. 12], may support information seeking. These features aim to support users' information seeking behaviours,

M. Masoodian et al. (Eds.): APCHI 2004, LNCS 3101, pp. 666–671, 2004.
© Springer-Verlag Berlin Heidelberg 2004

therefore, possibly addressing users' needs and increasing quality of search results in terms of relevance and user satisfaction.

It is hoped that this model may perhaps improve ways of developing systems and their interfaces with design features for supporting users' information seeking behaviours.

2   Objectives, Deliverables, and Methodology

Objectives, deliverables, and methodology to develop an IR interface with design features to support information seeking are described as follows:

- **Objective 1** surveys limitations in traditional IR systems as well as definitions and models of creativity and information seeking.

  Deliverables: A critique of limitations of IR systems as well as definitions and models of creativity and information seeking are presented.

  Methodology: An extensive literature review is conducted to survey and understand limitations of IR systems, definitions, and models of creativity and information seeking.

- **Objective 2** examines approaches to investigate relationships between creativity and information seeking and conducts pilot studies to understand these relationships.

  Deliverables: Different perspectives/approaches of investigating relationships between creativity and information seeking are presented.

  Methodology: By surveying established creativity and information seeking models, a mapping process is conducted to examine the different approaches to investigate relationships between creativity and information seeking. The mapping process involves analyzing and comparing similarities and differences between surveyed creativity and information seeking models.

- **Objective 3** designs and implements a prototype with design features to support users' information seeking behaviours.

  Deliverables: Propose a prototype with design features to support users' information seeking behaviours.

  Methodology: Investigate design features that support users' information seeking behaviours through techniques such as literature reviews, focus groups, and empirical studies.

  Develop a prototype with design features that supports users' information seeking behaviours.

- **Objective 4** evaluates and refines the prototype.

  Deliverables: Propose users' feedback and refine prototype to ensure it supports users' information seeking behaviours.

  Methodology: Evaluate prototype based on users' satisfaction and relevance of search results to task.

3   Contributions to Research

This research aims to contribute to the fields of IR, information seeking, and human-computer interaction (HCI). The survey of definitions and models of creativity provides scholars with new avenues of investigation on how creativity might help address limitations of traditional IR systems. Proposed approaches on investigating relationships between creativity and information seeking may benefit scholars by providing insights on different approaches of developing systems and interfaces for supporting users' information seeking behaviours.

4   Work Done So Far

4.1 Limitations of IR Systems and Models of Creativity and Information Seeking

To address Objective 1 and provide background for this work, limitations of traditional IR systems were reviewed. Traditional IR systems judge precision and recall based on a match between index and query terms. This mode of operation is the 'best-match' principle [2]. However, this method is limited as it does not consider the contextual nature of human judgment [5], it assumes users can specify their needs in a query, and that words used between indexers and users are similar [2].

To provide foundations for understanding creativity and information seeking, 3 models of creativity and 3 models of information seeking were reviewed [10]. The models of creativity reviewed are the systems' view of creativity, componential model of a creative process and the interactionist model of creative behavior. The models of information seeking reviewed are Wilson's model of information seeking behaviour, Kuhlthau's model of information search process, and Ells' behavioural model of information seeking.

The survey of limitations of IR systems provided insights on what features are currently lacking in IR interfaces and should be proposed to support users' information seeking behaviours. The review of models of creativity and information seeking provided a better understanding of creativity and information seeking so that features to support creativity and information may be conceptually derived.

4.2 Approaches for Investigating Creativity and Information Seeking

Holistic Model of Creativity
To address Objective 2, we propose a holistic model of creativity [10] by synthesizing established models of creativity [e.g., [1]] as definitions of creativity differ. This model defines creativity from the following four perspectives and forms the definition of creativity for this work:

- The creative process. The creative process consists of four stages:
    i)   *Preparation.* The individual collects all necessary data to solve the problem.
    ii) *Incubation.* The individual unconsciously works on the problem.
    iii) *Illumination.* Possible ideas start to surface to consciousness.
    iv) *Verification.* The idea is worked into a communicable form.

- <u>The creative person.</u> He/she should have imagination, independence, and divergent thinking.
- <u>The creative product.</u> The product should be novel and valuable.
- <u>The creative environment.</u> The environment should support collaboration as idea generation occurs out of relationships with others.

Five Approaches for Investigating Creativity and Information Seeking

The four perspectives indicated in the holistic model of creativity inspire the five approaches of investigating creativity and information seeking. The approaches are:

- <u>"Process" approach.</u> To accomplish an information seeking task, the creative person goes through various stages in information seeking. To investigate this perspective, it may be necessary to map established creativity models [e.g., [1]] to information seeking models [e.g., [7]]. This enhances understanding of information seeking by including concepts from creativity.
- <u>"Person" approach.</u> The extent of a person's creativity may affect his/her information seeking behaviour. Hence, it may be interesting to investigate if creativity is a product of "nature" or "nurture" and how his/her creativity may affect his/her information seeking behaviour.
- <u>"Environment" approach.</u> Features in an IR system may support/hinder a person's creativity and information seeking behaviour. This perspective may be investigated by mapping design features to interface design to support users' information seeking behaviour.
- <u>"Product" approach.</u> The way the environment supports information seeking may affect the creativity of the product (i.e., quality of search results). To investigate this perspective, it may be interesting to compare the quality of search results obtained from IR systems with and without supportive features.
- <u>"Task" approach.</u> To provide context for understanding users' creativity and information seeking behavior, the task approach was included. Based on the task, the way a person exhibits his/her creativity and information seeking skills may vary. One way to investigate this perspective is to find out how different tasks affect the ways he/she exhibits creativity and information seeking.

4.3 Using Pilot Studies to Elicit Conceptual Design Features

To address Objective 3, a mapping of established "creativity" models to "information seeking" models was conducted to provide understanding of information seeking with concepts from creativity [10]. Using this understanding, design features to support information seeking were brainstormed with 2 information specialists [8]. Initial proposed features were evaluated with 6 IR systems to examine if these systems provided proposed features to support information seeking.

A pilot study was conducted to understand subjects' information seeking behaviours while using Google to complete a task. Subjects' interaction with Google and information seeking behaviours were analyzed using Claims Analysis [4] and Interaction Framework [6] to elicit design features for information seeking.

Findings suggested that Google provides design features that could support information seeking. However, it does not provide an integrated environment. Hence, more can be done to possibly strengthen Google's support by incorporating other design features highlighted in our pilot study [9].

5   On-Going Work

The second and third year of the PhD will concentrate mostly on the "environment" approach. This approach was selected as related works in creativity usually address users' creative traits and provide an environment for the creative process to take place. These environments either support the creative process in a general manner [e.g. [3]] or provide support for the creative process in an "artistic" domain, such as product design and image manipulation [e.g. [13]]. Moreover, modern user interfaces do not explicitly support users' creative process that requires experimentation, exploration of variations, and continual evaluation of one's progress. Instead, a linear progression through tasks is imposed, providing a poor fit for creative pursuits [13]. Our work differs from these works and attempts to address the nature of creative pursuits by developing an IR interface with design features that closely supports users' information seeking behaviour which may be iterative and context dependent.

In the next phase of the PhD, we will concentrate on Objective 3 involving design requirements. To make ideas concrete in that interface with proposed design features may better support users' information seeking, we are exploring a variety of ways to capture design requirements for implementation of a prototype as proof of concept:

1. More detailed examination of established creativity and information seeking models to conceptually propose design features with information specialists. This is continued work done in the first year [8].
2. Examine existing literature on "creative" design features. Shneiderman [12] proposes eight ways to improve software to support human creative processes. Selker [11] proposes general guidelines and issues to consider in interface design to improve users' creativity. These works provide insights on design features and guidelines to consider when designing interfaces to support creativity. Some of these guidelines and features may be useful to support users' information seeking behaviour and may be used in our work.
3. Observe users interacting with an IR system to understand their information seeking behaviours to elicit supportive design features. This will be an extension of the initial pilot study with more subjects involved [9]. Interviews may also be conducted to understand their needs and requirements.
4. Elicit design features by examining existing IR systems to see what features are lacking and may be included in our work.

Finally, Objective 4 involves carrying out usability evaluations on the prototype

Acknowledgements

I would like to thank my supervisors, Dr. Yin-Leng Theng and Dr. Dion Hoe-Lian Goh, and Professor Schubert Foo for their valuable feedback and comments.

References

1. Amabile, T. M. (1990). Within you, without you: The social psychology of creativity, and beyond. In M. A. Runco & R. S. Albert (Eds.) *Theories of creativity* (pp. 61-91). California, U.S.A: Sage Publications.
2. Belkin, N.J., Oddy, R. N. and Brooks, H., ASK for Information Retrieval: Part I. Background and Theory. *Journal of Documentation*, 1982. **38**(2): p.61-71.
3. Burleson, W., Developing a Framework for HCI Influences on Creativity, *Proc. HCII 2003, Vol. 2, Theory and Practice (Part II)*, C. Stephanidis, J. Jacko (Eds.), pp.1168-1172.
4. Carroll, J. (2000). *Making Use: Scenario-Based Design of Human-Computer Interactions*. The MIT Press.
5. Case, D. O. (2002). *Looking for Information: A Survey of Research on Information Seeking, Needs, and Behaviour*. California, USA: Elsevier Science.
6. Dix, A., Finlay, J., Abowd, G, and Beale, R. (1998). *Human-Computer Interaction*. London, England: Prentice Hall.
7. Ellis, D., Cox, D. and Hall, K. A Comparison of Information Seeking Patterns of Researchers in the Physical and Social Sciences. *Journal of Documentation*, 1993. **49**(4), p. 356-369.
8. Lee, S. S., Theng, Y. L. & Goh, D. H. L. (2003). Creative Information Seeking and Information Retrieval Environments. *Proc. ICADL 2003*, p. 398-410.
9. Lee, S. S., Theng, Y. L. & Goh, D. H. L. (2004). Creative Information Seeking and Interface Design. *Proc. APCHI 2004*, Paper accepted.
10. Lee, S. S., Theng, Y. L. & Goh, D. H. L. (2003). *Creative Information Seeking Part I: A conceptual framework*. Manuscript accepted for publication.
11. Selker, T., Fostering Motivation and Creativity for Computer Users, *Proc. HCII 2003, Vol. 2, Theory and Practice (Part II)*, C. Stephanidis, J. Jacko (Eds.), p.1303-1306.
12. Shneiderman, B. (2002). Creativity Support Tools: A Tutorial Overview. *Creativity and Cognition 2002*, p. 1- 2.
13. Terry, M. and Mynatt, E. (2002). Recognising Creative Needs in User Interface Design. *Creativity and Cognition 2002*, p. 38 - 44.
14. Weisberg, R. W. (1993). *Creativity Beyond the Myth of Genius*. New York: W.H. Freeman and Company.

Understanding Interaction Experience in Mobile Learning

Fariza Hanis Abdul Razak

Computing Department
Lancaster University, Lancaster, LA1 4YR United Kingdom
abdulraz@comp.lancs.ac.uk

Abstract. The convergence of mobile technology and e-learning has generated considerable excitement among both practitioners and academics. Mass media continually promotes novel idea about m-learning. Content developers also continue to deliver learning on wireless, mobile learning devices based on their often abstract conceptions of what the 'generalised' learners might want to learn. We are now seeing the adoption of e-learning into m-learning without a clear understanding of motivations and circumstances surrounding m-learning and m-learners. This research looks into interaction experience that is believed to play a significant role in the development of usable m-learning.

Keywords. M-learning, e-learning, interaction experience, HCI, mobile environment

1 Mobile Learning Context

The workforce has become much more mobile than before: about 50% of all employees now spend up to 50% of their time outside the office. In fact, many full time learners (like those in schools and higher learning education) are also very mobile. There is evidence that people would like to make more use of this "empty time" for learning purposes. M-learning (mobile learning) is designed to fit with the unique work style requirements of the mobile workforce. Mobile workers need to continually enhance their knowledge and skills in order to address immediate problems. This new type of learning is to empower people to manage their own learning in a variety of contexts throughout their lifetimes [1].

M-learning doesn't replace traditional learning; it just represents another way of learning using a new technology. In fact, the fundamentals of learning still don't change with m-learning:

1. Learning more effective when active. A course built around actively "doing" will be better than passively reading from the screen.
2. Individual learning styles. Some learners prefer reading, others might prefer observing, doing, or being coached, and the preferred method of learning can change depending on the context.

M. Masoodian et al. (Eds.): APCHI 2004, LNCS 3101, pp. 672-674, 2004.

3. Learner controls learning. Content should be presented in such way that the learner understands and controls the information flow. The Instructor, whether human or computer, is a learning facilitator.

2 Research Problem

Although m-learning is a natural evolution of e-learning, to effectively build and deliver m-learning requires rethinking, reinvestigating, and re-evaluating the human-computer interaction in the m-learning environment. Existing e-learning frameworks may not work very well with m-learning: the interaction experience in m-learning is different from other types of learning. Learning with mobile devices constitutes a new learning-interaction experience: a lot is still unknown about the m-learning experience. Although some research in m-learning has discussed some aspects of mobile experiences [2], the discussion did not really focus on the understanding of what constitutes interaction experiences in the mobile environment. It is believed that interaction experience can be an important, mediating towards the successs of m-learning.

3 My Research

My research is aimed at understanding interaction experience in m-learning by examining a broad range of aspects of m-learners, their environments, and relationships. I hope that this research will serve as a base for development of an m-learning experience framework. This research is broken into two main areas: understanding of interaction experience in the mobile environment and the development of m-learning content.

3.1 Understanding of Interaction Experience in the Mobile Environment

To understand the interaction experience in the mobile environment, I am investigating three important components:

1. Understanding of the mobile learners – including their characteristics, psychological (affective and cognitive), and physical capability.
2. Understanding of the m-learning environment – the motivations and circumstances surrounding mobile device use and adoption; and how and why people adopt m-learning.
3. Understanding of the mobile experience – completely different from desktop experience as it has specific characteristics that need to be factored into the design of a mobile application.

3.2 Development of M-learning Content

When developing m-learning content, it is important to balance effective learning and adoption of mobile and web technology, which has advantages and limitations.

Learning Object Methodology will be applied in this development, because it allows a designer to create learning content in chunks. The chunks allow flexibility in terms of how they can be used together and separately [3]. Other key development issues include:

1. User interface – including task flow, predictability and consistency, and ease of use.
2. Battery life – balance between applications and battery consumption.
3. Modality – different devices support multiple kinds of modalities, each behaving differently.
4. Interruption – how well the application handles interruption and resumes interaction later.

4 Conclusion

Understanding interaction experience is not an entirely new area in HCI, but there is no agreed framework that can actually guide designers and developers towards the development of usable m-learning systems.

There is considerable work to be accomplished on many fronts – HCI, mobile technology, learning communities, and content development – before the potential of m-learning comes to fruition. Although this research may not provide a perfect solution to the current problem, it can at least offer some promise especially to the HCI and learning communities.

References

1. Bentley, T.: Learning Beyond the Classroom. Education For A Changing World. (1998) 177–193
2. Trevor, J., Hilbert, D. M., Schilit, B. N., Tzu, K. K.: From Desktop to Phonetop: An UI For Web Interaction on Very Small Devices. In ACM UIST (2001)
3. IEEE Learning Object Metadata (2002). See http://ltsc.ieee.org/wg12/

User Experience in Interactive Computer Game Development

Tracey Sellar

User Experience Lab
School of Computer and Information Sciences
Auckland University of Technology
New Zealand
tracey.sellar@aut.ac.nz

Abstract. This paper outlines PhD research into user experience in interactive computer game development. The study will investigate how usability methods and approaches can be adapted and extended to evaluate and improve the user experience of gaming systems. The research will focus on exploring ways to evaluate fun and engaging user experiences, and on identifying how to provide useful, valid, timely, cost-efficient feedback on user experience to game development teams. A range of research methods is proposed including case studies with industry stakeholders, contextual and lab-based user experience evaluations with gamers, and action research within a games company. Research findings will inform the development of a practical evaluation model and tools to support game experience design practices and product development.

Keywords. Interactive computer game development, usability methods, user experience.

1 Introduction

Interactive computer game development is a rapidly growing worldwide industry. According to the Entertainment Software Association, revenue from computer and video game software more than doubled in the U.S. from 3.2 billion dollars in 1995 to 6.9 billion dollars in 2002 [1], with over 225 million games being sold in 2001 [2]. Interactive game industry growth is set to continue as advances in technology contribute to rich, immersive entertainment experiences, uptake of online gaming increases, hardware prices decrease, and the audience for games broadens. However, within this optimistic environment, we are currently seeing discord within the games industry. Games developers are going out of business, development schedules are lengthening, budgets are expanding to cater to new technologies and changing user expectations, and publishers are consolidating and taking fewer risks on projects, leading to a reliance on licensed game concepts and sequels, and mid-development cancellation of projects. In response to uncertainty in the industry, developers are now focusing on fundamental issues: how do we expand the market to reach a wider

M. Masoodian et al. (Eds.): APCHI 2004, LNCS 3101, pp. 675-681, 2004.
© Springer-Verlag Berlin Heidelberg 2004

games audience? How do we know what works for gamers? How do we make successful games?

Game playing is a voluntary activity; a game needs to capture interest early and motivate a user to keep playing over extended periods of time. Effective human computer interface design is crucial for engaging users in the immersive experience of computer games. However, usability researchers report that user-centred design principles have not reached the same level of usage or awareness in game design and development as they have in other electronic applications, such as productivity application software [3]. This raises the question of why user-centred design is not integrated into an industry that is focused on designing fun experiences and entertaining audiences? At a time when game companies are searching for a better understanding of their audiences' needs there are ways that user experience methods and approaches can add value to game development.

Clanton [4] divides the Human Computer Interaction (HCI) of a computer game into three levels, the *game interface* (the control peripherals and user interface), the *game mechanics* (the game physics), and the *gameplay* (discovering and achieving goals in the game). Games share similar usability considerations to other software applications in the user interface and interaction mechanisms. Game menu screens and selection options are more satisfying for users when they are easy to use and interact with. The importance of usable game interface design was highlighted in a report by Lazzaro [5] which stated that players have abandoned games altogether because of interface difficulties. Likewise, game interaction mechanisms, which range from hand held controllers and steering wheels, to mobile phone input mechanisms and motion sensitive controllers, need to be easy to learn, intuitive, comfortable, and perform effectively if their use is going to reflect positively on the overall gaming experience. Pagulayan et al [3] similarly concluded as a result of game usability testing that, "the ease of use of a game's controls and interface is closely related to fun ratings for that game".

There are however, unique challenges in gameplay design and evaluation, which suggest a need to explore new approaches to usability. The ISO 9241-11 definition of usability includes three independent measures including effectiveness, efficiency and satisfaction [6]. In the case of video game usability, effectiveness and efficiency, although key measures for user interface and interaction, are not necessarily prominent criteria for gameplay evaluation (See [7] for discussion). User satisfaction is, on the other hand, critical to the success of interactive games. In order to capture user interest, a game needs to engage and involve users from the outset of play. In order to sustain user interest, games need to provide reward and challenge. Consumer loyalty can be quickly eroded by poor user interface or unintuitive gameplay [8]. By seeking to understand the user experience during gameplay, usability methods can be adapted or extended to gather quality data and improve overall game design.

There has been a change in the conceptualisation of usability within the research community in recent years. This changing approach to usability is reflected in Thomas and Macredies' [9] concept of the *new usability*. The *new usability* conceives of usability as being about "consumer experience" rather than "ease of use". Traditionally, usability has been concerned with "making systems easy to learn and easy to use" [10]. As mentioned, these conventional usability characteristics may no longer be adequate when evaluating the overall user experience of gaming systems. Interactive games are often finely tuned in their design so as to be challenging or frustrating during gameplay. The design complexity and expectation of users creates a game that requires dedication and perseverance to master over a period of time, rather than being easy to use. At the same time, it is crucial to find ways to evaluate user experience as, "input from users becomes necessary to distinguish good challenges from incomprehensible design" [3].

Research is currently being undertaken into measuring intangible aspects of user experience such as "fun", "enjoyment", or whether a product is desirable enough to purchase [11]. A "Funology" workshop at CHI 2002 raised the question: "how can HCI address value, engagement, aesthetics and emotion...what methods can we develop or adapt to gather data?" [12]. A recent book, *Funology: From Usability to Enjoyment* collated research from leading HCI figures to address whether traditional usability approaches are too limited and need to be extended to encompass enjoyment, engagement, empowerment and emotion [13]. Nielsen's assessment of what is required is simply, "we need much better methods for testing enjoyable aspects of user interfaces", as cited in [13].

Clanton [4] states that the game design community is devoted to iterative design and testing to optimise for fun. Although this is the case in most game studios, conventional game testing methods such as beta testing and quality assurance (QA) play testing do not necessarily provide the best possible target user feedback with which to make informed design decisions. Beta testing typically occurs towards the end of development and can provide feedback that is too late and insufficiently granular enough to take action on [14]. Play testing within a QA team provides valuable information, however, the focus is generally on software functionality, bugs and crashes, and as it relies on feedback from experienced gamers it does not truly represent the consumer experience.

New technological developments in gaming are leading to an increased need to understand and evaluate the consumer experience of games and gaming products e.g. online console and PC gaming, emergent gameplay, wireless handheld gaming, and Sony EyeToy™. Games researchers are responding to this need with studies on the appeal of games peripherals [15] and positive affect in games [16]. Recent games research into affect and emotion has investigated ways to evaluate physiological responses during gameplay to determine positive emotional experiences [17]. One of the next steps proposed by games researchers is to explore ways to elicit deeper and more varied emotion in players [18]. The research directions for game development and HCI converge on this topic. Identifying ways to design and evaluate optimal user experiences will enable both game developers *and* software developers to create products that engage and empower their end users.

2   Aims of the Research

The proposed research seeks to investigate the following question: How can usability methods and approaches be adapted and extended to evaluate and improve the user experience of gaming systems? The study will focus on exploring ways to evaluate fun and engaging user experiences, and on identifying how to provide useful, valid, timely, cost-efficient feedback on user experience to game development teams.

There are three central areas of investigation, which include:
• Building an understanding of user experience in games
• Developing insight into games industry dynamics and development processes
• Formulating usability methods and approaches for evaluating user experience in game development

The findings from this research will lead to the development of a practical model to evaluate user experience, which will be implemented in a game development environment(s) and refined through iteration.

2.1   Building an Understanding of User Experience in Games

At the 2002 Games Forum held in Wellington, New Zealand, industry representatives spoke of the need to find out what makes a user continue playing a game and what motivates them to come back to the game. Preliminary investigations will explore these user motivations in the context of the broader gaming experience.

The social dynamics, needs, perceptions, and use contexts of users strongly influence the gaming experience. For example, game playing is no longer a purely individual entertainment experience. Online gaming communities connect remote users in multi-player gameplay and provide strong feedback loops through forums. User communities are vocal and proactive about usability in gaming and collaborate to develop software modifications to customise and improve games. Game designers and developers also take part in user forums to identify feature requirements and introduce new design ideas. In understanding the broad picture of user gaming environments, we can begin to formulate usability approaches with which to effectively evaluate user experience.

2.2   Developing Insight into Games Industry Dynamics and Processes

An understanding of the structure, constraints, perceptions and drivers of the games industry is required in order to inform the use of user experience approaches and methods that will add value to game development.

Primary stakeholders in the games industry include publishers, console manufacturers, and independent developers. The industry demands placed on independent game studios are vast. To sign a publishing deal, developers must bring their game concept to demo status before a publisher will consider it, requiring a budget of $500,000-$1 million [19]. Developers may be involved in creating content for more than ten different game genres, with each genre requiring a different variety of skills. In addition, game development schedules are lengthy, ranging from one to five years, which can result in prohibitive production costs for independent game studios. The realities of the development process mean that sections of a game are completed at different times and in a different order than consumers will actually experience them [3]. This impacts on how, when, and what types of evaluations can be scheduled in order to deliver quality, timely, and useful feedback to development teams.

2.3   Formulating Usability Methods and Approaches for Use in Game Development

Usability methods and approaches need to work effectively for developers within actual industry environments. Preliminary discussions with the games industry have revealed a wide variance in game development processes, and have highlighted the strong budgetary constraints faced by small development studios. User experience methods therefore need to be flexible and cost-efficient if they are to be accepted and effectively integrated into under resourced production schedules. It is anticipated that such methods, if they are adaptable and can be used in a variety of development environments and with different game formats, will provide significant value for game developers, improve user experience, and add value to the end product.

3   Research Approach

A range of research methods will be applied to increase rigour and validity of the study. These will include interviews, observations, usability evaluations, focus groups and questionnaires. The choice of method(s) will depend on the availability of primary and secondary research data and will be directly influenced by the level and type of industry involvement with the research. As the New Zealand games industry is small, a high level of buy-in to the research will be pivotal to the effectiveness and success of this approach.

A case study or studies of gaming companies will be undertaken to provide an understanding of design and evaluation processes within game development settings. An examination of existing industry practices and dynamics will inform ways that user experience methods can be applied and adapted to complement and support the development process. Key stakeholders in the game production process will be interviewed and where possible work practices will be observed, to ensure the research reflects industry needs and valued outcomes are produced. Interviewees will include game producers, designers and developers, to discuss production strategies, process, and user experience design; quality assurance (QA) leads and testers, to build an understanding of the cross over between usability, user experience and QA; and third party service providers who conduct game focus group testing. Additional interviews will be conducted, where feasible, with game publishers and console manufacturers.

Contextual and lab-based studies will be carried out to provide research data on game user experience. Contextual studies of game players will enable user behaviour to be observed in context of use. Users will also be invited to participate in usability evaluations where human computer interaction and user experience of interactive games will be explored. A games evaluation facility has been set up at the User Experience Lab at Auckland University of Technology in order to conduct evaluations with game players. Usability facilitation techniques will be used to elicit user feedback, including think-aloud protocol, observation, and in situ interviewing. Audio-visual game data will be captured either on video or digitally, and techniques for evaluating data will be investigated, such as Omodei et als' cued-recall debrief method [20]. Usability methods for evaluating mobile and wireless game devices will also be examined. An exploratory approach will be applied to methods of collecting user feedback in order to investigate ways of adapting and extending usability techniques to meet the specific needs and challenges of game evaluation. Initial data collection will address audio, visual, and interactive game elements [21]. User data will be supplemented by expert reviews of games conducted by user experience practitioners, which will provide an opportunity to examine Federoff's [7] work in this area.

The findings from industry research and user experience studies will inform the development of a practical model to assess user experience, and the creation of a set of evaluation tools. The model and tools will be tested and iterated within industry environments by evaluating game prototypes and concepts during development. This approach may involve action research as applied research within one of the case study companies. In collaboration with company stakeholders, usability methods and approaches would be introduced into a game development environment and investigated in a series of iterative cycles. The use of an action research methodology would be dependent on finding a game company that is interested in the research and prepared to be involved with the study.

4   Conclusions

PhD progress to date has centred on building an understanding of the New Zealand and international games industry, developing industry and research contacts, and gaining an awareness of the role of usability and user experience practices and processes within interactive computer game development. Challenges have been encountered with industry interactions. In particular, many organisations understandably protect and treat their development processes as intellectual property, which limits access to information. An approach I am investigating with regard to this is the use of Non Disclosure Agreements. Resource constraints in small game studios can also deter companies from involvement in research collaboration. One way I am addressing this situation is by communicating my early findings to industry to demonstrate the benefits of the research. Already developers are showing interest in the study; small studios are eager to gain competitive advantage in a highly competitive industry, and ultimately, all developers want to create successful games.

References

1.   Entertainment Software Association. (2003). Historical Sales Figures. Retrieved February 11, 2003, from http://www.idsa.com/pressroom.html. Now available from http://www.theesa.com/ffbox7.html

2.   Interactive Digital Software Association. (2002, May). *Essential Facts About the Computer and Video Game Industry.* Retrieved February 11, 2003. Now available from http://www.theesa.com/IDSABooklet.pdf

3.   Pagulayan, R. J., Keeker, K., Wixon, D., Romero, R. L., & Fuller, T. (2002). User-centred design in games. In J. Jacko and A. Sears (Eds.), *Handbook for Human-Computer Interaction in Interactive Systems.* Mahwah, NJ: Lawrence Erlbaum Associates, Inc.

4.   Clanton, C. (1998). An Interpreted Demonstration of Computer Game Design, *Proceedings of ACM CHI 98 Conference on Human Factors in Computing Systems: Summary,* 18-23 April, pp.1-2.

5.   Lazzaro, N. (2004). Why We Play Games: Four Keys to More Emotion in Player Experiences, *Proceedings of the Game Developers Conference 2004,* 22-26 March.

6.   ISO 9241-11. Ergonomic requirements for office work with visual display terminals (VDTs) – Part 11: Guidance on usability. (1998). *International Organization for Standardization.*

7.   Federoff, M. (2002). *Heuristics and Usability Guidelines for the Creation and Evaluation of Fun in Video Games,* Unpublished Masters Dissertation, Department of Telecommunications, Indiana University.

8.   Lowe, C. (Undated). Key barriers to fully engaging majority-market gamers. Retrieved February 23, 2003, from http://www.gamesbiz.net/keynotes.asp

9.   Thomas, P., & Macredie, R. D. (2002). Introduction to The New Usability, *ACM Transactions on Computer-Human Interaction,* Vol. 9, No. 2, June, pp. 69-73.

10.   Preece, J., Rogers, Y., Sharp, H., Benyon, D., Holland, S., & Carey, T. (1994). *Human-Computer Interaction,* Addison-Wesley, p. 14.

11.   Benedek, J., & Miner, T. (2002). Measuring Desirability: New methods for evaluating desirability in a usability lab setting, *Usability Professionals' Association 2002 Conference Proceedings.*

12.   Monk, A. F., Hassenzahl, M., Blythe, M., & Reed, D. (2002). Funology: Designing Enjoyment, *SIGCHI Bulletin,* September/October, p. 11.

13.   Blythe, M., Overbeeke, K., Monk, A., & Wright, P. (Eds.). (2003). *Funology: From Usability to Enjoyment,* Kluwer Academic Publishers, The Netherlands.

14.   Fulton, B. (2002). Beyond Psychological Theory: Getting Data that Improve Games, *Proceedings of the Game Developers Conference 2002,* 21-23 March.

15.   Johnson, D., Gardner, J., Wiles, J., Sweetser, P., & Hollingsworth, K. (2002). The Inherent Appeal of Physically Controlled Peripherals. *International Workshop on Entertainment Computing, 2002.*

16.   Johnson, D., & Wiles, J. (2001). Effective Affective User Interface Design in Games, *Conference for Affective Human Factors Design, 2001.*

17.   Bentley, T., Johnston, L., & von Baggo, K. (2003). Affect: Physiological Responses During Computer Use, *OZCHI 2003 Conference Proceedings.*

18.   Sykes, J. (2004, January). Affective Gaming. Retrieved January 27, 2004, from http://www.igda.org/columns/ivorytower

19.   O'Leary, C. (2002). *Game On: NZ. Growing the Interactive Games Industry in New Zealand,* Industry New Zealand, p. 20. Retrieved October 14, 2003, from http://www.nzte.govt.nz/common/files/gameon-oct2002.pdf

20.   Omodei, M. M., Wearing, A. J., & McLennan, J. (1998). Head-mounted video recording: A methodology for studying naturalistic decision making. In R. Fline., M. Strub., E. Salas., & L. Martin (Eds.), *Decision Making Under Stress: Emerging themes and applications,* Aldershot, pp.137-146.

21.   Rollings, A., & Adams, E. (2003). *Andrew Rollings and Ernest Adams on Game Design.* New Riders Publishing.

Using Patterns to Guide User Interface Development

Elizabeth G. Todd

Institute of Information Sciences & Technology
Massey University
Palmerston North, New Zealand
e.todd@massey.ac.nz

Abstract. User Interface patterns have the potential to guide the development of conceptual user interface models. A pattern management tool, which would enable development and maintenance of collections of patterns and their use by user interface developers, is proposed. Preliminary results have identified six questions that can be used for describing the internal validity of a user interface pattern language.

Keywords: user interface, use case, pattern languages, conceptual design

1 Introduction

The purpose of this research is to investigate the development of conceptual graphical user interface models guided by selecting appropriate patterns from a pattern language. A software engineer should be able to move from a use-case to browse a pattern collection and by exploring the links between the patterns identify user interface descriptions which along with user interface elements [10] can be developed into UI models that are independent of implementation details. It is envisaged that these UI models will use a method similar to Constantine's [2] canonical abstract prototypes. Users will be able to explore the look and feel of these prototypes to validate the design. It should then be possible to develop realistic prototypes using different implementations.

2 Context

It is axiomatic that users of a specific software product will judge the quality of the software by the interface therefore the UI must be validated by them. UI patterns have the potential to provide users and developers with a common 'language' leading to better communication when determining and validating user-interface requirements.

A UI pattern as defined by Borchers is "*a structured textual and graphical description of a proven solution to a recurring design problem*" [1, p8]. And, van Duyne, Landay and Hong say that "*Patterns communicate insights into design problems, capturing the essence of the problems and their solutions in a compact form.*

M. Masoodian et al. (Eds.): APCHI 2004, LNCS 3101, pp. 682-686, 2004.

They describe the problem in depth, the rationale for the solution, how to apply the solution, and some of the trade-offs in applying the solution" [4, p19]. These definitions complement each other; van Duyne *et al.* focus on pattern content and stress their use as an aid to communication while Borchers' identifies the structured presentation of the content which includes illustrative elements. Patterns provide the reader with a solution to a recurring problem.

The literature concerning UI patterns has mainly concentrated on the development and reporting of sets of UI related patterns [1, 4, 6, 12]. More recently, some authors have suggested methods on how to use patterns when developing an application [4, 6]. A pattern language is a collection of related patterns. The relationships between the patterns in a pattern language should be synergistic, in that the language should provide an understanding of the design domain that is greater than just the individual patterns. A pattern language is considered to be a layered hierarchy as can be seen by Borchers' definition *"A pattern language is a hierarchy of design patterns ordered by their scope. High-level patterns address large-scale design issues and reference lower level patterns to describe their solution."* [1, p8]

3 Research Method

The research method is to be based on Morrison, Morrison and Moore's [7] product driven research method. This method is about the researcher *"... creating unique or innovative products. Researchers first observe or predict an organisational problem or class of problems, and then build an innovative product to address them."* [7, p14] They suggest Nunamaker, Chen and Purdin's Model [8] as suitable, for guiding product-driven research. They suggest that the system is developed and then evaluated using *"research techniques such as laboratory and field experiments and case studies"* [8, p15]. An iterative approach is taken, so that system rework and/or enhancement is based on the results of evaluation. For this product-driven research method Morrison *et al.* identified two goals: to develop new technologies to help organise function more productively, and to advance theory on the use and impacts of these new technologies. [7, p15]

How would a proof be provided to show that the new technology meets these goals? Morrison *et al.* say that this is very difficult to do. For practitioners involved in this type of research, market acceptance is seen as a form of proof (*e.g.* take-up of email is used as an example). In a research environment alternative forms of proof may include one or more of:

o   Experiments using small numbers of senior students.
o   Academic argument based on current literature that justifies the development by identifying the "benefits, drawbacks, and their underlying needs"
o   Practical workshops to elicit expert feed back.
o   Trials of the tool in a workplace environment.

4 Research Question

One goal of this research project is the development of a Computer Aided Software Engineering (CASE) tool that uses a UI pattern language to guide development of UI models based on a UI method such as CONDUIT (**Con**ceptual **D**esign of **U**ser **Inter**faces). CONDUIT is an enhancement of the Unified Process that enables the developer to create high-level user interface descriptions from textual use-cases early in the software development life cycle [10]. The tool should provide facilities for managing the UI pattern language including aiding the development of a valid pattern language. The software engineer should be able to visualize and manipulate the language's content, then extract the relevant patterns to develop a sub-set of related patterns for guiding specific UI development. The tool may be usable for teaching UI practices to Software Engineering students.

The key question guiding this research is: *Can a useful tool be developed that uses Use Case definitions and User Interface patterns to guide a Software Engineer in the development of a useful conceptual model of a user interface?* From this question, four areas have been identified as needing further investigation:
1. structuring and navigating collections of patterns;
2. using patterns for guiding user interface modeling;
3. methods for developing conceptual models of user interfaces, and
4. CASE tools that use patterns as a guide for software development.

Investigation of the UI pattern language literature found that most publications have concentrated on the development and reporting of UI patterns and little has been written on how to use these patterns together when developing a system. Although there has been some effort in providing mechanisms for evaluating individual patterns there appears to be very little guidance on how to evaluate groups of related patterns variously termed pattern catalogues or pattern languages. Initial research has concentrated on answering the question: What makes a good user interface pattern language?

5 Preliminary Results

Initial research investigated using two UI pattern collections [4], [12] that include questions for guiding the selection of patterns to analyze existing interfaces. One outcome of this exercise was the realisation that the links guiding selections of further patterns were confused. Given that "*The fact that individual patterns are integrated into pattern languages ... enables the collection for patterns to operate generatively, each pattern showing the sub-patterns required to resolve more detailed design issues, in the context of the larger design*" [9, p5], this finding lead to the question: What attributes define a quality UI pattern language?

Three types of validation that require consideration when evaluating a pattern language were identified: the validity of the individual patterns, the external validation of a pattern language and the internal validation of a pattern language. The UI development community has provided procedures for evaluating individual patterns but there appears to be very little guidance on how to evaluate pattern catalogues or pattern languages. External validation is related to the human experience as users interact with the system and the user interface elements change in response to their activity [3]. Internal validation examines the connectivity between the levels in the language's hierarchy to determine the "ability to combine" to describe higher order patterns [11].

After identifying potential questions for testing the internal validity of a pattern language [13], a number of case studies were carried out to investigate whether these questions could be used to establish the internal validity of a number of existing UI pattern collections. This research resulted in the rewording of the six questions and the identification of criteria for describing the internal validity of a pattern language [14]. To guide the definition of the internal validity of a pattern language the questions have been further refined to take into account the pattern language mark-up language (PLML) which was defined at the patterns workshop CHI2003 [5].

1: *Do the contains and is-contained-by links between the patterns form a map?* This criterion can be presented as a participation rate; if all patterns are linked into the map then that is a one hundred percent participation rate.

2: *Does the contains map match the is-contained-by map?* An idealised map can be created from the language map where every contains-link and is-contained-by-link is assumed to be defined correctly in the related patterns section. The is-contained-by map links patterns that are used with others to instantiate the 'parent' pattern. The contained map defines the potential parent or context patterns. Two metrics defining the difference between the is-contained-by map and the idealised map and similarly between the contained map and the idealised map provide a measure of how well the two maps match.

3: *Can the map be ordered into a hierarchy of levels?* Once one or more roots have been identified then the number of levels below the root can be counted. A level is only counted if it includes more than one pattern.

4: *Can the levels be used to describe a user interface at different degrees of granularity (scale)?* Currently this criterion is defined-by-example, that is, by providing a hierarchy of descriptions based on the levels identified by question 3.

5: *How 'rich' are the links within each level of the hierarchy?* A relative scale for describing the richness of language maps has been developed. The categories identified are: None, Unknown, Minimal, Developed-in-one-level, Developing and Rich.

6: *Can the patterns be organised using different classifications of categories thereby providing alternative viewpoints?* - Trying to define a metric for this question has raised more questions: What is the difference between a linked subset or sub-language and an alternative view? How many patterns have to participate in a view? Do the patterns in a viewpoint have to be linked? Are the links the same as those for the language map?

6   Future Work

If successful, an outcome of this research will be a CASE tool that uses UI patterns to facilitate development of UI models. This CASE tool may be based on the user interface design method, CONDUIT as the synergistic properties of a "good" user interface pattern language will further enhance this method. Such a tool requires a pattern management component which has facilities for creating, editing and linking patterns into a pattern language structure. Additional work is required to identify the different kinds of links that occur between patterns and determine which ones should be used when defining the language map. Understanding how UI patterns can be categorised and the nature of the different types of link may lead to the definition of a suitable set of criteria for determining how to evaluate Test 6.

As a number of the on-line UI pattern collections have now been converted to PLML it is anticipated that the pattern management tool will be able to access these pattern collections. Further research into related technologies such as RDF and ontology languages such as OWL is required. The core of a UI pattern is the definition of the problem-solution pair [5]. If the pattern language that links problem-solution pairs forms a meta-language, and possibly the kernel of a user interface ontology, then these tools may enable different forms of reasoning about UI patterns.

References

1. Borchers, J. O.: A Pattern Approach to Interaction Design. Wiley, England (2001)
2. Constantine, L. L.: Canonical Abstract Prototypes for Abstract Visual and Interaction Design. DSV-IS'2003, LINCS. Springer-Verlag, Berlin (2003)
3. Cooper, A., Riemann, R.: About Face 2.0. Wiley, Indiana (2003)
4. van Duyne, D. K., J. A. Landay, et al.: The Design of Sites - Patterns principles and processes for crafting a customer-centered web experience. Addison-Wesley, Boston (2003)
5. Fincher, S.: Perspectives on HCI Patterns. Interfaces: 56. (2003)
6. Graham, I.: A Pattern Language for Web Usability. Addison-Wesley, Great Britain (2003)
7 Morrison, J., Morrison, M., Moore, S. Systems Development in MIS Research: Roles, Approaches and Strategies. Journal of Computer Information Systems Summer (1997)
8 Nunamaker, J. F., Chen, M. Purdin, T. Systems Development in Information Systems Research. Journal of Management (1990)
9. Pemberton, L. The Promise of Pattern Languages for Interaction Design. Human Factors Symposium, Loughborough, UK (2000) http://www.it.bton.ac.uk/staff /lp22/HF2000.html. Accessed Oct 2003
10. Phillips, C., Kemp, E.: CONDUIT: A Method for the Conceptual Design of User Interfaces within the Rational Unified Process. CHINZ. ACM, Dunedin, NZ (2003)
11. Salingaros, N.: The Structure of Pattern Languages. Architectural Research Quarterly (2000)
12. Tidwell, J.: Interaction Design Patterns. PLOP. Illinois (1998)
13. Todd, E., Kemp, E. & Phillips, C. Validating User Interface Pattern Languages. CHINZ. ACM, Dunedin, NZ (2003)
14. Todd, E., Kemp, E., Phillips, C.: What makes a good User Interface pattern language? In: Cockburn, A. (ed): Conferences in Research and Practice in Information Technology, Vol. 28 (AUIC). Australian Computer Society, Dunedin, NZ (2004)

Multimodal Cues for Object Manipulation in Augmented and Virtual Environments

Mihaela A. Zahariev

Human Motor Systems Laboratory, School of Kinesiology
Simon Fraser University, Burnaby, B.C., Canada, V5A 1S6
mzaharia@sfu.ca

Abstract. The purpose of this work is to investigate the role of multimodal, especially auditory displays on human manipulation in augmented environments. We use information from all our sensory modalities when interacting in natural environments. Despite differences among the senses, we use them in concert to perceive and interact with multimodally specified objects and events. Traditionally, human-computer interaction has focused on graphical displays, thus not taking advantage of the richness of human senses and skills developed though interaction with the physical world [1]. Virtual environments have the potential to integrate all sensory modalities, to present the user with multiple inputs and outputs, and to allow the user to directly acquire and manipulate augmented or virtual objects. With the increasing availability of haptic and auditory displays, it is important to understand the complex relationships amongst different sensory feedback modalities and how they affect performance when interacting with augmented and virtual objects. Background and motivation for this research, questions and hypotheses, and some preliminary results are presented. A plan for future experiments is proposed.

1 Background

Significant research has been done on the roles of visual and haptic information in the planning and execution of prehension in natural environments [2]. The visual system provides crucial information about object properties relevant for prehension, such as size, shape and orientation, and also about the movement of one's hand towards the object. The haptic system provides information about object properties such as weight and texture, confirms target acquisition, modulates grip force for stable grasp, and is also used to detect collisions of the held object with other objects. Visual information is normally present before and during prehension, while haptic information is only present after contact with the object is made. Both visual and haptic systems assess object properties, although with different degrees of accuracy [3].

The roles of visual and haptic feedback on manipulative performance have also been examined in computer-generated environments. Virtual environments have the potential to integrate different sensory modalities and to allow the user to directly acquire and manipulate augmented or virtual objects. Improvements have been made with regards to real-time interaction, the quality of the displays, the introduction of multimodal interfaces, and the immersion of the human user in the computer-generated environment.

M. Masoodian et al. (Eds.): APCHI 2004, LNCS 3101, pp. 687–691, 2004.
© Springer-Verlag Berlin Heidelberg 2004

Virtual environments may be however just approximations of their physical, real-world counterparts. Specifically, the quality and availability of visual and haptic sensory feedback are often degraded, which can negatively impact human manipulative performance. On the other hand, computer-generated environments have great flexibility in their use of different sensory modalities, offering the possibility to enhance the available feedback and to substitute feedback that would normally be available through other modalities. One sensory modality that requires more detailed examination is the auditory modality.

Sounds provide important perceptual cues in both natural and computer-generated environments, including warning and feedback signals, information about object properties, such as location, type of material or texture of objects, and also about making contact [4], [5], [6]. Moreover, auditory interfaces can increase the realism of a simulated environment, providing the user with a richer experience. Research on multimodal perceptual performance points to the benefit of deliberately adding sound to haptic interfaces. Texture perception, for example, is a multisensory task in which information from several sensory modalities is available: haptics, vision and audition. In a bimodal texture identification task with a probe, touch-produced sound cues were found to be incorporated in the judgments of roughness. [5]. Impact sounds were also found to influence the haptic perception of stiffness with a probe [7].

Little research has been directed to the effects of auditory cues on motor performance. Force feedback was successfully substituted by auditory cues for detection of object contact and in peg-in-hole tasks in teleoperation [6]; enhancing haptic feedback with auditory cues was found to improve performance on a reach, grasp and place task [8].

2 Research Goals and Proposed Experiments

This work will examine how, when and what kind of sensory information is useful for improving performance on reach, grasp, and manipulation tasks. The goal is to investigate the role of sensory information when grasping and manipulating virtual or augmented objects in computer-generated environments, and specifically, the role of auditory information, and its interaction with visual and haptic information. Research questions include the following: Are auditory cues used for planning and execution of hand movements? What kind of auditory cues are relevant for prehension? How do they affect manipulative performance? How do auditory cues interact with other sensory cues? Does the presentation of information to more than one modality enhance performance? Can auditory cues successfully enhance or replace cues from other sensory modalities?

Different types of auditory cues will be used in both direct and remote manipulation tasks, alone or in combination with graphic and haptic cues. The cues will occur at different points in the task, such as when making or breaking contact between hand and object, or between the held object and other objects or surfaces. Besides contact information, auditory cues related to object properties such as type of material, weight and texture will be investigated. Auditory cues can provide redundant feedback, incongruent feedback, or substitutive feedback. To infer planning and control processes, in addition to movement times, we examine three-dimensional kinematic measures, such as peak velocities and their time of occurrence, aperture profiles, as well as gripping forces.

2.1 Preliminary Work

We investigated the effects of combined auditory, graphic and haptic contact information on a reach, grasp and place task in an augmented environment [8]. Auditory and graphic cues were presented alone or in combination when grasping or placing an object on the table. Haptic contact information was available to subjects, as the physical object was always present. The cues enhanced information about making contact between hand and object during grasp, or between object and table during place.

Experimental Set-Up. The experiment was conducted in the Enhanced Virtual Hand Laboratory, illustrated in Figure 1. An upside down SGI monitor displays an image on a half-silvered mirror that lies between the tabletop and computer screen. The image is reflected by the mirror so that it appears as a graphical image on the table surface. Infrared emitting diodes (IREDs) were used in conjunction with a dual-sensor OPTO-TRAK 3-D motion analysis system (Northern Digital Inc., Waterloo, Canada) to sample and record the 3-D movement of subjects. Subjects wore CrystalEYES googles so that the reflected image appeared 3-D, and headphones to hear the auditory cue. IREDs were placed on the goggles, on the subject's right hand, and on the object. Markers on the goggles drove the stereoscopic, head-coupled graphics display. The auditory and graphic cues were triggered either by force sensors on the object to be grasped, or by object position.

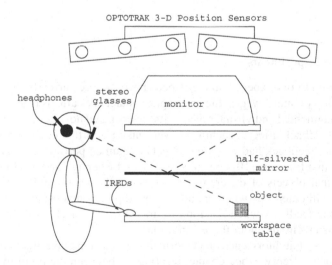

Fig. 1. Experimental Setup of the Enhanced Virtual Hand Laboratory

Results. We expected that movements would be affected after the occurrence of cues, that is, the cues would act as feedback. However, movements were affected during the reach phase, before the cues were provided. Compared to only haptic contact information, reaching movements were faster, with a higher peak velocity with redundant auditory, but not graphic, contact cues, as illustrated in Figure 2(a) and 2(b). Moreover, reaching movements were faster, with a higher peak velocity when the cues occurred when the hand touched the object, compared to when the object contacted the table. (More detailed results have been reported in [8]). In brief, these results suggest the benefits of adding auditory cues for enhancing manipulative performance in an augmented environment.

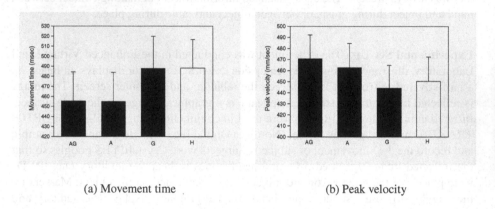

           (a) Movement time   (b) Peak velocity

Fig. 2. Kinematic measures for the reach phase. AG: auditory and graphic; A: auditory; G: graphic; H: haptic only contact cues

2.2   Future Experiments

As a follow-up to our experiment described above, we are currently investigating how the availability of auditory, graphic and haptic contact cues affects reaching movements to acquire augmented and virtual objects. [9] investigated how the availability of visual and haptic feedback affects reaching movements in a virtual environment. Both haptic and visual feedback had profound effects on human performance. An unexpected finding was that Fitts law [10] does not always hold when making reaching movements towards virtual objects of different sizes, specifically when haptic feedback was removed. We will determine whether auditory or graphic contact cues could successfully replace haptic feedback when reaching to grasp virtual objects of different sizes, and whether Fitts law holds under these conditions.

The effects of auditory cues on performance will also be investigated in the context of laparoscopic surgery. Since contact information between the tip of the tool and the target object is greatly reduced, compared to direct manipulation with the bare hands [11], it would be interesting to examine the effects of enhancing contact information between the tip of the laparoscopic tool and target object with auditory cues. Also, auditory cues could provide information about the magnitude of force applied by the tool to target tissues. Auditory cues may be beneficial for both performance and learning of laparoscopic tasks and skills.

3 Implications

By gaining understanding of the role of visual, haptic and auditory information for interaction in computer-generated environments, it will be possible to provide users with the most effective information at the most appropriate times. The results of this work have implications for understanding multisensory information processing and its role in the planning and execution of reaching, grasping and manipulation tasks, and also for the design of multimodal displays in interactive augmented and virtual environments, such as laparoscopic surgery training simulators.

References

[1] Ishii, H., Ullmer, B.: Tangible bits: Towards seamless interfaces between people, bits and atoms. In: Proceedings of the Conference on Human Factors in Computing Systems, CHI 97. Volume 47. (1997) 381–391

[2] MacKenzie, C.L., Iberall, T.: The Grasping Hand. Amsterdam: Elsevier-North Holland (1994)

[3] Klatsky, R.L., Lederman, S.J., Reed, C.: There's more to touch than meets the eye: the salience of object attributes for haptics with and without vision. Journal of Experimental Psychology: General 116 (1987) 356–369

[4] Klatsky, R.L., Pai, D.K., Krotkov, E.P.: Perception of material from contact sounds. Presence: Teleoperators and Virtual Environments 9 (2000) 399–410

[5] Lederman, S.J., Klatzky, R.L., Morgan, T., Hamilton, C.: Integrating multimodal information about surface texture via a probe: relative contributions of haptic and touch-produced sounds. In: Proceedings of the 10th annual Symposium on haptic interfaces for virtual environment and teleoperator systems, IEEE VR'02. (2002) 97–104

[6] Massimino, M.J., Sheridan, T.B.: Sensory substitution for force feedback in teleoperation. Presence: Teleoperators and Virtual Environments 2 (1993) 344–352

[7] DiFranco, D.W., Beauregard, G.L., Srinivasan, M.A.: The effect of auditory cues on the haptic perception of stiffness in virtual environments. In Rizzoni, G., ed.: Proceedings of the ASME Dynamic Systems and Control Division, DSC. Volume 61. (1997) 17–22

[8] Zahariev, M.A., MacKenzie, C.L.: Auditory, graphical and haptic contact cues for a reach, grasp, and place task in an augmented environment. In: Proceedings of the Fifth International Conference on Multimodal Interfaces, ICMI 03, ACM Press (2003) 273–276

[9] Mason, A.H., Walji, M.A., Lee, E.J., Mackenzie, C.L.: Reaching movements to augmented and graphic objects in virtual environments. In: Proceedings of the Conference on Human Factors in Computing Systems, CHI 2001, ACM Press (2001) 426–433

[10] Fitts, P.M.: The information capacity of the human motor system in controlling the amplitude of movement. Journal of Experimental Psychology 47 (1954) 381–391

[11] Den Boer, K.T., Herder, J.L., Sjoerdsma, W.: Sensitivity of laparoscopic dissectors. what can you feel? Surg Endosc 13 (1999) 869–873

Author Index

Abdul Razak, Fariza Hanis, 672
Al-Shehri, Saleh A., 1
Alam, Jaimee, 231
Alexander, Samuel, 641
Aoyagi, Shigemi, 441
Asai, Kikuo, 9
Ayatsuka, Yuji, 19

Baggo, Karola von, 521
Balbo, Sandrine, 620
Barr, Pippin, 111
Baumgartner, Valentina-Johanna, 252
Beale, Russell, 30
Bentley, Todd, 521
Benwell, George, 589
Biddle, Robert, 111, 262
Bidwell, Nicola J., 40
Billinghurst, Mark, 143
Bladh, Thomas, 50
Brown, Judy, 262
Burmeister, Oliver, 521
Byun, Un Sik, 211

Campbell, Malcolm, 540
Candy, Linda, 60
Carr, David A., 50
Casiez, Géry, 70
Catarci, Tiziana, 615
Chaillou, Christophe, 70
Chatfield, Craig, 570
Cho, Dong-sub, 171
Choi, Hoo-Gon, 201
Choi, Hyoukryeol, 201
Choi, Jeong-Dan, 81
Choi, Jin-Seong, 163
Choong, Yow Kin, 451
Colbert, Martin, 91

Demming, Geanbry, 575
Draheim, Dirk, 101
Duignan, Matthew, 111

Edmonds, Ernest, 60

Foo, Schubert Shou-Boon, 604
Francis, Caroline, 646

Goh, Dion Hoe-Lian, 604
Green, Richard, 121
Gunes, Hatice, 583

Häkkilä, Jonna, 570
Han, Dongil, 133
Hauber, Jeorg, 143
Hayes, Jared, 589
Henderson, Sarah, 651
Hendley, Robert J., 30
Hewlett, Cindy, 369
Hong, Sang Hyuk, 201
Howard, Steve, 180, 349
Hwang, Chi-Jeong, 81

Iga, Soichiro, 153
Iizuka, Kazuhisa, 409
Iwata, Mitsuru, 471, 481

Jamieson, John, 511
Jan, Tony, 583
Jang, Byung-Tae, 81
Jeon, Jae Wook, 201
Jeong, Hyuk, 163
Johnston, Lorraine, 521

Kane, Bridget, 656
Kemp, Elizabeth, 231, 594
Kemp, Raymond, 594
Khoo, Eugene Aik Min, 599
Kim, Douglas Jihoon, 211
Kim, Jong-Sung, 163
Kim, Yung Bok, 171
Kimani, Stephen, 615
Kinshuk, 511
Kishino, Fumio, 305
Kitamura, Yoshifumi, 305
Kjeldskov, Jesper, 180, 191
Kohno, Michimune, 19
Komatsu, Yoichiro, 471
Kondo, Kimio, 9
Kurihara, Satoshi, 441
Kwak, Mira, 171

Larssen, Astrid Twenebowa, 661
Lee, Dong-Seok, 211

Lee, Seongil, 201
Lee, Shu-Shing, 604, 666
Leung, Ying K., 625
Li, Lei, 221
Lim, Kee Yong, 599
Lindgaard, Gitte, 625
Lueg, Christopher P., 40
Luz, Saturnino, 656
Lyons, Paul, 231, 241, 283

Marcus, Aaron, 252
Matsumoto, Toshiko, 481
McGavin, Mike, 262
Miller, Ralph R., 610
Mirabella, Valeria, 615
Miura, Motoki, 272, 399
Mizoguchi, Fumio, 317
Mohanarajah, Thevalojinie, 594
Moore, Antoni, 589
Moretti, Giovanni, 241, 283
Mori, Joji, 531
Mugridge, Rick, 631
Mullane, Aaron, 620
Myhill, Carl, 293

Naito, Satoshi, 305
Nataraj, Mitra, 631
Nishiyama, Hiroyuki, 317
Noble, James, 111, 262

Obayashi, Makoto, 317
Ohno, Saiko, 153
Osawa, Noritaka, 9
Overmyer, Scott P., 610

Parviainen, Jyrki, 328
Patsula, Peter J., 338
Paynter, John, 501
Pearce, Jon M., 349
Phillips, Chris, 221, 231
Piccardi, Massimo, 583
Piekarski, Wayne, 420
Pilgrim, Chris J., 625
Plénacoste, Patricia, 70
Pryke, Andy, 30

Raikundalia, Gitesh K., 491
Raisamo, Jukka, 359
Raisamo, Roope, 328, 359
Regenbrecht, Holger, 143
Rekimoto, Jun, 19

Robertson, Toni, 369
Ryu, Jeha, 560

Sainio, Nina, 328
Sarrafzadeh, Abdolhossein, 641
Sas, Corina, 379
Sato, Daisuke, 399
Sato, Koji, 441
Sato, Shuhei, 389
Scholl, Jeremiah, 50
Scogings, Chris, 221
Sellar, Tracey, 675
Shiba, Haruya, 550
Shibayama, Etsuya, 389
Shimamura, Kazunori, 550
Shizuki, Buntarou, 272, 399, 409
Singh, Darryl, 631
Skov, Mikael B., 191
Slay, Hannah, 420
Smith, Wally, 431
Sugawara, Toshiharu, 441
Sugimoto, Yuji Y., 9
Sunny, Sanju, 451

Takada, Toshihiro, 441
Takahashi, Shin, 389
Tanaka, Jiro, 272, 399, 409
Tang, Kuo-Hao Eric, 461
Tano, Shun'ichi, 471, 481
Theng, Yin-Leng, 604
Thomas, Bruce, 420
Todd, Elizabeth G., 682
Tran, Minh Hong, 491
Tsai, Li-Chen, 461
Tsui, Tina Wai Chi, 501

Verhaart, Michael, 511
Vernik, Rudi, 420

Weber, Gerald, 101
Wilson, Mark, 283
Wong, B.L. William, 589
Woo, Daniel, 531
Wood-Bradley, Guy, 540

Yamaguchi, Takumi, 550
Yang, Yun, 491
Yoon, Jungwon, 560

Zahariev, Mihaela A., 687
Zajicek, Mary, 636